Oracle SQL by Example

Third Edition

Oracle SQL by Example

Third Edition

ALICE RISCHERT

PRENTICE HALL
PTR

PRENTICE HALL
Professional Technical Reference
Upper Saddle River, New Jersey 07458
www.phptr.com

Library of Congress Cataloging-in-Publication Data

Rischert, Alice.
   Oracle SQL by example / Alice Rischert.-- 3rd ed.
     p. cm. -- (Prentice Hall PTR Oracle series)
   Rev. ed. of: Oracle SQL interactive workbook, 2003.
   Includes indexes.
   ISBN 0-13-145131-6
  1. SQL (Computer program language) 2. Oracle (Computer file)
I. Rischert, Alice. Oracle SQL interactive workbook. II. Title. III. Series.

   QA76.73.S67R57 2004
   005.13'3--dc22   2004107600

Editorial/production supervision: Jessica Balch (Pine Tree Composition, Inc.)
Cover design director: Jerry Votta
Cover design: Talar Boorujy
Art director: Gail Cocker-Bogusz
Interior design: Meg Van Arsdale
Manufacturing buyer: Dan Uhrig
Senior project editor: Kristy Hart
Publisher: Jeffery Pepper
Marketing manager: Kate Hargett
Editorial assistant: Linda Ramagnano
Full-service production coordinator: Anne R. Garcia

© 2004 Pearson Education, Inc.
Publishing as Prentice Hall Professional Technical Reference
Upper Saddle River, NJ 07458

Prentice Hall books are widely used by corporations and government agencies
for training, marketing, and resale.

For information regarding corporate and government bulk discounts, please contact:
Corporate and Government Sales (800)382-3419 or corpsales@pearsontechgroup.com

Other company and product names mentioned herein are the trademarks
or registered trademarks of their respective owners.

Printed in the United States of America
10   9   8   7   6   5   4   3   2

ISBN 0-13-145131-6

Pearson Education Ltd., *London*
Pearson Education Australia Pty, Limited, *Sydney*
Pearson Education Singapore, Pte. Ltd.
Pearson Education North Asia Ltd., *Hong Kong*
Pearson Education Canada, Ltd., *Toronto*
Pearson Educación de Mexico, S.A. de C.V.
Pearson Education—Japan, *Tokyo*
Pearson Education Malaysia, Pte. Ltd.

To my daughter, Kirsten, and my parents, Albert and Hilde

About Prentice Hall Professional Technical Reference

With origins reaching back to the industry's first computer science publishing program in the 1960s, Prentice Hall Professional Technical Reference (PH PTR) has developed into the leading provider of technical books in the world today. Formally launched as its own imprint in 1986, our editors now publish over 200 books annually, authored by leaders in the fields of computing, engineering, and business.

Our roots are firmly planted in the soil that gave rise to the technological revolution. Our bookshelf contains many of the industry's computing and engineering classics: Kernighan and Ritchie's *C Programming Language,* Nemeth's *UNIX System Administration Handbook,* Horstmann's *Core Java,* and Johnson's *High-Speed Digital Design.*

PH PTR acknowledges its auspicious beginnings while it looks to the future for inspiration. We continue to evolve and break new ground in publishing by providing today's professionals with tomorrow's solutions.

PRENTICE
HALL
PTR

CONTENTS

FOREWORD

THE ANCIENT PROBLEM

The year was AD 1680; the place was the Levant—a region on the eastern shores of the Mediterranean. The political climate was stable enough to allow peaceful trade among nations. Seaports were bustling with merchants who were making profits by expanding their markets outside of their country of origin. They met many challenges in travel, as well as in adapting to other cultures and customs. A major obstacle was communication. As a seller of goods, your best chance for top sales is to target people whose language you know but how can you sell something if you cannot extol its virtues to your potential customer? Sign language and written symbols can be quite effective, but are not nearly as personal and understandable as the spoken word. The problem with spoken language in a situation like this is that there are many languages to master.

THE ANCIENT SOLUTION

The solution that emerged from this problem in the classical world has been used by people of many lands throughout history: use a common language when gathered in a multicultural environment. In the Levant, the common language that developed was a combination of Italian, Spanish, French, Greek, Arabic, and Turkish. This language, called *Lingua Franca*, became a standard in many ports as merchants used it to successfully communicate with their customers and fellow traders. Those who learned and mastered this language became the most effective and successful business people. Although Lingua Franca is now extinct, the term *lingua franca* is applied to any hybrid language used for communication between people of diverse native languages and cultures.

THE MODERN-DAY PROBLEM

In today's information technology (IT) industry, we face a similar situation. Companies are solving their data management requirements using relational and object-relational databases. Businesses have found these databases to offer the best features and most robust environments. The challenges that companies are facing when using databases are mainly in creating flexible and efficient human interfaces. Customized interface application development takes much in the way of effort and resources if it is to properly address the requirements of the business.

IT professionals who are tasked with creating modern database systems must rely on their training and expertise, both in designing the proper database storage objects and in programming the most efficient application programs. In the recent past, developers of relational and object-relational systems have used procedural programming languages such as COBOL, Fortran, and C to create application programs that access data. Regardless of the procedural language used, there is an additional language embedded in these procedural programs. This language offers a standard way to define and manipulate the data structures in a relational or object-relational database. It is the lingua franca of database technology— Structured Query Language (SQL). With SQL, developers using diverse base languages, database software, hardware, and operating systems can effectively communicate with the database in a standard way. A standard language means that the written code is understood easily and can be supported fully and enhanced quickly. This is the promise of SQL, and this promise has been fulfilled successfully for decades in countless relational database application programs.

The problem today is not the lack of a common language, as was the case in ancient times before lingua franca. SQL is the common language. The problem today is in the assimilation and proper use of this language. As the computer industry continues its logarithmic growth, the number of application developers increases similarly. Each new developer who writes programs that need to access a relational database must be trained in the lingua franca. In the recent past, with a smaller number of new developers, this was a manageable feat. When a new developer was in training, she or he would learn both a procedural programming language and the database language embedded in it—SQL.

Today, the trend in IT solutions is toward object orientation. Object-oriented analysis, design, and programming have come of age and, according to popular opinion, are now the best ways to create computer systems. This means that C++ and Java, which are object-oriented languages, are replacing the traditional procedural languages as the choice for building new systems. From the perspective of the database management system, this is merely a shift in the main programming language that the developer uses to interface with the user. The core database language, SQL, is still required and is of key importance.

However, something fundamental has been lost in this paradigm shift to object orientation. That something is a solid background in SQL. This problem persists for many reasons. Unfortunately, IT management professionals everywhere are employing Java programmers who do not have a solid grasp of the SQL language. This arrangement works up to a point, but there is, eventually, a collision with a brick wall. In many situations, this consultant has had to break into the SQL code used in a Java program only to find inefficient or incorrect use of the SQL language. Misunderstanding or misuse of the SQL language can have adverse effects on the program's efficiency and, without proper testing, can adversely affect production data systems, many of which are critical to the functioning of the business. On the other hand, proper use of SQL can result in application programs that are simpler to create and maintain and that are most efficient in data storage and data access.

THE MODERN-DAY SOLUTION

The solution to the problem of misunderstanding the lingua franca of databases is simple—an increased focus on learning the foundations and abilities of SQL and the correct methods for coding SQL programs. Time and money spent in training on the basics of SQL are time and money well spent. There are many ways to learn a subject like SQL. In this writer's experience of over 20 years as a trainer in the IT and other industries, the best learning experience comes from a multifaceted approach. Human beings learn in different ways, and using different approaches to present the same subject ensures that the subject will be mastered. In addition, the repetition of concepts and material in different formats ensures a thorough understanding of the subject. Research has shown that repetition and variety are proven learning techniques.

What Ms. Rischert has accomplished in this book is the epitome of the solution for the correct understanding of SQL. This book will be useful for seasoned IT professionals who need to study the language more completely or who just need a refresher on the concepts and thought processes of using SQL, as well as for those who are new to the subject and want to learn it in the right way.

The author applies the teaching principles of variety and repetition in a multifaceted approach to the subject. This approach allows the student of the subject to totally master the basics as well as the best ways to use the language. All core SQL subjects are treated with this approach, which includes a brief description of the concept followed by simple and easy-to-grasp examples. Examples make the concepts real and allow the reader to quickly master the subject.

The very best way to learn the concepts of any new technology is to be tasked with an application development project that uses that technology. However, a project in the real-world workplace is not the right place to learn—the stakes are too high and the pressure too great. This book gives you a taste of real-world application development needs and processes by assigning a series of labs in each chapter to apply the knowledge gained from the conceptual discussion and examples. The book then provides the solutions to these problems so that you can check your work. Proper use of these sections will lead you to a solid mastery of the language and give you the ability to use this lingua franca successfully to solve real-world business problems. This type of mastery will serve you well in whatever type of database programming environment you find yourself.

Peter Koletzke
Quovera
Redwood Shores, CA
May 2004

ACKNOWLEDGMENTS

A few months after the second edition of the book was published, the effort for the new edition started. While the changes to this third edition were not as far reaching as in the previous edition, it nevertheless required a tremendous amount of research and testing to include the new and changed functionality of Oracle 10*g*. The request for an update of the book turned out to be a rewrite of a number of topics and the addition of many new exercises.

I am privileged to acknowledge a number of individuals who contributed along the way by offering suggestions, corrections, guidance, ideas, comments, and advice. Some people who contributed to the previous edition were again available to help out. In particular, I would like to express my appreciation for the tremendous efforts by Dan Diaz and Bernard Dadario. They reviewed many chapters for accuracy to ensure the functionality worked exactly as described. Their excellent comments, together with the efforts and suggestions of Mitch Murov and Gnana Supramaniam, are reflected in the book. Mauro Bottalico researched some of Oracle's latest object-oriented features. Daniel Liao once again helped create some of the wonderful graphic illustrations.

A number of readers and some current and past students at Columbia University's Database Application Design and Development program sent in comments, corrections, and suggestions. There are too many individuals to acknowledge, but all their contributions were extremely helpful and very much appreciated.

I am particularly grateful to Jeff Pepper at Prentice Hall for initiating and believing in this project and for putting up with delays due to so many unexpected circumstances. The beta versions of the software presented special challenges. Chapters that were completed had to be revised after the functionality changed and then again after the production version was released. Anne Garcia at Prentice Hall and Jessica Balch at Pine Tree Composition ensured that all corrections made it in the book.

Lynn Snyder and Sheila Cepero at Oracle were helpful in getting answers to follow-up questions and bug reports; their efforts alleviated some of the frustrations of Oracle beta software and first-draft documentation. Peter Linsley at Oracle was very helpful in demystifying some of the regular expression functionality.

I would also like to thank those individuals who helped with the second edition of the book as many of their contributions continue to be reflected this work. Thank you Ben Rosenzweig, Gordon Green, Richard Kamm, Susan Hesse, Tom Phips, and Alex Morrison. Thanks to the faculty and staff of Columbia University's Computer Technology and Application program, in particular Dr. Art Langer and Dennis Green.

Lonnie Blackwood and Dean Dinnebeil kept my schedule manageable during the book-writing process; thanks for understanding the many demands that were placed on me during this time. Thanks to my colleagues at XWare/Ecteon who unwittingly provided some of the material. Their questions, problems, and challenges provided the framework for some of the book.

Douglas Scherer offered his wonderful encouragement and insight with each edition of this book. Peter Koletzke has been a dear friend and supporter for so many years and we often found ourselves discussing the challenges of writing about beta software as Peter completed his work on yet another JDeveloper book. His enthusiasm and encouragements once again helped me see the light at the end of the tunnel.

Thank you to the Garcia families; they all have given me invaluable support over the last few years. My parents, sisters Irene and Christa, and my brother Guenter deserve a great deal of thanks for all their tremendous advice and encouragement. Spooky, our little kitty, for entertaining me with her acrobatic performances, which gave me the needed breaks and laughs. Finally, I owe most of my thanks to my lovely daughter, Kirsten. Thanks for your understanding, love, and doing so well in school. It really really made writing this book easier. You are such a great kid!

Alice Rischert

ABOUT THE AUTHOR

Alice Rischert is the chair of Columbia University's Database Application Development and Design program, where she teaches classes in Oracle SQL, PL/SQL, and database design. Ms. Rischert's wide-ranging technology experience encompasses systems integration, database architecture, and project management for a number of companies in the United States, Europe, and Asia. Ms. Rischert has worked with Oracle since Version 5, and she has presented on SQL and PL/SQL topics at Oracle conferences.

INTRODUCTION

The SQL language is the de facto standard language for relational databases, and Oracle's database server is the leading relational database on the market today. *Oracle SQL by Example, third edition,* presents an introduction to the Oracle SQL language in a unique and highly effective format. Rather than being a reference book, it guides you through the basic skills until you reach a mastery of the language. The book challenges you to work through hands-on guided tasks rather than read through descriptions of functionality. You will be able to retain the material more easily, and the additional example questions reinforce and further enhance the learning experience.

WHO THIS BOOK IS FOR

This book is intended for anyone requiring a background in Oracle's implementation of the SQL language. In particular, application developers, system designers, and database administrators will find many practical and representative real-world examples. Students new to Oracle will gain the necessary experience and confidence to apply their knowledge in solving typical problems they face in the work situation. Individuals already familiar with Oracle SQL but wishing a firmer foundation or those interested in the new Oracle 10g features will discover many of the useful tips, tricks, and information.

The initial audience for the book was the students of the Oracle SQL class at Columbia University's Computer Technology and Applications program. The student body has a wide-ranging level of technology experience. Their questions, learning approaches, and feedback provided the framework for this book. Many students cited the hands-on exercises as critical to their understanding of database technology and the SQL language and continuously asked for more examples and additional challenging topics. This book shares much of the material presented in the classroom and looks at the various angles of many solutions to a particular issue.

The book begins with the basic concepts of relational databases, the SQL*Plus environment, and SQL; it then gradually deepens the knowledge. A reader who already has some fundamental understanding of SQL will benefit from reading this book as it allows him or her to gain a better insight to writing alternative SQL statements. After performing the exercises in this book, you will harness the power of SQL and utilize much of Oracle's SQL functionality.

WHAT MAKES THIS BOOK DIFFERENT

This book encourages the reader to learn by doing; this requires active participation by performing the exercises. Ultimately, the reward is a thorough understanding of SQL and a high level of comfort dealing with the real-world Oracle SQL topics. Performing the exercises help with the retention of the material, and the Self-Review and Test Your Thinking sections further test your understanding and offer additional challenges. The companion Web site contains solutions to the Test Your Thinking exercises and includes additional exercises and answers.

The book's focus is to give the readers examples of how the SQL language is commonly used, with many exercises supporting the learning experience. Unlike other SQL books, this book discusses Oracle's specific implementation of the language. Learning the language alone is not enough. The book also teaches you how to adopt good habits and educates you about many Oracle-specific technology features that are essential to successful systems development. The examples are derived from a sample database that takes you through the typical tasks you will encounter when working with an Oracle database.

This book is *not* a reference book, but rather it teaches SQL by illustrating its use through many examples. Use the index to look up previously discussed concepts or refer back to certain topics. The best way to learn the SQL language is to perform the exercises and compare your answers with the sample answers and accompanying explanations.

This book does not cover the entire Oracle SQL syntax, but emphasizes the essentials of the most frequently used features with many examples to reinforce the learning. Some of Oracle's syntax options are too numerous, and many are very infrequently used; including them all would make the book swell by a several hundred additional pages. Instead, I have concentrated on those that you will use most. After performing the exercises, you will also have gained sufficient knowledge to read up and understand the Oracle documentation, if needed. I hope that you will enjoy this learning experience and come away with the knowledge you hoped to gain.

HOW THIS BOOK IS ORGANIZED

Each chapter of the book is divided into labs covering a particular topic. The objective of each lab is defined at its beginning, with brief examples that introduce the reader to the covered concepts.

Following the lab's introductory examples are exercises that are the heart of the lab. They reinforce and expand the reader's knowledge of the subject. Each exercise consists of a series of steps to follow to perform specific tasks or particular questions that are designed to help you discover the important aspects of the SQL language. The answers to these questions are given at the end of the exercises, along with more in-depth discussion of the concepts explored.

After you perform the exercises and compare the answers with the sample queries, answers, and explanations, the lab ends with multiple-choice Self-Review Questions. These are meant to test that you have understood the material covered in the lab. The answers to these questions appear in Appendix A. There are additional Self-Review questions at this book's companion Web site.

At the end of each chapter, the Test Your Thinking section reinforces and combines all the topics learned in labs, and solidifies your skills. The answers to these questions are found on the companion Web site for this book.

LAYOUT OF A CHAPTER

```
Chapter
        Lab
                Exercises
                Exercise Answers (with detailed discussion)
                Self-Review Questions
        Lab ...
        Test Your Thinking Questions
```

The chapters should be completed in sequence because concepts covered in earlier chapters are required for the completion of exercises in later chapters.

ABOUT THE COMPANION WEB SITE

The companion Web site is located at http://authors.phptr.com/rischert3e. Here you will find a number of very important things:

1. Installation files you need before you begin reading the book.
2. Answers to the Test Your Thinking questions.
3. Additional Self-Review questions.
4. Additional resources such as links, tips, and errata.

INSTALLATION FILES

All of the exercises and questions are based on a sample schema called STUDENT. The required files to install this STUDENT schema and the installation instructions can be downloaded from the Web site.

TEST YOUR THINKING

The answers to the Test Your Thinking sections are found at the Web site.

ADDITIONAL SELF-REVIEW QUESTIONS

The Web site will have many other features, such as additional Self-Review questions, a message board, and periodically updated information about the book.

 Visit the companion Web site and download the required files before starting the labs and exercises.

WHAT YOU WILL NEED

To complete the exercises you need the following:

> The Oracle® database software
> Oracle's SQL*Plus software or a Web browser
> Access to the Internet

ORACLE 10*g*

Oracle 10*g* is Oracle's latest version of the relational database software and its flagship product. You can use either the Personal Edition or Enterprise Edition. Various beta versions of the Enterprise edition of Oracle 10*g* were used to create the exercises for this book.

If you have a previous version of the Oracle database, you will be able to complete a large majority of the exercises; however, some syntax options and features are only available in Oracle 10*g*.

If you don't have the latest release of the Oracle software available, you can obtain a trial copy from Oracle's Web site at www.oracle.com. You have the option of either downloading the Personal or Enterprise editions or purchasing a CD pack from the Oracle store (http://oraclestore.oracle.com) for a nominal fee.

ORACLE SQL*PLUS SOFTWARE OR WEB BROWSER

You can perform all the exercises in this book with Oracle's SQL*Plus software. Alternatively, you can use *i*SQL*Plus, a Web-based version, which does not require the installation of the Oracle SQL*Plus software on your individual machine. Only a browser is necessary. The *i*SQL*Plus version simplifies the editing and offers a superior display of the result. However, *i*SQL*Plus does not allow certain functionality and this is pointed out where applicable. For a list of unsupported commands refer to Appendix C, "SQL*Plus Command Reference." Instead of SQL*Plus, you can also use alternate SQL execution environments and a list is available in Appendix H, "Resources."

ACCESS TO THE INTERNET

You will need access to the Internet so that you can access the companion Web site: http://authors.phptr.com/rischert3e. Here you will find files that are necessary to install the sample STUDENT schema.

ABOUT THE STUDENT SCHEMA

Throughout this book, you access data from a sample schema called STUDENT, which contains information about a computer education program. The schema was designed to record data about instructors, courses, students, and their respective enrollments and grades.

After you download the installation files to create the schema within your Oracle database, you will be able to follow the exercises in the book. In Chapter 1, "SQL and Data," you are introduced to the relational concepts necessary to read the schema diagram. Appendix D, "Student Database Schema," shows you a graphical representation of the schema, and Appendix E, "Table and Column Descriptions," lists descriptive information about each table and column.

CONVENTIONS USED IN THIS BOOK

There are several conventions used in this book to make your learning experience easier. These are explained here.

 This icon denotes advice and useful information about a particular topic or concept from the author to you, the reader.

 This icon flags tips that are especially helpful tricks that will save you time or trouble—for instance, a shortcut for performing a particular task or a method that the author has found useful.

 Computers are delicate creatures and can be easily damaged. Likewise, they can be dangerous to work on if you're not careful. This icon flags information and precautions that not only save you headaches in the long run, but may even save you or your computer from harm.

 Passages referring to the book's companion Web site are flagged with this icon. The companion Web site is located at http://authors.phptr.com/rischert3e.

ERRATA

I have made every effort to make sure there are no errors in the text and code. However, to err is human. As part of the companion Web site, you will find corrections as they're spotted. If you find an error that has not been reported, please let me know by contacting me at ar280@yahoo.com. You comments and suggestions are greatly appreciated.

CHAPTER I

SQL AND DATA

What is SQL? SQL (pronounced *sequel*) is an acronym for *Structured English QUEry Language,* a standardized language used to access and manipulate data. The history of SQL corresponds closely with the development of relational databases concepts published in a paper by Dr. E. F. Codd at IBM in 1970. He applied mathematical concepts to the specification of a method for data storage and access; this specification, which became the basis for relational databases, was intended to overcome the physical dependencies of the then-available database systems. The SQL language (originally called "System R" in the prototype and later called "SEQUEL") was developed by the IBM Research Laboratory as a standard language to use with relational databases. In 1979 Oracle, then called Relational Software, Inc., introduced the first commercially available implementation of a relational database incorporating the SQL language. The SQL language evolved with many additional syntax expansions incorporated into the American National Standards Institute (ANSI) SQL standards developed since. Individual database vendors continuously added extensions to the language, which eventually found their way into the latest ANSI standards used by relational databases today. Large-scale commercial implementations of relational database applications started to appear in the mid to late 1980s as early implementations were hampered by poor performance. Since then, relational databases and the SQL language have continuously evolved and improved.

Before you begin to use SQL, however, you must know about data, databases, and relational databases. What is a database? A *database* is an organized collection of data. A *database management system* (DBMS) is software that allows the creation, retrieval, and manipulation of data. You use such systems to maintain patient data in a hospital, bank accounts in a bank, or inventory in a warehouse. A *relational database management system* (RDBMS) provides this functionality within the context of the relational database theory and the rules defined for relational databases by Codd. These rules, called "Codd's Twelve Rules," later expanded to include additional rules, describe goals for database management systems to cope with ever-challenging and demanding database requirements. Compliance with Codd's Rules has been a major challenge for database vendors and early versions of relational databases complied with only a handful of the rules.

Today, SQL is accepted as the universal standard database access language. Databases using the SQL language are entrusted with managing critical information affecting many aspects of our daily lives. Most applications developed today use a relational database and Oracle continues to be one of the largest and most popular database vendors. Although relational databases and the SQL language are already over 30 years old, there seems to be no slowing down of the popularity of the language. Learning SQL is probably one of the best long-term investments you can make for a number of reasons:

- SQL is used by most commercial database applications.
- Although the language has evolved over the years with a large array of syntax enhancements and additions, most of the basic functionality has remained essentially unchanged.
- SQL knowledge will continue to be a fundamental skill because there is currently no mature and viable alternative language that accomplishes the same functionality.
- Learning Oracle's specific SQL implementation allows you great insight into the feature-rich functionality of one of the largest and most successful database vendors.

Understanding relational database concepts provides you with the foundation for understanding the SQL language. Those unfamiliar with relational concepts or interested in a refresher will receive an overview of basic relational theories in the next two labs. If you are already familiar with relational theory, you can skip the first two labs and jump directly to Lab 1.3, "The STUDENT Schema Diagram." The STUDENT database manages student enrollment data at a fictional university. Lab 1.3 teaches you about the organization and relationships of the STUDENT database, which is used throughout the exercises in this book.

LAB 1.1

DATA, DATABASES, AND THE DEFINITION OF SQL

LAB OBJECTIVES

After this lab, you will be able to:
✔ Identify and Group Data
✔ Define SQL
✔ Define the Structures of a RDBMS: Tables, Columns, Rows, and Keys

Data is all around you—you make use of it every day. Your hair may be brown, your flight leaves from gate K10, you try to get up in the morning at 6:30 A.M. Storing data in related groups and making the connections among them are what databases are all about.

You interact with a database when you withdraw cash from an ATM machine, order a book from a Web site, or check stock quotes on the Internet. The switch from the information processing society to the knowledge management society will be facilitated by databases. Databases provide a major asset to any organization by helping it run its business, and databases represent the backbones of the many technological advances we enjoy today.

Before the availability of relational databases, data was stored in individual files that could not be accessed unless you knew a programming language. Data could not be combined easily and modifications to the underlying database structures were extremely difficult. The Relational Model conceived by E. F. Codd provided the framework to solve a myriad of these and many other database problems. Relational databases offer *data independence,* meaning a user does not need to know on which hard drive and file a particular piece of information is stored. The RDBMS provides users with *data consistency* and *data integrity.* For example, if an employee works in the Finance department and we know that he can only work for one department, there should not be duplicate department records or contradicting data in the database. As you work through this lab, you will discover many of these useful and essential features. Let's start with a discussion of the terminology used in relational databases.

TABLES

A relational database stores data in tables. Tables typically contain data about a single subject. Each table has a unique name that signifies the contents of the data. For example, you can store data about books you read in a table called BOOK.

COLUMNS

Columns in a table organize the data further and a table consists of at least one column. Each column represents a single, low-level detail about a particular set of data. The name of the column is unique within a table and identifies the data you find in the column. For example, the BOOK table may have a column for the title, publisher, date the book was published, and so on. The order of the columns is unimportant because SQL allows you to display data in any order you choose.

ROWS

Each row usually represents one unique set of data within this table. For example, the row in Figure 1.1 with the title "The Invisible Force" is unique within the BOOK table. All the columns of the row represent respective data for the row. Each intersection of a column and row in a table represents a value, and some do not, as you see in the PUBLISH_DATE column. The value is said to be *NULL*. Null is an unknown value, so it's not even blank spaces. Nulls cannot be evaluated or compared because they are unknown.

PRIMARY KEY

When working with tables, you must understand how to uniquely identify data within a table. This is the purpose of the *primary key*; it uniquely identifies a row within a table, which means that you find one, and only one, row in the table by

BOOK Table

BOOK_ID	TITLE	PUBLISHER	PUBLISH_DATE	
1010	The Invisible Force	Literacy Circle		
1011	Into The Sky	Prentice Hall	10/02	◄── Row
1012	Making It Possible	Life Books	2/99	

Column

Figure 1.1 ■ Example of the BOOK table.

CUSTOMER_ID	CUSTOMER_NAME	ADDRESS	PHONE	ZIP
2010	Movers, Inc.	123 Park Lane	212-555-1212	10095
2011	Acme Mfg. Ltd.	555 Broadway	212-566-1212	10004
2012	ALR Inc.	50 Fifth Avenue	212-999-1212	10010

PRIMARY KEY

Figure 1.2 ■ Primary key example.

looking for the primary key value. Figure 1.2 shows an example of the CUSTOMER table with the CUSTOMER_ID as the primary key of the table.

At first glance you may think that the CUSTOMER_NAME column can serve as the primary key of the CUSTOMER table because it is unique. However, it is entirely possible to have customers with the same name. Therefore, the CUSTOMER_NAME column is not a good choice for the primary key. Sometimes the unique key is a system-generated sequence number; this type of key is called a *synthetic* or *surrogate key*. The advantage of such a surrogate key is that it is unique and does not have any inherent meaning or purpose; therefore, it is not subject to changes. In this example, the CUSTOMER_ID column is such a surrogate key.

It is best to avoid any primary keys that are subject to updates as they cause unnecessary complexity. For example, the phone number of a customer is a poor example of a primary key column choice. Though it may possibly be unique within a table, phone numbers can change and then cause a number of problems with updates of other columns that reference this column.

A table may have only one primary key, which consists of one or more columns. If the primary key contains multiple columns, it is referred to as a *composite primary key* or *concatenated primary key*. (Choosing appropriate keys is discussed more in Chapter 11, "Create, Alter, and Drop Tables.") Oracle does not require that every table have a primary key, and there may be cases where it is not appropriate to have one. However, it is strongly recommended that most tables have a primary key.

FOREIGN KEYS

If you store the customer and the customer's order information in one table, the customer's name and address is repeated for each order. Figure 1.3 depicts such a table. Any change to the address requires the update of all the rows in the table for that individual customer.

If, however, the data is split into two tables (CUSTOMER and ORDER as shown in Figure 1.4) and the customer's address needs to be updated, only one row in the CUSTOMER table needs to be updated. Furthermore, splitting data this way avoids data inconsistency whereby the data differs between the different rows.

ID	CUSTOMER_ NAME	ADDRESS	PHONE	ZIP	ORDER ID	ORDER_ DATE	TOTAL_ ORDER
2010	Movers, Inc.	123 Park Lane	212-555-1212	10095	100	12/23/01	$500
2010	Movers, Inc.	123 Park Lane	212-555-1212	10095	102	7/20/02	$100
2010	Movers, Inc.	123 Park Lane	212-555-1212	10095	103	8/25/02	$400
2010	Movers, Inc.	123 Park Lane	212-555-1212	10095	104	9/20/02	$200
2011	Acme Mfg. Ltd.	555 Broadway	212-566-1212	10004	105	8/20/02	$900
2012	ALR Inc.	50 Fifth Avenue	212-999-1212	10010	101	01/05/02	$600

Figure 1.3 ■ **Example of CUSTOMER data mixed with ORDER data.**

Eliminating redundancy is one of the key concepts in relational databases and this process, referred to as *normalization*, is discussed shortly.

Figure 1.4 illustrates how the data is split into two tables to provide data consistency. In this example, the CUSTOMER_ID becomes a *foreign key* column in the ORDER table. The foreign key is the column that links the CUSTOMER and ORDER table together. You can find all orders for a particular customer by looking for the particular CUSTOMER_ID in the ORDER table. The CUSTOMER_ID corresponds to a single row in the CUSTOMER table that provides the customer-specific information. The foreign key column CUSTOMER_ID happens to have the same column name in the ORDER table. This makes it easier to recognize the fact that the tables share common column values. Often the foreign key column and the primary key have identical column names, but it is not required. You will

▼ PRIMARY KEY   CUSTOMER

CUSTOMER_ID	CUSTOMER_NAME	ADDRESS	PHONE	ZIP
2010	Movers, Inc.	123 Park Lane	212-555-1212	10095
2011	Acme Mfg. Ltd.	555 Broadway	212-566-1212	10004
2012	ALR Inc.	50 Fifth Avenue	212-999-1212	10010

▼FOREIGN KEY

ORDER_ID	CUSTOMER_ID	ORDER_ DATE	TOTAL_ ORDER
100	2010	12/23/01	$500
102	2010	7/20/02	$100
103	2010	8/25/02	$400
104	2010	9/20/02	$200
105	2011	8/20/02	$900
101	2012	01/05/02	$600

ORDER

Figure 1.4 ■ **Primary and foreign key relationship between CUSTOMER and ORDER tables.**

learn more about foreign key columns with the same and different names and how to create foreign key relationships in Chapter 11, "Create, Alter, and Drop Tables." Chapter 6, "Equijoins," teaches you how to combine results from the two tables using SQL.

 You connect and combine data between tables in a relational database via common columns.

SQL LANGUAGE COMMANDS

You work with the tables, rows, and columns using the SQL language. SQL allows you to query data, create new data, modify existing data, and delete data. Within the SQL language you can differentiate between individual sublanguages, which are a collection of individual commands.

For example, the *Data Manipulation Language* (DML) commands allow you to query, insert, update, or delete data. SQL allows you to create new database structures such as tables or modify existing ones; this subcategory of SQL language commands is called the *Data Definition Language* (DDL). Using the SQL language you can control access to the data using *Data Control Language* (DCL) commands. Table 1.1 shows you different language categories with examples of their respective SQL commands.

One of the first statements you will execute is the SELECT command, which allows you to query data. For example, to retrieve the TITLE and PUBLISHER columns from the BOOK table you may issue a SELECT statement such as the following:

```
SELECT title, publisher
   FROM book
```

The INSERT command lets you add new rows to a table. The next command shows you an example of an INSERT statement that adds a row to the BOOK table. The row contains the values Oracle SQL as a book title, a BOOK_ID of 1013, and a publish date of 12/02 with Prentice Hall as the publisher.

Table 1.1 ■ Overview of SQL Language Commands

Description	SQL Commands
Data Manipulation	SELECT, INSERT, UPDATE, DELETE, MERGE
Data Definition	CREATE, ALTER, DROP, TRUNCATE, RENAME
Data Control	GRANT, REVOKE
Transaction Control	COMMIT, ROLLBACK, SAVEPOINT

```
INSERT INTO book
(book_id, title, publisher, publish_date)
VALUES
(1013, 'Oracle SQL', 'Prentice Hall', '12/02')
```

To create new tables you use the CREATE TABLE command. The following statement illustrates how to create a simple table called AUTHOR with three columns. The first column, called AUTHOR_ID, holds numeric data; the FIRST_NAME and LAST_NAME columns contain alphanumeric character data.

```
CREATE TABLE author
(author_id    NUMBER,
 first_name   VARCHAR2(30),
 last_name    VARCHAR2(30))
```

You can manipulate the column definitions of a table with the ALTER TABLE command. This allows you to add or drop columns. You can also create primary and foreign key constraints on a table. Constraints enforce business rules within the database. For example, a primary key constraint can enforce the uniqueness of the AUTHOR_ID column in the AUTHOR table.

To grant SELECT and INSERT access to the AUTHOR table, you issue a GRANT command. It allows the user Scott to retrieve and insert data in the AUTHOR table.

```
GRANT SELECT, INSERT ON author TO scott
```

Starting with Chapter 2, "SQL: The Basics," you will learn how to execute the SELECT command against the Oracle database; Chapter 10, "Insert, Update, and Delete," will teach you the details of data manipulation and transaction control; and Chapter 11, "Create, Alter, and Drop Tables," introduces you to the creation of tables and the definition of constraints to enforce the required business rules. Chapter 14, "Security," discusses how to control the access to data and the various Oracle database features.

LAB 1.1 EXERCISES

1.1.1 IDENTIFY AND GROUP DATA

a) Give three examples of types of data.

b) What groupings of data do you use in your daily life?

c) Give an example of a database system you use outside of the workplace and explain how it helps you.

1.1.2 DEFINE SQL

a) What is SQL and why is it useful?

b) Try to match each of the SQL commands on the left with a verb from the list on the right.

1. CREATE   a. manipulate
2. UPDATE   b. define
3. GRANT   c. control

c) Why do you think it is important to control access to data in a database?

1.1.3 DEFINE THE STRUCTURES OF A RDBMS: TABLES, COLUMNS, ROWS, AND KEYS

a) How is data organized in a relational database?

b) Do you think it's possible to have a table with no rows at all?

c) Figure 1.5 displays a listing of an EMPLOYEE and a DEPARTMENT table. Identify the columns you consider to be primary keys and foreign keys for the tables.

EMPLOYEE_ID	FIRST_NAME	LAST_NAME	SALARY	DEPT_NO
230	Kyle	Hsu	80,000	40
231	Kirsten	Soehner	130,000	50
232	Madeline	Dimitri	70,000	40
234	Joshua	Hunter	90,000	20

DEPT_NO	DEPARTMENT_NAME
20	Finance
40	Human Resources
50	Sales
60	Information Systems

Figure 1.5 ■ EMPLOYEE and DEPARTMENT tables.

LAB 1.1 EXERCISE ANSWERS

1.1.1 ANSWERS

a) Give three examples of types of data.

Answer: The answer to this question will vary depending on your choices.

A circle, square, and triangle are all data about geometrical shapes. Your mother, father, and sister are data about your immediate family members. Fiction, comedy, cookbook, and computer are all data about types of books.

b) What groupings of data do you use in your daily life?

Answer: The answer to this question will vary depending on your situation.

I use my address book daily. It contains addresses and phone numbers of friends, relatives, and coworkers. I also keep a running to-do list of tasks at work, which groups together the tasks I have completed, as well as separately grouping those tasks I have yet to do.

When grouping data, each piece of data should be related to the others. A person's physical appearance is typically described by more than just brown hair; that person may also have green eyes, be 6 feet tall, and be of the female sex. In my address book, I group together a person's name, address, and telephone number. I may keep a separate address book for my business contacts that would group together the person's name, company name, work telephone number, fax number, and email address.

c) Give an example of a database system you use outside of the workplace and explain how it helps you.

Answer: Again, the answer to this question will vary depending on your situation.

When I'm in a record store, I often use a computerized information kiosk to search for information about an album, such as where it is located in the store. Another example is an ATM machine, where I can inquire about my account balance.

1.1.2 ANSWERS

a) What is SQL and why is it useful?

Answer: SQL, the Structured Query Language, is a standardized relational database access language. It is useful because it allows a user to query, manipulate, define, and control data in a RDBMS.

The SQL language is sanctioned by ANSI, which determines standards on all aspects of the SQL language, including datatypes. However, most relational database products, including Oracle, have their own extensions to the ANSI standard, providing additional functionality within their respective products by further extending the use of SQL.

b) Try to match each of the SQL commands on the left with a verb from the list on the right:

Answer: The following shows how these commands match with the appropriate verb.

1. CREATE ⟶ a. manipulate
2. UPDATE ⟶ b. define
3. GRANT ⟶ c. control

DML is used to *manipulate* data, with the SELECT, INSERT, UPDATE, and DELETE commands. (Note that in some of Oracle's own documentation, the SELECT command is not part of the DML language but is considered Data Retrieval Language.) DDL is used to *define* objects such as tables with the CREATE, ALTER, and DROP commands. DCL is used to *control* access privileges in a RDBMS, such as with the GRANT and REVOKE commands to give or remove privileges. These SQL commands are written and executed against the database using a software program. In this workbook, Oracle's SQL*Plus program or *i*SQL*Plus with your Web browser is used to communicate these commands to the RDBMS. The use of SQL*Plus and SQL commands will be covered in Chapter 2, "SQL: The Basics."

c) Why do you think it is important to control access to data in a database?

Answer: Data can contain sensitive information to which some users should have limited access privileges. Some users may be allowed to query certain data but not change it, while others are allowed to add data to a database, but not delete it. By controlling access to data, the security of the data is assured for all users. You learn about safeguarding your data in Chapter 14, "Security."

1.1.3 ANSWERS

a) How is data organized in a relational database?

Answer: Data is organized by placing like pieces of information together in a table that consists of columns and rows.

For example, the data found in a library is typically organized in several ways to facilitate finding a book. Figure 1.6 shows information specific to books. The data is organized into columns and rows; the columns represent a type of data (title vs. genre), and the rows contain data. A table in a database is organized in the same way. You might call this table BOOK; it contains information related to books only. Each intersection of a column and row in a table represents a value.

Searching for a book by location might yield this excerpt of data shown in Figure 1.7. This set of columns and rows represents another database table called LOCATION, with information specific to locations in a library.

TITLE	AUTHOR	ISBN#	GENRE	LOCATION_ID
Magic Gum	Harry Smith	0-11-124456-2	Computer	D11
Desk Work	Robert Jones	0-11-223754-3	Fiction	H24
Beach Life	Mark Porter	0-11-922256-8	Juvenile	J3
From Here to There	Gary Mills	0-11-423356-5	Fiction	H24

Figure 1.6 ■ BOOK table.

The advantage to storing information about books and their locations separately is that information is not repeated unnecessarily, and maintenance of the data is much easier.

For instance, two books in the BOOK table have the same LOCATION_ID, H24. If the floor, section, and shelf information were also stored in the BOOK table, this information would be repeated for each of the two book rows. In that situation, if the floor of LOCATION_ID H24 changed, both of the rows in the BOOK table would have to change. Instead, by storing the location information separately, the floor information only has to change once in the LOCATION table.

The two tables (BOOK and LOCATION) have a common column between them, namely LOCATION_ID. In a relational database, SQL can be used to query information from more than one table at a time, making use of the common column they contain by performing a *join*. The join allows you to query both the BOOK and LOCATION tables to return a list of book titles together with floor, section, and shelf information to help you locate the books easily.

LOCATION_ID	FLOOR	SECTION	SHELF
D11	1	3	1
H24	2	2	3
J3	3	1	1

Figure 1.7 ■ LOCATION table.

b) Do you think it's possible to have a table with no rows at all?

Answer: Yes, it is possible, though clearly it is not very useful to have a table with no data.

c) Figure 1.5 displays a listing of an EMPLOYEE and its respective DEPARTMENT table. Identify the columns you consider to be primary keys and foreign keys for the tables.

Answer: The primary key of the EMPLOYEE table is the EMPLOYEE_ID. The primary key of the DEPARTMENT table is DEPT_NO. The DEPT_NO is also the foreign key column of EMPLOYEE table and is common between the two tables.

In the DEPT_NO column of the EMPLOYEE table you can ONLY enter values that exist in the DEPARTMENT table. The DEPARTMENT table is the parent table from which the child table, the EMPLOYEE table, gets its DEPT_NO values. Establishing a foreign key relationship highlights the benefit of *referential integrity*. Only valid primary key values from the parent table are allowed in the child's foreign key column, therefore avoiding *orphan rows* (child rows without parent rows). For example, you cannot enter a DEPT_NO of 10 in the EMPLOYEE table if such a value does not exist in the DEPARTMENT table.

Note that the DEPARTMENT table contains one row with the department number of 60, which does not have any corresponding employees. The referential integrity rule allows a parent without child(ren), but does not allow a child without a parent because this would be considered an orphan row. You will learn how to establish primary key and foreign key relationships in Chapter 11, "Create, Alter, and Drop Tables."

LAB 1.1 SELF-REVIEW QUESTIONS

In order to test your progress, you should be able to answer the following questions.

1) A university's listing of students and the classes they are enrolled in is an example of a database system.

   a) _____ True
   b) _____ False

2) A table must always contain both columns and rows.

   a) _____ True
   b) _____ False

3) SQL is software that interacts with a relational database.

   a) _____ True
   b) _____ False

4) More than one user can be connected to a database at the same time.

   a) _____ True
   b) _____ False

5) Referential integrity ensures that each value in a foreign key column of the child table links back to a matching primary key value in the parent table.

   a) _____ True
   b) _____ False

Answers appear in Appendix A, Section 1.1.

LAB 1.2

TABLE RELATIONSHIPS

LAB OBJECTIVES

After this lab, you will be able to:

✔ Read a Schema Diagram
✔ Identify Data Normalization Rules and Table Relationships
✔ Understand the Database Development Context

Although this is a book about SQL, you must understand the basic concepts, terminology, and issues involving database design to be able to understand why tables are organized in specific ways. This lab will introduce you to the practical aspects of designing tables and determining their respective relationships to each other.

DATA NORMALIZATION

The objective of *normalization* is the elimination of redundancy in tables, therefore avoiding any future data manipulation problems. There are a number of different rules for minimizing duplication of data, which are formulated into the various *normal forms*.

The rules verify that the columns you placed in the tables do in fact belong there. You design your tables, the appropriate columns, and the matching primary and foreign keys to comply with these rules. This process is called normalization. The normalization rules will be quite intuitive after you have read through the examples in this lab. Although there are many normalization rules, the *five normal forms* and the *Boyce–Codd normal form* (BCNF) are the most widely accepted. This lab will discuss the first three normal forms because programmers and analysts typically don't bother normalizing beyond third normal form—with the exception of experienced database designers.

FIRST NORMAL FORM

For a table to be in *first normal form*, all repeating groups must be removed and placed in a new table. The example in Figure 1.8 illustrates the repeating groups in the BOOK table. The table has the location information of various warehouses across the country where the title is stocked. The location is listed in three columns as LOCATION_1 LOCATION_2, and LOCATION_3.

BOOK Table

BOOK_ID	TITLE	RETAIL_PRICE	LOCATION_1	LOCATION_2	LOCATION_3
1010	The Invisible Force	29.95	New York	San Francisco	
1011	Into The Sky	39.95	Chicago		
1012	Making It Possible	59.95	Miami	Austin	New York

Figure 1.8 ■ Repeating group.

Imagine the scenario when you have more than three locations for a book. To avoid this and other problems, the database designer will move the location information to a separate table named BOOK_LOCATION, as illustrated in Figure 1.9. This design is more flexible and allows the storing of books at an unlimited number of locations.

BOOK Table

BOOK_ID	TITLE	RETAIL_PRICE
1010	The Invisible Force	29.95
1011	Into The Sky	39.95
1012	Making It Possible	59.95

BOOK_LOCATION Table

BOOK_ID	LOCATION
1010	New York
1010	San Francisco
1011	Chicago
1012	Miami
1012	Austin
1012	New York

Figure 1.9 ■ Tables in first normal form.

SECOND NORMAL FORM

Second normal form states that all nonkey columns must depend on the entire primary key, not just part of it. This form only applies to tables that have composite primary keys. Figure 1.10 shows the BOOK_AUTHOR table with both the

BOOK_ID	AUTHOR_ID	ROYALTY_SHARE	AUTHOR_PHONE_NO
10001	900	100	212-555-1212
10002	901	75	901-555-1212
10002	900	25	212-555-1212
10003	902	100	899-555-1212

Figure 1.10 ■ Violation of second normal form in the BOOK_AUTHOR table.

BOOK_ID and AUTHOR_ID as the composite primary key. In this example, authors with the ID 900 and 901 coauthored the book with the ID of 10002. If you add the author's phone number to the table, the second normal form is violated because the phone number is dependent only on the AUTHOR_ID, not on the BOOK_ID. Note ROYALTY_SHARE is dependent completely on the combination of both columns because the percentage of the royalty varies from book to book and is split among authors.

THIRD NORMAL FORM

The *third normal form* goes a step further than the second normal form: It states that every nonkey column must be a fact about the primary key column. The third normal form is quite intuitive. Figure 1.11 shows a table that violates third normal form. The PUBLISHER_PHONE_NO column is not dependent on the primary key column BOOK_ID but on the PUBLISHER_NAME column. Therefore, it should not be part of the BOOK table.

Instead, the publisher's phone number should be stored in a separate table called PUBLISHER. This has the advantage that when a publisher's phone number is updated, it only needs to be updated in one place, rather than all occurrences of this publisher in the BOOK table. Removing the PUBLISHER_PHONE_NO column eliminates redundancy and avoids any possibilities of data inconsistencies (see Figure 1.12).

The BOOK table can also benefit by introducing a surrogate key, such as a PUBLISHER_ID. Such a key is not subject to changes and is easily referenced in any additional tables that may need to refer to data about the publisher.

BOOK Table

BOOK_ID	TITLE	PUBLISHER_NAME	PUBLISH_DATE	PUBLISHER_PHONE_NO
1010	The Invisible Force	Literacy Circle	12/01	801-111-1111
1011	Into The Sky	Prentice Hall	10/02	999-888-1212
1012	Making It Possible	Life Books	2/99	777-555-1212
1013	Wonders of the World	Literacy Circle	5/99	801-111-1111

Figure 1.11 ■ Violation of third normal form.

BOOK Table

BOOK_ID	TITLE	PUBLISHER_ID	PUBLISH_DATE
1010	The Invisible Force	1	12/01
1011	Into The Sky	2	10/02
1012	Making It Possible	3	2/99
1013	Wonders of the World	1	5/99

PUBLISHER Table

PUBLISHER_ID	PUBLISHER_NAME	PUBLISHER_PHONE_NO
1	Literacy Circle	801-111-1111
2	Pen Books	999-888-1212
3	Life Books	777-555-1212

Figure 1.12 ■ Tables in third normal form.

BOYCE–CODD NORMAL FORM, FOURTH NORMAL FORM, AND FIFTH NORMAL FORM

The Boyce-Codd normal form is an even more elaborate version of the third normal form and deals with deletion anomalies. The *fourth normal form* tackles potential problems when three or more columns are part of the unique identifier and their dependencies to each other. The *fifth normal form* splits the tables even further apart to eliminate all redundancy. These different normal forms are beyond the scope of this book; for more details, please consult one of the many excellent books on database design.

TABLE RELATIONSHIPS

When two tables have a common column or columns, the tables are said to have a *relationship* between them. The *cardinality* of a relationship is the actual number of occurrences for each entity. We will explore one-to-one, one-to-many, and many-to-many relationships.

ONE-TO-MANY RELATIONSHIP (1:M)

Figure 1.13 shows the CUSTOMER table and the ORDER table. The common column is CUSTOMER_ID. The link between the two tables is a *one-to-many* relationship, the most common type of relationship. This means that "one" individual customer can have "many" order rows in the ORDER table. This relationship represents the business rule that "one customer can place one or many orders (or no orders)." Reading the relationship in the other direction, an order is associated with only one customer row (or no customer rows). In other words, "each order may be placed by one and only one customer."

CUSTOMER Table

PRIMARY KEY▾

CUSTOMER_ID	CUSTOMER_NAME	ADDRESS	PHONE	ZIP
2010	Movers, Inc.	123 Park Lane	212-555-1212	10095
2011	Acme Mfg Ltd.	555 Broadway	212-566-1212	10004
2012	ALR Inc.	50 Fifth Avenue	212-999-1212	10010

**LAB
1.2**

ORDER Table

PRIMARY KEY▾   ▾FOREIGN KEY

ORDER_ID	CUSTOMER_ID	ORDER_DATE	TOTAL_ORDER_AMOUNT
100	2010	12/23/01	$500
101	2012	01/05/02	$600
102	2010	07/20/02	$100
103	2010	08/25/02	$400
104	2010	09/20/02	$200

Figure 1.13 ■ One-to-many relationship example between CUSTOMER and ORDER table.

ONE-TO-ONE RELATIONSHIP (1:1)

One-to-one relationships exist in the database world, but they are not typical because most often data from both tables are combined into one table for simplicity. Figure 1.14 shows an example of a *one-to-one* relationship between the PRODUCT table and the PRODUCT_PRICE table. For every row in the PRODUCT table you may find only "one" matching row in the PRODUCT_PRICE table. And for every row in the PRODUCT_PRICE table there is "one" matching row in the

PRODUCT

▾PRIMARY KEY

PRODUCT_ID	PRODUCT_NAME	MANUFACTURER
10001	Bolt	ACME, Inc.
10002	Screw	KR Mfg.
10003	Nail	ABC, Ltd.

PRODUCT_PRICE

▾FOREIGN KEY & PRIMARY KEY

PRODUCT_ID	RETAIL_PRICE	IN_STOCK_QTY
10001	$0.45	10,000
10002	$0.02	20,000
10003	$0.10	50,000

Figure 1.14 ■ One-to-one relationship example.

PRODUCT table. If the two tables are combined, the RETAIL_PRICE and IN_STOCK_QTY columns can be included in the PRODUCT table.

MANY-TO-MANY RELATIONSHIP (M:M)

The examination of Figure 1.15 reveals a *many-to-many* relationship between the BOOK and AUTHOR tables. One book can have one or more authors and one author can write one or more books. The relational database model requires the resolution of many-to-many relationships into one-to-many relationship tables. This is done by creating an *associative table* (also called an *intersection table*). The solution in this example is achieved via the BOOK_AUTHOR table. Figure 1.16 shows the columns of this table.

The BOOK_AUTHOR table lists the individual author(s) for each book and shows, for a particular author, the book(s) he or she wrote. The primary key of the BOOK_AUTHOR table is the combination of both columns: the BOOK_ID column and the AUTHOR_ID column. These two columns represent the concatenated primary key that uniquely identifies a row in the table. As you may recall from the previous lab, multicolumn primary keys are referred to as a composite or concatenated primary key. Additionally, the BOOK_AUTHOR table has the AUTHOR_ID and the BOOK_ID as two individual foreign keys linking back to the AUTHOR and the BOOK table, respectively.

The BOOK_AUTHOR table contains an additional column, the ROYALTY_SHARE column. It identifies the royalty percentage for each author for an individual book. When there are multiple authors, the percentage of the royalty is split; in the case of a sole author the share is 100%. This column is appropriately located in the BOOK_AUTHOR table as the values are relevant for the combination of the BOOK_ID and AUTHOR_ID. This combination of columns uniquely identifies both a book and an author and the respective percentage share of the royalty.

BOOK

BOOK_ID	TITLE	RETAIL_PRICE
10001	Call in the Dark	39.95
10002	The Spy	29.95
10003	Perspectives	59.95

Primary Key → (BOOK_ID)

AUTHOR

AUTHOR_ID	FIRST_NAME	LAST_NAME
900	King	John
901	Oats	Heather
902	Turrow	Stephen

Primary Key → (AUTHOR_ID)

Figure 1.15 ■ Many-to-many relationship example.

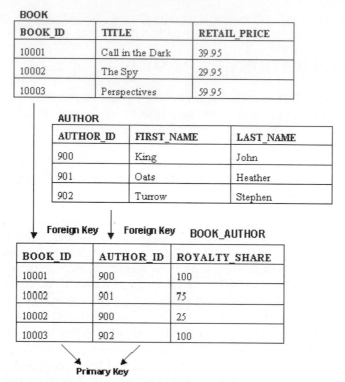

Figure 1.16 ■ Associative BOOK_AUTHOR table that resolves the many-to-many relationship.

DRAWING RELATIONSHIPS

For clarity of meaning and conceptual consistency, it is useful to show table relationships using drawings (called *schema diagrams*) and there are a number of standard notations for this type of diagram. For example, Figure 1.17 illustrates one of the ways to graphically depict the relationship between tables. The convention used in this book for a one-to-many relationship is a line with a "crow's foot" (fork) on one end indicating the "many" side of the relationship; at the other end, a "single line" depicts the "one" side of the relationship. You will see the use of the *crow's-foot notation* throughout this book. Software diagramming programs that support the graphical display of relational database models often allow you to choose your notation preference.

CARDINALITY AND OPTIONALITY

The cardinality expresses the ratio of a parent and child table from the perspective of the parent table. It describes how many rows you may find between the two tables for a given primary key value. For example, in Figure 1.13 you saw a one-to-many relationship between the CUSTOMER and ORDER tables and the relationship ratio is expressed in the form of a 1:M ratio.

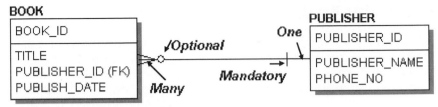

Figure 1.17 ■ Crow's foot notation.

Graphical relationship lines indicate the *optionality* of a relationship, whether a row is required or not (mandatory or optional). Specifically, optionality shows if one row in a table can exist without a row in the related table.

Figure 1.17 shows a one-to-many relationship between the PUBLISHER (parent) and the BOOK (child). Examining the relationship line on the "many" end, you notice a "circle" identifying the *optional relationship* and a crow's foot indicating "many." The symbols indicate that a publisher *may* publish zero, one, or many books. You use the word "may" to indicate that the relationship is *optional* and allows a publisher to exist without a corresponding value in the BOOK table.

The relationship line also reads the other way. The solid line on the PUBLISHER end of the line indicates the "one" side, a "vertical bar" intersects it and this bar identifies a *mandatory relationship*. You read this direction of the relationship as "One book *must* be published by one and only one publisher." This means a row in the BOOK table must always have the PUBLISHER_ID value filled in. It cannot be null because that means unknown and indicates there is no associated PUBLISHER row.

The "(FK)" symbol next to the PUBLISHER_ID column indicates that this is a foreign key column. In this diagram, the primary key is separated from the other columns with a line; you observe the BOOK_ID and the PUBLISHER_ID as the primary keys or unique identifiers.

Figure 1.18 shows an optional relationship on both sides; a book may be published by zero or one publisher. Effectively, this means the value in the PUBLISHER_ID column in BOOK is optional. Reading the relationship from the PUBLISHER, you can say that "one publisher may publish zero, one, or many books" (which is identical to Figure 1.17).

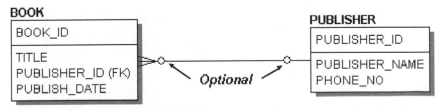

Figure 1.18 ■ Optional relationship on both sides.

REAL-WORLD BUSINESS PRACTICE

You will typically see only these two types of relationships: First, mandatory on the "one" side and optional on the "many" end as in Figure 1.17; and second, optional on both ends as in Figure 1.18. Only rarely will you find other types of relationships. For example, mandatory relationships on both sides are infrequently implemented—this means that rows must be inserted in both tables simultaneously. Occasionally, you will find one-to-one relationships, but most often the columns from both tables are combined into one table. Many-to-many relationships are not allowed in the relational database; they must be resolved via an associative or intersection table into one-to-many relationships.

LABELING RELATIONSHIPS

To clarify and explain the nature of the relationship on the diagram, it's useful to add a label or name with a verb on the relationship line. Figure 1.19 shows an example of a labeled relationship. For the utmost clarity, a relationship should be labeled on both sides. You then read it as: "One PUBLISHER may publish zero, one, or many BOOKs; and one BOOK must be published by one and only one PUBLISHER." This kind of labeling makes the relationship perfectly clear and states the relationship in terms that a business user can understand.

IDENTIFYING AND NONIDENTIFYING RELATIONSHIPS

In an *identifying relationship,* the foreign key is propagated to the child entity as the primary key. This is in contrast to a *nonidentifying relationship,* in which the foreign key becomes one of the nonkey columns. Nonidentifying relationships may accept a null value in the foreign key column.

Figure 1.20 depicts some of the tables used in the lab; the many-to-many relationship between the BOOK and AUTHOR tables is now resolved to the associative table called BOOK_AUTHOR. If a graphical representation of a table's box has *rounded edges,* it means that the relationship is *identifying.* Effectively, one of the foreign keys became the primary key or part of the primary key. In the case of the BOOK_AUTHOR table, both foreign key columns constitute the primary key and both columns may not be null because a primary key is never null.

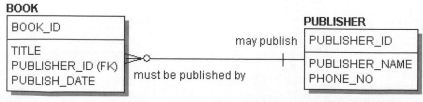

Figure 1.19 ■ **Labeled relationship between BOOK and PUBLISHER.**

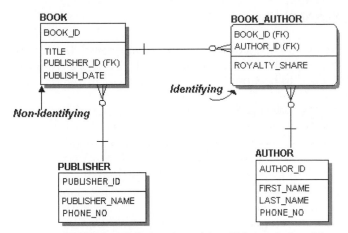

Figure 1.20 ■ Identifying and nonidentifying relationships.

The relationship between the PUBLISHER and BOOK tables is nonidentifying, as indicated by the sharp edges. The foreign key column PUBLISHER_ID is not part of the primary key. The foreign key columns of a nonidentifying relationship may be either NULL or NOT NULL. In this instance, you can determine if a null is allowed by checking if the relationship is optional or mandatory. Although the foreign key column allows null values in non-identifying relationships, here the relationship depicts a single bar on the relationship line. Effectively, for every row in the BOOK table there must be a corresponding row in the PUBLISHER table and the PUBLISHER_ID column of the BOOK table cannot be null.

DATABASE DEVELOPMENT CONTEXT

Now that you are familiar with the some of the relational database terminology and its core concepts, you are ready to learn about how all this information fits into the context of database development. From the initial idea of an application until the final system implementation, the data model is continuously refined. Figure 1.21 indicates the essential phases of the development project with respect to the database.

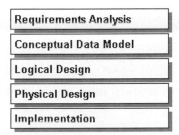

Figure 1.21 ■ Database development and design phases.

REQUIREMENTS ANALYSIS

Initially, the process starts off with gathering data requirements that identify the needs and wants of the users. One of the outputs of this phase is a list of individual data elements that need to be stored in the database.

CONCEPTUAL DATA MODEL

The *conceptual data model* logically groups the major data elements from the requirements analysis into individual *entities*. An entity is just something of significance for which you need to store data. For example, all data related to books such as the title, publish date, and retail price are placed in the book entity. Data elements such as the author's name and address are part of the author entity. The individual data elements are referred to as *attributes*.

You designate a *unique identifier* or *candidate key* that uniquely distinguishes a row in the entity. Notice that in this conceptual data model we use the terms entity, attribute, and candidate key or unique identifier instead of table, column, and primary key, respectively.

Noncritical attributes are not included in the model to emphasize the business meaning of those entities, attributes, and relationships. Many-to-many relationships are acceptable and not resolved. The diagram of the conceptual model is useful to communicate the initial understanding of the requirements to business users. The conceptual model gives no consideration to the implementation platform or database software. Many projects skip the conceptual model and go directly to the logical model.

LOGICAL DATA MODEL

The purpose of the *logical data model* is to show that all of the entities, their respective attributes, and the relationship between entities represent the business requirements without considering technical issues. The focus is entirely on business problems and considers a design that accommodates growth and change. The entities and attributes require descriptive names and documentation of their meaning. Labeling and documenting the relationships between entities clarify the business rules between them.

The diagram may show the datatype of an attribute in general terms such as text, number, and date. In many logical design models you will find foreign key columns identified: in others they are implied.

The complete model is called the *logical data model* or *Entity Relationship Diagram* (ERD). At the end of the analysis phase the entities are fully normalized, the unique identifier for each entity is determined, and any many-to-many relationships are resolved into associative entities.

PHYSICAL DATA MODEL

The *physical data model*, also referred to as the *schema diagram,* is a graphical model of the physical design implementation of the database. This physical schema diagram is what the programmers and you will use to learn about the database and the relationship between the tables. In Lab 1.3 you will be introduced to the STUDENT schema diagram used throughout this workbook.

This physical data model is derived from the fully normalized logical model. Before the actual implementation (installation) of the physical data model in the database, multiple physical data models may exist. They represent a variety of alternative physical database designs that consider the performance implications and application constraints. One of the physical design models will be implemented in the database. The schema diagram graphically represents the chosen implemented physical data model; it is specific to a particular RDBMS product such as Oracle.

Figure 1.22 depicts the schema diagram of the book publishing database discussed in this chapter. It shows the structure of the tables with their respective columns, and it illustrates the relationships between the tables.

The physical data model has a different terminology than the conceptual or logical data model. The physical data model refers to tables instead of entities; the individual pieces of data are columns instead of attributes in the logical model.

TRANSFER FROM LOGICAL TO PHYSICAL MODEL

The transfer from the logical to the physical models—which ultimately means the actual implementation in a database as tables, columns, primary keys, foreign keys, indexes, and so on—requires a number of steps and considerations. The entities identified in the logical data model are resolved to physical tables; the entity name is often identical to the table name. Some designers use singular

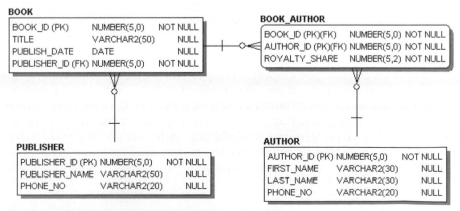

Figure 1.22 ■ Book publishing database diagram.

names for entities and plural names for tables; others abbreviate the entity names when implementing the physical model to follow certain business naming standards. Frequently, the physical data model includes additional tables for specific technical implementation requirements and programming purposes such as a report queue table or an error log table.

As mentioned, attributes become columns with names being either identical or following business naming conventions and abbreviations. The columns are associated with the database software vendor's specific datatypes, which considers valid column lengths and restrictions. Individual data entry formats are determined (e.g., phone numbers must be in numeric format with dashes between). Rules for maintaining data integrity and consistency are created and physical storage parameters for individual tables are determined. You will learn about these and many other aspects of creating these restrictions in Chapter 11, "Create, Alter, and Drop Tables." Sometimes additional columns are added that were never in the logical design with the purpose of storing precalculated values; this is referred to as *denormalization,* which we will discuss shortly.

Another activity that occurs in the physical data design phase is the design of indexes. *Indexes* are database objects that facilitate speedy access to data with the help of a specific column or columns of a table. Placing indexes on tables is necessary to optimize efficient query performance, but indexes have the negative impact of requiring additional time for insert, update, or delete operations. Balancing the trade-offs with the advantages requires careful consideration of these factors, including knowledge in optimizing SQL statements and an understanding of the features of a particular database version. You will learn more about different types of indexes and the success factors of a well-placed index strategy in Chapter 12, "Views, Indexes, and Sequences."

Database designers must be knowledgeable and experienced in many aspects of programming, design, and database administration to fully understand how design decisions impact cost, system interfaces, programming effort, and future maintenance.

    Poor physical database design is very costly and difficult to correct.

You may wonder how the graphical models you see in this book are produced. Specific software packages allow you to visually design the various models, and they allow you to display different aspects of it such as showing only table names or showing table names, columns, and their respective datatypes. Many of these tools even allow you to generate the DDL SQL statements to create the tables. For a list of software tools that allow you to visually produce the diagrams, see the book's Web site at http://authors.phptr.com/rischert3e and Appendix H, "Resources."

DENORMALIZATION

Denormalization is the act of adding redundancy to the physical database design. Typically, logical models are fully normalized or at least in third normal form. When designing the physical model, database designers must weigh the benefit of eliminating all redundancy with data split into many tables against potentially poor performance when these many tables are joined.

Therefore, database designers, also called database architects, sometimes purposely add redundancy to their physical design. Only experienced database designers should do denormalization. Increasing redundancy may greatly increase the overall programming effort because now many copies of the same data must be kept in sync; however, the time it takes to query data may be less.

In some applications, particularly data warehousing applications where massive amounts of detailed data are stored and summarized, denormalization is required. *Data warehouse applications* are database applications that benefit users that need to analyze large data sets from various angles and use this data for reporting and decision-making purposes. Typically, the source of the data warehouse is historical transaction data, but it can also include data from various other sources for the purpose of consolidating data. For example, the purchasing department of a supermarket chain could determine how many turkeys to order for a specific store on the week before Thanksgiving or use the data to determine what promotional offers have the largest sales impact on stores with certain customer demographics.

The primary purpose of a data warehouse is to query, report, and analyze data. Therefore, redundancy is encouraged and necessary for queries to perform efficiently.

LAB 1.2 EXERCISES

1.2.1 READ A SCHEMA DIAGRAM

    a) Describe the nature of the relationship between the ORDER_HEADER table and the ORDER_DETAIL table (Figure 1.23).

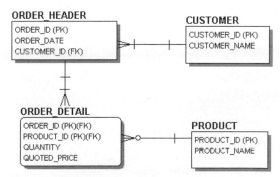

Figure 1.23 ■ **Order tables.**

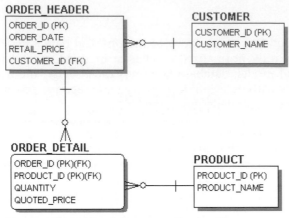

Figure 1.24 ■ Not fully normalized table.

1.2.2 IDENTIFY DATA NORMALIZATION RULES AND TABLE RELATIONSHIPS

a) One of the tables in Figure 1.24 is not fully normalized. Which normal form is violated? Draw a new diagram.

b) How would you change Figure 1.24 to add information about the sales representative who took the order?

c) How would you change Figure 1.25 if an employee does not need to belong to a department?

d) Based on Figure 1.25, why do you think the social security number (SSN) column should not be the primary key of the EMPLOYEE table?

1.2.3 UNDERSTAND THE DATABASE DEVELOPMENT CONTEXT

a) Figures 1.26 and 1.27 depict the logical and physical model of a fictional movie rental database. What differences do you notice between the following entity relationship diagram and the physical schema diagram?

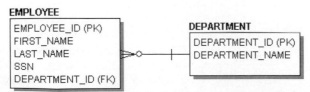

Figure 1.25 ■ EMPLOYEE to DEPARTMENT relationship.

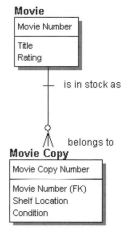

is in stock as

belongs to

Movie Copy

Movie Copy Number
Movie Number (FK)
Shelf Location
Condition

Figure 1.26 ■
Logical Data Model.

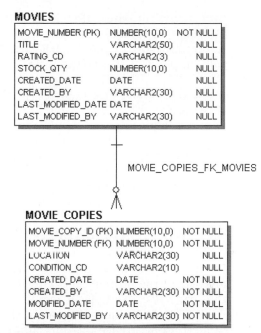

MOVIE_COPIES_FK_MOVIES

Figure 1.27 ■ Physical Data Model.

LAB 1.2 EXERCISE ANSWERS

1.2.1 ANSWERS

a) Describe the nature of the relationship between the ORDER_HEADER table and the ORDER_DETAIL table (Figure 1.23).

Answer: The relationship depicts a mandatory one-to-many relationship between the ORDER_HEADER and the ORDER_DETAIL tables. The ORDER_HEADER table contains data found only once for each order, such as the ORDER_ID, the CUSTOMER_ID, and the ORDER_DATE. The ORDER_DETAIL table holds information about the individual order lines of an order. One row in the ORDER_HEADER table must have one or many order details. One ORDER_DETAIL row must have one and only one corresponding row in the ORDER_HEADER table.

MANDATORY RELATIONSHIP ON BOTH ENDS

The mandatory relationship indicates from the ORDER_HEADER to ORDER_DETAIL that a row in the ORDER_HEADER table cannot exist unless a row in ORDER_DETAIL is created simultaneously. This is a "chicken and egg" problem whereby a row in the ORDER_HEADER table cannot be created without an ORDER_DETAIL row and vice versa. In fact, it really doesn't matter as long as you create the rows within one transaction. Furthermore, you must make sure that every row in the ORDER_HEADER table has at least one row in the ORDER_DETAIL table and rows in the ORDER_DETAIL table have exactly one corresponding row in the ORDER_HEADER table. There are various ways to physically implement this relationship.

Another example of a mandatory relationship on the figure is the relationship between ORDER_HEADER and CUSTOMER. You can see the bar on the many side of the relationship as an indication for the mandatory row. That means a customer must have placed an order before a row in the CUSTOMER table is saved, and an order can only be placed by a customer.

However, for most practical purposes a mandatory relationship on both ends is rarely implemented unless there is a very specific and important requirement.

NO DUPLICATES ALLOWED

On the previous diagrams, such as Figure 1.23, you noticed that some foreign keys are part of the primary key. This is frequently the case in associative entities; in this particular example, it requires the combination of ORDER_ID and PRODUCT_ID to be unique. Ultimately, the effect is that a single order containing the same product twice is not allowed. Figure 1.28 lists sample data in the ORDER_DETAIL table for ORDER_ID 345 and PRODUCT_ID P90, which violates the primary key and is therefore not allowed. Instead, you must create one order with a quantity of 10 or create a second order with a different ORDER_ID so the primary key is not violated. You will learn about how Oracle responds with error messages when you attempt to violate the primary key constraint and other types of constraints in Chapter 10, "Insert, Update, and Delete."

ORDER_DETAIL Table

ORDER_ID	PRODUCT_ID	QUANTITY	QUOTED_PRICE
123	P90	5	$50
234	S999	9	$12
345	P90	7	$50
345	X85	3	$10
345	P90	3	$50

Figure 1.28 ■ Sample data of the ORDER_DETAIL table.

1.2.2 ANSWERS

a) One of the tables in Figure 1.24 is not fully normalized. Which normal form is violated? Draw a new diagram.

Answer: The third normal form is violated on the ORDER_HEADER table. The RETAIL_PRICE column belongs to the PRODUCT table instead (Figure 1.29).

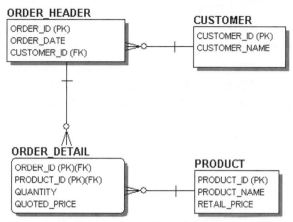

Figure 1.29 ■ Fully normalized tables.

Third normal form states that every nonkey column must be a fact about the primary key column, which is the ORDER_ID column in the ORDER_HEADER table. This is clearly not the case in the ORDER_HEADER table, as the RETAIL PRICE column is not a fact about the ORDER_HEADER and does not depend upon the ORDER_ID; it is a fact about the PRODUCT. The QUOTED_PRICE column is included in the ORDER_DETAIL table because the price may vary over time, from order to order, and from customer to customer. (If you want to track any changes in the retail price, you may want to create a separate table, called PRODUCT_PRICE_HISTORY, that keeps track of the retail price per product and the effective date of each price change.) Table 1.2 provides a review of the normal forms.

Table 1.2 ■ The Three Normal Forms

Description	Rule
First Normal Form (1NF)	No repeating groups are permitted
Second Normal Form (2NF)	No partial key dependencies are permitted
Third Normal Form (3NF)	No nonkey dependencies are permitted.

b) How would you change Figure 1.24 to add information about the sales representative who took the order?

Answer: As you see in Figure 1.30, you need to add another table that contains the sales representative's name, SALES_REP_ID, and any other important information. The SALESREP_ID then becomes a foreign key in the ORDER_HEADER table.

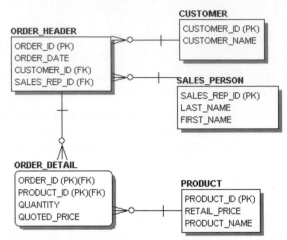

Figure 1.30 ■ **ORDER_HEADER** with **SALES_REP_ID** column.

c) How would you change Figure 1.25 if an employee does not need to belong to a department?

Answer: You change the relationship line on the DEPARTMENT table end to make it optional. This has the effect that the DEPARTMENT_ID column on the EMPLOYEE table can be null; that is, a value is not required (Figure 1.31).

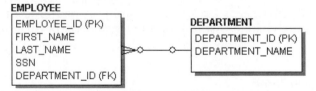

Figure 1.31 ■ **EMPLOYEE to DEPARTMENT** with optional relationship line.

d) Based on Figure 1.25, why do you think the social security number (SSN) column should not be the primary key of the EMPLOYEE table?

Answer: The requirement for a primary key is that it is unique, not subject to updates, and not null.

Although the SSN is unique, there have been incidents (though rare) of individuals with the same SSN or individuals who had to change their SSN. It is conceivable to have an employee without a SSN assigned yet (e.g., a legal alien with a work permit), hence the column is null. There is a myriad of reasons for not using a SSN, therefore it's best to create a surrogate or artificial key.

1.2.3 ANSWERS

a) Figures 1.26 and 1.27 depict the logical and physical model of a fictional movie rental database. What differences do you notice between the following entity relationship diagram and the physical schema diagram?

Answer: You can spot a number of differences between the logical model (entity relational diagram) and the physical model (schema diagram). While some logical and physical models are identical, these figures exhibit distinguishing differences you may find in the real world.

The entity name of the logical model is singular versus plural for the table name on the physical model. Some table names have special prefixes that denote the type of application the table belongs to. For example, if a table belongs to the purchase order system, it may be prefixed with PO_; if it belongs to the accounts payable system, the prefix is AP_; and so on. In the logical model, the spaces are allowed for table and column names. Typically, in Oracle implementations, table names are defined in uppercase and use the underscore (_) character to separate words.

Although the logical model may include the datatypes, here the datatype (such as DATE, VARCHAR2, NUMBER) shows on the physical model only. The physical model also indicates if a column allows NULL values.

The attribute and column names differ between the two models. For example, the RATING attribute changed to RATING_CD, which indicates the values are encoded, such as, for example, "PG" rather than a descriptive "Parental Guidance" value. Designers create or follow established naming conventions and abbreviations for consistency. Naming conventions can help describe the type of values stored in the column.

The STOCK_QTY is another example of using the abbreviation QTY to express that the column holds a quantity of copies. Notice this column is absent from the logical model; it is a *derived column*. The quantity of movies for an individual movie title could be determined from the MOVIE_COPIES table. The database designer deliberately denormalized the table by adding this column. This simplifies any queries that determine how many copies of this particular title exist. Rather than issuing another query that counts the number of rows in the MOVIE_COPIES for the specific title, this column can be queried. Adding a derived column to a table requires that the value stays in sync with the data in the related table (MOVIE_COPIES in this case). The synchronization can be accomplished by writing a program that is executed from the end user's screen. Alternatively, the developer could write a trigger on the table that automatically updates the STOCK_QTY value whenever a new row is added or deleted on the MOVIE_COPIES table for each individual title. (For an example of a table trigger, refer to Chapter 12, "Create, Alter, and Drop Tables.")

The schema diagram prominently exhibits columns that did not exist in the logical data model, namely CREATED_DATE, MODIFIED_DATE, CREATED_BY, and MODIFIED_BY. Collectively, these columns are sometimes referred to as "audit columns." They keep information about when a row was created and last changed together with the respective user that executed this action.

On the logical data model the relationship is labeled in both directions. On the physical model, the name of the foreign key constraint between the tables is listed instead. You may find that some physical models depict no label at all. There are no set standards for how a physical or logical model must graphically look and therefore the diagrams produced by various software vendors that offer diagramming tools not only look different, they also allow a number of different display options.

LAB 1.2 SELF-REVIEW QUESTIONS

In order to test your progress, you should be able to answer the following questions.

1) An entity relationship diagram depicts entities, attributes, and tables.

   a) _____ True
   b) _____ False

2) The crow's foot depicts the M of a 1:M relationship.

   a) _____ True
   b) _____ False

3) Repeating groups are a violation of the first normal form.

   a) _____ True
   b) _____ False

4) The logical model is derived from the schema diagram.

   a) _____ True
   b) _____ False

5) The concept of denormalization deals with eliminating redundancy.

   a) _____ True
   b) _____ False

6) When you issue a SQL statement, you are concerned with the logical design of the database.

   a) _____ True
   b) _____ False

7) In a mandatory relationship, null values are not allowed in the foreign key column.

    a) _____ True
    b) _____ False

8) A nonidentifying relationship means that the foreign key is propagated as a non-key attribute in the child entity or child table.

    a) _____ True
    b) _____ False

Answers appear in Appendix A, Section 1.2.

**LAB
1.2**

L A B   1 . 3

THE STUDENT
SCHEMA DIAGRAM

L A B   O B J E C T I V E S

After this lab, you will be able to:
- ✔ Understand the STUDENT Schema Diagram and Identify Table Relationships

Throughout this book, the database for a school's computer education program is used as a case study upon which all exercises are based. If you have worked through the previous two labs, you know that the schema diagram is a model of data that reflects the relationships among data in a database. The name of the case study schema diagram is STUDENT. Before you begin to write SQL statements against the database, it is important to familiarize yourself with the diagram. You can find this graphical representation in Appendix D, "Student Database Schema."

In this book you will be frequently referring to the STUDENT schema diagram shown in Appendix D, "STUDENT Database Schema." Rather than flipping back and forth, you may find it more convenient to print out the schema diagram from the companion Web site of this book located at http://authors.phptr.com/rischert3e.

THE STUDENT TABLE

Examine the STUDENT schema diagram and locate the STUDENT table. This table contains data about individual students, such as their names, addresses, employers, and dates they registered in the program.

DATATYPES

Next to each column name in the diagram you find the datatype of the column. Each column contains a different kind of data, which can be classified by a datatype. You will notice that the FIRST_NAME column is of datatype VARCHAR2(25). This means that a variable length of (with a maximum of 25) alphanumeric characters (letters or numbers) may be stored in this column. Another datatype, the CHAR datatype, also stores alphanumeric data, but is a fixed-length datatype and pads any unused space in the column with blanks until it reaches the defined column length. The STUDENT_ID column is of datatype NUMBER with a maximum number of eight integer digits and no decimal place digits; the column is the primary key as denoted with the "(PK)" symbol. Oracle also provides a DATE datatype (as seen on the CREATED_DATE and MODIFIED_DATE columns) that stores both the date and time. You will learn more about the various datatypes in the next chapter.

Next to each column, the schema diagram indicates if a column allows NULL values. A NULL value is an unknown value. A space or value of zero is not the same as NULL. When a column in a row is defined as allowing NULL values, it means that a column does not need to contain a value. When a column is defined as NOT NULL it must always contain a value.

You will observe that the STUDENT table does not show the city and state. This information can be looked up via the foreign key column ZIP as indicated with the "(FK)" symbol after the column name. The ZIP column is a NOT NULL column and requires that every student row have a corresponding zip code entered.

THE COURSE TABLE

The COURSE table lists all the available courses that a student may take. The primary key of the table is the COURSE_NO column. The DESCRIPTION column shows the course description and the COST column lists the dollar amount charged for the enrollment in the course. The PREREQUISITE column displays the course number that must be taken as a prerequisite to this course. This column is a foreign key column and its values refer back the COURSE_NO column. Only valid COURSE_NO values may be listed in this column. The relationship line of the COURSE table to itself represents a *recursive* or *self-referencing relationship*.

RECURSIVE RELATIONSHIP

As the term recursive or self-referencing relationship implies, a column in the COURSE table refers back to another column in the same table. The PREREQUISITE column refers back to the COURSE_NO column, which provides the list of acceptable values (also referred to as a *domain*) for the PREREQUISITE column. Because the relationship is optional, the foreign key column PREREQUISITE column allows null. Recursive relationships are always optional relationships; otherwise, there is no starting point in the hierarchy.

Figure 1.32 lists an excerpt of data from the COURSE table. Notice that the courses with the COURSE_NO column values of 10 and 20 do not have a value in the PREREQUISITE column: Those are the courses that a student must take to be able to take any subsequent courses (unless equivalent experience can be substituted). Course number 20 is a prerequisite course for course number 100, Hands-On-Windows, and course number 140, Structured Analysis. You will explore more about the intricacies of recursive relationships in Chapter 15, "Regular Expressions and Hierarchical Queries."

COURSE_NO	DESCRIPTION	PREREQUISITE	...
10	DP Overview		...
20	Intro to Computers		...
100	Hands-On Windows	20	...
140	Structured Analysis	20	...
25	Intro to Programming	140	...
...	...	...	...

Figure 1.32 ■ Data from the COURSE table.

THE SECTION TABLE

The SECTION table includes all the individual sections a course may have. An individual course may have zero, one, or many sections, each of which can be taught at different rooms, times, and by different instructors. The primary key of the table is the SECTION_ID. The foreign key that links back to the COURSE table is the COURSE_NO column. The SECTION_NO column identifies the individual section number. For example, for the first section of a course, it contains the number 1; the second section lists the number 2, and so on. The two columns, COURSE_NO and SECTION_NO, also uniquely identify a row, but SECTION_ID has been created instead. This SECTION_ID column is called a surrogate key because it does not have any meaning to the user.

The column START_DATE_TIME shows the date and time the section meets for the first time. The LOCATION column lists the classroom. The CAPACITY column shows the maximum number of students that may enroll in this section. The INSTRUCTOR_ID column is another foreign key column within the SECTION table; it links back to the INSTRUCTOR table. The relationship between the SECTION and the INSTRUCTOR table indicates that an instructor must always be assigned to a section. The INSTRUCTOR_ID column of the SECTION table may never be null and when you read the relationship from the opposite end, you can say that an individual instructor may teach zero, one, or multiple sections.

The relationship line leading from the COURSE table to the SECTION table means that a course may have zero, one, or multiple sections. Conversely, every individual section *must* have a corresponding row in the COURSE table.

Relationships between tables are based on *business rules*. In this case, the business rule is that a course can exist without a section, but a section cannot exist unless it is assigned to a course. As mentioned, this is indicated with the bar (|) on the other end of the relationship line. Most of the child relationships on the schema diagram are considered mandatory relationships (with two exceptions); this dictates that the foreign key columns in the child table must contain a value (must be NOT NULL) and that value must correspond to a row in the parent table via its primary key value.

THE INSTRUCTOR TABLE

The INSTRUCTOR table lists information related to an individual instructor, such as name, address, phone, and zip code. The ZIP column is the foreign key column to the ZIPCODE table. The relationship between the INSTRUCTOR and the ZIPCODE is an optional relationship so a null value in the ZIP column is allowed. For a given ZIP column value, there is one and only one value in the ZIPCODE table. For a given ZIP value in the ZIPCODE table you may find zero, one, or many of the same value in the INSTRUCTOR table. Another foreign key relationship exists to the SECTION table: An instructor may teach zero, one, or multiple sections, and an individual section can be taught by one and only one instructor.

THE ZIPCODE TABLE

The primary key of ZIPCODE is the ZIP column. For an individual zip code, it allows you to look up the corresponding CITY and STATE column values. The datatype of this column is VARCHAR2 and not a NUMBER, because it allows you to enter leading zeros. Both the STUDENT and the INSTRUCTOR table reference the ZIPCODE table. The relationship between the ZIPCODE and STUDENT tables is mandatory: For every ZIP value in the STUDENT table there must be a corresponding value in the ZIPCODE table, and for one given zip code, there may be zero, one, or multiple students with that zip code. In contrast, the relationship between the INSTRUCTOR and ZIPCODE table is optional; the ZIP column of the INSTRUCTOR table may be null.

WHAT ABOUT DELETE OPERATIONS?

Referential integrity does not allow deletion of a primary key value in a parent table that exists in a child as a foreign key value. This would create orphan rows in the child table. There are many ways to handle deletes and you will learn about this topic and the effects of the deletes on other tables in Chapter 10, "Insert, Update, and Delete."

THE ENROLLMENT TABLE

The ENROLLMENT table is an intersection table between the STUDENT and the SECTION table. It lists the students enrolled in the various sections. The primary key of the table is a composite primary key consisting of the STUDENT_ID and SECTION_ID columns. This unique combination does not allow a student to register for the same section twice. The ENROLL_DATE column contains the date the student registered for the section and the FINAL_GRADE column lists the student's final grade. The final grade is to be computed from individual grades such as quizzes, homework assignments, and so on.

The relationship line between the ENROLLMENT and STUDENT tables indicates that one student may be enrolled in zero, one, or many sections. For one row of the ENROLLMENT table you can find one and only one corresponding row in the STUDENT table. The relationship between the ENROLLMENT and SECTION table shows that a section may have zero, one, or multiple enrollments. A single row in the ENROLLMENT table always links back to one and only one row in the SECTION table.

THE GRADE_TYPE TABLE

The GRADE_TYPE table is a lookup table for other tables as it relates to grade information. The table's primary key is the GRADE_TYPE_CODE column that lists the unique category of grade, such as MT, HW, PA, and so on. The DESCRIPTION column describes the abbreviated code. For example, for the GRADE_TYPE_CODE of MT you will find the description Midterm, for HW you will see Homework.

THE GRADE TABLE

This table lists the grades a student received for an individual section. The primary key columns are STUDENT_ID, SECTION_ID, GRADE_TYPE_CODE, and GRADE_CODE_OCCURRENCE. For an individual student you will find all the grades related to the section the student is enrolled in. For example, the listed grades may include the midterm grade, individual quizzes, final examination grade, and so on. For some grades (e.g., quizzes, homework assignments) there may be multiple grades and the sequence number is shown in the GRADE_CODE_OCCURRENCE column. Figure 1.33 displays an excerpt of data from the GRADE table. The NUMERIC_GRADE column lists the actual grade received. This grade may be converted to a letter grade with the help of the GRADE_CONVERSION table discussed later.

From the relationship between the ENROLLMENT and GRADE table, you can learn that rows only exist in the GRADE table if the student is actually enrolled in the section listed in the ENROLLMENT table. In other words, it is not possible for a student to have grades for a section in which he or she is not enrolled. The

STUDENT_ID	SECTION_ID	GRADE_ TYPE_ CODE	GRADE_ CODE_ OCCURRENCE	NUMERIC_ GRADE	...
221	104	FI	1	77	...
221	104	HM	1	76	...
221	104	HM	2	76	...
221	104	HM	3	86	...
221	104	HM	4	96	...
221	104	MT	1	90	...
221	104	PA	1	83	...
221	104	QZ	1	84	...
221	104	QZ	2	83	...
...	...	...	...	...	...

Figure 1.33 ■ Data from the GRADE table.

foreign key columns STUDENT_ID and SECTON_ID from the ENROLLMENT table enforce this relationship.

THE GRADE_TYPE_WEIGHT TABLE

The GRADE_TYPE_WEIGHT table aids in computation of the final grade a student receives for an individual section. This table lists how the final grade for an individual section is computed. For example, the midterm may constitute 50 percent of the final grade, all the quizzes 10 percent, and the final examination 40 percent. If there are multiple grades for a given GRADE_TYPE_CODE, the lowest grade may be dropped if the column DROP_LOWEST contains the value "Y." The final grade is determined by using the individual grades of the student and section in the GRADE table in conjunction with this table. This computed final grade value is stored in the FINAL_GRADE column of the ENROLLMENT table discussed previously. (The FINAL_GRADE column is a derived column. As mentioned, the values to compute this number are available in the GRADE and GRADE_TYPE_WEIGHT tables, but because the computation of this value is complex, it is stored to simplify queries.)

The primary key of this table consists of the SECTION_ID and GRADE_TYPE_CODE columns. A particular GRADE_TYPE_CODE value may exist zero, one, or multiple times in the GRADE_TYPE_WEIGHT table. For every row of the GRADE_TYPE_WEIGIIT table you will find one and only one corresponding GRADE_TYPE_CODE value in the GRADE_TYPE table.

The relationship between the GRADE_TYPE_WEIGHT table and the SECTION table indicates that a section may have zero, one, or multiple rows in the GRADE_TYPE_WEIGHT table for a given SECTION_ID value. For one SECTION_ID value in the GRADE_TYPE_WEIGHT table there must always be one and only one corresponding value in the SECTION table.

THE GRADE_CONVERSION TABLE

The purpose of the GRADE_CONVERSION table is to convert a number grade to a letter grade. The table does not have any relationship with any other tables. The column LETTER_GRADE contains the unique grades, such as A+, A, A-, B, and so forth. For each of these letter grades, there is an equivalent number range. For example, for the letter B, the range is 83 through 86 and is listed in the MIN_GRADE and MAX_GRADE columns.

 You can find the individual table and column descriptions of all the tables listed in the STUDENT schema diagram in Appendix E, "Table and Column Descriptions."

LAB 1.3 EXERCISES

1.3.1 UNDERSTAND THE SCHEMA DIAGRAM AND IDENTIFY TABLE RELATIONSHIPS

a) What does the STUDENT schema diagram represent?

b) Does the STUDENT schema diagram tell you where a student lives? Explain.

c) What four columns are common to all tables in the STUDENT schema diagram?

d) What is the primary key of the COURSE table?

e) How many primary keys does the ENROLLMENT table have? Name the column(s).

f) How many foreign keys does the SECTION table have?

g) Will a foreign key column in a table accept any data value? Explain using the STUDENT and ZIPCODE tables.

h) If the relationship between the ZIPCODE and STUDENT tables were optional, what would have to change in the STUDENT table?

i) From what domain of values (what column in what table) do you think the PREREQUISITE column of the COURSE table gets its values?

j) Explain the relationship(s) the ENROLLMENT table has to other table(s).

LAB 1.3 EXERCISE ANSWERS

1.3.1 ANSWERS

a) What does the STUDENT schema diagram represent?

Answer: The STUDENT schema diagram is a graphical representation of tables in a relational database.

A schema diagram is a useful tool during the software development lifecycle. English-like words should be used to name tables and columns so that anyone, whether developer or end-user, can look at a schema diagram and grasp the meaning of data, and the relationships among them, represented there. Developers study it to understand the design of a database, long before they put hands to keyboard to develop a system, and end-users can use it to understand how their data is stored.

b) Does the STUDENT schema diagram tell you where a student lives? Explain.

Answer: No. The STUDENT schema diagram tells you how data is organized in a relational database: the names of tables, the columns in those tables, and the relationship among them. It cannot tell you what actual data looks like. You use the SQL language to interact with a relational database to view, manipulate, and store the data in the tables.

c) What four columns are common to all tables in the STUDENT schema diagram?

Answer: The four columns are CREATED_BY, CREATED_DATE, MODIFIED_BY, and MODIFIED_DATE.

Database tables often contain columns similar to these four to create an audit trail. These columns are designed to identify who first created or last modified a row of a table and when the action occurred. You will typically find these columns only on the physical schema diagram, not on the logical model. Some of these values in the columns can be filled in automatically by writing triggers. You will see an example of a table trigger in Chapter 12, "Create, Alter, and Drop Tables." (Triggers are described in further detail in another book in this series called *Oracle PL/SQL by Example*, 3/e, by Benjamin Rosenzweig and Elena Silvestrova; Prentice Hall, 2004.)

d) What is the primary key of the COURSE table?

Answer: The primary key of the COURSE table is the column COURSE_NO.

You can identify the primary key with the "PK" symbol listed next to the column. In general a primary key uniquely identifies a row in a table, and the column or columns of the primary key are defined as NOT NULL.

e) How many primary keys does the ENROLLMENT table have? Name the column(s).

Answer: A table can have only one primary key. The primary key of the ENROLLMENT table consists of the two columns STUDENT_ID and SECTION_ID.

As mentioned earlier, a primary key uniquely identifies a single row in a table. In the case of the ENROLLMENT table, two columns uniquely identify a row and create a composite primary key.

Looking at the schema diagram you also notice that these two columns are also foreign keys. The STUDENT_ID column is the foreign key to the STUDENT table and the SECTION_ID is the foreign key to the SECTION table. Both foreign key relationships are identifying relationships.

f) How many foreign keys does the SECTION table have?

Answer: Two. The foreign keys of the SECTION table are COURSE_NO and INSTRUCTOR_ID.

g) Will a foreign key column in a table accept any data value? Explain using the STUDENT and ZIPCODE tables.

Answer: No. A foreign key must use the values of the primary key it references as its domain of values.

The ZIP column is the primary key in the ZIPCODE table. The STUDENT table references this column with the foreign key ZIP column. Only values that exist in the ZIP column of the ZIPCODE table can be valid values for the ZIP column of the STUDENT table. If you attempt to create a row or change an existing row in the STUDENT table with a zip code not found in the ZIPCODE table, the foreign key constraint on the STUDENT table will reject it.

In general, a foreign key is defined as being a column, or columns, in the child table. This column refers back to the primary key of another table, referred to as the parent table.

The primary key values are the domain of values for the foreign key column. A *domain* is a set of values that shows the possible values a column can have. The primary key values of the parent table are the only acceptable values that may appear in the foreign key column in the other table. (Domains are not only used in context with primary key and foreign key relationships, but can also be used for a list of values that may not be stored in a table. For example, common domains include Yes/No, Gender: Male/Female/Unknown, Weekday: Sun/Mon/Tue/Wed/Thu/Fri/Sat.)

h) If the relationship between the ZIPCODE and STUDENT tables were optional, what would have to change in the STUDENT table?

Answer: The foreign key column ZIP in the STUDENT table would have to be defined as allowing NULL values. It is currently defined as NOT NULL. The relationship should be indicated as optional instead of mandatory as shown in Figure 1.34.

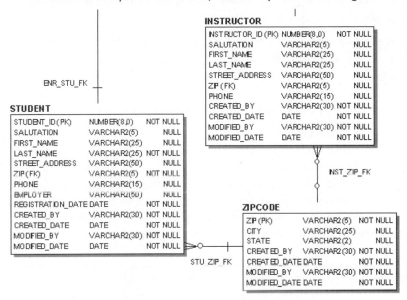

Figure 1.34 ■ **The relationships of the ZIPCODE table.**

There is such an optional relationship between the INSTRUCTOR and ZIPCODE tables. All the nonnull values of ZIP in the INSTRUCTOR table must be found in the ZIPCODE table.

i) From what domain of values (what column in what table) do you think the PRE-REQUISITE column of the COURSE table gets its values?

Answer: From the COURSE_NO column in the COURSE table.

In this case, the PREREQUISITE column refers back to the COURSE_NO column, which provides the domain of values for the PREREQUISITE column. A prerequisite is valid only if it is also a valid course number in the COURSE table. This relationship is shown in Figure 1.35.

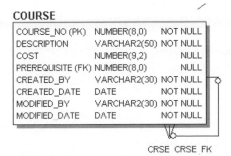

Figure 1.35 ■ **The self-referencing relationship of the COURSE table.**

j) Explain the relationship(s) the ENROLLMENT table has to other table(s).

Answer: The STUDENT table and the SECTION table are the parent tables of the ENROLLMENT table. The ENROLLMENT table is one of the parent tables of the GRADE table.

As shown in Figure 1.36, the relationship between the STUDENT and SECTION tables signifies a student may be enrolled in zero, one, or many sections. One individual student can be enrolled in one specific section only once, otherwise the unique combination of the two columns in the ENROLLMENT table would be violated. The combination of these two foreign key columns represents the primary key of the ENROLLMENT table.

The relationship of the ENROLLMENT table as the parent of the GRADE table shows that for an individual student and her or his enrolled section there may be zero, one, or many grades. The primary key columns of the ENROLLMENT table (STUDENT_ID and SECTION_ID) are foreign keys in the GRADE table that become part of the GRADE table's composite primary key. Therefore, only enrolled students may have rows in the GRADE as indicated with the optional line. If a row in GRADE exists, it must be for one specific enrollment in a section for one specific student.

**LAB
1.3**

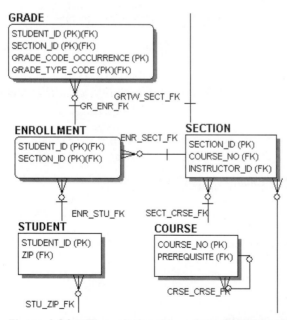

Figure 1.36 ■ The relationships of the ENROLLMENT table.

Note: In some cases, the foreign keys become part of a table's primary key, as in the ENROLLMENT or the GRADE table. If a composite primary key contains many columns (perhaps more than four or five), a surrogate key may be considered for simplicity. The decision to use a surrogate key is based on the database designer's understanding of how data is typically accessed by the application programs.

LAB 1.3 SELF-REVIEW QUESTIONS

In order to test your progress, you should be able to answer the following questions.

LAB
1.3

1) What role(s) does the STUDENT_ID column play in the GRADE table? Check all that apply.

   a) _____ Part of composite primary key
   b) _____ Primary key
   c) _____ Foreign key

2) The GRADE_TYPE table does not allow values to be NULL in any column.

   a) _____ True
   b) _____ False

3) The number of columns in a table matches the number of rows in that table.

   a) _____ True
   b) _____ False

4) The SECTION table has no foreign key columns.

   a) _____ True
   b) _____ False

5) A table can contain 10 million rows.

   a) _____ True
   b) _____ False

6) A primary key may contain NULL values.

   a) _____ True
   b) _____ False

7) A column name must be unique within a table.

   a) _____ True
   b) _____ False

8) If a table is a child table in three different one-to-many relationships, how many foreign key columns does it have?

   a) _____ One
   b) _____ Exactly three
   c) _____ Three or more

9) Referential integrity requires the relationship between foreign key and primary key to maintain values from the same domain.

   a) _____ True
   b) _____ False

10) A foreign key may be NULL.

   a) _____ True
   b) _____ False

11) Orphan rows are not allowed in the relational model.

   a) _____ True
   b) _____ False

Answers appear in Appendix A, Section 1.3.

CHAPTER 1

TEST YOUR THINKING

The projects in this section are meant to have you utilize all of the skills that you have acquired throughout this chapter. The answers to these projects can be found at the companion Web site to this book, located at *http://authors.phptr.com/rischert3e*. Visit the Web site periodically to share and discuss your answers.

In this chapter you learned about data, how data are organized in tables, and how the relationships among them are depicted in a schema diagram. Based on your newly acquired knowledge, design a schema diagram based on the fictional ACME Construction Company. Draw on your own work experience to design the following components.

1)   Draw boxes for these three tables: EMPLOYEE, POSITION, and DEPARTMENT.
2)   Create at least three columns for each of the tables and designate a primary key for each table.
3)   Create relationships among the tables that make sense to you. At least one table should have a self-referencing relationship. Hint: Be sure to include the necessary foreign key columns.
4)   Think about which columns should NOT allow NULL values.

C H A P T E R   2

SQL: THE BASICS

C H A P T E R   O B J E C T I V E S

In this chapter, you will learn about:

Now that you are familiar with the concepts of databases and schema diagrams, you are ready to start with hands-on exercises. You will learn the basics of SQL*Plus, the software tool that allows you to execute statements against the Oracle database. After you familiarize yourself with SQL*Plus, you will be ready to write SQL statements, or queries, to retrieve the data. SQL statements can range from very simple to highly complex; they can be a few words long or a few hundred words long. In this chapter, you begin by writing simple SQL statements, but you will be able to build longer, more complex SQL queries very quickly.

L A B   2 . 1

THE SQL*PLUS ENVIRONMENT

L A B   O B J E C T I V E S

After this lab, you will be able to:
- ✔ Identify Oracle's Client/Server Software
- ✔ Login and Logout of SQL*Plus

Oracle software runs on many different operating systems and hardware environments. You can use the SQL*Plus software under three different architectural configurations: as a stand-alone machine, in a client–server setup, or as *i*SQL*Plus within a three-tier architecture. Another piece of Oracle software, called SQL*Net (Version 7), Net8 (Version 8), or Oracle Net (Version 9*i* and 10*g*), provides the required communication protocol to the server.

STAND-ALONE ENVIRONMENT

SQL*Plus may be run in a stand-alone environment, where both the SQL*Plus client software and the Oracle database software reside on the same physical machine. This is the case when you install both the Oracle database server and the SQL*Plus software on your individual computer.

CLIENT–SERVER

A common setup is a client–server environment, also referred to as two-tier architecture, where a client communicates with the server. In this type of environment, Oracle's SQL*Plus tool resides on a client computer such as a PC or Unix workstation; the Oracle RDBMS software resides on a server. Figure 2.1 shows such a client–server architecture.

The client sends SQL statements to the server, and the server responds back with the result set. The job of the database server involves listening and managing many clients' requests, because in this configuration there are often multiple client machines involved.

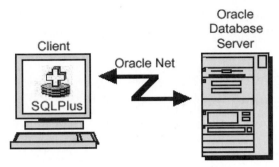

Figure 2.1 ■ Client–server architecture.

Instead of Oracle's SQL*Plus program, the client machine may run any other program with the ability to execute SQL statements against a database (e.g., Visual
Basic or a custom-built Java program). For the client computer's programs to communicate with the Oracle database server, the individual client machine is typically configured with the Oracle Net software, or the client may establish an Open
Database Connectivity (ODBC) connection.

THREE-TIER ARCHITECTURE

Starting with Oracle 8.1.7, you can use the *i*SQL*Plus interface in a Web browser
to access the Oracle database. It performs the same actions as SQL*Plus. The
advantage of *i*SQL*Plus is that you don't need to install and configure the
SQL*Plus program or Oracle Net software on your client machine. As long as you
use a compatible browser on your machine and know the URL of the Oracle HTTP
server, you can access the database. As with any connection, you obviously need
a valid user account and password.

Figure 2.2 shows the three-tiered architecture of an *i*SQL*Plus configuration. The
first tier is the client's Web browser, and the middle tier is the Oracle HTTP server
(Web server) that receives requests from the browser and forwards them via Oracle
Net to the third tier, the Oracle database server. The Oracle Web server returns

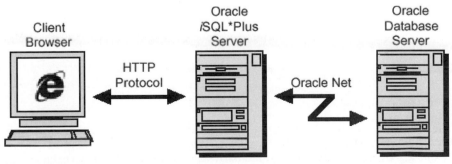

Figure 2.2 ■ Three-tier architecture.

results from the database server back to the Web browser for display. The three tiers may be on one machine but are typically on three different ones.

SQL AND THE ORACLE DATABASE SERVER

In the midst of all this software lies the SQL language. SQL commands are sent from the client software, also known as the *front end,* to the server, or *back end.* These commands send instructions to the server to tell it what services to provide. The server responds by sending back a result to the client, where it is displayed by the client software. Figure 2.3 shows a SQL statement that queries the DESCRIPTION column of the COURSE table. The SQL statement is sent to the Oracle server and the result is displayed by SQL*Plus.

USER ID AND PASSWORD

To connect to the database and communicate via SQL*Plus, you must have a user ID that has been created for you. For the purposes of all examples in this book, you use the user name STUDENT and the password LEARN. Note that the user ID and password are not case sensitive.

If you have not yet created the STUDENT schema according to the instructions on the companion Web site located at http://authors. phptr.com/rischert3e, you will not be able to log in with the STUDENT user ID and the LEARN password. You may want to continue to read through this lab first, create the STUDENT schema, and then perform the exercises in this lab.

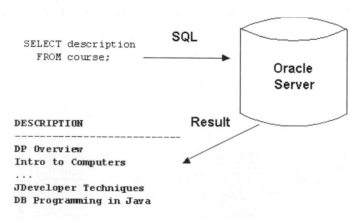

```
SELECT description            SQL
    FROM course;
                                            Oracle
                                            Server

DESCRIPTION                   Result
-------------------------
DP Overview
Intro to Computers
...
JDeveloper Techniques
DB Programming in Java

30 rows selected.
```

Figure 2.3 ■ **SQL and the Oracle database server.**

ACCESSING THE ORACLE DATABASE SERVER

You can access the Oracle server through various front-end tools. This book will discuss the use of Oracle's own SQL*Plus software (available as a graphical Windows environment and as a command line interface) and the browser-based *i*SQL*Plus.

This lab will teach you some of the basics of SQL*Plus, as this tool is almost always found in any Oracle database environment. The log on screens for SQL*Plus and the browser-based *i*SQL*Plus are slightly different, but easily understood. You can use either SQL*Plus or *i*SQL*Plus to execute your SQL statements, or perhaps you chose another front-end query tool that also allows you to enter SQL commands. (The companion Web site to this book lists other alternative query tools.) Differences between SQL*Plus or *i*SQL*Plus are pointed out to you as you work through the book. You can assume that with very few exceptions the functionality of *i*SQL*Plus and SQL*Plus are very similar, if not identical.

 When working through this book, you have a choice to use either a browser and access iSQL*Plus or use the SQL*Plus software installed on your machine.

SQL*PLUS CLIENT FOR WINDOWS

If the SQL*Plus program is installed on your Windows machine, you can access it by choosing Programs, then Oracle, Application Development, and SQL Plus. This launches the program and displays the Log On dialog box similar to Figure 2.4. Enter as the User Name STUDENT and as the Password LEARN.

If your database is installed on the same machine as your SQL*Plus client, you don't need to enter a value in the Host String field. If you are connecting to a

Figure 2.4 ■ Windows graphical user interface log on dialog box.

remote Oracle database, enter the Oracle Net connection string supplied to you by your Oracle database administrator and recorded in your TNSNAMES.ORA file. You will learn more about this special file later.

Figure 2.5 shows how your screen looks once you have successfully connected to the server. Effectively, you have established a connection with the Oracle database as the user STUDENT. The client and the server may now communicate with each other.

When you see the SQL> command prompt, SQL*Plus is ready to accept your commands and you may begin to type. This is the default prompt for SQL*Plus.

To log out, either type EXIT or QUIT and press enter. Alternatively, you can choose Exit from the File menu or simply use your mouse to close the window.

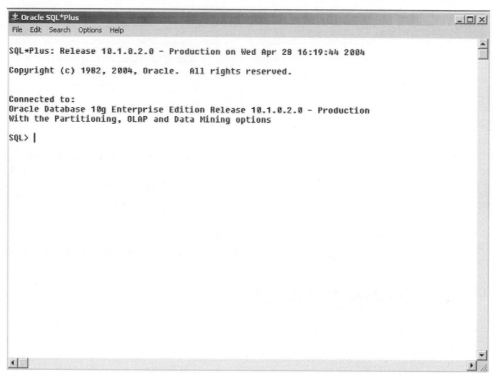

Figure 2.5 ■ SQL*Plus prompt.

CONNECTING WITH A WEB BROWSER: *i*SQL*PLUS

Instead of the SQL*Plus software program, you can also use the Web-based version called *i*SQL*Plus. To access the *i*SQL*Plus interface through your Web browser, you enter a URL. A Log on dialog similar to Figure 2.6 will appear. Here, the URL is http://scooby:5560/isqlplus and will obviously be different for your individual installation.

A valid URL to connect to *i*SQL*Plus is in the form of http://machine_name .domain:port/isqlplus. For example, http://mymachine.acme.com:5560/isqlplus is an example of a URL format. As part of the default Oracle installation, you will usually see the *i*SQL*Plus port number displayed. If you are unsure about your specific port number, try the default port 5560.

Also notice in Figure 2.6 that the domain is not shown, only the machine name scooby. Because the machine is on a local network, you can omit the domain. Instead of the name of the machine, you can also enter the IP address. If your Oracle database server is on your own machine and you want to access *i*SQL*Plus, you can substitute localhost instead and your URL will read http://localhost: 5560/isqlplus. Alternatively, you can use the IP address of 127.0.0.1.

Enter the user ID and password in the appropriate boxes. You don't need to supply the Connection Identifier (also called Host string) to connect to the default database instance.

Figure 2.7 displays the screen you see once you have successfully logged in. Notice the *i*SQL*Plus Workspace and the message "Connected as STUDENT@orcl" on the upper right-hand side of the screen. This indicates the name of the login user,

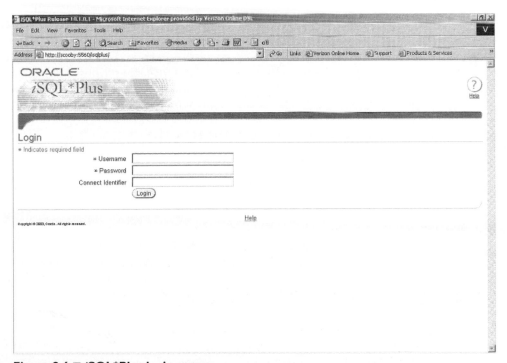

Figure 2.6 ■ *i*SQL*Plus login screen.

Figure 2.7 ■ *i*SQL*Plus Workspace.

which is STUDENT, and the name of the Oracle database instance you are connected to, called ORCL.

At the Enter statements text box, also referred to as the input area, you can enter
commands. If you want to run a script (e.g., the script you need to execute to generate the STUDENT schema), you can enter the path and name of the script or
click the Load Script button to locate the script. Once the script is loaded into the
input area, you can edit the script or simply click the Execute button to execute
the script. To logout and return to the Login screen, click on the Logout icon.

STARTING THE *i*SQL*PLUS APPLICATION SERVER

For the Windows environment, the *i*SQL*Plus application server is installed as a
Windows service as part of the default Oracle database server installation and
usually started automatically.

For other operating systems—or if you prefer to start *i*SQL*Plus from the command prompt—use the following syntax `%oracle_home%\bin\isqlplusctl
start`. For example, if C:\ORACLE\ORA10 is your Windows Oracle home direc-
tory where the files for the Oracle database and application server are installed,
you start the *i*SQL*Plus application server with this command `C:\oracle\
ora10\bin\isqlplusctl start`.

Refer to the companion Web site for more information on general *i*SQL*Plus installation and configuration questions.

COMMAND-LINE INTERFACES FOR SQL*PLUS

In place of a graphical user interface such as SQL*Plus for Windows or *i*SQL*Plus, you may use a command-line interface. A command-line interface is available with every Oracle version. Frequently, you will use this interface in operating systems such as Linux or Unix. Even Windows has a command-line interface and you will see it displayed in Figure 2.8. All SQL*Plus and SQL commands operate for this interface just the same. Note that depending on the operating system, your editor, as well as the cut and paste commands, may be different.

To invoke SQL*Plus, you type `sqlplus` at the respective operating system's command prompt. For Windows you start SQL*Plus by typing `C.\> sqlplus` from the Windows command prompt. In this example, the username and password is supplied to start SQL*Plus. You can also enter `sqlplus` and you will be prompted for the user name and password or `sqlplus student`, which will prompt for the password.

THE REMOTE DATABASE AND COMMON
LOG-ON PROBLEMS

Often the database resides on a machine other than your client machine, or you have a choice of accessing different databases. In these cases you need to supply the name of the database in the Host String box of the Log On dialog box (see Figure 2.9) or the Connection Identifier box in *i*SQL*Plus. For example, to connect to a database called ITCHY you have enter this name in the Host String box.

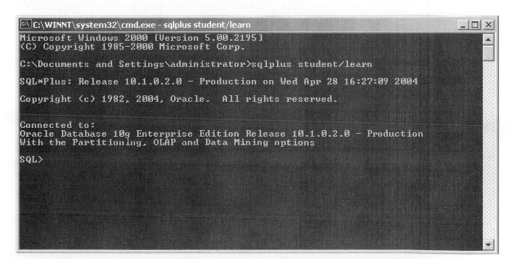

```
C:\WINNT\system32\cmd.exe - sqlplus student/learn                    _ □ X
Microsoft Windows 2000 [Version 5.00.2195]
(C) Copyright 1985-2000 Microsoft Corp.

C:\Documents and Settings\administrator>sqlplus student/learn

SQL*Plus: Release 10.1.0.2.0 - Production on Wed Apr 28 16:27:09 2004

Copyright (c) 1982, 2004, Oracle.  All rights reserved.


Connected to:
Oracle Database 10g Enterprise Edition Release 10.1.0.2.0 - Production
With the Partitioning, OLAP and Data Mining options

SQL>
```

Figure 2.8 ■ Command line-based SQL*Plus under the Windows operating system.

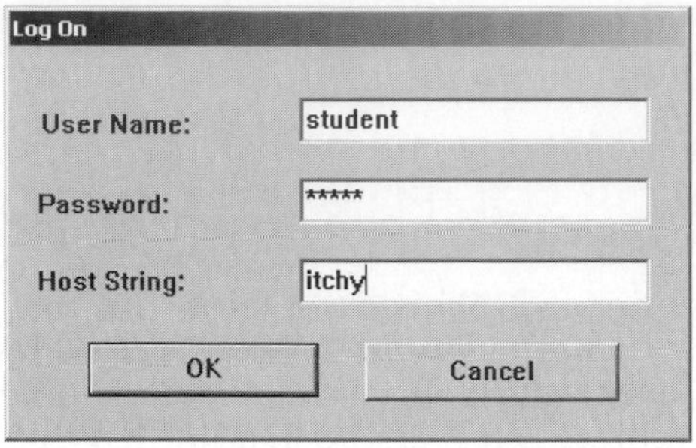

Figure 2.9 ■ SQL*Plus Windows graphical user interface log on dialog box.

The host string matches an entry in a file called TNSNAMES.ORA, which lists the database's IP address (or the machine name) and database instance name.

Essentially, the TNSNAMES.ORA file is a file containing a list of databases with their respective technical connection information. Your database administrator can help you with the configuration and setup of this file if you have a remote database setup.

Following is an excerpt of a TNSNAMES.ORA file. The entries in your file will obviously vary. If you supply the host string ITCHY at log in, SQL*Plus will look up the ITCHY entry in the TNSNAMES.ORA file. The HOST entry shows the IP address (if you use a TCP/IP network), which is listed as 169.254.147.245. Alternatively, you can enter the machine name. The SID entry identifies the name of the Oracle instance; here the instance is called ORCL. (When you install Oracle with the default options, you will be asked to supply such an instance name [SID]. A common default name is ORCL.)

```
ITCHY =
  (DESCRIPTION =
    (ADDRESS_LIST =
      (ADDRESS =
        (PROTOCOL = TCP)
        (Host = 169.254.147.245)
        (Port = 1521)
      )
    )
    (CONNECT_DATA = (SID = ORCL)
    )
  )
SCRATCHY =
  (DESCRIPTION =
    (ADDRESS_LIST =
      (ADDRESS = (PROTOCOL = TCP)(HOST = milly.columbia.edu)(PORT = 1521))
    )
    (CONNECT_DATA =
```

```
    (SERVER = DEDICATED)
    (SERVICE_NAME = scraty.columbia.edu)
  )
)
```

Your TNSNAMES.ORA file may contain an entry called DEFAULT. If you do not supply a Host String in the Log On dialog box, you will be connected to the database listed under the DEFAULT option. Note, depending on your individual setup, you may at times need to specify or omit the .WORLD suffix next to the host name (such as ITCHY.WORLD or simply ITCHY) in the TNSNAMES.ORA file. Additionally, Oracle 9*i* and 10*g* installations allow the use the format of the second entry called SCRATCHY. It uses a service name instead of the SID.

If you are using an Oracle 10*g* client such as SQL*Plus for Windows, you can use a new feature called easyconnect. It allows you to make a connection without the entry being present in the TNSNAMES.ORA file. For example, you can connect to SCRATCHY by using this connect identifier in the Host String box: `milly.columbia.edu:1521/scraty.columbia.edu`. It lists the machine name called MILLY.COLUMBIA.EDU followed by the port number (the default port of the Oracle database is typically 1521), followed by the service name SCRATY.COLUMBIA.EDU.

COMMON LOG-ON PROBLEMS

Although we cannot possibly list all the errors and solutions to all log-on problems, here are two very common Oracle error messages.

A TNS error usually deals with the connectivity between the server and the client. The following message is displayed if the connect identifier could not be resolved. This may be due to an invalid host string. Check the values and retry.

```
ORA-12154: TNS: could not resolve the connect identifier specified
```

The next error occurs if you entered the wrong password or user name when the Oracle server attempted to authenticate you as a valid user. Double-check the spelling of your user name, which is STUDENT, and password, which is LEARN. (If you cannot log on with this ID and password, check the readme.txt file regarding the installation of the STUDENT schema.)

```
    ORA-01017: invalid username/password; logon denied
```

EXITING FROM SQL*PLUS OR *i*SQL*PLUS

There are a number of ways to exit SQL*Plus. You can type EXIT or select Exit from the File menu in the SQL*Plus Windows version. For *i*SQL*Plus, you click the Logout icon rather than typing EXIT as this will free up system resources. Exiting ends the session and the STUDENT user is no longer connected to the database.

However, there may be other client machines connected to the Oracle database; the server software continues to run, regardless of whether a client is connected to it.

CREATING THE STUDENT SCHEMA

Now that you know how to log on to the Oracle database using SQL*Plus or *i*SQL*Plus, this is a good time to read the readme.txt file you downloaded from the Web site located at http://authors.phptr.com/rischert3e and create the STUDENT schema if you have not already done so.

Unless specifically mentioned, we will not differentiate between SQL*Plus and *i*SQL*Plus commands because many are almost identical. For a list of unsupported commands see Appendix C, "SQL*Plus Command Reference."

 All commands in SQL*Plus require the user to press the Enter key to execute them. In iSQL*Plus you always need to press the Execute button. The reminder to press the Enter key or the Execute button will not be included in the rest of the examples and exercises in this book.

LAB 2.1 EXERCISES

2.1.1 IDENTIFY ORACLE'S CLIENT/SERVER SOFTWARE

a) Identify which piece of Oracle software is the client, which is the server, and how they communicate with each other.

b) What is the role of SQL between client and server?

2.1.2 LOGIN AND LOGOUT OF SQL*PLUS

a) Once you have logged into SQL*Plus (not *i*SQL*Plus) with the user ID STUDENT and password LEARN, what information does the SQL*Plus screen show you? (If you do not have access to SQL*Plus, please answer the question by referring to Figure 2.5.)

b) What do you learn when you type DESCRIBE student and press Enter? If you use *i*SQL*Plus, click the Execute button instead of pressing Enter.

c) Execute the following command and describe what you see:
SHOW ALL.

LAB 2.1 EXERCISE ANSWERS

2.1.1 ANSWERS

a) Identify which piece of Oracle software is the client, which is the server, and how they communicate with each other.

Answer: SQL*Plus or the browser displaying iSQL*Plus is the client and the Oracle RDBMS is the server. In an Oracle 9i or 10g environment, Oracle Net is the protocol that facilitates the communications.

b) What is the role of SQL between client and server?

Answer: SQL commands are issued from the client, telling the server to perform specific actions. The server sends back the results of those instructions to the client software, where they are displayed.

2.1.2 ANSWERS

a) Once you have logged into SQL*Plus (not iSQL*Plus) with the user ID STUDENT and password LEARN, what information does the SQL*Plus screen show you? (If you do not have access to SQL*Plus, please answer the question by referring to Figure 2.5.)

Answer: The screen shows which version of SQL*Plus you are using, the current date and time, Oracle copyright information, and the version of the Oracle database you are connected to. After this information is displayed, you see the SQL> command prompt. At this prompt you are able to enter commands.

PL/SQL is another Oracle language addressed in a separate book in this series *Oracle PL/SQL by Example* by Benjamin Rosenzweig and Elena Silvestrova (Prentice Hall, 2004).

b) What do you learn when you type DESCRIBE student and press Enter? If you use iSQL*Plus, click the Execute button instead of pressing Enter.

Answer: You find out about the structure of the STUDENT table, specifically its column names, whether those columns allow nulls and the datatype of each column.

To write SQL statements, you need to know a table's column names and their datatypes. The SQL*Plus DESCRIBE command displays this information and shows if a column does not allow null values.

Many SQL*Plus commands may be abbreviated. For instance, DESCRIBE may be shortened to DESC. Retype the command using this abbreviation and compare the results. Figure 2.10 displays the result of the DESCRIBE command executed in SQL*Plus.

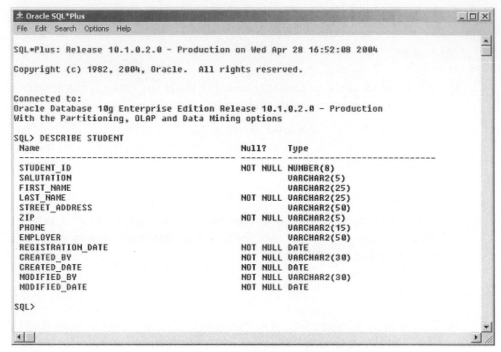

Figure 2.10 ■ Executing the SQL*Plus DESCRIBE command.

 SQL*Plus is not case sensitive; the user ID, password, and SQL*Plus commands may all be entered in either upper or lowercase, or a combination of the two. Throughout this book, they are in uppercase for easy identification. In the next lab you will learn about formatting your SQL statements and when it is appropriate to capitalize words.

COMMON DATATYPES

Every column in Oracle must have a datatype, which determines what type of data can be stored.

DATE

The DATE datatype is used to store date and time information. By default the display format for a date is DD-MON-YY. For example, July 4, 2003 displays as 04-JUL-03. There are a number of functions you can use to change the display format or to show the time, which you will learn about in "Chapter 4, Date and Conversion Functions."

NUMBER

Columns with the datatype NUMBER only allow numerical data; no text, hyphens, or dashes are allowed. A column defined as NUMBER(5,2) can have a maximum of three digits before the decimal point and two digits after the decimal point. The first digit (5) is called the *precision;* the second digit (2) is referred to as the *scale.* The smallest allowed number is –999.99 and the largest is 999.99. A column definition with a zero scale such as NUMBER(5) or NUMBER(5,0) allows integers in the range from –99,999 to 99,999.

VARCHAR2 AND CHAR

The VARCHAR2 and CHAR datatypes store alphanumeric data (e.g., text, numbers, special characters, etc.). VARCHAR2 is the variable length datatype and the most commonly used alphanumeric datatype; its maximum size is 4,000 characters. The main difference between VARCHAR2 and CHAR is that the CHAR datatype is a fixed-length datatype and any unused room is blank padded with spaces.

For example, a column defined as CHAR(10) and containing the four-character length value of JOHN in a row will have six blank characters padded at the end to make the total length 10 spaces. (If the column is stored in a VARCHAR2(10) column instead, it stores four characters only.) A CHAR column can store up to 2,000 characters.

The CLOB database allows you to store large amounts of textual data. It replaces the LONG datatype, which is desupported in Oracle 10*g.*

OTHER

Datatypes such as BFILE or BLOB require access through specific purpose functions in very highly specialized ways that go beyond the objectives of this book. In addition to the datatypes mentioned, Oracle also has additional datatypes to support specific national character sets (e.g., NCLOB, NVARCHAR2), intermedia datatypes, and spatial (geographic) data. Oracle also gives you the ability to create your own customized object datatypes.

Refer to Appendix I, "Oracle Datatypes," for a detailed listing of the various datatypes. For most SQL operations, you typically use the NUMBER, VARCHAR2, and various DATE-related datatypes. They are the most commonly used datatypes where the vast majority of data is stored.

c) Execute the following command and describe what you see: SHOW ALL.

Answer: You will see a list of SQL*Plus environmental variables and their current settings. Using the SET command, many of them can be changed to suit your needs for a SQL*Plus session, which is defined as the time in between when you log in and log out of SQL*Plus. When you start your next SQL*Plus session, however, all commands will be set back to their defaults.

It is important to note here that SQL*Plus commands, such as SHOW and DESCRIBE, are *not* part of the SQL language. You will begin to type SQL commands using the SQL*Plus tool in the next lab.

If you use *i*SQL*Plus, you can change the environment variables and settings by clicking the Preferences icon.

LAB 2.1 SELF-REVIEW QUESTIONS

In order to test your progress, you should be able to answer the following questions.

1) The DESC command displays column names of a table.

    a) _____ True
    b) _____ False

2) Anyone can connect to an Oracle database as long as he or she has the SQL*Plus software.

    a) _____ True
    b) _____ False

3) The SQL*Plus command SHOW USER displays your login name.

    a) _____ True
    b) _____ False

4) Typing SHOW RELEASE at the prompt displays the version number of SQL*Plus you are using.

    a) _____ True
    b) _____ False

5) The COST column of the COURSE table is defined as NUMBER(9,2). The maximum cost of an individual course is 9,999,999.99.

    a) _____ True
    b) _____ False

Answers appear in Appendix A, Section 2.1.

LAB 2.2

THE ANATOMY
OF A SELECT STATEMENT

LAB OBJECTIVES

After this lab, you will be able to:

✔ Write a SQL SELECT Statement
✔ Use DISTINCT in a SQL Statement

THE SELECT STATEMENT

When you write a SQL query, it is usually to answer a question such as "How many students live in New York?" or "Where, and at what time, does the Unix class meet?" A SQL *SELECT statement,* or SQL *query,* is used to answer these questions. A SELECT statement can be broken down into a minimum of two parts: the *SELECT list* and the *FROM clause.* The SELECT list usually consists of the column or columns of a table(s) from which you want to display data. The FROM clause states on what table or tables this column or columns are found. Later in this chapter, you will learn some of the other clauses that can be used in a SELECT statement.

HOW DO YOU WRITE A SQL QUERY?

Before formulating the SELECT statement, you must first determine the table where the information is located. A study of the schema diagram reveals that the COURSE table provides descriptions of courses. (You can also refer to Appendix E, "Table and Column Descriptions.")

The following SELECT statement provides a list of course descriptions:

**LAB
2.2**

```
SELECT description
  FROM course
```

The SELECT list shows the single column called DESCRIPTION, which contains this information. The DESCRIPTION column is found on the COURSE table as specified in the FROM clause. When the statement is executed, the result set is a list of all the values found in the DESCRIPTION column of the COURSE table:

DESCRIPTION

DP Overview
Intro to Computers
...
JDeveloper Techniques
DB Programming in Java

30 rows selected.

 Many of the result sets displayed throughout this book do not list all the rows. This is denoted with a line of "..." in the middle of the output. Typically, you will see the beginning and the ending rows of the result set and the number of rows returned. The resulting output of the SQL command is displayed in a bold font to easily distinguish the output from the commands you enter.

EXECUTING THE SQL STATEMENT

SQL*Plus does not require a new line for each clause, but it requires the use of a semicolon (;) at the end of each SQL statement to execute it. (Figure 2.11 shows the result of the execution of the previously mentioned SQL query in SQL*Plus.) Alternatively, the forward slash (/) may be used on a separate line to accomplish the same. In *i*SQL*Plus a semicolon or forward slash is not required, you only need to press the Execute button:

```
SQL> SELECT description
  2      FROM course;
```
Or:
```
SQL> SELECT description
  2      FROM course
  3    /
```

 *The SQL*Plus commands such as DESC or SHOW USER discussed in the previous lab are not SQL commands and therefore do not require a semicolon or forward slash.*

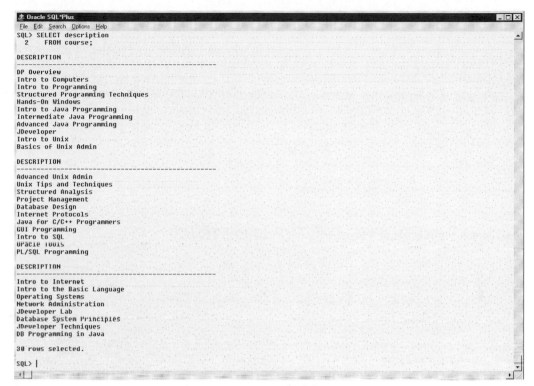

Figure 2.11 ■ Executing the SELECT statement in SQL*Plus.

RETRIEVING MULTIPLE COLUMNS

To retrieve a list of course descriptions and the cost of each course, include the COST column in the SELECT list:

```
SELECT description, cost
  FROM course
DESCRIPTION                     COST
------------------------------- ----
DP Overview                     1195
Intro to Computers              1195
...
JDeveloper Techniques           1195
DB Programming in Java

30 rows selected.
```

When you want to display more than one column in the SELECT list, separate the columns with commas. It is good practice to include a space after the comma for readability. The order of columns in a SELECT list will determine the order in which the columns are displayed in the output.

SELECTING ALL COLUMNS

You can also select all columns in a table with the asterisk (*) wildcard character. This is handy so you don't have to type all columns in the SELECT list. The columns are displayed in the order in which they are defined in the table. This is the same order you see when you use the SQL*Plus DESCRIBE command. If you execute this command you will notice that the columns wrap in SQL*Plus (not *i*SQL*Plus) as there is not sufficient room to display them in one line. You will learn how to format the output shortly.

```
SELECT *
  FROM course
```

ELIMINATING DUPLICATES WITH DISTINCT

The use of DISTINCT in the SELECT list eliminates duplicate data in the result set. The following SELECT statement retrieves the last name and the corresponding zip code for all rows of the INSTRUCTOR table.

```
SELECT last_name, zip
  FROM instructor
```

LAST_NAME	ZIP
Hanks	10015
Wojick	10025
Schorin	10025
Pertez	10035
Morris	10015
Smythe	10025
Chow	10015
Lowry	10025
Frantzen	10005
Willig	

10 rows selected.

Notice that there are 10 rows, yet only nine instructors have zip codes. Instructor Willig has a NULL value in the ZIP column. If you want to show only the distinct zip codes of the table, you write the following SELECT statement. The last row shows the NULL value.

```
SELECT DISTINCT zip
  FROM instructor
```

ZIP
10005
10015

```
10025
10035
```

```
5 rows selected.
```

 By definition, a NULL is an unknown value, and a NULL does not equal another NULL. However, there are exceptions: If you write a SQL query using DISTINCT, SQL will consider a NULL value equal to another NULL value.

From Chapter 1, "SQL and Data," you already know that a primary key is always unique or distinct. Therefore, the use of DISTINCT in a SELECT list containing the primary key column(s) is unnecessary. The ZIP column in the INSTRUCTOR table is not the primary key and can therefore contain duplicate values.

DISPLAYING THE NUMBER OF ROWS RETURNED

You may notice that SQL*Plus sometimes does not show the number of rows returned by the query, but rather depends on the feedback settings for your SQL*Plus session. Typically, the feedback is set to 6 or more rows. In the previous example the feedback was set to 1, which displays the feedback line even when there is only one row returned. You will find this setting useful if your result set returns less than the default six rows and if any of the rows return nulls, which display as a blank. Otherwise, you may think it is not a row or value. To display the exact number of rows returned until you exit SQL*Plus, enter the SQL*Plus command:

```
SET FEEDBACK 1
```

To display your current settings use the SHOW ALL command or simply SHOW FEEDBACK. (If you want to retain certain SQL*Plus settings, you can create a login.sql file for your individual computer in a client–server setup. You can also create a glogin.sql file for all users if you want all to have the identical settings or if you use *i*SQL*Plus. See the companion Web site for more information.)

SQL STATEMENT FORMATTING CONVENTIONS

You will notice that the SQL statements presented in this and all other books in this series follow a common format. The use of uppercase for SELECT, FROM, and other Oracle keywords is for emphasis only, and distinguishes them from table and column names, which you see in the SQL statement as lowercase letters. A standard format enhances the clarity and readability of your SQL statements and helps you detect errors more easily. Refer to Appendix B, "SQL Formatting Guide," for the formatting guidelines used throughout.

CANCELLING A COMMAND AND PAUSING THE OUTPUT

If you want to stop a command while the statement is still executing, you can press CTRL+C in SQL*Plus for Windows or the Cancel button in *i*SQL*Plus.

If your result in SQL*Plus is fairly large, you can examine the output by scrolling up and down. If you wish to look at the rows one screen at a time, use the SQL*Plus SET PAUSE ON command. This commands displays one screen at a time and to change the number of lines displayed per screen to use the SET PAGESIZE n command where *n* is the number of rows per page. To continue to the next screen, press the Enter key in SQL*Plus. If you want to stop scrolling through the screens and return to the SQL> prompt, press CTRL + C. Remember to issue the SET PAUSE OFF command to stop the feature when you are done!

In *i*SQL*Plus you can choose to display only a specific number of rows per page by clicking on Preferences, Interface Configuration, Output Page Setup, and then Multiple Pages. If the output has more than the specified number of rows, you will see a Next Page button that lets you move to the next page of rows.

LAB 2.2 EXERCISES

2.2.1 WRITE A SQL SELECT STATEMENT

  a) Write a SELECT statement to list the first and last names of all students.

  b) Write a SELECT statement to list all cities, states, and zip codes.

  c) Describe the result set of the following SQL statement:

```
SELECT *
  FROM grade_type
```

2.2.2 USE DISTINCT IN A SQL STATEMENT

  a) Why are the result sets of each of the following SQL statements the same?

```
SELECT letter_grade
  FROM grade_conversion

SELECT DISTINCT letter_grade
  FROM grade_conversion
```

  b) Explain the result set of the following SQL statement:

```
SELECT DISTINCT cost
  FROM course
```

c) Explain what happens, and why, when you execute the following SQL statement:

```
SELECT DISTINCT course_no
  FROM class
```

LAB 2.2 EXERCISE ANSWERS

2.2.1 ANSWERS

a) Write a SELECT statement to list the first and last names of all students.

Answer: The SELECT list contains the two columns that provide the first and last names of students; the FROM clause lists the STUDENT table where these columns are found.

```
SELECT first_name, last_name
  FROM student
FIRST_NAME                      LAST_NAME
------------------------------  ----------
George                          Eakheit
Leonard                         Millstoin
. . .
Kathleen                        Mastandora
Angela                          Torres

268 rows selected.
```

You will also notice many rows are returned; you can examine each of the rows by scrolling up and down. There are many SET options in SQL*Plus that allow you to change the headings and the overall display of the data. As you work your way through this book, you will examine and learn about the most important SQL*Plus settings.

b) Write a SELECT statement to list all cities, states, and zip codes.

Answer: The SELECT list contains the three columns that provide the city, state, and zip code; the FROM clause contains the ZIPCODE table where these columns are found.

```
SELECT city, state, zip
  FROM zipcode
CITY                            ST ZIP
------------------------------  -- --------
Santurce                        PR 00914
```

```
North Adams                    MA 01247
...
New York                       NY 10005
New York                       NY 10035

227 rows selected.
```

c) Describe the result set of the following SQL statement:

```
SELECT *
  FROM grade_type
```

*Answer: All columns and rows of the GRADE_TYPE table are returned in the result set. If you use iSQL*Plus, your result will look similar to Figure 2.12. If you use SQL*Plus, your result may resemble the first listing of SQL output in Figure 2.13.*

FORMATTING YOUR RESULT: THE SQL*PLUS COLUMN AND FORMAT COMMANDS

If you are using SQL*Plus, not *i*SQL*Plus, you will notice that the result set is difficult to read when data "wraps" itself onto the next line. The result may look similar to the screen you see in Figure 2.13. This will often occur when your SELECT

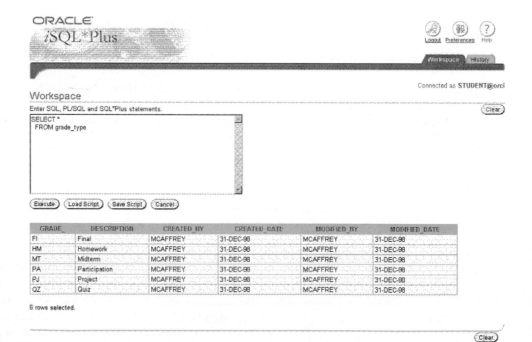

Figure 2.12 ■ SELECT statement against the GRADE_TYPE table issued in *i*SQL*Plus.

```
Oracle SQL*Plus
File  Edit  Search  Options  Help

SQL> SELECT *
  2     FROM grade_type
  3  /

GR DESCRIPTION                                  CREATED_BY                     CREATED_D
-- ------------------------------------------   ----------------------------   ---------
MODIFIED_BY                     MODIFIED_
------------------------------  ---------
FI Final                                        MCAFFREY                       31-DEC-98
MCAFFREY                        31-DEC-98

HM Homework                                     MCAFFREY                       31-DEC-98
MCAFFREY                        31-DEC-98

MT Midterm                                      MCAFFREY                       31-DEC-98
MCAFFREY                        31-DEC-98

PA Participation                                MCAFFREY                       31-DEC-98
MCAFFREY                        31-DEC-98

PJ Project                                      MCAFFREY                       31-DEC-98
MCAFFREY                        31-DEC-98

QZ Quiz                                         MCAFFREY                       31-DEC-98
MCAFFREY                        31-DEC-98

6 rows selected.

SQL> COL description FORMAT A13
SQL> COL created_by FORMAT A8
SQL> COL modified_by FORMAT A8
SQL> /

GR DESCRIPTION     CREATED_ CREATED_D MODIFIED MODIFIED_
-- -------------   -------- --------- -------- ---------
FI Final           MCAFFREY 31-DEC-98 MCAFFREY 31-DEC-98
HM Homework        MCAFFREY 31-DEC-98 MCAFFREY 31-DEC-98
MT Midterm         MCAFFREY 31-DEC-98 MCAFFREY 31-DEC-98
PA Participation   MCAFFREY 31-DEC-98 MCAFFREY 31-DEC-98
PJ Project         MCAFFREY 31-DEC-98 MCAFFREY 31-DEC-98
QZ Quiz            MCAFFREY 31-DEC-98 MCAFFREY 31-DEC-98

6 rows selected.

SQL>
```

Figure 2.13 ■ **SELECT issued in SQL*Plus for Windows.**

**LAB
2.2**

statement contains multiple columns. To help you view the output more easily, SQL*Plus offers a number of formatting commands.

The SQL*Plus COLUMN command allows you to specify format attributes for specific columns. Because the SQL statement contains three alphanumeric columns, format each using these SQL*Plus commands:

```
COL description FORMAT A13
COL created_by FORMAT A8
COL modified_by FORMAT A8
```

When you re-execute the SQL statement, the result is more readable, as you see in the last result set shown in Figure 2.13.

The DESCRIPTION column is formatted to display a maximum of 13 characters; the CREATED_BY and MODIFIED_BY columns are formatted to display 8 characters. If the values in the columns do not fit into the space allotted, the data will wrap within the column. The column headings get truncated to the specified length.

The format for the column stays in place until you either respecify the format for the columns, specifically clear the format for the column, or exit SQL*Plus. To clear all the column formatting, execute the CLEAR COLUMNS command in SQL*Plus.

The two DATE datatype columns of this statement, CREATED_DATE and MODI-FIED_DATE, are not formatted by the COL command. By default, Oracle displays all DATE datatype columns with a 9-character width. You will learn about formatting columns with the DATE datatype in Chapter 4, "Date and Conversion Functions."

FORMATTING NUMBERS

If the column is of a NUMBER datatype column, you can change the format with a *format model* in the COLUMN command. For example, the 9 in the format model 999.99 represents the numeric digits, so the number 100 is displayed as 100.00. You can add dollar signs, leading zeros, angle brackets for negative numbers, and round values to format the display to your desire.

```
COL cost FORMAT $9,999.99
SELECT DISTINCT cost
  FROM course
        COST
----------
 $1,095.00
 $1,195.00
 $1,595.00


4 rows selected.
```

If you did not allot sufficient room for the number to fit in the column, SQL*Plus will show a # symbol instead.

```
COL cost FORMAT 999.99
   COST
-------
#######
#######
#######


4 rows selected.
```

For more SQL*Plus COLUMN FORMAT commands, see Appendix C, "SQL*Plus Command Reference."

Throughout this book you notice that the output is displayed in SQL*Plus rather than iSQL*Plus format. The reason for this is simply that it takes up less space in the book.

2.2.2 ANSWERS

a) Why are the result sets of each of the following SQL statements the same?

```
SELECT letter_grade
   FROM grade_conversion

SELECT DISTINCT letter_grade
   FROM grade_conversion
```

Answer: The result sets are the same because the data values in the LETTER_GRADE column in the GRADE_CONVERSION table are not repeated; the LETTER_GRADE column is the primary key of the table, so by definition its values are already distinct.

b) Explain the result set of the following SQL statement:

```
SELECT DISTINCT cost
   FROM course
```

Answer: The result set contains four rows of distinct costs in the COURSE table, including the NULL value.

```
SET FEEDBACK 1

SELECT DISTINCT cost
   FROM course
        COST
-----------
        1095
        1195
        1595


4 rows selected.
```

Note that if you changed the feedback SQL*Plus environment variable to 1, using the SQL*Plus command SET FEEDBACK 1, the result will include the "4 rows selected." statement. There is one row in the COURSE table containing a null value in the COST column. Even though null is an unknown value, DISTINCT recognizes one or more null values in a column as one distinct value when returning a result set.

c) Explain what happens, and why, when you execute the following SQL statement:

```
SELECT DISTINCT course_no
   FROM class
```

Answer: Oracle returns an error because a table named CLASS does not exist.

```
FROM class
     *
ERROR at line 2:
ORA-00942: table or view does not exist
```

The asterisk in the error message indicates the error in the query. SQL is an exacting language. As you learn to write SQL, you will inevitably make mistakes. It is important to pay attention to the error messages returned to you from the database to learn from and correct your mistakes. This Oracle error message tells you that you referenced a table or a view does not exist in this database schema. (Views are discussed in Chapter 12, "Views, Indexes, and Sequences.") Correct your SQL statement and execute it again.

LAB 2.2 SELF-REVIEW QUESTIONS

In order to test your progress, you should be able to answer the following questions.

1) The column names listed in the SELECT list must be separated by commas.

  a) _____ True
  b) _____ False

2) A SELECT list may contain all the columns in a table.

  a) _____ True
  b) _____ False

3) The asterisk may be used as a wildcard in the FROM clause.

  a) _____ True
  b) _____ False

4) The following statement contains an error:

```
SELECT courseno
   FROM course
```

  a) _____ True
  b) _____ False

Answers appear in Appendix A, Section 2.2.

LAB 2.3

EDITING A SQL STATEMENT

LAB OBJECTIVES

After this lab, you will be able to:

✔ Edit a SQL Statement Using SQL*Plus Commands
✔ Edit a SQL Statement Using an Editor
✔ Save, Retrieve, and Run a SQL Statement in iSQL*Plus

THE LINE EDITOR

In iSQL*Plus you can easily edit your statement just as any text. Sometimes you may not have access to iSQL*Plus, therefore you must learn how to write and edit a statement using the SQL*Plus line editor.

When using SQL*Plus, you may have noticed that typing the same SQL statement over and over again to make a small change quickly becomes very tedious. You can use SQL*Plus's line editor to change your statement, indicating which line to change, then use a command to execute the change.

At the SQL prompt, type and execute the following statement to retrieve a list of course numbers:

```
SELECT course_no
   FROM course
```

SQL*Plus stores the last SQL command you typed in what is referred to as the *SQL buffer.* You can re-execute a statement by just pressing the "/", which reruns the command. The statement stays in the buffer until you enter another SQL command. Use the SQL*Plus LIST command, or simply the letter L, to list the contents of the buffer. The semicolon or the slash, both of which execute the statement, are not stored in the buffer. The asterisk next to the number 2 indicates this is the current line in the buffer.

```
SQL>LIST
  1 SELECT course_no
  2*   FROM course
```

For example, if you want to retrieve a list of descriptions instead, simply change the column `course_no` to `description` using the line editor. To make a change, indicate to the line editor which line to make current. To change it to the first line, type the number 1 at the SQL prompt:

```
SQL> 1
  1* SELECT course_no
```

Just the first line of the two-line statement is displayed, and the asterisk indicates this is now the current line in the buffer. You can make a change to that line with the CHANGE command:

```
SQL>CHANGE/course_no/description
```

The newly changed line is presented back to you:

```
  1* SELECT description
```

The CHANGE command is followed by a forward slash, followed by the text you want to change, and separated from the new text with another forward slash. The abbreviated command for the CHANGE command is the letter C. You are now ready to execute your statement to produce the new result set. Because you are not typing the statement for the first time, you cannot use the semicolon. Type a forward slash to execute the statement instead. The forward slash will always execute the current SQL statement in the buffer. Remember that certain commands you have learned so far, such as the LIST command, are not SQL, but SQL*Plus commands. Only SQL statements are saved in the buffer, never SQL*Plus commands.

USING AN EDITOR IN SQL*PLUS FOR WINDOWS

Although handy, using SQL*Plus's line editor capabilities can still be tedious, especially as your SQL statements grow in size and complexity. You may also want to save some statements for later use. This is where a *text editor* becomes useful. A text editor is a software program with no ability to format the text, such as with boldface or italics. Notepad, a text editor that comes with the Microsoft Windows operating systems, is one example of a text editor and is referenced in this book. Any other text editor will work just as well. For more about setting the default editor in SQL*Plus, see Appendix C, "SQL*Plus Command Reference."

To use a text editor in SQL*Plus for Windows or a SQL*Plus version with the command line interface, simply execute the EDIT or ED command. This command will *invoke*, or open, the default editor currently set in SQL*Plus. When you use the EDIT command at the SQL prompt, SQL*Plus will stay open in the background and your text editor will be in the foreground, automatically displaying the SQL statement in the buffer. The file already has a name, which can also be set as a default in SQL*Plus. For quick editing of statements, simply make your changes here, save the file, and exit Notepad, which brings you back to SQL*Plus. If you wish to save the file for future reference, while still in Notepad select Save As to save the file with a different name and any extension you wish. It is common to save SQL files with a .sql extension.

If your editor puts a .txt after the file name (effectively creating a myfile.sql.txt file), change the Save As type to *All Files* instead of *Text documents (*.txt)*. Another way to ensure the file contains a .sql extension is to enclose the entire file name in quotes, (e.g., "myfile.sql" or if you want to include the path "c:\examples\ myfile.sql"). Figure 2.14 displays the Save As dialog in SQL*Plus.

 *Notice that when you invoke an editor, the SQL statement ends with a forward slash on a separate line at the end. SQL*Plus adds this character to the file so the file can be executed in SQL*Plus. When*

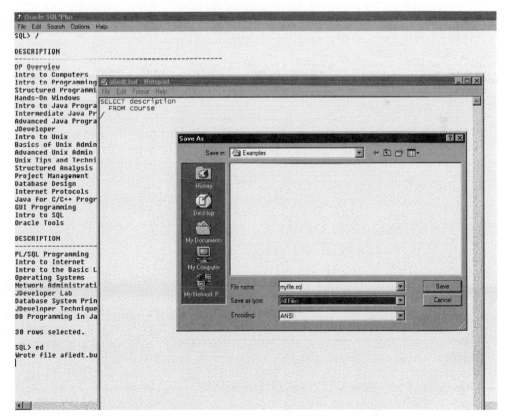

Figure 2.14 ■ Use of the Notepad text editor in SQL*Plus for Windows.

> *you invoke the editor from SQL*Plus, you can't go back to the SQL*Plus screen until you close the editor.*

Type the following statement:

```
SELECT *
  FROM course
```

Now edit the file in Notepad and select Save As to save a second file with the name myfile2.sql. Exit Notepad and type and execute a new, different SQL statement:

```
SELECT state
  FROM zipcode
```

This statement is now in the buffer; however, you can execute a different SQL statement, such as the one you saved in myfile2.sql, with the START or @ command.

```
SQL>@myfile2
```

If the myfile2.sql file is stored in a directory other than the default directory, you need to specify the drive and directory name. You can also specify a valid URL such as @http://script.repository/alice/myfile2.sql.

```
SQL>@c:\examples\myfile2
```

The statement in the file runs, producing a result set. Because the file already contains a forward slash, the SQL statement is executed automatically. If you save myfile2 with an extension other than .sql, you must type the file name and extension. If you want to change myfile2 again, simply type the following. Notepad will open with myfile2.sql containing your SQL statement.

```
ED c:\examples\myfile2
```

CHANGING THE DEFAULT DIRECTORY OF SQL*PLUS FOR WINDOWS

Whenever you execute a script or save a file in SQL*Plus without specifying a directory, it is assumed to be in the default directory. Typically, this directory is named similar to C:\oracle\product\10.1.0\Db_2\BIN or C:\oracle\ora10\BIN. To change it to a different directory, such as the c:\guest directory, you need to create a shortcut. Modify the properties of the shortcut (see Figure 2.15) on the desktop to change the Start in field to the value c:\guest and then click OK. Whenever you invoke SQL*Plus through the shortcut, the c:\guest directory will be your default directory. If you are unsure how to create a shortcut in your Windows operating system, refer to the Windows documentation that came with your system. (Another way to change your default

Figure 2.15 ■ Changing the default directory in SQL*Plus for Windows.

directory is by modifying your Windows registry. Only make these modifications if you are sufficiently knowledgeable about the Windows operating system. For more information, see Oracle's *SQL*Plus User's Guide and Reference Manual.*)

COPYING AND PASTING STATEMENTS IN SQL*PLUS FOR WINDOWS

SQL*Plus for Windows allows you to copy and paste statements. You can open an editor such as Notepad in a separate window (without invoking it from SQL*Plus with the EDIT command) and enter your statements. Then select the text and copy the statement (CTRL + C or Copy from the Edit menu) and paste it into SQL*Plus using the Paste menu option or the CTRL + V command key.

EDITING IN *i*SQL*PLUS

Editing a SQL statement in *i*SQL*Plus is rather intuitive. You can enter the statements in the input area, also called the Workspace, and make changes using the delete and backspace keys or simply cut and paste. To save a statement to a text file, click on the Save Script button. You can reload the file later using the Load Script button. *i*SQL*Plus has a History tab that allows you to see the previously issued statements. Alternatively, you can also click the History link.

Figure 2.16 shows the last four statements that were issued. By default, at most the last ten statements or scripts are shown; you can increase this number when

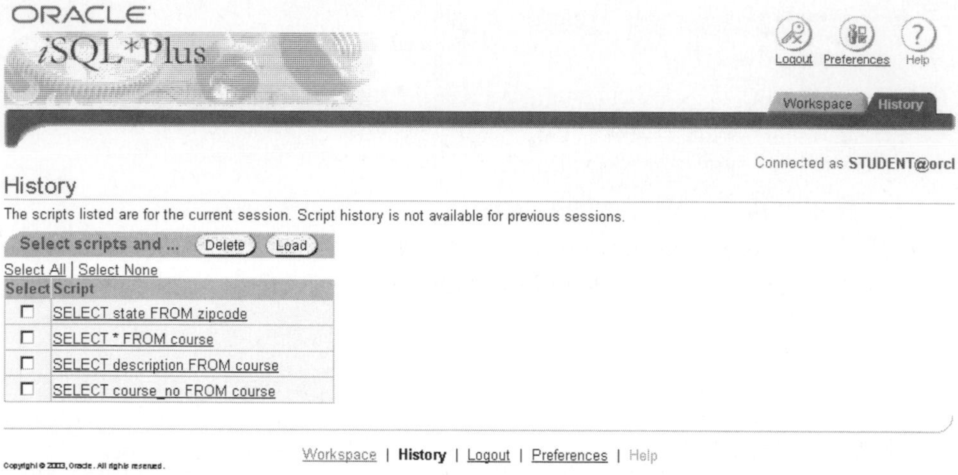

ORACLE

*i*SQL*Plus

Logout Preferences Help

Workspace History

Connected as **STUDENT@orcl**

History

The scripts listed are for the current session. Script history is not available for previous sessions.

Select scripts and ...   (Delete) (Load)

Select All | Select None

Select	Script
☐	SELECT state FROM zipcode
☐	SELECT * FROM course
☐	SELECT description FROM course
☐	SELECT course_no FROM course

Copyright © 2003, Oracle. All rights reserved.   Workspace | **History** | Logout | Preferences | Help

Figure 2.16 ■ History screen.

choosing Preferences, Interface Configuration, and then History Size. A history is only available for the duration of your current session. If you want to retain your statements after logout, you want to consider saving them to a file.

To run an individual statement, check the Select button and click the Load icon to bring the statement into the Workspace. You can load multiple statements at once, be sure to end each statement with a semicolon or a forward slash. You'll learn more about running multiple statements shortly.

PREFERENCES SCREEN

Either the Preferences icon on top or the Preference link on the bottom of the screen displays the Preferences screen. It allows you to customize your *i*SQL*Plus interface and execution environmental variables. Here you can change your password, modify the number of statements retained in the History screen, or change your display output location and page setup preferences. The menu choices on the left show Script Formatting, Script Execution, and Database Administration. These options allow you to change SQL*Plus environmental variables. You can leave them at their default setting. Most of these variables have equivalent SET commands that can be executed both in SQL*Plus and *i*SQL*Plus. You will learn more about these settings in Chapter 13, "The Data Dictionary and Advanced SQL*Plus Commands."

DIFFERENCES BETWEEN SQL*PLUS AND *i*SQL*PLUS

Throughout this book you will see both SQL*Plus and *i*SQL*Plus mentioned. For the most part the functionality between the two products is identical and does not impact on the result set, other than a different graphical output. If you are unclear if a certain SQL*Plus command performs identical in *i*SQL*Plus, refer to Appendix C, "SQL*Plus Command Reference."

Overall, there are a small number of differences between the two products, particularly with respect to edits of SQL statements and the display of data. You will find these differences highlighted in Table 2.1.

   *Unless specifically pointed out, all the mentioned SQL*Plus commands apply to both SQL*Plus and iSQL*Plus.*

**LAB
2.3**

Table 2.1 ■ Differences between SQL*Plus and *i*SQL*Plus

SQL*Plus	*i*SQL*Plus
Requires installation of SQL*Plus and Oracle Net software on individual machine.	No need to install special software, only browser is required.
Runs on individual workstation or on the server.	Runs from a browser, which is typically a workstation with access to the Web server where *i*SQL*Plus is running.
Editing via line editor or with your own editor.	Editing in the Workspace box.
SET commands control environmental variables that effect default formats and interface configuration settings among others.	Most of the SET commands can also be issued in *i*SQL*Plus. (See Appendix C, "SQL*Plus Command Reference" for differences). Alternatively, you can use the Preferences menu to modify the values.
Use the @ or START command to run scripts from a file or a URL.	For the @ or START command, only the URL format is supported.
Columns may not fit the whole width of your screen. Use various SQL*Plus formatting commands to make them display on one line.	The browser automatically handles the formatting of columns to fit the width of the screen.
To recall any previously issued statements use the SAVE command, write the statement to file, or scroll back and cut and paste.	To recall any previous statement, use the History tab, History link, or save the statement to file.

LAB 2.3 EXERCISES

 If you have access to only SQL*Plus but not iSQL*Plus or vice versa, just perform the exercises that are applicable for the specific environment. Exercises 2.3.1 and 2.3.2 use SQL*Plus only, not iSQL*Plus.

2.3.1 EDIT A SQL STATEMENT USING SQL*PLUS COMMANDS

**LAB
2.3**

Type and execute the following SQL statement (use SQL*Plus, not *i*SQL*Plus):

```
SELECT employer
  FROM student
```

a) Using SQL*Plus commands, change the column `employer` to `registration_date` and execute the statement again.

b) Using SQL*Plus commands, add a second column, `phone`, to the statement you changed. Display the PHONE column first, then the REGISTRATION_DATE column, in the result set.

2.3.2 EDIT A SQL STATEMENT USING AN EDITOR

Perform these exercises using SQL*Plus, not *i*SQL*Plus.

a) Invoke the editor and change the statement in your buffer to the following. Then save the file and execute it in SQL*Plus.

```
SELECT salutation, first_name, last_name, phone
  FROM instructor
```

b) Edit the preceding statement, which is now in your buffer, save it as inst.sql, and use the START or @ command to execute it in SQL*Plus.

c) Edit inst.sql, save it as inst.x, and use the START or @ command to execute it in SQL*Plus.

2.3.3 SAVE, RETRIEVE, AND RUN A SQL STATEMENT IN *i*SQL*PLUS

a) Enter the following SELECT statement into the Workspace area and execute the statement. Then save the statement in a file called state_zip.sql and press the Clear button.

```
SELECT DISTINCT state
  FROM zipcode
```

b) Click the Load Script button and then the Browse... button and locate the state_zip.sql file you just saved. Then press the Load button to load it into the Workspace. Execute the statement.

c) Explain the difference between the SQL language and SQL*Plus or *i*SQL*Plus.

LAB 2.3 EXERCISE ANSWERS

2.3.1 ANSWERS

Type and execute the following SQL statement (use SQL*Plus, not *i*SQL*Plus):

```
SELECT employer
  FROM student
```

a) Using SQL*Plus commands, change the column employer to registration_date and execute the statement again.

Answer: Select the first line in the buffer, then use the CHANGE command to change EMPLOYER to REGISTRATION_DATE.

Type 1 to select the first line in the buffer:

```
SQL.> 1
  1* SELECT employer
```

Then use the CHANGE command:

```
SQL> c/employer/registration_date
  1* SELECT registration_date
```

Type L to list the changed statement:

```
SQL> L
  1 SELECT registration_date
  2*   FROM student
```

If you care to run the query, you can do so with the forward slash "/", which then executes the statement currently in the buffer.

b) Using SQL*Plus commands, add a second column, phone, to the statement you changed. Display the PHONE column first, then the REGISTRATION_DATE column, in the result set.

Answer: You must again select the first line in the buffer, then use the CHANGE command to add the PHONE column to the SELECT list.

Type 1 to select the first line in the buffer:

```
SQL> 1
  1* SELECT registration_date
```

Then use the CHANGE command:

```
C/SELECT/SELECT phone,
```

Here, the CHANGE command will replace SELECT with SELECT phone, (including the comma), changing your statement to the following:

```
1 SELECT phone, registration_date
2*  FROM student
```

The result set will display phone first, then the registration date:

```
PHONE              REGISTRAT
---------------    ---------
201-555-5555       18-FEB-03
201-555-5555       22-FEB-03
...
718-555-5555       22-FEB-03
718-555-5555       28-JAN-03

268 rows selected.
```

The CHANGE command looks for the first occurrence, from left to right, of the text you wish to change. When it locates it, it replaces this occurrence with the new text you wish to change it to.

OTHER USEFUL LINE EDITOR COMMANDS

Besides the CHANGE and LIST commands, the SQL*Plus line editor has a number of other commands. For example, to add another column to the SQL statement you use the APPEND command. The statement currently in the buffer lists as follows:

```
SQL> L
1 SELECT phone, registration_date
2*  FROM student
```

First choose the line to which you want to add at the end, then use the A command and add the text you want to append. In the following example the ", last_name" text was added to the statement.

```
SQL> 1
  1* SELECT phone, registration_date
SQL> A , last_name
  1* SELECT phone, registration_date, last_name
```

Another useful command is the INPUT command; it adds a new line after the current line. To insert the text ", first_name" on the next line, use the INPUT or I command. SQL*Plus prompts you for a new line and you enter the text and press Enter. SQL*Plus prompts you once more for another new line and if you are finished adding, you press Enter again to indicate that you are done.

```
SQL> 1
  1* SELECT phone, registration_date, last_name
SQL> I
  2i        , first_name
  3i
SQL> L
  1  SELECT phone, registration_date, last_name
  2        , first_name
  3*    FROM student
```

If you need to insert the line before line 1, enter a 0 (zero) followed by a space and text. Use the DEL command if you want to delete lines in the buffer. To delete line 2, you enter:

```
SQL> DEL 2
SQL> L
  1  SELECT phone, registration_date, last_name
  2*    FROM student
```

You can also save the statement using the SQL*Plus SAVE command. In the next example, the SQL query is saved in the c:\guest directory under the file name myexample.sql; if you don't specify the extension, by default it will be .sql.

```
SQL> SAVE c:\guest\myexample
Created file c:\guest\myexample
```

You do not need to type a semicolon or forward slash, it will automatically be added. The statement can now be run either with the START or @ command. If you subsequently write other SQL statements and the statement is no longer in the SQL buffer, you can load it back into the buffer with the GET command. (The .sql extension is optional). You can then re-execute the statement with the forward slash.

```
SQL> GET c:\guest\myexample
  1  SELECT phone, registration_date, last_name
  2*    FROM student
```

2.3.2 ANSWERS

a) Invoke the editor and change the statement in your buffer to the following. Then save the file and execute it in SQL*Plus.

```
SELECT salutation, first_name, last_name, phone
   FROM instructor
```

Answer: Use the EDIT *command to edit the file and execute the changed statement in SQL*Plus with the forward slash.*

b) Edit the preceding statement, which is now in your buffer, save it as inst.sql, and use the START or @ command to execute it in SQL*Plus.

Answer: Use the EDIT *command to edit the file and save it as inst.sql. Execute the changed statement in SQL*Plus with the* START *or* @ *command.*

```
SQL>@inst.sql
```

c) Edit inst.sql, save it as inst.x, and use the START or @ command to execute it in SQL*Plus.

Answer: At the SQL prompt, type EDIT, *edit the file in your editor, save the file as inst.x, exit the editor, type at the SQL>prompt the command* @inst.x *to execute the changed statement.*

Because you saved the file with an extension other than .sql, you must explicitly reference both the file name and its extension. If you want to edit this file, you must type EDIT inst.x at the SQL prompt.

2.3.3 ANSWERS

a) Enter the following SELECT statement into the Workspace area and execute the statement. Then save the statement in a file called state_zip.sql and press the Clear button.

```
SELECT DISTINCT state
   FROM zipcode
```

Answer: When you execute this statement, it returns a list of the state abbreviations from the ZIPCODE table. When you click on the Save Script button, a message box informs you that the file is transferred from the Web browser to your individual computer. Click the Save button to save it on your computer (see Figure 2.17).

After you click the Save button you are prompted to enter the file name. You see a suggested file name, but change it to state_zip.sql instead and change the Save

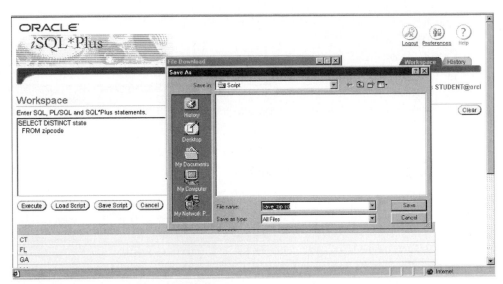

Figure 2.17 ■ Save a file in *iSQL*Plus.

as type to "All Files". The term *script* is just another word for command file containing one or multiple commands.

If you click the Clear button, the input area and output area are cleared, but note the SQL buffer is not cleared and it will still list the last statement if you were to enter the LIST command.

b) Click the Load Script button and then the Browse… button and locate the state_zip.sql file you just saved. Then press the Load button to load it into the Workspace. Execute the statement.

Answer: When you click the Browse. . . button, you will see a dialog box that displays the directory and file name similar to Figure 2.18. Then you need to press the Load button to transfer the file into the Workspace for execution. Afterwards, you can click the Execute button to run the statement. It is useful to save a file, if you want to retain the statement. iSQL*Plus retains a history of SQL statements you can access after you have cleared the screeen, but it is no longer available after your session ends.

RUNNING MULTIPLE STATEMENTS IN *iSQL*PLUS

You can run multiple SQL statements in *iSQL*Plus. For example, if you want to run the following two statements, you either place them in a script file or simply type them into the input area. Just be sure to end every statement with either a semicolon or a forward slash at the beginning of a separate line. Note: you don't need a semicolon or forward slash for the last statement unless you run the statements inside a script file. In this case you must end each statement with either

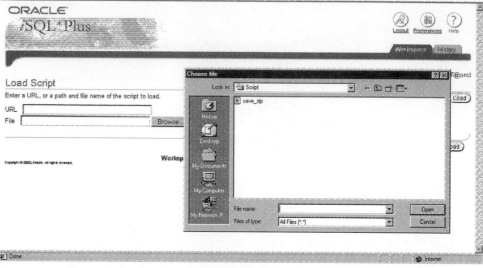

Figure 2.18 ■ The Choose file dialog in *iSQL*Plus.

one. Therefore, it is a good habit to place either the semicolon or forward slash after each statement.

In Figure 2.19, you see two query results. One shows the distinct zip codes for all instructors, and the second result is a listing of first and last names for all students. The second statement does not quite fit on one screen, but you can scroll down to see the rest.

Connected as STUDENT@orcl

Workspace   (Clear)

Enter SQL, PL/SQL and SQL*Plus statements.

```
SELECT DISTINCT zip
  FROM instructor
/
SELECT last_name, first_name
  FROM student
```

(Execute) (Load Script) (Save Script) (Cancel)

ZIP
10005
10015
10025
10035

LAST_NAME	FIRST_NAME
Cadet	Austin V.
M. Orent	Frank
Winnicki	Yvonne

Figure 2.19 ■ Executing multiple SQL statements.

Be careful, do not add both a semicolon and a forward slash to the same statement, otherwise it will be executed twice. For example, the next SQL statement will be executed twice.

```
SELECT DISTINCT zip
   FROM zipcode;
/
```

COMMENTS IN SQL SCRIPTS

Placing comments or remarks into a SQL script is very useful when you revisit the script later. It helps document the purpose, thoughts, and ideas or simply lists the author and creation date. You must identify the comment; otherwise you will receive an error when running the command. You can distinguish between two different types of comments: a single-line comment denoted with double dashes or a multiline comment spawning multiple lines, which starts with an opening comment like this, /*, and ends with a closing comment, which looks like this, */.

Following is an example of a script file that includes comments, but comments can also be embedded within the SQL statement itself.

```
/* Multi-line comment
Homework #2
By: Kirsten Sochner
Date created: 4/30/2002
*/

-- Answer #1:  This is a single-line comment!
SELECT DISTINCT state
   FROM zipcode;

-- Answer #2:
COL cost FORMAT $9,999.99
SELECT DISTINCT cost
   FROM course;

-- Answer #3:
SELECT instructor_id, -- Comment within a SQL statement!
       zip
   FROM instructor;
```

Note that SQL*Plus also has a REMARK command abbreviated as REM that allows single-line comments. This command is not recognized as a comment when your SQL statement is executed in an environment other than SQL*Plus or *i*SQL*Plus; it can also not be embedded in a SQL statement. Use the single-line and double-line comments mentioned previously instead!

c) Explain the difference between the SQL language and SQL*Plus or iSQL*Plus.

*Answer: SQL is a language that allows you to retrieve, manipulate, define, and control access to the database. SQL*Plus and iSQL*Plus are environments in which to execute the SQL statements and display the results.*

iSQL*Plus is the Web-based version of SQL*Plus and both programs are Oracle proprietary products. You can use other software programs to execute your SQL statements against an Oracle database. If you want to format your results in special ways use the SQL*Plus commands such as COLUMN FORMAT. If you don't execute the commands in iSQL*Plus or SQL*Plus these formatting commands are not available and you will need to use specific SQL functions to achieve somewhat similar results. Some of these SQL functions are discussed in the next chapter.

LAB 2.3 SELF-REVIEW QUESTIONS

In order to test your progress, you should be able to answer the following questions.

1) You can save a SQL statement to the SQL buffer for it to be referenced later.

   a) _____ True
   b) _____ False

2) After typing a SQL statement, you can execute it with either the semicolon or the forward slash.

   a) _____ True
   b) _____ False

3) You cannot save a .sql file to the A: drive.

   a) _____ True
   b) _____ False

4) The SQL*Plus START command can execute what is in the SQL buffer.

   a) _____ True
   b) _____ False

Answers appear in Appendix A, Section 2.3.

LAB 2.4

THE WHERE CLAUSE: COMPARISON AND LOGICAL OPERATORS

LAB OBJECTIVES

After this lab, you will be able to:
- ✔ Use Comparison and Logical Operators in a WHERE Clause
- ✔ Use NULL in a WHERE Clause

The *WHERE clause,* also called the *predicate,* provides the power to narrow down the scope of data retrieved. In fact, most SQL statements you write will contain a WHERE clause.

COMPARISON OPERATORS

Comparison operators compare expressions. An *expression* can be a column of any datatype, a *string* or *text literal* (sometimes referred to as a *text constant* or *character literal*), a number, or any combination of these. An expression can also be a *function* or *mathematical computation,* which you will learn about in Chapter 3, "Character, Number, and Miscellaneous Functions." An expression always results in a value.

TESTING FOR EQUALITY AND INEQUALITY

Comparison operators compare one expression with another expression. One of the most commonly used comparison operators is the *equal* operator, denoted by the = symbol. For example, if you are asked to provide the first name, last name, and phone number of a teacher with the last name of Schorin, you write the following SQL statement:

```
SELECT first_name, last_name, phone
  FROM instructor
 WHERE last_name = 'Schorin'
FIRST_NAME LAST_NAME  PHONE
---------- ---------- ----------
Nina       Schorin    2125551212

1 row selected.
```

Here, the column LAST_NAME is the left side of the equation and the text literal 'Schorin' is the right side. Single quotes are used around the text literal 'Schorin'. This statement will only retrieve rows from the INSTRUCTOR table that satisfy this condition in the WHERE clause. In this case, only one row is retrieved.

When you describe the INSTRUCTOR table, you see the datatype of the LAST_NAME column is VARCHAR2. This means the data contained in this column is alphanumeric. When two values are compared to each other, they must be of the same datatype; otherwise, Oracle returns an error. You will learn more about converting from one datatype to another in Chapter 4, "Date and Conversion Functions."

```
SQL> DESCR instructor
 Name                                     Null?    Type
 ---------------------------------------- -------- ------------
 INSTRUCTOR_ID                            NOT NULL NUMBER(8)
 SALUTATION                                        VARCHAR2(5)
 FIRST_NAME                                        VARCHAR2(25)
 LAST_NAME                                         VARCHAR2(25)
 STREET_ADDRESS                                    VARCHAR2(50)
 ZIP                                               VARCHAR2(5)
 PHONE                                             VARCHAR2(15)
 CREATED_BY                               NOT NULL VARCHAR2(30)
 CREATED_DATE                             NOT NULL DATE
 MODIFIED_BY                              NOT NULL VARCHAR2(30)
 MODIFIED_DATE                            NOT NULL DATE
```

SQL is case insensitive when it comes to column names, table names, and keywords such as SELECT. (There are some exceptions with regard to column names and table names. For more information see Chapter 11, "Create, Alter, and Drop Tables.") When you compare a text literal to a database column, the case of the data must match exactly. The syntax of the following statement is correct, but it does not yield any rows because the instructor's last name is obviously not in the correct case.

```
SELECT first_name, last_name, phone
  FROM instructor
 WHERE last_name = 'schorin'
```

no rows selected

Just as equality is useful, so is inequality.

```
SELECT first_name, last_name, phone
  FROM instructor
 WHERE last_name <> 'Schorin'
```

FIRST_NAME	LAST_NAME	PHONE
Fernand	Hanks	2125551212
Tom	Wojick	2125551212
...		
Marilyn	Frantzen	2125551212
Irene	Willig	2125551212

9 rows selected.

All rows except the one with the last name of 'Schorin', are retrieved. Inequality can also be expressed with the != notation.

THE GREATER THAN AND LESS THAN OPERATORS

The comparison operators >, <, >=, and <= can all be used to compare values in columns. In the following example, the >=, or *greater than or equal to,* operator is used to retrieve a list of course descriptions whose cost is greater than or equal to 1195:

```
SELECT description, cost
  FROM course
 WHERE cost >= 1195
```

DESCRIPTION	COST
DP Overview	1195
Intro to Computers	1195
...	
Database System Principles	1195
PL/SQL Programming	1195

26 rows selected.

The value 1195 is not enclosed in single quotes because it is a number literal.

THE BETWEEN COMPARISON OPERATOR

The BETWEEN operator tests for a range of values:

```
SELECT description, cost
  FROM course
 WHERE cost BETWEEN 1000 AND 1100
DESCRIPTION                        COST
--------------------------------   ----
Unix Tips and Techniques           1095
Intro to Internet                  1095
Intro to the Basic Language        1095

3 rows selected.
```

BETWEEN is inclusive of both values defining the range; the result set includes courses that cost 1000 and 1100 and everything in between. The lower end of the range must be listed first.

If you use *i*SQL*Plus then your result may look similar to Figure 2.20. Note that the result is identical; the only difference is the formatting.

DESCRIPTION	COST
Unix Tips and Techniques	1095
Intro to Internet	1095
Intro to the Basic Language	1095

Figure 2.20 ■ *i*SQL*Plus result.

BETWEEN is most useful for number and date comparisons, but it can also be used for comparing text strings in alphabetical order. Date comparisons are discussed in Chapter 4, "Date and Conversion Functions."

THE IN OPERATOR

The IN operator works with a *list of values,* separated by commas, contained within a set of parentheses. The following query looks for courses where the cost is either 1095 or 1595.

```
SELECT description, cost
  FROM course
 WHERE cost IN (1095, 1595)
DESCRIPTION                           COST
------------------------------------  ----
Structured Programming Techniques     1595
Unix Tips and Techniques              1095
```

```
Intro to Internet                           1095
Intro to the Basic Language                 1095
```

4 rows selected.

THE LIKE OPERATOR

Another very useful comparison operator is LIKE, which performs pattern-matching using the percent (%) or underscore (_) characters as wildcards. The percent wildcard is used to denote multiple characters, while the underscore wildcard is used to denote a single character. The next query retrieves rows where the last name begins with the uppercase letter S and ends in anything else:

```
SELECT first_name, last_name, phone
  FROM instructor
 WHERE last_name LIKE 'S%'
```

FIRST_NAME	LAST_NAME	PHONE
Nina	Schorin	2125551212
Todd	Smythe	2125551212

2 rows selected.

The % character may be placed at the beginning, end, or anywhere within the literal text, but always within the single quotes. This is also true of the underscore wildcard character, as in this statement:

```
SELECT first_name, last_name
  FROM instructor
 WHERE last_name LIKE '_o%'
```

FIRST_NAME	LAST_NAME
Tom	Wojick
Anita	Morris
Charles	Lowry

3 rows selected.

The WHERE clause returns only rows where the last name begins with any character, but the second letter must be a lowercase o. The rest of the last name is irrelevant.

NEGATING USING NOT

All the previously mentioned operators can be negated with the NOT comparison operator; for example, NOT BETWEEN, NOT IN, NOT LIKE.

```
SELECT phone
  FROM instructor
 WHERE last_name NOT LIKE 'S%'
```

In the SQL statement the LAST_NAME column used in the WHERE clause doesn't appear in the SELECT list. There is no rule about columns in the WHERE clause having to exist in the SELECT list.

The LIKE operator works well for simple pattern matching. If your pattern is more complex, you may want to consider using Oracle's regular expression functionality discussed in Chapter 15, "Regular Expressions and Hierarchical Queries."

EVALUATING NULL VALUES

Recall that NULL means an unknown value. The IS NULL and IS NOT NULL operators evaluate whether a data value is NULL or not. The following SQL statement returns courses that do not have a prerequisite:

```
SELECT description, prerequisite
  FROM course
 WHERE prerequisite IS NULL
DESCRIPTION                           PREREQUISITE
------------------------------------  ------------
DP Overview
Intro to Computers
Java for C/C++ Programmers
Operating Systems

4 rows selected.
```

Null values represent the unknown; a null cannot be equal or unequal to any value or to another null. Therefore, always use the IS NULL or IS NOT NULL operator when testing for nulls. There are a few exceptions when nulls are treated differently and a null can be equal to another null. One such example is the use of DISTINCT (see Lab 2.2). You will learn about the exceptions in the treatment of nulls throughout this book.

OVERVIEW OF COMPARISON OPERATORS

The comparison operators you have learned about so far are sometimes referred to as predicates or search conditions. A predicate is an expression that results in either a true, false, or unknown value. Table 2.2 provides you with a list of the

Table 2.2 ■ SQL Comparison Operators

Comparison Operator	Definition
=	Equal
!=, <>	Not equal
>, >=	Greater than, greater than or equal to
<, <=	Less than, less than or equal to
BETWEEN . . . AND . . .	Inclusive of two values
LIKE	Pattern matching with wildcard characters % and _
IN (. . .)	List of values
IS NULL	Test for null values

most common comparison operators. You will learn about additional operators such as EXISTS, ANY, SOME, ALL in Chapter 7, "Subqueries," and the OVERLAPS operator in Chapter 4, "Date and Conversion Functions." All these operators can be negated with the NOT logical operator.

LOGICAL OPERATORS

To harness the ultimate power of the WHERE clause, comparison operators can be combined with the help of the *logical operators* AND and OR. These logical operators are also referred to as *boolean operators*. They group expressions, all within the same WHERE clause of a single SQL statement.

For example, the following SQL query combines two comparison operators with the help of the AND boolean operator. The result shows rows where a course costs 1095 and the course description starts with the letter I:

```
SELECT description, cost
  FROM course
 WHERE cost = 1095
   AND description LIKE 'I%'
DESCRIPTION                             COST
--------------------------------------- ----
Intro to Internet                       1095
Intro to the Basic Language             1095

2 rows selected.
```

With just the = operator in the WHERE clause, the result set contains three rows. With the addition of the AND description LIKE 'I%', the result is further reduced to two rows.

PRECEDENCE OF LOGICAL OPERATORS

When AND and OR are used together in a WHERE clause, the AND operator always takes precedence over the OR operator, meaning any AND conditions are evaluated first. If there are multiple operators of the same precedence, the left operator is executed before the right. You can manipulate the precedence in the WHERE clause with the use of parentheses. In the following SQL statement, the AND and OR logical operators are combined:

```
SELECT description, cost, prerequisite
  FROM course
 WHERE cost = 1195
   AND prerequisite = 20
    OR prerequisite = 25
```

DESCRIPTION	COST	PREREQUISITE
Hands-On Windows	1195	20
Structured Analysis	1195	20
Project Management	1195	20
GUI Programming	1195	20
Intro to SQL	1195	20
Intro to the Basic Language	1095	25
Database System Principles	1195	25

```
7 rows selected.
```

The preceding SQL statement selects any record that has either a cost of 1195 and a prerequisite of 20, or just has a prerequisite of 25 no matter what the cost. The sixth row, `Intro to the Basic Language`, is selected because it satisfies the OR expression `prerequisite = 25`. The seventh row, `Database System Principles`, only satisfies one of the AND conditions, not both. However, the row is part of the result set because it satisfies the OR condition.

Here is the same SQL statement, but with parentheses to group the expressions in the WHERE clause:

```
SELECT description, cost, prerequisite
  FROM course
 WHERE cost = 1195
   AND (prerequisite = 20
      OR prerequisite = 25)
```

DESCRIPTION	COST	PREREQUISITE
Database System Principles	1195	25
Hands-On Windows	1195	20
Structured Analysis	1195	20
Project Management	1195	20

LAB 2.4

```
GUI Programming                      1195           20
Intro to SQL                         1195           20

6 rows selected.
```

The first expression selects only courses where the cost is equal to 1195. If the pre-requisite is either 25 or 20, then the second condition is also true. Both expressions need to be true for the row to be displayed. These are the basic rules of logical operators. If two conditions are combined with the AND operator, both conditions must be true; if two conditions are connected by the OR operator, only one of the conditions needs to be true for the record to be selected.

The result set returns six rows instead of seven. The order in which items in the WHERE clause are evaluated is changed by the use of parentheses and results in a different output.

 To ensure that your SQL statements are clearly understood, it is always best to use parentheses.

NULLS AND LOGICAL OPERATORS

SQL uses *tri-value logic*; this means a condition can evaluate to true, false, or unknown. (This is in contrast to boolean logic, where a condition must be either true or false.) A row gets returned when the condition evaluates to true. The following query returns rows from the COURSE table starting with the words Intro to as the description *and* a value equal or larger than 140 in the PREREQUISITE column.

```
SELECT description, prerequisite
  FROM course
 WHERE description LIKE 'Intro to%'
   AND prerequisite >= 140
DESCRIPTION                          PREREQUISITE
----------------------------------   ------------
Intro to Programming                          140
Intro to Unix                                 310

2 rows selected.
```

Rows with a null value in the PREREQUISITE column are not included because null is an unknown value. This null value in the column is not equal or greater to 140. Therefore, the row Intro to Computers does not satisfy *both* conditions and is excluded from the result set. Following is the list of course descriptions with null values in the PREREQUISITE column. It shows the row Intro to Computers with a null value in the PREREQUISITE column.

```
SELECT description, prerequisite, cost
  FROM course
 WHERE prerequisite IS NULL
DESCRIPTION                    PREREQUISITE       COST
---------------------------    ----------------   ----
Operating Systems                                 1195
Java for C/C++ Programmers                        1195
DP Overview                                       1195
Intro to Computers                                1195

4 rows selected.
```

The AND truth table in Table 2.3 illustrates the combination of two conditions with the AND operator. Only if *both* conditions are true is a row returned for output. In this example, with the prerequisite being null, the condition is unknown and therefore the row not included in the result. The comparison against a null value yields unknown unless you specifically test for it with the IS NULL or IS NOT operators.

Table 2.3 ■ AND Truth Table

AND	TRUE	FALSE	UNKNOWN
TRUE	TRUE	FALSE	UNKNOWN
FALSE	FALSE	FALSE	FALSE
UNKNOWN	UNKNOWN	FALSE	UNKNOWN

For the OR condition, just *one* of the conditions needs to be true. Again, let's examine how nulls behave under this scenario using the same query, but this time with the OR operator. The Intro to Computers course is now listed because it satisfies the 'Intro to%' condition only. In addition, you will notice that rows such as DB Programming in Java do not start with the 'Intro to' as the description, but satisfy the second condition, which is a prerequisite of greater or equal to 140.

```
SELECT description, prerequisite
  FROM course
 WHERE description LIKE 'Intro to%'
    OR prerequisite >= 140
DESCRIPTION                          PREREQUISITE
---------------------------------    ------------
DB Programming in Java                        350
Database Design                               420
Internet Protocols                            310
Intro to Computers
```

```
Intro to Internet                           10
Intro to Java Programming                   80
Intro to Programming                       140
Intro to SQL                                20
Intro to Unix                              310
Intro to the Basic Language                 25
JDeveloper Techniques                      350
Oracle Tools                               220
Structured Programming Techniques          204

13 rows selected.
```

Table 2.4 shows the truth table for the OR operator; it highlights the fact that just one of the conditions need be true for the row to be returned in the result set. It is irrelevant if the second condition evaluates to false or unknown.

Table 2.4 ■ OR Truth Table

OR	TRUE	FALSE	UNKNOWN
TRUE	TRUE	TRUE	TRUE
FALSE	TRUE	FALSE	UNKNOWN
UNKNOWN	TRUE	UNKNOWN	UNKNOWN

When you negate a condition with the NOT operator and the value you are comparing against is a null value, it also results in a null (see Table 2.5). The following query demonstrates that none of the null prerequisites are included in the result set.

```
SELECT description, prerequisite
   FROM course
  WHERE NOT prerequisite >= 140
DESCRIPTION                          PREREQUISITE
------------------------------------ ------------
Intro to Internet                              10
GUI Programming                                20
Intro to SQL                                   20
Hands-On Windows                               20
Structured Analysis                            20
Project Management                             20
Intro to the Basic Language                    25
Database System Principles                     25
PL/SQL Programming                             80
Intro to Java Programming                      80
Intermediate Java Programming                 120
```

```
Advanced Java Programming              122
JDeveloper                             122
JDeveloper Lab                         125
Basics of Unix Admin                   130
Network Administration                 130
Advanced Unix Admin                    132
Unix Tips and Techniques               134

18 rows selected.
```

Table 2.5 ■ NOT Truth Table

NOT	TRUE	FALSE	UNKNOWN
NOT	FALSE	TRUE	UNKNOWN

LAB 2.4

LAB 2.4 EXERCISES

2.4.1 USE COMPARISON AND LOGICAL OPERATORS IN A WHERE CLAUSE

a) Write a SELECT statement to list the last names of students living either in zip code 10048, 11102, or 11209.

b) Write a SELECT statement to list the first and last names of instructors with the letter "i" (either uppercase or lowercase) in their last name living in the zip code 10025.

c) Does the following statement contain an error? Explain.

```
SELECT last_name
  FROM instructor
 WHERE created_date = modified_by
```

d) What do you observe when you execute the following SQL statement?

```
SELECT course_no, cost
  FROM course
 WHERE cost BETWEEN 1500 AND 1000
```

e) Execute the following query and determine how many rows the query returns.

```
SELECT last_name, student_id
  FROM student
 WHERE ROWNUM <= 10
```

2.4.2 USE NULL IN A WHERE CLAUSE

a) Write a SELECT statement to list descriptions of courses with prerequisites and cost less than 1100.

b) Write a SELECT statement to list the cost of courses without a prerequisite; do not repeat the cost.

LAB 2.4 EXERCISE ANSWERS

2.4.1 ANSWERS

a) Write a SELECT statement to list the last names of students living either in zip code 10048, 11102, or 11209.

Answer: The SELECT statement selects a single column and uses the IN comparison operator in the WHERE clause.

```
SELECT last_name
  FROM student
 WHERE zip IN ('10048', '11102', '11209')
LAST_NAME
---------------
Masser
Allende
Winnicki
Wilson
Williams
McLean
Lefkowitz

7 rows selected.
```

The statement can also be written using the equal operator (=), in combination with the logical operator OR, and yields the same result set:

```
SELECT last_name
  FROM student
 WHERE zip = '10048'
    OR zip = '11102'
    OR zip = '11209'
```

There will be times when a SELECT statement can be written more than one way. The preceding statements are logically equivalent.

LAB
2.4

b) Write a SELECT statement to list the first and last names of instructors with the letter "i" (either uppercase or lowercase) in their last name living in the zip code 10025.

Answer: The SELECT statement selects two columns and uses the LIKE, =, and the AND and OR logical operators, combined with parentheses, in the WHERE clause.

```
SELECT first_name, last_name
  FROM instructor
 WHERE (last_name LIKE '%i%' OR last_name LIKE '%I%')
   AND zip = '10025'
FIRST_NAME                          LAST_NAME
-------------------------           ---------
Tom                                 Wojick
Nina                                Schorin

2 rows selected.
```

The LIKE operator must be used twice in this example because there is no way of knowing whether there is an upper or lowercase 'i' anywhere in the last name. You must test for both conditions, which cannot be done using a single LIKE operator. If one of the OR conditions is true, the expression is true.

If you need to search for the actual % symbol within a column value, you can use a SQL function or an escape character. You learn more about this in Chapter 3, "Character, Number, and Miscellaneous Functions."

c) Does the following statement contain an error? Explain.

```
SELECT last_name
  FROM instructor
 WHERE created_date = modified_by
```

Answer: Yes. The two columns in the WHERE clause are not the same datatype and the Oracle database returns an error when this statement is executed.

You will get an error similar to the following when you execute the statement.

```
SQL> SELECT last_name
  2    FROM instructor
  3   WHERE created_date = modified_by
  4  /
 WHERE created_date = modified_by
                  *
ERROR at line 3:
ORA-01858: a non-numeric character was found where a numeric was expected
```

There are times when the datatypes of columns do not agree and you need to convert from one datatype to another. You will learn about these circumstances in Chapter 4, "Date and Conversion Functions." (In this exercise example, data conversion is not fruitful because the data in these two columns is of a very different nature.)

d) What do you observe when you execute the following SQL statement?

```
SELECT course_no, cost
  FROM course
 WHERE cost BETWEEN 1500 AND 1000
no rows selected
```

Answer: The query returns no rows. Although there are courses that cost between 1000 and 1500, the BETWEEN clause requires the lower end of the range to be listed first. If the query is rewritten as follows, it returns rows.

```
SELECT course_no, cost
  FROM course
 WHERE cost BETWEEN 1000 AND 1500
```

BETWEEN AND TEXT LITERALS

As mentioned previously, BETWEEN is most often used for numbers and dates, which you will learn about in Chapter 4, "Date and Conversion Functions." You can apply the BETWEEN functions to text columns as you see in the next example, which utilizes the BETWEEN operator with text literals W and Z. The query lists the student's ID and the last name. Notice any students whose last name begins with the letter "Z" are not included, because the STUDENT table has no student with a last name of the single letter "Z". If a student's last name was spelled "waldo", this student would not be included in the result, because the WHERE clause is only looking for last names that fall between the uppercase letters of W and Z.

```
SELECT student_id, last_name
  FROM student
 WHERE last_name BETWEEN 'W' AND 'Z'
STUDENT_ID LAST_NAME
---------- ---------
       142 Waldman
...
       241 Yourish

11 rows selected.
```

If you are looking for "waldo", regardless of the case, use the OR operator to include both conditions.

```
SELECT student_id, last_name
  FROM student
 WHERE last_name BETWEEN 'W' AND 'Z'
    OR last_name BETWEEN 'w' AND 'z'
```

Here is another example of how you can use the BETWEEN and the >= and <= operators with text literals.

```
SELECT description
  FROM grade_type
 WHERE description BETWEEN 'Midterm' and 'Project'
```

This would be equivalent to:

```
SELECT description
  FROM grade_type
 WHERE description >= 'Midterm'
   AND description <= 'Project'
```

DESCRIPTION

Midterm
Participation
Project

3 rows selected.

e) Execute the following query and determine how many rows the query returns.

```
SELECT last_name, student_id
  FROM student
 WHERE ROWNUM <= 10
```

Answer: The query returns ten rows. The WHERE clause uses the pseudocolumn ROWNUM, which restricts the result to the first ten or less rows. A pseudocolumn is not a real column that exists on a table; you can select the column, but you cannot manipulate its value.

LAST_NAME	STUDENT_ID
Kocka	230
Jung	232
Mulroy	233
Brendler	234
Carcia	235
Tripp	236
Frost	237
Snow	238

```
Scrittorale                        240
Yourish                            241
```

10 rows selected.

The next statement shows the value of the ROWNUM pseudocolumn column in the SELECT list. The first row displays the ROWNUM value of 1,the second the ROWNUM value of 2, and so on. The ROWNUM pseudocolumn is useful if you want to limit the number of rows returned by a query. You will see additional examples of this and other pseudocolumns in subsequent chapters.

```
SELECT ROWNUM, last_name, student_id
   FROM student
 WHERE ROWNUM <= 10
     ROWNUM LAST_NAME                        STUDENT_ID
 ---------- ------------------------------ ----------
          1 Kocka                                 230
          2 Jung                                  232
          3 Mulroy                                233
          4 Brendler                              234
...
          9 Scrittorale                           240
         10 Yourish                               241
```

10 rows selected.

2.4.2 ANSWERS

a) Write a SELECT statement to list descriptions of courses with prerequisites and cost less than 1100.

Answer: The SELECT statement uses the IS NOT NULL and less than (<) comparison operators in the WHERE clause.

```
SELECT description, cost, prerequisite
   FROM course
 WHERE prerequisite IS NOT NULL
   AND cost < 1100
DESCRIPTION                              COST PREREQUISITE
------------------------------------- ---- ------------
Intro to Internet                      1095           10
Intro to the Basic Language            1095           25
Unix Tips and Techniques               1095          134
```

3 rows selected.

Both conditions need to be true for the row to be returned. If the one of the conditions is not met, the row simply is not selected for output.

b) Write a SELECT statement to list the cost of courses without a prerequisite; do not repeat the cost.

Answer: The SELECT statement selects a single column in combination with DISTINCT, and uses the IS NULL comparison operator in the WHERE clause.

```
SELECT DISTINCT cost
  FROM course
 WHERE prerequisite IS NULL
       COST
----------
       1195

1 row selected.
```

LAB 2.4 SELF-REVIEW QUESTIONS

In order to test your progress, you should be able to answer the following questions.

1) Comparison operators always compare two values only.

a) _____ True
b) _____ False

2) The BETWEEN operator uses a list of values.

a) _____ True
b) _____ False

3) The following statement is incorrect:

```
SELECT first_name, last_name
  FROM student
 WHERE employer = NULL
```

a) _____ True
b) _____ False

4) The following statement is incorrect:

```
SELECT description
  FROM course
 WHERE cost NOT LIKE (1095, 1195)
```

a) _____ True
b) _____ False

5) The following statement is incorrect:

```
SELECT city
  FROM zipcode
 WHERE state != 'NY'
```

a) _____ True
b) _____ False

6) The following statement returns rows in the STUDENT table where the last name begins with the letters SM.

```
SELECT last_name, first_name
  FROM student
 WHERE last_name = 'SM%'
```

a) _____ True
b) _____ False

Answers appear in Appendix A, Section 2.4.

LAB
2.4

LAB 2.5

THE ORDER BY CLAUSE

LAB OBJECTIVES

After this lab, you will be able to:

✔ Custom Sort Query Results

USING THE ORDER BY CLAUSE

Recall from Chapter 1, "SQL and Data," that data is not stored in a table in any particular order. In all of the examples used thus far, the result sets display data in the order in which they happen to be returned from the database. However, you may want to view data in a certain order and the ORDER BY clause accomplishes this by ordering the data any way you wish.

For example, the following statement retrieves a list of course numbers and descriptions for courses without a prerequisite, in alphabetical order by their descriptions:

```
SELECT course_no, description
  FROM course
 WHERE prerequisite IS NULL
 ORDER BY description
COURSE_NO DESCRIPTION
--------- --------------------------
       10 DP Overview
       20 Intro to Computers
      146 Java for C/C++ Programmers
      310 Operating Systems

4 rows selected.
```

By default, when the ORDER BY is used, the result set is sorted in *ascending* order; or you can be explicit by adding the abbreviation ASC after the column. If descending order is desired, the abbreviation DESC is used after the column in the ORDER BY clause:

```
SELECT course_no, description
  FROM course
 WHERE prerequisite IS NULL
 ORDER BY description DESC
```

COURSE_NO	DESCRIPTION
310	Operating Systems
146	Java for C/C++ Programmers
20	Intro to Computers
10	DP Overview

4 rows selected.

Instead of listing the name of the column to be ordered, you can list the sequence number of the column in the SELECT list. The next SQL statement returns the same result as the prior SQL statement, but uses a different ORDER BY clause. The number 2 indicates the second column of the SELECT list.

```
SELECT course_no, description
  FROM course
 WHERE prerequisite IS NULL
 ORDER BY 2 DESC
```

A result set can be sorted by more than one column. The columns you wish to sort by need only be included in the ORDER BY clause, separated by commas. The ORDER BY clause is always the last clause in an SQL statement.

COLUMN ALIAS

A column alias can be used in the SELECT list to give a column or value an alias; it can also make the result much easier to read. In next example, different forms of a column alias are used to take the place of the column name in the result set. An alias may also contain one or more words or be spelled in exact case when enclosed in double quotes. The optional keyword AS can precede the alias name.

```
SELECT first_name first,
       first_name "First Name",
       first_name AS "First"
  FROM student
 WHERE zip = '10025'
```

FIRST	First Name	First
Jerry	Jerry	Jerry
Nicole	Nicole	Nicole
Frank	Frank	Frank

3 rows selected.

To format the column with the SQL*Plus COLUMN format, you must specify the alias in quotes as well. For example:

```
COL "First" FORMAT A13
```

You can also use the column alias to order by a specific column.

```
SELECT first_name first, first_name "First Name",
       first_name AS "First"
  FROM student
 WHERE zip = '10025'
 ORDER BY "First Name"
```

FIRST	First Name	First
Frank	Frank	Frank
Jerry	Jerry	Jerry
Nicole	Nicole	Nicole

3 rows selected.

DISTINCT AND ORDER BY

The ORDER BY clause often contains columns listed in the SELECT clause, but it is also possible to ORDER BY columns that are not selected. One exception is columns qualified using the DISTINCT keyword—if the SELECT list contains DISTINCT, the column(s) the keyword pertains to must also be listed in the ORDER BY clause.

The next example shows that the STUDENT_ID column is not a column listed in the DISTINCT SELECT list and therefore results in an Oracle error message.

```
SQL> SELECT DISTINCT first_name, last_name
  2    FROM student
  3   WHERE zip = '10025'
  4   ORDER BY student_id
  5  /
 ORDER BY student_id
          *
 ERROR at line 4:
 ORA-01791: not a SELECTed expression
```

NULL VALUES AND ORDER BY

The following statement orders the COST column by the default sort order. Note that the row with a COST column value of NULL is the last row in the sort order.

```
SELECT DISTINCT cost
  FROM course
ORDER BY cost
      COST
----------
      1095
      1195
      1595
```

4 rows selected.

You can change the default ordering of the nulls with the NULLS FIRST or NULLS LAST option in the ORDER BY clause as you see in the next statement. Here the requested order is to list the NULL value first followed by the other values in the default ascending sort order.

```
SELECT DISTINCT cost
  FROM course
ORDER BY cost NULLS FIRST
      COST
----------

      1095
      1195
      1595
```

4 rows selected.

**LAB
2.5**

UNDERSTANDING ORACLE ERROR MESSAGES

As you begin to learn SQL, you will inevitably make mistakes when writing statements. Oracle returns an error number and error message to inform you of your mistake. Some error messages are easy to understand; others are not. While we cannot anticipate every possible error you may encounter, you will see that throughout the book I point out common mistakes. Here are some general guidelines when dealing with Oracle errors.

1. READ THE ORACLE ERROR MESSAGE CAREFULLY

Oracle will tell you on which line the error occurred.

```
SQL> SELECT salutation, first_name, las_name
  2    FROM student
  3   WHERE first_name = 'John'
  4  /
```

```
SELECT salutation, first_name, las_name
                                    *
ERROR at line 1:
ORA-00904: "LAS_NAME": invalid identifier
```

In this example the error is very easy to spot and the error message is self-explanatory. One of the column names is invalid, and Oracle points out the error by indicating the line number. The error is on line 1, and the asterisk indicates in what position within the line the error is found; it is the misspelled LAST_NAME column name.

2. RESOLVE ONE ERROR AT A TIME

Sometimes you may have multiple errors in a single SQL statement. The Oracle *parser*, which checks the syntax of all statements, starts checking from the end of the entire statement.

```
SQL> SELECT salutation, first_name, las_name
  2    FROM studen
  3    WHER first_name = 'John'
  4  /
  WHER first_name = 'John'
      *
ERROR at line 3:
ORA-00933: SQL command not properly ended
```

This type of error message may leave you clueless as to what could be wrong with this query. In fact, the statement contains three errors, one in each line. Because the parser works its way backwards, it complains about the first error on line 3. The position of the asterisk suggests that there is something wrong with the spelling of the FIRST_NAME column. But in fact, it is spelled correctly; otherwise, you would see the ORA-00904 invalid identifier error listed as in one of the previous examples complaining about the incorrect column name. The WHERE key word is missing the letter E; therefore, Oracle cannot interpret what you are attempting to do.

After you correct this error, you will see line 2 reported, exemplifying how the parser works its way backward.

```
SQL> SELECT salutation, first_name, las_name
  2    FROM studen
  3    WHERE first_name = 'John'
  4  /
  FROM studen
       *
ERROR at line 2:
ORA-00942: table or view does not exist
```

Here the table name is misspelled and Oracle indicates that such a table does not exist.

The last error in the statement is found on line 1 and is the misspelled LAST_NAME column name. The parser will report this error as the last error. If you are unsure about the spelling of a column or table name, you can always use the DESCRIBE SQL*Plus command to list the column names and their respective data types, or you can refer to Appendix D, "Student Database Schema," for a list of table and column names.

3. DOUBLE-CHECK THE SYNTAX OF YOUR STATEMENT

Simple typos, such as a stray period or comma, a missing space, or single quote, can cause very strange and seemingly unrelated error message that may have nothing to do with the problem. Therefore, carefully reread the statement or simply retype it. After looking at a statement for a long time, the error may not be apparent. Perhaps put it aside, take a break, and look at it with a fresh mind later, or ask someone for help in spotting the error.

4. LOOK UP THE ORACLE ERROR NUMBER

You can look up the Oracle error number in the *Oracle Database Error Messages Manual*. If the error starts with an ORA message type, it is typically a database-related error, whereas an error with an SP2 prefix indicates a SQL*Plus or *i*SQL*Plus specific error. Once you found the error in the manual, you will see the reason for the error and a recommended action on how to correct it. The recommended action may be general or very specific, once again depending on what type of error occurred.

Initially, the challenge may be finding the correct manual to look up the error message. Following are some suggestions on how to find this information. Besides looking at the online documentation that comes with your Oracle software and which is either found on your CDs or installed on your machine, you can also find the online manual on the Oracle Technology Network (OTN) Web site. Oracle offers a free subscription to the site, which includes a number of features such as access to the online manuals and discussion groups. The URL for OTN is http://otn.oracle.com; you must register first to become a member. Also refer to Appendix H, "Navigating through the Oracle Documentation" and Appendix G, "Resources." These appendixes offer you tips on how to find the needed information.

In some operating systems such as Unix, Linux, and VMS, you can also use the Oracle program called oerr to look up the error message from the operating system prompt. This does not work in the Windows environment. For example, to look up the ORA-00939 error you type at the Unix operating system prompt (indicated with the $ sign):

```
$ oerr ora 00939
00939, 00000, " too many arguments for function"
// *Cause: The function was referenced with too many arguments.
// *Action: Check the function syntax and specify only the
//          required number of arguments.
$
```

**LAB
2.5**

LAB 2.5 EXERCISES

2.5.1 CUSTOM SORT QUERY RESULTS

a) Write a SELECT statement to list each city and zip code in New York or Connecticut. Sort the result in ascending order by zip code.

b) Write a SELECT statement to list course descriptions and their prerequisite course numbers, sorted in ascending order by description. Do not list courses without a prerequisite.

c) Show the salutation, first, and last name of students with the last name Grant. Order the result by salutation in descending order and the first name in ascending order.

d) Execute the following query. What do you observe about the last row returned by the query?

```
SELECT student_id, last_name
  FROM student
 ORDER BY last_name
```

LAB 2.5 EXERCISE ANSWERS

2.5.1 ANSWERS

a) Write a SELECT statement to list each city and zip code in New York or Connecticut. Sort the result in ascending order by zip code.

Answer: The SELECT statement selects two columns, uses the equal operator and OR logical operator to combine expressions in the WHERE clause, and uses ORDER BY with a single column to sort the results in ascending order.

```
SELECT city, zip
  FROM zipcode
 WHERE state = 'NY'
    OR state = 'CT'
 ORDER BY zip
```

CITY	ZIP
Ansonia	06401
Middlefield	06455
...	

```
Hicksville                    11802
Endicott                      13760
```

142 rows selected.

Alternatively, the WHERE clause can be written as:

```
WHERE state IN ('NY', 'CT')
```

b) Write a SELECT statement to list course descriptions and their prerequisite course numbers, sorted in ascending order by description. Do not list courses without a prerequisite.

Answer: The following query shows the use of the IS NOT NULL comparison operator in the WHERE clause. The result is sorted by the DESCRIPTION column in ascending order.

```
SELECT description, prerequisite
  FROM course
 WHERE prerequisite IS NOT NULL
 ORDER BY description
DESCRIPTION                              PREREQUISITE
-------------------------------------    ------------
Advanced Java Programming                        122
Advanced Unix Admin                              132
...
Structured Programming Techniques                204
Unix Tips and Techniques                         134
```

26 rows selected.

**LAB
2.5**

Alternatively, the ORDER BY clause can be written as:

```
ORDER BY 1
```

You can even use the column alias.

```
SELECT description "Descr", prerequisite
  FROM course
 WHERE prerequisite IS NOT NULL
 ORDER BY "Descr"
```

In most of the previous examples, you see the SELECT list is taking up one line only. By spreading it over several lines, it sometimes makes it easier to read and this is perfectly acceptable formatting. By putting elements in the SELECT list on separate lines, you control exactly when the next line begins and indent it for easy readability below the line above it. The following SELECT statement has multiple columns in the SELECT list.

```
SELECT description, prerequisite,
       cost, modified_date
  FROM course
 WHERE prerequisite IS NOT NULL
 ORDER BY description
DESCRIPTION                      PREREQUISITE COST MODIFIED_
-------------------------------- ------------ ---- ---------
Advanced Java Programming                 122 1195 05-APR-03
...
Unix Tips and Techniques                  134 1095 05-APR-03

26 rows selected.
```

c) Show the salutation, first, and last name of students with the last name Grant. Order the result by salutation in descending order and the first name in ascending order.

Answer: The ORDER BY clause contains two columns, the SALUTATION and the FIRST_NAME. The salutation is sorted first in descending order. Within each salutation, the first name is sorted in ascending order.

```
SELECT salutation, first_name, last_name
  FROM student
 WHERE last_name = 'Grant'
 ORDER BY salutation DESC, first_name ASC
SALUT FIRST_NAME         LAST_NAME
----- ------------------ ---------
Ms.   Eilene             Grant
Ms.   Verona             Grant
Mr.   Omaira             Grant
Mr.   Scott              Grant

4 rows selected.
```

Again, you can write the query also with this ORDER BY clause:

```
ORDER BY 1 DESC, 2 ASC
```

Or to use the default order for the second column, which is ASC and can be omitted:

```
ORDER BY 1 DESC, 2
```

If you give your column a column alias, you can also use the column alias in the ORDER BY clause.

```
SELECT salutation "Sal", first_name "First Name",
       last_name "Last Name"
  FROM student
```

```
WHERE last_name = 'Grant'
ORDER BY "Sal" DESC, "First Name" ASC
```

Sal	First Name	Last Name
Ms.	Eilene	Grant
Ms.	Verona	Grant
Mr.	Omaira	Grant
Mr.	Scott	Grant

4 rows selected.

d) Execute the following query. What do you observe about the last row returned by the query?

```
SELECT student_id, last_name
   FROM student
ORDER BY last_name
```

Answer: The student with the STUDENT_ID of 206 has the last name entered in lowercase. When ordering the result set, the lowercase letters are listed after the uppercase letters.

STUDENT_ID	LAST_NAME
119	Abdou
399	Abdou
...	
184	Zuckerberg
206	annunziato

268 rows selected.

LAB 2.5 SELF-REVIEW QUESTIONS

In order to test your progress, you should be able to answer the following questions.

1) The following is the correct order of all clauses in this SELECT statement:

```
SELECT ...
   FROM ...
ORDER BY ...
WHERE ...
```

a) _____ True

b) _____ False

2) You must explicitly indicate whether an ORDER BY is ascending.

    a) _____ True
    b) _____ False

3) The following statement is correct:

```
SELECT *
  FROM instructor
 ORDER BY phone
```

    a) _____ True
    b) _____ False

4) The following statement is incorrect:

```
SELECT description "Description",
          prerequisite AS prereqs,
          course_no "Course#"
  FROM course
 ORDER BY 3, 2
```

    a) _____ True
    b) _____ False

5) You can order by a column you have not selected.

    a) _____ True
    b) _____ False

Answers appear in Appendix A, Section 2.5.

**LAB
2.5**

CHAPTER 2

TEST YOUR THINKING

The projects in this section are meant to have you utilize all of the skills that you have acquired throughout this chapter. The answers to these projects can be found at the companion Web site to this book, located at http://authors.phptr.com/rischert3e. Visit the Web site periodically to share and discuss your answers.

1) Invoke an editor from SQL*Plus; create a file called first.sql containing an SQL statement that retrieves data from the COURSE table for courses that cost 1195, and whose descriptions start with 'Intro', sorted by their prerequisites.

2) Create another file called second.sql that retrieves data from the STUDENT table for students whose last names begin with 'A', 'B', or 'C', and who work for 'Competrol Real Estate', sorted by their last names.

3) Create yet another file called third.sql that retrieves all the descriptions from the GRADE_TYPE table, for rows that were modified by the user MCAFFREY.

4) Execute each of the files, in the order they were created.

CHAPTER 3

CHARACTER, NUMBER, AND MISCELLANEOUS FUNCTIONS

Functions are a useful part of the SQL language. They can transform data in a way that is different from the way it is stored in a database. A function is a type of formula whose result is one of two things: either a *transformation,* such as changing the name of a student to uppercase letters, or *information,* such as the length of a word in a column. Most functions share similar characteristics, including a name, and typically at least one input parameter, also called *argument,* inside a pair of matching parentheses:

```
function_name(input_parameter)
```

All functions in this chapter and next chapter are performed on a single row. This chapter discusses the character, number, and miscellaneous functions. Chapter 4, "Date and Conversion Functions," discusses the date-related functions together with datatype conversion functions. Single-row functions are in contrast to aggregate functions, which are performed against multiple rows. You will learn about aggregate functions in Chapter 5, "Aggregate Functions, GROUP BY, and HAVING."

127

DATATYPES

Each value in Oracle has a datatype associated with it. A datatype determines its respective attributes and acceptable values. For example, you cannot enter a text value into a NUMBER datatype column or enter an invalid date such as 32-DEC-2002 into the DATE column. In most SQL operations, you use the NUMBER, VARCHAR2, and DATE datatypes. These are the commonly used datatypes where the vast majority of data is stored. In this chapter you will concentrate on functions related to the character and numeric data.

HOW TO READ A SYNTAX DIAGRAM

In this lab and the following chapters you will learn about many essential SQL functions and commands. The syntax of the individual commands or functions is listed together with many examples of usage. Table 3.1 lists the symbols that describe the syntax usage.

Table 3.1 ■ Syntax Symbols

Symbol	Usage
[ ]	Square brackets enclose syntax options.
{ }	Braces enclose items of which only one is required.
|	The vertical bar denotes options.
. . .	The three dots indicate that the preceding expression can be repeated.
Delimiters	Delimiters other than brackets, braces, bars, or the three dots must be entered exactly as shown on the syntax. Examples of such delimiters are commas, parentheses, and so on.
CAPS	Words in capital letters indicate the Oracle keywords that identify the individual elements of the SQL command or the name of the SQL function. The case of the keyword or command does not matter, but for readability is in uppercase letters.
UNDERLINE	Default values are underlined.

LAB 3.1

CHARACTER FUNCTIONS

LAB OBJECTIVES

After this lab, you will be able to:
- ✔ Use a Character Function in a SQL Statement
- ✔ Concatenate Strings

All character functions require alphanumeric input parameters. The input can be a *text literal* or *character literal*, sometimes referred to as a *string* or *text constant*, or a column of datatype VARCHAR2, CHAR, or CLOB. Text literals are always surrounded by single quotes. This lab discusses the most frequently used character functions.

THE LOWER FUNCTION

The LOWER function transforms data into lowercase. The next query shows how both a column and a text constant serve as individual parameters for the LOWER function:

```
SELECT state, LOWER(state), LOWER('State')
  FROM zipcode
ST LO LOWER
-- -- -----
PR pr state
MA ma state
...
NY ny state
NY ny state

227 rows selected.
```

The first column in the SELECT list displays the STATE column in the ZIPCODE table without any transformation. The second column uses the LOWER function to display the values of the STATE column in lowercase letters. The third column of the

SELECT list transforms the text constant 'State' into lowercase letters. Text constants used in a SELECT statement are repeated for every row of resulting output.

THE UPPER AND INITCAP FUNCTIONS

The UPPER function is the exact opposite of the LOWER function and transforms data into uppercase. The INITCAP function capitalizes the first letter of a word.

```
SELECT UPPER(city), state, INITCAP(state)
  FROM zipcode
 WHERE zip = '10035'
UPPER(CITY)                     ST IN
------------------------------  -- --
NEW YORK                        NY Ny

1 row selected.
```

The syntax of the UPPER, LOWER, and INITCAP function is listed here:

```
UPPER(char)
LOWER(char)
INITCAP(char)
```

THE LPAD AND RPAD FUNCTIONS

The LPAD and RPAD functions also transform data: They *left pad* and *right pad* strings, respectively. When you pad a string, you add to it. These functions can add characters, symbols, or even spaces to string to your result set. Unlike the LOWER, UPPER, or INITCAP functions, these functions take more than one parameter as their input.

This SELECT statement displays cities right padded with asterisks and states left padded with dashes:

```
SELECT RPAD(city, 20, '*') "City Name",
       LPAD(state, 10, '-') "State Name"
  FROM zipcode
City Name             State Name
--------------------  ----------
Santurce************  -------PR
North Adams*********  -------MA
...
New York************  -------NY
New York************  -------NY

227 rows selected.
```

The CITY column is right padded with the asterisk '*' character up to a length of 20 characters. The STATE column is left padded with '-' up to a total length of 10 characters. Both the LPAD and RPAD functions use three parameters, separated by commas. The first input parameter accepts either a text literal or a column of datatype VARCHAR2 or CHAR. The second argument specifies the total length the string should be padded to. The third optional argument indicates the character(s) the string should be padded with. If this parameter is not specified, the string is padded with spaces by default.

The syntax for the LPAD and RPAD functions is this:

```
LPAD(char1, n [, char2])
RPAD(char1, n [, char2])
```

Char1 is the string to perform the function on, n represents the length the string should be padded to, and char2 is the optional parameter (denoted by the brackets) used to specify which character(s) to pad the string with. The next SELECT statement shows an example of the LPAD function with the third optional argument missing, thus left padding the column with spaces.

```
SELECT LPAD(city, 20) AS "City Name"
  FROM zipcode
City Name
--------------------
           Santurce
        North Adams
...
           New York
           New York

227 rows selected.
```

THE DUAL TABLE

DUAL is a table unique to Oracle. It contains a single row and a single column called DUMMY and holds no significant data of its own. It can be used in conjunction with functions to select values that do not exist in tables, such as text literals or today's date.

```
SQL> DESCR dual
 Name                           Null?    Type
 ------------------------------ -------- -----------
 DUMMY                                   VARCHAR2(1)
```

A single row is always returned in the result set. In some of the subsequent SQL examples you are not concerned with specific rows, but instead use literals to demonstrate the purpose of the function.

```
SELECT *
  FROM dual
D
-
X

1 row selected.
```

THE LTRIM, RTRIM, AND TRIM FUNCTIONS

LTRIM and RTRIM are the opposite of LPAD and RPAD because they *trim*, or remove, unwanted characters, symbols, or spaces in strings. In this example, you see the use of the DUAL table to trim the zero (0) from the left, the right, and both sides. If both the left and right sides of the string are trimmed, you need to nest the function. The result of one function provides the input for the other function.

```
SELECT LTRIM('0001234500', '0') left,
       RTRIM('0001234500', '0') right,
       LTRIM(RTRIM('0001234500', '0'), '0') both
  FROM dual
LEFT      RIGHT      BOTH
-------   --------   -----
1234500   00012345   12345

1 row selected.
```

Here is the syntax for the LTRIM and RTRIM functions. The optional parameter char2 is used to specify which character(s) to trim from the string. If char2 is not specified, then the string is trimmed of spaces.

```
LTRIM(char1 [, char2])
RTRIM(char1 [, char2])
```

The TRIM function removes leading characters, trailing characters, or both, effectively doing the job of LTRIM and RTRIM in one function. If you want the function to act like LTRIM, specify LEADING as the first parameter; for RTRIM, use the TRAILING option; for both, specify either the BOTH keyword or omit it altogether.

The syntax for TRIM is as follows. The char1 indicates the *single* character to be removed; char2 is the string to be trimmed. If you don't specify char1, blank spaces are assumed.

```
TRIM([LEADING|TRAILING|BOTH] char1 FROM char2)
```

The next example shows the use of LEADING, TRAILING, and BOTH (if neither LEADING nor TRAILING is specified); the result is identical to the previous query:

```
SELECT TRIM(LEADING '0' FROM '0001234500') leading,
       TRIM(TRAILING '0' FROM '0001234500') trailing,
       TRIM('0' FROM '0001234500') both
   FROM dual
LEADING TRAILING BOTH
------- -------- -----
1234500 00012345 12345

1 row selected.
```

To trim blank spaces only, you can use this syntax:

```
TRIM(char2)
```

Here is an example of a string with blank characters. Note only leading and trailing blanks are trimmed and blank spaces in the middle of the string are ignored.

```
SELECT TRIM('   00012345  00  ') AS "Blank Trim"
   FROM dual
Blank Trim
------------
00012345  00

1 row selected.
```

THE SUBSTR FUNCTION

SUBSTR is another function that transforms a string, returning a *substring* or *subset* of a string, based on its input parameters. The following query displays student last names, the *first* five characters of those last names, and the *remaining* characters of those last names in the third column:

```
SELECT last_name,
       SUBSTR(last_name, 1, 5),
       SUBSTR(last_name, 6)
   FROM student
LAST_NAME                 SUBST SUBSTR(LAST_NAME,6)
------------------------- ----- -------------------------
Eakheit                   Eakhe it
Millstein                 Mills tein
...
Mastandora                Masta ndora
Torres                    Torre s

268 rows selected.
```

The SUBSTR function's first input parameter is a string; the second is the start position of the subset; the third is optional, indicating the length of the subset. If the third parameter is not used, the default is to display the remainder of the string. Here is the syntax for SUBSTR:

```
SUBSTR(char1, starting_position [, substring_length])
```

Note that if starting_position is a negative number, Oracle starts counting from the end of the string.

THE INSTR FUNCTION

INSTR, meaning *in string,* looks for the occurrence of a string inside another string, returning the starting position of the search string within the target string. Unlike the other string functions, INSTR does not return another string, but a number instead. This query displays course descriptions and the position in which the first occurrence of the string 'er', if any, in the DESCRIPTION column appears:

```
SELECT description, INSTR(description, 'er')
  FROM course
DESCRIPTION                      INSTR(DESCRIPTION,'ER')
------------------------------   -----------------------
DP Overview                                            6
Intro to Computers                                    16
...
JDeveloper Techniques                                  9
DB Programming in Java                                 0

30 rows selected.
```

As you can see in the first row of the result set, the string 'er' starts in the sixth position of the DP Overview. The last row, DB Programming in Java, does not contain an 'er' string, therefore the result is 0. The syntax for INSTR is:

```
INSTR(char1, char2 [,start_position [, occurrence]])
```

INSTR can take two optional input parameters. The third parameter allows you to specify the start position for the search. The fourth parameter specifies which occurrence of the string to look for. When these optional parameters are not used, the default value is 1.

THE LENGTH FUNCTION

The following SQL statement selects a text literal from the DUAL table in conjunction with the LENGTH function, which determines the length of a string expressed as a number.

```
SELECT LENGTH('Hello there')
  FROM dual
LENGTH('HELLOTHERE')
-------------------
                 11
```

1 row selected.

FUNCTIONS IN WHERE AND ORDER BY CLAUSES

The use of functions is not restricted to the SELECT list; they are also used in other SQL clauses. In a WHERE clause, a function restricts the output to rows that only evaluate to the result of the function. In an ORDER BY clause, rows are sorted based on the result of a function. The next query uses the SUBSTR function in the WHERE clause to search for student last names that begin with the string 'Mo'. The arguments are the LAST_NAME column of the STUDENT table, starting with the first character of the column for a length of two characters.

```
SELECT first_name, last_name
  FROM student
 WHERE SUBSTR(last_name, 1, 2) = 'Mo'
FIRST_NAME                  LAST_NAME
--------------------------- ---------
Edgar                       Moffat
Angel                       Moskowitz
Vinnie                      Moon
Bernadette                  Montanez
```

4 rows selected.

Alternatively, you can achieve the same result by replacing the SUBSTR function with this WHERE clause:

```
WHERE last_name LIKE 'Mo%'
```

The following SQL statement selects student first and last names, where the value in the FIRST_NAME column contains a period, and also orders the result set based on the length of students' last names:

```
SELECT first_name, last_name
  FROM student
 WHERE INSTR(first_name, '.') > 0
 ORDER BY LENGTH(last_name)
FIRST_NAME                  LAST_NAME
--------------------------- ---------
Suzanne M.                  Abid
D.                          Orent
```

```
...
V.                        Saliternan
Z.A.                      Scrittorale

21 rows selected.
```

NESTED FUNCTIONS

As you have seen on the example of LPAD and RPAD, functions can be nested within each other. Nested functions are evaluated starting from the inner function and working outward. The following example shows you the CITY column formatted in uppercase, right padded with periods.

```
SELECT RPAD(UPPER(city), 20,'.')
  FROM zipcode
 WHERE state = 'CT'
RPAD(UPPER(CITY),20,
--------------------
ANSONIA.............
MIDDLEFIELD.........
...
STAMFORD............
STAMFORD............

19 rows selected.
```

Here is a more complicated but useful example. You may have noticed that middle initials in the STUDENT table are entered in the same column as the first name. To separate the middle initial from the first name, nest the SUBSTR and INSTR functions. First, determine the position of the middle initial's period in the FIRST_NAME column with the INSTR function. From this position, deduct the number one. This brings you to the position before the period, where the middle initial starts, which is where you want the SUBSTR function to start. The WHERE clause only selects rows where the third or any subsequent character of the first name contains a period.

```
SELECT first_name,
       SUBSTR(first_name, INSTR(first_name, '.')-1) mi,
       SUBSTR(first_name, 1, INSTR(first_name, '.')-2) first
  FROM student
 WHERE INSTR(first_name, '.') >= 3
FIRST_NAME                     MI    FIRST
------------------------       ----  ------
Austin V.                      V.    Austin
John T.                        T.    John
...
```

```
Suzanne M.              M.    Suzanne
Rafael A.               A.    Rafael
```

7 rows selected.

For example, in the row for `Austin V.`, the position of the period (.) is 9, but you need to start at 8 to include the middle initial letter. The last column of the result lists the first name without the middle initial. This is accomplished by starting with the first character of the string and ending the string before the position where the middle initial starts. The key is to determine the ending position of the string with the INSTR function and count back two characters.

 When using nested functions, a common pitfall is to misplace matching parentheses or forget the second half of the pair altogether. Start by writing a nested function from the inside out. Count the number of left parentheses and make sure it matches the number of right parentheses.

CONCATENATION

Concatenation connects strings *together* to become one. Strings can be concatenated to produce a single column in the result set. There are two methods of concatenation in Oracle: One is with the CONCAT function, the other is with the concatenation operator (||), also known as two *vertical bars* or *pipe symbol*. The syntax of the CONCAT function is this:

```
CONCAT(char1, char2)
```

When you want to concatenate cities and states together using the CONCAT function you can use the function as follows:

```
SELECT CONCAT(city, state)
  FROM zipcode
CONCAT(CITY,STATE)
------------------
SanturcePR
North AdamsMA
...
New YorkNY
New YorkNY

227 rows selected.
```

The result set is difficult to read without spaces between cities and states. The CONCAT function takes only two parameters. By using the || operator, you can easily concatenate several strings:

```
SELECT city||state||zip
  FROM zipcode
CITY||STATE||ZIP
------------------
SanturcePR00914
North AdamsMA01247
...
New YorkNY10005
New YorkNY10035

227 rows selected.
```

For a result set that is easier to read, concatenate the strings with spaces and separate the CITY and STATE columns with a comma:

```
SELECT city||', '||state||' '||zip
  FROM zipcode
CITY||','||STATE||''||ZIP
-------------------------
Santurce, PR  00914
North Adams, MA   01247
...
New York, NY   10005
New York, NY   10035

227 rows selected.
```

THE REPLACE FUNCTION

The REPLACE function literally *replaces* a string with another string. In the following example, when the string 'hand' is found within the string 'My hand is asleep', it is replaced by the string 'foot':

```
SELECT REPLACE('My hand is asleep', 'hand', 'foot')
  FROM dual
REPLACE('MYHANDISA
------------------
My foot is asleep

1 row selected.
```

The following is the syntax for the REPLACE function:

```
REPLACE(char, if, then)
```

The second parameter looks to see if a string exists within the first parameter. If so, then it displays the third parameter. If the second parameter value is not found, then the original string is displayed:

```
SELECT REPLACE('My hand is asleep', 'x', 'foot')
  FROM dual
REPLACE('MYHANDISA
------------------
My hand is asleep

1 row selected.
```

THE TRANSLATE FUNCTION

Unlike REPLACE, which replaces an entire string, the TRANSLATE function provides a one-for-one character substitution. For instance, it allows you to determine if all the phone numbers in the STUDENT table follow the same format. In the next query, TRANSLATE substitutes the '#' character for every character from '0' to '9'. Then the values are checked against the '###-###-####' format.

```
SELECT phone
  FROM student
 WHERE TRANSLATE(
       phone, '0123456789',
              '##########') <> '###-###-####'

no rows selected
```

If any phone number is entered in an invalid format, such as 'abc-ddd-efgh' or '555-1212', the query returns the row(s) with the incorrect phone format. The following is the syntax for the TRANSLATE function:

```
TRANSLATE(char, if, then)
```

THE SOUNDEX FUNCTION

The SOUNDEX function allows you compare differently spelled words that phonetically sound alike. The next query uses the SOUNDEX function to display students where the last name sounds like Martin.

```
SELECT student_id, last_name
  FROM student
 WHERE SOUNDEX(last_name) = SOUNDEX('MARTIN')
STUDENT_ID LAST_NAME
---------- ---------
       110 Martin
```

```
324 Marten
393 Martin
```

3 rows selected.

WHICH CHARACTER FUNCTION SHOULD YOU USE?

It's easy to confuse character functions. When deciding which one to use, ask yourself exactly what is needed in your result set. Are you looking for the position of a string in a string? Do you need to produce a subset of a string? Do you need to know how long a string is? Or do you need to replace a string with something else? Table 3.2 lists the character functions discussed in this lab.

Table 3.2 ■ Character Functions

Function	Purpose
LOWER(char)	Converts to lowercase
UPPER(char)	Converts to uppercase
INITCAP(char)	Capitalizes the first letter
LPAD(char1, n [, char2])	Left pads
RPAD(char1, n [, char2])	Right pads
LTRIM(char1 [, char2])	Left trims
RTRIM(char1 [, char2])	Right trims
TRIM([LEADING|TRAILING|BOTH] char1 FROM char2)	Trims leading, trailing or both sides
SUBSTR(char1, starting_position [, substring_length])	Cuts out a piece of the string
INSTR(char1, char2 [, starting-position [, occurrence]])	Determines starting location of a string
LENGTH(char)	Returns length of a string
CONCAT(char1, char2)	Concatenates two strings
REPLACE(char, if, then)	Replaces string with another string
SOUNDEX(char)	Returns phonetic representation
TRANSLATE(char, if, then)	Substitutes individual character

SEARCHING, REPLACING, AND VALIDATING TEXT

In addition to the LIKE operator and the character functions SUBSTR and INSTR, Oracle offers additional search capabilities that come in the form of Oracle Text and regular expressions.

Oracle Text expands the text search capabilities with word and theme searching using the operators CONTAINS, CATSEARCH, and MATCH. The database will return ranked results based on the requested search. You can specify combinations of words with the AND and OR operators and use wildcards. You can search for documents that contain words that share the same stem, words that are located close to each other, or words that evolve around the same theme. The *Oracle Text Reference* manual and the *Oracle Text Application Developer's Guide* contain more information on this functionality.

Oracle 10*g* introduces regular expression functionality in the database. A regular expression is a notation for describing a pattern. This regular expression implementation significantly expands the functionality of the LIKE operator and the INSTR, SUBSTR, and REPLACE functions to search, replace, and validate patterns. You will learn more about the sophisticated capabilities of regular expressions within the context of the Oracle database in Chapter 15, "Regular Expressions and Hierarchical Queries."

LAB 3.1 EXERCISES

3.1.1 USE A CHARACTER FUNCTION IN A SQL STATEMENT

a) Execute the following SQL statement. Based on the result, what is the purpose of the INITCAP function?

```
SELECT description "Description",
       INITCAP(description) "Initcap Description"
  FROM course
 WHERE description LIKE '%SQL%'
```

b) Write the question answered by the following SQL statement.

```
SELECT last_name
  FROM instructor
 WHERE LENGTH(last_name) >= 6
```

c) Describe the result of the following SQL statement. Pay particular attention to the negative number parameter.

```
SELECT SUBSTR('12345', 3),
       SUBSTR('12345', 3, 2),
       SUBSTR('12345', -4, 3)
  FROM dual
```

d) Based on the result of the following SQL statement, describe the purpose of the LTRIM and RTRIM functions.

```
SELECT zip, LTRIM(zip, '0'), RTRIM(ZIP, '4')
  FROM zipcode
 ORDER BY zip
```

e) What do you observe when you execute the next statement? How would you change the statement to achieve the desired result?

```
SELECT TRIM('01' FROM '01230145601')
  FROM dual
```

f) What is the result of the following statement?

```
SELECT TRANSLATE('555-1212', '0123456789',
                              '#########')
  FROM dual
```

g) Write the SQL statement to retrieve those students that have a last name with the lowercase letter 'o' occurring three or more times.

h) The following statement determines how many times the string 'ed' occurs in the phrase 'Fred fed Ted bread, and Ted fed Fred bread.' Explain how this is accomplished.

```
SELECT (
        LENGTH('Fred fed Ted bread, and Ted fed Fred bread.') -
        LENGTH(REPLACE(
               'Fred fed Ted bread, and Ted fed Fred bread.', 'ed', NULL))
       ) /2 AS occurr
  FROM dual
    OCCURR
----------
         6

1 row selected.
```

3.1.2 CONCATENATE STRINGS

a) Write a SELECT statement that returns each instructor's last name, followed by a comma and a space, followed by the instructor's first name, all in a single column in the result set.

b) Using functions in the SELECT list, WHERE, and ORDER BY clauses, write the SELECT statement that returns course numbers and course descriptions from the COURSE table and looks like the following result set:

```
Description
------------------------------------
204.......Intro to SQL
130.......Intro to Unix
230.......Intro to Internet
20........Intro to Computers
25........Intro to Programming
120.......Intro to Java Programming
240.......Intro to the Basic Language

7 rows selected.
```

LAB 3.1 EXERCISE ANSWERS

3.1.1 ANSWERS

a) Execute the following SQL statement. Based on the result, what is the purpose of the INITCAP function?

```
SELECT description "Description",
       INITCAP(description) "Initcap Description"
  FROM course
 WHERE description LIKE '%SQL%'
```

Answer: The INITCAP function capitalizes the first letter of a word and forces the remaining characters to be lowercase.

The result set contains two rows, one displaying a course description as it appears in the database and one displaying each word with only the first letter capitalized. Words are delimited by nonalphanumeric characters or spaces.

```
Description              Initcap Description
----------------------   --------------------
Intro to SQL             Intro To Sql
PL/SQL Programming        Pl/Sql Programming

2 rows selected.
```

b) Write the question answered by the following SQL statement.

```
SELECT last_name
  FROM instructor
 WHERE LENGTH(last_name) >= 6
```

Answer: The question answered by the query could be phrased like this: "Which instructors have last names longer than six characters?"

```
LAST_NAME
----------------
Wojick
Schorin
...
Frantzen
Willig

7 rows selected.
```

The LENGTH function returns the length of a string, expressed as a number. The LENGTH function takes only a single input parameter, as in the following syntax:

```
LENGTH(char)
```

c) Describe the result of the following SQL statement. Pay particular attention to the negative number parameter.

```
SELECT SUBSTR('12345', 3),
       SUBSTR('12345', 3, 2),
       SUBSTR('12345', -4, 3)
  FROM dual
```

Answer: The first column takes the characters starting from position three until the end, resulting in the string '345'. The second SUBSTR function also starts at position three but ends after two characters, and therefore returns '34'. The third column has a negative number as the first parameter. It counts from the end of the string to the left four characters; thus the substring starts at position 2 and for a length of three characters, resulting in '234'.

```
SUB SU SUB
--- -- ---
345 34 234

1 row selected.
```

d) Based on the result of the following SQL statement, describe the purpose of the LTRIM and RTRIM functions.

```
SELECT zip, LTRIM(zip, '0'), RTRIM(ZIP, '4')
  FROM zipcode
 ORDER BY zip
```

Answer: The LTRIM and RTRIM functions left trim and right trim strings based on the function's parameters. With the three columns in the result set side by side, you see the differences: the first column shows the ZIP column without modification, the second with ZIP left-trimmed of its 0s, and the third with ZIP right-trimmed of its 4s.

```
ZIP    LTRIM RTRIM
-----  ----- -----
00914 914    0091
01247 1247   01247
...
43224 43224 4322
48104 48104 4810


227 rows selected.
```

e) What do you observe when you execute the next statement? How would you change the statement to achieve the desired result?

```
SELECT TRIM('01' FROM '01230145601')
   FROM dual
```

Answer: The query results in an error indicating that only one character can be trimmed at a time. This query attempts to trim two characters, which are 0 and 1. Nest the LTRIM and RTRIM functions to achieve the desired result.

```
SQL> SELECT TRIM('01' FROM '01230145601')
  2     FROM dual
  3  /
SELECT TRIM('01' FROM '01230145601')
         *
ERROR at line 1:
ORA-30001: trim set should have only one character
```

To trim multiple characters, use the LTRIM and RTRIM functions instead of TRIM. If you tried the REPLACE function, you will notice that it will replace all occurrences of the '01' string, not just the first and last.

```
SELECT LTRIM('01230145601', '01') left,
       RTRIM('01230145601', '01') right,
       RTRIM(LTRIM('01230145601', '01'), '01') both,
       REPLACE('01230145601', '01') replace
   FROM dual
LEFT        RIGHT       BOTH      REPLA
---------   ---------   -------   -----
230145601   012301456   2301456   23456

1 row selected.
```

f) What is the result of the following statement?

```
SELECT TRANSLATE('555-1212', '0123456789',
                             '##########')
   FROM dual
```

Answer: It returns the result ###-#####. The TRANSLATE function is a character substitution function. The listed SQL statement uses each of the characters of the string '555-1212' to look up the corresponding character and then returns this character. One of the uses for this function is to determine if data is entered in the correct format.

```
TRANSLAT
--------
###-####
```

```
1 row selected.
```

USING TRANSLATE FOR PATTERN SEARCH

The TRANSLATE function also comes in handy when you need to perform a pattern search using the LIKE operator and you are looking for the actual wildcard characters % or _. Assume you need to query the STUDENT table and you want to find any students where the student's employer spells his or her name similar to the pattern 'B_B'. The underscore has to be taken as a literal underscore, not as a wildcard. Qualifying employer names are 'Bayer B_Biller' or 'ABCB_Bellman'. Unfortunately, no such employer names exist in the STUDENT database, but there are occasions when data entry errors occur and you need to figure out which are the offending rows. The following query will check if such an employer with the pattern 'B_B' exists in the table:

```
SELECT student_id, employer
  FROM student
 WHERE TRANSLATE(employer, '_', '+') LIKE '%B+B%'
```

As you can see, the TRANSLATE function performs this trick. Here the underscore is replaced with the plus sign and then the LIKE function is applied with the replaced plus sign in the character literal.

USING INSTR FOR PATTERN SEARCH

Another way to solve this query would be to use the INSTR function.

```
SELECT student_id, employer
  FROM student
 WHERE INSTR(employer, 'B_B') > 0
```

THE ESCAPE CHARACTER AND THE LIKE OPERATOR

Yet another way to determine any such employers in the STUDENT table is with the escape character functionality in conjunction with the LIKE operator. In the next example, the backslash (\) is selected as the escape character to indicate that the underscore character following the character is to be interpreted as a literal underscore and not as the wildcard underscore.

```
SELECT student_id, employer
  FROM student
 WHERE employer LIKE '%B\_B%' ESCAPE '\'
```

The new regular expressions functionality in Oracle 10*g* allows sophisticated pattern searches with the REGEXP_LIKE operator. You will find out more about these capabilities in Chapter 15, "Regular Expressions and Hierarchical Queries."

g) Write the SQL statement to retrieve those students that have a last name with the lowercase letter 'o' occurring three or more times.

Answer: The INSTR function determines the third or more occurrence of the lowercase letter o in the LAST_NAME column of the STUDENT table.

The INSTR function has two required parameters; the rest are optional and default to 1. The first parameter is the string or column where the function needs to be applied and where you are looking to find the desired values. The second parameter identifies the search string; here you are looking for the letter 'o'. The third parameter determines at which starting position the search must occur. The last parameter specifies which occurrence of the string is requested.

If the INSTR function finds the desired result it returns the starting position of the searched value. The WHERE clause condition looks for those rows where the result of the INSTR function is greater than 0.

```
SELECT student_id, last_name
  FROM student
 WHERE INSTR(last_name, 'o', 1, 3) > 0
STUDENT_ID LAST_NAME
---------- ---------
       280 Engongoro
       251 Frangopoulos
       254 Chamnonkool

3 rows selected.
```

h) The following statement determines how many times the string 'ed' occurs in the phrase 'Fred fed Ted bread, and Ted fed Fred bread.' Explain how this is accomplished.

```
SELECT (
        LENGTH('Fred fed Ted bread, and Ted fed Fred bread') -
        LENGTH(REPLACE(
               'Fred fed Ted bread, and Ted fed Fred bread', 'ed', NULL))
       ) /2 AS occurr
  FROM dual
```

```
   OCCURR
----------
        6
```

1 row selected.

Answer: The nesting of the REPLACE and LENGTH functions determines that there are 6 occurrences of the string 'ed' in the phrase.

To understand the statement, it's best to break down the individual components of the statement: The first function determines the length of this tongue twister. The next component nests the LENGTH and REPLACE functions. The REPLACE function replaces every occurrence of 'ed' with a null. Effectively, the result string looks like this:

```
SELECT REPLACE('Fred fed Ted bread, and Ted fed Fred
bread', 'ed', NULL)
   FROM dual
REPLACE('FREDFEDTEDBREAD,ANDTE
-----------------------------
Fr f T bread, and T f Fr bread
```

1 row selected.

Then the LENGTH function determines the length of the reduced string. If you deduct the total length of the entire string from the length of the reduced string and divide the result by 2 (the number of letters in the string 'ed'), you determine the total number of occurrences.

3.1.2 ANSWERS

a) Write a SELECT statement that returns each instructor's last name, followed by a comma and a space, followed by the instructor's first name, all in a single column in the result set.

Answer: The instructor's last name, a comma and a space, and the instructor's first name are all concatenated using the || symbol.

```
SELECT last_name||', '||first_name
   FROM instructor
LAST_NAME||','||FIRST_NAME
--------------------------
Hanks, Fernand
Wojick, Tom
...
Frantzen, Marilyn
```

```
Willig, Irene

10 rows selected.
```

b) Using functions in the SELECT list, WHERE, and ORDER BY clauses, write the SELECT statement that returns course numbers and course descriptions from the COURSE table and looks like the following result set:

```
Description
-------------------------------------
204.......Intro to SQL
130.......Intro to Unix
230.......Intro to Internet
20........Intro to Computers
25........Intro to Programming
120.......Intro to Java Programming
240.......Intro to the Basic Language

7 rows selected.
```

Answer: The RPAD function right pads the COURSE_NO column with periods, up to 10 characters long; it is then concatenated with the DESCRIPTION column. The INSTR function is used in the WHERE clause to filter on descriptions starting with the string 'Intro'. The LENGTH function is used in the ORDER BY clause to sort the result set by ascending (shortest to longest) description length.

```
SELECT RPAD(course_no, 10, '.')||description
       AS "Description"
  FROM course
 WHERE INSTR(description, 'Intro') = 1
 ORDER BY LENGTH(description)
```

The same result can be obtained without the use of the INSTR function, as in the following WHERE clause:

```
WHERE description LIKE 'Intro%'
```

As you can see, concatenation combined with functions is a powerful way to quickly produce result sets that are useful and easy to read.

LAB 3.1 SELF-REVIEW QUESTIONS

In order to test your progress, you should be able to answer the following questions.

1) Functions that operate on single values can only have one input parameter.

   a) _____ True
   b) _____ False

2) The DUAL table can be used for testing functions.

a) _____ True
b) _____ False

3) The same function can be used twice in a SELECT statement.

a) _____ True
b) _____ False

4) The following SELECT statement contains an error:

```
SELECT UPPER(description)
  FROM LOWER(course)
```

a) _____ True
b) _____ False

5) The RTRIM function is useful for eliminating extra spaces in a string.

a) _____ True
b) _____ False

6) Which one of the following string functions tells you how many characters are in a string?

a) _____ INSTR
b) _____ SUBSTR
c) _____ LENGTH
d) _____ REPLACE

7) Which result will the following query return?

```
SELECT TRIM('   Mary Jones   ')
  FROM dual
```

a) _____ Mary Jones
b) _____ Mary Jones
c) _____ MaryJones
d) _____ The query returns an error.

8) The functions INSTR, SUBSTR, and TRIM are all single-row functions.

a) _____ True
b) _____ False

9) Which character function returns a specified portion of a character string?

a) _____ INSTR
b) _____ LENGTH
c) _____ SUBSTR
d) _____ INSTRING

10) Character functions never return results in the datatype NUMBER.

a) _____ True
b) _____ False

Answers appear in Appendix A, Section 3.1.

LAB 3.2

NUMBER FUNCTIONS

LAB OBJECTIVES

After this lab, you will be able to:
✔ Use Number Functions and Perform Mathematical Computations

Number functions are valuable tools for operations such as rounding numbers or computing the absolute value of a number. There are several single-row number functions in Oracle; the most useful ones are discussed here.

THE ABS FUNCTION

The ABS function computes the *absolute value* of a number, measuring its magnitude:

```
SELECT 'The absolute value of -29 is '||ABS(-29)
  FROM dual
'THEABSOLUTEVALUEOF-29IS'||ABS(
-------------------------------
The absolute value of -29 is 29

1 row selected.
```

ABS takes only a single input parameter, and its syntax is this:

```
ABS(value)
```

THE SIGN FUNCTION

The SIGN function tells you the *sign* of a value, returning a number 1 for positive numbers, −1 for negative numbers, or 0 for a zero. The following example compares SIGN with the ABS function:

```
SELECT -14, SIGN(-14), SIGN(14), SIGN(0), ABS(-14)
  FROM dual
       -14 SIGN(-14) SIGN(14)    SIGN(0)   ABS(-14)
--------- --------- ----------- -------- --------
       -14       -1           1        0        14
```

1 row selected.

SIGN also takes only a single input parameter, and its syntax is this:

```
SIGN(value)
```

 Most single-row functions return NULL when a NULL is the input parameter.

ROUND AND TRUNC FUNCTIONS

ROUND and TRUNC are two useful functions that *round* and *truncate* (or cut off) values, respectively, based on a given number of digits of precision. The next SELECT statement illustrates the use of ROUND and TRUNC, which both take two input parameters. Observe the differences in the result.

```
SELECT 222.34501,
       ROUND(222.34501, 2),
       TRUNC(222.34501, 2)
  FROM dual
  222.34501 ROUND(222.34501,2) TRUNC(222.34501,2)
--------- ------------------ ------------------
  222.34501             222.35             222.34
```

1 row selected.

Here, ROUND (222.34501,2) rounds the number 222.34501 to two digits to the right of the decimal, rounding the result up to 222.35, following the normal convention for rounding. In contrast, TRUNC has cut off all digits beyond two digits to the right of the decimal, resulting in 222.34. ROUND and TRUNC can be used to affect the left side of the decimal as well by passing a negative number as a parameter:

```
SELECT 222.34501,
       ROUND(222.34501, -2),
       TRUNC(222.34501, -2)
  FROM dual
```

```
222.34501 ROUND(222.34501,-2) TRUNC(222.34501,-2)
--------- ------------------- -------------------
222.34501                 200                 200
```

1 row selected.

Here is the syntax for both ROUND and TRUNC:

```
ROUND(value [, precision])
TRUNC(value [, precision])
```

Numbers with decimal places may be rounded to whole numbers by omitting the second parameter, or specifying a precision of 0:

```
SELECT 2.617, ROUND(2.617), TRUNC(2.617)
  FROM dual
2.617 ROUND(2.617) TRUNC(2.617)
----- ------------ ------------
2.617            3            2
```

1 row selected.

You can use the TRUNC and ROUND function not only on values of the NUMBER datatype but also on the DATE datatype, discussed in Chapter 4, "Date and Conversion Functions."

THE FLOOR AND CEIL FUNCTIONS

The CEIL function returns the smallest integer greater than or equal to a value; the FLOOR function returns the largest integer equal to or less than a value. These functions perform much like the ROUND and TRUNC functions without the optional precision parameter.

```
SELECT FLOOR(22.5), CEIL(22.5), TRUNC(22.5), ROUND(22.5)
  FROM dual
FLOOR(22.5) CEIL(22.5) TRUNC(22.5) ROUND(22.5)
----------- ---------- ----------- -----------
         22         23          22          23
```

1 row selected.

The syntax for the FLOOR and CEIL functions is:

```
FLOOR(value)
CEIL(value)
```

THE MOD FUNCTION

MOD is a function returning the *modulus,* or the remainder, of a value divided by another value. It takes two input parameters, as in this SELECT statement:

```
SELECT MOD(23, 8)
  FROM dual
MOD(23,8)
----------
        7
```

1 row selected.

The MOD function divides 23 by 8 returning a remainder of 7. Here is the syntax for MOD:

```
MOD(value, divisor)
```

The MOD function is particularly useful if you want to determine if a value is odd or even. If you divide by 2 and the remainder is a zero, this indicates that the value is even; if the remainder is 1, it means that the value is odd.

THE NUMBER VERSUS THE BINARY_FLOAT AND BINARY_DOUBLE DATATYPES

Oracle 10*g* added two new number datatypes: They are BINARY_FLOAT and BINARY_DOUBLE. A floating-point number consists of three components: a *sign,* the signed *exponent,* and a *significand.*

Oracle's floating-point numbers support the IEEE standard for binary floating-point arithmetic, just like Java and XML. Computations on floating-point values can be sometimes in the order of five to ten times faster than NUMBER because the floating-point datatypes use the native instruction set supplied by the hardware vendor. Compared to the NUMBER datatype, the floating-point datatypes use up less space for values stored with significant precision. Also the BINARY_DOUBLE datatype supports a wider range of values. The special operators IS [NOT] NAN and IS [NOT] INFINITE check for is "not a number" (NAN) and infinity respectively.

If an operation involves a mix of different numeric datatypes, the operation is performed in datatype with the highest precedence. The order of precedence is BINARY_DOUBLE, BINARY_FLOAT, and then NUMBER. For example, if the operation includes a NUMBER and a BINARY_DOUBLE, the value of the NUMBER datatype is implicitly converted to the BINARY DOUBLE datatype. Oracle offers various functions that allow conversions to and from different datatypes; they are discussed in Lab 4.5.

THE ROUND FUNCTION AND FLOATING-POINT NUMBERS

The ROUND function takes on a slightly different behavior if the datatype of the input parameter is not of NUMBER, but of either BINARY_FLOAT or BINARY_DOUBLE datatype. In this case, the ROUND function rounds towards the nearest even value.

```
SELECT ROUND(3.5), ROUND(3.5f), ROUND(4.5), ROUND(4.5f)
  FROM dual
ROUND(3.5) ROUND(3.5F) ROUND(4.5) ROUND(4.5F)
---------- ----------- ---------- -----------
         4    4.0E+000          5    4.0E+000

1 row selected.
```

THE REMAINDER FUNCTION

The new Oracle 10*g* REMAINDER function calculates the remainder according to the IEEE specification. The syntax is as follows:

```
REMAINDER(value, divisor)
```

The difference to the MOD function is that MOD uses FLOOR in its computations versus the REMAINDER function, which uses ROUND. The next example shows that the results between the MOD and REMAINDER function can be different:

```
SELECT MOD(23,8), REMAINDER(23,8)
  FROM DUAL
 MOD(23,8) REMAINDER(23,8)
---------- ---------------
         7              -1

1 row selected.
```

Effectively, the computation of the MOD function is (23-(8*FLOOR(23/8))) and the computation of the REMAINDER is (23-(8*ROUND(23/8))) as illustrated by the next statement.

```
SELECT (23-(8*FLOOR(23/8))) AS mod,
       (23-(8*ROUND(23/8))) AS remainder
  FROM DUAL
```

```
        MOD REMAINDER
----------- ---------
          7        -1
```

1 row selected.

WHICH NUMBER FUNCTION SHOULD YOU USE?

Table 3.3 lists the functions discussed in this lab. Sometimes you may nest these functions within other functions. As you progress through the following chapters, you will see specifically the usefulness of some of these function to write sophisticated SQL statements.

In Chapter 16, "Exploring Data Warehousing Features," you will learn more about additional number functions that help you solve analytical and statistical problems. For example, these functions can help you determine rankings such as the grades of the top 20 students or compute the median cost of all courses.

ARITHMETIC OPERATORS

The four mathematical operators (addition, subtraction, multiplication, and division) may be used in a SQL statement and can be combined.

Each of the four operators is used with course costs. Notice that one of the distinct course costs is null; here the computation with a null value yields another null.

Table 3.3 ■ Number Functions

Function	Purpose
ABS(value)	Returns absolute value
SIGN(value)	Returns sign of a value such as 1, –1, and 0
MOD(value, divisor)	Returns modulus
REMAINDER (value, divisor)	Returns remainder according to IEEE specification
ROUND(value [, precision])	Rounds value
TRUNC(value [, precision])	Truncates value
FLOOR(value)	Returns largest integer
CEIL(value)	Returns smallest integer

```
SELECT DISTINCT cost, cost + 10,
       cost - 10, cost * 10, cost / 10
  FROM course
     COST    COST+10    COST-10    COST*10 COST/10
 ---------- --------- --------- --------- -------
     1095      1105       1085      10950   109.5
     1195      1205       1185      11950   119.5
     1595      1605       1585      15950   159.5
```

4 rows selected.

Parentheses are used to group computations, indicating precedence of the operators. The following SELECT statement returns distinct course costs increased by 10%. The computation within the parentheses is evaluated first, followed by the addition of the value in the COST column, resulting in a single number. NULL values can be replaced with a default value. You will learn about this topic in Lab 3.3.

```
SELECT DISTINCT cost + (cost * .10)
  FROM course
COST+(COST*.10)
---------------
        1204.5
        1314.5
        1754.5
```

4 rows selected.

LAB 3.2 EXERCISES

3.2.1 USE NUMBER FUNCTIONS AND PERFORM MATHEMATICAL COMPUTATIONS

a) Describe the effect of the negative precision as a parameter of the ROUND function in the following SQL statement.

```
SELECT 10.245, ROUND(10.245, 1), ROUND(10.245, -1)
  FROM dual
```

b) Write a SELECT statement that displays distinct course costs. In a separate column, show the COST increased by 75% and round the decimals to the nearest dollar.

c) Write a SELECT statement that displays distinct numeric grades from the GRADE table and half those values expressed as a whole number in a separate column.

LAB 3.2 EXERCISE ANSWERS

3.2.1 ANSWERS

a) Describe the effect of the negative precision as a parameter of the ROUND function in the following SQL statement.

```
SELECT 10.245, ROUND(10.245, 1), ROUND(10.245, -1)
  FROM dual
```

Answer: A negative precision rounds digits to the left of the decimal point.

```
   10.245 ROUND(10.245,1) ROUND(10.245,-1)
--------- --------------- ----------------
   10.245            10.2               10
```

1 row selected.

For example, to round to the nearest hundreds, you can use a precision of -2. To round to the nearest thousands, use the precision parameter of -3, and so on. The next example illustrates the result of these negative parameters.

```
SELECT ROUND(120.09, -2), ROUND(1444.44, -3)
  FROM dual
ROUND(120.09,-2) ROUND(1444.44,-3)
---------------- -----------------
             100              1000
```

1 row selected.

b) Write a SELECT statement that displays distinct course costs. In a separate column, show the COST increased by 75% and round the decimals to the nearest dollar.

Answer: The SELECT statement uses multiplication and the ROUND function.

```
SELECT DISTINCT cost, cost*1.75, ROUND(cost*1.75)
  FROM course
     COST COST*1.75 ROUND(COST*1.75)
--------- --------- ----------------
     1095   1916.25             1916
     1195   2091.25             2091
     1595   2791.25             2791
```

4 rows selected.

c) Write a SELECT statement that displays distinct numeric grades from the GRADE table and half those values expressed as a whole number in a separate column.

Answer: The SELECT statement uses division to derive the value that is half the original value. The resulting value becomes the input parameter for the ROUND function. The displayed output shows a whole number because the ROUND function does not have any precision parameter specified.

```
SELECT DISTINCT numeric_grade, ROUND(numeric_grade / 2)
  FROM grade
NUMERIC_GRADE ROUND(NUMERIC_GRADE/2)
------------- ----------------------
           70                      35
           71                      36
...
           98                      49
           99                      50
```

30 rows selected.

Here, a mathematical computation is combined with a function. Be sure to place computations correctly, either inside or outside the parentheses of a function, depending on the desired result. In this case, if the / 2 were on the outside of the ROUND function, a very different result occurs, not the correct answer to the task that was posed.

LAB 3.2 SELF-REVIEW QUESTIONS

In order to test your progress, you should be able to answer the following questions.

1) Number functions can be nested.

    a) _____ True
    b) _____ False

2) The ROUND function can take only the NUMBER datatype as a parameter.

    a) _____ True
    b) _____ False

3) The following SELECT statement is incorrect:

```
SELECT capacity - capacity
   FROM section
```

a) _____ True
b) _____ False

4) What does the following function return?

```
SELECT LENGTH(NULL)
   FROM dual
```

a) _____ 4
b) _____ 0
c) _____ Null

Answers appear in Appendix A, Section 3.2.

L A B   3 . 3

MISCELLANEOUS SINGLE-ROW FUNCTIONS

L A B   O B J E C T I V E S

After this lab, you will be able to:
- ✔ Apply Substitution Functions and Other Miscellaneous Functions
- ✔ Utilize the Power of DECODE Function and the CASE Expression

In this lab you will learn about substitution functions to replace nulls with default values. You will also utilize the DECODE function and the CASE expression—these functions are destined to become your favorites, they allow you to perform powerful *if then else* comparisons.

THE NVL FUNCTION

The NVL function replaces a NULL value with a default value. NULLs represent a special challenge when used in calculations. A computation with an unknown value yields another unknown value, as you see in the following example.

```
SELECT 60+60+NULL
  FROM dual
60+60+NULL
---------------

1 row selected.
```

To avoid this problem, you can use the NVL function to substitute the NULL for another value.

```
NVL(input_expression, substitution_expression)
```

The NVL function requires two parameters: an input expression (i.e., a column, literal, or a computation) and a substitution expression. If the input expression does *not* contain a NULL value, the input parameter is returned. If the input parameter does contain a NULL value, then the substitution parameter is returned.

In the following example, the substitution value is the number literal 1000. The NULL is substituted with 1000, resulting in the output 1120.

```
SELECT 60+60+NVL(NULL, 1000)
  FROM dual
60+60+NVL(NULL,1000)
-------------------
               1120

1 row selected.
```

LAB
3.3

When you substitute a value, the datatype of the substituted value must agree with the datatype of the input parameter. The next example uses the NVL function to substitute any NULL values with 'Not Applicable' in the PREREQUISITE column. An error is encountered when the statement is executed because the datatypes of the two parameters are different. The substitution parameter is a text literal, and the column PREREQUISITE is defined as a NUMBER datatype.

```
SELECT course_no, description,
       NVL(prerequisite, 'Not Applicable') prereq
  FROM course
 WHERE course_no IN (20, 100)
NVL(prerequisite, 'Not Applicable') prereq
                 *
ERROR at line 2:
ORA-01722: invalid number
```

The error indicates Oracle cannot convert the text literal 'Not Applicable' into a NUMBER. To overcome this problem, transform the output of the PREREQUISITE column into a VARCHAR2 datatype using the TO_CHAR datatype conversion function. This function takes a NUMBER or DATE datatype and converts it into a string.

```
SELECT course_no, description,
       NVL(TO_CHAR(prerequisite), 'Not Applicable') prereq
  FROM course
 WHERE course_no IN (20, 100)
COURSE_NO DESCRIPTION          PREREQ
--------- -------------------- --------------
      100 Hands-On Windows     20
       20 Intro to Computers   Not Applicable

2 rows selected.
```

THE COALESCE FUNCTION

The COALESCE function is similar to the NVL function, yet with an additional twist. Instead of specifying one substitution expression for a null value, you can optionally evaluate multiple substitution columns or substitution expressions. The syntax is:

```
COALESCE(input_expression, substitution_expression_1,
[, substitution_expression_n])
```

The next SQL query shows the case of multiple substitution expressions, two substitutions to be precise. A table called GRADE_SUMMARY, which is not part of the STUDENT schema, illustrates the idea.

The structure of the GRADE_SUMMARY TABLE is as follows:

```
SQL> DESCR grade_summary
 Name                             Null?     Type
 -------------------------------- --------- ---------
 STUDENT_ID                                 NUMBER(8)
 MIDTERM_GRADE                              NUMBER(3)
 FINALEXAM_GRADE                            NUMBER(3)
 QUIZ_GRADE                                 NUMBER(3)
```

The resulting output of the Coalesce column shows that if the midterm grade is null, the final exam grade is substituted. If the final exam grade is also null then the grade for the quiz is substituted. You notice that this is the case with student 678 where both the MIDTERM_GRADE and the FINALEXAM_GRADE column values are null, therefore the value in the QUIZ_GRADE column is substituted. For student 999 all the column values are null, therefore the COALESCE function returns a null value.

```
SELECT student_id, midterm_grade, finalexam_grade, quiz_grade,
     COALESCE(midterm_grade, finalexam_grade, quiz_grade) "Coalesce"
  FROM grade_summary
```

STUDENT_ID	MIDTERM_GRADE	FINALEXAM_GRADE	QUIZ_GRADE	Coalesce
123	90	50	100	90
456	80	95		80
678			98	98
789		78	85	78
999				

```
5 rows selected.
```

(Note that the GRADE_SUMMARY table is a denormalized table, not what we recommend you design unless you have a very good reason to denormalize, but the purpose here is to illustrate the functionality of COALESCE. If you wish, you can create this table by downloading an additional script from the companion Web site located at http://authors.phptr.com/rischert3e.)

The following is an example using the COALESCE function with just a one substitution expression, which is equivalent to the NVL function discussed previously. The TO_CHAR function is necessary because the datatypes of the expressions do not agree. In this case, the PREREQUISITE column is of datatype NUMBER. The "Not Applicable" string is a character constant. You can use the TO_CHAR conversion function to make the two datatypes equivalent. The TO_CHAR function and conversion functions in general are covered in greater detail in Chapter 4, "Date and Conversion Functions."

```
SELECT course_no, description,
       COALESCE(TO_CHAR(prerequisite), 'Not Applicable') prereq
  FROM course
 WHERE course_no IN (20, 100)
COURSE_NO DESCRIPTION             PREREQ
--------- -------------------- --------------
      100 Hands-On Windows     20
       20 Intro to Computers   Not Applicable

2 rows selected.
```

THE NVL2 FUNCTION

The NVL2 function is yet another extension of the NVL function. It checks for both not null and null values and has three parameters versus NVL's two parameters. The syntax for the function is as follows:

```
NVL2(input_expr, not_null_substitution_expr, null_substitution_expr)
```

If the input expression is not null, the second parameter of the function, the `not_null_substitution_expr`, is returned. If the input expression is null, then the last parameter, the `null_substitution_expr`, is returned instead. This query shows how the NVL2 function works. The distinct course costs are displayed; if the value in the COST column is not null, the literal `exists` is displayed; otherwise the result displays the word `none`.

```
SELECT DISTINCT cost,
       NVL2(cost, 'exists', 'none') "NVL2"
  FROM course
       COST NVL2
---------- ------
       1095 exists
       1195 exists
```

```
              1595 exists
                   none

4 rows selected.
```

THE NULLIF FUNCTION

The NULLIF function is different because it generates null values. The function compares two expressions; if the values are equal, the function returns a null; otherwise, the function returns the first expression. The following SQL statement returns null for the NULLIF function if the values in the columns CREATED_DATE and MODIFIED_DATE are equal. This is the case for the row with the STUDENT_ID of 150. Both date columns are exactly the same, therefore the result of the NULLIF function is null. For the row with a STUDENT_ID of 340, the columns contain different values, therefore the first substitution expression is displayed. In this example, you see the use of the TO_CHAR function together with a DATE datatype as the input parameter. This allows the display of dates as formatted character strings. This functionality is explained in greater detail in Chapter 4, "Date and Conversion Functions."

```
SELECT student_id,
       TO_CHAR(created_date, 'DD-MON-YY HH24:MI:SS') "Created",
       TO_CHAR(modified_date, 'DD-MON-YY HH24:MI:SS') "Modified",
       NULLIF(created_date, modified_date) "Null if equal"
  FROM student
 WHERE student_id IN (150, 340)
STUDENT_ID Created             Modified            Null if e
---------- ------------------- ------------------- ---------
       150 30-JAN-03 00:00:00  30-JAN-03 00:00:00
       340 19-FEB-03 00:00:00  22-FEB-03 00:00:00  19-FEB-03

2 rows selected.
```

The syntax for the NULLIF function is as follows:

```
NULLIF(expression1, equal_expression2)
```

THE NANVL FUNCTION

The new 10*g* function NANVL is used only for the BINARY_FLOAT and BINARY_DOUBLE floating point datatypes. The function returns a substitution value in case the input value is a NaN (not a Number). In the following query output, the last row contains such a value. In this instance, the NANVL function's second parameter substitutes the value zero. (Note the FLOAT_TEST table is part of an additional script containing sample tables and it is available for download from the companion Web site.)

```
SELECT test_col, NANVL(test_col, 0)
  FROM float_test
  TEST_COL NANVL(TEST_COL,0)
---------- ------------------
   5.0E+000          5.0E+000
   2.5E+000          2.5E+000
        Nan                 0

3 rows selected.
```

The NANVL function's input and substitution values are numeric and the syntax is as follows:

```
NANVL(input_value, substitution_value)
```

THE DECODE FUNCTION

The DECODE function substitutes values based on a condition using *if then else* logic. If a value is equal to another value, the substitution value is returned. If the value compared is not equal to any of the listed expressions, an optional default value can be returned. The syntax code for the DECODE function is:

```
DECODE (if_expr, equals_search,
        then_result [,else_default])
```

Note that the search and result values can be repeated.

In the following query, the text literals 'New York' and 'New Jersey' are returned when the state is equal to 'NY' or 'NJ', respectively. If the value in the STATE column is other than 'NY' or 'NJ', a null value is displayed. The second DECODE function shows the use of the *else* condition. In the case of 'CT', the function returns the value 'Other'.

```
SELECT DISTINCT state,
       DECODE(state, 'NY', 'New York',
                     'NJ', 'New Jersey') no_default,
       DECODE(state, 'NY', 'New York',
                     'NJ', 'New Jersey',
                           'OTHER') with_default
  FROM zipcode
WHERE state IN ('NY','NJ','CT')
```

```
ST  NO_DEFAULT WITH_DEFAU
--  ---------- ----------
CT             OTHER
NJ  New Jersey New Jersey
NY  New York   New York
```

```
3 rows selected.
```

THE DECODE FUNCTION AND NULLS

If you want to specifically test for the null value, you can use the keyword NULL. The following SQL statement shows for instructors with a null value in the ZIP column the text `"NO zipcode!"`. Although one null does not equal another null, for the purpose of the DECODE function, null values are treated as equals.

```
SELECT instructor_id, zip,
       DECODE(zip, NULL, 'NO zipcode!', zip) "Decode Use"
  FROM instructor
 WHERE instructor_id IN (102, 110)
```

```
INSTRUCTOR_ID ZIP   Decode Use
------------- ----- -----------
          110       NO zipcode!
          102 10025 10025
```

```
2 rows selected.
```

THE DECODE FUNCTION AND COMPARISONS

The DECODE function does not allow greater than or less than comparisons; however, combining the DECODE function with the SIGN function overcomes this shortcoming.

The following SELECT statement combines the DECODE and SIGN functions to display the course cost as 500 for courses that cost less than 1195. If the course cost is greater than or equal to 1195, the actual cost is displayed. The calculation of the value in the COST column minus 1195 results in a negative number, a positive number, a zero, or null. The SIGN function determines the sign of the calculation and returns respectively –1, +1, 0, or null. The DECODE function checks if the result equals –1. If so, this indicates that the cost is less than 1195 and the DECODE function returns 500; otherwise the regular cost is shown. See Chapter 16, "Exploring Data Warehousing Features," for additional examples on the DECODE and SIGN functions.

```
SELECT course_no, cost,
       DECODE(SIGN(cost-1195),-1, 500, cost) newcost
  FROM course
 WHERE course_no IN (80, 20, 135, 450)
 ORDER BY 2
```

COURSE_NO	COST	NEWCOST
135	1095	500
20	1195	1195
80	1595	1595
450		

4 rows selected.

THE SEARCHED CASE EXPRESSION

A searched CASE expression is extremely powerful and can be utilized in many ways in SQL. It can be used in the SELECT list, the WHERE clause, the ORDER BY clause, as a parameter of a function, or anywhere an expression is allowed. Using a CASE expression is, in many cases, easier to understand, less restrictive, and more versatile than the DECODE function. For example, the following query accomplishes the same result as the previous query.

```
SELECT course_no, cost,
       CASE WHEN cost <1195 THEN 500
            ELSE cost
       END "Test CASE"
  FROM course
 WHERE course_no IN (80, 20, 135, 450)
 ORDER BY 2
```

COURSE_NO	COST	Test CASE
135	1095	500
20	1195	1195
80	1595	1595
450		

4 rows selected.

Each CASE expression starts with the keyword CASE and ends with the keyword END; the ELSE clause is optional. A condition is tested with the WHEN keyword; if the condition is true, the THEN clause is executed. The result of the query shows 500 in the column labeled "Test CASE" when the value in the COST column is less than 1195, otherwise it just displays the value of the COST column. Following is the syntax of the searched CASE expression:

```
CASE {WHEN condition THEN return_expr
      [WHEN condition THEN return_expr]... }
      [ELSE else_expr]
END
```

The next example expands the WHEN condition of the CASE expression with multiple conditions being tested. The first condition checks whether the value in the COST column is less than 1100; when true, the result evaluates to 1000. If the value in the COST column is equal to or greater than 1100, but less than 1500, the value in the COST column is multiplied by 1.1, increasing the cost by 10%. If the value in the COST column is null, then the value zero is the result. If none of the conditions are true, the ELSE clause is returned.

```
SELECT course_no, cost,
       CASE WHEN cost <1100 THEN 1000
            WHEN cost >=1100 AND cost <1500 THEN cost*1.1
            WHEN cost IS NULL THEN 0
            ELSE cost
       END "Test CASE"
  FROM course
 WHERE course_no IN (80, 20, 135, 450)
 ORDER BY 2
```

COURSE_NO	COST	Test CASE
135	1095	1000
20	1195	1314.5
80	1595	1595
450		0

4 rows selected.

The CASE expression lets you evaluate if-then-else conditions more simply than the DECODE function.

NESTING CASE EXPRESSIONS

A CASE expression can be nested further with additional CASE expressions as shown in the next example. An additional row with the COURSE_NO of 230 is included in this query to demonstrate the result of the nested expression. This nested expression is evaluated only if the COST is less than 1100. If this expression is true, the value of the PREREQUISITE column is checked; if it is either 10 or 50, the cost is cut in half. If the PREREQUISITE column does not have the value of 10 or 50, just the value in the COST is displayed.

```
SELECT course_no, cost, prerequisite,
       CASE WHEN cost <1100 THEN
                 CASE WHEN prerequisite IN (10, 50) THEN cost/2
                      ELSE cost
                 END
            WHEN cost >=1100 AND cost <1500 THEN cost*1.1
            WHEN cost IS NULL THEN 0
            ELSE cost
       END "Test CASE"
  FROM course
```

```
WHERE course_no IN (80, 20, 135, 450, 230)
ORDER BY 2
```

COURSE_NO	COST	PREREQUISITE	Test CASE
230	1095	10	547.5
135	1095	134	1095
20	1195		1314.5
80	1595	204	1595
450		350	0

5 rows selected.

CASE EXPRESSION IN THE WHERE CLAUSE

CASE expressions are allowed anywhere expressions are allowed; the following example shows a CASE expression in the WHERE clause. It multiplies the CAPACITY column by the result of the CASE expression that returns either 2, 1.5, or null depending on the starting letter of the value in the LOCATION column. Only if the result of the CASE expression is greater than 30 the row is chosen for output.

```
SELECT DISTINCT capacity, location
   FROM section
WHERE capacity*CASE
          WHEN SUBSTR(location, 1,1)='L' THEN 2
          WHEN SUBSTR(location, 1,1)='M' THEN 1.5
          ELSE NULL
       END  > 30
```

CAPACITY	LOCATION
25	L210
...	
25	M500

8 rows selected.

DATATYPE INCONSISTENCIES

You may come across the following error message when executing the CASE expression or the DECODE function. It indicates that the return datatype of the first condition does not agree with the datatype of the subsequent conditions. As you notice the first CASE condition returns a NUMBER datatype, the second condition returns the character string "Room too small".

```
SQL> SELECT section_id, capacity,
  2         CASE WHEN capacity >=15 THEN capacity
  3              WHEN capacity < 15 THEN 'Room too small'
  4         END AS "Capacity"
```

```
  5    FROM section
  6    WHERE section_id IN (101, 146, 147)
  7  /
     WHEN capacity < 15 THEN 'Room too small'
                           *
ERROR at line 3:
ORA-00932: inconsistent datatypes
```

You match the two datatypes with a conversion function. The next example shows the use of the TO_CHAR conversion function to convert the values of the CAPACITY column to a character datatype.

```
SELECT section_id, capacity,
       CASE WHEN capacity >=15 THEN TO_CHAR(capacity)
            WHEN capacity < 15 THEN 'Room too small'
       END AS "Capacity"
  FROM section
 WHERE section_id IN (101, 146, 147)
```

SECTION_ID	CAPACITY	Capacity
147	15	15
146	25	25
101	10	Room too small

```
3 rows selected.
```

SIMPLE CASE EXPRESSION

If your conditions are testing for equality only, you can use the simple CASE expression. It has the following syntax.

```
CASE {expr WHEN comparison_expr THEN return_expr
           [WHEN comparison_expr THEN return_expr]...}
           [ELSE else_expr]
END
```

The next statement shows such an example. The query checks the value in the COST column to see if it equals the different amounts, and, if true, the appropriate THEN expression is executed.

```
SELECT course_no, cost,
       CASE cost WHEN 1095 THEN cost/2
                 WHEN 1195 THEN cost*1.1
                 WHEN 1595 THEN cost
                 ELSE cost*0.5
       END "Simple CASE"
  FROM course
```

```
WHERE course_no IN (80, 20, 135, 450)
ORDER BY 2
COURSE_NO       COST Simple CASE
--------------- ---- -----------
        135     1095       547.5
         20     1195      1314.5
         80     1595        1595
        450
```

4 rows selected.

 Rather than hard-coding literals in the CASE expressions, you can use subqueries to read dynamic values from tables instead. You will learn more about this in Chapter 7, "Subqueries."

OVERVIEW OF MISCELLANEOUS FUNCTIONS AND CASE EXPRESSIONS

Table 3.4 lists the miscellaneous functions and CASE expressions discussed in this lab.

LAB 3.3 EXERCISES

3.3.1 APPLY SUBSTITUTION FUNCTIONS AND OTHER MISCELLANEOUS FUNCTIONS

a) List the last name, first name, and phone number of students who do not have a phone number. Display '212-555-1212' for the phone number.

b) For course numbers 430 and greater, show the course cost. Add another column reflecting a discount of 10% off the cost and substitute any NULL values in the COST column with the number 1000. The result should look similar to the following output.

```
COURSE_NO       COST       NEW
--------------- -------    ------
        430     1195       1075.5
        450                900
```

2 rows selected.

c) Write the query to accomplish the following output using the NVL2 function in the column 'Get this result'.

Table 3.4 ■ Miscellaneous Functions and the CASE Expressions

Function/Expression	Purpose
NVL(input_expression, substitution_expression)	Null value replacement
COALESCE(input_expression, substitution_expression_1, [, substitution_expression_*n*])	Null value replacement with multiple substitution expressions
NVL2(input_expr, not_null_substitution_expr, null_substitution_expr)	Null and not null substitution replacement
NULLIF(expression1, equal_expression2)	Returns null if the value of two expressions are identical, otherwise returns first expression
NANVL(input_value, substitution_value)	Returns substitution value in case of NaN (Not a Number) value.
DECODE (if_expr, equals_search, then_result [,else_default])	Substitution function based on if then else logic
CASE {WHEN cond THEN return_expr [WHEN cond THEN return_ expr]...} [ELSE else_expr] END	Searched CASE expression. It allows for testing of null values, and greater than and less than comparisons.
CASE {expr WHEN expr THEN return_expr [WHEN expr THEN return_expr]...} [ELSE else_expr] END	The simple CASE expression tests for equality only. No greater than, less than, or IS NULL comparisons are allowed.

**LAB
3.3**

```
ID NAME                PHONE         Get this result
----------------       -----------   -----------------
112 Thomas Thomas      201-555-5555  Phone# exists.
111 Peggy Noviello                   No phone# exists.

2 rows selected.
```

3.3.2 UTILIZE THE POWER OF THE DECODE FUNCTION AND THE CASE EXPRESSION

a) Rewrite the query from Exercise 3.3.1 c) using the DECODE function instead.

b) For course numbers 20, 120, 122, and 132, display the description, course number, and prerequisite course number. If the prerequisite is course number 120, display 200; if the prerequisite is 130, display 'N/A'. For courses with no prerequisites, display 'None'. Otherwise, list the current prerequisite. The result should look like the one listed below.

```
COURSE_NO DESCRIPTION                      ORIGINAL NEW
--------- ------------------------------   -------- ----
      132 Basics of Unix Admin                  130 N/A
      122 Intermediate Java Programming         120 200
      120 Intro to Java Programming              80 80
       20 Intro to Computers                        None
```

4 rows selected.

c) Display the student ID, zip code, and phone number for students with student IDs 145, 150, or 325. For those students living in the 212 area code and in zip code 10048, display 'North Campus'. List students living in the 212 area code but in a different zip code as 'West Campus'. Display students outside the 212 area code as 'Off Campus'. The result should look like the following output. *Hint:* The solution to this query requires nested DECODE functions or nested CASE expressions.

```
STUDENT_ID ZIP   PHONE            LOC
---------- ----- ---------------- ------------
       145 10048 212-555-5555     North Campus
       150 11787 718-555-5555     Off Campus
       325 10954 212-555-5555     West Campus
```

3 rows selected.

d) Display all the distinct salutations used in the INSTRUCTOR table. Order them alphabetically except for female salutations, which should be listed first. *Hint:* Use the DECODE function or CASE expression in the ORDER BY clause.

LAB 3.3 EXERCISE ANSWERS

3.3.1 ANSWERS

a) List the last name, first name, and phone number of students who do not have a phone number. Display '212-555-1212' for the phone number.

Answer: There are various solutions to obtain the desired result. The first determines the rows with a NULL phone number using the IS NULL operator. Then you apply the

NVL function to the column with the substitution string '212-555-1212'. The second solution uses the NVL function in both the SELECT and WHERE clauses. Another way to achieve the result is to use the COALESCE function.

```
SELECT first_name||' '|| last_name name,
       phone oldphone,
       NVL(phone, '212-555-1212') newphone
  FROM student
 WHERE phone IS NULL
```

NAME	OLDPHONE	NEWPHONE
Peggy Noviello		212-555-1212

1 row selected.

You can also retrieve the same rows by applying the NVL function in the WHERE clause.

```
SELECT first_name||' '|| last_name name,
       phone oldphone,
       NVL(phone, '212-555-1212') newphone
  FROM student
 WHERE NVL(phone, 'NONE') = 'NONE'
```

NAME	OLDPHONE	NEWPHONE
Peggy Noviello		212-555-1212

1 row selected.

The next query applies the COALESCE function to achieve the same result.

```
SELECT first_name||' '|| last_name name,
       phone oldphone,
       COALESCE(phone, '212-555-1212') newphone
  FROM student
 WHERE COALESCE(phone, 'NONE') ='NONE'
```

b) For course numbers 430 and greater, show the course cost. Add another column reflecting a discount of 10% off the cost and substitute any NULL values in the COST column with the number 1000. The result should look similar to the following output.

COURSE_NO	COST	NEW
430	1195	1075.5
450		900

2 rows selected.

Answer: Substitute 1000 for the null value, using the NVL function before applying the discount calculation. Otherwise, the calculation yields a NULL..

```
SELECT course_no, cost,
       NVL(cost,1000)*0.9 new
  FROM course
 WHERE course_no >= 430
```

You can also use the COALESCE function instead.

```
SELECT course_no, cost,
       COALESCE(cost,1000)*0.9 new
  FROM course
 WHERE course_no >= 430
```

c) Write the query to accomplish the following output using the NVL2 function in the column 'Get this result'.

```
ID NAME                  PHONE         Get this result
------------------       ------------  ------------------
112 Thomas Thomas 201-555-5555 Phone# exists.
111 Peggy Noviello                     No phone# exists.

2 rows selected.
```

Answer: If the input parameter is not null, the NVL2 function's second parameter is returned. If the input parameter is null, then the third parameter is used.

```
SELECT student_id id, first_name||' '|| last_name name,
       phone,
       NVL2(phone, 'Phone# exists.', 'No phone# exists.')
        "Get this result"
  FROM student
 WHERE student_id IN (111, 112)
```

3.3.2 ANSWERS

a) Rewrite the query from Exercise 3.3.1 c) using the DECODE function instead.

Answer: The DECODE function can easily be substituted for the NVL2 function or the NVL function, because you can test for a NULL value. In this result, the DECODE function checks if the value is null. If this is true, the No phone# exists *literal is displayed; otherwise, it shows* Phone# exists.

```
SELECT student_id, first_name||' '|| last_name name,
       phone,
       DECODE(phone, NULL, 'No phone# exists.', 'Phone# exists.')
        "Get this result"
```

```
FROM student
WHERE student_id IN (111, 112)
```

b) For course numbers 20, 120, 122, and 132, display the description, course number, and prerequisite course number. If the prerequisite is course number 120, display 200; if the prerequisite is 130, display 'N/A'. For courses with no prerequisites, display 'None'. Otherwise, list the current prerequisite. The result should look like the one listed below.

```
COURSE_NO DESCRIPTION                          ORIGINAL NEW
--------- ------------------------------------ -------- ----
      132 Basics of Unix Admin                      130 N/A
      122 Intermediate Java Programming             120 200
      120 Intro to Java Programming                  80 80
       20 Intro to Computers                            None

4 rows selected.
```

Answer: The solution can be achieved with either the CASE expression or the DECODE function.

SOLUTION USING THE CASE EXPRESSION

```
SELECT course_no, description, prerequisite "ORIGINAL",
       CASE WHEN prerequisite = 120 THEN '200'
            WHEN prerequisite = 130 THEN 'N/A'
            WHEN prerequisite IS NULL THEN 'None'
            ELSE TO_CHAR(prerequisite)
       END "NEW"
  FROM course
 WHERE course_no IN (20, 120, 122, 132)
 ORDER BY course_no DESC
```

The query checks for nulls with the IS NULL condition. The ELSE clause requires you to convert the NUMBER datatype into a VARCHAR2 using the TO_CHAR function, otherwise you receive an ORA-00932: inconsistent datatypes error, indicating that the output datatypes do not match. Oracle expects the datatype to be consistent with the same datatype as the first result expression, which is a string as indicated by the single quotes around the '200'.

If you attempt to use the simple CASE expression to solve the query, you will notice that the test for the null value cannot be accomplished because the simple CASE expression only allows testing for the equality (=). The IS NULL operator is not permitted and returns the error ORA-00936: missing expression.

```
SELECT course_no, description, prerequisite "ORIGINAL",
       CASE prerequisite WHEN 120 THEN '200'
                         WHEN 130 THEN 'N/A'
                         WHEN IS NULL THEN 'None'
                         ELSE TO_CHAR(prerequisite)
       END "NEW"
  FROM course
 WHERE course_no IN (20, 120, 122, 132)
 ORDER BY course_no DESC
       WHEN IS NULL THEN 'None'
                    *
ERROR at line 4:
ORA-00936: missing expression
```

SOLUTION USING THE DECODE FUNCTION

```
SELECT course_no, description, prerequisite "ORIGINAL",
       DECODE(prerequisite, 120, '200',
                            130, 'N/A',
                            NULL, 'None',
                            TO_CHAR(prerequisite)) "NEW"
  FROM course
 WHERE course_no IN (20, 120, 122, 132)
 ORDER BY course_no DESC
```

The solution is best approached in several steps. The PREREQUISITE column is of datatype NUMBER. If you replace it in the DECODE function with another NUMBER for prerequisite 120, Oracle expects to continue to convert to the same datatype for all subsequent replacements. As the other replacements ('N/A' and 'None') are text literals, you need to enclose the number 200 with single quotes to predetermine the datatype for all subsequent substitutions as a VARCHAR2.

For any records that have a null prerequisite, "None" is displayed. Although one null does not equal another null, for the purpose of the DECODE function, null values are treated as equals.

The explicit datatype conversion with TO_CHAR function on the PREREQUISITE is good practice, though if you omit it, Oracle will implicitly convert the value to a VARCHAR2 datatype. The automatic datatype conversion works in this example because the datatype is predetermined by the datatype of the first substitution value.

c) Display the student ID, zip code, and phone number for students with student IDs 145, 150, or 325. For those students living in the 212 area code and in zip code 10048, display 'North Campus'. List students living in the 212 area code but in a different zip code as 'West Campus'. Display students outside the 212 area code as 'Off Campus'. The result should look like the following output. *Hint:* The solution requires nested DECODE functions or nested CASE expressions.

```
STUDENT_ID ZIP    PHONE           LOC
---------- -----  --------------- ------------
       145 10048  212-555-5555    North Campus
       150 11787  718-555-5555    Off Campus
       325 10954  212-555-5555    West Campus
```

3 rows selected.

**LAB
3.3**

Answer: The CASE expressions can be nested within each other to allow for the required logic. A more complicated way to obtain the desired result is using nested DECODE statements; the output from one DECODE is an input parameter in a second DECODE function.

SOLUTION USING CASE EXPRESSION

```
SELECT student_id, zip, phone,
       CASE WHEN SUBSTR(phone, 1, 3) = '212' THEN
               CASE WHEN zip = '10048' THEN 'North Campus'
                    ELSE   'West Campus'
               END
           ELSE 'Off Campus'
       END loc
  FROM student
 WHERE student_id IN (150, 145, 325)
```

SOLUTION USING DECODE FUNCTION

```
SELECT student_id, zip, phone,
       DECODE(SUBSTR(phone, 1, 3), '212',
                  DECODE(zip, '10048', 'North Campus',
                                        'West Campus'),
              'Off Campus') loc
  FROM student
 WHERE student_id IN (150, 145, 325)
```

d) Display all the distinct salutations used in the INSTRUCTOR table. Order them alphabetically except for female salutations, which should be listed first. *Hint:* Use the DECODE function or CASE expression in the ORDER BY clause.

Answer: The DECODE function or the CASE expression is used in the ORDER BY clause to substitute a number for all female salutations, thereby listing them first when executing the ORDER BY clause.

```
SELECT DISTINCT salutation
  FROM instructor
 ORDER BY DECODE(salutation, 'Ms', 1,
                             'Mrs', 1,
                             'Miss', 1)
```

```
SALUT
-----
Ms
Dr
Hon
Rev
Mr

5 rows selected.
```

Or with the CASE expression:

```
SELECT DISTINCT salutation
    FROM instructor
    ORDER BY CASE salutation WHEN 'Ms' THEN '1'
                             WHEN 'Mrs' THEN '1'
                             WHEN 'Miss' THEN '1'
                             ELSE salutation
             END
```

The ASCII equivalent number of '1' is less than the ASCII equivalent of 'Dr', or any other salutation. Therefore, Ms is listed first in the sort order. ASCII stands for American Standard Code for Information Interchange and deals with common formats.

To display the decimal representation of the first character of a string, use the ASCII function. Here is an example query of how you can determine the ASCII number of various values.

```
SELECT ASCII('1') "1", ASCII('0') "ZERO", ASCII('D') "D",
       ASCII('a') "a", ASCII('A') "A"
    FROM dual
           1           ZERO          D           a  A
--------------- ----------- --------- --------- --
          49            48         68        97 65

1 row selected.
```

LAB 3.3 SELF-REVIEW QUESTIONS

In order to test your progress, you should be able to answer the following questions.

1) A calculation with a null always yields another null.

    a) _____ True
    b) _____ False

2) The following query is valid.

```
SELECT NVL(cost, 'None')
  FROM course
```

a) _____ True
b) _____ False

3) The NVL2 function updates the data in the database.

a) _____ True
b) _____ False

4) The DECODE function lets you perform if-then-else functionality within the SQL language.

a) _____ True
b) _____ False

5) The DECODE function cannot be used in the WHERE clause of a SQL statement.

a) _____ True
b) _____ False

6) CASE expressions can be used in the ORDER BY clause of a SELECT statement.

a) _____ True
b) _____ False

7) The functions discussed in this lab can be used on the VARCHAR2 datatype only.

a) _____ True
b) _____ False

Answers appear in Appendix A, Section 3.3.

CHAPTER 3

TEST YOUR THINKING

The projects in this section are meant to have you utilize all of the skills that you have acquired throughout this chapter. The answers to these projects can be found at the companion Web site to this book, located at: http://authors.phptr.com/rischert3e. Visit the Web site periodically to share and discuss your answers.

1) Write the SELECT statement that returns the following output. Be sure to use spaces and punctuation exactly as you see them. (Use the SQL*Plus commands SET FEEDBACK OFF and SET HEADING OFF to turn off the number of rows displayed at the end of the statement and to turn off the column headings. Be sure to reset these options to their defaults when you are done. For more explanations on SQL*Plus commands, refer to Appendix C, "SQL*Plus Command Reference.")

```
Instructor: R. Chow...... Phone: 212-555-1212
Instructor: M. Frantzen.. Phone: 212-555-1212
Instructor: F. Hanks..... Phone: 212-555-1212
Instructor: C. Lowry..... Phone: 212-555-1212
Instructor: A. Morris.... Phone: 212-555-1212
Instructor: G. Pertez.... Phone: 212-555-1212
Instructor: N. Schorin... Phone: 212-555-1212
Instructor: T. Smythe.... Phone: 212-555-1212
Instructor: I. Willig.... Phone: 212-555-1212
Instructor: T. Wojick.... Phone: 212-555-1212
```

2) Rewrite the following query to replace all occurrences of the string 'Unix' with 'Linux'.

```
SELECT 'I develop software on the Unix platform'
  FROM dual
```

3) Determine which student does not have the first letter of her or his last name capitalized. Show the STUDENT_ID and LAST_NAME columns.

4) Check if any of the phone numbers in the INSTRUCTOR table have been entered in the (###)###-#### format.

5) Explain the functionality of the following query:

```
SELECT section_id, capacity,
       CASE WHEN MOD(capacity, 2) <> 0 THEN 'Odd capacity'
            ELSE 'Even capacity'
       END "Odd or Even "
  FROM section
 WHERE section_id IN (101, 146, 147)
```

CHAPTER 4

DATE AND CONVERSION FUNCTIONS

CHAPTER OBJECTIVES

In this chapter, you will learn about:

In this chapter you will gain an understanding of Oracle's two date-related categories of datatypes: the datetime datatypes and the interval datatypes.

The datetime datatypes keep track of both date and time; they consist of the individual datatypes DATE, TIMESTAMP, TIMESTAMP WITH TIME ZONE, and TIMESTAMP WITH LOCAL TIME ZONE. In the first two labs you will learn about the most popular datatype—the DATE datatype. Lab 4.3 introduces you to the other three datatypes, which contain fractional seconds and time zone values. Table 4.1 shows an overview of the datetime datatypes.

The interval datatypes are the topic of Lab 4.4; they express differences between dates and times. The Oracle-supported interval datatypes are INTERVAL YEAR TO MONTH and INTERVAL DAY TO SECOND and they are listed in Table 4.2.

In the chapter's final lab you will become familiar with datatype conversion functions; they allow you convert a literal or column from one datatype to another. Like character and number functions, all conversion and date-related functions are single-row functions.

The SQL novice often finds date and conversion functions challenging, but the many examples in the labs will help you master these functions and avoid the common pitfalls.

Table 4.1 ■ Overview of Datetime Datatypes

Datatype	Fractional Seconds	Time Zone	Lab
DATE	No	No	4.1, 4.2
TIMESTAMP	Yes	No	4.3
TIMESTAMP WITH TIME ZONE	Yes	Yes	4.3
TIMESTAMP WITH LOCAL TIME ZONE	Yes	Yes	4.3

Table 4.2 ■ Overview of Interval Datatypes

Datatype	Supported Time Differences
INTERVAL YEAR TO MONTH	Years and months
INTERVAL DAY TO SECOND	Days, hours, minutes, and seconds

L A B   4 . 1

APPLYING ORACLE'S DATE FORMAT MODELS

L A B   O B J E C T I V E S

After this lab, you will be able to:
- ✔ Compare a Text Literal to a DATE Column
- ✔ Apply Format Models

When working with an Oracle database, you will inevitably need to query columns containing dates. Oracle's DATE datatype consists of a *date and time,* that are stored in an internal format that keeps track of the century, year, month, day, hour, minute, and second.

CHANGING THE DATE DISPLAY FORMAT

When you query a DATE datatype column, Oracle typically displays it in the default format DD-MON-YY as in the following query.

```
SELECT last_name, registration_date
  FROM student
 WHERE student_id IN (123, 161, 190)
LAST_NAME  REGISTRAT
---------  ---------
Affinito   03-FEB-03
Grant      02-FEB-03
Radicola   27-JAN-03

3 rows selected.
```

To change the display format of the column REGISTRATION_DATE, you use the TO_CHAR function together with a format model, also referred to as a *format mask.* The result shows the registration date in both the default date format and in the MM/DD/YYYY format.

```
SELECT last_name, registration_date,
       TO_CHAR(registration_date, 'MM/DD/YYYY')
       AS "Formatted"
  FROM student
 WHERE student_id IN (123, 161, 190)
  LAST_NAME       REGISTRAT Formatted
  ---------       --------- ----------
  Affinito        03-FEB-03 02/03/2003
  Grant           02-FEB-03 02/02/2003
  Radicola        27-JAN-03 01/27/2003

3 rows selected.
```

The TO_CHAR conversion function changes the DATE datatype into text and applies a format mask. As you see from the syntax listed in Table 4.3, the function takes a DATE datatype as the first parameter; the second optional parameter is for the format mask. In Table 4.4 you will find commonly used elements of date format masks.

The TO_DATE function does just the opposite of the TO_CHAR function—it converts a text literal into a DATE datatype.

The next SQL statement shows the same student record with the date and time formatted in various ways. The first format model is Dy, which shows the abbreviated day of the week in mixed format. The next format model is DY, and it

Table 4.3 ■ Date Related Conversion Functions

Function	Purpose	Return Datatype
TO_CHAR(date [,format_mask])	Converts datetime datatypes into VARCHAR2 to display it in a different format than the default date format. (The TO_CHAR function can be used with other datatypes besides the DATE, see Lab 4.5).	VARCHAR2
TO_DATE(char [,format_mask])	Converts a text literal to a DATE datatype. As with all other date-related conversion functions, the format_mask is optional if the literal is in the default format; otherwise, a format mask must be specified.	DATE

Table 4.4 ■ Commonly Used Elements of the DATE Format Model

Format	Description
YYYY	Four-digit year.
YEAR	Year spelled out.
RR	Two-digit year based on century. If two-digit year is between 50 and 99, then it's the previous century; if the year is between 00 and 49, it's the current century.
MM	Two-digit month.
MON	Three-letter abbreviation of the month in capital letters.
MONTH	Month spelled out in capital letters and padded with blanks.
Month	Month spelled with first letter in caps and padded with blanks to a length of nine characters.
DD	Numeric day (1–31).
DAY	Day of the week in capital letters and padded with blanks to a length of nine characters.
DY	Three letter abbreviation of the day of the week in caps.
D	Day of the week number (1–7). Sunday is day 1, Monday is day 2, and so forth.
DDD	Day of the year (1–366).
DL	Day long format; equivalent to 'fmDay, Month DD, YYYY'.
HH or HH12	Hours (0–12).
HH24	Hours in military format (0–23).
MI	Minutes (0–59).
SS	Seconds (0–59).
SSSSS	Seconds past midnight (0–86399).
AM or PM	Meridian indicator.
TS	Short time format; the equivalent format mask is 'HH:MI:SS AM'.
WW	Week of the year (1–53).
W	Week of the month (1–5).
Q	Quarter of the year.

returns the uppercase version. The fourth column has the month spelled out, but notice the extra spaces after the month. Oracle pads the month with up to nine spaces, which may be useful when you choose to align the month columns. If you want to eliminate the extra spaces, use the fill mask *fm*. You will see some examples of this format mask shortly. The last column shows only the time.

```
SELECT last_name,
       TO_CHAR(registration_date, 'Dy') AS "1.Day",
       TO_CHAR(registration_date, 'DY') AS "2.Day",
       TO_CHAR(registration_date, 'Month DD, YYYY')
          AS "Look at the Month",
       TO_CHAR(registration_date, 'HH:MI pm') AS "Time"
  FROM student
 WHERE student_id IN (123, 161, 190)
LAST_NAME 1.Da 2.Da Look at the Month  Time
--------- ---- ---- ------------------ --------
Affinito  Mon  MON  February  03, 2003 12:00 am
Grant     Sun  SUN  February  02, 2003 12:00 am
Radicola  Mon  MON  January   27, 2003 12:00 am

3 rows selected.
```

USING SPECIAL FORMAT MASKS

Here is a more elaborate example, which uses the *fm* mask to eliminate the extra spaces between the month and the date in the second column of the following result set. In addition, this format mask uses the *th* suffix on the day (dd) mask to include the "st", "nd", "rd," and "th" in lowercase after each number. The third and last column spells out the date using the *sp* format parameter with the first letter capitalized by using the Dd format. Also notice you can add a text literal, as in this case with the "of" text.

```
SELECT last_name,
       TO_CHAR(registration_date, 'fmMonth ddth, YYYY')
       "Eliminating Spaces",
       TO_CHAR(registration_date, 'Ddspth "of" fmMonth')
       "Spelled out"
  FROM student
 WHERE student_id IN (123, 161, 190)
LAST_NAME  Eliminating Spaces  Spelled out
---------  ------------------  -------------------------
Affinito   February 3rd, 2003  Third of February
Grant      February 2nd, 2003  Second of February
Radicola   January 27th, 2003  Twenty-Seventh of January

3 rows selected.
```

Table 4.5 shows you additional examples of how the format models can be used.

Table 4.5 ■ Date Format Model Examples

Format Mask	Example
DD-Mon-YYYY HH24:MI:SS	12-Apr-2003 17:00:00 (Note that the case matters!)
MM/DD/YYYY HH:MI pm	04/12/2003 5:00 pm
Month	April
fmMonth DDth, YYYY	April 12th, 2003
Day	Sunday
DY	SUN
Qth YYYY	2nd 2003 (This shows the 2nd quarter of 2003)
Ddspth	Twelfth (Spells out the date)
DD-MON-RR	12-APR-03 (More on the RR format later in this lab)

HOW TO PERFORM A DATE SEARCH

Often you need to query data based on certain date criteria. For example, if you need to look for all those students who registered on January 22, 2003, you write a SQL statement similar to the following:

```
SELECT last_name, registration_date
  FROM student
 WHERE registration_date = TO_DATE('22-JAN-2003', 'DD-MON-YYYY')
LAST_NAME                      REGISTRAT
------------------------       ---------
Crocitto                       22-JAN-03
Landry                         22-JAN-03
...
Sethi                          22-JAN-03
Walter                         22-JAN-03

8 rows selected.
```

In the WHERE clause, the text literal '22-JAN-2003' is converted to a DATE datatype using the TO_DATE function and the format model. The TO_DATE function helps Oracle understand the text literal based on the supplied format mask. The text literal is converted to the DATE datatype, which is then compared to the

REGISTRATION_DATE column, also of datatype DATE. Now you are comparing identical datatypes.

It is best to inform Oracle about the format of your text literal via the format mask, otherwise Oracle will not be able to interpret the text literal correctly and will return the following error message indicating that the text literal and the associated format mask do not agree.

```
SELECT last_name, registration_date
  FROM student
 WHERE registration_date = TO_DATE('22/01/2003', 'DD-MON-YYYY')
WHERE registration_date = TO_DATE('22/01/2003', 'DD-MON-YYYY')
                              *
ERROR at line 3:
ORA-01843: not a valid month
```

IMPLICIT CONVERSION AND DEFAULT DATE FORMAT

In some cases Oracle will implicitly perform a conversion of the text literal to the DATE datatype because the text literal is in the default date format. The next SQL statement shows you such an example. The text literal is the default date format mask, which typically is DD-MON-YYYY and DD-MON-RR, so the implicit conversion is performed automatically by Oracle. The default date format can be changed with the initialization parameter NLS_DATE_FORMAT in your Oracle database initialization file (also referred to as init.ora file) and your Windows Registry.

```
    SELECT last_name, registration_date
      FROM student
     WHERE registration_date = '22-JAN-2003'
    LAST_NAME                  REGISTRAT
    ------------------------   ---------
    Crocitto                   22-JAN-03
    Landry                     22-JAN-03
    ...
    Sethi                      22-JAN-03
    Walter                     22-JAN-03

    8 rows selected.
```

The same result can also be achieved with this WHERE clause. Note that this will only work if your Oracle installation has the DD-MON-RR format model as the NLS_DATE_FORMAT default date format.

```
    WHERE registration_date = '22-JAN-03'
```

It is best to explicitly use the TO_DATE function when converting a text literal! You will see the advantages of doing so as you go through some of the exercises.

THE RR DATE FORMAT MASK AND THE PREVIOUS CENTURY

Although the year 2000 is long behind us, you still have to deal with dates in the prior century. For example, the next statement retrieves all rows in the GRADE_TYPE table that were created on December 31, 1998. You will notice the century is missing in the WHERE clause.

```
SELECT grade_type_code, description, created_date
  FROM grade_type
 WHERE created_date = '31-DEC-98'
GR DESCRIPTION          CREATED_D
-- -------------------- ---------
FI Final                31-DEC-98
HM Homework             31-DEC-98
MT Midterm              31-DEC-98
PA Participation        31-DEC-98
PJ Project              31 DEC 98
QZ Quiz                 31-DEC-98

6 rows selected.
```

The query will only return rows if your Oracle installation includes the DD-MON-RR format mask. This special RR format mask interprets the two-digit year from 50 until 99 as the prior century, which currently is for years from 1950 through 1999. Two-digit year numbers from 00 until 49 are interpreted as the current century, that is, as years 2000 through 2049.

You can also see what your session settings are by issuing this query, which returns session attributes.

```
SELECT SYS_CONTEXT ('USERENV', 'NLS_DATE_FORMAT')
  FROM dual
SYS_CONTEXT('USERENV','NLS_DATE_FORMAT')
-------------------------------------------
DD-MON-RR

1 row selected.
```

If your default format mask is set to DD-MON-YY instead, Oracle interprets '31-DEC-98' as '31-DEC-2098', which is obviously not the desired result. Therefore, it's always best to be specific and to include the four-digit year in your WHERE clause. If your queries do not interpret the century correctly (usually Oracle versions prior to 8.1.7), visit the companion Web site located at http://authors.phptr.com/rischert3e for more details.

The next query illustrates how a two-digit year gets interpreted with the RR format mask. The text literals '17-OCT-67' and '17-OCT-17' are converted to a DATE datatype with the format mask DD-MON-RR. Then the TO_CHAR function converts the DATE datatype back to text but this time with a four-digit year. Effectively, the two-digit year 67 is interpreted as 1967 and the two-digit year literal 17 is interpreted as 2017.

```
SELECT TO_CHAR(TO_DATE('17-OCT-67','DD-MON-RR'),'YYYY') "1900",
       TO_CHAR(TO_DATE('17-OCT-17','DD-MON-RR'),'YYYY') "2000"
  FROM dual
1900 2000
---- ----
1967 2017

1 row selected.
```

DON'T FORGET ABOUT THE TIME

As previously mentioned, the Oracle DATE datatype includes the time. You can query records for a specific time or ignore the time altogether. The next SQL statement displays the time as part of the result set. If no time component was included when the data was entered, Oracle assumes the time is midnight, which is 12:00:00 AM, or 00:00:00 military time (HH24 time format mask). The WHERE clause retrieves only those rows where the column has a value of January 22, 2003 midnight; other records with a different time are not returned, should any exist.

```
SELECT last_name,
       TO_CHAR(registration_date, 'DD-MON-YYYY HH24:MI:SS')
  FROM student
 WHERE registration_date = TO_DATE('22-JAN-2003', 'DD-MON-YYYY')
LAST_NAME                    TO_CHAR(REGISTRATION
-----------------------      --------------------
Crocitto                     22-JAN-2003 00:00:00
Landry                       22-JAN-2003 00:00:00
...
Sethi                        22-JAN-2003 00:00:00
Walter                       22-JAN-2003 00:00:00

8 rows selected.
```

TIME AND THE TRUNC FUNCTION

You already learned about the TRUNC function in connection with the NUMBER datatype in Chapter 3, "Character, Number, and Miscellaneous Functions." The TRUNC function can also take a DATE datatype as an input parameter, which interprets the time as midnight (i.e. 12:00:00 AM). The next example shows the TRUNC function applied to the ENROLL_DATE column. This has the effect that the records are included no matter what the time, as long as the date is February 7, 2003.

```
SELECT student_id, TO_CHAR(enroll_date, 'DD-MON-YYYY HH24:MI:SS')
  FROM enrollment
 WHERE TRUNC(enroll_date) = TO_DATE('07-FEB-2003', 'DD-MON-YYYY')
STUDENT_ID TO_CHAR(ENROLL_DATE,
---------- --------------------
       140 07-FEB-2003 10:19:00
       141 07-FEB-2003 10:19:00
...
       158 07-FEB-2003 10:19:00
       159 07-FEB-2003 10:19:00

20 rows selected.
```

THE ANSI DATE AND ANSI TIMESTAMP FORMATS

Instead of using Oracle's date literals, you can specify a date in the ANSI format listed in the next example. This format contains no time portion and must be listed exactly in the format YYYY-MM-DD with the DATE keyword prefix.

```
SELECT student_id, TO_CHAR(enroll_date, 'DD-MON-YYYY HH24:MI:SS')
  FROM enrollment
 WHERE enroll_date >= DATE '2003-02-07'
   AND enroll_date <  DATE '2003-02-08'
```

If you want to include the time portion, use the ANSI TIMESTAMP keyword. The literal must be in the ANSI TIMESTAMP format, which is defined as YYYY-MM-DD HH24:MI:SS.

```
SELECT student_id, TO_CHAR(enroll_date, 'DD-MON-YYYY HH24:MI:SS')
  FROM enrollment
 WHERE enroll_date >= TIMESTAMP '2003-02-07 00:00:00'
   AND enroll_date <  TIMESTAMP '2003-02-08 00:00:00'
```

LAB 4.1 EXERCISES

4.1.1 COMPARE A TEXT LITERAL TO A *DATE* COLUMN

a) Display the course number, section ID, and starting date and time for sections that were taught on May 4, 2003.

b) Show the student records that were modified on or before January 22, 2003. Display the date the record was modified and each student's first and last name concatenated in one column.

4.1.2 APPLY FORMAT MODELS

a) Display the course number, section ID, and starting date and time for sections that start on Tuesdays.

b) List the section ID and starting date and time for all sections that begin and end in July 2003.

c) Determine the day of the week for December 31, 1899.

d) Execute the following statement. Write the question to obtain the desired result. Pay particular attention to the ORDER BY clause.

```
SELECT 'Section '||section_id||' begins on '||
       TO_CHAR(start_date_time, 'fmDay')||'.' AS "Start"
  FROM section
 WHERE section_id IN (146, 127, 121, 155, 110, 85, 148)
 ORDER BY TO_CHAR(start_date_time, 'D')
```

LAB 4.1 EXERCISE ANSWERS

4.1.1 ANSWERS

a) Display the course number, section ID, and starting date and time for sections that were taught on May 4, 2003.

Answer: To display a DATE column in a nondefault format, use the TO_CHAR function. To compare a text literal to a DATE column, use the TO_DATE function. It is best to always use the four-digit year and the format mask when using the TO_DATE function. This is good practice and not subject to year interpretations or ambiguities if the default date format is different.

```
SELECT course_no, section_id,
       TO_CHAR(start_date_time, 'DD-MON-YYYY HH24:MI')
  FROM section
 WHERE start_date_time >= TO_DATE('04-MAY-2003', 'DD-MON-YYYY')
   AND start_date_time < TO_DATE('05-MAY-2003', 'DD-MON-YYYY')
COURSE_NO SECTION_ID TO_CHAR(START_DAT
--------- ---------- -----------------
       25         88 04-MAY-2003 09:30
      100        144 04-MAY-2003 09:30
      120        149 04-MAY-2003 09:30
      122        155 04-MAY-2003 09:30
```

4 rows selected.

The returned result set displays the starting date and time using the TO_CHAR function and the specified format mask in the SELECT list. In the WHERE clause the text literals '04-MAY-2003' and '05-MAY-2003' are transformed into the DATE datatype with the TO_DATE function. Because no format mask for the time is specified, Oracle assumes the time is midnight, which is 12:00:00 AM, or 00:00:00 military time (HH24 time format mask). The WHERE clause retrieves only those rows where the START_DATE_TIME column has values on or after '04-MAY-2003 12:00:00 AM' and before '05-MAY-2003 12:00:00 AM'.

You can also include the time in your WHERE clause, such as in the following example. It is irrelevant if you choose AM or PM in the display 'DD-MON-YYYY HH:MI:SS AM' format mask for the display of the result, but obviously not in the WHERE clause with the actual date string listed as '04-MAY-2003 12:00:00 AM' and '04-MAY-2003 11:59:59 PM'.

```
SELECT course_no, section_id,
       TO_CHAR(start_date_time, 'DD-MON-YYYY HH24:MI')
  FROM section
 WHERE start_date_time >= TO_DATE('04-MAY-2003 12:00:00 AM',
                                  'DD-MON-YYYY HH:MI:SS AM')
   AND start_date_time <= TO_DATE('04-MAY-2003 11:59:59 PM',
                                  'DD-MON-YYYY HH:MI:SS AM')
```

The next SQL query returns the same result when the following WHERE clause is used instead. Here, note that Oracle has to perform the implicit conversion of the text literal into a DATE datatype.

```
 WHERE start_date_time >= '04-MAY-2003'
   AND start_date_time <  '05-MAY-2003'
```

The next WHERE clause returns the same result again, but Oracle has to perform the implicit conversion and pick the correct century.

```
WHERE start_date_time >= '04-MAY-03'
  AND start_date_time <  '05-MAY-03'
```

You can use the TRUNC function to ignore the timestamp.

```
SELECT course_no, section_id,
       TO_CHAR(start_date_time, 'DD-MON-YYYY HH24:MI')
  FROM section
 WHERE TRUNC(start_date_time) = TO_DATE('04-MAY-2003', 'DD-MON-YYYY')
```

The next WHERE clause is another valid alternative; however, the previous WHERE clause is preferable because it explicitly specifies the text literal to DATE datatype conversion together with the format mask and includes the four-digit year.

```
WHERE TRUNC(start_date_time) = '04-MAY-03'
```

 When you modify a database column with a function in the WHERE clause, such as the TRUNC function on the database column START_DATE_TIME, you cannot take advantage of an index should one exist on the column, unless it is a function-based index. Indexes speed up the retrieval of the data; you will learn more about the performance advantages of indexes in Chapter 12, "Views, Indexes, and Sequences."

The next statement does not return the desired rows. Only rows that have a START_DATE_TIME of midnight on May 4, 2003 qualify and because there are no such rows, no rows are selected for output.

```
SELECT course_no, section_id,
       TO_CHAR(start_date_time, 'DD-MON-YYYY HH24:MI')
  FROM section
 WHERE start_date_time = '04-MAY-03'
```

no rows selected

The ANSI format is listed in the next example. The ANSI DATE format must be specified exactly in the format YYYY-MM-DD with the DATE keyword prefix; note that it does not have a time component.

```
SELECT course_no, section_id,
       TO_CHAR(start_date_time, 'DD-MON-YYYY HH24:MI')
  FROM section
 WHERE start_date_time >= DATE '2003-05-04'
   AND start_date_time <  DATE '2003-05-05'
```

Alternatively, you can apply the TRUNC function on the START_DATE_TIME column, but just be aware of the possible performance impact mentioned previously.

```
SELECT course_no, section_id,
       TO_CHAR(start_date_time, 'DD-MON-YYYY HH24:MI')
  FROM section
 WHERE TRUNC(start_date_time) = DATE '2003-05-04'
```

If you want to include the time, use the ANSI TIMESTAMP keyword. The literal must be exactly in the ANSI TIMESTAMP format defined as YYYY-MM-DD HH24:MI:SS.

```
SELECT course_no, section_id,
       TO_CHAR(start_date_time, 'DD-MON-YYYY HH24:MI')
  FROM section
 WHERE start_date_time >= TIMESTAMP '2003-05-04 00:00:00'
   AND start_date_time <  TIMESTAMP '2003-05-05 00:00:00'
```

ERROR WHEN ENTERING THE WRONG FORMAT

Any attempt to change the predetermined format or the use of the wrong keyword results in an error, as you see in the next example. For this query to work, the TIMESTAMP keyword must be used instead of the DATE keyword, because the literal is in the ANSI TIMESTAMP format.

```
SELECT course_no, section_id,
       TO_CHAR(start_date_time, 'DD-MON-YYYY HH24:MI')
  FROM section
 WHERE start_date_time >= DATE '2003-05 04 00:00:00'
   AND start_date_time <  DATE '2003-05-05 00:00:00'
 WHERE start_date_time >= DATE '2003-05-04 00:00:00'
                               *
ERROR at line 4:
ORA-01861: literal does not match format string
```

b) Show the student records that were modified on or before January 22, 2003. Display the date the record was modified and each student's first and last name concatenated in one column.

Answer: The query compares the MODIFIED_DATE column to the text literal. The text literal may be in either the Oracle default format or, better yet, formatted with the TO_DATE function and the appropriate four-digit year format model.

```
SELECT first_name||' '||last_name fullname,
       TO_CHAR(modified_date, 'DD-MON-YYYY HH:MI P.M.')
       "Modified Date and Time"
  FROM student
 WHERE modified_date < TO_DATE('01/23/2003','MM/DD/YYYY')
```

FULLNAME	Modified Date and Time
Fred Crocitto	22-JAN-2003 12:00 A.M.

```
J. Landry                     22-JAN-2003 12:00 A.M.
...
Judy Sethi                    22-JAN-2003 12:00 A.M.
Larry Walter                  22-JAN-2003 12:00 A.M.

8 rows selected.
```

As previously mentioned, it is best practice to explicitly use the TO_DATE function to convert the text literal into a DATE datatype. It does not really matter which format mask you use (in this case MM/DD/YYYY was used in the WHERE clause) as long as the date literal agrees with the format mask. This allows Oracle to interpret the passed date correctly. Be sure to include the century to avoid ambiguities.

Another possible solution is the following WHERE clause utilizing the TRUNC function:

```
WHERE TRUNC(modified_date) <= TO_DATE('01/22/2003','MM/DD/YYYY')
```

4.1.2 Answers

a) Display the course number, section ID, and starting date and time for sections that start on Tuesdays.

Answer: The SQL statement shows all the sections that start on Tuesday by using the DY format mask, which displays the abbreviated day of the week in capitalized letters.

```
SELECT course_no, section_id,
       TO_CHAR(start_date_time, 'DY DD-MON-YYYY')
  FROM section
 WHERE TO_CHAR(start_date_time, 'DY') = 'TUE'
COURSE_NO SECTION_ID TO_CHAR(START_DATE_TIME,'DYDD-MON
---------- ---------- -------------------------------
        25         86 TUE 10-JUN-2003
       220         98 TUE 15-APR-2003
...
       100        143 TUE 03-JUN-2003
       122        152 TUE 29-APR-2003

12 rows selected.
```

THE FILL MODE

Some of the format masks are tricky. For example, if you choose the 'Day' format mask, you must specify the correct case and add the extra blanks to fill it up to a total length of nine characters. The following query does not return any rows.

```
SELECT course_no, section_id,
       TO_CHAR(start_date_time, 'Day DD-Mon-YYYY')
  FROM section
 WHERE TO_CHAR(start_date_time, 'Day') = 'Tuesday'
```

no rows selected

Use the *fill mode (fm)* with the format mask to suppress the extra blanks:

```
SELECT course_no, section_id,
       TO_CHAR(start_date_time, 'Day DD-Mon-YYYY')
  FROM section
 WHERE TO_CHAR(start_date_time, 'fmDay') = 'Tuesday'
COURSE_NO SECTION_ID TO_CHAR(START_DATE_TIME,'DAYDD-MON-YYYY')
--------- ---------- -----------------------------------------
       25         86 Tuesday   10-Jun-2003
      220         98 Tuesday   15-Apr-2003
...
      100        143 Tuesday   03-Jun-2003
      122        152 Tuesday   29-Apr-2003
```

12 rows selected.

b) List the section ID and starting date and time for all sections that begin and end in July 2003.

Answer: In the SQL language there are often several different solutions that deliver the same result set. Examine the various correct solutions and avoid the pitfalls.

SOLUTION ONE:

```
SELECT section_id,
       TO_CHAR(start_date_time, 'DD-MON-YYYY HH24:MI:SS')
  FROM section
 WHERE start_date_time >= TO_DATE('07/01/2003', 'MM/DD/YYYY')
   AND start_date_time <  TO_DATE('08/01/2003', 'MM/DD/YYYY')
SECTION_ID TO_CHAR(START_DATE_T
---------- --------------------
        81 24-JUL-2003 09:30:00
        85 14-JUL-2003 10:30:00
...
       147 24-JUL-2003 09:30:00
       153 24-JUL-2003 09:30:00
```

14 rows selected.

You see that this first solution takes the time into consideration. It retrieves those rows that start on July 1, 2003 at midnight or thereafter ("≥="); the AND condition identifies the rows that have a START_DATE_TIME prior to August 1, 2003.

The following query will *not* yield the correct result if you have a section that starts on July 31, 2003 any time after midnight. The TO_DATE function converts the string to a DATE datatype and sets the time stamp to 12:00:00 A.M. Therefore, a section starting on July 31, 2003 at 18:00 is not considered part of the range.

```
SELECT section_id,
       TO_CHAR(start_date_time, 'DD-MON-YYYY HH24:MI:SS')
  FROM section
 WHERE start_date_time BETWEEN
       TO_DATE('07/01/2003', 'MM/DD/YYYY')
   AND TO_DATE('07/31/2003', 'MM/DD/YYYY')
```

SOLUTION TWO:

This solution includes the 24-hour time format mask.

```
SELECT section_id,
       TO_CHAR(start_date_time, 'DD-MON-YYYY HH24:MI:SS')
  FROM section
 WHERE start_date_time BETWEEN
       TO_DATE('07/01/2003', 'MM/DD/YYYY')
   AND TO_DATE('07/31/2003 23:59:59', 'MM/DD/YYYY HH24:MI:SS')
```

This WHERE clause can also be used to obtain the desired output: The query ignores the time on the column START_DATE_TIME completely.

```
 WHERE TRUNC(start_date_time) BETWEEN
       TO_DATE('07/01/2003', 'MM/DD/YYYY')
   AND TO_DATE('07/31/2003', 'MM/DD/YYYY')
```

The following WHERE clause also returns the correct result because the literals are in the correct Oracle default format mask. However, it is best not to rely on Oracle's implicit conversion and to specify the conversion function together with the four-digit year.

```
WHERE TRUNC(start_date_time) BETWEEN '1-JUL-03' AND '31-JUL-03'
```

 Always think about the time when you compare dates.

AVOID THIS COMMON ERROR

Another common source of errors when using dates is applying the wrong datatype conversion function, as illustrated in this example:

```
SELECT section_id,
       TO_CHAR(start_date_time, 'DD-MON-YYYY HH24:MI:SS')
  FROM section
 WHERE TO_CHAR(start_date_time, 'DD-MON-YYYY HH24:MI:SS')
       >= '01-JUL-2003 00:00:00'
   AND TO_CHAR(start_date_time, 'DD-MON-YYYY HH24:MI:SS')
       <= '31-JUL-2003 23:59:59'
SECTION_ID TO_CHAR(START_DATE_T
---------- --------------------
        79 14-APR-2003 09:30:00
        80 24-APR-2003 09:30:00

...

       155 04-MAY-2003 09:30:00
       156 15-MAY-2003 09:30:00

78 rows selected.
```

The column START_DATE_TIME is converted to a character column in the WHERE clause and then compared to the text literal. The problem is that the dates are no longer compared. Instead, the character representation of the text literal and the character representation of the contents in column START_DATE_TIME in the format 'DD-MON-YYYY HH24:MI:SS' are compared.

A column value such as '14-APR-2003 09:30:00' is inclusive of the text literals '01-JUL-2003 00:00:00' and '31 JUL 2003 23:59:59' because the first digit of the column value 1 falls within the range of the characters 0 and 3. Therefore, the condition is true, but we know that April 14, 2003 is not in this date range.

This leads into a brief discussion about character comparison semantics. To illustrate the effect of character comparisons further, look at the next hypothetical examples. The query checks whether the text literal 9 is between the text literals 01 and 31, evaluated by the first digit, 0 and 3, and it returns no row, which indicates that it does not fall in this range.

```
SELECT *
  FROM dual
 WHERE '9' BETWEEN '01' AND '31'

no rows selected
```

With this knowledge, you can try the text literals. As you can see the comparison of text literals used in the query with the wrong datatype makes this condition true; however, not if you compared the DATE datatype values, because we know that April 14, 2003 does not fall in the month of July 2003. In conclusion, remember to make sure your datatype conversion does not cause incorrect results!

```
SELECT *
  FROM dual
 WHERE '14-APR-2003 09:30:00' BETWEEN '01-JUL-2003 00:00:00'
                                  AND '31-JUL-2003 23:59:59'
D
-
X

1 row selected.
```

 Be sure to choose the correct datatype conversion function in your WHERE clause.

TO_CHAR FUNCTION VERSUS TO_DATE FUNCTION

The TO_DATE function converts text to the DATE datatype, typically used in the WHERE clause of a SELECT statement. The TO_CHAR function converts a DATE datatype to text, typically used in the SELECT clause to format the result. You can also use TO_CHAR to query for specifics in a format mask. For example, to find which sections meet on Tuesday, you use the TO_CHAR function in the WHERE clause as seen in the answer to exercise 4.1.2 (a) and listed here once again:

```
SELECT course_no, section_id,
       TO_CHAR(start_date_time, 'Day DD-Mon-YYYY')
  FROM section
 WHERE TO_CHAR(start_date_time, 'fmDay') = 'Tuesday'
```

c) Determine the day of the week for December 31, 1899.

Answer: The day of the week is Sunday.

You need to nest conversion functions by using the TO_DATE function to convert the text literal to a DATE datatype, then the TO_CHAR function to display the day of the week.

First, you translate the text literal '31-DEC-1899' using the format mask 'DD-MON-YYYY' into the Oracle DATE datatype. Then apply the TO_CHAR formatting function to convert the date into any format you wish, in this case to show the day of the week.

```
SELECT TO_CHAR(TO_DATE('31-DEC-1899', 'DD-MON-YYYY'),'Dy')
  FROM dual
TO_
--
Sun

1 row selected.
```

d) Execute the following statement. Write the question to obtain the desired result. Pay particular attention to the ORDER BY clause.

```
SELECT 'Section '||section_id||' begins on '|| TO_CHAR(start_date_time,
       'fmDay')||'.' AS "Start"
  FROM section
 WHERE section_id IN (146, 127, 121, 155, 110, 85, 148)
 ORDER BY TO_CHAR(start_date_time, 'D')
```

Answer: Your answer may be phrased similar to the following:"Display the day of the week when the sections 146, 127, 121, 155, 110, 85, and 148 start. Order the result by the day of the week starting with Sunday."

The result of the query will look similar to this result. Notice the statement uses the D format mask to order by the day of the week. This format assigns the number 1 for Sunday, 2 for Monday, and so on.

```
Start
-------------------------------
Section 155 begins on Sunday.
Section 85 begins on Monday.
Section 110 begins on Tuesday.
Section 121 begins on Wednesday.
Section 127 begins on Thursday.
Section 146 begins on Friday.
Section 148 begins on Saturday.

7 rows selected.
```

LAB 4.1 SELF-REVIEW QUESTIONS

In order to test your progress, you should be able to answer the following questions.

1) The TRUNC function on a date without a format model truncates the time stamp to 12:00:00 A.M.

    a) _____ True
    b) _____ False

2) Converting a text literal to a DATE format requires using the TO_CHAR function.

    a) _____ True
    b) _____ False

3) The format mask 'Dy' displays Monday as follows:

    a) _____ MON
    b) _____ Monday
    c) _____ MONDAY
    d) _____ Mon

4) Choose the format mask that displays "December 31st, 1999".

    a) _____ DD-MON-YYYY
    b) _____ MONTH DDth, YYYY
    c) _____ fmMONTH DD, YYYY
    d) _____ Month fmDD, YYYY
    e) _____ fmMonth ddth, yyyy

5) The SQL query displays the distinct hours and minutes from the SECTION table's START_DATE_TIME column.

```
SELECT DISTINCT TO_CHAR(start_date_time, 'HH24:MM')
  FROM section
```

    a) _____ True
    b) _____ False

Answers appear in Appendix A, Section 4.1.

LAB 4.2

PERFORMING DATE AND TIME MATH

LAB OBJECTIVES

After this lab, you will be able to:
✔ Understand the SYSDATE Function and Perform Date Arithmetic

THE SYSDATE FUNCTION

The SYSDATE function returns the computer operating system's current date and time and does not take any parameters. If you connect to the database server via a client machine, it returns the date and time of the machine hosting the database, not the date and time of your client machine. For example, if your client workstation is located in New York, your local time zone is *Eastern Standard Time* (EST); if you connect to a server in California, you will receive the server's *Pacific Standard Time* (PST) date and time. To include the time in the result, you use the TO_CHAR function together with the appropriate format mask.

```
SELECT SYSDATE, TO_CHAR(SYSDATE, 'DD-MON-YYYY HH24:MI')
  FROM dual
SYSDATE    TO_CHAR(SYSDATE,'
---------  ------------------
26-AUG-02 26-AUG-2002 10:38

1 row selected.
```

Using the SYSDATE function, you can determine the number of days until the year 2005. The following query subtracts today's date from January 1, 2005.

```
SELECT TO_DATE('01-JAN-2005','DD-MON-YYYY')-TRUNC(SYSDATE) int,
       TO_DATE('01-JAN-2005','DD-MON-YYYY')-SYSDATE dec
  FROM dual
       INT        DEC
---------- ----------
       859 858.560243
```

**LAB
4.2**

1 row selected.

To perform any date calculation, the column or text literal must be converted into the Oracle DATE datatype. For the first column, the text literal '01-JAN-2005' is converted into a DATE datatype using the TO_DATE function and the corresponding format mask. Because a time is not specified, the text literal '01-JAN-2005' is set to 00:00:00 military time (the equivalent of 12:00:00 AM). From this date, the operating system's date (result of the SYSDATE function) is subtracted. SYSDATE is nested inside the TRUNC function, which truncates the timestamp to 00:00:00. As a result, the column shows 859 days.

The second column of the returned result performs the identical operation; however, this expression does not use the TRUNC function on the SYSDATE function and therefore the time is factored into the calculation. The difference is now expressed in days with the time in decimal format. To display the decimal in hours or minutes, you can use the NUMTODSINTERVAL function discussed in the Lab 4.4.

THE ROUND FUNCTION

The ROUND function allows you to round days, months, or years. The following SQL statement lists the current date and time in the first column using the TO_CHAR function and a format mask. The next column shows the current date and time rounded to the next day. If the time stamp is at or past 12:00 noon and no format mask is supplied, the ROUND function rounds to the next day. The last column displays the date rounded to the nearest month using the MM format mask.

```
SELECT TO_CHAR(SYSDATE,'DD-MON-YYYY HH24:MI') now,
       TO_CHAR(ROUND(SYSDATE),'DD-MON-YYYY HH24:MI') day,
       TO_CHAR(ROUND(SYSDATE,'MM'),'DD-MON-YYYY HH24:MI')
       mon
  FROM dual
NOW                  DAY                  MON
-----------------    -----------------    -----------------
26-AUG-2002 10:33    26-AUG-2002 00:00    01-SEP-2002 00:00
```

1 row selected.

PERFORMING ARITHMETIC ON DATES

From the previous example on calculating the number of days until the year 2005, you know that you can perform arithmetic on a DATE datatype. In the following example, three hours are added to the current date and time. To determine tomorrow's date and time, simply add the number 1 to the SYSDATE function.

```
SELECT TO_CHAR(SYSDATE, 'MM/DD HH24:MI:SS') now,
       TO_CHAR(SYSDATE+3/24, 'MM/DD HH24:MI:SS')
       AS now_plus_3hrs,
       TO_CHAR(SYSDATE+1, 'MM/DD HH24:MI:SS') tomorrow,
       TO_CHAR(SYSDATE+1.5, 'MM/DD HH24:MI:SS') AS
       "36Hrs from now"
  FROM dual
NOW               NOW_PLUS_3HRS   TOMORROW        36Hrs from now
--------------    --------------  --------------  --------------
08/26 10:34:17    08/26 13:34:17  08/27 10:34:17  08/27 22:34:17

1 row selected.
```

The fraction 3/24 represents three hours; you can also express minutes as a fraction of 1440 (60 minutes × 24 hours = 1440, which is the total number of minutes in a day). For example, 15 minutes is 15/1440 or 1/96 or any equivalent fraction or decimal number.

Oracle has a number of functions to perform specific date calculations. To determine the date of the first Sunday of the year 2000, use the NEXT_DAY function as in the following SELECT statement.

```
SELECT TO_CHAR(TO_DATE('12/31/1999','MM/DD/YYYY'),
               'MM/DD/YYYY DY') "New Year's Eve",
       TO_CHAR(NEXT_DAY(TO_DATE('12/31/1999',
                                'MM/DD/YYYY'),
               'SUNDAY'),'MM/DD/YYYY DY')
       "First Sunday"
  FROM dual
New Year's Eve First Sunday
--------------  --------------
12/31/1999 FRI 01/02/2000 SUN

1 row selected.
```

The text string '12/31/1999' is first converted to a date. To determine the date of the next Sunday, the NEXT_DAY function is applied. Last, format the output with a TO_CHAR format mask to display the result in the 'MM/DD/YYYY DY' format.

THE EXTRACT FUNCTION

The EXTRACT function extracts the year, month, or day from a column of the DATE datatype column. The next example shows rows with April values in the START_DATE_TIME column and how the various elements of the DATE datatype can be extracted. Valid keyword choices are YEAR, MONTH, and DAY. You cannot extract hours, minutes, or seconds from the DATE datatype. These options are only available on the other datetime-related datatypes you will learn about in Lab 4.3.

```
SELECT TO_CHAR(start_date_time, 'DD-MON-YYYY') "Start Date",
       EXTRACT(MONTH FROM start_date_time) "Month",
       EXTRACT(YEAR FROM start_date_time) "Year",
       EXTRACT(DAY FROM start_date_time) "Day"
  FROM section
 WHERE EXTRACT(MONTH FROM start_date_time) = 4
 ORDER BY start_date_time
Start Date         Month        Year        Day
---------------  ----------  ----------  ---
09-APR-2003             4        2003     9
09-APR-2003             4        2003     9
...
29-APR-2003             4        2003    29
08-APR-2004             4        2004     8

21 rows selected.
```

Here you see another example of the EXTRACT function. It passes a text literal as the parameter, which is in ANSI DATE format.

```
SELECT EXTRACT(YEAR FROM DATE '2002-03-11') year,
       EXTRACT(MONTH FROM DATE '2002-03-11') month,
       EXTRACT(DAY FROM DATE '2002-03-11') day
  FROM dual
     YEAR      MONTH        DAY
  ---------  ---------  ---------
     2002         3         11

1 row selected.
```

Table 4.6 summarizes some of the most frequently used DATE calculation functions with their purposes and respective syntax.

Table 4.6 ■ Commonly Used Oracle Datetime-Related Calculation Functions

Function	Purpose	Return Datatype
ADD_MONTHS(date, integer)	Adds or subtracts number of months from a certain date.	DATE
MONTHS_BETWEEN (date2, date1)	Determines the number of months between two dates.	NUMBER
LAST_DAY(date)	Returns the last date of the month.	DATE
NEXT_DAY(date, day_of_the_week)	Returns the first day of the week that is later than the date parameter passed.	DATE
TRUNC(date)	Ignores the hours, minutes, and seconds on DATE datatype.	DATE
ROUND(date [,format_mask])	Rounds to various DATE components depending on the optional supplied format mask.	DATE
NEW_TIME(date, current_time_zone, new_time_zone)	Returns the date and time in another time zone; for example, EST (Eastern Standard Time), PST (Pacific Standard Time), PDT (Pacific Daylight Time).	DATE

Note that Oracle's time zone datatypes, discussed in Lab 4.3, handle conversions and computations related to various time zones with much more ease.

LAB 4.2 EXERCISES

4.2.1 UNDERSTAND THE *SYSDATE* FUNCTION AND PERFORM DATE ARITHMETIC

a) Determine the number of days between February 13, 1964 and the last day of the same month and year.

b) Compute the number of months between September 29, 1999 and August 17, 2003.

c) Add three days to your current date and time.

LAB 4.2 EXERCISE ANSWERS

4.2.1 ANSWERS

a) Determine the number of days between February 13, 1964 and the last day of the same month and year.

Answer: First convert the text literal 13-FEB-1964 to a DATE datatype, then use the LAST_DAY function. The date returned is February 29, 1964, which was a leap year. The difference between the two dates is 16 days.

```
SELECT LAST_DAY(TO_DATE('13-FEB-1964','DD-MON-YYYY')) lastday,
       LAST_DAY(TO_DATE('13-FEB-1964','DD-MON-YYYY'))
       - TO_DATE('13-FEB-1964','DD-MON-YYYY') days
  FROM dual
LASTDAY          DAYS
---------    ---------
29-FEB-64          16

1 row selected.
```

The LAST_DAY function takes a single parameter and accepts only parameters of the DATE datatype, either your column must be a DATE datatype column or you must convert it with the TO_DATE function.

b) Compute the number of months between September 29, 1999 and August 17, 2003.

Answer: The simplest solution is to use the MONTHS_BETWEEN function to determine the result.

```
SELECT MONTHS_BETWEEN(TO_DATE('17-AUG-2003','DD-MON-YYYY'),
       TO_DATE('29-SEP-1999','DD-MON-YYYY')) months
  FROM dual
        MONTHS
--------------
    46.6129032

1 row selected.
```

The MONTHS_BETWEEN function takes two dates as its parameters and returns a numeric value.

c) Add three days to your current date and time.

Answer: The answer will vary depending on when you execute this query. To add days to the current date and time, just add the number of days to the SYSDATE function.

```
SELECT TO_CHAR(SYSDATE, 'DD-MON-YYYY HH24:MI:SS') "Current",
       TO_CHAR(SYSDATE+3, 'DD-MON-YYYY HH24:MI:SS') "Answer"
  FROM dual
Current                 Answer
-------------------     -------------------
06-MAR-2002 23:12:02    09-MAR-2002 23:12:02

1 row selected.
```

If you have to add hours, you can express the hour as a fraction of the day. For example, five hours are SYSDATE+5/24. To find out yesterday's date, you can subtract days, thus the SELECT clause will read SYSDATE-1. You will see additional examples of computing differences between dates in Lab 4.4, which discusses the interval datatypes.

LAB 4.2 SELF-REVIEW QUESTIONS

In order to test your progress, you should be able to answer the following questions.

1) Using the ADD_MONTHS function, you can subtract months from a given date.

    a) _____ True
    b) _____ False

2) Which one of the following solutions adds 15 minutes to a given date?

    a) _____ SELECT SYSDATE+1/96 FROM dual
    b) _____ SELECT SYSDATE+1/128 FROM dual
    c) _____ SELECT TO_DATE(SYSDATE+1/128) FROM dual
    d) _____ SELECT TO_CHAR(SYSDATE+1/128, 'DD-MON-YYYY 24HH:MI')
             FROM dual

3) Choose the date that is calculated by the following query:

```
SELECT TO_CHAR(NEXT_DAY(TO_DATE('02-JAN-2000 SUN',
               'DD-MON-YYYY DY'), 'SUN'),
               'fmDay Month DD, YYYY')
   FROM dual
```

    a) _____ Sunday January 2, 2000
    b) _____ Monday January 3, 2000
    c) _____ Sunday January 9, 2000
    d) _____ None of the above dates
    e) _____ Invalid query

4) The next query gives you which of the following results?

```
SELECT ROUND(TO_DATE('2000/1/31 11:59', 'YYYY/MM/DD HH24:MI'))
   FROM dual
```

    a) _____ Returns an Oracle error message
    b) _____ 30-JAN-00
    c) _____ 31-JAN-00
    d) _____ 01-FEB-00

Answers appear in Appendix A, Section 4.2.

LAB 4.3

UNDERSTANDING TIMESTAMP AND TIME ZONE DATATYPES

LAB OBJECTIVES

After this lab, you will be able to:

✔ Use Oracle's Timestamp and Time Zone Datatypes

Starting with Oracle 9*i*, Oracle added additional datetime-related datatypes, which include fractional seconds and time zones. These datatypes are TIMESTAMP, TIMESTAMP WITH TIME ZONE, and TIMESTAMP WITH LOCAL TIME ZONE.

THE TIMESTAMP DATATYPE

The TIMESTAMP datatype allows you to store optional fractional seconds with a precision of up to 9; the default precision is 6. An example of a text literal in the default format looks like this: `'14-MAR-02 08.29.01.000123 AM'`. This represents the default format mask of 'DD-MON-RR HH.MI.SS.FF AM'. The fractional seconds are expressed with the FF format mask. To change the default precision of the fractional seconds, you add a number from 1 to 9 after the FF mask. For example, FF4 displays the fractional seconds with a four-digit precision.

Instead of using the Oracle default format model, you can represent the format mask of a literal with the ANSI TIMESTAMP format as follows: `TIMESTAMP '2002-03-14 08:29:01.000123'`. Again, 000123 are the fractional seconds showing a six-digit precision.

THE TIMESTAMP WITH TIME ZONE DATATYPE

Besides the date, time, and fractional seconds, the TIMESTAMP WITH TIME ZONE datatype includes the *time zone displacement value*. The time zone displacement, also called *time zone offset value,* is expressed as the difference (in hours and minutes) between your local time and the *Greenwich Mean Time* (GMT) now called *Coordinated Universal Time* (UTC). The earth divides into 24 times zones. The time zone along the prime meridian in Greenwich, England is commonly known as GMT, against which all other time zones are compared. At noon Greenwich time, it is midnight at the International Date Line in the Pacific.

The time zone displacement value is shown as a positive or negative number (i.e., –5:00), indicating the hours and minutes before or after UTC. Alternatively, the time zone can be expressed as a time zone region name such as America/New_York instead of –5:00. The TIMESTAMP WITH TIME ZONE datatype is useful when storing date and time information across geographic regions. Oracle stores all values of this datatype in UTC.

The time zone region of the database is determined at the time of the database creation. If you don't specify any, the time zone defaults to your operating system's time zone. If all of these choices are invalid, the default becomes UTC. To find out the time zone value of your database, use the DBTIMEZONE function. The query returns the time zone displacement value indicating that the time zone is 5 hours before UTC.

```
SELECT DBTIMEZONE
  FROM dual
DBTIME
------
-05:00

1 row selected.
```

The Whole Truth

Instead of returning the offset number for the time zone displacement as you see indicated by the –05:00, the default can be changed for all displacement offsets to a region name instead. The time zone region equivalent for EST (Eastern Standard Time) and EDT (Eastern Daylight Time) is 'America/New_York' and is listed in the V$TIMEZONE_NAMES data dictionary view, where you can find the list of valid time zone regions. (The data dictionary is a set of tables that provides information about the database. Data dictionary views are discussed in Chapter 13, "The Data Dictionary and Advanced SQL*Plus Commands." The server's time zone is determined at the creation of the database. It can be modified with an ALTER DATABASE statement. For more information on the CREATE and ALTER DATABASE statements, please see the *Oracle Administrator's Guide*.)

THE TIMESTAMP WITH LOCAL TIME ZONE DATATYPE

The TIMESTAMP WITH LOCAL TIME ZONE stores the date and time values of the database's own local time zone. When the user retrieves the data, the returned values are automatically converted to represent each individual user's time zone. In addition, the database does not store the time zone displacement value as part of the datatype and there is no text literal to represent this datatype.

When performing arithmetic on this datatype, Oracle automatically converts all values to UTC before doing the calculation and then converts the value back to the local time. This is in contrast to the TIMESTAMP WITH TIME ZONE datatype, where the values are always stored in UTC and a conversion is unnecessary.

DAYLIGHT SAVINGS

Oracle provides automatic support for daylight savings time and for boundary cases when the time switches. Typically, daylight savings time starts on the first Sunday in April and runs until the last Sunday in October; in Europe it starts a week earlier and ends at the same time.

DEFAULT FORMAT MASKS

Table 4.7 shows the datetime-related datatypes and their individual components together with default formats and example literals. Throughout this lab you will get to use these datatypes in different exercises.

Table 4.8 lists the valid range of values for the individual components of the datetime-related datatypes.

DATETIME FUNCTIONS

A listing of the datetime functions to determine the current date and time is shown in Table 4.9.

THE LOCALTIMESTAMP FUNCTION

The next SQL statement shows the use of the LOCALTIMESTAMP function, which returns the current date and time including the fractional sections in Oracle's TIMESTAMP format. This function considers the local user's *session* time; that is, if the database server is in San Francisco and the user is in New York, the time displayed is the user's local New York time.

Table 4.7 ■ Overview of Oracle Datetime-Related Datatypes

Datatype	Components	Default Formats

DATE	Century, Year, Month, Day, Hour, Minute, Second	Oracle Default Formats:
		`'DD-MON-RR'` and `'DD-MON-YYYY'`
		`'14-MAR-02'` and `'14-MAR-2002'`
		
		ANSI Formats:
		`DATE 'YYYY-MM-DD'`
		`DATE '2002-03-14'`
		`TIMESTAMP 'YYYY-MM-DD HH24:MI:SS'`
		`TIMESTAMP '2002-03-14 16:21:04'`

TIMESTAMP	Same as DATE with additional fractional seconds	Oracle Default Formats:
		`'DD-MON-RR HH.MI.SS.FF AM'`
		`'14-MAR-02 04.21.04.000001 PM'`
		`'DD-MON-YYYY HH.MI.SS.FF AM'`
		`'14-MAR-2002 04.21.04.000001 PM'`
		
		ANSI Format:
		`TIMESTAMP 'YYYY-MM-DD HH24:MI:SS.FF'`
		`TIMESTAMP '2003-03-14 16:31:04.000001'`

TIMESTAMP WITH TIME ZONE	Same as TIMESTAMP plus Time Zone Hour and Time Zone Minute (TZH:TZM) or Time Zone Region Name (TZR)	Oracle Default Formats with time offset values in hours and minutes:
		`'DD-MON-RR HH.MI.SS.FF AM TZH:TZM'`
		`'14-MAR-02 04.21.04.000001 PM -05:00'`
		`'DD-MON-YYYY HH.MI.SS.FF AM TZH:TZM'`
		`'14-MAR-2002 04.21.04.000001 PM -05:00'`
		
		Oracle Default Formats with time zone region:
		`'DD-MON-RR HH.MI.SS.FF AM TZR'`
		`'14-MAR-02 04.21.04.000001 PM America/New_York'`
		`'DD-MON-YYYY HH.MI.SS.FF AM TZR'`
		`'14-MAR-2002 04.21.04.000001 PM America/New_York'`
		
		ANSI Format with offset value:
		`TIMESTAMP 'YYYY-MM-DD HH24:MI:SS.FF TZH:TZM'`
		`TIMESTAMP '2002-03-14 16:21:04.000001 -5:00'`
		
		ANSI Format with time zone region:
		`TIMESTAMP 'YYYY-MM-DD HH:MI:SS.FF TZR'`
		`TIMESTAMP '2002-03-14 16:21:04.000001 America/New_York'`

TIMESTAMP WITH LOCAL TIME ZONE	Same components as the TIMESTAMP datatype	See TIMESTAMP.

LAB 4.3

Table 4.8 ■ Valid Value Ranges for Date and Time Components

Date Component	Valid Values
YEAR	−4712 − 9999 (excluding year 0)
MONTH	01 − 12
DAY	01 − 31
HOUR	00 − 23
MINUTE	00 − 59
SECOND	00 − 59 (optional precision up to 9 digits for TIMESTAMP, TIMESTAMP WITH TIME ZONE, and TIMESTAMP WITH LOCAL TIME ZONE)
TIMEZONE_HOUR	−12 − +13
TIMEZONE_MINUTE	00 − 59

```
SELECT LOCALTIMESTAMP
  FROM dual
LOCALTIMESTAMP
----------------------------
14-MAR-02 04.21.04.000001 PM

1 row selected.
```

THE SYSTIMESTAMP FUNCTION

When compared to the SYSDATE function, the SYSTIMESTAMP function includes fractional seconds with a default six-digit precision. Like the SYSDATE function it shows the *database's* time zone, not that of the client machine executing the function. The time zone displacement or offset in the following SQL statement is −05.00, indicating the time is 5 hours before the UTC, which in this example represents EST. The format mask is expressed in the format mask [+|-] TZH:TZM, which means it is either a positive or negative number together with the time zone hours and time zone minutes offset numbers.

```
SELECT SYSTIMESTAMP
  FROM dual
SYSTIMESTAMP
-----------------------------------
10-MAR-02 03.23.34.000000 PM -05:00

1 row selected.
```

Table 4.9 ■ **Session and Server Datetime Functions**

Function	Purpose	Return Datatype
CURRENT_DATE	Returns the date and time of the local *session* time zone in DATE datatype. (The local session time can be different than the server's date and time, if the client session is in a different time zone.)	DATE
CURRENT_TIMESTAMP [(optional_precision)]	Returns the individual's *session* date and time in the datatype TIMESTAMP WITH TIME ZONE value.	TIMESTAMP WITH TIME ZONE
DBTIMEZONE	Returns the time zone offset value of the database *server* time zone or time zone region name, depending on the setup of the database.	VARCHAR2
LOCALTIMESTAMP [(optional_precision)]	Returns in the TIMESTAMP format the current date and time in the local *session* time.	TIMESTAMP
SESSIONTIMEZONE	Returns the time zone offset value of the *session* time zone or the time zone region name, depending on the setup of the database.	VARCHAR2
SYSDATE	Returns the database *server* operating system current date and time.	DATE
SYSTIMESTAMP	Returns date, time, and six-digit fractional seconds and time zone of the *server*. This is similar to the SYSDATE function, but includes the fractional seconds and time zone.	TIMESTAMP WITH TIME ZONE

THE CURRENT_TIMESTAMP FUNCTION

The CURRENT_TIMESTAMP function returns the current *session's* time in the datatype TIMESTAMP WITH TIME ZONE value. It differs from the LOCALTIMESTAMP function in that the datatype is not TIMESTAMP, but TIMESTAMP WITH TIME ZONE and therefore includes the time zone displacement value.

```
SELECT CURRENT_TIMESTAMP, LOCALTIMESTAMP
  FROM dual
```

CURRENT_TIMESTAMP	LOCALTIMESTAMP
31-MAR-02 07.59.49.000000 PM -05:00	31-MAR-02 07.59.49.000000 PM

```
1 row selected.
```

THE CURRENT_DATE FUNCTION

The CURRENT_DATE function returns the date and time in the *session's* time zone. The returned values can be different than the values returned by the SYSDATE function. For example, if you execute a query on your machine located on the east coast against a database server that is located on the west coast, the SYSDATE function returns the date and time of the server in PST and the CURRENT_DATE function returns your local east coast date and time. Note that the return datatype of the CURRENT_DATE function is a DATE datatype.

```
SELECT TO_CHAR(CURRENT_DATE, 'DD-MON-YYYY HH:MI:SS PM')
  FROM dual
```

TO_CHAR(CURRENT_DATE,'D
01-APR-2002 02:37:11 AM

```
1 row selected.
```

You may wonder how the CURRENT_DATE function compares to the previously mentioned LOCALTIMESTAMP function. The difference is the return datatype of the function. CURRENT_DATE returns a DATE datatype and the LOCALTIMESTAMP function returns the TIMESTAMP datatype, which also includes the fractional seconds.

THE SESSIONTIMEZONE FUNCTION

Because an individual user may be in a different time zone than the server, you can execute different functions depending on what you want to accomplish. The SESSIONTIMEZONE returns the session's time zone displacement value; the DBTIMEZONE function returns the server's time zone displacement value.

The next statement shows the execution of the SESSIONTIMEZONE function; you notice it includes the time zone displacement value indicating the difference in hours and minutes between the UTC and your local time. The user's local time zone is determined by either the most recent ALTER SESSION statement setting the local time zone or by your operating system's time zone. If none of them are valid, the default is UTC.

```
SELECT SESSIONTIMEZONE
  FROM dual
SESSIONTIMEZONE
---------------
-05:00

1 row selected.
```

THE DBTIMEZONE FUNCTION

The DBTIMEZONE function is in contrast with the SESSIONTIMEZONE function. You can verify the database's local time zone with the DBTIMEZONE function. It displays the database server's time zone displacement value; if none has been set, it displays UTC as the default value.

```
SELECT DBTIMEZONE
  FROM dual
DBTIME
------
-05:00

1 row selected.
```

CHANGING THE LOCAL TIME ZONE

You can experiment with changing the time zone of your local machine and the effect on the discussed functions. For example, on the Windows operating system, you can change the time zone in the Control Panel by choosing the Date/Time Properties (as shown in Figure 4.1). If you change your default time zone to another time zone with a different time zone displacement value, you will notice that the results of the SESSIONTIMEZONE function are different. Make sure to log out of the current SQL*Plus session first, so the effects of the time zone change are visible. If you use *i*SQL*Plus, you will not notice any difference, because your browser checks the *i*SQL*Plus HTTP server and not your local machine for the time zone.

OVERRIDING THE INDIVIDUAL SESSION TIME ZONE

You can change the time zone for an individual session with the ALTER SESSION command. The setting remains until you exit the session. The following three example statements illustrate different ways you can change the time zone offset value. The first changes the value to a time zone region name, the second makes it equivalent to the database server's time zone, and the last resets it to the session's local time zone.

```
ALTER SESSION SET TIME_ZONE = 'America/New_York'
ALTER SESSION SET TIME_ZONE = dbtimezone
ALTER SESSION SET TIME_ZONE = local
```

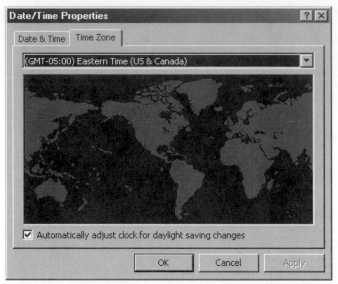

Figure 4.1 ■ Changing the time zone on the Windows operating system.

EXTRACT FUNCTIONS

Extracting functions allow you to pull out various components of the datetime datatypes, such as the YEAR, MONTH, and so on (see Table 4.10). Similar results may also be accomplished with the TO_CHAR function and the respective format mask discussed in Lab 4.2.

THE SYS_EXTRACT_UTC FUNCTION

The purpose of the SYS_EXTRACT_UTC function is to extract the UTC from a passed date and time value. The next example shows two equivalent date and time values when translated to UTC. Both are ANSI literals of the datatype TIMESTAMP WITH TIME ZONE.

```
TIMESTAMP '2002-03-11 7:00:00 -8:00'
TIMESTAMP '2002-03-11 10:00:00 -5:00'
```

The first timestamp shows March 11, 2002 at 7:00 A.M. PST, which is 8 hours before UTC. This value is identical to the next timestamp; it shows the same date with 10:00 A.M. EST local time, which is 5 hours before UTC. The 7:00 A.M. time on the west coast is identical to the 10:00 A.M. east coast as there is a three-hour time difference. When calculating the time in UTC, you will see that the two timestamps are identical in UTC. In fact, Oracle calculates the TIMESTAMP WITH TIME ZONE datatype always in UTC and then displays the local time with the time zone displacement.

Table 4.10 ■ Extracting Functions

Function	Purpose	Return Datatype
EXTRACT(YEAR FROM date)	Extracts year from a DATE datatype. Valid keyword choices are YEAR, MONTH, and DAY to extract the year, month, and day, respectively.	NUMBER
EXTRACT(YEAR FROM timestamp)	Extracts year from a TIMESTAMP datatype. Valid keyword choices are YEAR, MONTH, DAY, HOUR, MINUTE, SECOND to extract the year, month, day, hour, minute, and seconds including fractional seconds, respectively.	NUMBER
EXTRACT(YEAR FROM timestamp_with_time_zone)	Valid keywords are YEAR, MONTH, DAY, HOUR, MINUTE, SECOND, TIMEZONE_HOUR, TIMEZONE_MINUTE, TIMEZONE_REGION, TIMEZONE_ABBR. The values are returned in UTC.	NUMBER for TIMEZONE_REGION (If TIMEZONE_ABBR is passed, the EXTRACT function returns VARCHAR2)
SYS_EXTRACT_UTC (timestamp with time zone)	Returns the date and time in UTC	TIMESTAMP WITH TIME ZONE
TZ_OFFSET(time_zone)	Returns the time difference between UTC and passed time zone value	VARCHAR2

LAB
4.3

```
SELECT SYS_EXTRACT_UTC(TIMESTAMP '2002-03-11 7:00:00 -8:00')
          "West coast to UTC",
       SYS_EXTRACT_UTC(TIMESTAMP '2002-03-11 10:00:00 -5:00')
          "East coast to UTC"
  FROM dual
West coast to UTC                East coast to UTC
-------------------------------  -------------------------------
11-MAR-02 03.00.00.000000000 PM  11-MAR-02 03.00.00.000000000 PM

1 row selected.
```

THE EXTRACT FUNCTION
AND THE TIMESTAMP DATATYPE

The following SQL statement extracts the various components of this datatype including the seconds. You cannot extract the fractional seconds only, they are included as part of the SECOND keyword specification. The passed TIMESTAMP literal is in the ANSI TIMESTAMP default format.

```
SELECT EXTRACT(HOUR FROM TIMESTAMP '2002-03-11 15:48:01.123') hour,
       EXTRACT(MINUTE FROM TIMESTAMP '2002-03-11 15:48:01.123') minute,
       EXTRACT(SECOND FROM TIMESTAMP '2002-03-11 15:48:01.123') second,
       EXTRACT(YEAR FROM TIMESTAMP '2002-03-11 15:48:01.123') year,
       EXTRACT(MONTH FROM TIMESTAMP '2002-03-11 15:48:01.123') month,
       EXTRACT(DAY FROM TIMESTAMP '2002-03-11 15:48:01.123') day
  FROM dual
```

HOUR	MINUTE	SECOND	YEAR	MONTH	DAY
15	48	1.123	2002	3	11

```
1 row selected.
```

EXTRACT AND THE TIMESTAMP
WITH TIME ZONE DATATYPE

Following are examples of the EXTRACT function that illustrate how to pull out the various components of the TIMESTAMP WITH TIME ZONE datatype. Important to note here is that when using EXTRACT on this datatype, all date and time values are returned in UTC, not the time displayed by default in the column.

The next example shows just a few of the components. When examining the result you see that the column labeled HOUR displays the time as 21, which is 9 P.M., but the actual local time is stored as 4 P.M. in the column named COL_TIMESTAMP_W_TZ. This is a clear indication that the EXTRACT function uses UTC.

```
SELECT col_timestamp_w_tz,
       EXTRACT(YEAR FROM col_timestamp_w_tz) year,
       EXTRACT(MONTH FROM col_timestamp_w_tz) month,
       EXTRACT(DAY FROM col_timestamp_w_tz) day,
       EXTRACT(HOUR FROM col_timestamp_w_tz) hour,
       EXTRACT(MINUTE FROM col_timestamp_w_tz) min,
       EXTRACT(SECOND FROM col_timestamp_w_tz) sec
  FROM date_example
```

COL_TIMESTAMP_W_TZ	YEAR	MONTH	DAY	HOUR	MIN	SEC
24-MAR-02 04.25.32.000000 PM -05:00	2002	3	24	21	25	32

```
1 row selected.
```

The keywords TIMEZONE_HOUR and TIMEZONE_MINUTE allow you to display the time zone displacement value expressed in hours and minutes. The TIME-ZONE_REGION and TIMEZONE_ABBR keywords indicate the time zone region information spelled out or in abbreviated format. If a region has not been setup for your database or results in ambiguity, you will see the value UNKNOWN, as in this example.

```
SELECT col_timestamp_w_tz,
       EXTRACT(TIMEZONE_HOUR FROM col_timestamp_w_tz) tz_hour,
       EXTRACT(TIMEZONE_MINUTE FROM col_timestamp_w_tz) tz_min,
       EXTRACT(TIMEZONE_REGION FROM col_timestamp_w_tz) tz_region,
       EXTRACT(TIMEZONE_ABBR FROM col_timestamp_w_tz) tz_abbr
  FROM date_example
```

```
COL_TIMESTAMP_W_TZ                   TZ_HOUR TZ_MIN TZ_REGION TZ_ABBR
---------------------------------    ------- ------ --------- -------
24-MAR-02 04.25.32.000000 PM -05:00       -5      0 UNKNOWN   UNK
```

```
1 row selected.
```

THE DATE_EXAMPLE TABLE

In the two previous SQL statements you may have noticed the use of a table called DATE_EXAMPLE to illustrate the different date variants. This table is not part of the STUDENT schema but can be created based on the additional script, available for download from the companion Web site. Listed here are the columns of the DATE_EXAMPLE table and their respective datatypes.

```
SQL> DESCR date_example
 Name                           Null?    Type
 ------------------------       -------- ---------------------------
 COL_DATE                                DATE
 COL_TIMESTAMP                           TIMESTAMP(6)
 COL_TIMESTAMP_W_TZ                      TIMESTAMP(6) WITH TIME ZONE
 COL_TIMESTAMP_W_LOCAL_TZ                TIMESTAMP(6) WITH LOCAL TIME
```

The first column named COL_DATE is of the familiar DATE datatype. The second column, called COL_TIMESTAMP, includes fractional seconds with a six-digit precision. The third column, called COL_TIMESTAMP_W_TZ, additionally contains the time zone offset. Last, the fourth column is defined as the TIMESTAMP WITH LOCAL TIME ZONE datatype.

CONVERSION FUNCTIONS

To query against a column of the new datatype, you need to state any literal in the default format listed in Table 4.7 or use a function shown in Table 4.11 to convert the literal to the desired datatype. In the previous labs you became familiar with the TO_CHAR and the TO_DATE functions. The TO_TIMESTAMP and

TO_TIMESTAMP_TZ work in a similar way. The TO_CHAR and TO_DATE functions are listed for completeness.

The next statement queries the DATE_EXAMPLE table and converts the text literal into a TIMESTAMP WITH TIME ZONE datatype to be able to compare the value against the column COL_TIMESTAMP_W_TZ of the same datatype.

**LAB
4.3**

```
SELECT col_timestamp_w_tz
  FROM date_example
 WHERE col_timestamp_w_tz = TO_TIMESTAMP_TZ
               ('24-MAR-02 04.25.32.000000 PM -05:00',
                'DD-MON-RR HH.MI.SS.FF AM TZH:TZM')
```

Table 4.11 ■ Datetime-Related Conversion Functions

Function	Purpose	Return Datatype
TO_TIMESTAMP(char [,format_mask])	Converts text to the TIMESTAMP datatype based on format mask (this works similar to the TO_DATE function).	TIMESTAMP
TO_TIMESTAMP_TZ(char [,format_mask])	Converts text or a database column of VARCHAR2 or CHAR datatype to TIMESTAMP WITH TIME ZONE datatype based on format mask.	TIMESTAMP WITH TIME ZONE
TO_DATE(char [,format_mask])	Converts text to a DATE datatype. As with all other datetime-related conversion functions, the format_mask is optional if the value is in the default format; otherwise, a format mask must be specified.	DATE
TO_CHAR(date [,format_mask])	Converts all datetime-related datatypes into VARCHAR2 to display it in a different format than the default date format. (The TO_CHAR function can be used with other datatypes; see Lab 4.5).	VARCHAR2
FROM_TZ(timestamp, hour_min_offset)	Converts a TIMESTAMP value into a TIMESTAMP WITH TIME ZONE datatype. An example of the hour_min_offset value (time zone displacement value) is '+5:00' or it can be a time zone region name such as 'America/New_York'.	TIMESTAMP WITH TIME ZONE

Note that Oracle does not provide a conversion function to convert to a TIMESTAMP WITH LOCAL TIME ZONE datatype. Use the CAST function discussed in Lab 4.5 instead.

```
COL_TIMESTAMP_W_TZ
-------------------------------------
24-MAR-02 04.25.32.000000 PM -05:00

1 row selected.
```

DATETIME EXPRESSION

A datetime expression can be a column of datatype TIMESTAMP WITH TIME ZONE, TIMESTAMP WITH LOCAL TIME ZONE, TIMESTAMP, or an expression that results in any of the three datatypes.

LAB 4.3

The expression can be shown in various time zones with the keywords AT TIME ZONE. The next example illustrates the value of 24-MAR-02 04.25.32.000000 P.M. -05:00 in the COL_TIMESTAMP_W_TZ column displayed in the Los Angeles local time instead. The expression uses the time zone region name 'America/Los_Angeles' after the keywords AT TIME ZONE.

```
SELECT col_timestamp_w_tz AT TIME ZONE 'America/Los_Angeles'
  FROM date_example
COL_TIMESTAMP_W_TZATTIMEZONE'AMERICA/LOS_ANGELES
-------------------------------------------------
24-MAR-02 01.25.32.000000 PM AMERICA/LOS_ANGELES

1 row selected.
```

The syntax of the datetime expression is as follows:

```
datetime_value_expr AT {
  LOCAL |
  TIME ZONE{'[+|-]hh:mm' |
            DBTIMEZONE |
            SESSIONTIMEZONE |
            'time_zone_name'}}
```

Besides showing the time in the local time zone, you can also choose a specific time zone displacement in the TZH:TZM format. Other syntax alternatives are DBTIMEZONE, which returns the value in the database server's time zone. The SESSIONTIMEZONE shows the session's time zone and the time zone name for a time zone region name.

The next example displays the same column expressed in the database server's time zone with the DBTIMEZONE keyword.

```
SELECT col_timestamp_w_tz AT TIME ZONE DBTIMEZONE
  FROM date_example
```

```
COL_TIMESTAMP_W_TZATTIMEZONEDBTIMEZONE
---------------------------------------
24-MAR-02 04.25.32.000000 PM -05:00
```

```
1 row selected.
```

Compared to the NEW_TIME function mentioned in Lab 4.2, the datetime expression is more versatile because it allows a greater number of time zone values.

LAB 4.3 EXERCISES

4.3.1 USE ORACLE'S TIMESTAMP AND TIME ZONE DATATYPES

a) Describe the default display formats of the result returned by the following SQL query.

```
SELECT col_date, col_timestamp, col_timestamp_w_tz
  FROM date_example
```

```
COL_DATE   COL_TIMESTAMP                 COL_TIMESTAMP_W_TZ
---------  ----------------------------  -----------------------------------
24-MAR-02  24-MAR-02 04.25.32.000000 PM  24-MAR-02 04.25.32.000000 PM -05:00
```

```
1 row selected.
```

b) Explain the result of the following SELECT statement. Are there alternate ways to rewrite the query's WHERE clause?

```
SELECT col_timestamp
  FROM date_example
 WHERE col_timestamp = '24-MAR-02 04.25.32.000000 PM'
```
```
COL_TIMESTAMP
----------------------------
24-MAR-02 04.25.32.000000 PM
```

```
1 row selected.
```

c) What function can you utilize to display the seconds component of a TIMESTAMP datatype column?

d) What do you observe about the text literal of the following query's WHERE clause?

```
SELECT col_timestamp_w_tz
  FROM date_example
 WHERE col_timestamp_w_tz = '24-MAR-02 04.25.32.000000 PM -05:00'
```

COL_TIMESTAMP_W_TZ

24-MAR-02 04.25.32.000000 PM -05:00

1 row selected.

> **e)** The following sets of SQL statements are issued against the
> database server. Explain the results.

```
SELECT SESSIONTIMEZONE
  FROM dual
```
SESSIONTIMEZONE

-05:00

1 row selected.

```
SELECT col_timestamp_w_tz, col_timestamp_w_local_tz
  FROM date_example
```
COL_TIMESTAMP_W_TZ	**COL_TIMESTAMP_W_LOCAL_TZ**
24-MAR-02 04.25.32.000000 PM -05:00	**24-MAR-02 04.25.32.000000 PM**

1 row selected.

```
ALTER SESSION SET TIME_ZONE = '-8:00'
```
Session altered.

```
SELECT col_timestamp_w_tz, col_timestamp_w_local_tz
  FROM date_example
```
COL_TIMESTAMP_W_TZ	**COL_TIMESTAMP_W_LOCAL_TZ**
24-MAR-02 04.25.32.000000 PM -05:00	**24-MAR-02 01.25.32.000000 PM**

1 row selected.

```
ALTER SESSION SET TIME_ZONE = '-5:00'
```
Session altered.

Lab 4.3 Exercise Answers

4.3.1 Answers

a) Describe the default display formats of the result returned by the following SQL query.

```
SELECT col_date, col_timestamp, col_timestamp_w_tz
  FROM date_example
COL_DATE  COL_TIMESTAMP                   COL_TIMESTAMP_W_TZ
--------- ----------------------------    -----------------------------------
24-MAR-02 24-MAR-02 04.25.32.000000 PM 24-MAR-02 04.25.32.000000 PM -05:00

1 row selected.
```

Answer: This query returns the default display format values of three columns: COL_DATE, COL_TIMESTAMP, and COL_TIMESTAMP_W_TZ.

You are already familiar with the DD-MON-RR DATE default format listed in the right column. The default display format for the Oracle TIMESTAMP datatype is DD-MON-RR HH.MI.SS.FF AM as shown in the second column. The third column, named COL_TIMESTAMP_W_TZ, also shows the time zone displacement value in the default format +/- TZH:TZM. (All the default display formats can be changed with the NLS_TIMESTAMP_FORMAT and NLS_TIMESTAMP_TZ_FORMAT parameters in the Oracle database initialization file or with an ALTER SESSION statement. An ALTER SESSION statement changes certain values for the user's current session. These temporary settings remain until the user disconnects his session; i.e., exits from SQL*Plus or from any other program that created the session.)

b) Explain the result of the following SELECT statement. Are there alternate ways to rewrite the query's WHERE clause?

```
SELECT col_timestamp
  FROM date_example
 WHERE col_timestamp = '24-MAR-02 04.25.32.000000 PM'
COL_TIMESTAMP
----------------------------
24-MAR-02 04.25.32.000000 PM

1 row selected.
```

Answer: The query shows the use of the TIMESTAMP datatype. There are alternative ways available to achieve the same result. As you learned previously in context with the DATE datatype, it is always preferable to explicitly perform the datatype conversion instead of using the default text literal. The following query uses the TO_TIMESTAMP function to convert the text literal into an Oracle TIMESTAMP datatype and it uses the matching format masks. The FF format mask represents the fractional seconds; the AM format mask indicates the time listed in the AM/PM format, not the 24-hour military time format.

```
SELECT col_timestamp
  FROM date_example
 WHERE col_timestamp =
       TO_TIMESTAMP('24-MAR-2002 04:25:32.000000 PM',
                    'DD-MON-YYYY HH:MI:SS.FF AM')
```

If you exclude the fractional seconds together with the FF format mask, the fractional seconds are implied to be zero, as you can see in the next example.

```
SELECT col_timestamp
  FROM date_example
 WHERE col_timestamp =
       TO_TIMESTAMP('24-MAR-2002 04:25:32 PM',
                    'DD-MON-YYYY HH:MI:SS AM')
```

The following query using the ANSI TIMESTAMP format also returns the correct result.

```
SELECT col_timestamp
  FROM date_example
 WHERE col_timestamp = TIMESTAMP '2002-03-24 16:25:32.000000'
```

CONVERSION BETWEEN ORACLE DATE DATATYPES

You may wonder if you can apply any of the previously used TO_DATE format models to query the COL_TIMESTAMP column. The next SQL statement converts the text literal to a DATE datatype with the TO_DATE function. The DATE datatype is implicitly converted to the TIMESTAMP datatype. Because the fractional seconds in this example are equal to 000000, the result is considered equivalent and the row returned.

```
SELECT col_timestamp
  FROM date_example
 WHERE col_timestamp = TO_DATE('24-MAR-2002 04:25:32 PM',
                               'DD-MON-YYYY HH:MI:SS AM')
```

The following SQL statement shows what happens when you apply a TO_TIMESTAMP function to a DATE datatype column. Notice that the TO_TIMESTAMP function sets the time portion of the DATE column to midnight.

```
SELECT TO_TIMESTAMP(col_date) "TO_TIMESTAMP",
       TO_CHAR(col_date, 'DD-MON-YYYY HH24:MI')
       AS "DISPLAY DATE"
  FROM date_example
TO_TIMESTAMP             DISPLAY DATE
------------------------ ----------------
24-MAR-02 12.00.00 AM    24-MAR-2002 16:25

1 row selected.
```

c) What function can you utilize to display the seconds component of a TIME-STAMP datatype column?

Answer: You can use either the TO_CHAR or the EXTRACT function to display components such as the year, month, date, hour, minute, and seconds from the TIMESTAMP datatype columns.

The next SQL statement shows how they are used and their respective differences.

```
SELECT col_timestamp,
       TO_CHAR(col_timestamp, 'SS') AS "CHAR Seconds",
       EXTRACT(SECOND FROM col_timestamp) AS "EXTRACT Seconds"
  FROM date_example
COL_TIMESTAMP                      CHAR Seconds EXTRACT Seconds
---------------------------        ------------ ---------------
24-MAR-02 04.25.32.000000 PM 32                             32

1 row selected.
```

The first column displays the column's value in the default TIMESTAMP format; the second column utilizes the TO_CHAR function to display the seconds. If you want to include the fractional seconds, you need to add the FF format mask, which is omitted in this example. The third column shows the use of the EXTRACT function to return the seconds. You may notice the difference in the display of the result between the second and the third column. The TO_CHAR function returns the seconds as a string; the EXTRACT function returns the seconds as a NUMBER datatype. The fractional seconds are always included when using the SECOND keyword with this datatype, but because they are zero they are not shown in the result.

d) What do you observe about the text literal of the following query's WHERE clause?

```
SELECT col_timestamp_w_tz
  FROM date_example
 WHERE col_timestamp_w_tz = '24-MAR-02 04.25.32.000000 PM -05:00'
COL_TIMESTAMP_W_TZ
-----------------------------------
24-MAR-02 04.25.32.000000 PM -05:00

1 row selected.
```

Answer: This SQL statement queries the column called COL_TIMESTAMP_W_TZ using the default TIMESTAMP WITH TIMEZONE display format literal.

You may use other formats in the WHERE clause to accomplish the same. For example, you can use the TO_TIMESTAMP_TZ function to explicitly convert the text literal already in default format to a TIMESTAMP WITH TIME ZONE datatype.

```
SELECT col_timestamp_w_tz
  FROM date_example
 WHERE col_timestamp_w_tz =
       TO_TIMESTAMP_TZ('24-MAR-02 04.25.32.000000 PM -05:00')
```

If you choose a text literal not in default format, you must supply the format mask as illustrated in the next example. The TZH and TZM indicate the time zone displacement values in hours and minutes from UTC. In this example, the fractional seconds (FF) are not included because they are zero.

```
SELECT col_timestamp_w_tz
  FROM date_example
 WHERE col_timestamp_w_tz =
       TO_TIMESTAMP_TZ('24-MAR-2002 16:25:32 -05:00',
                       'DD-MON-YYYY HH24:MI:SS TZH:TZM')
```

The next WHERE clause uses the region name instead of the time zone offset number value. Region names are expressed in the TZR format mask.

```
SELECT col_timestamp_w_tz
  FROM date_example
 WHERE col_timestamp_w_tz =
       TO_TIMESTAMP_TZ('24-MAR-2002 16:25:32 America/New_York',
                       'DD-MON-YYYY HH24:MI:SS TZR')
```

You can retrieve valid time zone region names from the column TZNAME in the data dictionary view V$TIMEZONE_NAMES.

```
SELECT *
  FROM v$timezone_names
TZNAME                         TZABBREV
-------------------------      --------
Africa/Cairo                   LMT
...
America/Los_Angeles            PST
...
America/Chicago                CST
...
America/Denver                 MST
...
America/New_York               EST
...

1393 rows selected.
```

Alternatively, if you want to express the WHERE clause in PST, you can use the America/Los_Angeles region name and the actual hour literal needs to be changed from 16 to 13 to result in the same UTC:

```
WHERE col_timestamp_w_tz = TO_TIMESTAMP_TZ(
        '24-MAR-2002 13:25:32 America/Los_Angeles',
        'DD-MON-YYYY HH24:MI:SS TZR')
```

THE TZ_OFFSET FUNCTION

You can find out the time differences between the UTC and the individual time zones with the TZ_OFFSET function. Following is a query that illustrates the appropriate offset values. Note the query result is different when daylight savings time is in effect.

```
SELECT TZ_OFFSET('Europe/London') "London",
       TZ_OFFSET('America/New_York') "NY",
       TZ_OFFSET('America/Chicago') "Chicago",
       TZ_OFFSET('America/Denver') "Denver",
       TZ_OFFSET('America/Los_Angeles') "LA"
  FROM dual
```

London	NY	Chicago	Denver	LA
+01:00	-05:00	-06:00	-07:00	-08:00

```
1 row selected.
```

AVOID THIS COMMON ERROR

Here's one common mistake you can avoid in conjunction with the datetime-related datatypes. In the next query the HH24 mask is used simultaneously with the A.M./P.M. format mask. An Oracle error indicates that you must choose either HH24 or use the HH (or HH12) together with the A.M./P.M. mask to adjust the time to either 24-hour or 12-hour format.

```
SQL> SELECT col_timestamp_w_tz
  2    FROM date_example
  3   WHERE col_timestamp_w_tz =
  4         TO_TIMESTAMP_TZ('24-MAR-2002 16:25:32 PM -05:00',
  5                         'DD-MON-YYYY HH24:MI:SS PM TZH:TZM')
  6  /
                         'DD-MON-YYYY HH24:MI:SS PM TZH:TZM')
                          *
ERROR at line 5:
ORA-01818: 'HH24' precludes use of meridian indicator
```

e) The following sets of SQL statements are issued against the database server. Explain the results.

```
SELECT SESSIONTIMEZONE
  FROM dual
SESSIONTIMEZONE
---------------
-05:00

1 row selected.
```

```
SELECT col_timestamp_w_tz, col_timestamp_w_local_tz
  FROM date_example
COL_TIMESTAMP_W_TZ                   COL_TIMESTAMP_W_LOCAL_TZ
------------------------------------ ----------------------------
24-MAR-02 04.25.32.000000 PM -05:00  24-MAR-02 04.25.32.000000 PM

1 row selected.
```

```
ALTER SESSION SET TIME_ZONE = '-8:00'
Session altered.
```

```
SELECT col_timestamp_w_tz, col_timestamp_w_local_tz
  FROM date_example
COL_TIMESTAMP_W_TZ                   COL_TIMESTAMP_W_LOCAL_TZ
------------------------------------ ----------------------------
24-MAR-02 04.25.32.000000 PM -05:00  24-MAR-02 01.25.32.000000 PM

1 row selected.
```

```
ALTER SESSION SET TIME_ZONE = '-5:00'
Session altered.
```

Answer: The results are explained below each statement.

This query determines the session's current time zone offset value, which is –5 hours before UTC. When daylight savings time is in effect the time zone offset value changes.

```
SELECT SESSIONTIMEZONE
  FROM dual
SESSIONTIMEZONE
---------------
-05:00

1 row selected.
```

The subsequent query of the exercise returns the currently stored values in the columns of the datatypes TIMESTAMP WITH TIME ZONE and TIMESTAMP WITH LOCAL TIME ZONE. Notice that the date and timestamps are identical in both columns. They represent the same date and time.

```
SELECT col_timestamp_w_tz, col_timestamp_w_local_tz
  FROM date_example
COL_TIMESTAMP_W_TZ                      COL_TIMESTAMP_W_LOCAL_TZ
-----------------------------------     ----------------------------
24-MAR-02 04.25.32.000000 PM -05:00 24-MAR-02 04.25.32.000000 PM
```

1 row selected.

LAB 4.3

Now the session's time zone is changed to be equivalent to the west coast time zone, which is 8 hours before UTC. This statement helps simulate a user's query result on the west coast.

```
ALTER SESSION SET TIME_ZONE = '-8:00'
Session altered.
```

The individual database user's local session time zone can be changed for the duration of the session with the ALTER SESSION command. When the user exits the session, the values are no longer effective. Alternatively, this could also be achieved by changing the user's operating system time zone value, but the ALTER SESSION commands will always override the operating system settings.

The query is reissued and when you compare the two column values, you notice that the second column with the datatype TIMESTAMP WITH LOCAL TIME ZONE shows a different value. The local time stamp is adjusted to the local west coast time.

```
SELECT col_timestamp_w_tz, col_timestamp_w_local_tz
  FROM date_example
COL_TIMESTAMP_W_TZ                      COL_TIMESTAMP_W_LOCAL_TZ
-----------------------------------     ----------------------------
24-MAR-02 04.25.32.000000 PM -05:00 24-MAR-02 01.25.32.000000 PM
```

1 row selected.

The next statement resets the time zone to its initial time zone offset value to −5:00 as determined by the SESSIONTIMEZONE function issued previously.

```
ALTER SESSION SET TIME_ZONE = '-5:00'
Session altered.
```

When you reissue the query against the DATE_EXAMPLE table, you notice the local time is back to its original value.

```
SELECT col_timestamp_w_tz, col_timestamp_w_local_tz
  FROM date_example
COL_TIMESTAMP_W_TZ                      COL_TIMESTAMP_W_LOCAL_TZ
----------------------------------- ----------------------------
24-MAR-02 04.25.32.000000 PM -05:00 24-MAR-02 04.25.32.000000 PM

1 row selected.
```

When the user exits the SQL*Plus session, these ALTER SESSION settings are no longer in effect. The ALTER SESSION settings only persist during the duration of the session.

LAB 4.3 SELF-REVIEW QUESTIONS

In order to test your progress, you should be able to answer the following questions.

1) What datatype will the following function return?

```
SELECT FROM_TZ(col_timestamp, '+5:00')
  FROM date_example
FROM_TZ(COL_TIMESTAMP,'+5:00')
-------------------------------------------
24-MAR-02 04.25.32.000000 PM +05:00

1 row selected.
```

  a) _____ DATE
  b) _____ TIMESTAMP
  c) _____ TIMESTAMP WITH TIME ZONE
  d) _____ Returns an Oracle error message

2) The ALTER SESSION statement can change the session's time zone.

  a) _____ True
  b) _____ False

3) The TIMESTAMP WITH LOCAL TIME ZONE datatype displays the local date and time.

  a) _____ True
  b) _____ False

4) The time zone displacement value indicates the time difference to UTC.

  a) _____ True
  b) _____ False

5) The TIMESTAMP WITH LOCAL TIME ZONE datatype allows fractional seconds.

   a) _____ True
   b) _____ False

6) The following query displays five fractional seconds.

```
SELECT TO_CHAR(SYSTIMESTAMP, 'HH:MI:SS.FF5')
  FROM dual
```

   a) _____ True
   b) _____ False

Answers appear in Appendix A, Section 4.3.

LAB 4.4

PERFORMING CALCULATIONS WITH THE INTERVAL DATATYPES

LAB OBJECTIVES

After this lab, you will be able to:
✔ Understand the Functionality of the Interval Datatypes

THE INTERVAL DATATYPES

Oracle has two interval datatypes; they are INTERVAL YEAR TO MONTH and INTERVAL DAY TO SECOND. These datatypes store the difference between two date values. Table 4.12 provides you with an overview of the two datatypes and respective example literals.

USING INTERVALS

You can use intervals for calculations such as in the next example where an interval of one year and six months is added to a student's registration date. The interval is represented as the literal '01-06'. The TO_YMINTERVAL function converts this text literal to the INTERVAL YEAR TO MONTH datatype. The result of the query shows the graduation date as one year and six months after the REGISTRATION_DATE.

```
SELECT student_id, registration_date,
       registration_date+TO_YMINTERVAL('01-06') "Grad. Date"
  FROM student
 WHERE student_id = 123
STUDENT_ID REGISTRAT Grad. Dat
---------- --------- ---------
       123 27-JAN-03 27-JUL-04
```

```
1 row selected.
```

Table 4.12 ■ Interval Datatypes

Datatype	Purpose and Example Literals
INTERVAL YEAR [(year_precision)] TO MONTH	Values are expressed in years and months. The default year precision is 2. Literal examples: INTERVAL '3-2' YEAR TO MONTH (3 years and 2 months) INTERVAL '2' YEAR (2 years) INTERVAL '4' MONTH (4 months) INTERVAL '36' MONTH (36 months or 3 years)
INTERVAL DAY [(day_precision)] TO SECOND [(fractional_seconds_ precision)]	Values are expressed in days, hours, minutes, and seconds. The default value for the day precision is 2, the fractional seconds precision has a six-digit default value. Literal examples: INTERVAL '30' DAY (30 days) INTERVAL '200' DAY (3) (300 days. Because the literal exceeds the default DAY precision of 2 you need to explicitly specify the precision.) INTERVAL '12:51' HOUR TO MINUTE (12 hours and 51 minutes) INTERVAL '15' MINUTE (15 minutes) INTERVAL '3 5:10:15.10' DAY TO SECONDS (3 days, 5 hours, 10 minutes, 15 seconds, and 10 fractional seconds) Note the components must be contiguous; for example, you cannot skip the MINUTE component between the HOUR and SECOND component.

Table 4.13 ■ Valid Value Ranges for Interval Components

Interval Component	Valid Values
YEAR	Positive or negative integer, default precision is 2.
MONTH	00–11 Note that the 12th month will be converted to a year.
DAY	Positive or negative integer, default precision is 2.
HOUR	00–23
MINUTE	00–59
SECOND	00–59 (Plus optional precision up to 9-digit fractional seconds).

The interval datatypes have individual components as listed in Table 4.13.

EXTRACT AND INTERVALS

Just like with the other datetime datatypes, you can use the EXTRACT function to extract specific components. This query retrieves the minutes.

```
SELECT EXTRACT(MINUTE FROM INTERVAL '12:51' HOUR TO MINUTE)
  FROM dual
EXTRACT(MINUTEFROMINTERVAL'12:51'HOURTOMINUTE)
-----------------------------------------------
                                             51

1 row selected.
```

The interval datatypes allows a number of useful functions listed in Table 4.14.

The next example expresses the time difference between the columns START_DATE_TIME and CREATED_DATE of the SECTION table. The first row of the output indicates that the difference between the two dates is the decimal result of 97.3958333 days; according to the fourth column where the NUMTODSINTERVAL function is applied, this translates into 97 days, 9 hours, 29 minutes, and 59.999999999 seconds.

```
SELECT DISTINCT TO_CHAR(created_date, 'DD-MON-YY HH24:MI')"CREATED_DATE",
                TO_CHAR(start_date_time, 'DD-MON-YY HH24:MI')"START_DATE_TIME",
                start_date_time-created_date"Decimal",
                NUMTODSINTERVAL(start_date_time created_date, 'DAY')"Interval"
  FROM section
ORDER BY 3
```

Table 4.14 ■ Useful Interval Functions

Function	Purpose	Return Datatype
TO_YMINTERVAL(char)	Convert a text literal to an INTERVAL YEAR TO MONTH datatype	INTERVAL YEAR TO MONTH
TO_DSINTERVAL(char)	Convert a text literal to an INTERVAL DAY TO SECOND datatype	INTERVAL DAY TO SECOND
NUMTOYMINTERVAL (number, 'YEAR') NUMTOYMINTERVAL (number, 'MONTH')	Convert a number to an INTERVAL YEAR TO MONTH literal	INTERVAL YEAR TO MONTH
NUMTODSINTERVAL (number, 'DAY')	Convert a number to an INTERVAL DAY TO SECOND literal. Instead of the DAY parameter you can pass the HOUR, MINUTE, or SECOND instead.	INTERVAL DAY TO SECOND
EXTRACT(MINUTE FROM interval_ datatype)	Extract specific components (i.e., YEAR, MONTH, DAY, HOUR, MINUTE, SECOND).	NUMBER

```
CREATED_DATE      START_DATE_TIME    Decimal Interval
---------------   ---------------    ----------  -----------------------------
02-JAN-03 00:00   09-APR-03 09:30    97.3958333  +000000097 09:29:59.999999999
02-JAN-03 00:00   14-APR-03 09:30    102.395833  +000000102 09:29:59.999999999
...
02-JAN-03 00:00   24-JUL-03 09:30    203.395833  +000000203 09:29:59.999999999
02-JAN-03 00:00   08-APR-04 09:30    462.395833  +000000462 09:29:59.999999999

29 rows selected.
```

INTERVAL EXPRESSION

As an alternative to the NUMTODSINTERVAL or the NUMTOYMINTERVAL function you can use an *interval expression,* which can be either DAY TO SECOND or YEAR TO MONTH. The next example shows as the first column the value of datatype TIMESTAMP in the COL_TIMESTAMP column of the DATE_EXAMPLE table. The second column subtracts from the SYSTIMESTAMP function the COL_TIMESTAMP column and displays the difference as an interval of DAY TO SECOND, resulting in a difference of 108 days, 19 hours, 30 minutes, and 48 seconds. (The value of SYSTIMESTAMP at the time of the query was 11-JUL-02 11.56.20.000000 AM -04:00. Note that the precision is set to 4 to allow for larger numbers.)

```
SELECT col_timestamp, SYSTIMESTAMP,
       (SYSTIMESTAMP - col_timestamp) DAY(4) TO SECOND
       "Interval Day to Second"
    FROM date_example
```

```
COL_TIMESTAMP              Interval Day to Second
--------------------       -------------------------
24-MAR-02 04.25.32 PM      +0108 19:30:48.000000

1 row selected.
```

If the same query is displayed as a YEAR TO MONTH interval instead, you will see this result displayed as zero years and 4 months.

```
SELECT col_timestamp,
       (SYSTIMESTAMP - col_timestamp) YEAR TO MONTH
       "Interval Year to Month"
  FROM date_example
COL_TIMESTAMP              Interval Year to Month
--------------------       ----------------------
24-MAR-02 04.25.32 PM      +00-04

1 row selected.
```

DETERMINING OVERLAPS

The OVERLAPS functionality is implemented in Oracle but not documented. The OVERLAPS operator is useful to determine if two time periods overlap. For example, you can use this operator to determine if a planned meeting conflicts with other scheduled meetings.

The next example table is called MEETING and contains three columns: a MEETING_ID column and two columns that determine the start and end date and time of a meeting.

```
SQL> DESCR meeting
 Name                      Null?     Type
 ----------------------    -------   ----------
 MEETING_ID                          NUMBER(10)
 MEETING_START                       DATE
 MEETING_END                         DATE
```

The table has two rows, as you see from the following SELECT statement.

```
SELECT meeting_id,
       TO_CHAR(meeting_start, 'DD-MON-YYYY HH:MI PM') "Start",
       TO_CHAR(meeting_end, 'DD-MON-YYYY HH:MI PM') "End"
  FROM meeting
MEETING_ID Start                  End
---------- --------------------   --------------------
         1 01-JUL-2002 09:30 AM   01-JUL-2002 10:30 AM
         2 01-JUL-2002 03:00 PM   01-JUL-2002 04:30 PM

2 rows selected.
```

If you want to find out if a particular date and time conflicts with any of the already scheduled meetings, you can issue this SQL query with the OVERLAPS operator. This operator is used just like any of the other comparison operators in the WHERE clause of a SQL statement. Here it compares the column pair MEETING_START and MEETING_END with the date and time 01-JUL-2002 3:30 PM and a two-hour interval. The row that overlaps is returned in the output.

```
SELECT meeting_id,
       TO_CHAR(meeting_start, 'DD-MON-YYYY HH:MI PM') "Start",
       TO_CHAR(meeting_end, 'DD-MON-YYYY HH:MI PM') "End"
  FROM meeting
 WHERE (meeting_start, meeting_end)
       OVERLAPS
       (TO_DATE('01-JUL-2002 3:30PM', 'DD-MON-YYYY HH:MI PM'),
        INTERVAL '2' HOUR)
MEETING_ID Start                End
---------- -------------------- --------------------
         2 01-JUL-2002 03:00 PM 01-JUL-2002 04:30 PM
```

1 row selected.

Alternatively, if you want to find out which meetings do NOT conflict, you can negate the predicate with the NOT logical operator as shown in the next example.

```
SELECT meeting_id,
       TO_CHAR(meeting_start, 'DD-MON-YYYY HH:MI PM') "Start",
       TO_CHAR(meeting_end, 'DD-MON-YYYY HH:MI PM') "End"
  FROM meeting
 WHERE NOT (meeting_start, meeting_end)
       OVERLAPS
       (TO_DATE('01-JUL-2002 3:30PM', 'DD-MON-YYYY HH:MI PM'),
        INTERVAL '2' HOUR)
MEETING_ID Start                End
---------- -------------------- --------------------
         1 01-JUL-2002 09:30 AM 01-JUL-2002 10:30 AM
```

1 row selected.

The syntax for OVERLAPS is as follows:

```
event OVERLAPS event
```

Whereby `event` is either of the following:

```
(start_event_date_time, end_event_start_time)
```

Or:

```
(start_event_date_time, interval_duration)
```

LAB 4.4 EXERCISES

4.4.1 UNDERSTAND THE FUNCTIONALITY OF THE INTERVAL DATATYPES

a) Explain the result of this SQL statement.

```
SELECT section_id "ID",
       TO_CHAR(created_date, 'MM/DD/YY HH24:MI')
         "CREATED_DATE",
       TO_CHAR(start_date_time, 'MM/DD/YY HH24:MI')
         "START_DATE_TIME",
       NUMTODSINTERVAL(start_date_time-created_date, 'DAY')
         "Interval"
  FROM section
 WHERE NUMTODSINTERVAL(start date time-created date, 'DAY')
       BETWEEN INTERVAL '100' DAY(3) AND INTERVAL '120' DAY(3)
 ORDER BY 3
 ID CREATED_DATE    START_DATE_TIM Interval
--- --------------- -------------- ------------------------------
 79 01/02/03 00:00  04/14/03 09:30 +000000102 09:29:59.999999999
 87 01/02/03 00:00  04/14/03 09:30 +000000102 09:29:59.999999999
...
152 01/02/03 00:00  04/29/03 09:30 +000000117 09:29:59.999999999
125 01/02/03 00:00  04/29/03 09:30 +000000117 09:29:59.999999999

17 rows selected.
```

**LAB
4.4**

b) Explain the result of the following SQL statements. What do you observe?

```
SELECT NUMTODSINTERVAL(360, 'SECOND'),
       NUMTODSINTERVAL(360, 'MINUTE')
  FROM dual
NUMTODSINTERVAL(360,'SECOND') NUMTODSINTERVAL(360,'MINUTE')
----------------------------- -----------------------------
+000000000 00:06:00.000000000 +000000000 06:00:00.000000000

1 row selected.

SELECT NUMTODSINTERVAL(360, 'HOUR'),
       NUMTODSINTERVAL(360, 'DAY')
  FROM dual
NUMTODSINTERVAL(360,'HOUR')    NUMTODSINTERVAL(360,'DAY')
----------------------------- -----------------------------
+000000015 00:00:00.000000000 +000000360 00:00:00.000000000

1 row selected.
```

LAB 4.4 EXERCISE ANSWERS

4.4.1 ANSWERS

a) Explain the result of this SQL statement.

```
SELECT section_id,
       TO_CHAR(created_date, 'MM/DD/YY HH24:MI')
         "CREATED_DATE",
       TO_CHAR(start_date_time, 'MM/DD/YY HH24:MI')
         "START_DATE_TIME",
       NUMTODSINTERVAL(start_date_time-created_date, 'DAY')
         "Interval"
  FROM section
 WHERE NUMTODSINTERVAL(start_date_time-created_date, 'DAY')
       BETWEEN INTERVAL '100' DAY(3) AND INTERVAL '120' DAY(3)
 ORDER BY 3
```

```
SECTION_ID CREATED_DATE    START_DATE_TIM Interval
---------- --------------  -------------- -----------------------------
        79 01/02/03 00:00  04/14/03 09:30 +000000102 09:29:59.999999999
        87 01/02/03 00:00  04/14/03 09:30 +000000102 09:29:59.999999999
...
       152 01/02/03 00:00  04/29/03 09:30 +000000117 09:29:59.999999999
       125 01/02/03 00:00  04/29/03 09:30 +000000117 09:29:59.999999999
```

17 rows selected.

> *Answer: The query shows four columns: the SECTION_ID, the CREATED_DATE, the START_DATE_TIME (the date and time a section starts), and the "Interval" column. This last column expresses the difference between the START_DATE_TIME column and the CREATED_DATE column in days, hours, minutes, and seconds using the NUM-TODSINTERVAL function. Without this function the calculation will return the time portion as a decimal. The WHERE clause of the query retrieves rows with a time difference value between 100 and 120 days. The ORDER BY clause sorts the result by the START_DATE_TIME column values.*

The WHERE clause uses both the NUMTODSINTERVAL function and the INTER-VAL expression and checks if the result falls BETWEEN the INTERVAL literals 100 and 120 days. Because the INTERVAL DAY has a default precision of 2, you must include the three-digit precision.

b) Explain the result of the following SQL statements. What do you observe?

```
SELECT NUMTODSINTERVAL(360, 'SECOND'),
       NUMTODSINTERVAL(360, 'MINUTE')
  FROM dual
NUMTODSINTERVAL(360,'SECOND') NUMTODSINTERVAL(360,'MINUTE')
----------------------------- -----------------------------
+000000000 00:06:00.000000000 +000000000 06:00:00.000000000

1 row selected.

SELECT NUMTODSINTERVAL(360, 'HOUR'),
       NUMTODSINTERVAL(360, 'DAY')
  FROM dual
NUMTODSINTERVAL(360,'HOUR')   NUMTODSINTERVAL(360,'DAY')
----------------------------- -----------------------------
+000000015 00:00:00.000000000 +000000360 00:00:00.000000000

1 row selected.
```

LAB 4.4

Answer: The SQL statements illustrate how a number literal is translated to an interval using the NUMSTODSINTERVAL function with various parameter options.

The first SQL statement shows the number literal of 360 converted into seconds in the first column. The second column translates it into minutes. From the result, you will notice that 360 seconds are now 6 minutes as indicated with the 00:06:00 interval. The second column shows the 360 minutes converted into 6 hours as shown with the interval 06:00:00.

The second statement again performs the same conversion; this time the number literal represents hours, which are translated into 15 days. The second column shows 360 days with the interval +000000360 00:00:00.000000000.

LAB 4.4 SELF-REVIEW QUESTIONS

In order to test your progress, you should be able to answer the following questions.

1) The TO_YMINTERVAL function converts a text literal to an INTERVAL DAY TO SECOND datatype.

    a) _____ True
    b) _____ False

2) The NUMTODSINTERVAL function converts a number to an INTERVAL YEAR TO MONTH datatype.

    a) _____ True
    b) _____ False

3) The EXTRACT function is not valid for the INTERVAL YEAR TO MONTH datatype.

    a) _____ True
    b) _____ False

4) The following interval literal is invalid.

```
INTERVAL '5 10:30:10.00' DAY TO SECOND
```

    a) _____ True
    b) _____ False

Answers appear in Appendix A, Section 4.4.

**LAB
4.4**

CONVERTING FROM ONE DATATYPE TO ANOTHER

LAB OBJECTIVES

After this lab, you will be able to:
- ✔ Convert between Different Datatypes
- ✔ Format Data

You know the good old phrase, "You can't compare apples to oranges." SQL works just the same way. When you compare two values or columns they must be of the same datatype or of a compatible datatype. Sometimes Oracle can implicitly convert from one datatype to the other. It is preferable to explicitly specify the conversion with a function to avoid any ambiguities or errors when your SQL statement is executed.

DATATYPE CONVERSION

You have already learned about implicit conversion in the context of the datetime functions discussed in the previous labs. In the following SQL statement the WHERE clause compares a text literal against the numeric COURSE_NO column. When Oracle compares a character datatype, in this case the text literal '350', against the NUMBER datatype, which is the COURSE_NO column, Oracle implicitly converts the character data to a NUMBER. This works perfectly as you see from the query result.

```
SELECT course_no, description
  FROM course
 WHERE course_no = '350'
COURSE_NO DESCRIPTION
--------- --------------
      350 JDeveloper Lab

1 row selected.
```

Clearly, in this example, you have control over the literal and can simply change the text literal '350' to a NUMBER to avoid the implicit conversion. Such a change becomes more difficult or impossible when you are working within a programming language where you may not have influence over the datatype of a supplied value. Inevitably, things can go wrong, as you see illustrated in this example table called CONVERSION_EXAMPLE. (This table is not part of the STUDENT schema, but can be downloaded from the companion Web site.)

```
SQL> DESCR conversion_example
 Name                          Null?     Type
 -------------------- -------- -----------
 COURSE_NO                               VARCHAR2(9)
```

The following SELECT statement retrieves all the rows from the table. Notice that the COURSE_NO column in this table is of datatype VARCHAR2 and therefore it accepts both numeric as well as alphanumeric entries. The table contains two rows, one with the value of 123 and another with the value xyz.

```
SELECT *
  FROM conversion_example
COURSE_NO
---------
123
xyz

2 rows selected.
```

To illustrate the effects of the implicit data conversion, first query the row with the value of 123 in the COURSE_NO column. As you can see, this statement executes flawlessly because the COURSE_NO column is a VARCHAR2 column and the text literal 123 is enclosed in single quotes.

```
SELECT *
  FROM conversion_example
 WHERE course_no = '123'
COURSE_NO
---------
123

1 row selected.
```

The next query does not enclose the literal in single quotes; in fact, it now represents a number literal. Oracle implicitly converts the COURSE_NO column to a NUMBER datatype resulting in an ORA-01722 invalid number error. This error occurs because all the values in the COURSE_NO column are now implicitly converted into the NUMBER datatype. But this conversion cannot be completed because one of the rows, the row with the value xyz, obviously cannot be converted into a NUMBER. Therefore, the query does not return any rows.

```
SELECT *
  FROM conversion_example
 WHERE course_no = 123
ERROR:
ORA-01722: invalid number

no rows selected
```

To avoid this error, it is always best to explicitly specify the conversion function to make sure that the datatypes agree. You accomplish the conversion with the TO_CHAR function; it converts the passed parameter into a character datatype as you see in the next following SQL statement.

```
SELECT *
  FROM conversion_example
 WIIERE coursc_no - TO_CHAR(123)
```

You may wonder why you would bother even adding the TO_CHAR function if you can just enclose the values with quotes. Clearly, the easiest solution is to simply enclose the value with single quotes, but as previously mentioned, you may encounter cases where you do not have control over the literal or when you are comparing one table's column against another table's column.

THE CAST FUNCTION

The CAST function also converts from one datatype to another. It can be applied to Oracle's most commonly used built-in datatypes (i.e., VARCHAR2, CHAR, NUMBER, and the datetime variants) or with a user-defined datatype or subquery. (The creation of user-defined datatypes is beyond the scope of this book. You will learn about subqueries in Chapter 7, "Subqueries.")

The syntax for the CAST function is as follows:

```
CAST(expression AS datatype)
```

Following are examples of how CAST is used with Oracle's familiar datatypes. The SELECT statement contains CAST instead of the TO_CHAR function. When converting to a VARCHAR2 or CHAR datatype, also referred to as *casting*, you need to specify the length. Here it is three characters long.

```
SELECT *
  FROM conversion_example
 WHERE course_no = CAST(123 AS VARCHAR2(3))
```

The next query casts the text literal 29-MAR-02 into a DATE datatype in the first column and as a TIMESTAMP WITH LOCAL TIME ZONE datatype in the second column.

```
SELECT CAST('29-Mar-02' AS DATE),
       CAST('29-MAR-02' AS TIMESTAMP WITH LOCAL TIME ZONE)
  FROM dual
CAST('29- CAST('29-MAR-02'ASTIMESTAMPWITHLOCALTIMEZONE)
--------- ---------------------------------------------
29-MAR-02 29-MAR-02 12.00.00.000000 AM

1 row selected.
```

You can use the CAST not only in the SELECT list, but also in the WHERE clause.

```
SELECT section_id,
       TO_CHAR(start_date_time, 'DD-MON-YYYY HH24:MI:SS')
  FROM section
 WHERE start_date_time >= CAST('01-JUL-2003' AS DATE)
   AND start_date_time <  CAST('01-AUG-2003' AS DATE)
```

The following statement casts the literal '04-JUL-2002 10:00:00 AM', shown in the default format, into the TIMESTAMP datatype, because the FROM_TZ function requires this datatype as the first parameter. The FROM_TZ function (discussed in Lab 4.3) converts the TIMESTAMP value into a TIMESTAMP WITH TIME ZONE datatype. The chosen time zone for date literal is the time zone region name 'America/New_York'. The AT TIME ZONE keywords of the resulting expression display the value in the local Los Angeles time.

```
SELECT FROM_TZ(CAST('04-JUL-2002 10:00:00 AM' AS TIMESTAMP),
       'America/New_York') AT TIME ZONE 'America/Los_Angeles'
       "FROM_TZ Example"
  FROM dual
FROM_TZ Example
--------------------------------------------------
04-JUL-02 07.00.00.000000 AM AMERICA/LOS_ANGELES

1 row selected.
```

The next example illustrates the use of CAST on intervals. The text literal '1-6' is converted into the INTERVAL YEAR TO MONTH datatype. As always, there are multiple ways to accomplish the same functionality in the SQL language; here the TO_YMINTERVAL function performs the identical function. This function requires a NUMBER datatype as input parameter. (See also Table 4.14 in Lab 4.4.)

```
SELECT CAST('1-6' AS INTERVAL YEAR TO MONTH) "CAST",
       TO_YMINTERVAL('1-6') "TO_YMINTERVAL",
       NUMTOYMINTERVAL(1.5, 'YEAR') "NUMTOYMINTERVAL"
  FROM dual
```

```
CAST    TO_YMINTERVAL NUMTOYMINTERVAL
------  ------------- ---------------
+01-06 +000000001-06 +000000001-06
```

```
1 row selected.
```

Following is an example of a SQL statement that casts the COST column of the COURSE table into a BINARY_FLOAT datatype. Alternatively, you can also use the TO_BINARY_FLOAT conversion function.

```
SELECT CAST(cost AS BINARY_FLOAT) AS cast,
       TO_BINARY_FLOAT(cost) AS to_binary_float
  FROM course
 WHERE course_no < 80
      CAST TO_BINARY_FLOAT
---------- ---------------
1.195E+003      1.195E+003
1.195E+003      1.195E+003
1.195E+003      1.195E+003
```

```
3 rows selected.
```

CAST VERSUS ORACLE'S CONVERSION FUNCTIONS

You may wonder why you should use the CAST instead of any of the other Oracle conversion functions. The CAST function is ANSI SQL:1999 compliant, so there is no need to learn multiple Oracle-specific functions. However, some of Oracle's built-in datatypes, such as the various LOB types, LONG RAWs, and LONGs, cannot be converted from one datatype to another using CAST. Instead, you must use Oracle's individual conversion functions. One disadvantage of the CAST function is casting into VARCHAR2 and CHAR datatypes because they need to be constrained to a determined length. The TO_DATE function and TO_CHAR functions are overall very versatile as they allow you a large variety of different format model choices. So you may choose whichever functions fit your specific requirements.

Table 4.15 provides you with an overview of Oracle conversion functions. In this lab you will concentrate on the TO_NUMBER, TO_CHAR, and CAST functions. In previous labs you already learned about the TO_DATE and the TO_CHAR conversion functions as well as conversion functions related to datetime and interval datatypes (see Table 4.11 Datetime-Related Conversion Functions, and Table 4.14, Useful Interval Functions).

FORMATTING DATA

The TO_CHAR conversion function is useful not only for data conversions between different datatypes, but also for formatting data. In the next SQL statement you see how a format mask can be applied with this function. To display a

Table 4.15 ■ Frequently Used Datatype Conversion Functions

Function	Purpose
TO_NUMBER(char [, format_mask])	Converts a VARCHAR2 or CHAR to a NUMBER.
TO_BINARY_FLOAT(expression [,format_mask])	Converts a character or numeric value to BINARY_FLOAT.
TO_BINARY_DOUBLE(expression [,format_mask])	Converts a character or numeric value to BINARY_DOUBLE.
TO_CHAR(datetime [, format_mask])	Converts a datetime value to a VARCHAR2.
TO_CHAR(number [, format_mask])	Converts a NUMBER to a VARCHAR2
TO_CLOB(char)	Converts a VARCHAR2 or CHAR to a CLOB.
TO_DATE(char [, format_mask])	Converts a VARCHAR2, CHAR, or NUMBER to a DATE.
CAST(expression AS datatype)	Converts from one datatype to another. Can be used for Oracle's most commonly used datatypes and for user-defined datatypes.

**LAB
4.5**

formatted result for the COST column, for instance, you can apply the format mask '999,999'. The values in the COST column are then formatted with a comma separating the thousands.

```
SELECT course_no, cost,
       TO_CHAR(cost, '999,999') formatted
  FROM course
 WHERE course_no < 25
COURSE_NO      COST FORMATTED
--------- --------- -----------
       10      1195     1,195
       20      1195     1,195

2 rows selected.
```

The conversion function used in the SELECT statement does not modify the values stored in the database, but rather performs a "temporary" conversion for the purpose of executing the statement. In Chapter 2, "SQL: The Basics," you learned about the SQL*Plus COLUMN FORMAT command, which achieves the same result. However, if you execute the SQL statement from a program other than SQL*Plus or *i*SQL*Plus, the COLUMN command is not available and you must use the TO_CHAR function to format the result.

The following statement shows both the effects of the SQL*Plus COLUMN FORMAT command and the TO_CHAR function. The column labeled "SQL*PLUS" is formatted with the COL "SQL*Plus" FORMAT 999,999 command, the last column labeled "CHAR" is formatted with the TO_CHAR function.

```
COL "SQL*PLUS" FORMAT 999,999

SELECT course_no, cost "SQL*PLUS",
       TO_CHAR(cost, '999,999') "CHAR"
  FROM course
 WHERE course_no < 25
COURSE_NO SQL*PLUS CHAR
--------- -------- --------
       10    1,195    1,195
       20    1,195    1,195

2 rows selected.
```

Table 4.16 gives an overview of the most popular NUMBER format models in conjunction with the TO_CHAR function.

Table 4.16 ■ Common NUMBER Format Models

Format Mask	Example Value	Applied TO_CHAR Function	Result
999,990.99	.45	TO_CHAR(.45, '999,990.99')	0.45 (Note the leading zero)
$99,999.99	1234	TO_CHAR(1234, '$99,999.99')	$1,234.00
0999	123	TO_CHAR(123, '0999')	0123
L9999.99	1234.99	TO_CHAR(1234.99, 'L9999.99')	$1234.99 (local currency)
L99G999D99	1234.56	TO_CHAR(1234.56, 'L99G999D99')	$1,234.56 (local values for: currency, group, and decimal separators)
999PR	-123	TO_CHAR(-123, '999PR')	<123>
999MI	-123	TO_CHAR(-123, '999MI')	123-
999s	-123	TO_CHAR(-123, '999s')	123-
s999	-123	TO_CHAR(-123, 's999')	-123
999	123.59	TO_CHAR(123.59, '999')	124 (Note the rounding)

Notice that rounding can be accomplished not only with the ROUND function but also with a format model.

LAB 4.5 EXERCISES

4.5.1 CONVERT BETWEEN DIFFERENT DATATYPES

Type and execute the following query:

```
SELECT zip, city
  FROM zipcode
 WHERE zip = 10025
```

a) Rewrite the query using the TO_CHAR function in the WHERE clause.

b) Rewrite the query using the TO_NUMBER function in the WHERE clause.

c) Rewrite the query using CAST in the WHERE clause.

4.5.2 FORMAT DATA

a) Write the SQL statement that displays the following result. Note the last column in the result shows the formatted COST column with a leading dollar sign and a comma to separate the thousands. Include the cents in the result as well.

```
COURSE_NO      COST FORMATTED
---------  ---------  ------------
      330       1195   $1,195.00

1 row selected.
```

b) List the COURSE_NO and COST columns for courses that cost more than 1500. In a third, fourth, and fifth column show the cost increased by 15%. Show the increased cost columns, one with a leading dollar sign and separate the thousands, and in another column show the same formatting but rounded to the nearest dollar. The result should look similar to the following output.

```
COURSE_NO     OLDCOST     NEWCOST     FORMATTED       ROUNDED
----------  ----------  ----------  -------------  -------------
       80         1595     1834.25     $1,834.25      $1,834.00

1 row selected
```

c) Based on the previous question, write the query to achieve this result. Use the fm format mask to eliminate the extra spaces.

```
Increase
-----------------------------------------------------------
The price for course# 80 has been increased to $1,834.25.

1 row selected.
```

LAB 4.5 EXERCISE ANSWERS

4.5.1 ANSWERS

Type and execute the following query:

```
SELECT zip, city
   FROM zipcode
  WHERE zip = 10025
```

a) Rewrite the query using the TO_CHAR function in the WHERE clause.

Answer: The TO_CHAR function converts the number literal to a VARCHAR2 datatype, which makes it equal to the VARCHAR2 datatype of the ZIP column.

```
SELECT zip, city
   FROM zipcode
  WHERE zip = TO_CHAR(10025)
ZIP    CITY
-----  --------
10025 New York

1 row selected.
```

b) Rewrite the query using the TO_NUMBER function in the WHERE clause.

Answer: The VARCHAR2 datatype of the ZIP column is converted to a NUMBER datatype by applying the TO_NUMBER function. Oracle then compares it to the number literal 10025.

```
SELECT zip, city
   FROM zipcode
  WHERE TO_NUMBER(zip) = 10025
ZIP    CITY
-----  --------
10025 New York

1 row selected.
```

When you compare the results of the SQL statements from answers a and b, they are identical. Answer b is less desirable because a function is applied to a database column in the WHERE clause. This disables the use of any indexes that may exist on the ZIP column and may require Oracle to read every row in the table instead of looking up the value in the index. Applying functions to database columns in the SELECT clause does not affect performance.

 It is best to explicitly specify the datatype conversion functions—your statements are easier to understand and the behavior predictable. Oracle's algorithms for implicit conversion may be subject to change across versions and products, and implicit conversion can have a negative impact on performance if the queried column is indexed. You will learn about indexes in Chapter 12, "Views, Indexes, and Sequences," and about performance considerations in Chapter 17, "SQL Optimization."

c) Rewrite the query using CAST in the WHERE clause.

Answer: You can write the query in one of the following ways.

```
SELECT zip, city
  FROM zipcode
 WHERE CAST(zip AS NUMBER) = 10025
```

Or as:

```
SELECT zip, city
  FROM zipcode
 WHERE zip = CAST(10025 AS VARCHAR2(5))
```

If you specify a too short length of the VARCHAR2 datatype, you will receive an error similar to this:

```
SELECT zip, city
  FROM zipcode
 WHERE zip = CAST(10025 AS VARCHAR2(3))
WHERE zip = CAST(10025 AS VARCHAR2(3))
                *
ERROR at line 3:
ORA-25137: Data value out of range
```

In the next SQL query result, observe the way SQL*Plus displays the result of a NUMBER column versus the result in a character type column. In the output you see as the first column the ZIP column in datatype VARCHAR2. It is left aligned, just like the VARCHAR2 column CITY. In general, values of the NUMBER datatype are always right aligned in SQL*Plus; character values are always left aligned.

```
SELECT zip, TO_NUMBER(zip) "TO_NUMBER",
       CAST(zip AS NUMBER) "CAST", city
  FROM zipcode
 WHERE zip = '10025'
ZIP      TO_NUMBER      CAST CITY
-------  -------------- --------------
10025            10025 10025 New York

1 row selected.
```

4.5.2 ANSWERS

a) Write the SQL statement that displays the following result. Note the last column in the result shows the formatted COST column with a leading dollar sign and a comma to separate the thousands. Include the cents in the result as well.

```
COURSE_NO      COST FORMATTED
---------- ---------- ------------
       330      1195    $1,195.00

1 row selected.
```

Answer: The TO_CHAR function, together with the format mask in the SELECT clause of the statement, achieves the desired formatting.

```
SELECT course_no, cost,
       TO_CHAR(cost, '$999,999.99') Formatted
  FROM course
 WHERE course_no = 330
```

b) List the COURSE_NO and COST columns for courses that cost more than 1500. In a third, fourth, and fifth column show the cost increased by 15%. Show the increased cost columns, one with a leading dollar sign and separate the thousands, and in another column show the same formatting but rounded to the nearest dollar. The result should look similar to the following output.

```
COURSE_NO    OLDCOST    NEWCOST FORMATTED    ROUNDED
---------- ---------- ---------- ------------ ------------
        80       1595    1834.25   $1,834.25    $1,834.00
1 row selected
```

Answer: An increase of 15% means a multiplication of the column COST by 1.15. You can round to the nearest dollar with the ROUND function.

```
SELECT course_no, cost oldcost,
       cost*1.15 newcost,
       TO_CHAR(cost*1.15, '$999,999.99') formatted,
       TO_CHAR(ROUND(cost*1.15), '$999,999.99') rounded
  FROM course
 WHERE cost > 1500
```

Alternatively, the identical result is achieved with the format mask '$999,999', which omits the digits after the decimal point and rounds the cents as shown in the next statement:

```
SELECT course_no, TO_CHAR(ROUND(cost*1.15), '$999,999.99') rounded,
       TO_CHAR(cost*1.15, '$999,999') "No Cents"
  FROM course
 WHERE cost > 1500
```

COURSE_NO	ROUNDED	No Cents
80	$1,834.00	$1,834

1 row selected.

c) Based on the previous question, write the query to achieve this result. Use the fm format mask to eliminate the extra spaces.

```
Increase
-----------------------------------------------------------
The price for course# 80 has been increased to $1,834.25.
```

1 row selected.

Answer: The following query achieves the desired result set. The fm format mask eliminates the blank padding.

```
SELECT 'The price for course# '||course_no||' has been increased to '||
       TO_CHAR(cost*1.15, 'fm$999,999.99')||'.'
       "Increase"
  FROM course
 WHERE cost > 1500
```

LAB 4.5 SELF-REVIEW QUESTIONS

In order to test your progress, you should be able to answer the following questions. There may be more than one correct answer, so choose all that apply.

1) Which SQL statement results in an error?

a) _____ `SELECT TO_CHAR('123') FROM dual`
b) _____ `SELECT TO_CHAR(123) FROM dual`
c) _____ `SELECT TO_NUMBER('001.99999') FROM dual`
d) _____ `SELECT TO_NUMBER('A123') FROM dual`
e) _____ `SELECT TO_CHAR('A123') FROM dual`
f)_____ `SELECT TO_NUMBER(' 000123 ') FROM dual`

2) Which of the following NUMBER format masks are valid?

a) _____ `SELECT TO_CHAR(1.99,'9,9999.9X') FROM dual`
b) _____ `SELECT TO_CHAR(1.99,'A99.99) FROM dual`
c) _____ `SELECT TO_CHAR(1.99,'$000.99') FROM dual`
d) _____ `SELECT TO_CHAR(1.99,'999.99') FROM dual`
e) _____ `SELECT TO_CHAR(1.99,'.99') FROM dual`

3) Explicit datatype conversion is preferable to Oracle's implicit conversion.

a) _____ True
b) _____ False

4) The TO_CHAR, TO_NUMBER, and TO_DATE conversion functions are single-row functions.

a) _____ True
b) _____ False

**LAB
4.5**

5) How can you correct the following SQL error message?

```
SQL> SELECT *
  2    FROM conversion_example
  3   WHERE course_no = CAST(123 AS VARCHAR2)
  4  /
 WHERE course_no = CAST(123 AS VARCHAR2)
                                        *
ERROR at line 3:
ORA-00906: missing left parenthesis
```

a) _____ Change the datatype to a CHAR
b) _____ Add a column length definition
c) _____ Choose a different aggregate function
d) _____ This query does not make sense

Answers appear in Appendix A, Section 4.5.

CHAPTER 4

TEST YOUR THINKING

The projects in this section are meant to have you utilize all of the skills that you have acquired throughout this chapter. The answers to these projects can be found at the companion Web site to this book, located at http://authors.phptr.com/rischert3e. Visit the Web site periodically to share and discuss your answers.

1)   Display all the sections where classes start at 10:30 A.M.

2)   Write the query to accomplish the following result. The output shows you all the days of the week where sections 83, 86, and 107 start. Note the order of the days.

```
DAY    SECTION_ID
----   ----------
Mon           107
Tue            86
Wed            83

3 rows selected.
```

3)   Select the distinct course costs of all the courses. If the course cost is unknown, substitute a zero. Format the output with a leading $ sign and separate the thousands with a comma. Display two digits after the decimal point. The query's output should look like the following result:

```
COST
-----------
     $0.00
 $1,095.00
 $1,195.00
 $1,595.00

4 rows selected.
```

4)   List all rows of the GRADE_TYPE table that were created in the year 1998.

5) What, if anything, is wrong with the following SQL statement?

```
SELECT zip + 100
  FROM zipcode
```

6) For the students enrolled on January 30, 2003, display the columns STUDENT_ID and ENROLL_DATE.

7) Execute the following SQL statements. Explain the individual statements.

```
SELECT SESSIONTIMEZONE, CURRENT_TIMESTAMP
  FROM dual;
ALTER SESSION SET TIME_ZONE = '-8:00';
SELECT SESSIONTIMEZONE, CURRENT_TIMESTAMP
  FROM dual;
ALTER SESSION SET TIME_ZONE = '-5:00';
```

AGGREGATE FUNCTIONS, GROUP BY, AND HAVING

CHAPTER OBJECTIVES

In this chapter, you will learn about:

In the last two chapters, you learned about character functions, number functions, date functions, and miscellaneous functions, all *single-row* functions. In this chapter, you will learn about *aggregate functions,* which work on *groups of rows*. The most commonly used aggregate functions are discussed in this chapter. Aggregate functions allow you to generate summary data for a group of rows to obtain totals, averages, counts, minimum values, and maximum values. In Chapter 16, "Exploring Data Warehousing Features," you will learn about advanced SQL aggregation topics involving the ROLLUP and CUBE operators.

L A B   5 . 1

AGGREGATE FUNCTIONS

L AB   O BJECTIVES

After this lab, you will be able to:
✔ Use Aggregate Functions in a SQL Statement

Aggregate functions do just as you would expect: They *aggregate,* or group togeth-er, data to produce a single result. Questions such as "How many students are reg-istered?" and "What is the average cost of a course?" can be answered by using aggregate functions. You count the individual students to answer the first ques-tion, and you calculate the average cost of all courses to answer the second. In each case, the result is a single answer based on several rows of data.

THE COUNT FUNCTION

One of the most common aggregate functions is the COUNT function, which lets you count values in a table. The function takes a single parameter, which can be a column in a table of any datatype and can even be the asterisk (*) wildcard. The following SELECT statement returns the number of rows in the ENROLLMENT table:

```
SELECT COUNT(*)
  FROM enrollment
COUNT(*)
---------
      226

1 row selected.
```

COUNT AND NULLS

The COUNT function is useful for determining whether a table has data. If the result set returns the number 0 when using COUNT(*), it means there are no rows in the table, even though the table exists.

Following is an example of the COUNT function used with a database column as a parameter. The difference is that COUNT(*) counts rows that contain null values, whereas COUNT with a column excludes rows that contain nulls.

```
SELECT COUNT(final_grade), COUNT(section_id), COUNT(*)
  FROM enrollment
COUNT(FINAL_GRADE) COUNT(SECTION_ID)  COUNT(*)
------------------ ------------------ ---------
                 1                226       226
```

1 row selected.

The FINAL_GRADE column in the ENROLLMENT table allows null values, and there is only one row with a value in the FINAL_GRADE column. Therefore, the result of the function is 1. COUNT(section_id) returns the same number as the COUNT(*) because the SECTION_ID column contains no nulls.

COUNT AND DISTINCT

DISTINCT is often used in conjunction with aggregate functions to determine the number of distinct values. There are 226 rows in the ENROLLMENT table, but 64 distinct section IDs. Several students are enrolled in the same section; some individual section IDs exist more than once in the ENROLLMENT table.

```
SELECT COUNT(DISTINCT section_id), COUNT(section_id)
  FROM enrollment
COUNT(DISTINCTSECTION_ID) COUNT(SECTION_ID)
------------------------- -----------------
                       64               226
```

1 row selected.

THE SUM FUNCTION

The SUM function adds values together for a group of rows. The following example adds up all the values in the CAPACITY column of the SECTION table. The result is the total capacity of all sections. If any values in the CAPACITY column contain a null, these values are ignored.

```
SELECT SUM(capacity)
  FROM section
SUM(CAPACITY)
-------------
         1652
```

1 row selected.

THE AVG FUNCTION

The AVG function returns the average of a group of rows. In the following example, the average capacity of each section is computed. Any nulls in the CAPACITY column are ignored. To substitute nulls with a zero, use the NVL or COALESCE function discussed in Chapter 3, "Character, Number, and Miscellaneous Functions."

```
SELECT AVG(capacity), AVG(NVL(capacity,0))
  FROM section
AVG(CAPACITY) AVG(NVL(CAPACITY,0))
------------- --------------------
    21.179487            21.179487

1 row selected.
```

In this example, there are no sections with null values in the CAPACITY column; therefore, the result of the two functions is identical.

THE MIN AND MAX FUNCTIONS

The MIN and MAX functions are opposites of each other, providing the minimum and maximum values, respectively, in a group of rows: The result shows the lowest value in the CAPACITY column of the SECTION; this value is 10 and the highest value is 25.

```
SELECT MIN(capacity), MAX(capacity)
  FROM section
MIN(CAPACITY) MAX(CAPACITY)
------------- -------------
           10            25

1 row selected.
```

MIN AND MAX WITH OTHER DATATYPES

The previous example operated on the CAPACITY column, which is of the NUMBER datatype. The MIN and MAX functions can take other datatypes as a parameter. The next example shows the use with the DATE datatype and displays the first and last registration date in the STUDENT table.

```
SELECT MIN(registration_date) "First", MAX(registration_date) "Last"
  FROM student
First     Last
--------- ---------
22-JAN-03 23-FEB-03

1 row selected.
```

A less frequently used datatype for the MIN and MAX functions is the VARCHAR2 datatype. This query shows the minimum or maximum value of the DESCRIP-TION column and returns the first and last values in an alphabetized list of values.

```
SELECT MIN (description) AS MIN, MAX (description) AS MAX
  FROM course
MIN                              MAX
-------------------------------  -------------------------
Advanced Java Programming        Unix Tips and Techniques

1 row selected.
```

(The capital letter "A" is equal to the ASCII value 65, "B" is 66, and so on. Lowercase letters, numbers, and characters all have their own ASCII values. Therefore, MIN and MAX can be used to evaluate a character's respective first and last letters in alphabetical order.)

AGGREGATE FUNCTIONS AND NULLS

All the aggregate functions you have learned about so far ignore null values except for the COUNT(*) function. Use the NVL or COALESCE function to substitute for any null values. Aggregate functions always return a row. Even if the query returns no rows, the result is simply one row with a null value; the COUNT function always returns either a zero or a number.

AGGREGATE FUNCTIONS AND CASE

Placing a CASE expression within an aggregate function can be useful, if you want to manipulate or select specific values before applying the aggreate function. For example, the following SQL statement shows the computation of the average course cost. If the value in the PREREQUISITE column is null the value in the COST column is multiplied by 1.1; if the value is equal to 20, it is multiplied by 1.2; in all other cases the value retrieved in the COST column remains unchanged.

```
SELECT AVG(CASE WHEN prerequisite IS NOT NULL THEN cost*1.1
                WHEN prerequisite = 20 THEN cost*1.2
                ELSE cost
           END) AS avg
  FROM course
        AVG
----------
1301.81034

1 row selected.
```

AGGREGATE FUNCTION SYNTAX

Table 5.1 lists the most commonly used aggregate functions and their corresponding syntax. As you may notice, you can use the DISTINCT keyword with all these functions to only evaluate the distinct values. The ALL keyword is the default option and evaluates all rows. The DISTINCT keyword is really only useful for the AVG, SUM, and COUNT functions.

Table 5.1 ■ Commonly Used Aggregate Functions

Function	Purpose
COUNT({* | [DISTINCT|ALL] expression)	Counts number of rows. The wildcard (*) option includes duplicates and null values.
SUM([DISTINCT|ALL] value)	Computes total of a value, ignores nulls.
AVG([DISTINCT|ALL] value)	Average of a value, ignores nulls.
MIN([DISTINCT|ALL] expression)	Determines the minimum value of an expression, ignores nulls.
MAX([DISTINCT|ALL] expression)	Determines the maximum value of an expression, ignores nulls.

LAB 5.1 EXERCISES

5.1.1 USE AGGREGATE FUNCTIONS IN A SQL STATEMENT

a) Write a SELECT statement to determine how many courses do not have a prerequisite.

b) Write a SELECT statement to determine the total number of students enrolled. Count students only once, no matter how many courses they are enrolled in.

c) Determine the average cost for all courses. If the course cost contains a null value, substitute the value 0.

d) Write a SELECT statement to determine the date of the most recent enrollment.

LAB 5.1 EXERCISE ANSWERS

5.1.1 ANSWERS

a) Write a SELECT statement to determine how many courses do not have a pre-requisite.

Answer: The COUNT function is used to count the number of rows in the COURSE table where the values in the PREREQUISITE column are null.

```
SELECT COUNT(*)
  FROM course
 WHERE prerequisite IS NULL
  COUNT(*)
---------
        4
```

```
1 row selected.
```

b) Write a SELECT statement to determine the total number of students enrolled. Count students only once, no matter how many courses they are enrolled in.

Answer: DISTINCT is used in conjunction with the COUNT function to count distinct students, regardless of how many times they appear in the ENROLLMENT table.

```
SELECT COUNT(DISTINCT student_id)
  FROM enrollment
COUNT(DISTINCTSTUDENT_ID)
-------------------------
                      165
```

```
1 row selected.
```

c) Determine the average cost for all courses. If the course cost contains a null value, substitute the value 0.

Answer: Both the NVL and the COALESCE function substitute any null value with a zero. The NVL or COALESCE function must be nested inside the AVG function.

```
SELECT AVG(NVL(cost, 0))
  FROM course
AVG(NVL(COST,0))
----------------
          1158.5
```

```
1 row selected.
```

or:

```
SELECT AVG(COALESCE(cost, 0))
   FROM course
```

If you do not substitute the nulls for the zero value, the average course cost returns a different, more accurate, result.

```
SELECT AVG(cost)
   FROM course
AVG(COST)
---------
1198.4483

1 row selected.
```

d) Write a SELECT statement to determine the date of the most recent enrollment.

Answer: The MAX function determines the most recent value in the ENROLL_DATE column of the ENROLLMENT table.

```
SELECT MAX(enroll_date)
   FROM enrollment
MAX(ENROL
---------
21-FEB-03

1 row selected.
```

LAB 5.1 SELF-REVIEW QUESTIONS

In order to test your progress, you should be able to answer the following questions.

1) How many of these functions are aggregate functions: AVG, COUNT, SUM, ROUND?

   a) _____ One
   b) _____ Two
   c) _____ Three
   d) _____ Four

2) Choose the correct question for the following SQL statement:

```
SELECT NVL(MAX(modified_date),
       TO_DATE('12-MAR-2005', 'DD-MON-YYYY'))
  FROM enrollment
```

a) _____ Display the date when a STUDENT table was last modified.

b) _____ Display the date a STUDENT record was last modified. Replace any null value with the date March 12, 2005.

c) _____ Show the date a record in the ENROLLMENT table was last modified. If the result returns a null value, display March 12, 2005.

d) _____ For all the ENROLLMENT records show the date 12-Mar-2005.

3) An aggregate function can be applied on a single row.

a) _____ True

b) _____ False

4) The following SQL statement contains an error:

```
SELECT AVG(*)
  FROM course
```

a) _____ True

b) _____ False

5) The following SQL statement determines the average of all capacities in the SECTION table:

```
SELECT AVG(DISTINCT capacity)
  FROM section
```

a) _____ True

b) _____ False

6) The following SQL statement contains an error:

```
SELECT SUM(capacity*1.5)
  FROM section
```

a) _____ True

b) _____ False

Answers appear in Appendix A, Section 5.1.

LAB 5.2

THE GROUP BY AND HAVING CLAUSES

LAB OBJECTIVES

After this lab, you will be able to:

✔ Use the GROUP BY and HAVING Clauses

THE GROUP BY CLAUSE

The GROUP BY clause determines how the rows are grouped. The aggregate function together with the GROUP BY clause shows the aggregate value for each group. For example, for all the different locations you can determine the number of rows or the average, minimum, maximum, or total capacity.

To understand the result of the GROUP BY clause without an aggregate function, compare it to that of the DISTINCT clause.

The following two queries will return the same result, which is a distinct listing of the values in the LOCATION column.

```
SELECT DISTINCT location
   FROM section
```

Or:

```
SELECT location
   FROM section
 GROUP BY location
LOCATION
--------
H310
L206
...
M311
```

M500

12 rows selected.

If you want to expand on this example and now include how many times each respective location value is listed in the SECTION table, you add the COUNT(*) function in the query.

```
SELECT location, COUNT(*)
  FROM section
 GROUP BY location
LOCATION    COUNT(*)
--------    ----------
H310               1
L206               1
L210              10
L211               3
L214              15
...
M500               1
```

12 rows selected.

Essentially, the GROUP BY clause and the aggregate function work hand-in-hand. Based on the distinct values as listed in the GROUP BY clause, the aggregate function returns the result.

We can further expand the SQL query to determine other values for the distinct LOCATION column. For example, the next statement adds the aggregate functions SUM, MIN, and MAX to the SELECT list. For each distinct location you see the total capacities with the SUM function, which adds up all the values in the CAPACITY column. The MIN and MAX functions return the minimum and maximum capacity for each respective location.

```
SELECT location, COUNT(*), SUM(capacity) AS sum,
       MIN(capacity) AS min, MAX(capacity) AS max
  FROM section
 GROUP BY location
LOCATION COUNT(*)    SUM    MIN    MAX
-------- --------  ------ ------ ------
H310            1      15     15     15
L206            1      15     15     15
L210           10     200     15     25
L211            3      55     15     25
L214           15     275     15     25
...
M500            1      25     25     25
```

12 rows selected.

You can validate the result of the query by looking at one of the rows. For example, the row with the LOCATION value of L211 has three rows according to the COUNT function. The total of all the values in the CAPACITY column is 55 (25 + 15 + 15). The minimum value of the CAPACITY column is 15 and the maximum value is 25.

```
SELECT location, capacity, section_id
  FROM section
 WHERE location = 'L211'
```

LOCATION	CAPACITY	SECTION_ID
L211	25	119
L211	15	133
L211	15	153

3 rows selected.

GROUPING BY MULTIPLE COLUMNS

The next query applies the aggregate functions to the distinct values of the LOCATION and the INSTRUCTOR_ID columns; therefore, the statement returns more rows than the previous GROUP BY query.

```
SELECT location, instructor_id,
       COUNT(*), SUM(capacity) AS sum,
       MIN(capacity) AS min, MAX(capacity) AS max
  FROM section
 GROUP BY location, instructor_id
```

LOCATION	INSTRUCTOR_ID	COUNT(*)	SUM	MIN	MAX
H310	103	1	15	15	15
L206	108	1	15	15	15
L210	101	1	15	15	15
L210	103	2	40	15	25
L210	104	1	25	25	25
L210	105	2	40	15	25
L210	106	1	25	25	25
L210	108	3	55	15	25
L214	102	4	70	15	25
...					
M500	102	1	25	25	25

39 rows selected.

When you examine the result, you notice there are six rows for the L210 location. For this location, each row has a different INSTRUCTOR_ID value. On each of these six distinct LOCATION and INSTRUCTOR_ID combinations, the aggregate functions are applied. For example, the first row has only one row with this

LOCATION and INSTRUCTOR_ID combination and the second row has two rows, as you see from the number in the COUNT(*) column. Once again, you can validate the result by issuing an individual query against the SECTION table.

```
SELECT location, instructor_id, capacity, section_id
  FROM section
 WHERE location = 'L210'
 ORDER BY 1, 2
LOCATION INSTRUCTOR_ID   CAPACITY SECTION_ID
-------- -------------  ---------- ----------
L210               101         15        117
L210               103         15         81
L210               103         25        150
L210               104         25         96
L210               105         25         91
L210               105         15        129
L210               106         25         84
L210               108         15         86
L210               108         15        155
L210               108         25        124

10 rows selected.
```

**LAB
5.2**

ORACLE ERROR ORA-00979

Every column you list in the SELECT list, except the aggregate function column itself, must be repeated in the GROUP BY clause. Following is the error Oracle returns when you violate this rule:

```
SQL> SELECT location, instructor_id,
  2         COUNT(*), SUM(capacity) AS sum,
  3         MIN(capacity) AS min, MAX(capacity) AS max
  4    FROM section
  5   GROUP BY location
  6  /
SELECT location, instructor_id,
                 *
ERROR at line 1:
ORA-00979: not a GROUP BY expression
```

The error message indicates that Oracle does not know how to process this query. The query lists the LOCATION and the INSTRUCTOR_ID column in the SELECT list, but only the LOCATION column in the GROUP BY clause. Essentially, Oracle is confused about the instruction. The GROUP BY clause lists only the LOCATION column, which determines the distinct values. But the statement fails to specify what to do with the INSTRUCTOR_ID column.

SORTING DATA

The GROUP BY clause groups the rows, but it does not necessarily sort the results in any particular order. To change the order, use the ORDER BY clause, which follows the GROUP BY clause. The columns used in the ORDER BY clause must appear in the SELECT list, which is unlike the normal use of ORDER BY. In the following example, the result is sorted in descending order by the total capacity. Note that you can also use the column alias in the ORDER BY clause.

```
SELECT location "Location", instructor_id,
       COUNT(location) "Total Locations",
       SUM(capacity) "Total Capacity"
  FROM section
 GROUP BY location, instructor_id
 ORDER BY "Total Capacity" DESC
```

THE HAVING CLAUSE

The purpose of the HAVING clause is to eliminate groups, just as the WHERE clause is used to eliminate rows. Using the previous example, the applied HAVING clause restricts the result set to locations with a total capacity value of more than 50 students.

```
SELECT location "Location", instructor_id,
       COUNT(location) "Total Locations",
       SUM(capacity) "Total Capacity"
  FROM section
 GROUP BY location, instructor_id
HAVING SUM(capacity) > 50
 ORDER BY "Total Capacity" DESC
```

Location	INSTRUCTOR_ID	Total Locations	Total Capacity
L509	106	5	115
L509	101	4	85
L507	101	3	75
L507	107	3	75
L509	105	3	75
...			
L214	106	3	55

14 rows selected.

THE WHERE AND HAVING CLAUSES

As previously mentioned, the HAVING clause eliminates groups that do not satisfy its condition. This is in contrast to the WHERE clause, which eliminates rows even before the aggregate functions and the GROUP BY and HAVING clauses are applied:

```
SELECT location "Location", instructor_id,
       COUNT(location) "Total Locations",
       SUM(capacity) "Total Capacity"
  FROM section
 WHERE section_no IN (2, 3)
 GROUP BY location, instructor_id
HAVING SUM(capacity) > 50
Location INSTRUCTOR_ID Total Locations Total Capacity
-------- ------------- --------------- --------------
L214               104               3             55

1 row selected.
```

The WHERE clause is executed by the database first, narrowing the result set to rows in the SECTION table where the SECTION_NO equals either 2 or 3 (i.e., the second or third section of a course). The next step is to group the result by the columns listed in the GROUP BY clause and to apply the aggregate functions. Last, the HAVING condition is tested against the groups. Only those rows with a total capacity of greater than 50 are returned in the result.

MULTIPLE CONDITIONS IN THE HAVING CLAUSE

The HAVING clause can use multiple operators to further eliminate any groups, as in this example. The columns used in the HAVING clause must be found either in the GROUP BY clause or they must be aggregate functions. In the following example, you notice that the aggregate COUNT function is not mentioned in the SELECT list, yet the HAVING clause refers to it. The second condition of the HAVING clause chooses only location groups with a starting value of L5. In this particular example, it is preferable to move this condition to the WHERE clause because it will eliminate the rows even before the groups are formed and therefore execute the statement faster.

```
SELECT location "Location",
       SUM(capacity) "Total Capacity"
  FROM section
 WHERE section_no = 3
 GROUP BY location
HAVING (COUNT(location) > 3
        AND location LIKE 'L5%')
```

```
Location   Total Capacity
---------- --------------
L507                  100
L509                  175
```

`2 rows selected.`

CONSTANTS AND FUNCTIONS WITHOUT PARAMETERS

Any constant, such as a text or number literal or a function that does not take any parameters, such as the SYSDATE function, may be listed in the SELECT list without being repeated in the GROUP BY clause. This does not cause the ORA-00979 error message. The next query shows the text literal 'Hello', the number literal 1, and the SYSDATE function in the SELECT list of the query. You will notice that these expressions do not need to be repeated in the GROUP BY clause.

```
SELECT 'Hello', 1, SYSDATE, course_no "Course #",
       COUNT(*)
  FROM section
 GROUP BY course_no
HAVING COUNT(*) = 5
```

```
'HELL          1 SYSDATE    Course #  COUNT(*)
----- --------- --------- --------- ---------
Hello          1 08-APR-02       100         5
Hello          1 08-APR-02       122         5
Hello          1 08-APR-02       125         5
```

`3 rows selected.`

ORDER OF THE CLAUSES

The HAVING clause can also appear before the GROUP BY clause, but this is rarely seen in practice.

```
SELECT course_no "Course #",
       AVG(capacity) "Avg. Capacity",
       ROUND(AVG(capacity)) "Rounded Avg. Capacity"
  FROM section
HAVING COUNT(*) = 2
 GROUP BY course_no
```

NESTING AGGREGATE FUNCTIONS

Aggregate functions can also be nested, as in the following example. The query returns the largest number of students that enrolled in an individual section. The COUNT function determines a count for all the sections based on the GROUP BY clause, which lists the SECTION_ID. Against this result, the MAX function is applied and it returns 12 as the largest of the values. In other words, 12 students is the largest number of students enrolled in an individual section.

```
SELECT MAX(COUNT(*))
  FROM enrollment
 GROUP BY section_id
MAX(COUNT(*))
-------------
           12

1 row selected.
```

TAKING AGGREGATE FUNCTIONS
AND GROUPS TO THE NEXT LEVEL

All of the SQL statements so far have focused on a single table. You will learn how to avoid potential pitfalls when joining tables and applying aggregate functions in Chapter 7, "Subqueries."

In Chapter 16, "Exploring Data Warehousing Features," you will learn about many additional aggregate and analytical functions such as MEDIAN and RANK, which allow you to analyze data even further. Some of this functionality permits you to avoid the ORA-00979 error through the use of a special analytical clause. Chapter 16 also introduces you to the ROLLUP and CUBE operators so that you can perform multilevel aggregations.

LAB 5.2 EXERCISES

5.2.1 USE THE GROUP BY AND HAVING CLAUSES

    a) Show a list of prerequisites and count how many times each appears in the COURSE table. Order the result by the PREREQUISITE column.

b) Write a SELECT statement showing student IDs and the number of courses they are enrolled in. Show only those enrolled in more than two classes.

c) Write a SELECT statement that displays the average room capacity for each course. Display the average expressed to the nearest whole number in another column. Use column aliases for each column selected.

d) Write the same SELECT statement as in the previous question except for courses with exactly two sections. Hint: Think about the relationship between the COURSE and SECTION tables, specifically how many times a course can be represented in the SECTION table.

LAB 5.2 EXERCISE ANSWERS

5.2.1 ANSWERS

a) Show a list of prerequisites and count how many times each appears in the COURSE table. Order the result by the PREREQUISITE column.

Answer: The COUNT function and GROUP BY clause are used to count distinct prerequisites. The last row of the result set shows the number of prerequisites with a null value.

```
SELECT prerequisite, COUNT(*)
  FROM course
 GROUP BY prerequisite
 ORDER BY prerequisite
PREREQUISITE  COUNT(*)
------------  ---------
         10          1
         20          5
...
        350          2
        420          1
                     4
```

17 rows selected.

NULLS AND THE GROUP BY CLAUSE

If there are null values in a column and you group on the column, all the null values are considered equal. This is different from the typical handling of nulls, where one null is not equal to another. The aforementioned query and result shows that there are four null prerequisites. The nulls always appear last in the default ascending sort order.

You can change the default ordering of the nulls with the NULLS FIRST option in the ORDER BY clause as you see in the next statement. When you look at the result set, you see that the nulls are now first, followed by the default ascending sort order.

```
SELECT prerequisite, COUNT(*)
  FROM course
 GROUP BY prerequisite
 ORDER BY prerequisite NULLS FIRST
PREREQUISITE   COUNT(*)
------------   ---------
                      4
         10           1
...
        350           2
        420           1

17 rows selected.
```

b) Write a SELECT statement showing student IDs and the number of courses they are enrolled in. Show only those enrolled in more than two classes.

Answer: To obtain the distinct students, use the STUDENT_ID column in the GROUP BY clause. For each of the groups, count records for each student with the COUNT function. Eliminate only those students enrolled in more than two sections from the groups with the HAVING clause.

```
SELECT student_id, COUNT(*)
  FROM enrollment
 GROUP BY student_id
HAVING COUNT(*) > 2
STUDENT_ID   COUNT(*)
----------   ---------
       124          4
       184          3
...
```

```
238        3
250        3
```

7 rows selected.

c) Write a SELECT statement that displays the average room capacity for each course. Display the average expressed to the nearest whole number in another column. Use column aliases for each column selected.

Answer: The SELECT statement uses the AVG function and the ROUND function. The GROUP BY clause ensures that the average capacity is displayed for each course.

```
SELECT course_no "Course #",
       AVG(capacity) "Avg. Capacity",
       ROUND(AVG(capacity)) "Rounded Avg. Capacity"
  FROM section
 GROUP BY course_no
```

Course #	Avg Capacity	Rounded Avg Capacity
10	15	15
20	20	20
25	22.777778	23
...		
350	21.666667	22
420	25	25
450	25	25

28 rows selected.

The previous SQL statement uses nested functions. Nested functions always work from the inside out, so the AVG(capacity) function is evaluated first, and its result is the parameter for the ROUND function. ROUND's optional precision parameter is not used, so the result of AVG(capacity) rounds to a precision of zero, or no decimal places.

A COMMON ERROR YOU CAN AVOID

Sometimes you may copy the columns from the SELECT list—with the exception of the aggregate function, of course—down to the GROUP BY clause. After all, cut and paste saves a lot of typing. You then may end up with an error such as the next one. The error message on ORA-00933 "SQL command not properly ended" may leave you clueless as to how to solve the problem.

```
SQL> SELECT course_no "Course #",
  2          AVG(capacity) "Avg. Capacity",
  3          ROUND(AVG(capacity)) "Rounded Avg. Capacity"
```

```
4     FROM section
5   GROUP BY course_no "Course #"
6  /
GROUP BY course_no "Course #"
               *
ERROR at line 5:
ORA-00933: SQL command not properly ended
```

Actually, to resolve the error, you must exclude column aliases in the GROUP BY clause. Notice how the "Course #" column alias remained in the GROUP BY clause.

 Column aliases are not allowed in the GROUP BY clause.

d) Write the same SELECT statement as in the previous question except for courses with exactly two sections. *Hint:* Think about the relationship between the COURSE and SECTION tables, specifically how many times a course can be represented in the SECTION table.

Answer:The HAVING clause is added to limit the result set to courses appearing exactly twice.

```
SELECT course_no "Course #",
       AVG(capacity) "Avg. Capacity",
       ROUND(AVG(capacity)) "Rounded Avg. Capacity"
  FROM section
 GROUP BY course_no
HAVING COUNT(*) = 2
```

Course #	Avg. Capacity	Rounded Avg. Capacity
132	25	25
145	25	25
146	20	20
230	13.5	14
240	12.5	13

5 rows selected.

Notice the COUNT(*) function in the HAVING clause does not appear as part of the SELECT list. You can eliminate any groups in the HAVING clause using aggregate functions, even if this aggregate function is not mentioned in the SELECT list.

LAB 5.2 SELF-REVIEW QUESTIONS

In order to test your progress, you should be able to answer the following questions.

LAB 5.2

1) Which column(s) must be included in the GROUP BY clause of the following SELECT statement?

```
SELECT NVL(MAX(final_grade),0), section_id,
       MAX(created_date)
  FROM enrollment
 GROUP BY _____
```

   a) _____ FINAL_GRADE
   b) _____ SECTION_ID
   c) _____ CREATED_DATE
   d) _____ All three
   e) _____ None of the above

2) You can combine DISTINCT and a GROUP BY clause in the same SELECT statement.

   a) _____ True
   b) _____ False

3) There is an error in the following SELECT statement.

```
SELECT COUNT(student_id)
  FROM enrollment
 WHERE COUNT(student_id) > 1
```

   a) _____ True
   b) _____ False

4) How many rows in the following SELECT statement will return a null prerequisite?

```
SELECT prerequisite, COUNT(*)
  FROM course
 WHERE prerequisite IS NULL
 GROUP BY prerequisite
```

   a) _____ None
   b) _____ One
   c) _____ Multiple

5) Determine the error in the following SELECT statement.

```
SELECT COUNT(*)
  FROM section
 GROUP BY course_no
```

a) _____ No error
b) _____ Line 1
c) _____ Line 2
d) _____ Line 3

Answers appear in Appendix A, Section 5.2.

CHAPTER 5

TEST YOUR THINKING

The projects in this section are meant to have you utilize all of the skills that you have acquired throughout this chapter. The answers to these projects can be found at the companion Web site to this book, located at: *http://authors.phptr.com/rischert3e*. Visit the Web site periodically to share and discuss your answers.

1)   List the order in which the WHERE, GROUP BY, and HAVING clauses are executed by the database in the following SQL statement.

```
SELECT section_id, COUNT(*), final_grade
  FROM enrollment
 WHERE TRUNC(enroll_date) >
       TO_DATE('2/16/2003', 'MM/DD/YYYY')
 GROUP BY section_id, final_grade
HAVING COUNT(*) > 5
```

2)   Display a count of all the different course costs in the COURSE table.

3)   Determine the number of students living in zip code 10025.

4)   Show all the different companies for which students work. Display only companies where more than four students are employed.

5)   List how many sections each instructor teaches.

6)   Formulate the question for the following statement:

```
SELECT COUNT(*), start_date_time, location
  FROM section
 GROUP BY start_date_time, location
HAVING COUNT(*) > 1
```

7)   Determine the highest grade achieved for the midterm within each section.

8)   A table called CUSTOMER_ORDER contains 5,993 rows with a total order amount of $10,993,333.98 based on the orders from 4,500 customers. Given this scenario, how many row(s) do you think the following query returns?

```
SELECT SUM(order_amount) AS "Order Total"
  FROM customer_order
```

CHAPTER 6

EQUIJOINS

So far, you have written SQL statements against a single table. In this chapter you will learn about joining tables, one of the most important aspects of the SQL language. The *equijoin* is by far the most common form of join and it allows you to connect two or more tables. Equijoins are based on equality of values in one or more columns. You will learn about other types of joins in Chapter 9, "Complex Joins."

LAB 6.1

THE TWO-TABLE JOIN

LAB OBJECTIVES

After this lab, you will be able to:
- ✔ Write Simple Join Constructs
- ✔ Narrow Down Your Result Set
- ✔ Understand the Cartesian Product

In this lab, you will join information from two tables into one meaningful result. Suppose you want to list the course number, course description, section number, location, and instructor ID for each section. This data is found in two separate tables: The course number and description are in the COURSE table; the SECTION table contains the course number, section number, location, and instructor ID. One approach is to query the individual tables and record the results on paper, then match every course number in the COURSE table with the corresponding course number in the SECTION table. The other approach is to formulate a SQL statement that accomplishes the join for you.

Figure 6.1 shows a partial listing of the COURSE table. Missing columns and rows are indicated with the three periods (...). The primary key of the COURSE table is the COURSE_NO.

Figure 6.2 shows a partial listing of the SECTION table. The COURSE_NO column is the foreign key to the COURSE table.

COURSE_NO	DESCRIPTION	...	MODIFIED_DATE
10	DP Overview	...	05-APR-03
20	Intro to Computers	...	05-APR-03
25	Intro to Programming	...	05-APR-03
80	Structured Programming Technique	...	05-APR-03
100	Hands-On Windows	...	05-APR-03
120	Intro to Java Programming	...	05-APR-03
...	...	...	...

Figure 6.1 ■ Excerpt of the COURSE table.

SECTION_ID	COURSE_NO	SECTION_NO	...	LOCATION
80	10	2	....	L214
81	20	2	....	L210
82	20	4	...	L214
83	20	7	...	L509
84	20	8	...	L210
85	25	1	...	M311
86	25	2	...	L210
87	25	3	...	L507
88	25	4	...	L214
89	25	5	...	L509
90	25	6	...	L509
91	25	7	...	L210
92	25	8	...	L509
93	25	9	...	L507
...	...	...	...	...
141	100	1	...	L214

Figure 6.2 ■ Excerpt of the SECTION table.

Examine the result set listed in Figure 6.3. For example, for course number 10, one section exists in the SECTION table. The result of the match is one row. Looking at course number 20, Intro to Computers, you observe that this course has multiple rows in the SECTION table because there are multiple classes/sections for the same course. You may also notice that course number 80, Structured Programming Techniques, is missing from the result. This course number has no matching entry in the SECTION table and therefore this row is not in the result.

COURSE_NO	SECTION_NO	DESCRIPTION	LOCATION	INSTRUCTOR_ID
10	2	DP Overview	L214	102
20	2	Intro to Computers	L210	103
20	4	Intro to Computers	L214	104
20	7	Intro to Computers	L509	105
20	8	Intro to Computers	L210	106
25	1	Intro to Programming	M311	107
25	2	Intro to Programming	L210	108
25	3	Intro to Programming	L507	101
25	4	Intro to Programming	L214	102
25	5	Intro to Programming	L509	103
25	6	Intro to Programming	L509	104
25	7	Intro to Programming	L210	105
25	8	Intro to Programming	L509	106
25	9	Intro to Programming	L507	107
100	1	Hands-On Windows	L214	102
...	...	...	...	...

Figure 6.3 ■ Result of join between COURSE and SECTION table.

STEPS TO FORMULATE THE SQL STATEMENT

Before you write the SQL join statement, first choose the columns you want to include in the result. Next, determine the tables to which the columns belong. Then, identify the common columns between the tables.

Last, determine if there is a one-to-one or a one-to-many relationship among the column values. Joins are typically used to join between the primary key and the foreign key. In the previous example, the COURSE_NO column in the COURSE table is the primary key, and the column COURSE_NO in the SECTION table is the foreign key. This represents a one-to-many relationship between the tables. (When you join tables related through a many-to-many relationship, it yields a *Cartesian product*. There is more on the Cartesian product later in this chapter.)

Following is the SQL statement that achieves the result shown in Figure 6.3. It looks much like the previous SELECT statements you have written so far, but two tables, separated by commas, are listed in the FROM clause.

```
SELECT course.course_no, section_no, description,
       location, instructor_id
  FROM course, section
 WHERE course.course_no = section.course_no
```

The WHERE clause formulates the *join criteria*, also called the *join condition*, between the two tables using the common COURSE_NO column. Since this is an equijoin, the values in the common columns must equal each other for a row to be displayed in the result set. Each COURSE_NO value from the COURSE table must match a COURSE_NO value from the SECTION table. To differentiate between columns of the same name, *qualify* the columns by prefixing the column with the table name and a period. Otherwise, Oracle returns an error—"ORA-00918: column ambiguously defined."

Instead of displaying the COURSE_NO column from the COURSE table in the SELECT list, you can use the COURSE_NO column from the SECTION table. Because it is an equijoin, it returns the same result.

The Whole Truth

The order in which the tables are listed in the FROM clause can have an effect on the efficiency of the SQL statement, but it has no effect on the query result. You will learn about this in Chapter 17, "SQL Optimization."

TABLE ALIAS

Instead of using the table name as a prefix to differentiate between the columns, you can use a *table alias,* which qualifies the table using a short abbreviation.

```
SELECT c.course_no, s.section_no, c.description,
       s.location, s.instructor_id
  FROM course c, section s
 WHERE c.course_no = s.course_no
```

The table alias names are arbitrary. However, you cannot use any Oracle *reserved words.* (Reserved words have a special meaning in the SQL language or in the Oracle database and are typically associated with a SQL command. For example, SELECT and WHERE are reserved words.) It is best to keep the name short and simple, as in this example. The COURSE table has the alias c, and the SECTION table has the alias s.

 To easily identify the source table of a column and to improve the readability of a join statement, it is best to qualify all column names with the table alias. Furthermore, this avoids any future ambiguities that may arise if a new column with the same name is added later. Without a qualified table alias, a subsequently issued SQL statement referencing both tables results in the Oracle error message "ORA-00918: column ambiguously defined."

NARROWING DOWN YOUR RESULT SET

The previous SQL statement lists all the rows in the SECTION and COURSE tables with matching COURSE_NO values. If you want to narrow down the criteria to specific rows, you can expand the WHERE clause to include additional conditions. The next statement chooses only those courses and their respective sections where the DESCRIPTION column starts with the text "Intro to".

```
SELECT c.course_no, s.section_no, c.description,
       s.location, s.instructor_id
  FROM course c, section s
 WHERE c.course_no = s.course_no
   AND c.description LIKE 'Intro to%'
```

NULLS AND JOINS

In an equijoin, a null value in the common column has the effect that the row is not included in the result. Look at the foreign key column ZIP on the INSTRUCTOR table, which allows nulls.

First, query for records with a null value.

```
SELECT instructor_id, zip, last_name, first_name
  FROM instructor
 WHERE zip IS NULL
INSTRUCTOR_ID ZIP   LAST_NAME  FIRST_NAME
------------- ----- ---------- ----------
          110       Willig     Irene
```

1 row selected.

Next, formulate the join to the ZIPCODE table via the ZIP column. Observe that instructor Irene Willig does not appear in the result.

```
SELECT i.instructor_id, i.zip, i.last_name, i.first_name
  FROM instructor i, zipcode z
 WHERE i.zip = z.zip
INSTRUCTOR_ID ZIP   LAST_NAME  FIRST_NAME
------------- ----- ---------- ----------
          101 10015 Hanks      Fernand
          105 10015 Morris     Anita
          109 10015 Chow       Rick
          102 10025 Wojick     Tom
          103 10025 Schorin    Nina
          106 10025 Smythe     Todd
          108 10025 Lowry      Charles
          107 10005 Frantzen   Marilyn
          104 10035 Pertez     Gary
```

9 rows selected.

A null value is not equal to any other value, including another null value. In this case, the zip code of Irene Willig's record is null; therefore, this row is not included in the result. In Chapter 9, "Complex Joins," you will learn how to include null values by formulating an *outer join* condition.

ANSI JOIN SYNTAX

Starting with 9*i* Oracle implemented a number of additions to the SQL language to conform to many aspects of the ANSI SQL/92 and SQL:1999 standards. The advantage of the ANSI join syntax over the traditional comma-separated tables FROM clause is that SQL queries can run unmodified against other non-Oracle, ANSI compliant databases.

THE INNER JOIN

The term *inner join* is used to express a join that satisfies the join condition. Typically, the join condition is based on equality, thus creating an equijoin. (The inner join is in contrast to the outer join. Besides the matched rows, the outer join also includes the unmatched rows from two tables.)

The ANSI syntax, compared to the previously discussed join syntax, has a number of differences. One is the JOIN keyword, which replaces the comma between the tables and identifies the tables to-be-joined.

The keyword INNER is optional and typically omitted. To express a join condition, you can specify either the USING condition or the ON condition.

THE USING CONDITION   The USING condition, also referred as the USING clause, identifies the common column between the tables. Here the common column is the COURSE_NO column, which has the same name and compatible datatype in both tables. An equijoin is always assumed with the USING clause.

```
SELECT course_no, s.section_no, c.description,
       s.location, s.instructor_id
  FROM course c JOIN section s
 USING (course_no)
```

Alternatively, you can include the optional INNER keyword, and as mentioned, this is usually omitted.

```
SELECT course_no, s.section_no, c.description,
       s.location, s.instructor_id
  FROM course c INNER JOIN section s
 USING (course_no)
```

The following query will not execute because you cannot use a table alias name with this syntax. The USING syntax implies that the column names are identical. The Oracle error identifies the C.COURSE_NO column as the column in the USING clause with the problem.

```
SQL> SELECT course_no, s.section_no, c.description,
  2         s.location, s.instructor_id
  3    FROM course c JOIN section s
  4   USING (c.course_no)
  5  /
 USING (c.course_no)
        *
ERROR at line 4:
ORA-01748: only simple column names allowed here
```

The next query shows the COURSE_NO column in the SELECT list prefixed with the alias name, thus resulting in an error as well. This alias must also be eliminated to successfully run the query.

```
SQL> SELECT c.course_no, s.section_no, c.description,
  2          s.location, s.instructor_id
  3    FROM course c JOIN section s
  4*   USING (course_no)
SQL> /
SELECT c.course_no, s.section_no, c.description,
             *
ERROR at line 1:
ORA-25154: column part of USING clause cannot have qualifier
```

The next example illustrates the error you receive when you omit the parentheses around the column COURSE_NO in the USING clause.

```
SQL> SELECT c.course_no, s.section_no, c.description,
  2          s.location, s.instructor_id
  3    FROM course c JOIN section s
  4    USING course_no
  5   /
  USING course_no
        *
ERROR at line 4:
ORA-00906: missing left parenthesis
```

THE ON CONDITION   In case the column names on the tables are different, you use the ON condition, also referred to as the ON clause. The next query is identical in functionality to the previous query, but is now expressed with the ON condition and the column name is qualified with the alias both in the SELECT list as well as in the ON condition. This syntax allows for conditions other than equality and different column names; you will see many such examples in Chapter 9, "Complex Joins."

```
SELECT c.course_no, s.section_no, c.description,
       s.location, s.instructor_id
  FROM course c JOIN section s
    ON (c.course_no = s.course_no)
```

The pair of parentheses around the ON condition is optional. When comparing this syntax to the traditional join syntax there are not many differences other than the ON clause and the JOIN keyword.

ADDITIONAL **WHERE** CLAUSE CONDITIONS   The ON or the USING conditions let you specify the join condition separate from any other WHERE condition. One of the advantages of the ANSI join syntax is that it separates the join condition from the filtering WHERE clause condition.

```
SELECT c.course_no, s.section_no, c.description,
       s.location, s.instructor_id
  FROM course c JOIN section s
    ON (c.course_no = s.course_no)
 WHERE description LIKE 'B%'
```

THE NATURAL JOIN

The natural join joins the tables based on the columns with the same name and datatype. Here there is no need to prefix the column name with the table alias and the join is indicated with the keywords NATURAL JOIN. There is not even a mention of which column(s) to join. This syntax figures out the common columns between the tables. Any use of the ON or the USING clause is not allowed with the NATURAL JOIN keywords and the common columns may not list a table alias.

```
SELECT course_no, s.section_no, c.description,
       s.location, s.instructor_id
  FROM course c NATURAL JOIN section s
```

```
no rows selected
```

You may be surprised that the query does not return any result. However, when you examine the two tables you notice that the COURSE_NO column is not the only column with a common name. The columns CREATED_BY, CREATED_DATE, MODIFIED_BY, and MODIFIED_DATE are also common to both tables. These columns record the name of the last user updating a row and the original user creating the row, including the respective date and time. The SQL statement does not return any results because there are no rows that have identical values for all five common columns.

 Using the natural join within a program is somewhat risky. There is always a chance for columns to be added to the table in the future that happen to have the same column name, and you may not get the desired result. Therefore, the natural join works best for ad hoc queries, but not for repeated use within programs.

CARTESIAN PRODUCT

The Cartesian product is rarely useful in the real world. It usually indicates either the WHERE clause has no joining columns or that multiple rows from one table match multiple rows in another table; in other words, it indicates a many-to-many relationship.

To illustrate the multiplication effect of a Cartesian product, the following query joins the INSTRUCTOR table with the SECTION table. The INSTRUCTOR table contains 10 rows; the SECTION table has 78 rows. The multiplication of all the possible combinations results in 780 rows.

```
SELECT COUNT(*)
  FROM section, instructor
COUNT(*)
---------
      780
```

1 row selected.

Following is a partial listing of the rows showing all the different combinations of values between the two tables.

```
SELECT s.instructor_id s_instructor_id,
       i.instructor_id i_instructor_id
  FROM section s, instructor i
S_INSTRUCTOR_ID I_INSTRUCTOR_ID
--------------- ---------------
            101             101
            101             101
            101             101
            101             101
            101             101
            101             101
            101             101
            101             101
            101             101
            101             102
            101             102
            101             102
...
            108             110
            101             110
```

780 rows selected.

(If you wish to stop and examine the rows one screen at a time, you can use the SQL*Plus SET PAUSE ON command. This displays one screen at a time. To continue to the next screen, press the Enter key or the Next Page button in *i*SQL*Plus for *10g*. If you want to stop scrolling through the screens and return to the SQL> prompt, press CTRL + C. Remember to issue the SET PAUSE OFF command to stop the feature when you are done! Appendix C, "SQL*Plus Command Reference" has more details about the various SQL*Plus commands.)

THE ANSI STANDARD CROSS-JOIN

To formulate a Cartesian product using the ANSI JOIN syntax you use the keyword CROSS JOIN. It replaces the comma between the two tables. Because of the nature of the cross-join as the combination of all possible values, the SQL statement does not have a join criteria. The result is obviously identical to that of the Cartesian product.

```
SELECT COUNT(*)
  FROM section CROSS JOIN instructor
```

LAB 6.1 EXERCISES

6.1.1 WRITE SIMPLE JOIN CONSTRUCTS

a) For all students, display last name, city, state, and zip code. Show the result ordered by zip code.

b) Select the first and last names of all enrolled students and order by last name in ascending order.

6.1.2 NARROW DOWN YOUR RESULT SET

a) Execute the following SQL statement. Explain your observations about the WHERE clause and the resulting output.

```
SELECT c.course_no, c.description, s.section_no
  FROM course c, section s
 WHERE c.course_no = s.course_no
   AND c.prerequisite IS NULL
 ORDER BY c.course_no, s.section_no
```

b) Select the student ID, course number, enrollment date, and section ID for students who enrolled in course number 20 on January 30, 2003.

6.1.3 UNDERSTAND THE CARTESIAN PRODUCT

a) Select the students and instructors who live in the same zip code by joining on the common ZIP column. Order the result by the STUDENT_ID and INSTRUCTOR_ID columns. What do you observe?

LAB 6.1 EXERCISE ANSWERS

6.1.1 ANSWERS

a) For all students, display last name, city, state, and zip code. Show the result ordered by zip code.

Answer: The common column between the ZIPCODE table and the STUDENT table is the ZIP column. The ZIP column in both tables is defined as NOT NULL. For each row in the ZIPCODE table there may be zero, one, or multiple students living in one particular zip code. For each student's zip code there must be one matching row in the ZIPCODE table. Only those records that satisfy the equality condition of the join are returned.

```
SELECT s.last_name, s.zip, z.state, z.city
  FROM student s, zipcode z
 WHERE s.zip = z.zip
 ORDER BY s.zip
LAST_NAME                        ZIP   ST CITY
--------------------------       ----- -- ----------
Norman                           01247 MA North Adams
Kocka                            02124 MA Dorchester
...
Gilloon                          43224 OH Columbus
Snow                             48104 MI Ann Arbor

268 rows selected.
```

Because the ZIP column has the same name in both tables, you must qualify the column when you use the traditional join syntax. For simplicity, it is best to use an alias instead of the full table name because it saves you a lot of typing and improves readability. The ORDER BY clause lists the S.ZIP column, as does the SELECT clause. Choosing the Z.ZIP column instead of S.ZIP in the SELECT list or ORDER BY clause displays the same rows because the values in the two columns have to be equal to be included in the result.

You can also write the query with the ANSI join syntax instead and use the ON or the USING condition. If you use the ON condition, you must prefix the common columns with either their full table name or their table alias if one is specified.

```
SELECT s.last_name, s.zip, z.state, z.city
  FROM student s JOIN zipcode z
    ON (s.zip = z.zip)
 ORDER BY s.zip
```

If you choose the USING condition instead, do not alias the common column because this will cause an error.

```
SELECT s.last_name, zip, z.state, z.city
  FROM student s JOIN zipcode z
 USING (zip)
 ORDER BY zip
```

b) Select the first and last names of all enrolled students and order by last name in ascending order.

Answer: You need to join the ENROLLMENT and STUDENT tables. Only students who are enrolled have one or multiple rows in the ENROLLMENT table.

```
SELECT s.first_name, s.last_name, s.student_id
  FROM student s, enrollment e
 WHERE s.student_id = e.student_id
 ORDER BY s.last_name
```

FIRST_NAME	LAST_NAME	STUDENT_ID
Mardig	Abdou	119
Suzanne M.	Abid	257
...		
Salewa	Zuckerberg	184
Salewa	Zuckerberg	184
Salewa	Zuckerberg	184
Freedon	annunziato	206

226 rows selected.

Note that student Salewa Zuckerberg with STUDENT_ID 184 is returned three times. This is because Salewa Zuckerberg is enrolled in three sections. When the SECTION_ID column is included in the SELECT list, this fact becomes self-evident in the result set.

However, if you are not interested in the SECTION_ID and you want to only list the names without the duplication, use DISTINCT in the SELECT statement.

```
SELECT DISTINCT s.first_name, s.last_name, s.student_id
  FROM student s, enrollment e
 WHERE s.student_id = e.student_id
 ORDER BY s.last_name
```

The STUDENT_ID column is required in the SELECT clause because there may be students with the same first and last name but who are, in fact, different individuals. The STUDENT_ID column differentiates between these students; after all, it's the primary key that is unique to each individual row in the STUDENT table.

You may also notice that the student with the last name 'annunziato' is the last row. Because the last name is in lowercase, it has a higher sort order. (See Lab 3.3 regarding the sort order values and the ASCII function.)

If you use the ANSI syntax your SQL statement may look similar to this statement.

```
SELECT s.first_name, s.last_name, s.student_id
  FROM student s JOIN enrollment e
    ON (s.student_id = e.student_id)
 ORDER BY s.last_name
```

Or you may write the statement with the USING clause. In this particular query all aliases are omitted, which has the disadvantage that you cannot easily recognize the source table for each column.

```
SELECT first_name, last_name, student_id
  FROM student JOIN enrollment
 USING (student_id)
 ORDER BY last_name
```

6.1.2 ANSWERS

a) Execute the following SQL statement. Explain your observations about the WHERE clause and the resulting output.

```
SELECT c.course_no, c.description, s.section_no
  FROM course c, section s
 WHERE c.course_no = s.course_no
   AND c.prerequisite IS NULL
 ORDER BY c.course_no, section_no
```

Answer: This query includes both a join condition and a condition that restricts the rows to courses that have no prerequisite. The result is ordered by the course number and the section number.

```
COURSE_NO DESCRIPTION                       SECTION_NO
--------- ------------------------------    ----------
       10 DP Overview                                2
       20 Intro to Computers                         2
...
      146 Java for C/C++ Programmers                 2
      310 Operating Systems                          1

8 rows selected.
```

The COURSE and SECTION tables are joined to obtain the SECTION_NO column. The join requires the equality of values for the COURSE_NO columns in both tables. The courses without a prerequisite are determined with the IS NULL operator.

If the query is written with the ANSI join syntax and the ON clause, you see one advantage of the ANSI join syntax over the traditional join syntax. The ANSI join distinguishes the join condition from the filtering criteria.

```
SELECT c.course_no, c.description, s.section_no
  FROM course c JOIN section s
    ON (c.course_no = s.course_no)
 WHERE c.prerequisite IS NULL
 ORDER BY c.course_no, section_no
```

b) Select the student ID, course number, enrollment date, and section ID for students who enrolled in course number 20 on January 30, 2003.

Answer: The SECTION and ENROLLMENT tables are joined through their common column: SECTION_ID. This column is the primary key in the SECTION table and the foreign key column in the ENROLLMENT table. The rows are restricted to those records that have a course number of 20 and an enrollment date of January 30, 2003 by including this condition in the WHERE clause.

```
SELECT e.student_id, s.course_no,
       TO_CHAR(e.enroll_date,'MM/DD/YYYY HH:MI PM'),
       e.section_id
  FROM enrollment e JOIN section s
    ON (e.section_id = s.section_id)
 WHERE s.course_no = 20
   AND e.enroll_date >= TO_DATE('01/30/2003','MM/DD/YYYY')
   AND e.enroll_date < TO_DATE('01/31/2003','MM/DD/YYYY')
```

```
STUDENT_ID COURSE_NO TO_CHAR(ENROLL_DATE SECTION_ID
---------- --------- ------------------- ----------
       103        20 01/30/2003 10:18 AM         81
       104        20 01/30/2003 10:18 AM         81
```

2 rows selected.

Alternatively, you can use the USING clause or the more traditional join syntax, listed here.

```
SELECT e.student_id, s.course_no,
       TO_CHAR(e.enroll_date,'MM/DD/YYYY HH:MI PM'),
       e.section_id
  FROM enrollment e, section s
 WHERE e.section_id = s.section_id
   AND s.course_no = 20
   AND e.enroll_date >= TO_DATE('01/30/2003','MM/DD/YYYY')
   AND e.enroll_date < TO_DATE('01/31/2003','MM/DD/YYYY')
```

Note the WHERE clause considers the date and time values of the ENROLL_DATE column. There are alternative WHERE clause solutions, such as applying the TRUNC function on the ENROLL_DATE column. Refer to Chapter 4, "Date and Conversion Functions," for many examples on querying and displaying DATE datatype columns.

6.1.3 ANSWERS

a) Select the students and instructors who live in the same zip code by joining on the common ZIP column. Order the result by the STUDENT_ID and INSTRUCTOR_ID columns. What do you observe?

Answer: When you join the STUDENT and INSTRUCTOR tables, there is a many-to-many relationship, which causes a Cartesian product as a result.

```
SELECT s.student_id, i.instructor_id,
       s.zip, i.zip
  FROM student s, instructor i
 WHERE s.zip = i.zip
 ORDER BY s.student_id, i.instructor_id
STUDENT_ID INSTRUCTOR_ID ZIP   ZIP
---------- ------------- ----- -----
       163           102 10025 10025
       163           103 10025 10025
       163           106 10025 10025
       163           108 10025 10025
       223           102 10025 10025
       223           103 10025 10025
       223           106 10025 10025
       223           108 10025 10025
       399           102 10025 10025
       399           103 10025 10025
       399           106 10025 10025
       399           108 10025 10025

12 rows selected.
```

Initially, this query and its corresponding result may not strike you as a Cartesian product because the WHERE clause contains a join criteria. However, the relationship between the STUDENT and the INSTRUCTOR table does not follow the primary key/foreign key path, and therefore a Cartesian product is possible. A look at the schema diagram reveals that no primary key/foreign key relationship exists between the two tables. To further illustrate the many-to-many relationship between the ZIP columns, select those students and instructors living in zip code 10025 in separate SQL statements.

```
SELECT student_id, zip
  FROM student
 WHERE zip = '10025'
STUDENT_ID ZIP
---------- -----
       223 10025
       163 10025
       399 10025

3 rows selected.
```

```
SELECT instructor_id, zip
  FROM instructor
 WHERE zip = '10025'
INSTRUCTOR_ID ZIP
------------- -----
          102 10025
          103 10025
          106 10025
          108 10025
```

4 rows selected.

These results validate the solution's output: the Cartesian product shows the three student rows multiplied by the four instructors, which results in twelve possible combinations. You can rewrite the query to include the DISTINCT keyword to select only the distinct student IDs. The query can also be written with a *subquery* construct, which avoids the Cartesian product. You will learn about this in Chapter 7, "Subqueries."

JOINING ALONG THE PRIMARY/FOREIGN KEY PATH

You can also join along the primary/foreign key path by joining the STUDENT table to the ENROLLMENT table, then to the SECTION table, and last to the INSTRUCTOR table. This involves a multitable join, discussed in Lab 6.2. However, the result is different from the Cartesian product result because it shows only instructors who teach a section in which the student is enrolled. In other words, an instructor living in zip code 10025 is included in the result only if the instructor teaches that student also living in the same zip code. This is in contrast to the Cartesian product example, which shows all of the instructors and students living in the same zip code, whether the instructor teaches this student or not. You will explore the differences between these two examples once more in the Test Your Thinking section at the end of the chapter.

LAB 6.1 SELF-REVIEW QUESTIONS

In order to test your progress, you should be able to answer the following questions.

1) Find the error(s) in the following SQL statement.

```
1 SELECT stud.last_name, stud.first_name,
2        stud.zip, zip.zip, zip.state, zip.city,
3        TO_CHAR(stud.student_id)
4   FROM student stud, zipcode zip
5  WHERE stud.student_id = 102
6    AND zip.zip = '11419'
7    AND zip.zip = s.zip
```

a) _____ No error
b) _____ This is not an equijoin
c) _____ Lines 1, 2, 3
d) _____ Line 4
e) _____ Lines 5, 6
f) _____ Line 7

2) Find the error(s) in the following SQL statement.

```
1 SELECT s.*, zipcode.zip,
2        DECODE(s.last_name, 'Smith', szip,
3              UPPER(s.last_name))
4   FROM student s, zipcode
5  WHERE stud.zip = zipcode.zip
6    AND s.last_name LIKE 'Smi%'
```

a) _____ Lines 1 and 2
b) _____ Lines 1 and 4
c) _____ Line 3
d) _____ Lines 2 and 5
e) _____ Line 4

3) A table alias is the name of a duplicate table stored in memory.

a) _____ True
b) _____ False

4) To equijoin a table with another table involves matching the common column values.

a) _____ True
b) _____ False

5) Find the error(s) in the following SQL statement.

```
1 SELECT TO_CHAR(w.modified_date, 'dd-mon-yyyy'),
2         t.grade_type_code, description,
3         TO_NUMBER(TO_CHAR(number_per_section))
4   FROM grade_type t, grade_type_weight w
5  WHERE t.grade_type_code = w.grade_type_code_cd
6    AND ((t.grade_type_code = 'MT'
7      OR t.grade_type_code = 'HM'))
8    AND t.modified_date >=
9        TO_DATE('01-JAN-2003', 'DD-MON-YYYY')
```

a) _____ Lines 1 and 8
b) _____ Line 4
c) _____ Line 5
d) _____ Lines 6 and 7
e) _____ Lines 5, 6, 7

6) Given two tables, T1 and T2, and their rows as shown, which result will be returned by the following query?

```
SELECT t1.val, t2.val, t1.name, t2.location
  FROM t1, t2
 WHERE t1.val = t2.val
```

```
Table T1              Table T2
VAL NAME              VAL LOCATION
--- --------------    --- ---------
A   Jones             A   San Diego
B   Smith             B   New York
C   Zeta              B   New York
    Miller                Phoenix
```

a) _____

```
V V NAME        LOCATION
- - ----------  ---------
A A Jones       San Diego
B B Smith       New York
B B Smith       New York
    Miller      Phoenix
```

b) _____

```
V V NAME         LOCATION
- - ----------   ---------
A A Jones        San Diego
B B Smith        New York
B B Smith        New York
```

c) _____ None of the above

7) The USING clause of the ANSI join syntax always assumes an equijoin and identical column names.

   a) _____ True
   b) _____ False

8) The NATURAL JOIN keywords and the USING clause of the ANSI join syntax are mutually exclusive.

   a) _____ True
   b) _____ False

9) The common column used in the join condition must be listed in the SELECT list.

   a) _____ True
   b) _____ False

Answers appear in Appendix A, Section 6.1.

JOINING THREE
OR MORE TABLES

L A B   O B J E C T I V E S

After this lab, you will be able to:

✔ Join Three or More Tables
✔ Join with Multicolumn Join Criteria

You often have to join more than two tables to determine the answer to a query. In this lab, you will practice these types of joins. Additionally, you will join tables with multicolumn keys.

THREE OR MORE TABLE JOINS

The join example at the beginning of the chapter involved two tables: the COURSE and SECTION tables. The following SQL statement repeats this query and the result of the join (see Figure 6.4). To include the instructor's first and last name, you will expand this statement to join to a third table, the INSTRUCTOR table.

```
SELECT c.course_no, s.section_no, c.description,
       s.location, s.instructor_id
  FROM course c, section s
 WHERE c.course_no = s.course_no
```

Figure 6.5 shows a partial listing of the INSTRUCTOR table. The INSTRUCTOR_ID column is the primary key of the table and is the common column with the SECTION table. Every row in the SECTION table with a value for the INSTRUCTOR_ID column must have one corresponding row in the INSTRUCTOR table. A particular INSTRUCTOR_ID in the INSTRUCTOR table may have zero, one, or multiple rows in the SECTION table.

COURSE_NO	SECTION_NO	DESCRIPTION	LOCATION	INSTRUCTOR_ID
10	2	DP Overview	L214	102
20	2	Intro to Computers	L210	103
20	4	Intro to Computers	L214	104
20	7	Intro to Computers	L509	105
20	8	Intro to Computers	L210	106
25	1	Intro to Programming	M311	107
25	2	Intro to Programming	L210	108
25	3	Intro to Programming	L507	101
25	4	Intro to Programming	L214	102
25	5	Intro to Programming	L509	103
25	6	Intro to Programming	L509	104
25	7	Intro to Programming	L210	105
25	8	Intro to Programming	L509	106
25	9	Intro to Programming	L507	107
100	1	Hands-On Windows	L214	102
...	...	...	...	...

Figure 6.4 ■ Result of join between COURSE and SECTION tables.

To formulate the SQL statement, follow the same steps performed in Lab 6.1. First, determine the columns and tables needed for output. Then, confirm whether a one-to-one or a one-to-many relationship exists between the tables to accomplish the join. The changes to the previous SQL statement are indicated in bold.

```
SELECT c.course_no, s.section_no, c.description, s.location,
       s.instructor_id, i.last_name, i.first_name
  FROM course c, section s, instructor i
 WHERE c.course_no = s.course_no
   AND s.instructor_id = i.instructor_id
```

INSTRUCTOR_ID	LAST_NAME	FIRST_NAME	...
101	Hanks	Fernand	...
102	Wojick	Tom	...
103	Schorin	Nina	...
104	Pertez	Gary	...
105	Morris	Anita	...
106	Smythe	Todd	...
107	Frantzen	Marilyn	...
108	Lowry	Charles	...
109	Chow	Rick	...
110	Willig	Irene	...

Figure 6.5 ■ The INSTRUCTOR table.

The join yields the result shown in Figure 6.6. The three-table join result now includes the instructor's first and last name. For example, notice the INSTRUCTOR_ID with the 102 is listed multiple times in the SECTION table. This instructor teaches several sections; therefore, the INSTRUCTOR_ID's corresponding first and last names are repeated in the result.

ANSI JOIN SYNTAX FOR THREE AND MORE TABLE JOINS

The join across three tables can be expressed with the ANSI join syntax. Create the first join between the COURSE and SECTION tables via the JOIN keyword and the ON clause. To this result the next table and join condition are added. The set of parentheses around the ON clause is optional.

```
SELECT c.course_no, s.section_no, c.description, s.location,
       s.instructor id, i.last_name, i.first_name
  FROM course c JOIN section s
    ON (c.course_no = s.course_no)
  JOIN instructor i
    ON (s.instructor_id = i.instructor_id)
```

Alternatively, the query can be expressed with the USING clause. The table and column aliases in the SELECT and FROM clauses are optional, but the parentheses in the USING clause are required.

COURSE _NO	SECT NO	DESCRIPTION	LOCA	INST _ID	LAST_NAME	FIRST_NAME
10	2	DP Overview	L214	102	Wojick	Tom
20	2	Intro to Computers	L210	103	Schorin	Nina
20	4	Intro to Computers	L214	104	Pertez	Gary
20	8	Intro to Computers	L210	106	Smythe	Todd
20	7	Intro to Computers	L509	105	Morris	Anita
25	2	Intro to Programming	L210	108	Lowry	Charles
25	8	Intro to Programming	L509	106	Smythe	Todd
25	9	Intro to Programming	L507	107	Frantzen	Marilyn
25	1	Intro to Programming	M311	107	Frantzen	Marilyn
25	7	Intro to Programming	L210	105	Morris	Anita
25	6	Intro to Programming	L509	104	Pertez	Gary
25	5	Intro to Programming	L509	103	Schorin	Nina
25	4	Intro to Programming	L214	102	Wojick	Tom
25	3	Intro to Programming	L507	101	Hanks	Fernand
100	1	Hands-On Windows	L214	102	Wojick	Tom
...	...	...	...	...	...	...

Figure 6.6 ■ Result of join between COURSE, SECTION, and INSTRUCTOR tables.

```
SELECT course_no, s.section_no, c.description, s.location,
       instructor_id, i.last_name, i.first_name
  FROM course c JOIN section s
 USING (course_no)
  JOIN instructor i
 USING (instructor_id)
```

MULTICOLUMN JOINS

The basic steps of the multicolumn join do not differ from the previous examples. The only variation is to make multicolumn keys part of the join criteria.

One of the multikey column examples in the schema is the GRADE table. The primary key of the table consists of the four columns STUDENT_ID, SECTION_ID, GRADE_CODE_OCCURRENCE, and GRADE_TYPE_CODE. The GRADE table also has two foreign keys: the GRADE_TYPE_CODE column, referencing the GRADE_TYPE table, and the multicolumn foreign key STUDENT_ID and SECTION_ID, referencing the ENROLLMENT table.

To help you understand the data in the table, examine a set of sample records for a particular student. The student with ID 220 is enrolled in SECTION_ID 119 and has nine records in the GRADE table: four homework assignments (HM), two quizzes (QZ), one midterm (MT), one final examination (FI), and one participation (PA) grade.

```
SELECT student_id, section_id, grade_type_code type,
       grade_code_occurrence no,
       numeric_grade indiv_gr
  FROM grade
 WHERE student_id = 220
   AND section_id = 119
```

STUDENT_ID	SECTION_ID	TY	NO	INDIV_GR
220	119	FI	1	85
220	119	HM	1	84
220	119	HM	2	84
220	119	HM	3	74
220	119	HM	4	74
220	119	MT	1	88
220	119	PA	1	91
220	119	QZ	1	92
220	119	QZ	2	91

```
9 rows selected.
```

The next SQL query joins the GRADE table to the ENROLLMENT table to include the values of the ENROLL_DATE column in the result set. All the changes to the previous SQL query are indicated in bold.

```
SELECT g.student_id, g.section_id,
       g.grade_type_code type,
       g.grade_code_occurrence no,
       g.numeric_grade indiv_gr,
       TO_CHAR(e.enroll_date, 'MM/DD/YY') enrolldt
  FROM grade g, enrollment e
 WHERE g.student_id = 220
   AND g.section_id = 119
   AND g.student_id = e.student_id
   AND g.section_id = e.section_id
```

STUDENT_ID	SECTION_ID	TY	NO	INDIV_GR	ENROLLDT
220	119	FI	1	85	02/16/03
220	119	HM	1	84	02/16/03
220	119	HM	2	84	02/16/03
220	119	HM	3	74	02/16/03
220	119	HM	4	74	02/16/03
220	119	MT	1	88	02/16/03
220	119	PA	1	91	02/16/03
220	119	QZ	1	92	02/16/03
220	119	QZ	2	91	02/16/03

9 rows selected.

To join between the tables ENROLLMENT and GRADE, use both the SECTION_ID and STUDENT_ID columns. These two columns represent the primary key of the ENROLLMENT table and foreign key of the GRADE table, thus a one-to-many relationship between the tables exists.

The values for the ENROLL_DATE column are repeated, because for each individual grade you have one row showing the ENROLL_DATE in the ENROLLMENT table.

EXPRESSING MULTICOLUMN JOINS USING THE ANSI JOIN SYNTAX

A join involving multiple columns on a table requires the columns to be listed in the ON or the USING clause as a join criteria. The next SQL statement shows the ON clause.

```
SELECT g.student_id, g.section_id,
       g.grade_type_code type,
       g.grade_code_occurrence no,
       g.numeric_grade indiv_gr,
       TO_CHAR(e.enroll_date, 'MM/DD/YY') enrolldt
  FROM grade g JOIN enrollment e
    ON (g.student_id = e.student_id
   AND g.section_id = e.section_id)
```

LAB 6.2

```
WHERE g.student_id = 220
  AND g.section_id = 119
```

When you write the query with the USING clause, you list the join columns separated by commas.

```
SELECT student_id, section_id,
       grade_type_code type,
       grade_code_occurrence no,
       numeric_grade indiv_gr,
       TO_CHAR(enroll_date, 'MM/DD/YY') enrolldt
  FROM grade JOIN enrollment
 USING (student_id, section_id)
 WHERE student_id = 220
   AND section_id = 119
```

JOINING ACROSS MANY TABLES

Joining across multiple tables is repeating the same steps of a two-join or three-join table over again. The first two tables are joined and then the result is joined to each subsequent table using the common column(s). This is then repeated until all the tables are joined.

To join *n* tables together, you need at least *n*–1 join conditions. For example, to join five tables, at least four join conditions are required unless your join deals with tables containing multicolumn keys. You will obviously need to include these multicolumns as part of the join condition.

The Oracle optimizer determines the order in which the tables are joined based on the join condition, the indexes on the table, and the various statistics about the tables (such as number of rows or the number of distinct values in each column). The join order has a tremendous impact on the performance of multitable joins. You can learn more about this topic and how to influence the optimizer in Chapter 17, "SQL Optimization."

THE ANSI JOIN VERSUS THE TRADITIONAL JOIN SYNTAX

You may wonder which one of the join syntax options is better. The ANSI join syntax has a number of advantages.

1. It is easy to identify the join criteria and the filtering condition.
2. An accidental Cartesian product is avoided because you must

explicitly specify the join criteria, and any missing join conditions become evident because an error is generated.

3. The syntax is easy to read and understand.

4. The USING clause requires less typing, but the datatypes of the columns must match.

5. SQL is understood by other ANSI-compliant non-Oracle databases.

Although the traditional join syntax, with the columns separated by commas in the FROM clause and the join condition listed in the WHERE clause, may become the old way of writing SQL, you must nevertheless familiarize yourself with this syntax because millions of SQL statements already use it, and it clearly performs its intended purpose.

The ANSI join syntax has some distinct functional advantages over the traditional join syntax when it comes to outer joins, which you can learn about in Chapter 9, "Complex Joins."

DIFFERENT TYPES OF JOINS

Most of the joins you will come across are based on equality, with the equijoin being the most dominant. In this chapter you learned about equijoins; there are other types of joins you must become familiar with, most notably the self-join, the nonequijoin, and the outer join. (See Table 6.1 for a listing of the various types of joins.)

LAB 6.2 EXERCISES

6.2.1 JOIN THREE OR MORE TABLES

a) Display the student ID, course number, and section number of enrolled students where the instructor of the section lives in zip code 10025. Additionally, the course should not have any prerequisites.

b) Produce the mailing addresses for instructors who taught sections starting in June 2003.

c) List the student IDs of enrolled students living in Connecticut.

6.2.2 JOIN WITH MULTICOLUMN JOIN CRITERIA

a) Show all the grades student Fred Crocitto received for SECTION_ID 86.

Table 6.1 ■ Types of Joins

Join Type	Base of Join Condition	Learn About It	Syntax
Equijoin or Inner Join	Equality	This chapter	Traditional comma-separated join or ANSI JOIN syntax (including optional INNER keyword).
Natural Join	Equality	This chapter	NATURAL JOIN keyword.
Cross-Join or Cartesian Product	No join condition	This chapter	Traditional comma-separated with the missing join condition in the WHERE clause or CROSS JOIN keyword.
Self-Join	Equality	Chapter 9, "Complex Joins"	(See Equijoin or Inner Join).
Outer Join (left, right, full)	Equality and extending the result set	Chapter 9, "Complex Joins"	OUTER JOIN keywords or outer join operator(+).
Non-Equijoin	Nonequality of values	Chapter 9, "Complex Joins"	Traditional comma-separated join or ANSI join syntax with the ON clause. The join criteria is not based on equality.

b) List the final examination grades for all enrolled Connecticut students of course number 420. Note final examination does not mean final grade.

c) Display the LAST_NAME, STUDENT_ID, PERCENT_OF_FINAL_GRADE, GRADE_TYPE_CODE, and NUMERIC_GRADE columns for students who received 80 or less for their class project (GRADE_TYPE_CODE = 'PJ'). Order the result by student last name.

LAB 6.2 EXERCISE ANSWERS

6.2.1 ANSWERS

a) Display the student ID, course number, and section number of enrolled students where the instructor of the section lives in zip code 10025. Additionally, the course should not have any prerequisites.

Answer: This query involves joining four tables. The course number is found in the SEC-TION and COURSE tables, the PREREQUISITE column in the COURSE table. To deter-mine the zip code of an instructor, use the INSTRUCTOR table. To choose only enrolled students, join to the ENROLLMENT table.

```
SELECT c.course_no, s.section_no, e.student_id
  FROM course c, section s, instructor i, enrollment e
 WHERE c.prerequisite IS NULL
   AND c.course_no = s.course_no
   AND s.instructor_id = i.instructor_id
   AND i.zip = '10025'
   AND s.section_id = e.section_id
```

COURSE_NO	SECTION_NO	STUDENT_ID
10	2	128
146	2	117
146	2	140
...		
20	8	158
20	8	199

12 rows selected.

To obtain this result, build the four-table join just like any other join, step by step. First start with one of the tables, such as the COURSE table.

```
SELECT course_no
  FROM course
 WHERE prerequisite IS NULL
```

For each of these courses you find the corresponding sections when you join the COURSE table with the SECTION table. Notice the bolded additions to the SQL statement.

```
SELECT c.course_no, s.section_no
  FROM course c, section s
 WHERE c.prerequisite IS NULL
   AND c.course_no = s.course_no
```

Then include instructors who live in zip code 10025. The common column between SECTION and INSTRUCTOR is INSTRUCTOR_ID.

```
SELECT c.course_no, s.section_no
  FROM course c, section s, instructor i
 WHERE c.prerequisite IS NULL
   AND c.course_no = s.course_no
   AND s.instructor_id = i.instructor_id
   AND i.zip = '10025'
```

Finally, join the results of the ENROLLMENT table via the SECTION_ID column, which leads you to the solution shown previously.

Instead of using the traditional join syntax to obtain the result, you can opt for the ANSI join syntax instead. The query may look similar to the following statement.

```
SELECT course_no, section_no, student_id
  FROM course JOIN section
 USING (course_no)
  JOIN instructor
 USING (instructor_id)
  JOIN enrollment
 USING (section_id)
 WHERE prerequisite IS NULL
   AND zip = '10025'
```

Another possible alternative using the ANSI join syntax is listed next: It uses the ON condition instead.

```
SELECT c.course_no, s.section_no, e.student_id
  FROM course c JOIN section s
    ON (c.course_no = s.course_no)
  JOIN instructor i
    ON (s.instructor_id = i.instructor_id)
  JOIN enrollment e
    ON (s.section_id = e.section_id)
 WHERE c.prerequisite IS NULL
   AND i.zip = '10025'
```

b) Produce the mailing addresses for instructors who taught sections starting in June 2003.

Answer: This solution requires the join of three tables: You join the INSTRUCTOR, SECTION, and ZIPCODE tables to produce the mailing list.

```
SELECT i.first_name || ' ' ||i.last_name name,
       i.street_address, z.city || ', ' || z.state
```

```
        || ' ' || i.zip "City State Zip",
        TO_CHAR(s.start_date_time, 'MM/DD/YY') start_dt,
        section_id sect
   FROM instructor i, section s, zipcode z
  WHERE i.instructor_id = s.instructor_id
    AND i.zip = z.zip
    AND s.start_date_time >=
        TO_DATE('01-JUN-2003','DD-MON-YYYY')
    AND s.start_date_time <
        TO_DATE('01-JUL-2003','DD-MON-YYYY')
```

NAME	STREET_ADDRESS	City State Zip	START_DT	SECT
Fernand Hanks	100 East 87th	New York, NY 10015	06/02/03	117
Anita Morris	34 Maiden Lane	New York, NY 10015	06/11/03	83
Anita Morris	34 Maiden Lane	New York, NY 10015	06/12/03	91
Anita Morris	34 Maiden Lane	New York, NY 10015	06/02/03	113
...				
Gary Pertez	34 Sixth Ave	New York, NY 10035	06/12/03	90
Gary Pertez	34 Sixth Ave	New York, NY 10035	06/10/03	120
Gary Pertez	34 Sixth Ave	New York, NY 10035	06/03/03	143
Gary Pertez	34 Sixth Ave	New York, NY 10035	06/12/03	151

```
17 rows selected.
```

One of the first steps in solving this query is to determine the columns and tables involved. Look at the schema diagram in Appendix D, "Student Database Schema," or refer to the table and column comments listed in Appendix E, "Table and Column Descriptions."

In this example, the instructor's last name, first name, street address, and zip code are found in the INSTRUCTOR table. The CITY, STATE, and ZIP are columns in the ZIPCODE table. The join also needs to include the SECTION table because the column START_DATE_TIME lists the date and time on which the individual sections started. The next step is to determine the common columns. The ZIP column is the common column between the INSTRUCTOR and ZIPCODE tables. For every value in the ZIP column of the INSTRUCTOR table you have one corresponding ZIP value in the ZIPCODE table. For every value in the ZIPCODE table there may be zero, one, or multiple records in the INSTRUCTOR table. The join returns only the matching records.

The other common column is the INSTRUCTOR_ID in the SECTION and INSTRUCTOR tables. Only instructors who teach have one or more rows in the SECTION table. Any section that does not have an instructor assigned is not taught.

As always, the query can be expressed with one of the ANSI join syntax variations.

```
SELECT first_name || ' ' ||last_name name,
       street_address, city || ', ' || state
       || ' ' || zip "City State Zip",
       TO_CHAR(start_date_time, 'MM/DD/YY') start_dt,
       section_id sect
  FROM instructor JOIN section s
 USING (instructor_id)
  JOIN zipcode
 USING (zip)
 WHERE start_date_time >=TO_DATE('01-JUN-2003','DD-MON-YYYY')
   AND start_date_time < TO_DATE('01-JUL-2003','DD-MON-YYYY')
```

Looking at the result, notice there are instructors teaching multiple sections. To see only the distinct addresses, use the DISTINCT keyword and drop the START_DATE_TIME and SECTION_ID columns from the SELECT list.

c) List the student IDs of enrolled students living in Connecticut.

Answer: Only students enrolled in classes are in the result; any student who does not have a row in the ENROLLMENT table is not considered enrolled. The STUDENT_ID is the common column between the STUDENT and ENROLLMENT tables. The STATE column is in the ZIPCODE table. The common column between the STUDENT and the ZIPCODE tables is the ZIP column.

```
SELECT student_id
  FROM student JOIN enrollment
 USING (student_id)
  JOIN zipcode
 USING (zip)
 WHERE state = 'CT'
STUDENT_ID
----------
       220
       270
       270
...
       210
       154

13 rows selected.
```

Because students can be enrolled in more than one class, add the DISTINCT keyword if you want to display each STUDENT_ID once.

Following is the SQL statement expressed using the traditional join syntax.

```
SELECT s.student_id
  FROM student s, enrollment e, zipcode z
 WHERE s.student_id = e.student_id
   AND s.zip = z.zip
   AND z.state = 'CT'
```

6.2.2 ANSWERS

a) Show all the grades student Fred Crocitto received for SECTION_ID 86.

Answer: The grades for each section and student are stored in the GRADE table. The primary key of the GRADE table consists of the STUDENT_ID, SECTION_ID, GRADE_TYPE_CODE, and GRADE_CODE_OCCURRENCE columns. This means a student, such as Fred Crocitto, has multiple grades for each grade type.

```
SELECT s.first_name|| ' '|| s.last_name name,
       e.section_id, g.grade_type_code,
       g.numeric_grade grade
  FROM student s JOIN enrollment e
    ON (s.student_id = e.student_id)
  JOIN grade g
    ON (e.student_id = g.student_id
   AND e.section_id = g.section_id)
 WHERE s.last_name = 'Crocitto'
   AND s.first_name ='Fred'
   AND e.section_id = 86
```

The SQL statement using the traditional join syntax may look similar to this query.

```
SELECT s.first_name|| ' '|| s.last_name name,
       e.section_id, g.grade_type_code,
       g.numeric_grade grade
  FROM student s, enrollment e, grade g
 WHERE s.last_name = 'Crocitto'
   AND s.first_name ='Fred'
   AND e.section_id = 86
   AND s.student_id = e.student_id
   AND e.student_id = g.student_id
   AND e.section_id = g.section_id
```

NAME	SECTION_ID	GR	GRADE
Fred Crocitto	86	FI	85
...			
Fred Crocitto	86	QZ	90
Fred Crocitto	86	QZ	84
Fred Crocitto	86	QZ	97
Fred Crocitto	86	QZ	97

```
11 rows selected.
```

To build up the SQL statement step by step, you may want to start with the STU-DENT table and select the record for Fred Crocitto.

```
SELECT last_name, first_name
  FROM student
 WHERE last_name = 'Crocitto'
   AND first_name = 'Fred'
```

Next, choose the section with the ID of 86 in which Fred is enrolled. The common column between the two tables is STUDENT_ID.

```
SELECT s.first_name||' '|| s.last_name name,
       e.section_id
  FROM student s, enrollment e
 WHERE s.last_name = 'Crocitto'
   AND s.first_name = 'Fred'
   AND e.section_id = 86
   AND s.student_id = e.student_id
```

Then retrieve the individual grades from the GRADE table. The common columns between the GRADE table and the ENROLLMENT table are SECTION_ID and STU-DENT_ID. They represent the primary key in the ENROLLMENT table and are for-eign keys in the GRADE table. Both columns need to be in the WHERE clause.

If you want to expand the query, add the DESCRIPTION column of the GRADE_TYPE table for each GRADE_TYPE_CODE. The common column between the tables GRADE and GRADE_TYPE is GRADE_TYPE_CODE.

```
SELECT s.first_name||' '|| s.last_name name,
       e.section_id, g.grade_type_code grade,
       g.numeric_grade, gt.description
  FROM student s, enrollment e, grade g, grade_type gt
 WHERE s.last_name = 'Crocitto'
   AND s.first_name = 'Fred'
   AND e.section_id = 86
   AND s.student_id = e.student_id
   AND e.student_id = g.student_id
   AND e.section_id = g.section_id
   AND g.grade_type_code = gt.grade_type_code
```

If you also show the COURSE_NO column, join to the SECTION table via the ENROLLMENT table column SECTION_ID.

```
SELECT s.first_name||' '|| s.last_name name,
       e.section_id, g.grade_type_code,
       g.numeric_grade grade, gt.description,
       sec.course_no
  FROM student s, enrollment e, grade g, grade_type gt,
       section sec
```

```
WHERE s.last_name = 'Crocitto'
  AND s.first_name = 'Fred'
  AND e.section_id = 86
  AND s.student_id = e.student_id
  AND e.student_id = g.student_id
  AND e.section_id = g.section_id
  AND g.grade_type_code = gt.grade_type_code
  AND e.section_id = sec.section_id
```

```
NAME            SECTION_ID GR GRADE DESCRIPTION COURSE_NO
--------------- ---------- -- ----- ----------- ---------
Fred Crocitto           86 FI    85 Final              25
...
Fred Crocitto           86 QZ    90 Quiz               25
Fred Crocitto           86 QZ    84 Quiz               25
Fred Crocitto           86 QZ    97 Quiz               25
Fred Crocitto           86 QZ    97 Quiz               25

11 rows selected.
```

b) List the final examination grades for all enrolled Connecticut students of course number 420. Note final examination does not mean final grade.

Answer: This answer requires joining five tables. The needed joins are the ZIPCODE table with the STUDENT table to determine the Connecticut students and the STUDENT and ENROLLMENT tables to determine the SECTION_IDs in which the students are enrolled. From these SECTION_IDs you only include sections where the course number equals 420. This requires a join of the ENROLLMENT table to the SECTION table. Last, the ENROLLMENT table needs to be joined to the GRADE table to display the grades.

```
SELECT e.student_id, sec.course_no, g.numeric_grade
  FROM student stud, zipcode z,
       enrollment e, section sec, grade g
 WHERE stud.zip = z.zip
   AND z.state = 'CT'
   AND stud.student_id = e.student_id
   AND e.section_id = sec.section_id
   AND e.section_id = g.section_id
   AND e.student_id = g.student_id
   AND sec.course_no = 420
   AND g.grade_type_code = 'FI'
STUDENT_ID COURSE_NO NUMERIC_GRADE
---------- --------- -------------
       196       420            84
       198       420            85

2 rows selected.
```

You may list any of the columns you find relevant to solving the query. For this solution, the columns STUDENT_ID, COURSE_NO, and NUMERIC_GRADE were chosen.

Obviously, the query can be expressed with the ANSI join syntax here showing the USING clause.

```
SELECT student_id, course_no, numeric_grade
  FROM student JOIN zipcode
 USING (zip)
    JOIN enrollment
 USING (student_id)
   JOIN section
 USING (section_id)
   JOIN grade g
 USING (section_id, student_id)
 WHERE course_no = 420
   AND grade_type_code = 'FI'
   AND state = 'CT'
```

c) Display the columns LAST_NAME, STUDENT_ID, PERCENT_OF_FINAL_GRADE, GRADE_TYPE_CODE, and NUMERIC_GRADE for students who received 80 or less for their class project (GRADE_TYPE_CODE = 'PJ'). Order the result by student last name.

Answer: Join the tables GRADE_TYPE_WEIGHT, GRADE, ENROLLMENT, and STUDENT.

The column PERCENT_OF_FINAL_GRADE of the GRADE_TYPE_WEIGHT table stores the weighted percentage a particular grade has on the final grade. One of the foreign keys of the GRADE table is the combination of the GRADE_TYPE_CODE and SECTION_ID; these columns represent the primary key of the GRADE_TYPE_WEIGHT table.

To include the student's last name, you have two choices. Either follow the primary and foreign key relationships by joining the tables GRADE and ENROLLMENT via the STUDENT_ID and SECTION_ID columns, and then join the ENROLLMENT table to the STUDENT table via the STUDENT_ID column, or skip the ENROLLMENT table and join GRADE directly to the STUDENT table via the STUDENT_ID. Examine the first option of joining to the ENROLLMENT table and then joining it to the STUDENT table.

```
SELECT g.student_id, g.section_id,
       gw.percent_of_final_grade pct, g.grade_type_code,
       g.numeric_grade grade, s.last_name
  FROM grade_type_weight gw, grade g,
       enrollment e, student s
 WHERE g.grade_type_code = 'PJ'
```

```
      AND gw.grade_type_code = g.grade_type_code
      AND gw.section_id = g.section_id
      AND g.numeric_grade <= 80
      AND g.section_id = e.section_id
      AND g.student_id = e.student_id
      AND e.student_id = s.student_id
    ORDER BY s.last_name
```

STUDENT_ID	SECTION_ID	PCT	GR	GRADE	LAST_NAME
245	82	75	PJ	77	Dalvi
176	115	75	PJ	76	Satterfield
244	82	75	PJ	76	Wilson
248	155	75	PJ	76	Zapulla

4 rows selected.

SKIPPING THE PRIMARY/FOREIGN KEY PATH

The second choice is to join the STUDENT_ID from the GRADE table directly to the STUDENT_ID of the STUDENT table, thus skipping the ENROLLMENT table entirely. The following query returns the same result.

```
SELECT g.student_id, g.section_id,
       gw.percent_of_final_grade pct, g.grade_type_code,
       g.numeric_grade grade, s.last_name
  FROM grade_type_weight gw, grade g,
       student s
 WHERE g.grade_type_code = 'PJ'
   AND gw.grade_type_code = g.grade_type_code
   AND gw.section_id = g.section_id
   AND g.numeric_grade <= 80
   AND g.student_id = s.student_id
 ORDER BY s.last_name
```

STUDENT_ID	SECTION_ID	PCT	GR	GRADE	LAST_NAME
245	82	75	PJ	77	Dalvi
176	115	75	PJ	76	Satterfield
244	82	75	PJ	76	Wilson
248	155	75	PJ	76	Zapulla

4 rows selected.

This shortcut is perfectly acceptable, even if it does not follow the primary/foreign key relationship path. In this case, you can be sure not to build a Cartesian product as you can guarantee only one STUDENT_ID in the STUDENT table for every STUDENT_ID in the GRADE table. In addition, it also saves another join; thus, the query executes a little faster and takes up less resources, which is probably negligible with this small result set.

LAB 6.2 SELF-REVIEW QUESTIONS

In order to test your progress, you should be able to answer the following questions.

1) Which SQL statement shows the sections that have instructors assigned to them?

   a) _____

   ```
   SELECT c.course_no, s.section_id, i.instructor_id
     FROM course c, section s, instructor i
    WHERE c.course_no = s.course_no
      AND i.instructor_id = s.section_id
   ```

   b) _____

   ```
   SELECT c.course_no, s.section_id, i.instructor_id
     FROM course c, section s, instructor i
    WHERE c.course_no = s.course_no
      AND i.instructor_id = s.instructor_id
   ```

   c) _____

   ```
   SELECT course_no, section_id, instructor.instructor_id
     FROM section, instructor
    WHERE instructor.instructor_id = section.section_id
   ```

   d) _____

   ```
   SELECT c.section_id, i.instructor_id
     FROM course c, instructor i
    WHERE i.instructor_id = c.section_id
   ```

   e) _____

   ```
   SELECT c.course_no, i.instructor_id
     FROM course c JOIN instructor
    USING (instructor_id)
   ```

2) How do you resolve the Oracle error ORA-00918: column ambiguously defined?

   a) _____ Correct the join criteria and WHERE clause condition
   b) _____ Choose another column
   c) _____ Add the correct table alias
   d) _____ Correct the spelling of the column name

3) Joins involving multiple columns must always follow the primary/foreign key relationship path.

    a) _____ True
    b) _____ False

4) Find the error(s) in the following SQL statement.

```
1 SELECT g.student_id, s.section_id,
2         g.numeric_grade, s.last_name
3   FROM grade g,
4        enrollment e, student s
5  WHERE g.section_id = e.section_id
6    AND g.student_id = e.student_id
7    AND s.student_id = e.student_id
8    AND s.student_id = 248
9    AND e.section_id = 155
```

    a) _____ Line 1
    b) _____ Line 5
    c) _____ Line 6
    d) _____ Lines 5, 6
    e) _____ Lines 1, 5, 6
    f) _____ No error

5) Equijoins are the most common type of joins and are always based on equality of values.

    a) _____ True
    b) _____ False

6) To join four tables you must have at least three join conditions.

    a) _____ True
    b) _____ False

Answers appear in Appendix A, Section 6.2.

**LAB
6.2**

CHAPTER 6

TEST YOUR THINKING

The projects in this section are meant to have you utilize all of the skills that you have acquired throughout this chapter. The answers to these projects can be found at the companion Web site to this book, located at: *http://authors.phptr.com/rischert3e*. Visit the Web site periodically to share and discuss your answers.

1) Select the course description, section number, and location for sections meeting in location L211.

2) Show the course description, section number, and starting date and time of the courses Joseph German is taking.

3) List the instructor ID, last name of the instructor, and section ID of sections where class participation contributes to 25% of the total grade. Order the result by the instructor's last name.

4) Display the first and last names of students who received 99 or more points on their class project.

5) Select the grades for quizzes of students living in zip code 10956.

6) List the course number, section number, and instructor first and last names for classes with course number 350 as a prerequisite.

7) Write the questions for the following two SELECT statements. Explain the difference between the two results.

```
SELECT stud.student_id, i.instructor_id,
       stud.zip, i.zip
  FROM student stud, instructor i
 WHERE stud.zip = i.zip

SELECT stud.student_id, i.instructor_id,
       stud.zip, i.zip
  FROM student stud, enrollment e, section sec,
       instructor i
 WHERE stud.student_id = e.student_id
   AND e.section_id = sec.section_id
   AND sec.instructor_id = i.instructor_id
   AND stud.zip = i.zip
```

C H A P T E R   7

SUBQUERIES

A subquery is a SELECT statement nested in various clauses of a SQL statement. It allows you to use the output from one query as the input of another SQL statement. Subqueries make it easy to break down problems into logical and manageable pieces.

L A B   7 . 1

SIMPLE SUBQUERIES

LAB OBJECTIVES

After this lab, you will be able to:

✔ Write Subqueries in the WHERE and HAVING Clauses
✔ Write Subqueries Returning Multiple Rows
✔ Write Subqueries Returning Multiple Columns

As mentioned, a subquery allows you to break down a problem into individual components and solve it by nesting the queries. Although subqueries can be nested several levels deep, it is impractical beyond four or five levels. Subqueries are sometimes also referred to as *sub-SELECTs* or *nested SELECTs*.

Subqueries are not used just in SELECT statements, but in other SQL statements that allow subqueries as well (e.g., the WHERE clause of DELETE statements, the SET and WHERE clause of UPDATE statements, or part of the SELECT clause of INSERT statements). You use these SQL statements in Chapter 10, "Insert, Update, and Delete."

In this book, the subquery is referred to as the inner query and the surrounding statement is known as the outer query. In the simple subquery, the inner query is executed once, before the execution of the outer query. (This is in contrast to the correlated subquery, where the inner query executes repeatedly. You will learn to write correlated subqueries in Lab 7.2.)

SCALAR SUBQUERIES

The *scalar subquery* is also called the *single row subquery*; it returns a single column with one row. When you want to show the courses with the lowest course cost, you can write two separate queries. First, determine the lowest cost by applying the aggregate function MIN to the COST column of the COURSE table.

```
SELECT MIN(cost)
  FROM course
MIN(COST)
---------
     1095
```

1 row selected.

Then, write another SELECT statement that retrieves courses equaling the cost.

```
SELECT course_no, description, cost
  FROM course
 WHERE cost = 1095
COURSE_NO DESCRIPTION                               COST
--------- ---------------------------------------- ----
      135 Unix Tips and Techniques                 1095
      230 Intro to Internet                        1095
      240 Intro to the Basic Language              1095
```

3 rows selected.

The subquery construct simplifies the writing of two separate queries and the recording of the intermediate result. The following SQL statement nests the subquery determining the lowest course cost in the WHERE clause of the outer query. The inner query, which is the query determining the lowest cost from the COURSE table, is executed first. The result is fed to the outer query, which retrieves all the values that qualify.

```
SELECT course_no, description, cost
  FROM course
 WHERE cost =
       (SELECT MIN(cost)
          FROM course)
COURSE_NO DESCRIPTION                               COST
--------- ---------------------------------------- ----
      135 Unix Tips and Techniques                 1095
      230 Intro to Internet                        1095
      240 Intro to the Basic Language              1095
```

3 rows selected.

Instead of performing equality conditions, you may need to construct >, <, >=, <=, or <> comparisons against a set of rows. These comparisons will only work, just like the aforementioned statement, if the subquery returns a single row.

SUBQUERIES RETURNING MULTIPLE ROWS

Subqueries can return one or multiple rows. If a subquery returns a single row, the =, <, >, <=, >=, or <> operator may be used for comparison with the subquery. If multiple records are returned, the IN, ANY, ALL, or SOME operator must be used; otherwise, Oracle returns an error message.

The following query displays the course number, description, and cost of courses with a cost equal to the highest cost of all the courses. The highest cost requires the use of the aggregate function MAX. As you recall from Chapter 5, "Aggregate Functions, GROUP BY, and HAVING," aggregate functions when used alone without out the presence of any nonaggregate expressions in the SELECT list always return one row. The subquery returns the single value 1595. All the rows of the COURSE table are compared to this value to see if any rows have the same course cost. Only one record in the COURSE table equals this cost.

```
SELECT course_no, description, cost
  FROM course
 WHERE cost =
       (SELECT MAX(cost)
          FROM course)
COURSE_NO DESCRIPTION                            COST
--------- -------------------------------- ------
       80 Structured Programming Techniques   1595

1 row selected.
```

The next SQL statement is an example of a subquery that returns several rows.

```
SELECT course_no, description, cost
  FROM course
 WHERE cost =
       (SELECT cost
          FROM course
         WHERE prerequisite = 20)
ERROR at line 4:
ORA-01427: single-row subquery returns more than one row
```

Multiple rows of the subquery satisfy the criteria of a prerequisite course number equal to 20. Therefore, Oracle returns an error message. To eliminate the error, change the = operator of the outer query to the IN operator. The IN operator compares a list of values for equivalency. If any of the values in the list satisfy the condition, the record is included in the result set.

```
SELECT course_no, description, cost
  FROM course
```

```
WHERE cost IN
       (SELECT cost
          FROM course
         WHERE prerequisite = 20)
COURSE_NO DESCRIPTION                                COST
--------- ------------------------------------    ----
       10 DP Overview                              1195
       20 Intro to Computers                       1195
...
      122 Intermediate Java Programming            1195
      100 Hands-On Windows                         1195
```

25 rows selected.

You can also negate the criteria of the subquery and include only records with values that are not in the subquery's result. You accomplish this by applying the NOT IN operator.

```
SELECT course_no, description, cost
  FROM course
 WHERE cost NOT IN
       (SELECT cost
          FROM course
         WHERE prerequisite = 20)
COURSE_NO DESCRIPTION                                COST
--------- ------------------------------------    ----
       80 Structured Programming Techniques        1595
      135 Unix Tips and Techniques                 1095
      230 Intro to Internet                        1095
      240 Intro to the Basic Language              1095
```

4 rows selected.

 If the subquery returns multiple rows and you want to perform a comparison other than equality or inequality, use the ALL, ANY, and SOME operators discussed in Lab 7.4 to perform such comparisons.

Table 7.1 provides an overview of the various comparison operators available for subqueries. If your subquery returns more than one row, you have to choose a different operator than if your subquery retrieves at most one row only.

Table 7.1 ■ Comparison Operators for Subqueries

Comparison Operator	Subquery Returns One Row	Subquery Returns Multiple Rows
Equality	=	IN
Inequality	<>	NOT IN
Greater than	>	Use the ANY, ALL, SOME
Less than	<	operators (see Lab 7.4).
Greater than and equal	>=	
Less than and equal	<=	

NESTING MULTIPLE SUBQUERIES

You can nest one subquery within another subquery. The innermost query is always evaluated first, then the next higher one, and so on. The result of each subquery is fed into the enclosing statement.

The next query determines the last and first names of students enrolled in section number 8 of course number 20.

```
SELECT last_name, first_name
  FROM student
 WHERE student_id IN
       (SELECT student_id
          FROM enrollment
         WHERE section_id IN
               (SELECT section_id
                  FROM section
                 WHERE section_no = 8
                   AND course_no = 20))
```

LAST_NAME	FIRST_NAME
Limate	Roy
Segall	J.

2 rows selected.

The innermost nested subquery, the last subquery in the example, is executed first; it determines the SECTION_ID for section number 8 and course number 20. The surrounding query uses this resulting SECTION_ID in the WHERE clause to select student IDs from the ENROLLMENT table. These STUDENT_ID rows are fed to the outermost SELECT statement, which then displays the first and last names from the STUDENT table.

SUBQUERIES AND JOINS

Subqueries using the IN or = operator can often be expressed as an equijoin if the subquery does not contain an aggregate function. The following query can be transformed into an equijoin.

```
SELECT course_no, description
  FROM course
 WHERE course_no IN
        (SELECT course_no
           FROM section
          WHERE location = 'L211')
```
```
COURSE_NO DESCRIPTION
--------- ----------------------------
      142 Project Management
      125 JDeveloper
      122 Intermediate Java Programming

3 rows selected.
```

Here is the same query now expressed as an equijoin:

```
SELECT c.course_no, c.description
  FROM course c, section s
 WHERE c.course_no = s.course_no
   AND s.location = 'L211'
```

SUBQUERIES RETURNING MULTIPLE COLUMNS

SQL allows you to compare multiple columns in the WHERE clause to multiple columns of a subquery. The values in the columns must match both sides of the equation in the WHERE clause for the condition to be true. This means the datatype must be compatible and the number and order of columns must match.

For example, for each section, determine the students with the highest grade for their project (PJ). The following query does not accomplish this goal. It returns the highest project grade for each section, but does not list the individual student(s).

```
SELECT section_id, MAX(numeric_grade)
  FROM grade
 WHERE grade_type_code = 'PJ'
 GROUP BY section_id
```
```
SECTION_ID MAX(NUMERIC_GRADE)
---------- ------------------
        82                 77
        88                 99
...
```

```
    149                    83
    155                    92
```

8 rows selected.

The following query obtains the desired result by transforming the query into a subquery. The outer query displays the desired STUDENT_ID column and the WHERE clause compares the column pairs against the column pairs in the subquery.

```
SELECT student_id, section_id, numeric_grade
  FROM grade
 WHERE grade_type_code = 'PJ'
   AND (section_id, numeric_grade) IN
       (SELECT section_id, MAX(numeric_grade)
          FROM grade
         WHERE grade_type_code = 'PJ'
         GROUP BY section_id)
```

STUDENT_ID	SECTION_ID	NUMERIC_GRADE
245	82	77
166	88	99
...		
232	149	83
105	155	92

8 rows selected.

The execution steps are just like the previous simple subqueries. First, the innermost query is executed, determining the highest grade for each section. Then the pairs of columns are compared. If the column pair matches, Oracle displays the record.

If you were to write the query using literals instead of a subquery, the query would look like the following. It shows column pairs whereby the values of each expression pair is surrounded by parentheses.

```
SELECT student_id, section_id, numeric_grade
  FROM grade
 WHERE grade_type_code = 'PJ'
   AND (section_id, numeric_grade) IN
       ((82, 77),
        (88, 99),
   ...
        (149, 83),
        (155, 92))
```

SUBQUERIES AND NULLS

One easily overlooked behavior of subqueries is the occurrence of null values. The next example illustrates this subject on the COURSE table and the PREREQUISITE column. The first query shows a subquery that returns all the COURSE_ NO and PREREQUISITE column values for courses with the COURSE_NO of 120, 220, and 310 of the COURSE table. Note that the course number 310 has a null value for in the PREREQUISITE column, meaning that the individual course does not have any prerequisites.

```
SELECT course_no, prerequisite
  FROM course
 WHERE course_no IN (120, 220, 310)
COURSE_NO PREREQUISITE
--------- ------------
      120           80
      220           80
      310

3 rows selected.
```

If you use this result and now formulate a subquery for these rows specifically and negate it with NOT, you will notice an interesting result. The outer query does not return any rows despite the fact that there are rows with PREREQUISITE column values other than 80 and null.

```
SELECT course_no, prerequisite
  FROM course
 WHERE prerequisite NOT IN
       (SELECT prerequisite
          FROM course
         WHERE course_no IN (310, 220))

no rows selected
```

If you translate the result of the subquery into a list of values, you will see the same identical result. No rows are returned from the query because the condition evaluates to unknown when any member of the values in the list has a null.

```
SELECT course_no, prerequisite
  FROM course
 WHERE prerequisite NOT IN (80, NULL)

no rows selected
```

You typically only come across this type of scenario in subqueries; therefore, you must be aware of any NOT IN operator subqueries that can potentially return null values. The way to solve this null dilemma is to use the NOT EXISTS operator discussed in Lab 7.2. The next query will return the desired result.

```
SELECT course_no, prerequisite
   FROM course c
 WHERE NOT EXISTS
        (SELECT '*'
            FROM course
          WHERE course_no IN (310, 220)
            AND c.prerequisite = prerequisite)
```

The NVL or COALESCE functions are useful to deal with null values. You can substitute a default value and apply the function to both the subquery and the WHERE clause condition.

ORDER BY CLAUSE IN SUBQUERIES

The ORDER BY clause is not allowed inside a subquery with the exception of the inline view discussed in Lab 7.3. If you attempt to include an ORDER BY clause you will get an error message.

```
SELECT course_no, description, cost
   FROM course
 WHERE cost IN
        (SELECT cost
            FROM course
          WHERE prerequisite = 420
          ORDER BY cost)
          ORDER BY cost)
          *
ERROR at line 7:
ORA-00907: missing right parenthesis
```

It is not immediately apparent where the problem lies unless you already know about this rule. The message essentially indicates that an ORDER BY clause is not allowed in a subquery and that Oracle is expecting to see the right parenthesis signifying the closing of the subquery. An ORDER BY clause is certainly valid for the outer query, just not for the nested subquery.

You cannot use the ORDER BY clause inside a nested subquery. Another type of subquery, the inline view discussed in Lab 7.3, allows such a construct.

LAB 7.1 EXERCISES

7.1.1 WRITE SUBQUERIES IN THE WHERE AND HAVING CLAUSES

a) Write a SQL statement that displays the first and last names of students who registered first.

b) Show the sections with the lowest course cost and a capacity equal to or lower than the average capacity. Also display the course description, section number, capacity, and cost.

c) Select the course number and total capacity for each course. Show only the courses with a total capacity less than the average capacity of all the sections.

d) Choose the most ambitious students: Display the STUDENT ID for students enrolled in the most sections.

7.1.2 WRITE SUBQUERIES RETURNING MULTIPLE ROWS

a) Select the STUDENT_ID and SECTION_ID of enrolled students living in zip code 06820.

b) Display the course number and course description of the courses taught by instructor Fernand Hanks.

c) Select the last name and first name of students not enrolled in any class.

7.1.3 WRITE SUBQUERIES RETURNING MULTIPLE COLUMNS

a) Determine the STUDENT ID and last name of students with the highest FINAL_GRADE for each section. Also include the SECTION_ID and the FINAL_GRADE columns in the result.

b) Select the sections and their capacity where the capacity equals the number of students enrolled.

LAB 7.1 EXERCISE ANSWERS

7.1.1 ANSWERS

a) Write a SQL statement that displays the first and last names of students who registered first.

Answer: The query is broken down into logical pieces by first determining the earliest registration date of all students. The aggregate function MIN obtains the result in the subquery. The earliest date is compared to the REGISTRATION_DATE column for each student, and only records that are equal to the same date and time are returned.

```
SELECT first_name, last_name
  FROM student
 WHERE registration_date =
       (SELECT MIN(registration_date)
          FROM student)
```

FIRST_NAME	LAST_NAME
J.	Landry
Judith	Olvsade
...	
Larry	Walter
Catherine	Mierzwa

8 rows selected.

b) Show the sections with the lowest course cost and a capacity equal to or lower than the average capacity. Also display the course description, section number, capacity, and cost.

Answer: First, break down the problem into individual queries. Start by determining the average capacity of all sections and the lowest course cost of all courses. To compare both cost and capacity against the subqueries, the SECTION and COURSE tables require a join.

```
SELECT c.description, s.section_no, c.cost, s.capacity
  FROM course c, section s
 WHERE c.course_no = s.course_no
   AND s.capacity <=
       (SELECT AVG(capacity)
          FROM section)
   AND c.cost =
       (SELECT MIN(cost)
          FROM course)
```

DESCRIPTION	SECTION_NO	COST	CAPACITY
Intro to Internet	1	1095	12
Intro to Internet	2	1095	15
...			
Unix Tips and Techniques	2	1095	15
Unix Tips and Techniques	4	1095	15

6 rows selected.

c) Select the course number and total capacity for each course. Show only the courses with a total capacity less than the average capacity of all the sections.

Answer: To determine the total capacity per course, use the SUM function to add the values in the SECTION table's CAPACITY column. Compare the total capacity for each course to the average capacity for all sections and return those courses that have a total capacity less than the average capacity.

```
SELECT course_no, SUM(capacity)
  FROM section
 GROUP BY course_no
HAVING SUM(capacity) <
       (SELECT AVG(capacity)
          FROM section)
```

COURSE_NO	SUM(CAPACITY)
10	15
144	15

2 rows selected.

The solution shows only those courses and their respective capacities that satisfy the condition in the HAVING clause.

To determine the solution, first write the individual queries and then combine them. The following query first determines the total capacity for each course.

```
SELECT course_no, SUM(capacity)
  FROM section
 GROUP BY course_no
```

COURSE_NO	SUM(CAPACITY)
10	15
20	80
...	
420	25
450	25

28 rows selected.

The average capacity for all sections is easily obtained using the AVG function.

```
SELECT AVG(capacity)
  FROM section
```

AVG(CAPACITY)
21.179487

1 row selected.

d) Choose the most ambitious students: Display the STUDENT_ID for students enrolled in the most sections.

Answer: A count of records for each student in the ENROLLMENT table shows how many sections each student is enrolled in. Determine the most number of enrollments per student by nesting the aggregate functions MAX and COUNT.

```
SELECT student_id, COUNT(*)
  FROM enrollment
 GROUP BY student_id
HAVING COUNT(*) =
        (SELECT MAX(COUNT(*))
           FROM enrollment
          GROUP BY student_id)
```

STUDENT_ID	COUNT(*)
124	4
214	4

2 rows selected.

To reach the subquery solution, determine the number of enrollments for each student. Notice that the STUDENT_ID column is not listed in the SELECT list. Therefore, only the result of the COUNT function is shown.

```
SELECT COUNT(*)
  FROM enrollment
 GROUP BY student_id
```

COUNT(*)
2
1
...
2
2

165 rows selected.

The second query combines two aggregate functions to determine the highest number of sections any student is enrolled in. This subquery is then applied in the HAVING clause of the solution.

```
SELECT MAX(COUNT(*))
  FROM enrollment
 GROUP BY student_id
```

```
MAX(COUNT(*))
-------------
            4
```

1 row selected.

7.1.2 ANSWERS

a) Select the STUDENT_ID and SECTION_ID of enrolled students living in zip code 06820.

Answer: The IN operator is necessary because the subquery returns multiple rows.

```
SELECT student_id, section_id
  FROM enrollment
 WHERE student_id IN
       (SELECT student_id
          FROM student
         WHERE zip = '06820')
STUDENT_ID SECTION_ID
---------- ----------
       240         81
```

1 row selected.

Alternatively, you can write the query as a join and achieve the same result.

```
SELECT e.student_id, e.section_id
  FROM enrollment e, student s
 WHERE e.student_id = s.student_id
   AND s.zip = '06820'
```

b) Display the course number and course description of the courses taught by instructor Fernand Hanks.

Answer: To determine the courses taught by this instructor, nest multiple subqueries. This question can also be solved using an equijoin.

```
SELECT course_no, description
  FROM course
 WHERE course_no IN
       (SELECT course_no
          FROM section
         WHERE instructor_id IN
               (SELECT instructor_id
                  FROM instructor
                 WHERE last_name = 'Hanks'
                   AND first_name = 'Fernand'))
```

```
COURSE_NO DESCRIPTION
--------- ------------------------------
       25 Intro to Programming
      240 Intro to the Basic Language
...
      120 Intro to Java Programming
      122 Intermediate Java Programming
```

9 rows selected.

The alternative solution is an equijoin:

```
SELECT c.course_no, c.description
  FROM course c, section s, instructor i
 WHERE c.course_no = s.course_no
   AND s.instructor_id = i.instructor_id
   AND i.last_name = 'Hanks'
   AND i.first_name = 'Fernand'
```

c) Select the last name and first name of students not enrolled in any class.

Answer: Use the NOT IN operator to eliminate those student IDs not found in the ENROLLMENT table. The result is a listing of students with no rows in the ENROLLMENT table. They may be newly registered students that have not yet enrolled in any courses.

```
SELECT last_name, first_name
  FROM student
 WHERE student_id NOT IN
       (SELECT student_id
          FROM enrollment)
```

LAST_NAME	FIRST_NAME
Eakheit	George
Millstein	Leonard
...	
Larcia	Preston
Mastandora	Kathleen

103 rows selected.

You may wonder why the solution does not include the DISTINCT keyword in the subquery. It is not required and does not alter the result, nor change the efficiency of the execution. Oracle automatically eliminates duplicates in a list of values as a result of the subquery.

7.1.3 ANSWERS

a) Determine the STUDENT_ID and last name of students with the highest FINAL_GRADE for each section. Also include the SECTION_ID and the FINAL_GRADE columns in the result.

Answer: The solution requires pairs of columns to be compared. First, determine the subquery to show the highest grade for each section. Then match the result to the columns in the outer query.

```
SELECT s.student_id, s.last_name, e.final_grade,
       e.section_id
  FROM enrollment e, student s
 WHERE e.student_id = s.student_id
   AND (e.final_grade, e.section_id) IN
       (SELECT MAX(final_grade), section_id
          FROM enrollment
         GROUP BY section_id)
STUDENT_ID LAST_NAME   FINAL_GRADE SECTION_ID
---------- ----------  ----------- ----------
       102 Crocitto            92          89

1 row selected.
```

Note, there is no need to add a table alias to the subquery. Table aliases in sub queries are typically only used in correlated subqueries or in subqueries that contain joins. Correlated subqueries are discussed in Lab 7.2.

b) Select the sections and their capacity where the capacity equals the number of students enrolled.

Answer: The subquery determines the number of enrolled students per section. The resulting set is then compared to the column pair of SECTION_ID and CAPACITY.

```
SELECT section_id, capacity
  FROM section
 WHERE (section_id, capacity) IN
       (SELECT section_id, COUNT(*)
          FROM enrollment
         GROUP BY section_id)
SECTION_ID  CAPACITY
----------  --------
        99        12

1 row selected.
```

LAB 7.1 SELF-REVIEW QUESTIONS

In order to test your progress, you should be able to answer the following questions.

1) The ORDER BY clause is not allowed in subqueries.

a) _____ True
b) _____ False

2) Subqueries are used only in SELECT statements.

a) _____ True
b) _____ False

3) The most deeply nested, noncorrelated subquery always executes first.

a) _____ True
b) _____ False

4) What operator would you choose to prevent this Oracle error message?

```
ORA-01427: single-row subquery returns more than one row
```

a) _____ Use the >= operator
b) _____ Use the = operator
c) _____ Use the IN operator
d) _____ Use the <= operator

5) Subqueries can return multiple rows and columns.

a) _____ True
b) _____ False

Answers appear in Appendix A, Section 7.1.

L A B   7 . 2

CORRELATED SUBQUERIES

LAB OBJECTIVES

After this lab, you will be able to:
- ✔ Write Correlated Subqueries
- ✔ Write Correlated Subqueries Using the EXISTS and NOT EXISTS Operators

CORRELATED SUBQUERIES

Correlated subqueries are probably one of the most powerful, yet initially very difficult, concepts of the SQL language. Correlated subqueries are different from the simple subqueries discussed so far. First, they allow you to reference columns from the outer query in the subquery and second, they execute the inner query repeatedly. The subquery is called correlated because of the reference of a column from the outer query.

You use the correlated subquery when you need to review every row of the outer query against the result of the inner query. The inner query is executed repeatedly, each time specific to the correlated value of the outer query. This is in contrast to previous subquery examples, where the inner query is executed only once.

In the previous lab, one example illustrates how to determine the students with the highest grade for their project (PJ), within their respective sections. The solution is accomplished with the IN operator which compares the column pairs. The following SELECT statement repeats the solution.

```
SELECT student_id, section_id, numeric_grade
  FROM grade
 WHERE grade_type_code = 'PJ'
   AND (section_id, numeric_grade) IN
       (SELECT section_id, MAX(numeric_grade)
          FROM grade
         WHERE grade_type_code = 'PJ'
         GROUP BY section_id)
```

Here is the query rewritten as a correlated subquery.

```
SELECT student_id, section_id, numeric_grade
  FROM grade outer
 WHERE grade_type_code = 'PJ'
   AND numeric_grade =
       (SELECT MAX(numeric_grade)
          FROM grade
         WHERE grade_type_code = outer.grade_type_code
           AND section_id = outer.section_id)
STUDENT_ID SECTION_ID NUMERIC_GRADE
---------- ---------- -------------
       245         82            77
       166         88            99
...
       232        149            83
       105        155            92
```

8 rows selected.

This query is a correlated subquery because the inner query refers to columns from the outer query. The GRADE table is the parent query, or the outer query. For simplicity, a table alias of OUTER is used.

Now you can refer to columns of the outer query using the alias. In this example, the values of the column SECTION_ID of the outer query are compared to the values of the inner query. The inner query determines the highest project grade for the SECTION_ID and GRADE_TYPE_CODE values of the current outer row.

STEPS PERFORMED BY THE CORRELATED SUBQUERY

To select the correct records, the following steps are performed by Oracle:

1. Select a row from the outer query.
2. Determine the value of the correlated column(s).
3. Execute the inner query for each record of the outer query.
4. The result of the inner query is then fed to the outer query and evaluated. If it satisfies the criteria, the row is returned for output.
5. The next record of the outer query is selected and steps 2 through 4 are repeated until all the records of the outer query are evaluated.

Here are the steps in more detail.

STEP 1: SELECT A ROW FROM THE OUTER QUERY Choose a record in the outer query where the GRADE_TYPE_CODE equals 'PJ'. The row returned in this step will be further evaluated in the steps that follow.

```
SELECT student_id, section_id, numeric_grade
  FROM grade outer
 WHERE grade_type_code = 'PJ'
STUDENT_ID SECTION_ID NUMERIC_GRADE
---------- ---------- -------------
       105        155            92
       111        133            90
...
       245         82            77
       248        155            76
```

21 rows selected.

STEP 2: DETERMINE THE VALUE OF THE CORRELATED COLUMN(S) Starting with the first returned row with a STUDENT_ID 105, the value of the correlated column OUTER.SECTION_ID equals 155. For the column OUTER.GRADE_TYPE_CODE, the value is 'PJ'.

STEP 3: EXECUTE THE INNER QUERY Based on the correlated column values, the inner query is executed. It shows the highest grade for the respective section ID and grade type code.

```
SELECT MAX(numeric_grade)
  FROM grade
 WHERE grade_type_code = 'PJ'
   AND section_id = 155
MAX(NUMERIC_GRADE)
------------------
                92
```

1 row selected.

STEP 4: EVALUATE THE CONDITION Because the NUMERIC_GRADE equals 92, the row for STUDENT_ID 105 evaluates to true and is included in the result.

STEP 5: REPEAT STEPS 2 THROUGH 4 FOR EACH SUBSEQUENT ROW OF THE OUTER QUERY Evaluate the next row containing values STUDENT_ID 111 and SECTION_ID 133. The highest grade for the section and grade type code happens to be 92, but student 111 does not have a NUMERIC_GRADE equal to this value. Therefore, the row is not returned. Each row of the outer query repeats these steps until all the rows are evaluated.

```
SELECT MAX(numeric_grade)
  FROM grade
 WHERE grade_type_code = 'PJ'
   AND section_id = 133
MAX(NUMERIC_GRADE)
------------------
                92
```

1 row selected.

 Unlike the subqueries discussed in Lab 7.1 where the inner query is evaluated once, the correlated subquery executes the inner query repeatedly, once for each row in the outer table.

THE EXISTS OPERATOR

The EXISTS operator is used for correlated subqueries. It tests if the subquery returns at least one row. The EXISTS operator returns either true or false, never unknown. Because EXISTS tests only if a row exists, the columns shown in the SELECT list of the subquery are irrelevant. Typically, you use a single character text literal such as '1' or 'X' or the keyword NULL.

The following correlated subquery displays instructors where the INSTRUCTOR_ID has a matching row in the SECTION table. The result shows the INSTRUCTOR_ID, FIRST_NAME, LAST_NAME, and ZIP column values of instructors assigned to at least one section.

```
SELECT instructor_id, last_name, first_name, zip
  FROM instructor i
 WHERE EXISTS
       (SELECT 'X'
          FROM section
         WHERE i.instructor_id = instructor_id)
```

INSTRUCTOR_ID	LAST_NAME	FIRST_NAME	ZIP
101	Hanks	Fernand	10015
102	Wojick	Tom	10025
103	Schorin	Nina	10025
104	Pertez	Gary	10035
105	Morris	Anita	10015
106	Smythe	Todd	10025
108	Lowry	Charles	10025
107	Frantzen	Marilyn	10005

8 rows selected.

For every row of the INSTRUCTOR table, the outer query evaluates the inner query. It checks to see if the current row's INSTRUCTOR_ID value exists for the SECTION table's INSTRUCTOR_ID column. Only if a row with the appropriate value is found, the condition is true and the outer row is included in the result.

The query can also be written using the IN operator.

```
SELECT instructor_id, last_name, first_name, zip
  FROM instructor
 WHERE instructor_id IN
       (SELECT instructor_id
          FROM section)
```

Alternatively, you can write this query with an equijoin.

```
SELECT DISTINCT i.instructor_id, i.last_name,
       i.first_name, i.zip
  FROM instructor i JOIN section s
    ON i.instructor_id = s.instructor_id
```

Note that this equijoin solution allows you to list columns found on the SECTION table, whereas the subquery solution does not. The subquery has the advantage of breaking problems into individual pieces. Not all subqueries can be transformed into joins, such as subqueries containing an aggregate function.

THE NOT EXISTS OPERATOR

The NOT EXISTS operator is the opposite of the EXISTS operator; it tests if a matching row cannot be found. The next query displays the instructors not assigned to any section.

```
SELECT instructor_id, last_name, first_name, zip
  FROM instructor i
 WHERE NOT EXISTS
       (SELECT 'X'
          FROM section
         WHERE i.instructor_id = instructor_id)
```

INSTRUCTOR_ID	LAST_NAME	FIRST_NAME	ZIP
109	Chow	Rick	10015
110	Willig	Irene	

2 rows selected.

You cannot rewrite this particular query using an equijoin, but you can rewrite it with the NOT IN operator. However, the NOT IN operator does not always yield the same result if null values are involved, as you see in the following example.

NOT EXISTS VERSUS NOT IN

Display the INSTRUCTOR_ID, FIRST_NAME, LAST_NAME, and ZIP columns from the INSTRUCTOR table where there is no corresponding zip code in the ZIPCODE table. Note the ZIP column in the INSTRUCTOR table allows NULL values.

**LAB
7.2**

USING NOT EXISTS

```
SELECT instructor_id, last_name, first_name, zip
  FROM instructor i
 WHERE NOT EXISTS
        (SELECT 'X'
           FROM zipcode
          WHERE i.zip = zip)
```

INSTRUCTOR_ID	LAST_NAME	FIRST_NAME	ZIP
110	Willig	Irene	

1 row selected.

USING NOT IN

```
SELECT instructor_id, last_name, first_name, zip
  FROM instructor
 WHERE zip NOT IN
        (SELECT zip
           FROM zipcode)
```

no rows selected

As you can see, the difference between NOT EXISTS and NOT IN lies in the way NULL values are treated. Instructor Irene Willig's ZIP column contains a NULL value. The NOT EXISTS operator tests for NULL values, the NOT IN operator does not.

AVOIDING INCORRECT RESULTS
THROUGH THE USE OF SUBQUERIES

Many SQL statements perform joins, together with aggregate functions. When you join tables together, some values may be repeated as a result of a one-to-many relationship between the joined tables. If you apply an aggregate function to the resulting repeating values, the result of the calculation may be incorrect. The following example shows a listing of the total capacity for courses with enrolled students.

```
SELECT s.course_no, SUM(s.capacity)
  FROM enrollment e, section s
 WHERE e.section_id = s.section_id
 GROUP BY s.course_no
```

COURSE_NO	SUM(S.CAPACITY)
10	15
20	175
...	
420	50
450	25

25 rows selected.

To illustrate that the result is incorrect, look at the value for the CAPACITY column of COURSE_NO 20. The following query shows the capacity for each section, resulting in a total capacity of 80 students, rather than 175 students as seen on the previous result.

```
SELECT section_id, capacity
  FROM section
 WHERE course_no = 20
```

SECTION_ID	CAPACITY
81	15
82	15
83	25
84	25

4 rows selected.

A closer look at the effect of the join without the aggregate function reveals the problem.

```
SELECT s.section_id, s.capacity, e.student_id,
       s.course_no
  FROM enrollment e, section s
 WHERE e.section_id = s.section_id
   AND s.course_no = 20
 ORDER BY section_id
```

SECTION_ID	CAPACITY	STUDENT_ID	COURSE_NO
81	15	103	20
81	15	104	20
81	15	240	20
82	15	244	20
82	15	245	20
83	25	124	20

83	25	235	20
84	25	158	20
84	25	199	20

9 rows selected.

For each enrolled student, the capacity record is repeated as the result of the join. This is correct, because for every row in the ENROLLMENT table, the corresponding SECTION_ID is looked up in the SECTION table. But when the SUM aggregate function is applied to the capacity, the capacity value of every returned record is added to the total capacity for each course. To achieve the correct result, the query needs to be written as follows.

```
SELECT course_no, SUM(capacity)
  FROM section s
 WHERE EXISTS
        (SELECT NULL
            FROM enrollment e, section sect
           WHERE e.section_id = sect.section_id
             AND sect.course_no = s.course_no)
 GROUP BY course_no
```

COURSE_NO	SUM(CAPACITY)
10	15
20	80
...	
420	25
450	25

25 rows selected.

The outer query checks for every row if there is a matching COURSE_NO value in the subquery. If the COURSE_NO exists, the EXISTS operator evaluates to true and will include the row of the outer query in the result. The outer query sums up the values. The EXISTS operator solves this particular problem, but not all queries can be solved this way; some may need to be written using inline views (see Lab 7.3).

UNNESTING OF QUERIES

Sometimes Oracle implicitly transforms some subqueries into a join by unnesting the query as part of its optimization strategy. For example, in the background Oracle will rewrite the query if the primary and foreign keys exist on the tables and the join does not cause a Cartesian product or incorrect results because of an aggregate function in the SELECT clause.

Some subqueries cannot be unnested because the subquery contains an aggregate function, ROWNUM pseudocolumn (discussed in Lab 7.3), a set operator (see

Chapter 8, "Set Operators"), or because it is a correlated subquery that references a query that is not in the immediate outer query block.

SUBQUERY PERFORMANCE CONSIDERATIONS

When you initially learn SQL, your utmost concern must be about getting the correct result. Performance considerations should be secondary. However, as you get more experienced with the language or if you work with large data sets, you want to consider some of the effects of your constructed statements. As you have seen, sometimes you can achieve the same result with a join, a correlated subquery, or noncorrelated subquery.

As previously mentioned, under specific circumstances Oracle may automatically optimize your statement and implicitly transform your subquery to a join. This implicit transformation frequently results in better performance without your having to worry about applying any optimization techniques.

Performance benefits of one type of subquery over another type may be noticeable when working with very large volumes of data. To optimize subqueries, you must understand the key difference between the correlated and the noncorrelated subquery.

The correlated subquery evaluates the inner query for every row of the outer query, therefore, your optimization strategy should center on eliminating as many rows as possible from the outer query. This can be done by adding additional restricting criteria in the WHERE clause of the statement. The advantage of correlated subqueries is that they can use indexes should any exist on the correlated columns.

The noncorrelated subquery executes the inner query first and feeds this result to the outer query. Generally speaking, this query is best suited for situation where the inner query does not returns a very large result set and where no indexes exist on the compared columns.

If your query involves a NOT EXISTS condition, you cannot modify it to a NOT IN condition if the subquery can return null values. In many circumstances, the NOT EXISTS offers better performance because indexes are usually used.

Because the STUDENT schema contains a fairly small number of records, the difference in execution time is minimal. The illustrated alternate solutions allow you look at different ways to approach and solve problems. You may want to use those solutions as starting points for ideas and perform your own tests based on your distinct environment, data volume, and requirements.

Good performance is subject to many variables that can have a significant impact on the execution time of your statements. In Chapter 17, "SQL Optimization," you will learn more about the topic of SQL performance optimization.

LAB 7.2 EXERCISES

7.2.1 WRITE CORRELATED SUBQUERIES

**LAB
7.2**

a) Explain what the following correlated subquery accomplishes.

```
SELECT section_id, course_no
  FROM section s
 WHERE 2 >
        (SELECT COUNT(*)
           FROM enrollment
          WHERE section_id = s.section_id)
```

SECTION_ID	COURSE_NO
79	350
80	10
...	
145	100
149	120

27 rows selected.

b) Show the sections and their number of enrollments where the enrollment exceeds the capacity of the section, using a correlated subquery.

7.2.2 WRITE CORRELATED SUBQUERIES USING THE *EXISTS* AND *NOT EXISTS* OPERATORS

a) Write a SQL statement to determine the total number of students enrolled using the EXISTS operator. Count students enrolled in more than one course as one.

b) Show the STUDENT_ID, last name, and first name of students enrolled in three or more classes.

c) Which courses do not have sections assigned? Use a correlated subquery in the solution.

d) Which sections have no students enrolled? Use a correlated subquery in the solution and order the result by the course number in ascending order.

LAB 7.2 EXERCISE ANSWERS

7.2.1 ANSWERS

a) Explain what the following correlated subquery accomplishes.

```
SELECT section_id, course_no
  FROM section s
 WHERE 2 >
       (SELECT COUNT(*)
          FROM enrollment
         WHERE section_id = s.section_id)
SECTION_ID COURSE_NO
---------- ---------
        79       350
        80        10
...
       145       100
       149       120

27 rows selected.
```

Answer: The correlated subquery displays the SECTION_ID and COURSE_NO of sections with less than two students enrolled. It includes sections that have no students enrolled.

For each row of the SECTION table the number literal 2 is compared to the result of the COUNT(*) function of the inner subquery. For each row of the outer SECTION table with the S.SECTION_ID column being the correlated column, the inner query counts the number of rows for this individual SECTION_ID. If no enrollment is found for the particular section, the COUNT function returns a zero; the row satisfies the criteria that 2 is greater than zero and is included in the result set.

Let's look at one of the rows of the SECTION table, specifically, the row with the SECTION_ID value of 80. The inner query returns a count of 1.

```
SELECT COUNT(*)
  FROM enrollment
 WHERE section_id = 80
 COUNT(*)
---------
        1

1 row selected.
```

When the number 1 is compared in the WHERE clause of the outer query, you see that 2 > 1 is true; therefore, this section is returned in the result.

You can write two queries to verify that the result of the correlated query is correct. First, write a query that shows sections where the enrollment is less than 2 students. This query returns 13 rows.

```
SELECT section_id, COUNT(*)
  FROM enrollment
 GROUP BY section_id
HAVING COUNT(*) < 2
```

SECTION_ID	COUNT(*)
80	1
96	1
...	
145	1
149	1

13 rows selected.

Then write a second query to show the sections without any enrollments (i.e., the SECTION_ID does not exist in the ENROLLMENT table). To determine these sections, you can use the NOT IN operator because the SECTION_ID in the ENROLLMENT table is defined as NOT NULL.

```
SELECT section_id
  FROM section
 WHERE section_id NOT IN
       (SELECT section_id
          FROM enrollment)
```

SECTION_ID
79
93
...
136
139

14 rows selected.

The combination of the 13 and 14 rows from the last two queries returns a total of 27.

Alternatively, you can combine the results of the two queries with the UNION operator discussed in Chapter 8, "Set Operators."

b) Show the sections and their number of enrollments where the enrollment exceeds the capacity of the section, using a correlated subquery.

Answer: The correlated query solution executes the outer query's GROUP BY clause first; then for every group, the subquery is executed to determine if it satisfies the condition in the HAVING clause. Only sections where the number of enrolled students exceeds the capacity for the respective section are returned for output.

```
SELECT section_id, COUNT(*)
  FROM enrollment e
 GROUP BY section_id
HAVING COUNT(*) >
       (SELECT capacity
          FROM section
         WHERE e.section_id = section_id)
SECTION_ID  COUNT(*)
----------- --------
       101        12

1 row selected.
```

Alternatively, this can be solved using an equijoin and an aggregate function. The enrollment count is evaluated in the HAVING clause and compared with the capacity. The additional CAPACITY column in the output validates the correct result.

```
SELECT e.section_id, COUNT(*), s.capacity
  FROM enrollment e, section s
 WHERE e.section_id = s.section_id
 GROUP BY e.section_id, s.capacity
HAVING COUNT(*) > s.capacity
SECTION_ID  COUNT(*)  CAPACITY
----------- --------- --------
       101        12        10

1 row selected.
```

When you join tables and apply aggregate functions, be sure the resulting rows provide the correct result of the aggregate function.

7.2.2 ANSWERS

a) Write a SQL statement to determine the total number of students enrolled using the EXISTS operator. Count students enrolled in more than one course as one.

Answer: For every student, the query checks to see if a row exists in the ENROLLMENT table. If this is true, the record is part of the result set. After Oracle determines all the rows that satisfy the EXISTS condition, the aggregate function COUNT is applied to determine the total number of students.

```
SELECT COUNT(*)
  FROM student s
 WHERE EXISTS
        (SELECT NULL
           FROM enrollment
          WHERE student_id = s.student_id)
  COUNT(*)
---------
      165
```

1 row selected.

The same result can be obtained with the next query. Because the ENROLLMENT table may contain multiple STUDENT_IDS if the student is enrolled in several sections, you need to count the distinct occurrences of the STUDENT_ID to obtain the correct result.

```
SELECT COUNT(DISTINCT student_id)
  FROM enrollment
  COUNT(DISTINCT STUDENT_ID)
--------------------------
                       165
```

1 row selected.

b) Show the STUDENT_ID, last name, and first name of students enrolled in three or more classes.

Answer: There are four possible solutions; of those, only one uses the EXISTS operator. The other solutions are listed to illustrate alternate ways to obtain the same result set.

SOLUTION 1: CORRELATED SUBQUERY

```
SELECT first_name, last_name, student_id
  FROM student s
 WHERE EXISTS
        (SELECT NULL
           FROM enrollment
          WHERE s.student_id = student_id
          GROUP BY student_id
          HAVING COUNT(*) >= 3)
```

FIRST_NAME	LAST_NAME	STUDENT_ID
Daniel	Wicelinski	124
Roger	Snow	238
...		

| Salewa | Zuckerberg | 184 |
| Yvonne | Williams | 214 |

7 rows selected.

For each record in the STUDENT table, the inner query is executed to determine if the STUDENT_ID occurs three or more times in the ENROLLMENT table. The inner query's SELECT clause lists the NULL keyword, whereas in the previous examples, a text literal was selected. It is completely irrelevant what columns are selected in the subquery with the EXISTS and NOT EXISTS operators because these operators only check for the existence or nonexistence of rows.

SOLUTION 2: EQUIJOIN

```
SELECT first_name, last_name, s.student_id
  FROM enrollment e, student s
 WHERE e.student_id = s.student_id
 GROUP BY first_name, last_name, s.student_id
HAVING COUNT(*) >= 3
```

This solution joins the STUDENT and ENROLLMENT tables. Students enrolled multiple times are grouped into one row and the COUNT function counts the occurrences of each student's enrollment record. Only those having three or more records in the ENROLLMENT table are included.

Although Solution 2 achieves the correct result, you need to be aware of the dangers of aggregate functions in joins.

SOLUTION 3: IN SUBQUERY

This subquery returns only STUDENT_IDs with three or more enrollments. The result is then fed to the outer query.

```
SELECT first_name, last_name, student_id
  FROM student
 WHERE student_id IN
       (SELECT student_id
          FROM enrollment
         GROUP BY student_id
        HAVING COUNT(*) >= 3)
```

SOLUTION 4: ANOTHER CORRELATED SUBQUERY

The number literal 3 is compared to the result of the correlated subquery. It counts the enrollment records for each individual student. This solution is similar to the solution in Exercise 7.2.1a.

```
SELECT last_name, first_name, student_id
  FROM student s
 WHERE 3 <= (SELECT COUNT(*)
               FROM enrollment
              WHERE s.student_id = student_id)
```

c) Which courses do not have sections assigned? Use a correlated subquery in the solution.

Answer: For every course in the COURSE table, the NOT EXISTS condition probes the SECTION table to determine if a row with the same course number exists. If the course number is not found, the WHERE clause evaluates to true and the record is included in the result set.

```
SELECT course_no, description
  FROM course c
 WHERE NOT EXISTS
       (SELECT 'X'
          FROM section
         WHERE c.course_no = course_no)
```

COURSE_NO	DESCRIPTION
80	Structured Programming Techniques
430	JDeveloper Techniques

2 rows selected.

Note you can also write the query as follows:

```
SELECT course_no, description
  FROM course c
 WHERE NOT EXISTS
       (SELECT 'X'
          FROM section s
         WHERE c.course_no = s.course_no)
```

The SECTION table uses the table alias's which the S.COURSE_NO column refers to. This alias is not required; it simply clarifies the column's source table. When you use column(s) without an alias, it is understood that the column(s) refers to the table in the current subquery. However, you must use a table alias for the C.COURSE_NO column, referencing the COURSE_NO in the outer query; otherwise, the query is not correlated.

As an alternative, the same result can be obtained using the NOT IN operator. Because the COURSE_NO column in the SECTION table is defined as NOT NULL, the query returns the same result.

```
SELECT course_no, description
  FROM course
 WHERE course_no NOT IN
       (SELECT course_no
          FROM section)
```

d) Which sections have no students enrolled? Use a correlated subquery in the solution and order the result by the course number in ascending order.

Answer: The result contains only rows where the SECTION_ID does not exist in the ENROLLMENT table. The inner query executes for each row of the outer query.

```
SELECT course_no, section_id
  FROM section s
 WHERE NOT EXISTS
       (SELECT NULL
          FROM enrollment
         WHERE s.section_id = section_id)
 ORDER BY course_no
COURSE NO SECTION_ID
--------- ----------
       25         93
      134        129
...
      350         79
```

```
14 rows selected.
```

You can achieve the same result using the NOT IN operator because the SEC-TION_ID column in the ENROLLMENT table is defined as NOT NULL.

```
SELECT course_no, section_id
  FROM section
 WHERE section_id NOT IN
       (SELECT section_id
          FROM enrollment)
 ORDER BY course_no
```

LAB 7.2 SELF-REVIEW QUESTIONS

In order to test your progress, you should be able to answer the following questions.

1) The NOT EXISTS operator tests for occurrences of nulls.

    a) _____ True
    b) _____ False

2) In a correlated subquery the inner query is executed repeatedly.

    a) _____ True
    b) _____ False

3) The operators IN and EXISTS are somewhat equivalent.

    a) _____ True
    b) _____ False

4) Determine the correct question for the following SQL statement.

```
SELECT student_id, section_id
  FROM enrollment e
 WHERE NOT EXISTS
         (SELECT '1'
            FROM grade g
           WHERE e.section_id = section_id
             AND e.student_id = student_id)
```

    a) _____ Show the enrolled students and their respective sections that have grades assigned.
    b) _____ Determine the students and their sections where no grades have been assigned.
    c) _____ Determine which students are not enrolled.
    d) _____ Determine the students that are not enrolled and do not have grades.
    e) _____ This is an invalid query.

5) Always evaluate the result of a join first, before applying an aggregate function.

    a) _____ True
    b) _____ False

Answers appear in Appendix A, Section 7.2.

L A B   7 . 3

INLINE VIEWS AND SCALAR SUBQUERY EXPRESSIONS

LAB OBJECTIVES

After this lab, you will be able to:

✔ Write Inline Views and Write Scalar Subquery Expressions

INLINE VIEWS

Inline views, also referred to as queries in the FROM clause, allow you to treat a query as a virtual table or view. The following example illustrates the concept of the inline view.

```
SELECT e.student_id, e.section_id, s.last_name
  FROM (SELECT student_id, section_id, enroll_date
          FROM enrollment
         WHERE student_id = 123) e,
       student s
 WHERE e.student_id = s.student_id
STUDENT_ID SECTION_ID LAST_NAME
---------- ---------- ---------
       123         87 Radicola

1 row selected.
```

The inline view is written in the FROM clause of the query and enclosed within a set of parentheses; it has an alias called E. The result of this query is evaluated and executed first, and then the result is joined to the STUDENT table.

The inline view acts just like a virtual table, or, for that matter, like a view. A view is a query definition stored in the database that looks just like a table. It does not have any physical rows, because a view is actually a stored query that is only executed when the view is accessed. You learn more about views in Chapter 12, "Views, Indexes, and Sequences."

The difference between a view and an inline view is that the inline view does not need to be created and stored in the data dictionary. You can create this inline view or virtual table by placing your query into the FROM clause of a SQL statement.

Inline view queries may look very complicated, but are very easy to understand. They allow you to break down complex problems into simple queries. The following query uses two inline views to return the actual number of enrollments for course number 20 and joins this result to the capacity of the course. The actual and potential revenue is then computed by multiplying the course cost with the number of enrollments and the respective capacity of the course.

```
SELECT enr.num_enrolled "Enrollments",
       enr.num_enrolled * c.cost "Actual Revenue",
       cap.capacity "Total Capacity",
       cap.capacity * c.cost "Potential Revenue"
  FROM (SELECT COUNT(*) num_enrolled
          FROM enrollment e, section s
         WHERE s.course_no = 20
           AND s.section_id = e.section_id) enr,
       (SELECT SUM(capacity) capacity
          FROM section
         WHERE course_no = 20) cap,
       course c
 WHERE c.course_no = 20
```

Enrollments	Actual Revenue	Total Capacity	Potential Revenue
9	10755	80	95600

1 row selected.

The easiest way to understand the query is to look at the result set for each inline view. The first query, referenced with the alias ENR, returns the number of students enrolled in course number 20. It requires a join between the ENROLLMENT and the SECTION table, because the number of students enrolled per section is in the ENROLLMENT table and the COURSE_NO column is found in the SECTION table. The column joining the two tables is the SECTION_ID. The query returns one row and indicates that 9 students are enrolled in course number 20.

```
SELECT COUNT(*) num_enrolled
  FROM enrollment e, section s
 WHERE s.course_no = 20
   AND s.section_id = e.section_id
```

```
NUM_ENROLLED
------------
           9
```

1 row selected.

The second query, with the alias CAP, uses the aggregate function SUM to add all the values in the CAPACITY column for course number 20. Since the SUM function is an aggregate function, it returns one row with the total capacity of 80 for all the sections for course number of 20.

```
SELECT SUM(capacity) capacity
  FROM section
 WHERE course_no = 20
CAPACITY
---------
      80
```

1 row selected.

The last table in the FROM clause of the query is the COURSE table. This table holds the course cost to compute the actual revenue and the potential revenue. The query also retrieves one row.

Note that the results of the inline views, which are identified with the aliases ENR and CAP, are not joined together with the COURSE table, thus creating a Cartesian product. Because a multiplication of the number of rows from each involved inline view and table, 1*1*1, results in one row, this query returns the one row for course number 20. A join condition is not required in this case, but it can be added for clarification if so desired.

TOP-N QUERY

An example of a top-n query is a query allowing you to determine the top three students for a particular section. To accomplish this, you need to understand the use of the ROWNUM pseudocolumn.

This column returns a number indicating the order in which Oracle returns the rows from a table or set of tables. You can use ROWNUM to limit the number of rows returned, as in the following example. It returns the first five rows.

```
SELECT last_name, first_name
  FROM student
 WHERE ROWNUM <=5
LAST_NAME                      FIRST_NAME
------------------------------ ----------
Eakheit                        George
Millstein                      Leonard
```

Cadet	Austin V.
Zapulla	Tamara
Goldsmith	Jenny

5 rows selected.

A pseudocolumn is not a real column in a table; you can SELECT from this column, but you cannot manipulate its values. You will learn more about other pseudocolumns (e.g., LEVEL, NEXTVAL, CURRVAL, and ROWID) throughout this book.

Combining the ROWNUM pseudocolumn and an inline view help determine the three highest final examination grades of section 101 as illustrated with the following query.

```
SELECT ROWNUM, numeric_grade
   FROM (SELECT DISTINCT numeric_grade
           FROM grade
          WHERE section_id = 101
            AND grade_type_code = 'FI'
          ORDER BY numeric_grade DESC)
  WHERE ROWNUM <= 3
```

ROWNUM	NUMERIC_GRADE
1	99
2	92
3	91

3 rows selected.

The inline view selects the distinct values in the NUMERIC_GRADE column for all final examination grades where the SECTION_ID equals 101. This result is ordered by the NUMERIC_GRADE in descending order, with the highest NUMERIC_GRADE listed first. The outer query uses the ordered result of the inline view and the ROWNUM column to return only the first three. By ordering the results within the inline view this construct provides a method to both limit and order the number of rows returned. For even more sophisticated ranking functionality and on analytical and statistical functions refer to Chapter 16, "Exploring Data Warehousing Features."

PRACTICAL USES OF INLINE VIEWS

If your problem is very complex and challenging, inline views are sometimes the only way to solve the problem without violating any of the SQL syntax restrictions. Inline views allow you to break down the problem into individual queries and then combine the results through joins. If you want to write top-n queries without using any of the ranking functions (discussed in Chapter 16, "Exploring Data Warehousing Features"), you need to use an inline view.

SCALAR SUBQUERY EXPRESSIONS

You already learned about the scalar subquery, which is a query returning a single-column, single-row value. You can use a scalar subquery expression in most syntax that calls for an expression. The next examples show you how to use this functionality in the SELECT list, the WHERE clause, the ORDER BY clause of a query, a CASE expression, or as part of a function call.

SCALAR SUBQUERY EXPRESSION IN THE SELECT CLAUSE

This query returns all the Connecticut zip codes and a count of how many students live in each zip code. The query is correlated as the scalar subquery, and it is executed for each individual zip code. For some zip codes, no students are in the STUDENT table; therefore, the subquery's COUNT function returns a zero. (The query can also be written as an outer join discussed in Chapter 9, "Complex Joins.")

**LAB
7.3**

```
SELECT city, state, zip,
       (SELECT COUNT(*)
          FROM student s
         WHERE s.zip = z.zip) AS student_count
  FROM zipcode z
 WHERE state = 'CT'
```

CITY	ST	ZIP	STUDENT_COUNT
Ansonia	CT	06401	0
...			
Stamford	CT	06907	1

19 rows selected.

Note that scalar subquery expressions can become notoriously inefficient because Oracle can often execute table joins faster, particularly when scans of the entire result set are involved. Following is one example where the result of an equijoin is achieved using a scalar subquery.

```
SELECT student_id, last_name,
       (SELECT state
          FROM zipcode z
         WHERE z.zip = s.zip) AS state
  FROM student s
 WHERE student_id BETWEEN 100 AND 120
```

STUDENT_ID	LAST_NAME	ST
102	Crocitto	NY
...		
120	Alexander	NY

17 rows selected.

SCALAR SUBQUERY EXPRESSION IN THE WHERE CLAUSE

The next query is an example of a scalar subquery expression in the WHERE clause of a SELECT statement. The WHERE clause limits the result set to those students who enrolled in more courses than the average student. The equivalent equijoin is probably more efficient.

```
SELECT student_id, last_name
 FROM student s
 WHERE (SELECT COUNT(*)
          FROM enrollment e
         WHERE s.student_id = e.student_id) >
              (SELECT AVG(COUNT(*))
                 FROM enrollment
                GROUP BY student_id)
 ORDER BY 1
STUDENT_ID LAST_NAME
---------- ---------
       102 Crocitto
...
       283 Perkins

52 rows selected.
```

SCALAR SUBQUERY EXPRESSION IN THE ORDER BY CLAUSE

You may wonder why you need to ever execute a scalar subquery expression in the ORDER BY clause. The next example illustrates that you can sort by a column that does not even exist in the STUDENT table. The query lists the STUDENT_ID and LAST_NAME columns of those students with an ID between 230 and 235. The result is ordered by the number of sections a respective student is enrolled in. If you execute a separate query to verify the result, you will notice that student Brendler is enrolled in one section and the student called Jung in three sections.

```
SELECT student_id, last_name
  FROM student s
 WHERE student_id BETWEEN 230 AND 235
 ORDER BY (SELECT COUNT(*)
             FROM enrollment e
            WHERE s.student_id = e.student_id) DESC
STUDENT_ID LAST_NAME
---------- ---------
       232 Jung
...
       234 Brendler

5 rows selected.
```

SCALAR SUBQUERY EXPRESSION
AND THE CASE EXPRESSION

Scalar subquery expressions are particularly handy in CASE expressions or within the DECODE function. The following example demonstrates their extraordinarily powerful functionality. The SELECT statement lists the costs of courses with the COURSE_NO of 20 and 80. The column labeled "Test CASE" illustrates the result of the CASE expression.

Depending on the value of the COST column, a comparison against a scalar subquery expression is executed. For example, the COST column is compared to the average COST of all courses, and if the value in the COST column is less than or equal to that average, the value in the COST column is multiplied by 1.5.

LAB
7.3

The next WHEN comparison checks to see if the cost is equal to the highest course cost. If so, it displays the value of the COST column for COURSE_NO 20. Note that if the scalar subquery expression determines that the row with the COURSE_NO 20 does not exist, the scalar subquery expression will evaluate to a null.

```
SELECT course_no, cost,
       CASE WHEN cost <= (SELECT AVG(cost) FROM course) THEN
                         cost *1.5
            WHEN cost =  (SELECT MAX(cost) FROM course) THEN
                         (SELECT cost FROM course
                          WHERE course_no = 20)
            ELSE cost
       END "Test CASE"
  FROM course
 WHERE course_no IN (20, 80)
 ORDER BY 2
COURSE_NO       COST Test CASE
--------------- ---- ---------
       20       1195    1792.5
       80       1595      1195
```

2 rows selected.

The next example shows the use of the scalar subquery expression in the condition part of the CASE expression. The cost of course number 134, which happens to be 1195, is multiplied by 2, effectively doubling the cost. This result is then compared to see if it's less than or equal to the average cost of all courses.

```
SELECT course_no, cost,
       CASE WHEN (SELECT cost*2
                    FROM course
                   WHERE course_no = 134)
```

```
                                   <= (SELECT AVG(cost) FROM course) THEN
                                      cost *1.5
                    WHEN cost =   (SELECT MAX(cost) FROM course) THEN
                                  (SELECT cost FROM course
                                     WHERE course_no = 20)
                    ELSE cost
              END "Test CASE"
   FROM course
 WHERE course_no IN (20, 80)
 ORDER BY 2
    COURSE_NO      COST   Test CASE
    --------------- -----  ----------
             20     1195        1195
             80     1595        1195

2 rows selected.
```

SCALAR SUBQUERY EXPRESSIONS AND FUNCTIONS

The next example shows the use of the scalar subquery expression within a function. For every retrieved row, the UPPER function is executed, which in turn retrieves the respective student's last name from the STUDENT table. A join between the STUDENT and ENROLLMENT table to retrieve the same information is typically more efficient, but the example illustrates another of the many versatile uses of scalar subquery expressions.

```
SELECT student_id, section_id,
       UPPER((SELECT last_name
                FROM student
               WHERE student_id = e.student_id))
       "Last Name in Caps"
  FROM enrollment e
 WHERE student_id BETWEEN 100 AND 110
STUDENT_ID SECTION_ID Last Name in Caps
---------- ---------- ------------------
       102         86 CROCITTO
       102         89 CROCITTO
...
       110         95 MARTIN
       110        154 MARTIN

13 rows selected.
```

ERRORS IN SCALAR SUBQUERY EXPRESSIONS

Just like you learned in Lab 7.1, the scalar subquery expression must always return one row and one column. Otherwise the error message ORA-01427: single-row subquery returns more than one row is returned by Oracle. If you list multiple columns, you will receive the error message ORA-00913: too many values. If your subquery does not return any row, a null value is returned.

PERFORMANCE CONSIDERATIONS

While you have seen that scalar subquery expressions can be used anywhere expressions are allowed, their application may not be practical under all circumstances. For example, to display a value from another table, a join is frequently more efficient than a scalar subquery in the SELECT list. Because the scalar subquery expression will be evaluated for each row, you should try to eliminate as many rows as possible prior to the execution of the scalar subquery expression step. This can be achieved by adding additional restricting conditions to the WHERE clause. As always, there are many ways to achieve the same result using various SQL syntax option; this chapter illustrates the many different possibilities. Unfortunately, there is no specific set of guidelines you can follow that will ensure that your SQL statement executes in a timely manner. There are many variables that effect performance; however, the Oracle optimizer (discussed in Chapter 17, "SQL Optimization") typically does a pretty good job in efficiently processing your statement.

LAB 7.3 EXERCISES

7.3.1 WRITE INLINE VIEWS AND SCALAR SUBQUERY EXPRESSIONS

a) Write the query that displays the SECTION_ID and COURSE_NO columns along with the number of students enrolled for sections with the IDs of 93, 101, and 103. Utilize a scalar subquery to write the query. The result should look similar to the following output.

```
SECTION_ID COURSE_NO NUM_ENROLLED
---------- --------- ------------
        93        25            0
       103       310            4
       101       240           12
```

3 rows selected.

b) Write the exercise question that is answered by the following query.

```
SELECT g.student_id, section_id, g.numeric_grade,
       gr.average
  FROM grade g JOIN
       (SELECT section_id, AVG(numeric_grade) average
```

```
        FROM grade
       WHERE section_id IN (94, 106)
         AND grade_type_code = 'FI'
       GROUP BY section_id) gr
 USING (section_id)
 WHERE g.grade_type_code = 'FI'
   AND g.numeric_grade > gr.average
```

STUDENT_ID	SECTION_ID	NUMERIC_GRADE	AVERAGE
140	94	85	84.5
200	106	92	89
145	106	91	89
130	106	90	89

4 rows selected.

c) For each course number, display the total capacity of the individual sections. Include the number of students enrolled and the percentage of the course that is filled. The result should look similar to the following output.

COURSE_NO	TOTAL_CAPACITY	TOTAL_STUDENTS	Filled Percentage
240	25	13	52
230	27	14	51.85
...			
450	25	1	4
134	65	2	3.08

25 rows selected.

d) Determine the top five courses with the largest number of enrollments.

LAB 7.3 EXERCISE ANSWERS

7.3.1 ANSWERS

a) Write the query that displays the SECTION_ID and COURSE_NO columns along with the number of students enrolled for sections with the IDs of 93, 101, and 103. Utilize a scalar subquery to write the query. The result should look similar to the following output.

SECTION_ID	COURSE_NO	NUM_ENROLLED
93	25	0
103	310	4
101	240	12

3 rows selected.

Answer: This query uses a scalar subquery in the SELECT clause of the SQL statement. The scalar subquery is correlated and determines for each of the three SECTION_ID values the number of rows in the ENROLLMENT table.

```
SELECT section_id, course_no,
       (SELECT COUNT(*)
          FROM enrollment e
         WHERE s.section_id = e.section_id)
       AS num_enrolled
  FROM section s
 WHERE section_id IN (101, 103, 93)
```

b) Write the question that is answered by the following query.

```
SELECT g.student_id, section_id, g.numeric_grade,
       gr.average
  FROM grade g JOIN
       (SELECT section_id, AVG(numeric_grade) average
          FROM grade
         WHERE section_id IN (94, 106)
           AND grade_type_code = 'FI'
         GROUP BY section_id) gr
 USING (section_id)
 WHERE g.grade_type_code = 'FI'
   AND g.numeric_grade > gr.average
```

STUDENT_ID	SECTION_ID	NUMERIC_GRADE	AVERAGE
140	94	85	84.5
200	106	92	89
145	106	91	89
130	106	90	89

4 rows selected.

Answer: Show for sections 94 and 106 those students that have a final examination grade higher than the average for each respective section.

The inline view determines the average final examination grade for each of the sections 94 and 106. This query is executed first. The result is then joined with the GRADE table where the SECTION_ID column agrees. The filtering criteria is that the GRADE_TYPE_CODE column equals to 'FI', which stands for final examination grade, and the last condition chooses only those rows that have a grade higher than the average for each respective section.

c) For each course number, display the total capacity of the individual sections. Include the number of students enrolled and the percentage of the course that is filled. The result should look similar to the following output.

COURSE_NO	TOTAL_CAPACITY	TOTAL_STUDENTS	Filled Percentage
240	25	13	52
230	27	14	51.85
...			
450	25	1	4
134	65	2	3.08

25 rows selected.

Answer: The query uses inline views to retrieve the total capacity and number of students enrolled. The percentage filled column is calculated using the resulting values from the inline views and is used to order the result.

```
SELECT a.course_no, total_capacity, total_students,
       ROUND(100/total_capacity*total_students, 2)
       "Filled Percentage"
  FROM (SELECT COUNT(*) total_students, s.course_no
          FROM enrollment e, section s
         WHERE e.section_id = s.section_id
         GROUP BY s.course_no) a,
       (SELECT SUM(capacity) total_capacity, course_no
          FROM section
         GROUP BY course_no) b
 WHERE b.course_no = a.course_no
 ORDER BY "Filled Percentage" DESC
```

It helps to build the query step by step by looking at the individual queries. The first query, with the alias A, returns the total number of students enrolled for each course.

```
SELECT COUNT(*) total_students, s.course_no
  FROM enrollment e, section s
 WHERE e.section_id = s.section_id
 GROUP BY s.course_no
```

TOTAL_STUDENTS	COURSE_NO
1	10
9	20
...	

```
           2             420
           1             450
```

25 rows selected.

The second query, with the alias B, returns the total capacity for each course.

```
SELECT SUM(capacity) total_capacity, course_no
  FROM section
 GROUP BY course_no
TOTAL_CAPACITY COURSE_NO
-------------- ---------
           15        10
           80        20
...
           25       420
           25       450
```

28 rows selected.

Then, the two queries are joined by the common column, the COURSE_NO, using the aliases A and B assigned in the inline view queries. The outer query references the columns TOTAL_STUDENTS and TOTAL_CAPACITY. The ROUND function computes the percentage with a two-digit precision after the comma. The result is sorted by this percentage in descending order.

d) Determine the top five courses with the largest number of enrollments.

Answer: This question is solved with an inline view and the ROWNUM pseudocolumn.

```
SELECT ROWNUM Ranking, course_no, num_enrolled
  FROM (SELECT COUNT(*) num_enrolled, s.course_no
          FROM enrollment e, section s
         WHERE e.section_id = s.section_id
         GROUP BY s.course_no
         ORDER BY 1 DESC)
 WHERE ROWNUM <= 5
  RANKING COURSE_NO NUM_ENROLLED
--------- --------- ------------
        1        25           45
        2       122           24
        3       120           23
        4       140           15
        5       230           14
```

5 rows selected.

LAB 7.3 SELF-REVIEW QUESTIONS

In order to test your progress, you should be able to answer the following questions.

1) Scalar subquery expressions are not allowed in the GROUP BY clause.

a) _____ True
b) _____ False

2) Scalar subqueries return one or more rows.

a) _____ True
b) _____ False

3) Inline views are stored in the data dictionary.

a) _____ True
b) _____ False

4) The ROWNUM is an actual column in a table.

a) _____ True
b) _____ False

5) The ORDER BY clause is allowed in an inline view.

a) _____ True
b) _____ False

Answers appear in Appendix A, Section 7.3.

L A B 7 . 4

ANY, SOME, AND ALL OPERATORS IN SUBQUERIES

L A B   O B J E C T I V E S

After this lab, you will be able to:
✔ Use the ANY, SOME, and ALL Operators in Subqueries

You are already familiar with the IN operator, which compares a list of values for equality. The ANY, SOME, and ALL operators are related to the IN operator as they also compare against a list of values. Additionally, these operators allow >, <, >=, and <= comparisons.

The ANY operator checks whether any value in the list makes the condition true. The ALL operator returns rows if the condition is true for all the values in the list. The SOME operator is identical to ANY, and the two can be used interchangeably. Before applying these operators to subqueries, examine their effect on a simple list of values.

This query retrieves all the grades for SECTION_ID 84.

```
SELECT section_id, numeric_grade
  FROM grade
 WHERE section_id = 84
```

SECTION_ID	NUMERIC_GRADE
84	88
84	99
84	77
84	88

4 rows selected.

The familiar IN operator in the next SQL statement chooses all the grades that are either equal to 77 or equal to 99.

```
SELECT section_id, numeric_grade
  FROM grade
 WHERE section_id = 84
   AND numeric_grade IN (77, 99)
SECTION_ID NUMERIC_GRADE
---------- -------------
        84            99
        84            77
```

2 rows selected.

If you want to perform a comparison such as less than (<) against a list of values, use either the ANY, SOME, or ALL operator.

ANY AND SOME

This SQL query looks for any rows where the value in the NUMERIC_GRADE column is less than either value in the list.

```
SELECT section_id, numeric_grade
  FROM grade
 WHERE section_id = 84
   AND numeric_grade < ANY (80, 90)
SECTION_ID NUMERIC_GRADE
---------- -------------
        84            88
        84            88
        84            77
```

3 rows selected.

The query returns the NUMERIC_GRADE values 77 and 88. For the rows with the NUMERIC_GRADE of 88, the condition is true as 88 is less than 90, but the condition is not true for the value 80. However, because the condition needs to be true for any of the records compared in the list, the row is included in the result.

The following query performs a greater-than comparison with the ANY operator.

```
SELECT section_id, numeric_grade
  FROM grade
 WHERE section_id = 84
   AND numeric_grade > ANY (80, 90)
```

```
SECTION_ID NUMERIC_GRADE
---------- -------------
        84            88
        84            99
        84            88
```

3 rows selected.

Because the records with the NUMERIC_GRADE 88 are greater than 80, they are included. The NUMERIC_GRADE of 99 is greater than both 80 and 90, and therefore is also included in the result set, although just one of the conditions is sufficient to be included in the result set.

The ANY operator with the = operator is the equivalent of the IN operator. There are no rows that have a NUMERIC_GRADE of either 80 or 90.

```
SELECT section_id, numeric_grade
  FROM grade
 WHERE section_id = 84
   AND numeric_grade = ANY (80, 90)
```

no rows selected

The following query is the logical equivalent to the ANY operator.

```
SELECT section_id, numeric_grade
  FROM grade
 WHERE section_id = 84
   AND numeric_grade IN (80, 90)
```

no rows selected

ALL

The ALL operator returns true if every value in the list satisfies the condition. In the following example, all the records in the GRADE table must be less than 80 and 90. This condition is true only for the row with the NUMERIC_GRADE value of 77, which is less than both 80 and 90.

```
SELECT section_id, numeric_grade
  FROM grade
 WHERE section_id = 84
   AND numeric_grade < ALL (80, 90)
SECTION_ID NUMERIC_GRADE
---------- -------------
        84            77
```

1 row selected.

A SQL statement using <> ALL is equivalent to NOT IN.

```
SELECT section_id, numeric_grade
  FROM grade
 WHERE section_id = 84
   AND numeric_grade <> ALL (80, 90)
SECTION_ID NUMERIC_GRADE
---------- -------------
        84            88
        84            99
        84            77
        84            88
```

```
4 rows selected.
```

Whenever a subquery with the ALL operator fails to return a row, the query is automatically true. This is different from the ANY operator, which returns false.

LAB 7.4 EXERCISES

7.4.1 USE THE *ANY, SOME,* AND *ALL* OPERATORS IN SUBQUERIES

a) Write a SELECT statement to display the STUDENT_ID, SEC-TION_ID, and grade for students who received a final examination grade better than *all* of their individual homework grades.

b) Based on the result of question a, what do you observe about the row with the STUDENT_ID 102 and the SECTION_ID 89?

c) Select the STUDENT_ID, SECTION_ID, and grade of students who received a final examination grade better than *any* of their individual homework grades.

d) Based on question c, explain the result of the row with the STUDENT_ID 102 and the SECTION_ID 89.

LAB 7.4 EXERCISE ANSWERS

7.4.1 ANSWERS

a) Write a SELECT statement to display the STUDENT_ID, SECTION_ID, and grade for students who received a final examination grade better than *all* of their individual homework grades.

Answer: A correlated subquery is used to compare each individual student's final examination grade with his or her respective homework grades for a particular section. The output includes only those records where the final examination grade is higher than all of the homework grades.

```
SELECT student_id, section_id, numeric_grade
  FROM grade g
 WHERE grade_type_code = 'FI'
   AND numeric_grade > ALL
       (SELECT numeric_grade
          FROM grade
         WHERE grade_type_code = 'HM'
           AND g.section_id = section_id
           AND g.student_id = student_id)
```

STUDENT_ID	SECTION_ID	NUMERIC_GRADE
102	89	92
124	83	99
143	85	92
...		
215	156	90
283	99	85

96 rows selected.

To verify the result, use the STUDENT_ID 143 and SECTION_ID 85 as an example. The highest grade for all of the homework is 91 and the lowest is 81. The grade achieved in the final examination is 92.

```
SELECT student_id, section_id, grade_type_code,
       MAX(numeric_grade) max, MIN(numeric_grade) min
  FROM grade
 WHERE student_id = 143
   AND section_id = 85
   AND grade_type_code IN ('HM', 'FI')
 GROUP BY student_id, section_id, grade_type_code
```

STUDENT_ID	SECTION_ID	GR	MAX	MIN
143	85	FI	92	92
143	85	HM	91	81

2 rows selected.

The student with the ID of 143 enrolled in section 85 is correctly selected for output as it satisfies the condition that the final examination grade be greater than all of the homework grades.

The following query verifies that the student with the ID of 179 enrolled in section 116 has a lower grade in the final exam than in all the homework grades. Therefore, the row is not included in the set.

```
SELECT student_id, section_id, grade_type_code,
       MAX(numeric_grade) max, MIN(numeric_grade) min
  FROM grade
 WHERE student_id = 179
   AND section_id = 116
   AND grade_type_code IN ('HM', 'FI')
 GROUP BY student_id, section_id, grade_type_code
STUDENT_ID SECTION_ID GR MAX MIN
---------- ---------- -- --- ---
       179        116 FI  90  90
       179        116 HM  99  99

2 rows selected.
```

b) Based on the result of question a, what do you observe about the row with the STUDENT_ID 102 and the SECTION_ID 89?

Answer: Whenever the subquery with the ALL operator fails to return a row, the query is automatically true. Therefore, this student is also included in the result set.

The interesting aspect of the relationship between ALL and NULL is that here the student for this section has no homework grades, yet the row is returned for output.

```
SELECT student_id, section_id, grade_type_code,
       MAX(numeric_grade) max, MIN(numeric_grade) min
  FROM grade
 WHERE student_id = 102
   AND section_id = 89
   AND grade_type_code IN ('HM', 'FI')
 GROUP BY student_id, section_id, grade_type_code
STUDENT_ID SECTION_ID GR MAX MIN
---------- ---------- -- --- ---
       102         89 FI  92  92

1 row selected.
```

c) Select the STUDENT_ID, SECTION_ID, and grade of students who received a final examination grade better than *any* of their individual homework grades.

Answer: The ANY operator together with the correlated subquery achieves the desired result.

```
SELECT student_id, section_id, numeric_grade
  FROM grade g
 WHERE grade_type_code = 'FI'
   AND numeric_grade > ANY
       (SELECT numeric_grade
          FROM grade
         WHERE grade_type_code = 'HM'
           AND g.section_id = section_id
           AND g.student_id = student_id)
STUDENT_ID SECTION_ID NUMERIC_GRADE
---------- ---------- -------------
       102         86            85
       103         81            91
       143         85            92
...
       283         99            85
       283        101            88
```

157 rows selected.

Examine the grades for the homework and the final for STUDENT_ID 102 and SECTION_ID 86. This student's final grade of 85 is better than the homework grade of 82. The ANY operator tests for an OR condition, so the student and section are returned because only one of the homework grades has to satisfy the condition.

```
SELECT student_id, section_id, grade_type_code,
       numeric_grade
  FROM grade
 WHERE student_id = 102
   AND section_id = 86
   AND grade_type_code IN ('HM', 'FI')
 GROUP BY student_id, section_id, grade_type_code,
       numeric_grade
STUDENT_ID SECTION_ID GR NUMERIC_GRADE
---------- ---------- -- -------------
       102         86 FI            85
       102         86 HM            82
       102         86 HM            90
       102         86 HM            99
```

4 rows selected.

d) Based on question c, explain the result of the row with the STUDENT_ID 102 and the SECTION_ID 89.

Answer: This record is not returned because unlike the ALL operator, the ANY operator returns false.

The following example illustrates the effect of no records in the subquery on the ANY operator. The student 102 enrolled in SECTION_ID 89 has no homework grades, and, therefore, does not appear in question c's result set.

```
SELECT student_id, section_id, grade_type_code,
       numeric_grade
  FROM grade
 WHERE student_id = 102
   AND section_id = 89
   AND grade_type_code IN ('HM', 'FI')
STUDENT_ID SECTION_ID GR NUMERIC_GRADE
---------- ---------- -- -------------
       102         89 FI            92

1 row selected.
```

LAB 7.4 SELF-REVIEW QUESTIONS

In order to test your progress, you should be able to answer the following questions.

1) Are the operators NOT IN and <> ANY equivalent as illustrated in the following example?

```
SELECT 'TRUE'
  FROM dual
 WHERE 6 <> ANY (6, 9)

SELECT 'TRUE'
  FROM dual
 WHERE 6 NOT IN (6, 9)
```

a) _____ Yes
b) _____ No

2) The following queries are logically equivalent.

```
SELECT 'TRUE'
  FROM dual
 WHERE 6 IN (6, 9)

SELECT 'TRUE'
  FROM dual
 WHERE 6 = ANY (6,9)
```

a) _____ True
b) _____ False

3) The operators ANY and SOME are equivalent.

    a) _____ True
    b) _____ False

4) To perform any >=, <=, >, or < comparison with a subquery returning multiple rows, you need to use either the ANY, SOME, or ALL operator.

    a) _____ True
    b) _____ False

Answers appear in Appendix A, Section 7.4.

LAB
7.4

CHAPTER 7

TEST YOUR THINKING

The projects in this section are meant to have you utilize all of the skills that you have acquired throughout this chapter. The answers to these projects can be found at the companion Web site to this book, located at: *http://authors.phptr.com/rischert3e*. Visit the Web site periodically to share and discuss your answers.

1) Using a subquery construct, determine which sections the student Henry Masser is enrolled in.

2) Write the question for the following SELECT statement.

```
SELECT zip
  FROM zipcode z
 WHERE NOT EXISTS
       (SELECT '*'
          FROM student
         WHERE z.zip = zip)
   AND NOT EXISTS
       (SELECT '*'
          FROM instructor
         WHERE z.zip = zip)
```

3) Display the course number and description of courses with no enrollment. Also include courses that have no section assigned.

4) Can the ANY and ALL operators be used on the DATE datatype? Write a simple query to prove your answer.

5) If you have a choice to write either a correlated subquery or a simple non-correlated subquery, which one would you choose and why?

6) Determine the top three zip codes where most of the students live.

C H A P T E R   8

SET OPERATORS

Set operators combine two or more sets of data to produce a single result set. Oracle has four set operators: UNION, UNION ALL, MINUS, and INTERSECT. The UNION and UNION ALL operators combine results. The INTERSECT operator determines common rows. The MINUS operator shows differences between sets of rows.

The sets of data in a set operation are SELECT statements, as simple or as complex as SELECT statements can be written. When writing any set operation, there are two rules to remember:

- Each of the SELECT lists must contain the same number of columns.

- The matching columns in each of the SELECT lists must be the same datatype (Oracle considers CHAR and VARCHAR2 to be datatype compatible).

In this chapter you will use set operators to retrieve data from many tables throughout the STUDENT schema.

LAB 8.1

THE POWER OF UNION AND UNION ALL

**LAB
8.1**

LAB OBJECTIVES

After this lab, you will be able to:
✔ Use the UNION and UNION ALL Set Operators

The UNION operator is probably the most commonly used set operator. It combines two or more sets of data to produce a single set of data. Think of the UNION operator as two overlapping circles, as illustrated in Figure 8.1. The union of the two circles is everything from both circles. There are duplicates where they overlap, and there may even be duplicates within each set, but the final result shows these values only once. The UNION ALL operator includes these duplicates.

Imagine you need to create a phone list of all instructors and students. The following set operation uses the UNION operator to combine instructor and student names and phone numbers from the INSTRUCTOR and STUDENT tables into a single result set.

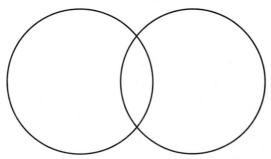

Figure 8.1 ■ UNION and UNION ALL set operators.

```
SELECT first_name, last_name, phone
  FROM instructor
 UNION
SELECT first_name, last_name, phone
  FROM student
```

FIRST_NAME	LAST_NAME	PHONE
A.	Tucker	203-555-5555
Adele	Rothstein	718-555-5555
...		
Z.A.	Scrittorale	203-555-5555
Zalman	Draquez	718-555-5555

276 rows selected.

The same three columns are selected from each table, effectively stacking the columns one on top of the other in the result set. The results are automatically sorted by the order in which the columns appear in the SELECT list.

Notice the result returns 276 rows, even though there are 268 student rows and 10 instructor rows. What happened to the other two rows? The following query shows duplicate rows in the STUDENT table.

```
SELECT first_name, last_name, phone, COUNT(*)
  FROM student
 GROUP BY first_name, last_name, phone
HAVING COUNT(*) > 1
```

FIRST_NAME	LAST_NAME	PHONE	COUNT(*)
Kevin	Porch	201-555-5555	2
Thomas	Edwards	201-555-5555	2

2 rows selected.

Because the UNION operator shows only distinct rows, both of the duplicate student rows appear just once in the result of the UNION set operation. To list all the instructors and students, including duplicates, there are two approaches. One approach is to add the ID of the INSTRUCTOR and STUDENT tables to the set operation, plus a text literal such as 'instructor' and 'student'. The other approach is to use the UNION ALL operator. UNION ALL includes any duplicates when sets of data are added. Think again of the two overlapping circles shown in Figure 8.1. UNION ALL not only adds the two sets of data, but includes the overlapping duplicates as well. Duplicates that may exist within each set are also included.

```
SELECT first_name, last_name, phone
  FROM instructor
 UNION ALL
```

```
SELECT first_name, last_name, phone
  FROM student
FIRST_NAME LAST_NAME            PHONE
---------- ----------------- ------------
Fernand    Hanks                2125551212
Tom        Wojick               2125551212
...
Kathleen   Mastandora           718-555-5555
Angela     Torres               718-555-5555

278 rows selected.
```

UNION ALL results in 278 rows, which includes the duplicates in the STUDENT table. Also, the result set is no longer sorted; UNION ALL does not perform a sort. Therefore, a query containing the UNION operator will be more time-consuming to execute than a query with the UNION ALL operator. Unless you have a reason to show only distinct rows, use UNION ALL instead of UNION because it will yield better performance.

ORDER BY AND SET OPERATIONS

Just like the result of any SELECT statement, the result of a set operation can be sorted using the ORDER BY clause. Instead of naming the column you want to sort the result by, refer to its position in the SELECT list instead. Consider what happens if you add the instructor and student IDs to the previous example using UNION and order the results by the LAST_NAME column:

```
SELECT instructor_id id, first_name, last_name, phone
  FROM instructor
 UNION
SELECT student_id, first_name, last_name, phone
  FROM student
 ORDER BY 3
      ID FIRST_NAME LAST_NAME           PHONE
--------- ---------- ----------------- ------------
     119 Mardig      Abdou               718-555-5555
     399 Jerry       Abdou               718-555-5555
...
     184 Salewa      Zuckerberg          718-555-5555
     206 Freedon     annunziato          718-555-5555

278 rows selected.
```

The ORDER BY clause can also refer to a column alias, such as id used for the first column. However, referring to the column position in the ORDER BY clause is ANSI-standard and is also independent of the column names in either SELECT statement.

With the addition of the instructor and student IDs, the unique combination of those IDs with first name, last name, and phone number now produces all 278 rows between the INSTRUCTOR and STUDENT tables.

The first columns in each of the individual SELECT statements, INSTRUCTOR_ID and STUDENT_ID, have different names but are of the same datatype. Oracle uses the alias to give the column in the result set to a meaningful name for both instructor and student IDs.

SQL will always take its cue from the topmost SELECT statement when naming columns in the result set. When you want the result set to display a specific column name that is not dependent on the names of columns listed in the topmost statement, you must use a column alias.

LAB 8.1 EXERCISES

8.1.1 USE THE UNION AND UNION ALL SET OPERATORS

a) Explain the result of the following set operation, and why it works.

```
SELECT first_name, last_name,
       'Instructor' "Type"
  FROM instructor
UNION
SELECT first_name, last_name,
       'Student'
  FROM student
```

b) Write a set operation, using the UNION set operator, to list all the zip codes in the INSTRUCTOR and STUDENT tables.

c) Write the question for the following set operation.

```
SELECT created_by
  FROM enrollment
UNION
SELECT created_by
  FROM grade
UNION
SELECT created_by
  FROM grade_type
UNION
SELECT created_by
  FROM grade_conversion
```

```
CREATED_BY
----------
ARISCHER
BMOTIVAL
BROSENZW
CBRENNAN
DSCHERER
JAYCAF
MCAFFREY

7 rows selected.
```

d) Explain the result of the following set operation:

```
SELECT course_no, description
  FROM course
 WHERE prerequisite IS NOT NULL
 ORDER BY 1
 UNION
SELECT course_no, description
  FROM course
 WHERE prerequisite IS NULL
```

e) What is wrong with the following set operation, and what do you have to change to make it work correctly?

```
SELECT instructor_id, last_name
  FROM instructor
 UNION
SELECT last_name, student_id
  FROM student
```

LAB 8.1 EXERCISE ANSWERS

8.1.1 ANSWERS

a) Explain the result of the following set operation, and why it works.

```
SELECT first_name, last_name,
       'Instructor' "Type"
  FROM instructor
 UNION
SELECT first_name, last_name,
       'Student'
  FROM student
```

Answer: The result set displays the first and last names of instructors and students. The third column identifies what type of person each is. 'Instructor' and 'Student' are both text literals and are in the same position in each SELECT list. Therefore, the two SELECT statements are row-compatible.

```
FIRST_NAME LAST_NAME                         Type
---------- ------------------------------    -------
A.         Tucker                            Student
Adele      Rothstein                         Student
...
Z.A.       Scrittorale                       Student
Zalman     Draquez                           Student

276 rows selected.
```

As your SELECT statements and set operations become more complex, it can be difficult to identify the data in your result sets accurately. This technique of identifying each row in the result set coming from one or the other set of data may be very useful.

b) Write a set operation, using UNION, to list all the zip codes in the INSTRUCTOR and STUDENT tables.

Answer: Two SELECT statements are combined using the UNION set operator for a result set displaying zip codes from both tables, eliminating any duplicates.

```
SELECT zip
  FROM instructor
 UNION
SELECT zip
  FROM student
ZIP
-----
01247
02124
...
43224
48104

149 rows selected.
```

c) Write the question for the following set operation.

```
SELECT created_by
  FROM enrollment
 UNION
SELECT created_by
  FROM grade
 UNION
```

```
SELECT created_by
  FROM grade_type
 UNION
SELECT created_by
  FROM grade_conversion
CREATED_BY
----------
ARISCHER
BMOTIVAL
BROSENZW
CBRENNAN
DSCHERER
JAYCAF
MCAFFREY

7 rows selected.
```

Answer: Create a list of users who created rows in the ENROLLMENT, GRADE, GRADE_TYPE, and GRADE_CONVERSION tables. Show each user name only once.

As mentioned in the beginning of this lab, set operators can be used with two or more sets of data. This exercise combines the data from four separate tables into a single result set, eliminating duplicates where they occur.

CONTROLLING THE SORT ORDER

Sometimes you want to choose a specific sort order. This can be accomplished with a literal by which you can order the result.

```
SELECT created_by, 'GRADE' AS SOURCE, 1 AS SORT_ORDER
  FROM grade
 UNION
SELECT created_by, 'GRADE_TYPE', 2
  FROM grade_type
 UNION
SELECT created_by, 'GRADE_CONVERSION', 3
  FROM grade_conversion
 UNION
SELECT created_by, 'ENROLLMENT', 4
  FROM enrollment
 ORDER BY 3
```

CREATED_BY	SOURCE	SORT_ORDER
ARISCHER	GRADE	1
BROSENZW	GRADE	1
CBRENNAN	GRADE	1
MCAFFREY	GRADE_TYPE	2
BMOTIVAL	GRADE_CONVERSION	3

| DSCHERER | ENROLLMENT | 4 |
| JAYCAF | ENROLLMENT | 4 |

7 rows selected.

d) Explain the result of the following set operation:

```
SELECT course_no, description
  FROM course
 WHERE prerequisite IS NOT NULL
 ORDER BY 1
 UNION
SELECT course_no, description
  FROM course
 WHERE prerequisite IS NULL
```

Answer: Oracle returns the following error message because the ORDER BY clause must be used at the end of a set operation.

```
ORA-00933: SQL command not properly ended
```

SQL always expects the ORDER BY clause to be the very last command in a SQL statement, including set operations. An ORDER BY clause logically has no purpose in the top most statement; it is applied only to the single set of data in the result set, which is a combination of all data from all SELECT statements in a set operation.

e) What is wrong with the following set operation, and what do you have to change to make it work correctly?

```
SELECT instructor_id, last_name
  FROM instructor
 UNION
SELECT last_name, student_id
  FROM student
```

Answer: Oracle returns an error: `ORA-01790: expression must have same datatype as corresponding expression.` *The datatypes of columns must be the same for columns in the same position in each SELECT list of a set operation. Either the order of the columns in the first or the second statement must be switched for the statement to work correctly.*

Sometimes the datatype of columns do not match because of the way the columns were created, in which case you can use the data conversion functions to change from one datatype to another.

DATATYPE CONVERSIONS AND NULLS

Sometimes you want to combine distinct result sets together with the UNION ALL operator and place a null value for those columns where you want to omit the value. The next example query uses the CAST function and the TO_DATE function to make sure the null columns agree with the same datatype and it avoids implicit datatype conversion.

```
SELECT DISTINCT salutation, CAST(NULL AS NUMBER),
       state, z.created_date
  FROM instructor i, zipcode z
 WHERE i.zip = z.zip
UNION ALL
SELECT salutation, COUNT(*),
       state, TO_DATE(NULL)
  FROM student s, zipcode z
 WHERE s.zip = z.zip
 GROUP BY salutation, state
```

SALUT	CAST(NULLASNUMBER)	ST	CREATED_D
DR		NY	03-AUG-03
HON		NY	03-AUG-03
...			
MS.	69	NY	
MS.	1	WV	
REV	1	NJ	

19 rows selected.

LAB 8.1 SELF-REVIEW QUESTIONS

In order to test your progress, you should be able to answer the following questions.

1) It is redundant to use DISTINCT in a UNION set operation.

    a) _____ True
    b) _____ False

2) Each of the SELECT statements in a set operation must have an ORDER BY clause when you want the results to be ordered.

    a) _____ True
    b) _____ False

3) A UNION set operation always returns the same result set as an equijoin.

   a) _____ True
   b) _____ False

4) You cannot use UNION to combine data from two tables that do not have a primary key/foreign key relationship.

   a) _____ True
   b) _____ False

5) There must be the same number of columns in each SELECT statement of a set operation.

   a) _____ True
   b) _____ False

Answers appear in Appendix A, Section 8.1.

LAB 8.2

THE MINUS AND INTERSECT SET OPERATORS

LAB OBJECTIVES

After this lab, you will be able to:
✔ Use the MINUS Set Operator
✔ Use the INTERSECT Set Operator

The MINUS set operator subtracts one set of data from another, identifying what data exists in one table but not the other. The INTERSECT set operator is the intersection of sets of data, identifying data common to all of them.

THE MINUS OPERATOR

The MINUS operation returns the difference between two sets. Effectively, you are subtracting one set from another set. The gray area of the circle in Figure 8.2 depicts the difference between the sets and indicates the data that is in one circle, but not in another.

The following set operation lists instructors not currently teaching any classes (sections).

```
SELECT instructor_id
  FROM instructor
 MINUS
SELECT instructor_id
  FROM section
INSTRUCTOR_ID
-------------
          109
          110

2 rows selected.
```

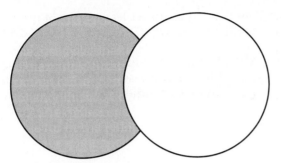

Figure 8.2 ■ The MINUS set operator.

Looking at the statements separately, the first SELECT statement returns the complete list of instructors.

```
SELECT instructor_id
  FROM instructor
INSTRUCTOR_ID
-------------
          101
          102
          103
          104
          105
          106
          109
          108
          107
          110

10 rows selected.
```

The second SELECT statement returns a distinct list of instructors currently teaching.

```
SELECT DISTINCT instructor_id
  FROM section
INSTRUCTOR_ID
-------------
          101
          102
          103
          104
          105
          106
          107
          108

8 rows selected.
```

Subtracting the second result set from the first result set leaves a list of instructors not currently teaching, which are the INSTRUCTOR_ID values of 109 and 110.

Just like the UNION set operator, MINUS eliminates duplicates when evaluating sets of data. Note DISTINCT is used in the preceding second SELECT statement when it is written separately. The following set operation implies distinct values in both SELECT statements.

```
SELECT created_by
  FROM enrollment
 MINUS
SELECT created_by
  FROM course
CREATED_BY
---------------
JAYCAF

1 row selected.
```

Written separately, the two SELECT statements use DISTINCT:

```
SELECT DISTINCT created_by
  FROM enrollment
CREATED_BY
-------------------------
DSCHERER
JAYCAF

2 rows selected.

SELECT DISTINCT created_by
  FROM course
CREATED_BY
---------------
DSCHERER

1 row selected.
```

The second SELECT statement results in the distinct value 'DSCHERER'. This is subtracted from the result of the first statement, which consists of the distinct values 'JAYCAF' and 'DSCHERER'. This results in the value 'JAYCAF' because 'JAYCAF' is not found in the COURSE table, only in the ENROLLMENT table. This type of statement whereby you retrieve data that exists in one table, but not in another, is sometimes referred to as an *antijoin*.

Be careful when positioning the SELECT statements in a MINUS set operation because their order makes a big difference. Be sure to place the set you want to subtract from first.

THE INTERSECT OPERATOR

The INTERSECT operator determines the common values between two sets. Figure 8.3 illustrates the two overlapping circles. The gray color indicates the area where the two circles intersect.

When you use INTERSECT instead of MINUS in the previous statement, the result is quite different:

```
SELECT created_by
  FROM enrollment
INTERSECT
SELECT created_by
  FROM course
CREATED_BY
---------------
DSCHERER

1 row selected.
```

The result set contains 'DSCHERER', which is the distinct value where the two sets overlap or intersect. Unlike MINUS, the order of the SELECT statements in an INTERSECT set operation does not matter.

INTERSECT INSTEAD OF EQUIJOINS

The INTERSECT set operator can replace the equijoin, which you learned about in Chapter 6, "Equijoins." The equijoin produces a result set that is the intersection of two or more tables, the same result as with INTERSECT.

Here is an equijoin that returns a list of course numbers for courses with corresponding sections:

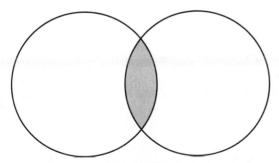

Figure 8.3 ■ **The INTERSECT set operator.**

```
SELECT DISTINCT c.course_no
  FROM course c, section s
 WHERE c.course_no = s.course_no
COURSE_NO
---------
       10
       20
...
      420
      450
```

28 rows selected.

This INTERSECT set operation returns the same result:

```
SELECT course_no
  FROM course
INTERSECT
SELECT course_no
  FROM section
COURSE_NO
---------
       10
       20
...
      420
      450
```

28 rows selected.

The drawback to using INTERSECT instead of an equijoin is that INTERSECT operates on all columns in each SELECT list of the set operation. Therefore, you cannot include columns that exist in one table and not the other.

EXECUTION ORDER OF SET OPERATIONS

The execution order for all set operations is from top to bottom. You will see the effect in the next following query. It consists of three tables called T1, T2, and T3. The query combines the values of table T1 and T2 and the subsequent MINUS operation compares this result to the values of T3. (These three tables are not found in the STUDENT schema unless you installed the additional tables from the companion Web site.)

```
SELECT col1
  FROM t1
UNION ALL
```

```
SELECT col2
   FROM t2
MINUS
SELECT col3
   FROM t3
      COL1
----------
      1
      4
```

2 rows selected.

You use parentheses to indicate a change the execution order as in the next following example. The query in parentheses is executed first; it determines the differences between T2 and T3. The UNION ALL operator combines the result with T1. As you notice the output it is quite different.

```
SELECT col1
   FROM t1
UNION ALL
(SELECT col2
   FROM t2
MINUS
SELECT col3
   FROM t3)
      COL1
----------
      1
      2
      3
      4
```

4 rows selected.

COMPARE TWO TABLES

Set operators are very useful if you need to determine the differences between two tables. For example, you want to compare test and production database tables or check data generated by a program to a previous state of the table. The following statement involves two tables. One is called OLD_TABLE, which contains the original state of the table, and the NEW_TABLE shows the data after the execution of various data manipulation statements. The queries inside the parentheses are executed first then the UNION ALL operation is performed. The SQL statement will return the differences between the two tables.

```
(SELECT *
   FROM old_table
 MINUS
 SELECT *
   FROM new_table)
UNION ALL
(SELECT *
   FROM new_table
 MINUS
 SELECT *
   FROM old_table)
```

Ideally, your tables have a primary key or unique key to uniquely identify the rows. If that's not the case, duplicate rows in the table may be possible. You may want to include the COUNT(*) function along with all the columns and a GROUP BY clause.

Another way to find out differences is to use Oracle's Flashback query. It allows you to list the changes performed between specific time intervals. You will learn more about this feature in Chapter 10, "Insert, Update, and Delete."

LAB 8.2 EXERCISES

8.2.1 USE THE MINUS SET OPERATOR

a) Explain the result of the following set operation.

```
SELECT course_no, description
  FROM course
 MINUS
SELECT s.course_no, c.description
  FROM section s, course c
 WHERE s.course_no = c.course_no
```

b) Use the MINUS set operator to create a list of courses and sections with no students enrolled. Add a column to the result set with the title Status and display the text No Enrollments in each row. Order the results by the COURSE_NO and SECTION_NO columns.

8.2.2 USE THE INTERSECT SET OPERATOR

a) Use the INTERSECT set operator to list all zip codes that are in both the STUDENT and INSTRUCTOR tables.

b) Use the INTERSECT set operator to list student IDs for students who are enrolled.

LAB 8.2 EXERCISE ANSWERS

8.2.1 ANSWERS

a) Explain the result of the following set operation.

```
SELECT course_no, description
  FROM course
 MINUS
SELECT s.course_no, c.description
  FROM section s, course c
 WHERE s.course_no = c.course_no
```

Answer: The set operation subtracts all courses having sections from all courses, resulting in the two courses without matching sections.

```
COURSE_NO DESCRIPTION
--------- --------------------------------
       80 Structured Programming Techniques
      430 JDeveloper Techniques

2 rows selected.
```

Another way to formulate the query is to write a subquery using the NOT IN or the NOT EXISTS operator:

```
SELECT course_no, description
  FROM course c
 WHERE NOT EXISTS
       (SELECT '*'
          FROM section
         WHERE c.course_no = course_no)
```

b) Use the MINUS set operator to create a list of courses and sections with no students enrolled. Add a column to the result set with the title `Status` and display the text `No Enrollments` in each row. Order the results by the COURSE_NO and SECTION_NO columns.

Answer: The first SELECT statement is the set of all courses with sections. The second SELECT statement subtracts the set of courses and sections having enrollments, leaving the difference of courses and sections without enrollments.

```
SELECT course_no, section_no, 'No Enrollments' "Status"
  FROM section
 MINUS
SELECT course_no, section_no, 'No Enrollments'
  FROM section s
```

```
WHERE EXISTS (SELECT section_id
                   FROM enrollment e
                  WHERE e.section_id = s.section_id)
ORDER BY 1, 2
COURSE_NO SECTION_NO Status
--------- ---------- --------------
       25          9 No Enrollments
      124          4 No Enrollments
...
      220          1 No Enrollments
      350          3 No Enrollments

14 rows selected.
```

This statement uses a trick to display No Enrollments in the result set. Even though it is not a column in either table, as long as it is in the first statement, there is a column for it in the result set. And, as long as it is in the second statement, it matches the first and, therefore, allows the MINUS to work correctly, subtracting one set from a similar set.

8.2.2 ANSWERS

a) Use the INTERSECT set operator to list all zip codes that are in both the STUDENT and INSTRUCTOR tables.

Answer: INTERSECT is used to find the intersection of distinct zip codes in the INSTRUCTOR and STUDENT tables.

```
SELECT zip
   FROM instructor
INTERSECT
SELECT zip
   FROM student
ZIP
-----
10025

1 row selected.
```

Be careful when deciding to use INTERSECT versus UNION. The key phrase in the question asked is "...zip codes that are in both...." INTERSECT achieves the intersection of both tables alone, whereas UNION returns all zip codes combined from both tables.

b) Use the INTERSECT set operator to list student IDs for students who are enrolled.

Answer: The intersection of student IDs in the STUDENT and ENROLLMENT tables yields all students who are enrolled.

```
SELECT student_id
  FROM student
INTERSECT
SELECT student_id
  FROM enrollment
STUDENT_ID
----------
       102
       103
...
       282
       283

165 rows selected.
```

LAB 8.2 SELF-REVIEW QUESTIONS

In order to test your progress, you should be able to answer the following questions.

1) The following two SELECT statements are equivalent and return the same rows.

```
SELECT student_id          SELECT student_id
  FROM enrollment            FROM student
MINUS                      MINUS
SELECT student_id          SELECT student_id
  FROM student               FROM enrollment
```

a) _____ True
b) _____ False

2) The SELECT statements in an INTERSECT set operation can contain a correlated subquery.

a) _____ True
b) _____ False

3) The following SQL statement executes without an error.

```
SELECT TO_CHAR(1)
  FROM dual
 MINUS
SELECT TO_NUMBER('1')
  FROM dual
```

a) _____ True
b) _____ False

4) It is redundant to use DISTINCT in either a MINUS or INTERSECT set operation.

    a) _____ True
    b) _____ False

Answers appear in Appendix A, Section 8.2.

C H A P T E R   8

TEST YOUR THINKING

The projects in this section are meant to have you utilize all of the skills that you have acquired throughout this chapter. The answers to these projects can be found at the companion Web site to this book, located at: *http://authors.phptr.com/rischert3e*. Visit the Web site periodically to share and discuss your answers.

1) List all the zip codes in the ZIPCODE table that are not used in the STUDENT or INSTRUCTOR tables. Write two different solutions, using set operators for both.

2) Write a SQL statement, using a set operator, to show which students enrolled in a section on the same day they registered.

3) Find the students that are not enrolled in any classes. Write three solutions: a set operation, a subquery, and a correlated subquery.

4) Show the students who have received grades for their classes. Write four solutions: a set operation, a subquery, a correlated subquery, and a join.

CHAPTER 9

COMPLEX JOINS

Outer joins and self-joins are extensions of the equijoin you learned about in Chapter 6, "Equijoins." The outer join includes the result rows returned by the equijoin, plus extra rows where no matches are found. The self-join, as implied by the name, joins a table to itself. This type of join is useful for tables with a self-referencing relationship or when you want to determine data inconsistencies.

You will see the usefulness of these types of joins for analyzing and exploring the relationships within your data.

LAB 9.1

OUTER JOINS

LAB OBJECTIVES

After this lab, you will be able to:

✔ Write Outer Joins with Two Tables
✔ Write Outer Joins with Three Tables

MISSING ROWS?

The outer join is similar to the equijoin because it returns all the records the equijoin returns. But it also returns records that are in one of the tables with no matching records in another table. The following is an equijoin and its result. The SQL statement returns all the rows where a match for the COURSE_NO column is found in both the COURSE and the SECTION tables.

```
SELECT course_no, description,
       section_id
  FROM course JOIN section
 USING (course_no)
 ORDER BY course_no
```

COURSE_NO	DESCRIPTION	SECTION_ID	COURSE_NO
10	DP Overview	80	10
20	Intro to Computers	81	20
...			
420	Database System Principles	108	420
450	DB Programming in Java	109	450

78 rows selected.

Some courses are not included in the result because there are no matching course numbers in the SECTION table. To determine those courses not assigned to any sections, write a NOT EXISTS subquery, a NOT IN subquery, or use the MINUS operator.

```
SELECT course_no, description
  FROM course c
 WHERE NOT EXISTS
        (SELECT 'X'
           FROM section
          WHERE c.course_no = course_no)
COURSE_NO DESCRIPTION
--------- --------------------------------
       80 Structured Programming Techniques
      430 JDeveloper Techniques

2 rows selected.
```

The previous equijoin did not return the two courses because there are no matches for course numbers 80 and 430 in the SECTION table. To include these courses in the result, you need to perform an outer join.

THE ANSI OUTER JOIN

The outer join is typically formed with one of three different syntax options. Either you can use the ANSI join syntax, Oracle's outer join operator denoted with the (+), or you can express the query as a UNION. This lab will teach you how to write the queries using various ways. Typically, it is best to use the ANSI outer join syntax as it greatly increases the SQL functionality and flexibility. It can also be easily understood by any non-Oracle databases and is not subject to the many limitations the Oracle-specific outer join operator imposes. If your SQL needs to run against Oracle versions prior to 9i, you have no choice but to use Oracle's outer join operator or a UNION ALL set operator.

The following query shows the use of the ANSI outer join syntax. The keywords LEFT OUTER are added to the JOIN keyword. It indicates that the rows in the table to the left side of the JOIN keyword are to be listed. This left table is the COURSE table and all rows are shown, including any rows where there is no matching COURSE_NO value in the SECTION table.

```
SELECT c.course_no, c.description,
       s.section_id, s.course_no
  FROM course c LEFT OUTER JOIN section s
    ON c.course_no = s.course_no
 ORDER BY c.course_no
COURSE_NO DESCRIPTION               SECTION_ID COURSE_NO
--------- ------------------------- ---------- ---------
       10 DP Overview                       80        10
       20 Intro to Computers                81        20
...
       80 Structured Programming
          Techniques
```

...

```
430 JDeveloper Techniques
450 DB Programming in Java          109          450
```

80 rows selected.

Look closely at the result for course numbers 80 and 430. These courses have no sections assigned. For example, COURSE_NO 430 of the COURSE table (c.course_no) shows the COURSE_NO value, but the COURSE_NO from the SECTION table (s.course_no) displays a null. The outer join displays null values for the columns s.course_no and s.section_id where no a match exists.

If you wanted to include all the rows in the SECTION table, you can also use the RIGHT OUTER JOIN syntax. This does not really make any sense when reviewing the schema diagram: You will notice that every row in the SECTION table must have a corresponding row in the COURSE table. Orphan rows, which are rows that exist in the SECTION table but not the COURSE table, are not allowed.

However, notice that if we switch the order of the tables to list the SECTION table first, you can write a RIGHT OUTER JOIN. This is essentially the same as the previous LEFT OUTER JOIN. The only difference is the order of the tables in the FROM clause and the RIGHT keyword. Based on the order of the tables in the FROM clause, you must choose either the RIGHT or the LEFT keyword to include all the rows of the outer joined table.

```
SELECT c.course_no, c.description,
       s.section_id, s.course_no
  FROM section s RIGHT OUTER JOIN course c
    ON c.course_no = s.course_no
 ORDER BY c.course_no
```

You can also write the outer join with another ANSI join syntax, such as the USING clause.

```
SELECT course_no, description,
       section_id
  FROM section RIGHT OUTER JOIN course
 USING (course_no)
 ORDER BY course_no
```

COURSE_NO	DESCRIPTION	SECTION_ID
10	DP Overview	80
20	Intro to Computers	81
...		
80	Structured Programming Techniques	
...		

```
430 JDeveloper Techniques
450 DB Programming in Java          109
```

80 rows selected.

Notice that the query and the returned result do not include both COURSE_NO columns because you are not allowed to alias the joined column when writing the query with the USING clause. The column now also contains a non-null value, unlike the previous result where the corresponding COURSE_NO column from the SECTION table showed a null. For the SECTION_ID column, you continue to see a null value as there obviously is no matching value in the SECTION table.

THE ORACLE OUTER JOIN OPERATOR (+)

The second way to express an outer join is with Oracle's outer join operator. The next query looks very much like the equijoin you are already familiar with, except for the (+) symbol next to the SECTION table's COURSE_NO column in the WHERE clause. Oracle uses the outer join operator (+) to indicate that nulls are shown for nonmatching rows. Exactly like the previous result set, you notice that for those rows of the COURSE table where a match does not exist in the SECTION table (course numbers 80 and 430), there are null values displayed the SECTION table columns.

You place the outer join operator on the table for which you want to return null column values when a match is not found. In this case, all the rows from the COURSE table are desired and for every row in the COURSE table for which a match cannot be found in the SECTION table, a null is shown. Therefore, the (+) operator is placed on the COURSE_NO column of the SECTION table.

```
SELECT c.course_no, c.description,
       s.section_id, s.course_no
  FROM course c, section s
 WHERE c.course_no = s.course_no(+)
 ORDER BY c.course_no
```

If the order of the tables in the FROM clause changes, the (+) operator still needs to remain on the S.COURSE_NO column. This syntax and the UNION ALL syntax are the only way to express outer joins in Oracle versions prior to Oracle 9i. If you have a choice, use the ANSI join syntax instead; it is easy and overall more flexible and functional.

THE OUTER JOIN AND THE UNION ALL OPERATOR

Alternatively, you can achieve the same result with two SQL statements: an equijoin and a correlated subquery with the results combined using the UNION ALL operator.

```
SELECT c1.course_no, c1.description,
       s.section_id, s.course_no
  FROM course c1, section s
 WHERE c1.course_no = s.course_no
UNION ALL
SELECT c2.course_no, c2.description,
       TO_NUMBER(NULL), TO_NUMBER(NULL)
  FROM course c2
 WHERE NOT EXISTS
       (SELECT 'X'
          FROM section
         WHERE c2.course_no = course_no)
```

In this example, the UNION ALL operator is used to combine the result of the equijoin (all courses with sections) with the result of the correlated subquery (courses with no match in the SECTION table). Duplicate rows are not returned between the two SELECT statements; each SELECT statement returns a different set. Therefore, it is more efficient to use UNION ALL rather than the UNION operator because the UNION ALL avoids the sort required by the UNION operator to eliminate the duplicates.

The TO_NUMBER datatype conversion is performed to match the datatypes of the columns in each of the SELECT statements in the set operation. Alternatively, you can substitute CAST(NULL AS NUMBER) for the TO_NUMBER(NULL) function.

FULL OUTER JOIN

A full outer join includes rows from both tables. Oracle does not support a full outer join with the (+) outer join operator. To accomplish a full outer join, you need to use either the ANSI FULL OUTER JOIN syntax or the UNION operator.

ANSI FULL OUTER JOIN

To fully illustrate the effects of an outer join, here are tables named T1 and T2 (not found in the STUDENT schema unless you installed the additional tables from the companion Web site) and the data in them. Table T1 has one numeric column named COL1 and table T2 also consists of a numeric column called COL2.

```
SELECT col1
  FROM t1
      COL1
---------
         1
         2
         3

3 rows selected.
```

```
SELECT col2
  FROM t2
    COL2
---------
        2
        3
        4
```

3 rows selected.

To understand the result of a full outer join on the tables T1 and T2, first write an outer join on table T1 with the following SELECT statement. This SELECT statement is referred to as a left outer join. The result includes all the rows from table T1.

```
SELECT col1, col2
  FROM t1 LEFT OUTER JOIN t2
    ON t1.col1 = t2.col2
    COL1 COL2
--------- ----
        1
        2    2
        3    3
```

3 rows selected.

The next SELECT statement returns all the rows from T2, whether a match is found or not. This outer join is a right outer join. All the rows on the right table are returned, including nonmatching rows.

```
SELECT col1, col2
  FROM t1 RIGHT OUTER JOIN t2
    ON t1.col1 = t2.col2
    COL1 COL2
--------- ----
        2    2
        3    3
             4
```

3 rows selected.

The full outer join includes all the rows from both tables, whether a match is found or not.

```
SELECT col1, col2
  FROM t1 FULL OUTER JOIN t2
    ON t1.col1 - t2.col2
```

```
    COL1 COL2
--------- ----
        1
        2    2
        3    3
             4
```

4 rows selected.

FULL OUTER JOIN USING THE UNION OPERATOR

You can also express the same full outer join using the Oracle outer join operator and combining the two SELECT statements with the UNION operator. The UNION operator eliminates the duplicate rows from the two statements.

```
SELECT col1, col2
  FROM t1, t2
 WHERE t1.col1 = t2.col2(+)
UNION
SELECT col1, col2
  FROM t1, t2
 WHERE t1.col1(+) = t2.col2
```

The first SELECT statement performs an outer join on the T1 table; the second SELECT statement performs an outer join on the T2 table. The result of each query is combined and duplicates are eliminated with the UNION operator.

LAB 9.1 EXERCISES

9.1.1 WRITE OUTER JOINS WITH TWO TABLES

a) Explain why Oracle returns an error message when you execute the following SELECT statement.

```
SELECT c.course_no, s.course_no, s.section_id,
       c.description, s.start_date_time
  FROM course c, section s
 WHERE c.course_no(+) = s.course_no(+)
```

b) Show the description of all courses with the prerequisite course number 350. Include the location where the sections meet in the result. Return course rows even if no corresponding row in the SECTION table is found.

c) Rewrite the following SQL statement using an outer join.

```
SELECT course_no, description
  FROM course c
 WHERE NOT EXISTS
        (SELECT 'X'
           FROM section
          WHERE c.course_no = course_no)
```

```
COURSE_NO DESCRIPTION
--------- --------------------------------
       80 Structured Programming Techniques
      430 JDeveloper Techniques
```

2 rows selected.

d) Show all the cities, state, and zip codes for Connecticut. Display a count of how many students live in each zip code. Order the result alphabetically by city. The result should look similar to the following output. Note, the column STUDENT_COUNT displays a zero when no student lives in a particular zip code.

```
CITY                        ST ZIP   STUDENT_COUNT
------------------------    -- ----- -------------
Ansonia                     CT 06401             0
Bridgeport                  CT 06605             1
...
Wilton                      CT 06897             0
Woodbury                    CT 06798             1
```

19 rows selected.

9.1.2 WRITE OUTER JOINS WITH THREE TABLES

a) Display the course number, description, cost, class location, and instructor's last name for all the courses. Also include courses where no sections or instructors have been assigned.

b) For students with the student ID of 102 and 301, determine the sections they are enrolled in. Also show the numeric grades and grade types they received, no matter if they are enrolled or received any grades.

LAB 9.1 EXERCISE ANSWERS

9.1.1 ANSWERS

a) Explain why Oracle returns an error message when you execute the following SELECT statement.

```
SELECT c.course_no, s.course_no, s.section_id,
       c.description, s.start_date_time
  FROM course c, section s
 WHERE c.course_no(+) = s.course_no(+)
```

Answer: The outer join symbol can be used only on one side of the equation, not both.

ERROR at line 4:
ORA-01468: a predicate may reference only one outer-joined table

This SQL statement attempts to include rows from the COURSE table for which no match exists in the SECTION table and include rows from the SECTION table where no match is found in the COURSE table. This is referred to as a full outer join; you want to include the rows from both tables, including those rows for which a match cannot be found in either table.

If you want to write such an outer join, you want to use the ANSI join syntax instead.

```
SELECT c.course_no, s.course_no, s.section_id,
       c.description, s.start_date_time
  FROM course c FULL OUTER JOIN section s
    ON c.course_no = s.course_no
```

When you look at the relationship between the SECTION and COURSE tables, you notice a section cannot exist unless a corresponding course exists. Therefore, finding any sections for which no course exists is impossible unless the foreign key constraint is disabled or dropped. (For information on how to create and drop foreign keys, see Chapter 11, "Create, Alter, and Drop Tables." To learn how to determine if the foreign keys are disabled or enabled, see Chapter 13, "The Data Dictionary and Advanced SQL* Plus Commands.")

b) Show the description of all courses with the prerequisite course number 350. Include the location where the sections meet in the result. Return course rows even if no corresponding row in the SECTION table is found.

Answer: To show all the courses with this prerequisite involves writing an outer join and applying an outer join to the COURSE table. For any records where no match in the SECTION table is found, null values are displayed for the respective SECTION table columns.

There are only two courses with a PREREQUISITE value of 350; they are course numbers 430 and 450.

```
SELECT course_no, description
  FROM course
 WHERE prerequisite = 350
```

```
COURSE_NO DESCRIPTION
--------- ----------------------
      430 JDeveloper Techniques
      450 DB Programming in Java
```

2 rows selected.

Only course number 450 has a matching course number in the SECTION table. Course number 430, JDeveloper Techniques, does not exist in the SECTION table.

```
SELECT section_id, course_no
  FROM section
 WHERE course_no IN (430, 450)
```
```
SECTION_ID  COURSE_NO
----------- ---------
        109       450
```

1 row selected.

The solution can be written as follows:

```
SELECT c.course_no cno, s.course_no sno,
       c.description,
       c.prerequisite prereq,
       s.location loc, s.section_id
  FROM course c LEFT OUTER JOIN section s
    ON c.course_no = s.course_no
 WHERE c.prerequisite = 350
```
```
CNO SNO DESCRIPTION                  PREREQ LOC  SECTION_ID
--- --- ----------------------       ------ ---- ----------
430     JDeveloper Techniques        350
450 450 DB Programming in Java       350 L507        109
```

2 rows selected.

Or:

```
SELECT c.course_no cno, s.course_no sno,
       c.description,
       c.prerequisite prereq,
       s.location loc, s.section_id
  FROM course c, section s
 WHERE c.course_no = s.course_no(+)
   AND c.prerequisite = 350
```

As you see from the result, the columns of the SECTION table, such as S.LOCATION (LOC as the column alias), S.COURSE_NO (SNO as the column alias), and S.SECTION_ID show null values for the unmatched row.

The solution can also be expressed with the USING clause. The COURSE_NO column does not have an alias and the result will show not show a null value for this column, even if it is not found in the SECTION table.

```
SELECT course_no cno,
       description,
       prerequisite prereq,
       location loc, section_id
  FROM course LEFT OUTER JOIN section
 USING (course_no)
 WHERE prerequisite = 350
```

ORACLE OUTER JOIN OPERATOR RESTRICTIONS

Oracle imposes a number of other restrictions and caveats when using the (+) outer join operator. For example, the outer join operator restricts the use of an outer joined column involving a subquery. You also cannot use the OR logical operator and IN comparison. If you incorrectly place the necessary (+) symbols on the correct WHERE clause conditions and join criteria, you will form an equijoin rather than an outer join. This occurs without warning, as you will see in the next following examples.

WHERE CONDITIONS AND THE ORACLE OUTER JOIN OPERATOR

There are some things you need to watch out for when you use Oracle's proprietary outer join operator, particularly when it comes to using conditions in WHERE clauses. The previously listed outer join is repeated for your reference. Note that the condition in the WHERE clause is applied to the PREREQUISITE column. This column is in the COURSE table, the outer joined table that includes all rows including nonmatching rows.

```
SELECT c.course_no cno, s.course_no sno,
       c.description,
       c.prerequisite prereq,
       s.location loc, s.section_id
  FROM course c, section s
 WHERE c.course_no = s.course_no(+)
   AND c.prerequisite = 350
```

The next SQL statement modifies the WHERE condition and adds a condition specific to the SECTION table. The query retrieves classes that only meet in S.LOCATION L507. Observe the output of the query and compare it to the previous result.

```
SELECT c.course_no cno, s.course_no sno,
       c.description,
       c.prerequisite prereq,
       s.location loc, s.section_id
  FROM course c, section s
 WHERE c.course_no = s.course_no(+)
   AND c.prerequisite = 350
   AND s.location = 'L507'
```

CNO	SNO	DESCRIPTION	PREREQ	LOC	SECTION_ID
450	450	DB Programming in Java	350	L507	109

```
1 row selected.
```

You may wonder what happened to course number 430? The course is no longer included in the result, even though the outer join operator is applied to return all the rows whether a match is found in the SECTION table or not.

When a WHERE clause contains a condition that compares a column from the outer joined table to a literal, such as the text literal 'L507', you also need to include the outer join operator on the column. Otherwise, Oracle returns only the results of the equijoin, rather than displaying nulls for the columns. The following query adds the outer join symbol to the LOCATION column.

```
SELECT c.course_no cno, s.course_no sno,
       c.description,
       c.prerequisite prereq,
       s.location loc, s.section_id
  FROM course c, section s
 WHERE c.course_no = s.course_no(+)
   AND c.prerequisite = 350
   AND s.location(+) = 'L507'
```

CNO	SNO	DESCRIPTION	PREREQ	LOC	SECTION_ID
430		JDeveloper Techniques	350		
450	450	DB Programming in Java	350	L507	109

```
2 rows selected.
```

These two records satisfy the condition of the prerequisite. The outer join operator applied to the S.LOCATION column includes records where either (a) the location equals L507, (b) the location is null, or (c) the location is different from L507. You will see an example shortly of why the location can be different.

Once you apply the outer join operator to a column on the outer joined table, you need to understand the order in which the conditions are processed. First, the records on the table where you want to include all the rows are processed. This is the condition prerequisite = 350. Next, the matching records in the SECTION table are identified. If a match is not found, the records with the prerequisite 350 are still returned. The next condition, `location(+) = 'L507'`, shows rows in the SECTION table that satisfy this condition; otherwise, a null is displayed.

What happens when you choose a different location, such as L210? Neither course meets in this location.

```
SELECT c.course_no cno, s.course_no sno,
       SUBSTR(c.description, 1,20),
       c.prerequisite prereq,
       s.location loc, s.section_id
  FROM course c, section s
 WHERE c.course_no = s.course_no(+)
   AND c.prerequisite = 350
   AND s.location(+) = 'L210'
```

CNO	SNO	DESCRIPTION	PREREQ	LOC	SECTION_ID
430		JDeveloper Techniques	350		
450		DB Programming in Java	350		

```
2 rows selected.
```

Here you see both courses with this prerequisite. This contrasts with the earlier output because now both the LOCATION and SECTION_ID columns display nulls. When the WHERE clause is evaluated, the PREREQUISITE condition is evaluated first, then matches are found in the SECTION table with the condition `location(+) = 'L210'`. Since none of the sections matches this LOCATION condition for this course number, nulls are shown for the SECTION_ID and the LOCATION.

WHERE CONDITIONS AND THE ANSI OUTER JOINS

When you compare the previous, proprietary Oracle syntax to the ANSI outer join syntax, you see that there are some differences. Following is the query of the first outer join with the condition `location = 'L507'`. The ANSI join returns the result of the equijoin, which is one row. This is not the desired result.

```
SELECT c.course_no cno, s.course_no sno,
       c.description,
       c.prerequisite prereq,
       s.location loc, s.section_id
  FROM course c LEFT OUTER JOIN section s
    ON c.course_no = s.course_no
 WHERE c.prerequisite = 350
   AND location = 'L507'
```

CNO	SNO	DESCRIPTION	PREREQ	LOC	SECTION_ID
450	450	DB Programming in Java	350	L507	109

```
1 row selected.
```

Instead, the query needs to be changed with the use of parentheses to obtain the correct result. The order of execution matters indeed, and the order is determined by the parentheses! The join on the COURSE_NO column together with the condition `location = 'L507'` is enclosed by parentheses; they determine that the join and LOCATION condition are executed first. This intermediate result includes all matching rows between the COURSE and SECTION tables based on the COURSE_NO column and those rows from the SECTION table where the LOCATION column has a value of L507.

```
SELECT c.course_no cno, s.course_no sno,
       c.description,
       c.prerequisite prereq,
       s.location loc, s.section_id
  FROM course c LEFT OUTER JOIN section s
    ON (c.course_no = s.course_no
   AND location = 'L507')
 WHERE c.prerequisite = 350
```

Here is an intermediate result listing of the join condition without the WHERE clause condition applied.

```
       ON (c.course_no = s.course_no
      AND location = 'L507')
  CNO SNO DESCRIPTION                     PREREQ LOC   SECTION_ID
  --- --- ------------------------------ ------ ----  ----------
  100 100 Hands-On Windows                   20 L507         144
  450 450 DB Programming in Java            350 L507         109
  ...
  350     JDeveloper Lab                    125
  430     JDeveloper Techniques             350
  220     PL/SQL Programming                 80
  230     Intro to Internet                  10

33 rows selected.
```

Based on this intermediate result set, the WHERE clause is applied; only rows with a prerequisite value of 350 are chosen for output and just two rows qualify for the final result. This works because the LOCATION column condition is part of the outer join criteria on the table for which nulls are to be displayed.

USING INLINE VIEWS AND OUTER JOINS You can also use inline views to gain control over the execution order. The same result can be obtained with the following query, which chooses all the rows from the COURSE table with a value of 350 in the PREREQUISITE column. This result set is then left outer joined with the inline view of the SECTION table, which retrieves only sections with a location column value of 'L507'.

```
SELECT c.course_no cno, s.course_no sno,
       c.description,
       c.prerequisite prereq,
       s.location loc, s.section_id
  FROM (SELECT *
          FROM course
         WHERE prerequisite = 350) c LEFT OUTER JOIN
       (SELECT * FROM section
         WHERE location = 'L507') s
    ON (c.course_no = s.course_no)
```

 WHERE clauses and outer joins may give you unexpected results unless you carefully craft your conditions. Inline views and the ANSI join syntax are best for complicated conditions because they allow you control over the execution order of the conditions and subsequent joins. ANSI joins are preferable over Oracle's proprietary outer join operator because the ANSI join syntax is less restrictive, easier to read, and allows your SQL statements to be portable to non-Oracle databases.

c) Rewrite the following SQL statement using an outer join.

```
SELECT course_no, description
  FROM course c
 WHERE NOT EXISTS
       (SELECT 'X'
          FROM section
         WHERE c.course_no = course_no)
```

```
COURSE_NO DESCRIPTION
--------- --------------------------------
       80 Structured Programming Techniques
      430 JDeveloper Techniques
```

```
2 rows selected.
```

Answer: A NOT EXISTS condition can be rewritten as an outer join condition by querying the SECTION table for nulls.

Your query can be written in many different ways. The following example shows the use of the (+) outer join operator:

```
SELECT c.course_no, c.description
  FROM course c, section s
 WHERE c.course_no = s.course_no(+)
   AND s.course_no IS NULL
```

Or you can write it with the ANSI outer join syntax and the USING clause.

```
SELECT course_no, description
  FROM course LEFT OUTER JOIN section
USING (course_no)
WHERE section_id IS NULL
```

d) Show all the cities, state, and zip codes for Connecticut. Display a count of how many students live in each zip code. Order the result alphabetically by city. The result should look similar to the following output. Note, the column STUDENT_COUNT displays a zero when no student lives in a particular zip code.

```
CITY                           ST ZIP   STUDENT_COUNT
------------------------------ -- ----- -------------
Ansonia                        CT 06401             0
Bridgeport                     CT 06605             1
...
Wilton                         CT 06897             0
Woodbury                       CT 06798             1

19 rows selected.
```

Answer: The query that achieves the correct solution requires the use of an outer join on the ZIPCODE table and the use of the aggregate function COUNT. When using an aggregate function together with outer joins, you must be careful to apply the aggregate function to the correct column.

```
SELECT city, state, z.zip,
       COUNT(s.zip) AS student_count
  FROM zipcode z LEFT OUTER JOIN student s
    ON (z.zip = s.zip)
 WHERE state = 'CT'
 GROUP BY city, state, z.zip
```

Notice the parameter in the COUNT function is the S.ZIP column instead of Z.ZIP. The COUNT function requires the STUDENT table's ZIP column as a parameter to ensure that if the zip code is not found in the STUDENT table, the COUNT function will return a zero.

Just for illustration of this important issue, the next query shows the result of both the Z.ZIP and the S.ZIP column in the SELECT list and as a parameter in the COUNT function. Notice that the SZIP column in the result is null and the column WRONG_VALUE has a count of one even though this zip code does not exist in the STUDENT table. The COUNT function for this column is counting the occurrence of the zip code in the ZIPCODE table, not the desired STUDENT table's zip code.

```
SELECT city, state, z.zip AS zzip, s.zip AS szip,
       COUNT(s.zip) AS student_count,
       COUNT(z.zip) AS wrong_value
  FROM zipcode z LEFT OUTER JOIN student s
    ON (z.zip = s.zip)
 WHERE state = 'CT'
 GROUP BY city, state, z.zip, s.zip
```

CITY	ST	ZZIP	SZIP	STUDENT_COUNT	WRONG_VALUE
Ansonia	CT	06401		0	1
...					
Woodbury	CT	06798	06798	1	1

19 rows selected.

ALTERNATIVE SOLUTION WITH A SCALAR SUBQUERY

The scalar subquery, discussed in Chapter 7, "Subqueries," can provide some simplicity and less chance for errors. The query is correlated as the scalar subquery is executed for each individual zip code. However, scalar subqueries can be notoriously inefficient because Oracle can often execute table joins more quickly, particularly when scans of the entire result set are involved.

```
SELECT city, state, zip,
       (SELECT COUNT(*)
          FROM student s
         WHERE s.zip = z.zip) AS student_count
  FROM zipcode z
 WHERE state = 'CT'
```

CITY	ST	ZIP	STUDENT_COUNT
Ansonia	CT	06401	0
...			
Stamford	CT	06907	1

19 rows selected.

9.1.2 ANSWERS

a) Display the course number, description, cost, class location, and instructor's last name for all courses. Also include courses where no sections or instructors have been assigned.

Answer: This outer join involves three tables: the COURSE, SECTION, and INSTRUCTOR tables. You want to include all the courses from the COURSE table, whether a section exists for it or not. Also, if no instructor is assigned to a section or no match is found, the rows of the SECTION table should still be included.

```
SELECT course_no cou, description, cost,
       location, last_name
  FROM course LEFT OUTER JOIN section
 USING (course_no)
  LEFT OUTER JOIN instructor
 USING (instructor_id)
 ORDER BY course_no
```

COU	DESCRIPTION	COST	LOCA	LAST_NAME
10	DP Overview	1195	L214	Wojick
20	Intro to Computers	1195	L210	Schorin
20	Intro to Computers	1195	L214	Pertez
20	Intro to Computers	1195	L509	Morris
20	Intro to Computers	1195	L210	Smythe
...				
430	JDeveloper Techniques	1195		
450	DB Programming in Java		L507	Hanks

80 rows selected.

When you review the result, recall from the previous examples that course number 430 does not have a section assigned. Therefore, the column LOCATION displays a null value. Also, the instructor's last name shows a null value, because there cannot be an instructor assigned if the row does not exist.

Alternatively, you can also use the Oracle outer join operator. The SQL statement will look similar to the following:

```
SELECT c.course_no cou, c.description, c.cost,
       s.location, i.last_name
  FROM course c, section s, instructor i
 WHERE c.course_no = s.course_no(+)
   AND s.instructor_id = i.instructor_id(+)
 ORDER BY c.course_no
```

The SELECT statement requires the outer join operator to be placed on the COURSE_NO column of the SECTION table. This indicates you want to see all the courses, whether there are corresponding sections or not. The outer join operator is also applied to the INSTRUCTOR_ID column of the INSTRUCTOR table. This directs Oracle to include rows from the SECTION table even if it doesn't find a matching record in the INSTRUCTOR table.

b) For students with the student ID of 102 and 301, determine the sections they are enrolled in. Also show the numeric grades and grade types they received, no matter if they are enrolled or received any grades.

Answer: You can write outer joins that include rows from all three tables: STUDENT, ENROLLMENT, and GRADE.

```
SELECT student_id, section_id, grade_type_code,
       numeric_grade
  FROM student LEFT OUTER JOIN enrollment
 USING (student_id)
  LEFT OUTER JOIN grade
 USING (student_id, section_id)
 WHERE student_id IN (102, 301)
```

Or:

```
SELECT s.student_id, en.section_id, grade_type_code,
       numeric_grade
  FROM student s LEFT OUTER JOIN enrollment en
    ON (s.student_id = en.student_id)
  LEFT OUTER JOIN grade g
    ON (s.student_id = g.student_id
   AND en.section_id = g.section_id)
 WHERE s.student_id IN (102, 301)
```

STUDENT_ID	SECTION_ID	GR	NUMERIC_GRADE
102	86	FI	85
102	86	HM	90
102	86	HM	99
102	86	HM	82
102	86	HM	82
102	86	MT	90
102	86	PA	85
102	86	QZ	90
102	86	QZ	84
102	86	QZ	97
102	86	QZ	97
102	89	FI	92
102	89	MT	91
301			

14 rows selected.

The student with ID 102 is enrolled and received grades. His rows are returned as part of an equijoin. However, student 301 is not enrolled in any section and does not have any grades.

You can also write the query using the traditional join syntax and the Oracle (+) outer join operator.

```
SELECT s.student_id, e.section_id, g.grade_type_code,
       g.numeric_grade
  FROM student s, enrollment e, grade g
 WHERE s.student_id IN (102, 301)
   AND s.student_id = e.student_id(+)
   AND e.student_id = g.student_id(+)
   AND e.section_id = g.section_id(+)
```

Because the outer join operator is applied to both the SECTION and the GRADE tables, STUDENT_ID 301 is included in the result. The condition `s.student_id IN (102, 301)` does not require an outer join operator because it is based on the STUDENT table, and this is the table from which you want all the rows that satisfy this condition.

LAB 9.1 SELF-REVIEW QUESTIONS

In order to test your progress, you should be able to answer the following questions.

1) A WHERE clause containing an outer join (+) operator cannot contain another condition with the OR operator, as in this example:

```
SELECT *
   FROM course c, section s
  WHERE c.course_no = s.course_no(+)
     OR c.course_no = 100
```

a) _____ True
b) _____ False

2) A column with the outer join (+) operator may not use the IN operator, as in this example:

```
SELECT *
   FROM course c, section s
  WHERE c.course_no = s.course_no(+)
    AND c.course_no(+) IN (100, 200)
```

a) _____ True
b) _____ False

3) An outer join between two tables returns all rows that satisfy the equijoin condition plus those records from the outer joined tables for which no matches are found.

a) _____ True
b) _____ False

4) Which of the WHERE clauses results in this error message?

```
SELECT c.course_no, s.course_no,
       SUBSTR(c.description, 1,20), s.start_date_time
   FROM course c, section s
```

ORA-01468: a predicate may reference only one outer joined table

a) _____ WHERE course_no = course_no
b) _____ WHERE c.course_no(+) = s.course_no
c) _____ WHERE c.course_no = s.course_no(+)
d) _____ WHERE c.course_no(+) = s.course_no(+)

Answers appear in Appendix A, Section 9.1.

LAB 9.2

SELF-JOINS

LAB OBJECTIVES

After this lab, you will be able to:
✔ Write Self-Joins and Detect Data Inconsistencies

Equijoins always join one or multiple tables. A self-join joins a table to itself by pretending there are different tables involved. This is accomplished by using table aliases. One table has one alias and the same table another alias. For the purpose of executing the query, Oracle treats them as two different tables.

Self-joins are quite useful to perform comparisons and to check for inconsistencies in data. Sometimes a self-join is needed to report on recursive relationships. Chapter 15, "Regular Expressions and Hierarchical Queries," covers detailed examples on hierarchical reporting of recursive relationships using the CONNECT BY operator.

One example that lends itself very well to showing the functionality of the self-join is the COURSE table. The PREREQUISITE column is a foreign key to the primary key column COURSE_NO of the COURSE table, reflecting a recursive relationship between the two columns. A PREREQUISITE is valid only if it is also a valid COURSE_NO; otherwise, the data manipulation operation on the table is rejected.

Many queries executed on the course table so far in this book typically only show the prerequisite number:

```
SELECT course_no, description, prerequisite
  FROM course
```

If you also want to show the description of the prerequisite, you will need to write a self-join. This is accomplished by pretending to have two separate tables via table aliases, such as C1 and C2. Join the PREREQUISITE column of table C1 with the COURSE_NO column of table C2. If matching records are found, the description of the prerequisite is displayed.

```
SELECT c1.course_no,
       c1.description course_descr,
       c1.prerequisite,
       c2.description pre_req_descr
  FROM course c1 JOIN course c2
    ON (c1.prerequisite = c2.course_no)
 ORDER BY 3
COURSE_NO COURSE_DESCR       PREREQUISITE PRE_REQ_DESCR
--------- ------------------ ------------ ------------------
      230 Intro to Internet           10 DP Overview
      100 Hands-On Windows            20 Intro to Computers
...
      450 DB Programming             350 JDeveloper Lab
      144 Database Design            420 Database Systems

26 rows selected.
```

Examine the first row, COURSE_NO 230, with the prerequisite course number of 10. The course description for course number 10 is DP Overview. This join works just like the equijoins you learned about in "Chapter 6, Equijoins." If a prerequisite is NULL or a match is not found, the self-join, just like the equijoin, does not return the record.

The self-join acts like other joins with primary key and foreign key columns. However, here the relationship is to the table itself. The PREREQUISITE column is a foreign key to the primary key COURSE_NO. The PREREQUISITE comes from the child table, and the COURSE_NO comes from the parent table. Every COURSE_NO may have zero or one PREREQUISITE. Note: To qualify as a prerequisite, the PREREQUISITE course number must be listed in the PREREQUISITE column for at least one or multiple courses.

The USING clause cannot be used with the self-join because the USING clause requires identical column names on both tables. This is obviously a problem, because the join needs to be executed on the columns PREREQUISITE and COURSE_NO.

The query can also be expressed in the traditional join format with the following SQL statement.

```
SELECT c1.course_no,
       c1.description course_descr,
       c1.prerequisite,
       c2.description pre_req_descr
  FROM course c1, course c2
 WHERE c1.prerequisite = c2.course_no
 ORDER BY 3
```

THE NON-EQUIJOIN

Occasionally, you need to construct joins that are not based on equality of values. The next query illustrates such an example using BETWEEN where you have values that fall into a range. The result shows a listing of grades for student ID 107 including the respective letter grade. The BETWEEN operator checks for each value in the NUMERIC_GRADE column to see if the individual grade is between the values found in the columns MIN_GRADE and MAX_GRADE of the GRADE_CONVERSION table. If a match is found, the corresponding letter grade is returned. For example, the first row of the result shows the value of 76 in the NUMERIC_GRADE column for a final examination. The appropriate letter grade for the value of 76 is a C.

**LAB
9.2**

```
SELECT grade_type_code, numeric_grade, letter_grade
  FROM grade g JOIN grade_conversion c
    ON (g.numeric_grade BETWEEN c.min_grade AND c.max_grade)
 WHERE g.student_id = 107
 ORDER BY 1, 2 DESC
GR NUMERIC_GRADE LE
-- ------------- --
FI            76 C
HM            96 A
HM            96 A
...
HM            73 C
MT            91 A-

12 rows selected.
```

You can express the query with the traditional join syntax instead.

```
SELECT grade_type_code, numeric_grade, letter_grade,
       min_grade, max_grade
  FROM grade g, grade_conversion c
 WHERE g.numeric_grade BETWEEN c.min_grade AND c.max_grade
   AND g.student_id = 107
 ORDER BY 1, 2 DESC
```

LAB 9.2 EXERCISES

9.2.1 WRITE SELF-JOINS AND DETECT DATA INCONSISTENCIES

a) For SECTION_ID 86, determine which students received a lower grade on their final than on their midterm. In your result, list the STUDENT_ID and the grade for the midterm and final.

b) Formulate the question for the following query.

```
SELECT DISTINCT a.student_id, a.first_name, a.salutation
   FROM student a, student b
  WHERE a.salutation <> b.salutation
    AND b.first_name = a.first_name
    AND a.student_id <> b.student_id
  ORDER BY a.first_name
```

c) Display the student ID, last name, and street address of students living at the same address and zip code.

d) Write a query showing the course number, course description, prerequisite, and description of the prerequisite. Include courses without any prerequisites. Note this requires a self-join and an outer join.

LAB 9.2 EXERCISE ANSWERS

9.2.1 ANSWERS

a) For SECTION_ID 86, determine which students received a lower grade on their final than on their midterm. In your result, list the STUDENT_ID and the grade for the midterm and final.

Answer: Using a self-join, you can compare the grade for the midterm with the grade for the final and determine if the final is lower than the midterm grade.

```
SELECT fi.student_id, mt.numeric_grade "Midterm Grade",
       fi.numeric_grade "Final Grade"
  FROM grade fi JOIN grade mt
    ON (fi.section_id = mt.section_id
   AND fi.student_id = mt.student_id)
 WHERE fi.grade_type_code = 'FI'
   AND fi.section_id = 86
   AND mt.grade_type_code = 'MT'
   AND fi.numeric_grade < mt.numeric_grade
STUDENT_ID Midterm Grade Final Grade
---------- ------------- -----------
       102            90          85
       108            91          76
       211            92          77

3 rows selected.
```

Notice three students have a lower grade in the final than the grade they achieved in the midterm. Using a self-join allows you to easily determine the correct result.

Imagine you are actually joining to a different table, even though it is really the same table. Visualize one table as the midterm table and the other as the final table, and the formulation of your SQL statement falls into place.

Start with the table representing the final grade for SECTION_ID 86. Then compare the result with the table representing the midterm grade (grade_type_code = 'MT'). Also join the STUDENT_ID and SECTION_ID to make sure you match the same individuals and section. Finally, compare the numeric grades between the midterm and final.

Using the traditional join syntax, you can also write the query as follows:

```
SELECT fi.student_id, mt.numeric_grade "Midterm Grade",
       fi.numeric_grade "Final Grade"
  FROM grade fi, grade mt
 WHERE fi.grade_type_code = 'FI'
   AND fi.section_id = 86
   AND mt.grade_type_code = 'MT'
   AND fi.section_id = mt.section_id
   AND fi.student_id = mt.student_id
   AND fi.numeric_grade < mt.numeric_grade
```

Alternatively, a somewhat similar solution can be obtained using the ANY operator and a correlated subquery (see Chapter 7, "Subqueries").

```
SELECT student_id, section_id, numeric_grade
  FROM grade g
 WHERE grade_type_code = 'FI'
   AND section_id = 86
   AND numeric_grade < ANY
       (SELECT numeric_grade
          FROM grade
         WHERE grade_type_code = 'MT'
           AND g.section_id = section_id
           AND g.student_id = student_id)
```

b) Formulate the question for the following query.

```
SELECT DISTINCT a.student_id, a.first_name, a.salutation
  FROM student a, student b
 WHERE a.salutation <> b.salutation
   AND a.first_name = b.first_name
   AND a.student_id <> b.student_id
 ORDER BY a.first_name
```

Answer: Determine the students who might have inconsistent salutations for their respective first names.

This self-join is used to check for errors and inconsistency of data. A number of students have different salutations for the same first name. For example, Kevin is both a female and male name. The same holds true for Daniel, Roger, and some other students as well.

```
STUDENT_ID FIRST_NAME                          SALUT
---------- ------------------------------      -----
       124 Daniel                              Mr.
       242 Daniel                              Mr.
       315 Daniel                              Ms.
...
       272 Kevin                               Ms.
       341 Kevin                               Mr.
       368 Kevin                               Mr.
       238 Roger                               Mr.
       383 Roger                               Ms.

17 rows selected.
```

The query self-joins by the first name and shows only those having a different salutation for the same name. Because there are multiple names for each table alias, this results in a Cartesian product. Eliminate any records where the STUDENT_IDs are identical with the condition a.student_id <> b.student_id. Duplicate rows are also eliminated using DISTINCT.

c) Display the student ID, last name, and street address of students living at the same address and zip code.

Answer: The self-join compares the street address and the zip code.

```
SELECT DISTINCT a.student_id, a.last_name,
       a.street_address
  FROM student a, student b
 WHERE a.street_address = b.street_address
   AND a.zip = b.zip
   AND a.student_id <> b.student_id
 ORDER BY a.street_address
STUDENT_ID LAST_NAME                STREET_ADDRESS
---------- ----------------------   --------------------
       390 Greenberg                105-34 65th Ave.  #6B
       392 Saliternan               105-34 65th Ave.  #6B
       234 Brendler                 111 Village Hill Dr.
       380 Krot                     111 Village Hill Dr.
...
       217 Citron                   PO Box 1091
       182 Delbrun                  PO Box 1091

22 rows selected.
```

The condition a.student_id <> b.student_id eliminates the student itself
from the result.

Alternatively, your ANSI join solution may be similar to the following SELECT
statement.

```
SELECT DISTINCT a.student_id, a.last_name,
       a.street_address
  FROM student a JOIN student b
    ON (a.street_address = b.street_address
   AND a.zip = b.zip
   AND a.student_id <> b.student_id)
 ORDER BY a.street_address
```

Or, your join and WHERE clause may look like this. It actually does not change
the result. The ON clause and the WHERE condition all need to be true and are
connected by the logical AND.

```
    ON (a.street_address = b.street_address
   AND a.zip = b.zip)
 WHERE a.student_id <> b.student_id
 ORDER BY a.street_address
```

You can also expand the query to include the city and state information for the
particular zip code by joining to a third table, the ZIPCODE table.

```
SELECT DISTINCT b.student_id id, b.last_name,
       b.street_address ||' '|| city || ', '
       || state address
  FROM student a, student b, zipcode z
 WHERE a.street_address = b.street_address
   AND a.zip = b.zip
   AND a.student_id <> b.student_id
   AND z.zip = b.zip
 ORDER BY address
 ID LAST_NAME     ADDRESS
 ---- ------------ ------------------------------------
 390 Greenberg    105-34 65th Ave.  #6B Forest Hills, NY
 392 Saliternan   105-34 65th Ave.  #6B Forest Hills, NY
 ...
 217 Citron       PO Box 1091 Ft. Lee, NJ
 182 Delbrun      PO Box 1091 Ft. Lee, NJ

 22 rows selected.
```

As always, there are many alternatives to achieve the same result; for example,
you can also write a subquery.

```
SELECT DISTINCT student_id id, last_name,
       street_address ||' '|| city || ', '
       || state address
  FROM student s, zipcode z
 WHERE s.zip = z.zip
   AND (street_address, s.zip) IN
       (SELECT street_address, zip
          FROM student
         GROUP BY street_address, zip
        HAVING COUNT(*) > 1)
 ORDER BY address
```

d) Write a query showing the course number, course description, prerequisite, and description of the prerequisite. Include courses without any prerequisites. Note this requires a self-join and an outer join.

Answer: The SELECT statement joins the courses and their corresponding prerequisites. It also includes those courses that do not have any prerequisites using an outer join, and displays a NULL for the prerequisite description column labeled PRE_REQ_DESCR.

```
SELECT c1.course_no,
       SUBSTR(c1.description, 1,15) course_descr,
       C1.prerequisite,
       SUBSTR(c2.description,1,15) pre_req_descr
  FROM course c1 LEFT OUTER JOIN course c2
    ON c1.prerequisite = c2.course_no
 ORDER BY 1
```

COURSE_NO	COURSE_DESCR	PREREQUISITE	PRE_REQ_DESCR
10	DP Overview		
20	Intro to Comput		
25	Intro to Progra	140	Structured Anal
...			
145	Internet Protoc	310	Operating Syste
146	Java for C/C++		
147	GUI Programming	20	Intro to Comput
...			
430	JDeveloper Tech	350	JDeveloper Lab
450	DB Programming	350	JDeveloper Lab

30 rows selected.

Using the traditional syntax, you can write the query as follows.

```
SELECT c1.course_no,
       SUBSTR(c1.description, 1,15) course_descr,
       C1.prerequisite,
       SUBSTR(c2.description,1,15) pre_req_descr
```

```
        FROM course c1, course c2
       WHERE c1.prerequisite = c2.course_no(+)
       ORDER BY 1
```

Or, you can even write the query with a UNION ALL.

```
    SELECT c1.course_no, c1.description course_descr,
           c1.prerequisite, c2.description pre_req_descr
      FROM course c1 JOIN course c2
        ON (c1.prerequisite = c2.course_no)
     UNION ALL
    SELECT course_no, description, prerequisite, NULL
      FROM course
     WHERE prerequisite IS NULL
```

LAB 9.2 SELF-REVIEW QUESTIONS

In order to test your progress, you should be able to answer the following questions.

1) A self-join requires you to always join the foreign key with the primary key in the same table.

a) _____ True
b) _____ False

2) Self-joins work only when you have a recursive relationship in your table.

a) _____ True
b) _____ False

3) You cannot use subqueries or ORDER BY clauses with self-joins.

a) _____ True
b) _____ False

4) A self-join joins a table to itself.

a) _____ True
b) _____ False

5) You need to use a table alias to be able to write a self-join.

a) _____ True
b) _____ False

Answers appear in Appendix A, Section 9.2.

CHAPTER 9

TEST YOUR THINKING

> The projects in this section are meant to have you utilize all of the skills that you have acquired throughout this chapter. The answers to these projects can be found at the companion Web site to this book, located at *http://authors.phptr.com/rischert3e*. Visit the Web site periodically to share and discuss your answers.

1) Write a query that shows all the instructors who live in the same zip code.

2) Are any of the rooms overbooked? Determine if any sections meet at the same date, time, and location.

3) Determine if there is any scheduling conflict for instructors: Are any instructors scheduled to teach one or more sections at the same date and time? Order the result by the INSTRUCTOR_ID and the starting date and time of the sections.

4) Show the course number, description, course cost, and section ID for courses that cost 1195 or more. Include courses that have no corresponding section.

5) Write a query that lists the section numbers and students IDs of students enrolled in classes held in location 'L210'. Include sections for which no students are enrolled.

INSERT, UPDATE, AND DELETE

CHAPTER OBJECTIVES

In this chapter, you will learn about:

In Chapters 1 through 9 you learned what data is and how to query and present data. In this chapter, you will learn how to modify the data in tables with the INSERT, UPDATE, DELETE, and MERGE statements, also known as Data Manipulation Language (DML). These statements give you the ability to create, change, or delete data from tables. In the first lab you will learn about creating data in tables with the different INSERT command options and how to make this change permanent. The second lab illustrates how to delete data and shows various ways to change existing data in the tables. Furthermore, you will learn about Oracle's locking and read-consistency features.

LAB 10.1

CREATING DATA AND TRANSACTION CONTROL

LAB OBJECTIVES

After this lab, you will be able to:
✔ Insert Data, Rollback and Commit Transactions

INSERTING DATA

The INSERT statement creates new data in a table. It can insert a single row or multiple rows (based on a subquery) into a table at one time.

INSERTING AN INDIVIDUAL ROW

The following INSERT statement inserts a row into the ZIPCODE table.

```
INSERT INTO zipcode
VALUES
   ('11111', 'Westerly', 'MA',
    USER, TO_DATE('18-JAN-2000', 'DD-MON-YYYY'),
    USER, SYSDATE)
```

When the statement is executed, Oracle responds with this message:

1 row created.

The INSERT INTO keywords always precede the name of the table into which you want to insert data. The VALUES keyword precedes a set of parentheses that enclose the values you want to insert. For each of the seven columns of the ZIP-CODE table there are seven corresponding values with matching datatypes in the INSERT statement separated by commas. The values in the list are in the same order as the columns when you DESCRIBE the ZIPCODE table. It is good practice to include a column list, nevertheless in case of future database changes. Following is the INSERT statement with the column list.

```
INSERT INTO zipcode
   (zip, city, state,
    created_by, created_date,
    modified_by, modified_date)
VALUES
   ('11111', 'Westerly', 'MA',
    USER, TO_DATE('18-JAN-2000', 'DD-MON-YYYY'),
    USER, SYSDATE)
```

The syntax of the single-row, single-table INSERT statement is:

```
INSERT INTO tablename [(column [, column]...)]
VALUES (expression|DEFAULT [,expression|DEFAULT]...)
```

As a reminder, the syntax convention for optional parts is enclosed in brackets denoted as [ ]. Keywords are in uppercase. The three dots(...) mean that the expression can be repeated. The vertical bar denotes options and the braces, {}, enclose items of which only one is required.

You notice from the INSERT statement into the ZIPCODE table that a text literal such as 'Westerly' is enclosed with single quotes and to insert a date requires the TO_DATE function with the format mask unless the date is in the default format (typically DD-MON-YYYY or DD-MON-RR).

The INSERT statement uses the SYSDATE function to insert the current date and time into the MODIFIED_DATE column. Similar to the SYSDATE function, the USER function is another function that does not take a parameter. It returns the schema name of the user logged in; in this case, the value STUDENT. This value is inserted in the CREATED_BY and MODIFIED_BY columns. You see the result of the USER function in the following example.

```
SELECT USER
   FROM dual
USER
---------------
STUDENT

1 row selected.
```

 The SQL*Plus SHOW USER *command also returns the schema name of the user logged in, but you cannot use this in an INSERT statement.*

Not all columns of the ZIPCODE table require values, only columns defined as NOT NULL. When you are not inserting data into all columns of a table, you must explicitly name the columns to insert data into. The following statement inserts values into just five of the seven columns in the ZIPCODE table; no data is inserted into the CITY and STATE columns.

```
INSERT INTO zipcode
   (zip, created_by, created_date,
    modified_by, modified_date)
VALUES
   ('11111', USER, SYSDATE, USER, SYSDATE)
```

Alternatively, the statement can be written to not explicitly list the columns and to insert NULL values in the columns instead.

```
INSERT INTO zipcode
VALUES
   ('11111', NULL, NULL, USER, SYSDATE, USER, SYSDATE)
```

Some columns may have default values defined as part of their column definition. Not listing the column in the INSERT statement automatically places the default value in the column, or you can also explicitly use the keyword DEFAULT.

INSERTING DATES AND TIMES

Inserting a value for any of the datetime datatypes is very similar to using these literals in the WHERE clause of a SELECT statement. Following is the structure of the DATE_EXAMPLE table used in Chapter 4, "Date and Conversion Functions."

```
SQL> DESCR date_example
 Name                          Null? Type
 ----------------------------- ----- ---------------------------
 COL_DATE                            DATE
 COL_TIMESTAMP                       TIMESTAMP(6)
 COL_TIMESTAMP_W_TZ                  TIMESTAMP(6) WITH TIME ZONE
 COL_TIMESTAMP_W_LOCAL_TZ            TIMESTAMP(6) WITH LOCAL TIME
                                     ZONE
```

This INSERT statement populates in the table; it explicitly converts the literals with the conversion functions into the respective datatype. The first column value is a DATE, and you use the TO_DATE function; the second value is a TIMESTAMP, and the literal is converted to this datatype with the TO_TIMESTAMP function. The third column value is of datatype TIMESTAMP WITH TIME ZONE and uses the corresponding TO_TIMESTAMP_TZ function to convert it into the correct datatype. Finally, the fourth column is the date and time in the local time zone. There is no specific conversion function for this datatype; it always displays the value in the local time.

```
INSERT INTO date_example
   (col_date,
    col_timestamp,
```

```
        col_timestamp_w_tz,
        col_timestamp_w_local_tz)
   VALUES
     (TO_DATE('24-MAR-2002 16:25:32',
              'DD-MON-YYYY HH24:MI:SS'),
      TO_TIMESTAMP('24-MAR-2002 16:25:32.0000000',
                   'DD-MON-YYYY  HH24:MI:SS.FF'),
      TO_TIMESTAMP_TZ('24-MAR-2002 16:25:32.0000000 -5:00',
                      'DD-MON-YYYY HH24:MI:SS.FF TZH:TZM'),
      TO_TIMESTAMP('24-MAR-2002 16:25:32.0000000',
                   'DD-MON-YYYY HH24:MI:SS.FF'))
```

ROUNDING OF NUMBERS

The next statement attempts to insert a value that exceeds in scale of the COST column of the COURSE table. The COST column is defined as NUMBER(9,2) and the inserted value is 50.57499.

```
INSERT INTO course
   (course_no, description, cost, prerequisite,
    created_by, created_date, modified_by, modified_date)
VALUES
   (900, 'Test Course', 50.57499, NULL,
    'Your name', SYSDATE, 'Your name', SYSDATE)
1 row created.
```

The INSERT statement proceeds successfully without any error, and the SELECT statement against the table reveals that Oracle rounds the number to 50.57.

```
SELECT cost, course_no
  FROM course
 WHERE course_no = 900
     COST COURSE_NO
--------- ---------
    50.57       900

1 row selected.
```

If the value exceeded the precision of the COST column, then you get an error like the next message. The precision is exceeded by one digit; the COST column is defined as NUMBER(9,2) with a two-digits scale, thus allowing a maximum number of seven digits left of the decimal point.

```
INSERT INTO course
   (course_no, description, cost, prerequisite,
    created_by, created_date, modified_by, modified_date)
VALUES
   (901, 'Test Course',12345678, NULL,
    'Your name', SYSDATE, 'Your name', SYSDATE)
```

```
(901, 'Test Course',12345678, NULL,
                    *
ERROR at line 5:
ORA-01438: value larger than specified precision allows for this column
```

INSERTING A FLOATING POINT NUMBER

The following INSERT statement adds a floating point number of the datatype BINARY_FLOAT into the FLOAT_TEST table. A literal of the BINARY_FLOAT datatype is followed by either an 'f' or 'F'.

```
INSERT INTO float_test
   (test_col)
VALUES
   (5f)
```

To indicate a BINARY_DOUBLE in a literal, follow it with a d or D. You can also use the conversion functions TO_BINARY_FLOAT and TO_BINARY_DOUBLE to ensure the correct datatype conversion.

If a value needs to be expressed as infinity or not a number (NaN), you use the special literals BINARY_FLOAT_NAN, BINARY_DOUBLE_NAN, BINARY_FLOAT_INFINITY, and BINARY_DOUBLE_INFINITY.

```
INSERT INTO float_test
   (test_col)
VALUES
   (BINARY_FLOAT_INFINITY)

SELECT *
   FROM float_test
TEST_COL
--------
5.0E+000
2.5E+000
     Nan
     Inf

4 rows selected.
```

INSERTS AND SCALAR SUBQUERIES

Scalar subqueries, which are defined as subqueries returning a single row and column, are allowed within the VALUE clause of an INSERT statement. The following example shows two scalar subqueries: One inserts the description of COURSE_NO 10 and concatenates it with the word Test; the second scalar subquery inserts the highest cost of any rows in the COURSE table into the COST column.

```
INSERT INTO course
   (course_no, description, cost,
    prerequisite, created_by, created_date,
    modified_by, modified_date)
VALUES
   (1000, (SELECT description||' - Test'
               FROM course
            WHERE course_no = 10),
    (SELECT MAX(cost)
       FROM course),
    20, 'MyName', SYSDATE,
    'MyName', SYSDATE)
```

Verify the result of the INSERT statement by querying the COURSE table for the
COURSE_NO equal to 1000.

```
SELECT description, cost, course_no
   FROM course
 WHERE course_no = 1000
```

DESCRIPTION	COST	COURSE_NO
DP Overview - Test	1595	1000

1 row selected.

INSERTING MULTIPLE ROWS

Another method for inserting data is to select data from another table via a subquery. The subquery may return one or multiple rows; thus, the INSERT statement
inserts one or multiple rows at a time. Suppose there is a table called
INTRO_COURSE in the STUDENT schema with columns similar to the COURSE
table; that is, the corresponding columns have a compatible datatype and column
length. They do not have to have the same column names or column order. The
following INSERT statement inserts data into the INTRO_COURSE table based on
a query against the rows of the COURSE table. According to the subquery's
WHERE clause, only those rows are chosen where the course has no prerequisite.

```
INSERT INTO intro_course
   (course_no, description_tx, cost, prereq_no,
    created_by, created_date, modified_by,
    modified_date)
SELECT course_no, description, cost, prerequisite,
       created_by, created_date, 'Melanie',
       TO_DATE('01-JAN-2001', 'DD-MON-YYYY')
   FROM course
 WHERE prerequisite IS NULL
```

The syntax for a multiple row INSERT based on a subquery is:

```
INSERT INTO tablename [(column [, column]...)]
subquery
```

INSERTING INTO MULTIPLE TABLES

While most often you use the single-table, single-row INSERT command, you may occasionally have a need to insert rows into multiple tables simultaneously. This feature is useful when data is transferred from other system sources and the destination is a data warehouse system where the data is consolidated and denormalized for the purpose of providing end users simple query access to this data. Another use for the multitable INSERT command is when you need to archive old data into separate tables.

Rather than executing multiple individual INSERT statements, the multitable INSERT is not only faster but allows additional syntax options, providing further flexibility by enabling the conditional insert of data and perhaps eliminating the need to write specific programs. There are two different types of multitable inserts: the INSERT ALL and the INSERT FIRST. The INSERT ALL can be divided into the unconditional INSERT and the conditional INSERT.

The next examples demonstrate multitable INSERT statements with the SECTION_HISTORY and the CAPACITY_HISTORY tables. You can add them to the STUDENT schema with the supplemental table scripts available from the companion Web site at *http://authors.phptr.com/rischert3e*.

THE UNCONDITIONAL INSERT ALL

The INSERT statement chooses the sections that started more than one year ago and inserts these rows into both tables—the SECTION_HISTORY and the CAPACITY_HISTORY tables. There is no condition on the INSERT statement, other than the WHERE clause condition that determines the rows to be selected from the SECTION table.

```
INSERT ALL
  INTO section_history
    VALUES (section_id, start_date_time, course_no, section_no)
  INTO capacity_history
    VALUES (section_id, location, capacity)
SELECT section_id, start_date_time, course_no, section_no,
       location, capacity
  FROM section
 WHERE TRUNC(start_date_time) < TRUNC(SYSDATE)-365
156 rows created.
```

THE CONDITIONAL INSERT ALL

The next statement chooses the same sections and inserts these rows into the tables depending on whether the individual INSERT condition is satisfied. For example, for a SECTION_ID value of 130 and a CAPACITY of 25, the statement will enter the row in both tables. If only one of the conditions is true, it inserts the row only into the table with the true condition. If both conditions are false, the selected row is not inserted into either of the tables.

```
INSERT ALL
 WHEN section_id BETWEEN 100 and 400 THEN
   INTO section_history
     VALUES (section_id, start_date_time, course_no, section_no)
 WHEN capacity >= 25 THEN
   INTO capacity_history
     VALUES (section_id, location, capacity)
SELECT section_id, start_date_time, course_no, section_no,
       location, capacity
  FROM section
 WHERE TRUNC(start_date_time) < TRUNC(SYSDATE)-365
106 rows created.
```

The syntax for the conditional INSERT ALL is as follows:

```
    INSERT ALL
    WHEN condition THEN
    insert_clause [insert_clause...]
    [WHEN condition THEN
    insert_clause [insert_clause...]...]
    [ELSE
    insert_clause [insert_clause...]]
    (query)
```

insert_clause:

```
    INTO tablename [(column [, column]...)]
    [VALUES (expression|DEFAULT[,expression|DEFAULT]...)]
```

THE CONDITIONAL INSERT FIRST

The INSERT FIRST statement evaluates the WHEN clauses in order; if the first condition is true, the row is inserted and subsequent conditions are no longer tested. For example, with a SECTION_ID value of 130 and a CAPACITY of 25, the statement will insert the row in the SECTION_HISTORY tables only because the first condition of the WHEN clause is satisfied. You can have an optional ELSE condition in case none of the conditions are true.

```
INSERT FIRST
 WHEN section_id BETWEEN 100 and 400 THEN
   INTO section_history
     VALUES (section_id, start_date_time, course_no, section_no)
 WHEN capacity >= 25 THEN
   INTO capacity_history
```

```
   VALUES (section_id, location, capacity)
SELECT section_id, start_date_time, course_no, section_no,
       location, capacity
  FROM section
 WHERE TRUNC(start_date_time) < TRUNC(SYSDATE)-365
71 rows created.
```

The syntax for the INSERT FIRST command is identical to that of the conditional INSERT ALL command except for the FIRST keyword instead of the ALL keyword.

THE PIVOTING INSERT ALL

The pivoting INSERT ALL statement is just like the unconditional INSERT ALL statement—it inserts the rows into multiple tables and it also does not have a WHEN condition. Here is the example of pivoting a table; that is, flipping it on its side. The following example table, called GRADE_DISTRIBUTION, has a count of the different grades per each section. The first row, with SECTION_ID of 400, shows 5 students with the letter grade A, 10 students with the letter grade B, 3 students with the letter grade C, and no D or F grade for any students of the section.

```
select *
  FROM grade_distribution
SECTION_ID GRADE_A GRADE_B GRADE_C GRADE_D GRADE_F
---------- ------- ------- ------- ------- -------
       400       5      10       3       0       0
       401       1       3       5       1       0
       402       5      10       3       0       1

3 rows selected.
```

Suppose you want to move the data into a more normalized table format. Then you can use a pivoting INSERT ALL statement. This example illustrates the inserting of the data into the table GRADE_DISTRIBUTION_NORMALIZED, which just lists the letter grade and the number of students. Here is the structure of the table. To insert the same data about SECTION_ID 400, five individual rows are needed.

```
SQL> DESCR grade_distribution_normalized
 Name                             Null?    Type
 -------------------------------- -------- -----------
 SECTION_ID                                NUMBER(8)
 LETTER_GRADE                              VARCHAR2(2)
 NUM_OF_STUDENTS                           NUMBER(4)
```

The following INSERT ALL statement transfers each individual selected row into the table, but in a normalized format whereby each grade is its own row.

```
INSERT ALL
   INTO grade_distribution_normalized
      VALUES (section_id, 'A', grade_a)
```

```
  INTO grade_distribution_normalized
     VALUES (section_id, 'B', grade_b)
  INTO grade_distribution_normalized
     VALUES (section_id, 'C', grade_c)
  INTO grade_distribution_normalized
     VALUES (section_id, 'D', grade_d)
  INTO grade_distribution_normalized
     VALUES (section_id, 'F', grade_f)
SELECT section_id, grade_a, grade_b,
       grade_c, grade_d, grade_f
  FROM grade_distribution
15 rows created.
```

When selecting from the GRADE_DISTRIBUTION_NORMALIZED table, you see the rows in a normalized format.

```
select *
  FROM grade_distribution_normalized
SECTION_ID LE NUM_OF_STUDENTS
---------- -- ---------------
       400 A                5
       401 A                1
       402 A                5
       400 D               10
...
       400 F                0
       401 F                0
       402 F                1

15 rows selected.
```

TRANSACTION CONTROL

Just as important as manipulating data is controlling when this change becomes permanent. DML statements are controlled within the context of a *transaction*. A transaction is a DML statement or group of DML statements that logically belong together, also referred to as a *logical unit of work*. The group of statements is defined by the commands COMMIT and ROLLBACK, in conjunction with the SAVEPOINT command.

COMMIT

The COMMIT command makes the change to the data permanent. Any previously uncommitted changes are now committed and cannot be undone. The effect of the COMMIT command is that it allows other sessions to see the data. The session issuing the DML command can always see the changes, but other sessions can only see the changes after you COMMIT. Another effect of a COMMIT is that locks for the changed rows are released and other users may perform changes on the rows. You will learn more about locking in Lab 10.2.

DDL statements, such as the CREATE TABLE command, or DCL statements, such as GRANT, implicitly issue a COMMIT to the database; there is no need to issue a COMMIT command. You learn about DDL commands in Chapter 11, "Create, Alter, and Drop Tables," and DCL commands in Chapter 14, "Security."

WHAT IS A SESSION?   A session is an individual connection to the Oracle database server. It starts as soon as the user is logged in and authenticated by the server with a valid login ID and password. The session ends when the user logs out with either a DISCONNECT command, an exit command to exit SQL*Plus, a click on the log off icon in *i*SQL*Plus, or when there is an abnormal termination, such as the system crashes or the user shuts off his or her or machine without properly exiting. An individual database user may be connected to multiple concurrent sessions simultaneously. For example, you can log into SQL*Plus multiple times, each time establishing an individual session. In *i*SQL*Plus you can start up multiple browser windows.

ROLLBACK

The ROLLBACK command undoes any DML statements back to the last COMMIT command issued. Any pending changes are discarded and any locks on the affected rows are released.

EXAMPLE OF A TRANSACTION

The following SQL statements all constitute a single transaction. The first INSERT statement starts the transaction and the ROLLBACK command ends it.

```
INSERT INTO zipcode
   (zip, city, state,
    created_by, created_date, modified_by, modified_date)
VALUES
   ('22222', NULL, NULL,
    USER, SYSDATE, USER, SYSDATE)
1 row created.

INSERT INTO zipcode
   (zip, city, state,
    created_by, created_date, modified_by, modified_date)
VALUES
   ('33333', NULL, NULL,
    USER, SYSDATE, USER, SYSDATE)
1 row created.

INSERT INTO zipcode
   (zip, city, state,
    created_by, created_date, modified_by, modified_date)
```

```
VALUES
   ('44444', NULL, NULL,
    USER, SYSDATE, USER, SYSDATE)
1 row created.
```

Now query the ZIPCODE table for the values inserted.

```
SELECT zip, city, state
  FROM zipcode
 WHERE zip IN ('22222', '33333', '44444')
ZIP   CITY                      ST
----- ------------------------ --
22222
33333
44444

3 rows selected.
```

Then, issue the ROLLBACK command and perform the same query.

```
ROLLBACK
Rollback complete.

SELECT zip, city, state
  FROM zipcode
 WHERE zip IN ('22222', '33333', '44444')

no rows selected
```

The values inserted are no longer in the ZIPCODE table; the ROLLBACK command prevents the values inserted by all three statements from being committed to the database. If a COMMIT command is issued between the first and second statements, the value '22222' would be found in the ZIPCODE table, but not the values '33333' and '44444'.

SAVEPOINT

The SAVEPOINT command allows you to save the result of DML transactions temporarily. The ROLLBACK command can then refer back to a particular SAVEPOINT and roll back the transaction up to that point; any statements issued after the SAVEPOINT are rolled back.

EXAMPLE OF A SAVEPOINT   Here are the same three DML statements used previously, but with SAVEPOINT commands issued in between.

```
INSERT INTO zipcode
   (zip, city, state,
    created_by, created_date, modified_by, modified_date)
VALUES
```

```
             ('22222', NULL, NULL,
              USER, SYSDATE, USER, SYSDATE)
1 row created.

SAVEPOINT zip22222
Savepoint created.

INSERT INTO zipcode
   (zip, city, state,
    created_by, created_date, modified_by, modified_date)
VALUES
   ('33333', NULL, NULL,
    USER, SYSDATE, USER, SYSDATE)
1 row created.

SAVEPOINT zip33333
Savepoint created.

INSERT INTO zipcode
   (zip, city, state,
    created_by, created_date, modified_by, modified_date)
VALUES
   ('44444', NULL, NULL,
    USER, SYSDATE, USER, SYSDATE)
1 row created.
```

Now query the ZIPCODE table for the values inserted.

```
SELECT zip, city, state
  FROM zipcode
 WHERE zip IN ('22222', '33333', '44444')
ZIP   CITY                          ST
----- ------------------------- --
22222
33333
44444

3 rows selected.
```

Then, issue the command ROLLBACK TO SAVEPOINT zip33333 and perform the same query.

```
ROLLBACK TO SAVEPOINT zip33333
Rollback complete.

SELECT zip, city, state
  FROM zipcode
 WHERE zip IN ('22222', '33333', '44444')
```

```
ZIP   CITY                      ST
----- ------------------------- --
22222
33333
```

```
2 rows selected.
```

All statements issued after the zip33333 savepoint are rolled back. When you rollback to the previous savepoint, the same result occurs, and so on.

```
ROLLBACK TO SAVEPOINT zip22222
Rollback complete.
```

```
SELECT zip, city, state
  FROM zipcode
 WHERE zip IN ('22222', '33333', '44444')
ZIP   CITY                      ST
----- ------------------------- --
22222
```

```
1 row selected.
```

The three statements still constitute a single transaction; however, it is possible to mark parts of the transaction with a SAVEPOINT in order to control when a statement is rolled back with the ROLLBACK TO SAVEPOINT command.

CONTROLLING TRANSACTIONS

It is important to control DML statements using COMMIT, ROLLBACK, and SAVEPOINT. If the three previous statements logically belong together—in other words, one does not make sense without the others occurring—then another session should not see the results until all three are committed at once. Until the user performing the inserts issues a COMMIT command, no other database users or sessions are able to see the changes. A typical example of such a transaction is the transfer from a savings account to a checking account. You obviously want to avoid the scenario where transactions from one account are missing and the balances are out of sync. Unless both data manipulations are successful, the change does not become permanent and visible to other users.

Oracle places a lock on a row whenever the row is manipulated through a DML statement. This prevents other users from manipulating the row until it is either committed or rolled back. Users can continue to query the row and see the old values until the row is committed.

STATEMENT-LEVEL ROLLBACK

If one individual statement fails in a series of DML statements, only this statement is rolled back and Oracle issues an implicit SAVEPOINT. The other changes remain until a COMMIT or ROLLBACK occurs to end the transaction.

The next example shows two SQL statements: the first INSERT statement executes successfully and the second fails.

```
INSERT INTO zipcode
   (zip, city, state,
    created_by, created_date, modified_by, modified_date)
VALUES
   ('99999', NULL, NULL,
    USER, SYSDATE, USER, SYSDATE)
1 row created.

INSERT INTO zipcode
   (zip, city, state,
    created_by, created_date, modified_by, modified_date)
VALUES
   (NULL, NULL, NULL,
    USER, SYSDATE, USER, SYSDATE)
INSERT INTO zipcode
*
ERROR at line 1:
ORA-01400: cannot insert NULL into
("STUDENT"."ZIPCODE"."ZIP")
```

The error message indicates the problem with the statement; it shows that a null value cannot be inserted into the ZIP column of the ZIPCODE table located in the STUDENT schema.

Only the second statement is rolled back. The first statement remains intact and uncommitted, as you see when executing the next query. The entire transaction ends when a ROLLBACK or COMMIT occurs.

```
SELECT zip
  FROM zipcode
 WHERE zip = '99999'
ZIP
-----
99999

1 row selected.
```

LAB 10.1 EXERCISES

10.1.1 INSERT DATA, ROLLBACK AND COMMIT TRANSACTIONS

a) Write and execute an INSERT statement to insert a row into the GRADE_TYPE table for a grade type of 'Extra Credit', identified by a code of 'EC'. Issue a COMMIT command afterward.

b) Explain what is wrong with the following INSERT statement. Hint: It is not the value COURSE_NO_SEQ.NEXTVAL, which inserts a value from a sequence, thus generating a unique number.

```
INSERT INTO course
   (course_no, description, cost)
VALUES
   (course_no_seq.NEXTVAL, 'Intro to Linux', 1295)
```

c) Execute the following SQL statement. Note that the SAMPLE clause chooses a random sample of 10 percent. Explain your observations and undo the change.

```
INSERT INTO instructor
 (instructor_id,
   salutation, first_name, last_name,
   street_address, zip, phone,
   created_by, created_date, modified_by, modified_date)
SELECT instructor_id_seq.NEXTVAL,
         salutation, first_name, last_name,
         street_address, zip, phone,
         USER, SYSDATE, USER, SYSDATE
   FROM student
SAMPLE (10)
```

d) Issue the following INSERT statements. Are the statements successful? If not, what do you observe?

```
INSERT INTO section
   (section_id, course_no, section_no,
    start_date_time,
    location, instructor_id, capacity, created_by,
    created_date, modified_by, modified_date)
VALUES
   (500, 90, 1,
    TO_DATE('03-APR-2002 15:00', 'DD-MON-YYYY HH24:MI'),
    'L500', 103, 50, 'Your name here',
    SYSDATE, 'Your name here', SYSDATE)

INSERT INTO instructor
   (last_name, salutation, instructor_id,
    created_by, created_date, modified_by, modified_date)
VALUES
   ('Spencer', 'Mister', 200,
    'Your name', SYSDATE, 'Your name', SYSDATE)
```

e) Insert the following row into the GRADE table and exit/logoff SQL*Plus or *i*SQL*Plus without issuing a COMMIT statement.

Log back into the server and query the GRADE table for the inserted row. What do you observe?

```
INSERT INTO grade
    (student_id, section_id, grade_type_code,
     grade_code_occurrence, numeric_grade, created_by,
     created_date, modified_by, modified_date)
VALUES
    (124, 83, 'MT',
     1, 90, 'MyName',
     SYSDATE, 'MyName', SYSDATE)
```

LAB 10.1 EXERCISE ANSWERS

10.1.1 ANSWERS

a) Write and execute an INSERT statement to insert a row into the GRADE_TYPE table for a grade type of 'Extra Credit', identified by a code of 'EC'. Issue a COMMIT command afterward.

Answer: All columns of the GRADE_TYPE table are identified as NOT NULL, so the INSERT statement needs to list all the columns and corresponding values.

```
INSERT INTO grade_type
    (grade_type_code, description,
     created_by, created_date, modified_by, modified_date)
VALUES
    ('EC', 'Extra Credit',
     USER, SYSDATE, USER, SYSDATE)
```
1 row created.

```
COMMIT
```
Commit complete.

It is not necessary to explicitly list the columns of the GRADE_TYPE table because values are supplied for all columns. However, it is good practice to name all the columns in the column list, because if additional columns are added in the future or the order of columns in the table changes, the INSERT statement will fail. This is particularly important when the INSERT statement is used in a program for repeated use.

b) Explain what is wrong with the following INSERT statement. Hint: It is not the value COURSE_NO_SEQ.NEXTVAL, which inserts a value from a sequence, thus generating a unique number.

```
INSERT INTO course
   (course_no, description, cost)
VALUES
   (course_no_seq.NEXTVAL, 'Intro to Linux', 1295)
```

Answer: The INSERT statement fails because it does not insert values into the NOT NULL columns CREATED_BY, CREATED_DATE, MODIFIED_BY, and MODIFIED_DATE in the COURSE table.

```
INSERT INTO course
              *
ERROR at line 1:
ORA-01400: cannot insert NULL into
("STUDENT"."COURSE"."CREATED_BY")
```

The Oracle error message informs you that the column CREATED_BY requires a value. The correct command includes the NOT NULL columns and is successfully executed when issued as follows:

```
INSERT INTO course
   (course_no, description, cost, created_date,
    modified_date, created_by, modified_by)
VALUES
   (course_no_seq.NEXTVAL, 'Intro to Linux', 1295, SYSDATE,
    SYSDATE, 'AliceRischert', 'AliceRischert')
1 row created
```

If you don't want to make this change permanent in the database, issue the ROLLBACK command.

```
ROLLBACK
Rollback complete.
```

The value supplied for the COURSE_NO column, COURSE_NO_SEQ.NEXTVAL, is not a text literal, number, or date. It is a value generated from a sequence called COURSE_NO_SEQ. A sequence is an Oracle database object that generates sequential numbers to ensure uniqueness whenever it is used, most commonly for generating primary keys. The keyword NEXTVAL indicates to Oracle to select the next value from the sequence. You learn more about sequences in Chapter 12, "Views, Indexes, and Sequences."

c) Execute the following SQL statement. Note that the SAMPLE clause chooses a random sample of 10 percent. Explain your observations and undo the change.

```
INSERT INTO instructor
 (instructor_id,
   salutation, first_name, last_name,
   street_address, zip, phone,
```

```
        created_by, created_date, modified_by, modified_date)
SELECT instructor_id_seq.NEXTVAL,
        salutation, first_name, last_name,
        street_address, zip, phone,
        USER, SYSDATE, USER, SYSDATE
    FROM student
SAMPLE (10)
```

Answer: This is an example of a multirow INSERT statement. The INSERT statement contains a SELECT clause that retrieves values from all columns of the STUDENT table and inserts them into the INSTRUCTOR table. While there is no WHERE clause present in this SELECT statement, it contains the SAMPLE clause, which randomly chooses 10 percent of the students as rows for the insert operation. The INSTRUCTOR_ID_SEQ is the name of the sequence that generates unique numbers. The pseudocolumn NEXTVAL retrieves the next value from the sequence. In this example, these generated unique numbers get inserted into the INSTRUCTOR_ID primary key column.

Be sure to undo the change afterwards with the ROLLBACK command.

```
ROLLBACK
Rollback complete.
```

d) Issue the following INSERT statements. Are the statements successful? If not, what do you observe?

```
INSERT INTO section
    (section_id, course_no, section_no,
     start_date_time,
     location, instructor_id, capacity, created_by,
     created_date, modified_by, modified_date)
VALUES
    (500, 90, 1,
     TO_DATE('03-APR-2002 15:00', 'DD-MON-YYYY HH24:MI'),
     'L500', 103, 50, 'Your name here',
     SYSDATE, 'Your name here', SYSDATE)

INSERT INTO instructor
    (last_name, salutation, instructor_id,
     created_by, created_date, modified_by, modified_date)
VALUES
    ('Spencer', 'Mister', 200,
     'Your name', SYSDATE, 'Your name', SYSDATE)
```

Answer: Both of the INSERT statements fail. You see the reason why after each individual statement is issued.

```
INSERT INTO section
    (section_id, course_no, section_no,
```

```
      start_date_time,
      location, instructor_id, capacity, created_by,
      created_date, modified_by, modified_date)
VALUES
   (500, 90, 1,
    TO_DATE('03-APR-2002 15:00', 'DD-MON-YYYY HH24:MI'),
    'L500', 103, 50, 'Your name here',
    SYSDATE, 'Your name here', SYSDATE)
INSERT INTO section
*
ERROR at line 1:
ORA-02291: integrity constraint (STUDENT.SECT_CRSE_FK)
violated - parent key not found
```

This statement fails because a parent row cannot be found. The foreign key constraint SECT_CRSE_FK is violated; that means a course number with the value of 500 does not exist in the COURSE table, thus the creation of an orphan row is prevented by the foreign key constraint. The constraint name is determined when you create a foreign key constraint, discussed in Chapter 12, "Create, Alter, and Drop Tables." Ideally, you want to name the constraint so that it is apparent which columns and tables are involved. If you are unsure which column and table the constraint references, you can query the data dictionary views USER_CONSTRAINTS or ALL_CONSTRAINTS discussed in Chapter 13, "The Data Dictionary and Advanced SQL*Plus Commands." Note also that the constraint name is prefixed with the STUDENT schema name; this is unrelated to the STUDENT table name.

The next INSERT statement also fails because it attempts to insert a value that is larger than the defined five-character width of the SALUTATION column of the INSTRUCTOR table. The value of 'Mister' is six characters long and therefore causes the following error message.

```
INSERT INTO instructor
   (last_name, salutation, instructor_id,
    created_by, created_date, modified_by, modified_date)
VALUES
   ('Spencer', 'Mister', 200,
    'Your name', SYSDATE, 'Your name', SYSDATE)
INSERT INTO instructor
            *
ERROR at line 1:
ORA-01401: inserted value too large for column
```

USING SPECIAL CHARACTERS IN SQL STATEMENTS

Some characters such as the ampersand or the single quote have a special meaning in SQL*Plus or within a SQL statement.

THE AMPERSAND (&) If you attempt to insert the following record, notice the message you will receive. Any attempt to insert or update a column with an ampersand is interpreted by Oracle as a substitution parameter for a SQL*Plus script and prompts you to enter a value. You will learn about this parameter in Chapter 13, "The Data Dictionary and Advanced SQL*Plus Commands." The & substitution parameter is specific to SQL*Plus or *i*SQL*Plus; you will not encounter such a prompt in other SQL execution environments.

```
INSERT INTO instructor
   (salutation, last_name, instructor_id,
    created_by, created_date, modified_by, modified_date)
VALUES
   ('Mr&Ms', 'Spencer', 300,
    'Your name', SYSDATE, 'Your name', SYSDATE)
Enter value for ms:
old    5:    ('Mr&Ms', 'Spencer', 300,
new    5:    ('Mr', 'Spencer', 300,


1 row created.


ROLLBACK
Rollback complete.
```

To temporarily turn off the substitution parameter functionality, you issue the SET DEFINE OFF command. Don't forget to reset it back to its default value with the SET DEFINE ON command.

```
SQL> SET DEFINE OFF
SQL> INSERT INTO instructor
  2     (salutation, last_name, instructor_id,
  3      created_by, created_date, modified_by, modified_date)
  4   VALUES
  5     ('Mr&Ms', 'Spencer', 300,
  6      'Your name', SYSDATE, 'Your name', SYSDATE)
  7   /
1 row created.

SQL> SET DEFINE ON
```

Alternatively, you can break the string into pieces and place the ampersand at the end of one string and then concatenate it with the remainder of the string,

```
INSERT INTO instructor
   (salutation, last_name, instructor_id,
    created_by, created_date, modified_by, modified_date)
VALUES
   ('Mr&'||'Ms', 'Spencer', 301,
    'Your name', SYSDATE, 'Your name', SYSDATE)
```

THE SINGLE QUOTE (') If you have another instructor named O'Neil, you need to use a double set of single quotes to make Oracle understand that this single quote is to be taken as a literal quote.

```
INSERT INTO instructor
   (salutation, last_name, instructor_id,
    created_by, created_date, modified_by, modified_date)
VALUES
   ('Mr.', 'O''Neil', 305,
    'Your name', SYSDATE, 'Your name', SYSDATE)
1 row created.

SELECT last_name
  FROM instructor
 WHERE instructor_id = 305
LAST_NAME
---------------
O'Neil

1 row selected.
```

In Oracle 10*g* you can choose alternate quoting as indicated with the letter q or Q. For example, the string 'O''Neil' can be written as q'!O'Neil!' whereby the q indicates the alternate quoting mechanism. The letter q or Q follows a single quote and the chosen quote delimiter. In this example the ! is the delimiter. The literal ends with the chosen delimiter and a single quote. As you see, O'Neil no longer requires two single quotes. You can choose any character as a delimiter except space, tab, and return. However, if the quote delimiter is [,{, <, or (, you must choose the corresponding closing delimiter.

```
INSERT INTO instructor
   (salutation, last_name, instructor_id,
    created_by, created_date, modified_by, modified_date)
VALUES
   ('Mr.', q'<O'Neil>', 305,
    'Your name', SYSDATE, 'Your name', SYSDATE)
```

e) Insert the following row into the GRADE table and exit/logoff SQL*Plus or *i*SQL*Plus without issuing a COMMIT statement. Log back into the server and query the GRADE table for the inserted row. What do you observe?

```
INSERT INTO grade
   (student_id, section_id, grade_type_code,
    grade_code_occurrence, numeric_grade, created_by,
    created_date, modified_by, modified_date)
VALUES
   (124, 83, 'MT',
    1, 90, 'MyName',
```

```
          SYSDATE, 'MyName', SYSDATE)
1 row created.
```

Answer: SQL*Plus and iSQL*Plus implicitly issue a COMMIT when you properly exit the program.

After you log back into the server and you query the GRADE table, you notice that the row exists, despite the missing COMMIT command. SQL*Plus and *i*SQL*Plus implicitly issue the COMMIT when you correctly exit the program by typing the EXIT or DISCONNECT command or by clicking the Logout icon in *i*SQL*Plus.

```
SELECT student_id, section_id, created_by, created_date
  FROM grade
 WHERE section_id = 83
   AND student_id = 124
   AND grade_type_code = 'MT'
   AND TRUNC(created_date) = TRUNC(SYSDATE)
STUDENT_ID SECTION_ID CREATED_BY CREATED_D
---------- ---------- ---------- ---------
       124         83 MyName     08-MAY-02

1 row selected.
```

The implicit commit behavior is part of Oracle's SQL*Plus programs; do not expect identical functionality in any other programs. Typically, you must explicitly commit or rollback your transactions. However, if you exit from either program by clicking the CLOSE button in the window, the INSERT statement will not COMMIT to the database. This is considered an abnormal exit and modified rows will be locked.

LOCKING OF ROWS THROUGH ABNORMAL TERMINATION

Rows may also become locked when a session abnormally terminates such as when the user reboots the machine without properly exiting or the application program connected to the database raises an unhandled exception. If you do not exit properly from your session, an uncommitted transaction may be pending and the row will be locked until Oracle eventually detects the dead session and rolls back the transaction. You can verify if in fact a lock is held on a particular row and table by querying the Oracle data dictionary views. Sometimes the Database Administrator (DBA) must intervene and manually release the lock if Oracle does not resolve the problem automatically.

 Clean exits and frequent commits are part of good habits that you should adopt; otherwise, locks will not be released and other users cannot make modifications to the same rows you changed.

Note the SQL*Plus command AUTOCOMMIT can be set to automatically commit every statement issued during a SQL*Plus session by typing SET AUTOCOMMIT ON or SET AUTOCOMMIT IMMEDIATE. This SQL*Plus command is dangerous because it means a ROLLBACK command issued during that session has no effect because every transaction is automatically committed. If you use *i*SQL*Plus, you may notice that after a period of inactivity you get a SP2-0864: Session has expired. Please log in again message. This is due to a timeout interval parameter set on *i*SQL*Plus. Typically, this interval is 30 minutes and can be changed. If you exceed the inactivity of the *i*SQL*Plus session, your uncommitted changes are automatically committed and the locks released.

LAB 10.1 SELF-REVIEW QUESTIONS

In order to test your progress, you should be able to answer the following questions.

1) A DML command automatically issues a COMMIT.

  a) _____ True
  b) _____ False

2) A statement-level rollback ends a transaction.

  a) _____ True
  b) _____ False

3) An INSERT statement can only insert one row at a time into a table.

  a) _____ True
  b) _____ False

4) A COMMIT or ROLLBACK command ends a transaction.

  a) _____ True
  b) _____ False

5) Uncommitted changes can be seen by all users.

  a) _____ True
  b) _____ False

6) A transaction is a logical unit of work.

  a) _____ True
  b) _____ False

Answers appear in Appendix A, Section 10.1.

LAB 10.2

UPDATING AND DELETING DATA

LAB OBJECTIVES

After this lab, you will be able to:
✔ Update Data
✔ Delete Data

UPDATING DATA

The UPDATE command manipulates existing data in a table. It always refers to a single table. For example, the following UPDATE statement updates the FINAL_GRADE column in the ENROLLMENT table to 90 for all students who enrolled in January 2003.

```
UPDATE enrollment
   SET final_grade = 90
 WHERE enroll_date >= TO_DATE('01/01/2003', 'MM/DD/YYYY')
   AND enroll_date < TO_DATE('02/01/2003', 'MM/DD/YYYY')
11 rows updated.
```

The keyword UPDATE always precedes the name of the table to be updated, and the SET keyword precedes the column or columns to be changed. An UPDATE statement can update all rows in a table at once, or just certain rows when restricted with a WHERE clause as in the previous example. The general syntax for the UPDATE command is as follows:

```
UPDATE tablename
SET {{(column[,column]...)=(subquery)|
       column={expression|(subquery)|DEFAULT}
     }[,{(column[,column]...)=(subquery)|
       column={expression|(subquery)|DEFAULT}
     }]...}
[WHERE condition]
```

UPDATING COLUMNS TO NULL VALUES

An UPDATE statement can also update columns with a NULL value. The following UPDATE statement sets the FINAL_GRADE column to NULL for all rows in the ENROLLMENT table.

```
UPDATE enrollment
    SET final_grade = NULL
```

Note the IS NULL operator is used only in a WHERE clause, not in the SET clause of an UPDATE statement.

COLUMN DEFAULT VALUE

A column may have a default value defined; this value is entered if an INSERT statement did not specify an explicit value for a column. Alternatively, you can use the DEFAULT keyword in the UPDATE or INSERT command to explicitly set the default value defined for the column. The NUMERIC_GRADE column of the GRADE table has such a default value of 0 defined. Examine the row before the change to the DEFAULT value.

```
SELECT numeric_grade
   FROM grade
  WHERE student_id = 211
    AND section_id = 141
    AND grade_type_code = 'HM'
    AND grade_code_occurrence = 1
NUMERIC_GRADE
-------------
           99

1 row selected.
```

To update the column to the default value of 0 for the first homework grade of student ID 211 in SECTION_ID 141, you issue the following UPDATE command.

```
UPDATE grade
    SET numeric_grade = DEFAULT
  WHERE student_id = 211
    AND section_id = 141
    AND grade_type_code = 'HM'
    AND grade_code_occurrence = 1
1 row updated.
```

Examine the result of the change by requerying the record. Notice that the column default value of 0 is now entered.

```
SELECT numeric_grade
  FROM grade
 WHERE student_id = 211
   AND section_id = 141
   AND grade_type_code = 'HM'
   AND grade_code_occurrence = 1
NUMERIC_GRADE
-------------
            0
```

1 row selected.

Now restore the value to the original value of 99 with the ROLLBACK command.

```
ROLLBACK
```
Rollback complete.

If you want to find out which columns have column default values, you query the data dictionary views called USER_TAB_COLUMNS or ALL_TAB_COLUMNS. They are discussed in greater detail in Chapter 13, "The Data Dictionary and Advanced SQL*Plus Commands." You will learn about the syntax to create column defaults in Chapter 12, "Create, Alter, and Drop Tables."

UPDATES AND THE CASE EXPRESSION

CASE expressions can be used anywhere expressions are allowed. The next example shows the CASE expression in the SET clause of the UPDATE statement. The FINAL_GRADE column of the ENROLLMENT table is updated whereby students enrolled in SECTION_ID 100 receive extra points for their FINAL_GRADE score.

```
UPDATE enrollment
   SET final_grade = CASE WHEN final_grade <=80 THEN
                               final_grade+5
                          WHEN final_grade > 80 THEN
                               final_grade+10
                 END
 WHERE section_id = 100
```

The CASE expression evaluates the current value of the FINAL_GRADE column. If the value is less than or equal to 80, the value of the FINAL_GRADE is increased by 5 points, if the value is greater than 80, the increase is 10 points. No provision is made for null values; they remain unchanged because they do not satisfy any of the WHEN conditions. A null value is not greater, less than, or equal to any value and there is no ELSE clause in this statement.

SUBQUERIES AND THE UPDATE COMMAND

An update can occur based on data from other tables using a subquery. The next example uses a subquery in the SET clause of the UPDATE command and it updates the ZIP column of INSTRUCTOR_ID 108 to be equal to the ZIP value of the state of Florida.

```
UPDATE instructor
   SET zip = (SELECT zip
                FROM zipcode
               WHERE state = 'FL')
 WHERE instructor_id = 108
```

In our ZIPCODE table the state of Florida has a single value in the ZIPCODE table.

```
SELECT zip
  FROM zipcode
 WHERE state = 'FL'
ZIP
-----
33431

1 row selected.
```

The result of the update effectively changes the zip code to 33431 for INSTRUCTOR_ID 108.

```
SELECT instructor_id, zip
  FROM instructor
 WHERE instructor_id = 108
INSTRUCTOR_ID ZIP
------------- -----
          108 33431

1 row selected.
```

SUBQUERIES RETURNING NULL VALUES

The following UPDATE query statement attempts to update the same instructor's zip code with a value for which you will not find any zip code in the ZIPCODE table.

```
UPDATE instructor
   SET zip = (SELECT zip
                FROM zipcode
               WHERE state = 'CA')
 WHERE instructor_id = 108
1 row updated.
```

When you issue the query to see the effect of the update, you notice that the sub-query returned a null value and therefore updated the ZIP column to a null.

```
SELECT instructor_id, zip
  FROM instructor
 WHERE instructor_id = 108
INSTRUCTOR_ID ZIP
------------- ---
          108

1 row selected.
```

SUBQUERIES RETURNING MULTIPLE VALUES

The next subquery returns multiple zip codes for the state of Connecticut. The error message indicates that the subquery returns multiple rows, which is not allowed for an equal sign (=) and therefore the UPDATE statement fails.

```
UPDATE instructor
   SET zip = (SELECT zip
                   FROM zipcode
                  WHERE state = 'CT')
 WHERE instructor_id = 108
   SET zip = (SELECT zip
                *
ERROR at line 2:
ORA-01427: single-row subquery returns more than one row
```

If you want just any one of the zip codes, no matter which one, you can utilize the MAX or MIN function. An aggregate function guarantees the return of a single row.

```
UPDATE instructor
   SET zip = (SELECT MAX(zip)
                   FROM zipcode
                  WHERE state = 'CT')
 WHERE instructor_id = 108
1 row updated.
```

UPDATES AND CORRELATED SUBQUERIES

The following statement updates the FINAL_GRADE column to 90 and the MOD-IFIED_DATE column to March 13, 2000 for those sections taught by the instructor Hanks.

```
UPDATE enrollment e
   SET final_grade = 90,
       modified_date = TO_DATE('13-MAR-2000', 'DD-MON-YYYY')
 WHERE EXISTS
```

```
(SELECT '*'
   FROM section s, instructor i
  WHERE e.section_id = s.section_id
    AND s.instructor_id = i.instructor_id
    AND i.last_name = 'Hanks')
```

As you see, you can use any of the SELECT statements you learned about to restrict the result set. In this example, a correlated subquery identifies the rows to be updated. A column from the outer table, in this case ENROLLMENT, is referenced in the subquery through the column E.SECTION_ID. Every row of the ENROLLMENT table is updated where a corresponding SECTION_ID is returned by the subquery. Just like other correlated subqueries, every row in the outer table, here the ENROLLMENT table, is examined and evaluated against the inner query. The update occurs for those rows where the condition of the correlated subquery evaluates to true.

AVOID THIS COMMON SCENARIO WITH CORRELATED SUBQUERIES

The following correlated update changes one column with a value from another table. Here are two example tables. TA and TB. The values from TA need to be updated to reflect changes made in TB. The query shows a listing of all the rows in the example table called TA.

```
SELECT *
  FROM ta
        ID COL1
--------- ----
        1 a
        2 b
        3 c
        4 d

4 rows selected.
```

This is a listing of all the rows in table TB. The idea of the correlated update is to update the rows of TA based on table TB by joining on the common column called ID.

```
SELECT *
  FROM tb
        ID COL2
--------- ----
        1 w
        2 x
        5 y
        6 z

4 rows selected.
```

When you execute the UPDATE statement and subsequently query table TA, you will notice that the rows with the ID 3 and 4 were updated with null values. The intention was to retain the original values.

```
UPDATE ta
   SET col1 = (SELECT col2
                   FROM tb
                   WHERE ta.id = tb.id)
```
4 rows updated.

```
SELECT *
   FROM ta
        ID COL1
--------- ----
        1 w
        2 x
        3
        4
```

4 rows selected.

The correlated update query does not have a WHERE clause; therefore, all the rows of table TA are evaluated. The correlated subquery returns a null value for any row that was not found in table TB. You can avoid this behavior and retain the values in COL1 by including only the rows found in table TB with an appropriate WHERE clause in the UPDATE statement.

```
ROLLBACK
```
Rollback complete.

```
UPDATE ta
   SET col1 = (SELECT col2
                   FROM tb
                   WHERE ta.id = tb.id)
 WHERE id IN (SELECT id
                   FROM tb)
```
2 rows updated.

A query against the TB table verifies that the desired updates are done correctly.

```
SELECT *
   FROM ta
        ID COL1
--------- ----
        1 w
        2 x
```

```
        3 c
        4 d
```

4 rows selected.

 Be sure to check your results before committing, especially when you perform complicated updates to a table.

UPDATES AND SUBQUERIES RETURNING MULTIPLE COLUMNS

Following are two example tables called EMPLOYEE and EMPLOYEE_CHANGE. The EMPLOYEE table holds a list of employees with their IDs, names, salaries, and titles. The purpose of the EMPLOYEE_CHANGE table is to hold all the changes that need to be made to the EMPLOYEE table. Perhaps the names, titles, and salary information comes from various other systems and are then recorded in the EMPLOYEE_CHANGE table that is to be used for updates to the master EMPLOYEE table.

```
SELECT *
  FROM employee
EMPLOYEE_ID NAME            SALARY TITLE
----------- --------------- ------ ---------
          1 John              1000 Analyst
          2 Mary              2000 Manager
          3 Stella            5000 President
          4 Fred               500 Janitor
```

4 rows selected.

```
SELECT *
  FROM employee_change
EMPLOYEE_ID NAME            SALARY TITLE
----------- --------------- ------ ----------
          1 John              1500 Programmer
          3 Stella            6000 CEO
          4 Fred               600 Clerk
          5 Jean               800 Secretary
          6 Betsy             2000 Sales Rep
```

5 rows selected.

The next statement updates both the SALARY and TITLE columns of the EMPLOYEE table with the corresponding values from the EMPLOYEE_CHANGE table for the employee with the ID of 4, which is Fred the Janitor. When you review the subquery of this UPDATE statement, you will notice the equal sign indicates that the subquery must return a single row.

```
UPDATE employee
   SET (salary, title) = (SELECT salary, title
                             FROM employee_change
                           WHERE employee_id = 4)
   WHERE employee_id = 4
1 row updated.
```

You now see the change and Fred now earns a different salary and has the title of Clerk.

```
SELECT *
   FROM employee
EMPLOYEE_ID NAME            SALARY TITLE
----------- --------------- ------ ---------
          1 John              1000 Analyst
          2 Mary              2000 Manager
          3 Stella            5000 President
          4 Fred               600 Clerk

4 rows selected.

ROLLBACK
Rollback complete.
```

Undo the change with the ROLLBACK command. The next example shows how to update all the rows in the EMPLOYEE table instead of just one individual employee.

```
UPDATE employee e
   SET (salary, title) =
       (SELECT salary, title
          FROM employee_change c
         WHERE e.employee_id = c.employee_id)
   WHERE employee_id IN (SELECT employee_id
                           FROM employee_change)
3 rows updated.
```

Notice three rows are updated and they are for the employees John, Stella, and Fred. The records for employees Jean and Betsy are not inserted into the EMPLOYEE table because the UPDATE statement just updates existing records and does not insert any new rows.

```
SELECT *
   FROM employee
EMPLOYEE_ID NAME            SALARY TITLE
----------- --------------- ------ ----------
          1 John              1500 Programmer
          2 Mary              2000 Manager
```

```
        3 Stella              6000 CEO
        4 Fred                 600 Clerk

4 rows selected.


ROLLBACK
Rollback complete.
```

MERGE: COMBINING INSERTS, UPDATES, AND DELETES

You can perform combined INSERT, UPDATE, and DELETE operations with the MERGE command using the following syntax:

```
MERGE INTO tablename
USING {query|tablename} ON (condition)
[WHEN MATCHED THEN UPDATE set_clause
     [DELETE condition]]
[WHEN NOT MATCHED THEN INSERT values_clause]
```

The table EMPLOYEE_CHANGE contains two additional rows, Jean and Betsy, not found in the EMPLOYEE table. The MERGE statement allows you to update the matching rows and lets you insert those rows found in the EMPLOYEE_CHANGE table but that are missing from the EMPLOYEE table.

```
MERGE INTO employee e
USING (SELECT employee_id, salary, title, name
         FROM employee_change) c
   ON (e.employee_id = c.employee_id)
WHEN MATCHED THEN
   UPDATE SET e.salary = c.salary,
              e.title = c.title
WHEN NOT MATCHED THEN
   INSERT (e.employee_id, e.salary, e.title, e.name)
   VALUES (c.employee_id, c.salary, c.title, c.name)
5 rows merged.
```

When you query the EMPLOYEE table you observe the changed values and the addition of the employees Jean and Betsy. Note that Mary did not have a record in the EMPLOYEE_CHANGE table; therefore, no modification to her record is performed.

```
SELECT *
  FROM employee
EMPLOYEE_ID NAME              SALARY TITLE
----------- --------------- ------ ---------
          1 John              1500 Programmer
          2 Mary              2000 Manager
```

```
     3  Stella          6000 CEO
     4  Fred             600 Clerk
     5  Jean             800 Secretary
     6  Betsy           2000 Sales Rep

6 rows selected.
```

Oracle 10*g* added an optional DELETE condition to the WHEN MATCHED THEN UPDATE clause of the MERGE command. It allows you to remove rows from the table during this operation. Only those rows are deleted that satisfy both the DELETE and the ON condition. It is important to note that the DELETE condition evaluates the rows based on the values after the update not the original values. The next statement adds the DELETE condition, which effectively deletes Stella from the EMPLOYEE table because her SALARY column value now equals to 6000.

```
ROLLBACK
Rollback complete.

MERGE INTO employee e
  USING (SELECT employee_id, salary, title, name
            FROM employee_change) c
    ON (e.employee_id = c.employee_id)
  WHEN MATCHED THEN
    UPDATE SET e.salary = c.salary,
               e.title = c.title
    DELETE WHERE salary = 6000
  WHEN NOT MATCHED THEN
    INSERT (e.employee_id, e.salary, e.title, e.name)
    VALUES (c.employee_id, c.salary, c.title, c.name)
5 rows merged.

SELECT *
  FROM employee
```

EMPLOYEE_ID	NAME	SALARY	TITLE
1	John	1500	Programmer
2	Mary	2000	Manager
4	Fred	600	Clerk
5	Jean	800	Secretary
6	Betsy	2000	Sales Rep

```
5 rows selected.
```

DELETING DATA

Data is removed from a table with the DELETE statement. It can delete all rows or just specific rows. The syntax is:

```
DELETE FROM tablename
[WHERE condition]
```

The following statement deletes all rows in the GRADE_CONVERSION table.

```
DELETE FROM grade_conversion
15 rows deleted.
```

When a ROLLBACK command is issued, the DELETE command is undone and the rows are back in the GRADE_CONVERSION table.

```
ROLLBACK
Rollback complete.

SELECT COUNT(*)
  FROM grade_conversion
 COUNT(*)
---------
       15

1 row selected.
```

REFERENTIAL INTEGRITY AND THE DELETE COMMAND

A DELETE operation on a row with dependent children rows has a different effect depending on how deletes on the foreign key are defined. There are three different ways you can specify a foreign key constraint with respect to deletes: restrict, cascade, or set null.

If you issue a DELETE on a parent table with associated children records and the foreign key constraint is set to ON DELETE CASCADE, the children are automatically deleted. If the foreign key constraint is set to ON DELETE SET NULL, the children rows are updated to a null value, providing the foreign key column of the child table allows nulls. The default option for a foreign key constraint with respect to deletes is restrict. It disallows the deletion of a parent if children rows exist. In this case you must delete the children rows first, before you delete the parent row.

 In the STUDENT schema all foreign key constraints are set to the default option, which restricts insert, update, and delete operations.

DELETES AND REFERENTIAL INTEGRITY IN ACTION

If a foreign key constraint is DELETE RESTRICT, you will not be able to delete any parent row, if any child records exist. In the following example, an attempt is made to delete the zip code 10025. Because the ZIP column of the ZIPCODE table is referenced as a foreign key column in the STUDENT table and the table contains student rows with this zip code, you cannot delete the row. Oracle prevents you from creating orphan rows and responds with an error message.

```
DELETE FROM zipcode
 WHERE zip = '10025'
DELETE FROM zipcode
*
ERROR at line 1:
ORA-02292: integrity constraint (STUDENT.INST_ZIP_FK)
violated - child record found
```

The constraint name error message consists of not only the constraint name but also the name of the schema, which in this case is the STUDENT schema. If you installed the tables into another user account, your schema name will be different. You will learn how to create constraints and specify constraint names in the next chapter.

A DELETE statement may delete rows in other tables. If the foreign key constraint specifies the ON DELETE CASCADE option, a delete of a parent row automatically deletes the associated child rows. Imagine that the referential integrity constraint between the STUDENT and ENROLLMENT tables is DELETE CASCADE. A DELETE statement would delete not only the individual STUDENT row, but also any associated ENROLLMENT rows.

To take the scenario a step further, suppose that the student also has records in the GRADE table. The delete will only be successful if the constraint between the ENROLLMENT table and the GRADE table is also DELETE CASCADE. Then the corresponding rows in the GRADE tables are deleted as well. If the delete is RESTRICT, the ORA-02292 error will appear, informing you to delete all the children records first.

As you know, the ZIPCODE table is not only referenced by the STUDENT table, but also by the INSTRUCTOR table. Suppose you have the ON DELETE SET NULL constraint as the foreign key. A delete of the zip code 10025 would cause an update of the ZIP column on the INSTRUCTOR table to a null value, providing the STUDENT table does not have this zipcode.

To find out which foreign keys have either the DELETE RESTRICT, the DELETE CASCADE, or SET NULL constraint, you can query the data dictionary views USER_CONSTRAINTS or ALL_CONSTRAINTS discussed in Chapter 13, "The Data Dictionary and Advanced SQL*Plus Commands."

THE SCHEMA DIAGRAM

Sometimes schema diagrams depicting the physical relationships between tables show the referential integrity rules in place. Three types of data manipulation operations are possible in SQL: INSERT, UPDATE, and DELETE. On some schema diagrams you may also find the letters I, U, and D, which are abbreviations for Insert, Update, and Delete, respectively. These abbreviated letters indicate the valid rules that these data manipulation operations must follow.

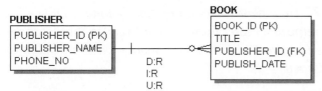

Figure 10.1 ■ Relationship between PUBLISHER and BOOK tables.

Figure 10.1 shows a schema diagram of the PUBLISHER and the BOOK table. The foreign key column PUBLISHER_ID is found in the BOOK table. A one-to-many, mandatory relationship exists between the PUBLISHER and BOOK tables. The I:R indicates that any INSERT operation filling in values in PUBLISHER_ID of the BOOK table is RESTRICTED to values found in the PUBLISHER table. By default most database systems require this condition when a foreign key is defined on a column.

The U:R notation indicates that any UPDATE to the PUBLISHER_ID column of the BOOK table is RESTRICTED to values found in the PUBLISHER table. Attempting to UPDATE an invalid value violates the U:R data integrity constraint and generates an error. Both the U:R and the I:R referential integrity rules are the default behaviors and often are not listed on schema diagrams.

The notation for the DELETE operation is listed as D:R, indicating that DELETE operations are restricted. Specifically, this means that you cannot delete a publisher row that is referenced in the BOOK table. If you were allowed to delete the row, you would not be able to tell the publisher of the book and you would create an orphan row. The relationship between the two tables is mandatory, indicating that a null value for the PUBLISHER_ID is not acceptable.

If instead you see a D:C notation, it depicts a DELETE CASCADE meaning a delete of a PUBLISHER row deletes any associated children rows in the BOOK table.

The D:N identifies the DELETE SET NULL. This means that upon the deletion of a PUBLISHER row any corresponding children rows are automatically set to null in the PUBLISHER_ID column of the BOOK table, providing nulls are allowed.

THE TRUNCATE COMMAND

The TRUNCATE command deletes all rows from a table, just like the DELETE command. However, the TRUNCATE command does not allow a WHERE clause and automatically issues a COMMIT. All rows are deleted without the ability to roll back the change.

```
TRUNCATE TABLE class
Table truncated.
```

The TRUNCATE statement works more quickly than a DELETE statement to remove all rows from a table because the database does not have to store the undo information in case a ROLLBACK command is issued.

If you attempt to TRUNCATE a table that is referenced by another table as a foreign key, Oracle will issue an error message indicating that this action is not allowed; otherwise, you may create orphan rows. You must disable the foreign key constraint first before you can succeed. Enabling and disabling constraints is discussed in Chapter 12, "Create, Alter, and Drop Tables."

```
TRUNCATE TABLE student
TRUNCATE TABLE student
                *
ERROR at line 1:
ORA-02266: unique/primary keys in table referenced by
enabled foreign keys
```

The Whole Truth

Oracle has the capability to attach triggers to tables that fire on DELETE, INSERT, and UPDATE commands. A table's triggers will not execute when the table is truncated. Triggers are written in the PL/SQL language and may perform sophisticated actions (i.e., recording changes to another table for auditing purpose or updating summary values on derived columns).

LOCKING

The real world scenario of a database system is one where many users are accessing data concurrently. Occasionally, users collide and want to manipulate the same piece of information. Locking ensures data consistency.

When you issue an INSERT, UPDATE, DELETE, or MERGE statement, Oracle automatically locks the modified rows. The lock prevents other sessions from making changes to these rows. The lock is released when the session initiating the change commits or rolls back. Other users or sessions may now modify the rows.

Queries do not place locks on rows. Data can always be queried despite being locked; however, other sessions can see the committed data only. After the successful commit of the transaction, the new change is visible to all sessions and the lock is released.

If a row is locked by a session, another session cannot acquire the lock and modify the row. The session attempting to acquire the locked row waits until the lock is released. The session might appear frozen while it waits. Users often think that perhaps their connection to the server dropped or that the DML operation is extremely slow. Users might terminate their session or reboot the machine, only to find out that if they retry the same action the session continues to behave identically. Oracle waits until the lock is released by the other session to proceed with the new change.

You should commit frequently, especially when you anticipate multiple users contending for the same row simultaneously.

THE LOST UPDATE PROBLEM

The WHERE clause of the next UPDATE statement lists not only the primary key column (the COURSE_NO column) but also includes the old COST column value.

```
UPDATE course
   SET cost = 800
 WHERE course_no = 25
   AND cost = 1195
```

Although this is may seem unnecessary, it can be helpful in case another user made changes to the values in the meantime. Then the UPDATE statement will not be successful and will return 0 rows updated. This indicates that the row containing the old value is no longer found. Many end-user application programs append the values displayed on a user's screen to the WHERE clause of an UPDATE statement. If the UPDATE returns with the 0 rows updated message, the program can alert the user that changes have been made and request the user to requery the data. This prevents the user from unknowingly overwriting data that changed since he or she last retrieved the data.

You may wonder why Oracle doesn't automatically lock the data to prevent such a situation or place locks on queries. Oracle releases the lock after the user issues a COMMIT or ROLLBACK. A SELECT does not cause any locks; the other user may have queried the data, updated the data, and issued a COMMIT immediately afterward. Therefore, any subsequent updates do not interfere with another user's UPDATE statement because the lock is already released.

While Oracle automatically takes care of locking, you can explicitly acquire a lock with the SELECT FOR UPDATE or the LOCK TABLE statement. This will override the default locking mechanism; however, this functionality is infrequently used in the real world. Oracle's implicit and automatic locking mechanism works very well for the vast majority of scenarios and adding the retrieved "old" values to the WHERE clause avoids overwriting any unwanted changes.

LOCKING OF ROWS BY DDL OPERATIONS

Locks are not just acquired on individual rows, but also on the entire table when a DDL operation such as ALTER TABLE or CREATE INDEX command is issued. A DML operation cannot update the table while the DDL operation is in progress (e.g., you cannot update rows while a table is being altered) and the same holds true for the reverse: A DDL command on a table cannot be executed if users are holding locks on the table (with some exceptions, such as the creation of online indexes discussed in Chapter 12, "Views, Indexes, and Sequences").

READ-CONSISTENCY OF DATA

Whenever a user changes data with a DML operation, Oracle keeps track of the old values on a rollback segment. If the user rolls back the transaction with the ROLLBACK command, Oracle reads the old values from the rollback segment and returns the data to the previous state.

WHAT IS A ROLLBACK SEGMENT OR THE UNDO TABLESPACE?

The UNDO tablespace contains the rollback segments that keep track of changes not yet committed. It allows users to issue the ROLLBACK command to restore the data to its original state. Uncommitted data is not permanent and therefore not ready for other users to see yet. Before any data is changed on the actual table, the change is written to the rollback segments first.

Figure 10.2 illustrates the visibility and timing of any changes made to the COST column of the COURSE table for two individual sessions. For example, session #2 updates the COST column value for COURSE_NO 20 to 2000 but does not COMMIT the change. Session #1 will still see the old values, which are retrieved from the rollback segments. Session #1, or any other session for that matter, will not see the data until the user performing the change makes it permanent by issuing a COMMIT.

THE SYSTEM CHANGE NUMBERS (SCN) AND MULTI-VERSIONING

When long-running queries and DML operations occur simultaneously, Oracle automatically handles this with the use of the System Change Number (SCN), a unique number, that tracks the order in which events occur. This feature enables queries to return a read-consistent result. For example, a query starts at 10:00 A.M., ends at 10:05 A.M., and during this time it computes the sum of all salaries for all employees. At 10:03 A.M. the salary of one employee is updated and a COMMIT is issued. What result does the query return? Because the query began before the UPDATE was issued, the result will return a read-consistent result based on the point in time when the query started, which is 10:00 A.M. When a query reads the newly changed salary row, it will recognize that the SCN of the UPDATE is issued after the start of the query and look for the old salary value on the rollback segment.

If you have very long-running queries, you may get an `ORA-1555 snapshot too old` error message; this indicates that Oracle had to overwrite the rollback information you are attempting to access and therefore cannot return a read-consistent result. Rollback data can be overwritten by other transactions when the previous

TIME	SESSION #1	SESSION #2
T1	SELECT cost FROM course WHERE course_no=20 **COST** `---------` **1195** **1 row selected.**	
T2		UPDATE course SET cost = 2000 WHERE course_no=20 **1 row updated.**
T3	SELECT cost FROM course WHERE course_no=20 **COST** `---------` **1195** **1 row selected.**	
T4		SELECT cost FROM course WHERE course_no=20 **COST** `---------` **2000** **1 row selected.**
T5		COMMIT **Commit complete.**
T6	SELECT cost FROM course WHERE course_no=20 **COST** `---------` **2000** **1 row selected.**	

Figure 10.2 ■ The effect of the COMMIT command.

transaction is committed or rolled back. When this rollback data is no longer available, the long-running query is looking for undo information that no longer exists and returns the error message. To eliminate this error, you can attempt to reissue the query, or, if there is a lot of activity on the system, you may need to increase the UNDO_RETENTION setting of the UNDO tablespace.

For more information on read-consistency, database recovery, and the management of the rollback/UNDO tablespace, refer to the *Oracle Database Administrator's Guide.*

FLASHBACK QUERIES

Oracle's flashback query feature allows you to look at values of a query at a specific time in the past, such as before specific DML statements occurred. This can be useful in case of a user's accidentally performing an unintended but committed DML change. Another possible application of the feature is to compare the current data against the previous day's data to see the changes. When using the flashback query you may specify either an explicit time expression (such as an interval or a specific timestamp value) or indicate an individual SCN. Data for flashback queries is kept only for a certain time period that is dependent on the undo management implemented by the DBA. You must familiarize yourself with the limitations of this feature. For example, issuing certain DDL commands, such as altering a table by dropping or modifying columns, invalidates the undo data for the individual table.

Following is an example that illustrates how you can use the flashback query feature. The SELECT statement returns the current value of the table before any changes occur. You see the cost of course number 20 displayed as 1195. The subsequent UPDATE statement changes the cost to 9999 and makes the change permanent with the COMMIT command.

```
SELECT course_no, cost
  FROM course
 WHERE course_no  = 20
COURSE_NO          COST
---------------- ----
            20 1195

1 row selected.

UPDATE course
   SET cost = 9999
 WHERE course_no = 20
1 row updated.

COMMIT
Commit complete.
```

STATEMENT-LEVEL FLASHBACK

The statement-level flashback ability allows the AS OF clause in the SELECT statement followed either by a TIMESTAMP value or a particular system change number (SCN). The next statement shows use of the TIMESTAMP clause to retrieve the value for the COST column for course number 20 as of August 1, 2003 at 4 P.M.

```
SELECT course_no, cost
   FROM course AS OF TIMESTAMP
    TO_TIMESTAMP('01-AUG-2003 04:00:00 PM',
               'DD-MON-YYYY HH:MI:SS AM')
  WHERE course_no = 20
COURSE_NO        COST
--------------- ----
           20 1195
```

1 row selected.

If flashback data is not available any more, Oracle will inform you with an ORA-08180: no snapshot found based on specified time error message. The syntax for the flashback query clause is as follows:

```
AS OF SCN|TIMESTAMP expr
```

If you want to run the flashback versions query by a specific SCN number, you can obtain the number with the next SQL statement. This may be useful to query the number before the start of a batch job and if anything goes wrong, you can query the changes easily.

```
SELECT DBMS_FLASHBACK.GET_SYSTEM_CHANGE_NUMBER
   FROM dual
GET_SYSTEM_CHANGE_NUMBER
------------------------
              4937491
```

1 row selected.

DETERMINING THE DATA CHANGES WITH A MINUS OPERATION   The next following statement retrieves the rows that were inserted or updated with different COST values in the COURSE table within the last 30 minutes. If you want to find out the updated and deleted data, reverse the two SELECT statements. If you prefer to see a detailed log of the changes, use the VERSIONS BETWEEN parameter discussed next.

```
SELECT *
   FROM course
  MINUS
SELECT *
   FROM course AS OF TIMESTAMP
        SYSTIMESTAMP - INTERVAL '30' MINUTE
```

RETRIEVING FLASHBACK HISTORY WITH THE VERSIONS PARAMETER

The Oracle 10*g* flashback query VERSIONS parameter allows you to retrieve the history of changes during a particular time period. For example, if the column value changes again, this time the COST is updated to 5555, you will see each individual change.

```
UPDATE course
   SET cost = 5555
 WHERE course_no = 20
1 row updated.


COMMIT
Commit complete.
```

The query uses the VERSIONS BETWEEN clause to determine the changes that occurred on the row within the last 10 minutes.

```
SELECT course_no, cost, VERSIONS_XID,
       VERSIONS_OPERATION
  FROM course
       VERSIONS BETWEEN TIMESTAMP
       SYSTIMESTAMP - INTERVAL '10' MINUTE
   AND SYSTIMESTAMP - INTERVAL '1' SECOND
 WHERE course_no = 20
```

COURSE_NO	COST	VERSIONS_XID	V
20	5555	0001001A000028B4	U
20	9999	00030028000028B7	U
20	1195		

3 rows selected.

Note the columns VERSIONS_XID and VERSIONS_OPERATION in the SELECT list; they are pseudocolumns that store the transaction reference information regarding the change and the type of change. The VERSIONS_OPERATION pseudocolumn indicates the type of data manipulation that took place (e.g., insert, update, or delete). The VERSIONS_XID column allows you to trace back the various modification details in the data dictionary view FLASHBACK_TRANSAC-TION_QUERY and you will see an example of this shortly. (Also refer to Chapter 13, "The Data Dictionary and Dynamic SQL Scripts," for more information about data dictionary views.) You can also see the timestamp of the changes along with other pseudocolumns that contain more details about DML changes in Table 10.1.

The syntax of this flashback query is as follows. Instead of the TIMESTAMP expression you can choose a specific system change number (SCN).

```
VERSIONS BETWEEN {SCN|TIMESTAMP} {expr|MINVALUE} AND {expr|MAXVALUE}
```

FLASHBACK TRANSACTION QUERY

The FLASHBACK_TRANSACTION_QUERY data dictionary contains not only details about the transaction, but also the SQL statement to undo the operation.

Table 10.1 ■ Version Query Pseudocolumns

Pseudocolumn	Description
VERSIONS_STARTTIME	Timestamp of the first version of the row.
VERSIONS_ENDTIME	Timestamp of the last version of the row.
VERSIONS_OPERATION	Displays the type of operation the row was subject to. Values are I (for INSERT), U (for UPDATE), and D (for DELETE).
VERSIONS_STARTSCN	The SCN for the first version of the row.
VERSIONS_ENDSCN	The SCN for the last version of the row.
VERSIONS_XID	Transaction ID generated by the change.

The following SQL*Plus DESCRIBE command shows the available columns. You will notice that the data dictionary references the XID column, which corresponds to the previously listed VERSIONS_XID pseudocolumn.

```
SQL> DESCRIBE flashback_transaction_query
 Name                      Null?      Type
 ------------------------- ---------- -------------
 XID                                  RAW(8)
 START_SCN                            NUMBER
 START_TIMESTAMP                      DATE
 COMMIT_SCN                           NUMBER
 COMMIT_TIMESTAMP                     DATE
 LOGON_USER                           VARCHAR2(30)
 UNDO_CHANGE#                         NUMBER
 OPERATION                            VARCHAR2(32)
 TABLE_NAME                           VARCHAR2(256)
 TABLE_OWNER                          VARCHAR2(32)
 ROW_ID                               VARCHAR2(19)
 UNDO_SQL                             VARCHAR2(4000)
```

The next statement lists one of the undo SQL statements for the table COURSE, which is owned by the STUDENT user. Note that the undo statement lists the ROWID pseudocolumn, which represents a unique way to identify a row within a table. There is more about the ROWID pseudocolumn in Chapter 12, "Views, Indexes, and Sequences."

```
SELECT undo_sql
  FROM flashback_transaction_query
 WHERE table_name = 'COURSE'
   AND table_owner = 'STUDENT'
```

```
UNDO_SQL
-----------------------------------------------
update "STUDENT"."COURSE" set "COST" = '1195'
 where ROWID = 'AAAKgzAAAAAAAAAAAA';
...
```

FLASHBACK TABLE AND FLASHBACK DATABASE

Oracle has additionally implemented two more flashback related commands. They are FLASHBACK TABLE and FLASHBACK DATABASE, which allow you to revert an individual table or an entire database respectively. Keep in mind that while the flashback choices provide a fallback option for application or user error, flashback data is only retained up to a specific period in time.

The following statement illustrates the FLASHBACK TABLE statement restoring the COURSE table to a state it was 5 minutes ago.

```
FLASHBACK TABLE course
   TO TIMESTAMP(SYSTIMESTAMP - INTERVAL '5' MINUTE)
Flashback complete.
```

To flashback a table or an entire database, you need special permissions discussed in Chapter 14, "Security." Furthermore, the FLASHBACK TABLE command does not work if you performed table structure changes (e.g. adding, dropping, or modifying table columns). Another requirement for the FLASHBACK TABLE command is that the table must have the ROW MOVEMENT option enabled. (This is done when a table is initially created or with the ALTER TABLE table_name ENABLE ROW MOVEMENT syntax.)

The syntax of the FLASHBACK TABLE command is as follows. The BEFORE DROP option will be discussed in the next chapter because it allows you to restore a dropped table.

```
FLASHBACK TABLE tablename [,tablename...] TO
{{SCN|TIMESTAMP} EXPR [ENABLE|DISABLE TRIGGERS]|
BEFORE DROP [RENAME TO newtablename]}
```

Although there are many options to correct unintentional errors, you must nevertheless have proper measures in place to protect your data against any accidents or failures so you can recover at any time. The database administrator is responsible for establishing, administering, and periodically testing the appropriate data safeguards and procedures.

PERFORMANCE CONSIDERATIONS WHEN WRITING DML STATEMENTS

Much like the index in a book, Oracle allows the creation of indexes on tables as they help speed up retrieval of rows. While the discussion on indexes takes place in Chapter 12, "Views, Indexes, and Sequences", you should be aware of the effect indexes have on the performance of your data manipulation statement.

Indexes can slow down data manipulation because they may require maintenance of the values within the indexes. For example, if an UPDATE operation affects an indexed column, the value in the index needs to be updated. A DELETE statement will require the entries in the index to be marked for deletion. An INSERT command will create index entries for all supplied column values where an index exists.

However, indexes can be beneficial for UPDATE or DELETE statements if the statement updates a small portion of the table and if it contains a WHERE clause that refers to an indexed column. Rather than looking through the entire table for the desired information, Oracle will find it quickly and perform the desired operation.

An index on the foreign key should be always be present if you update or delete the primary key on the parent table because referential integrity is maintained by temporarily locking the index on the child table rather than the entire child table. This greatly improves performance of the operation.

LAB 10.2 EXERCISES

10.2.1 UPDATE DATA

a) Using an UPDATE statement, change the location to B111 for all sections where the location is currently L210.

b) Update the MODIFIED_BY column with the user login name and update the MODIFIED_DATE column with a date of March 31, 2001, using the TO_DATE function for all the rows updated in exercise a.

c) Update instructor Irene Willig's zip code to 90210. What do you observe?

d) What does this query accomplish?

```
UPDATE enrollment e
   SET final_grade = (SELECT AVG(numeric_grade)
                        FROM grade g
                       WHERE e.student_id = g.student_id
                         AND e.section_id = g.section_id),
       modified_date = SYSDATE,
       modified_by = 'Your name here'
 WHERE student_id IN (SELECT student_id
                        FROM student
                       WHERE last_name like 'S%')
```

e) Update the first name from Rick to Nick for the instructor with the ID of 104.

f) Write and execute an UPDATE statement to update the phone numbers of instructors from 2125551212 to 212-555-1212 and the MODIFIED_BY and MODIFIED_DATE columns with the user logged in and today's date, respectively. Write a SELECT statement to prove the update worked correctly. Do not issue a COMMIT command.

g) Start another SQL*Plus session on your computer and login as STUDENT with the password LEARN while your current session is still open. Execute the same SELECT statement you executed in exercise f to prove your update worked correctly. Explain what data you see and why.

h) What do you think will be the result of the following statement?

```
MERGE INTO enrollment e
USING (SELECT AVG(numeric_grade) final_grade,
              section_id, student_id
         FROM grade
        GROUP BY section_id, student_id) g
   ON (g.section_id = e.section_id
   AND g.student_id = e.student_id)
  WHEN MATCHED THEN
    UPDATE SET e.final_grade = g.final_grade
  WHEN NOT MATCHED THEN
    INSERT (e.student_id, e.section_id, e.enroll_date,
            e.final_grade, e.created_by, e.created_date,
            e.modified_date, e.modified_by)
    VALUES (g.section_id, g.student_id, SYSDATE,
            g.final_grade, 'MERGE', SYSDATE,
            SYSDATE, 'MERGE')
```

10.2.2 DELETE DATA

a) Delete all rows from the GRADE_CONVERSION table. Then SELECT all the data from the table, issue a ROLLBACK command, and explain your observations.

b) If TRUNCATE is used in exercise a instead of DELETE, how would this change your observations? Caution: Do not actually execute the TRUNCATE statement unless you are prepared to reload the data.

c) Delete the row inserted in exercise 10.1.1a in the GRADE_TYPE table.

d) Formulate the question for the following query.

```
DELETE FROM enrollment
  WHERE student_id NOT IN
         (SELECT student_id
            FROM student s, zipcode z
           WHERE s.zip = z.zip
             AND z.city = 'Brooklyn'
             AND z.state = 'NY')
```

LAB 10.2 EXERCISE ANSWERS

10.2.1 ANSWERS

a) Using an UPDATE statement, change the location to B111 for all sections where the location is currently L210.

Answer: The UPDATE statement updates the LOCATION column in 10 rows of the SECTION table.

```
UPDATE section
   SET location = 'B111'
 WHERE location = 'L210'
10 rows updated.
```

Without the WHERE clause, all rows in the SECTION table are updated, not just ten rows. For example, if you want to make sure all students have their last names begin with a capital letter, issue the following UPDATE statement.

```
UPDATE student
   SET last_name = INITCAP(last_name)
```

UPDATES TO MULTIPLE TABLES

Typically, your UPDATE statement affects a single table. However, if the table has a trigger associated with it, it may fire if the certain conditions specified in the trigger are true. The code in the trigger may cause insert, updates, or deletes to other tables. Triggers can also add or modify values to rows you are changing. You can query the data dictionary view USER_TRIGGERS to see if any triggers are associated with your tables.

b) Update the MODIFIED_BY column with the user login name and update the MODIFIED_DATE column with a date of March 31, 2001, using the TO_DATE function for all the rows updated in exercise a.

Answer: The MODIFIED_BY column is updated with the USER function to reflect an update by the user logged in, namely STUDENT, and the MODIFIED_DATE column is updated using the TO_DATE function. The update is based on the previously updated location.

```
UPDATE section
   SET modified_by = USER,
       modified_date = TO_DATE('31-MAR-2001', 'DD-MON-YYYY')
 WHERE location = 'B111'
```
10 rows updated.

Instead of writing them as individual UPDATE statements, exercises a and b can be combined in a single UPDATE statement with the columns separated by commas.

```
UPDATE section
   SET location = 'B111',
       modified_by = USER,
       modified_date = TO_DATE('31-MAR-2001', 'DD-MON-YYYY')
 WHERE location = 'L210'
```

c) Update instructor Irene Willig's zip code to 90210. What do you observe?

Answer: The attempt to change the zip code to a value that does not exist in the ZIP-CODE table results in a referential integrity constraint error.

```
UPDATE instructor
   SET zip = '90210'
 WHERE last_name = 'Willig'
   AND first_name = 'Irene'
```
UPDATE instructor
*
ERROR at line 1:
ORA-02291: integrity constraint (STUDENT.INST_ZIP_FK)
violated - parent key not found

Oracle does not allow any invalid values in a column if the foreign key constraint exists and is enabled.

A query checking for this zip code in the ZIPCODE table retrieves no rows.

```
SELECT zip
  FROM zipcode
 WHERE zip = '90210'
```

no rows selected

UNIQUELY IDENTIFYING RECORDS

The WHERE clause in this statement lists the first and last name of the instructor, and it happens to be unique and sufficient to identify the individual. Imagine a scenario where you have instructors with the identical name, but who are in fact different individuals. When you perform manipulation of data, it is best to include the primary key value, such as the INSTRUCTOR_ID, to ensure that the correct row is changed.

d) What does this query accomplish?

```
UPDATE enrollment e
   SET final_grade = (SELECT AVG(numeric_grade)
                        FROM grade g
                       WHERE e.student_id = g.student_id
                         AND e.section_id = g.section_id),
       modified_date = SYSDATE,
       modified_by = 'Your name here'
 WHERE student_id IN (SELECT student_id
                        FROM student
                       WHERE last_name like 'S%')
```

Answer: This query updates the FINAL_GRADE, MODIFIED_DATE, and MODIFIED_BY columns of the ENROLLMENT table for students with the last name starting with the letter S. The computed average grade is based on the individual grades received by the student for the respective section.

The example illustrates a correlated UPDATE statement. The outer query identifies the students with the last name of beginning with S. For each individual outer row, the inner correlated subquery executes and computes the average of the individual grades from the GRADE table. The result is then updated in the FINAL_GRADE column of the ENROLLMENT table.

e) Update the first name from Rick to Nick for the instructor with the ID of 104.

Answer: The primary key column INSTRUCTOR_ID identifies the instructor uniquely and is therefore used in the WHERE clause. Additionally, it helps to add the old value of the FIRST_NAME column to the WHERE clause, in case any previous changes to the column have been made.

```
UPDATE instructor
   SET first_name = 'Nick'
 WHERE instructor_id = 109
   AND first_name = 'Rick'
1 row updated.
```

f) Write and execute an UPDATE statement to update the phone numbers of instructors from 2125551212 to 212-555-1212 and the MODIFIED_BY and MODIFIED_DATE columns with the user logged in and today's date, respectively. Write a SELECT statement to prove the update worked correctly. Do not issue a COMMIT command.

Answer: A single UPDATE statement updates three columns in ten rows simultaneously in the INSTRUCTOR table. The MODIFIED_BY column is updated with the USER func-

tion and the MODIFIED_DATE column is updated with the SYSDATE function entering today's date and time into the column.

```
UPDATE instructor
   SET phone = '212-555-1212',
       modified_by = USER,
       modified_date = SYSDATE
 WHERE phone = '2125551212'
10 rows updated.
```

```
SELECT instructor_id, phone, modified_by, modified_date
   FROM instructor
INSTRUCTOR_ID PHONE            MODIFIED_BY MODIFIED_
------------- ------------     ----------- ---------
          101 212-555-1212     STUDENT     09-MAY-03
          102 212-555-1212     STUDENT     09-MAY-03
...
          109 212-555-5555     STUDENT     09-MAY-03
          110 212-555-5555     STUDENT     09-MAY-03

10 rows selected.
```

g) Start another SQL*Plus session on your computer and login as STUDENT with the password LEARN while your current session is still open. Execute the same SELECT statement you executed in exercise f to prove your update worked correctly. Explain what data you see and why.

Answer: The session does not reflect the changes made. Any other database user or session cannot see the updated values in the INSTRUCTOR table until a COMMIT command is issued in the original session.

```
SELECT instructor_id, phone, modified_by, modified_date
   FROM instructor
INSTRUCTOR_ID PHONE            MODIFIED_BY MODIFIED_
------------- ------------     ----------- ---------
          101 2125551212       ESILVEST    02-JAN-03
          102 2125551212       ESILVEST    02-JAN-03
...
          109 2125555555       ESILVEST    02-JAN-03
          110 2125555555       ARISCHER    11-MAR-03

10 rows selected.
```

When you are ready to move on to the next exercise, please issue the ROLLBACK command in the first session to undo your changes.

h) What do you think will be the result of the following statement?

```
MERGE INTO enrollment e
USING (SELECT AVG(numeric_grade) final_grade, section_id, student_id
          FROM grade
         GROUP BY section_id, student_id) g
   ON (g.section_id = e.section_id
   AND g.student_id = e.student_id)
 WHEN MATCHED THEN
   UPDATE SET e.final_grade = g.final_grade
 WHEN NOT MATCHED THEN
   INSERT (e.student_id, e.section_id, e.enroll_date,
           e.final_grade, e.created_by, e.created_date,
           e.modified_date, e.modified_by)
   VALUES (g.section_id, g.student_id, SYSDATE,
           g.final_grade, 'MERGE', SYSDATE,
           SYSDATE, 'MERGE')
```

Answer: The MERGE statement will update the column FINAL_GRADE to the average grade per student and section based on the GRADE table. If the section and student is not found in the ENROLLMENT table the MERGE command will insert the row.

Actually, the INSERT part of the MERGE statement will probably never be executed because a row in the GRADE table cannot exist unless an ENROLLMENT row exists. The foreign key relationship between the two tables enforces this. In this instance, the following correlated subquery UPDATE will achieve the same result as the MERGE statement.

```
UPDATE enrollment e
   SET final_grade = (SELECT AVG(numeric_grade)
                        FROM grade g
                       WHERE g.section_id = e.section_id
                         AND g.student_id = e.student_id)
```

10.2.2 ANSWERS

a) Delete all rows from the GRADE_CONVERSION table. Then SELECT all the data from the table, issue a ROLLBACK command, and explain your observations.

Answer: A DELETE statement deletes all rows in the GRADE_CONVERSION table. A subsequently issued SELECT statement shows no rows in the table. Issuing a ROLLBACK un-does the delete. You can verify this by issuing another SELECT statement against the table.

```
DELETE FROM grade_conversion
15 rows deleted.

SELECT *
  FROM grade_conversion
no rows selected
```

```
ROLLBACK
Rollback complete.
```

b) If TRUNCATE is used in exercise a instead of DELETE, how would this change
your observations? Caution: Do not execute the TRUNCATE statement unless
you are prepared to reload the data.

*Answer: When TRUNCATE is used, the data cannot be rolled back; the ROLLBACK
statement has no effect. A subsequent SELECT statement reflects no rows in the
GRADE_CONVERSION table.*

```
TRUNCATE TABLE grade_conversion
Table truncated.

ROLLBACK
Rollback complete.

SELECT COUNT(*)
  FROM grade_conversion
 COUNT(*)
---------
        0

1 row selected.
```

 *Notice that when the ROLLBACK command is issued, Oracle returns
the* `Rollback complete` *message. This is misleading, because in
this case a rollback did not occur; the data is permanently deleted. Be
sure to use caution when using the TRUNCATE TABLE command.*

c) Delete the row inserted in exercise 10.1.1a in the GRADE_TYPE table.

Answer: A DELETE statement is written for the row where the grade type code is 'EC'.

```
DELETE FROM grade_type
 WHERE grade_type_code = 'EC'
1 row deleted.
```

d) Formulate the question for the following query.

```
DELETE FROM enrollment
 WHERE student_id NOT IN
        (SELECT student_id
           FROM student s, zipcode z
          WHERE s.zip = z.zip
            AND z.city = 'Brooklyn'
            AND z.state = 'NY')
```

Answer: Delete enrollment rows for all students except those who live in Brooklyn, NY.

The DELETE statement narrows down the records in the WHERE clause using a NOT IN subquery to find students who do not live in Brooklyn, NY. Alternatively, the DELETE statement can be rewritten as a correlated subquery using the NOT EXISTS operator, which under certain circumstances can execute faster.

```
DELETE FROM enrollment e
   WHERE NOT EXISTS
          (SELECT 'x'
             FROM student s, zipcode z
            WHERE s.zip = z.zip
              AND s.student_id = e.student_id
              AND z.city = 'Brooklyn'
              AND z.state = 'NY')
```

Because the STUDENT_ID in the STUDENT table is defined as NOT NULL, the NOT IN and NOT EXISTS statements are equivalent. For more information on the differences between NOT IN and NOT EXISTS see Chapter 7, "Subqueries," and Chapter 17, "SQL Optimization."

LAB 10.2 SELF-REVIEW QUESTIONS

In order to test your progress, you should be able to answer the following questions.

1) It is possible to restore rows deleted with a DELETE statement.

  a) _____ True
  b) _____ False

2) There is no syntax error in the following UPDATE statement.

```
UPDATE grade_type
   SET description = 'Exams'
 WHERE grade_type_code IN ('FI', 'MT')
```

  a) _____ True
  b) _____ False

3) The SELECT command always places locks on the retrieved rows.

  a) _____ True
  b) _____ False

4) Oracle achieves read-consistency by reading uncommitted data.

  a) _____ True
  b) _____ False

5) Oracle releases the lock of a row after the session issues a COMMIT or ROLL-BACK command.

    a) _____ True

    b) _____ False

Answers appear in Appendix A, Section 10.2.

CHAPTER 10

TEST YOUR THINKING

The projects in this section are meant to have you utilize all of the skills that you have acquired throughout this chapter. The answers to these projects can be found at the companion Web site to this book, located at *http://authors.phptr.com/rischert3e*. Visit the Web site periodically to share and discuss your answers.

1) Write and execute two INSERT statements to create rows into the ZIPCODE table for the following two cities: Newton, MA 02199; Cleveland, OH 43011. After your INSERT statements are successful, make the changes permanent.

2) Make yourself a student by writing and executing an INSERT statement to insert a row into the STUDENT table with data about you. Use one of the zip codes you inserted in exercise 1. Only insert values into the columns STUDENT_ID (use a value of '900'), FIRST_NAME, LAST_NAME, ZIP, REGISTRATION_DATE (use a date that is five days after today), CREATED_BY, CREATED_DATE, MODIFIED_BY, and MODIFIED_DATE. Issue a COMMIT command afterwards.

3) Write an UPDATE statement to update the data about you in the STUDENT table. Update the columns SALUTATION, STREET_ADDRESS, PHONE, and EMPLOYER. Be sure to also update the MODIFIED_DATE column and make the changes permanent.

4) Delete the row in the STUDENT table and the two rows in the ZIP-CODE table you created. Be sure to issue a COMMIT command afterward.

If you performed the exercises in this chapter, you will have changed data in most of the tables of the STUDENT schema. If you go back to the previous chapters and re-execute the queries, you may find that the results are different. Therefore, if you want to reload the tables and data, you can run the rebuildStudent.sql script. Refer to the readme file for more information on how to perform this step.

CHAPTER 11

CREATE, ALTER, AND DROP TABLES

CHAPTER OBJECTIVES

In this chapter, you will learn about:

This chapter introduces you to the Data Definition Language (DDL) commands associated with tables, the type of database object most frequently used. Table 11.1 provides you with an overview of other commonly used object types discussed in later chapters.

The DDL commands allow you to create, modify, and remove database objects. This chapter discusses the options available with respect to tables, which allow the manipulating of column definitions and constraints. Because database constraints enforce business rules and data integrity, understanding constraints such the as primary key, foreign key, check or unique constraints are essential to learning about a relational database.

 Keep in mind that all DDL statements automatically issue an implicit COMMIT.

505

Table 11.1 ■ Commonly Used Database Object Types

Database Object	Purpose	Find More Information
Table	Stores data	This chapter
View	Used for security and to hide complexity	Chapter 12
Index	Improves data access speed	Chapter 12
Sequence	Generates unique key values	Chapter 12
Synonym	Provides an alternative name for a database object	Chapter 14
Directory	Points to a directory location outside the Oracle database	This chapter
Stored Database Objects Created Using the PL/SQL Language		
Trigger	Individual PL/SQL program that executes on DML operations	
Function	Program that returns a single value	
Procedure	Accomplishes a specific task; the program may return zero, one, or many values	
Package	Collection of procedures, functions, or other PL/SQL constructs bundled together	

LAB 11.1

CREATING AND
DROPPING TABLES

LAB OBJECTIVES

After this lab, you will be able to:
- ✔ Create and Drop Tables
- ✔ Create Constraints

CREATING TABLES

Tables are created with the CREATE TABLE command and can be created in one of two ways. The first method is to specify the columns and their datatypes explicitly; the second method is to create a table based on an existing table.

The following statement creates a table called TOY, consisting of four columns. A NOT NULL constraint is specified for the DESCRIPTION column. The newly created table contains no data.

```
CREATE TABLE toy
    (toy_id              NUMBER(10),
     description         VARCHAR2(15) NOT NULL,
     last_purchase_date  DATE,
     remaining_quantity  NUMBER(6))
```

TABLE NAMES

A table name must be unique within a database schema; no other database object, such as another table, view, or a synonym, can have the same name. All database object names must be no longer than 30 characters; cannot include spaces or hyphens, but can have underscores; and must begin with a letter. The table name should describe the nature of the data contained in it; for consistency, choose either singular or plural names.

COLUMN NAMES

A column name must be unique within a table and should not exceed 30 characters. It should be descriptive of the values stored in the column. You can document the meaning of individual columns or tables in more detail with the COMMENT command discussed later in the chapter.

A column is defined not only by a name but also the datatype and length, where appropriate. When creating multiple columns a comma separates each column definition.

By default, table and column names are stored in the Oracle database in uppercase format. You can create table names and column names with mixed cases, special characters, and spaces if you use double quotes around the table and column names. This is rarely used and defies the conventions used by most Oracle database installations.

Many corporations have created their own standard column and naming conventions. Compliance with naming standards simplifies the task of identifying database objects for developers. Furthermore, it shortens the learning curve for individuals involved in the maintenance and support of the system.

 Be consistent with your table and column names in terms of abbreviations and the use of either the single or plural form.

To simplify the understanding of relationships among the tables use the identical column name for both the primary and foreign key columns whenever possible. For example, the STUDENT_ID foreign key column in the ENROLLMENT table references the primary key column of the same name in the STUDENT table.

Following is the simplified syntax of a CREATE TABLE statement. (Note that there are many more syntax options; only the most frequently used syntax choices are listed here.)

```
CREATE [GLOBAL TEMPORARY] TABLE tablename
  (columnname datatype [DEFAULT expr]
    [column_constraint_clause]
      [, columnname datatype [DEFAULT expr]
          [column_constraint_clause]...]
    [table_constraint_clause]
  )
```

```
[physical_storage_clause]
[ENABLE|DISABLE ROW MOVEMENT]
[temporary_table_clause]
[AS query]
```

The CREATE TABLE syntax shows that you must list the individual column name and the respective datatype; the default expression and a column constraint clause are optional. The column constraint clause has a number of individual syntax options that allow you to restrict the values in an individual column. Because a table actually doesn't consist of just one column, the syntax shows that the various syntax portions, consisting of column name, datatype, default expression, and column constraint clause, may be repeated for each subsequent column.

Besides an individual column constraint, a table may have table constraints that restrict one or multiple columns. Tables require physical storage with individual storage parameters defined in the storage clause. As previously mentioned, you can create a table based on another table; this is accomplished with the AS QUERY clause. Using the CREATE TABLE statement, you can create a temporary table with the GLOBAL TEMPORARY keywords and the use of a temporary_table_clause.

As you work your way through this lab, you will learn about all the different clauses and you will gain a good understanding about the fundamental functionality of the CREATE TABLE command.

COMMONLY USED ORACLE DATATYPES

Based on the nature of the type of data you want to store, you choose the appropriate datatype. This section will review Oracle's most commonly used datatypes.

CHARACTER DATA

Character data is stored in columns of datatype VARCHAR2, CHAR, LONG, or CLOB. When creating or altering a table, the VARCHAR2 and CHAR datatypes require a column length. The maximum length of a VARCHAR2 column is 4,000 characters. A fixed length CHAR column stores 2,000 characters at most. A name such as Smith stored in the LAST_NAME column defined as VARCHAR2(25) stores only 6 characters versus 25 characters in fixed-length CHAR(25) defined column because the CHAR adds trailing spaces. The LONG datatype stores up to 2 gigabytes of data in a single column; one LONG column per table is allowed, and you cannot use character functions on a LONG column. Oracle recommends the use of the CLOB datatype instead of LONG and the support of the datatype will be discontinued. CLOBs store up to 4 gigabytes of data and a table may have multiple CLOB columns. LONG and CLOB datatypes come with a number of restrictions related to the use of character functions you learned about in Chapter 3, "Character, Number and Miscellaneous Functions," most of which are overcome with Oracle Text, formerly known as ConText and *inter*Media Text. Using various operators it offers sophisticated full-text search capabilities.

NUMERIC DATA

The format of the NUMBER datatype is *NUMBER(p,s)*, whereby *p* is the *precision* (or total number of digits) and *s* is the *scale*. The scale represents the number of digits to the right of the decimal point. The NUMBER datatype can store up to 38 decimal digits of precision. The definition of NUMBER(5,2) on a column allows you to store values between –999.99 and 999.99. A number such as 1,000 is rejected, and a value such as 80.999 is rounded up to 81.00. Use the NUMBER datatype for data on which you need to calculate, not for phone numbers or zip codes. For example, in the STUDENT schema the ZIP column of the ZIPCODE table is stored as a VARCHAR2 rather than a NUMBER datatype because it requires leading zeros.

Oracle 10*g* added the BINARY_FLOAT and BINARY_DOUBLE datatypes to store floating-point numbers in 32-bit and 64-bit format. These datatypes are particularly useful if you require complex and/or fast arithmetic computations. Floating point numbers do not have a scale because the number of digits to the right of the decimal point is not restricted. Floating-point numbers can have a decimal anywhere from the first to the last digit or none at all.

DATE AND TIME

The DATE datatype stores the century, year, month, day, hour, minute, and second. It has its own internal format, which can be displayed using different format masks. You can store dates from January 1, 4712 BC to December 31, 4712 AD. The TIMESTAMP datatype includes additional fractional seconds and TIMESTAMP WITH TIME ZONE enables you to keep track of time across geographic regions. The TIMESTAMP WITH LOCAL TIME ZONE is concerned with the date and time in the local region only. The INTERVAL YEAR TO MONTH and INTERVAL DAY TO SECOND handle differences between dates.

BINARY DATA AND LARGE OBJECT DATA TYPES

Oracle allows you to save binary data such as images, audio, and video in datatypes called BLOB, RAW, LONG RAW, or BFILE. A BFILE datatype points to a binary operating system file.

INTEGRITY CONSTRAINTS

When creating tables, you typically create them with integrity constraints. These constraints enforce the business rules of a system. For instance, "The salary of an employee may not be a negative number," may be enforced with a check constraint on the salary column, or "An employee must have a unique social security number" is enforced with a NOT NULL constraint and a unique constraint.

Constraints ensure the data integrity and data consistency among all applications, no matter which program. They ease the burden of programming the business rules in individual applications because the database enforces the constraint.

The following CREATE TABLE statement creates a table called TAB1 with several types of constraints.

```
CREATE TABLE tab1
   (col1   NUMBER(10)    PRIMARY KEY,
    col2   NUMBER(4)     NOT NULL,
    col3   VARCHAR2(5)   REFERENCES zipcode(zip)
             ON DELETE CASCADE,
    col4   DATE          DEFAULT SYSDATE,
    col5   VARCHAR2(20)  UNIQUE,
    col6   NUMBER        CHECK(col6 < 100))
```

THE PRIMARY KEY CONSTRAINT

The first column of the table, COL1, has a PRIMARY KEY constraint, also referred to as an *entity integrity constraint*. The primary key ensures all values in this column are NOT NULL and are unique. This is enforced through a unique index automatically created by Oracle, unless an index already exists. (Indexes are discussed in Chapter 12, "Views, Indexes, and Sequences.") When the table TAB1 is created, Oracle automatically creates a name for this constraint, which looks something like this: SYS_C0030291. This constraint name is not terribly meaningful because it does not identify the table the constraint was created for or the constraint type. You learn how to name constraints shortly.

Every table usually has one primary key, consisting of one or more columns. The combination of all values in a multicolumn primary key, also called a concatenated primary key, must also be unique. Primary keys should be static, which means no updates are usually performed. The primary key values are typically created by a number-generating sequence. This type of key is also referred to as an *artificial* or *surrogate* key and has the advantage that these values are completely meaningless and therefore not subject to updates. As a primary key datatype, the NUMBER datatype is a better choice than the VARCHAR2 datatype because it is not prone to punctuation, case-sensitivity, and spelling mistakes, which make it more difficult to distinguish if two records are identical. Tables without a primary key should have at least a unique constraint.

THE UNIQUE CONSTRAINT

To enforce unique values on an individual or a group of columns, you create a unique constraint for a table. In this example, column COL5 has a UNIQUE constraint. Before determining the primary key, there are often alternate keys that are candidates for the primary key. Phone numbers or social security numbers are examples of alternate keys with unique constraints. However, these keys are often not chosen as the primary key because they may allow null values or the values are subject to updates. Often these keys are extremely useful for end users querying the data, and perhaps uniqueness may still need to be enforced through the unique constraint. Just like with a primary key constraint, Oracle automatically creates a unique index when a UNIQUE constraint is specified. The most distinguishing characteristic between the primary key constraint and the unique constraint is that a unique constraint allows null values.

THE FOREIGN KEY CONSTRAINT

The foreign key constraint, also referred to as *referential integrity constraint,* ensures that the values in the foreign key correspond to values of a primary key. The column COL3 contains a FOREIGN KEY constraint. The keyword REFERENCES, followed by the ZIPCODE table and the ZIP column in the ZIPCODE table in parentheses, indicates COL3 is a foreign key to the ZIP column of the ZIPCODE table. The FOREIGN KEY constraint indicates the domain of values for COL3; in other words, the only valid values for the COL3 column are zip codes found in the ZIP column of the ZIPCODE table and null values. Following is the excerpt from the previous CREATE TABLE statement, which shows the relevant foreign key constraint syntax.

```
CREATE TABLE tab1
...
   col3  VARCHAR2(5) REFERENCES zipcode(zip)
        ON DELETE CASCADE,
...
```

Alternatively, the foreign key can be created with this syntax; it does not mention the ZIP column. It is simply assumed that it is the primary key of the referenced table.

```
   col3  VARCHAR2(5) REFERENCES zipcode
        ON DELETE CASCADE,
```

When defining a FOREIGN KEY constraint on a table, the column name does not have to be identical to the column name it references. For example, COL3 is the foreign key name and ZIP is the referencing column name, but note that the datatype and length must agree. Foreign keys almost always reference primary keys, but occasionally may reference unique constraints. Foreign keys should usually be indexed and you will learn more about the purpose and syntax in Chapter 12, "Views, Indexes, and Sequences."

DELETES AND THE FOREIGN KEY

By default the foreign key constraint is of type DELETE RESTRICT; in effect, parent rows cannot be deleted if child rows exist. An ON DELETE CASCADE clause indicates that when a parent row is deleted, the corresponding row or rows in this child table will be deleted as well. In the previous SQL statement DELETE CASCADE is explicitly specified, so if a row in the ZIPCODE table is deleted, any rows with the same zip code are deleted from the TAB1 table.

Another possible clause for defining the delete behavior of the foreign key is the clause ON DELETE SET NULL. A delete of a zip code will update the corresponding child rows in TAB1 to null providing the COL3 column allows null values.

RECURSIVE RELATIONSHIP

A *recursive relationship* is also known as a self-referencing relationship; the PREREQUISITE and the COURSE_NO columns of the COURSE table are an example where a foreign key references the primary key constraint of the same table. A recursive relationship is enforced just like any other foreign key; you will see an example how you create such a relationship later in the chapter.

THE CHECK CONSTRAINT

Check constraints enforce logical expressions on column(s), which must evaluate to true for every row in the table. The COL6 column has a CHECK constraint, constraining the column to values less than 100. Note that a null value is allowed, as the column does not have a not null constraint.

```
CREATE TABLE tab1
...
    col6  NUMBER CHECK(col6 < 100))
...
```

Here is another example of a check constraint. The following constraint on a column called STATE restricts the values to the states listed in the IN clause.

```
state VARCHAR2(20) CHECK(state IN
    ('NY','NJ','CT','FL','CA'))
```

THE NOT NULL CHECK CONSTRAINT

The column COL2 contains a check constraint you are already familiar with, namely NOT NULL. Any inserts or changes to data changing the values in this column to NULL are rejected.

```
CREATE TABLE tab1
...
    col2  NUMBER(4) NOT NULL,
...
```

Alternatively, the check constraint can also be written like this, but the previous form is simpler.

```
    col2  NUMBER(4) CHECK (col2 IS NOT NULL),
```

You define the NOT NULL constraints for columns that must always contain a value. For example, the LAST_NAME column of the INSTRUCTOR table is defined as a NOT NULL column and therefore you cannot create or update a row in the INSTRUCTOR table unless a value exists in the column.

THE DEFAULT COLUMN OPTION

The column COL4 specifies a DEFAULT option, which is not a constraint. When a row is inserted into TAB1 and no value is supplied for COL4, SYSDATE is inserted by default.

```
CREATE TABLE tab1
...
    col4  DATE DEFAULT SYSDATE,
...
```

In INSERT statements the keyword DEFAULT explicitly specifies the default value, or if the column is omitted in the statement. In an UPDATE statement the DEFAULT keyword resets a column value to the default value. Refer to Lab 11.2 for more examples.

A default value can be created for any column except for the column or columns of the primary key. Often you choose a default value that represents a typical value. You may combine a default value with a NOT NULL constraint to avoid null values in columns. For example, if the typical COST of a course is 1095, you may want to create such a default value for this column. Another effect of default values and the NOT NULL constraint is that if you want to retrieve costs that are less than 1595 or null, you don't have to write this query:

```
SELECT *
  FROM course
 WHERE NVL(cost,0) < 1595
```

Instead you simplify the query to the following statement. In Lab 11.2 exercises you learn more about the factors to take into consideration when defining columns as null versus not null.

```
WHERE cost < 1595
```

NAMING CONSTRAINTS

Applying names to all constraints is a good habit you must adopt; it simplifies identifying constraint errors and avoids confusion and further research. Following is an example of how to name constraints in a CREATE TABLE statement.

```
CREATE TABLE tab1
  (col1  NUMBER(10),
   col2  NUMBER(4) CONSTRAINT tab1_col2_nn NOT NULL,
   col3  VARCHAR2(5),
   col4  DATE DEFAULT SYSDATE,
   col5  VARCHAR2(20),
   col6  NUMBER,
   CONSTRAINT tab1_pk PRIMARY KEY(col1),
   CONSTRAINT tab1_zipcode_fk FOREIGN KEY(col3)
      REFERENCES zipcode(zip),
   CONSTRAINT tab1_col5_col6_uk UNIQUE(col5, col6),
   CONSTRAINT tab1_col6_ck CHECK(col6 < 100),
   CONSTRAINT tab1_col2_col6_ck CHECK(col2 > 100 AND col6 >20))
```

Table created.

Some of the constraint names are next to each column; these are column-level constraints. The constraint names at the end of the statement are table-level constraints each of which are separated by commas. Constraint names cannot exceed 30 characters and must be unique within the user's schema. In this example the constraint names consist of the name of the table and column (or an abbreviated version) and a two-letter abbreviation identifying the type of constraint.

Ideally, you follow a standard naming convention determined by your organization. In this book, the convention for naming primary key constraints is the name of the table plus the _PK suffix. The foreign key constraint contains the abbreviated name of the child table, then the parent table and the _FK suffix. The unique constraint lists the table name and the columns plus the _UK suffix. Often you must abbreviate table and column names; otherwise, you exceed the 30-character constraint name limit. The last constraint, a CHECK constraint called TAB1_COL6_CK, contains the name table and column name plus the _CK suffix.

All the examples listed here show the constraints added at the time of the table creation. In Lab 11.2 you will see how to add constraints after the table exists.

 It is best to name constraints explicitly, for clarity and to manipulate them more easily, as you see in Lab 11.2. Also, when a SQL statement, such as an INSERT, UPDATE, or DELETE statement violates a constraint, Oracle returns an error message with the name of the constraint, making it easy to identify the source of the error.

TABLE-LEVEL AND COLUMN-LEVEL CONSTRAINTS

Constraints are defined on two possible levels—either on the column level or on the table level. A column-level constraint refers to a single column and is defined together with the column. A table-level constraint references one or multiple columns and is defined separately after the definition of all the columns. Column-level constraints are also referred to as *inline constraints* and table-level constraints are called *out-of-line constraints*.

All constraints can be defined at the table level except for the NOT NULL constraint. You must use a table-level constraint if you are constraining more than one column.

The general syntax for the column constraint clause is listed as follows: It shows the not null, primary, foreign, unique, and check constraint options.

```
[CONSTRAINT constraintname]
 [NULL|NOT NULL] |
 [REFERENCES tablename [(columnname)]
   [ON DELETE {CASCADE|ON DELETE SET NULL}] |
 [[UNIQUE|PRIMARY KEY]
   [USING INDEX
    [(CREATE INDEX indexname
       ON tablename (columnname[,columnname...])]
         [storage_clause])]] |
 [CHECK (check_condition)]
 [ENABLE|DISABLE]
 [VALIDATE|NOVALIDATE]
```

The constraint name is optional and must be preceded with the keyword CON-STRAINT. Unless you specify otherwise, your column allows nulls; the underline indicates that this is the default. The foreign key constraint is defined with the REFERENCES keyword; it has two choices with regard to deletes as indicated with the vertical bar or pipe symbol (|). One is the ON DELETE CASCADE keyword, the other is the ON DELETE SET NULL. If you don't list either of these two choices, the deletion of rows is restricted—that is, your delete is only successful if no child rows exist. Because the unique and primary key constraint automatically create a unique index, you can use an optional index clause to explicitly create an index with predefined storage parameters. This allows you to define the index on a different tablespace (which is often on a different physical device) for better performance.

The next constraint option is the check constraint syntax. You see that the check condition is within a set of parentheses. All constraints can be either disabled or enabled (the default). The VALIDATE and NOVALIDATE options indicate if the constraint is enforced for existing and new data or only for subsequently created data.

The table-level constraint is listed after the column definitions. The syntax is listed here:

```
[CONSTRAINT constraintname]
  [UNIQUE (columnname[,columnname...])|
   PRIMARY KEY (columnname[,columnname...])]
     [USING INDEX
     [CREATE INDEX indexname ON tablename (columnname[,columnname...])]
       [storage_clause]] |
  [FOREIGN KEY (columnname[,columnname...])]
     REFERENCES tablename [(columnname[,columnname...])]
     [ON DELETE {CASCADE|ON DELETE SET NULL}] |
  [CHECK (check_condition)]
  [ENABLE|DISABLE]
  [VALIDATE|NOVALIDATE]
```

WHAT ARE BUSINESS RULES?

Constraints enforce rules and procedures in organizations. For example, a rule that a student must have a last name is enforced through a NOT NULL constraint. Another rule may state that students must live in a valid zip code and this rule can be imposed with a referential integrity constraint to the ZIPCODE table and a NOT NULL constraint on the ZIP column of the STUDENT table. You can apply a check constraint to make sure course costs fall within a certain range. The datatype of a column determines what kind of data is allowed for entry and perhaps the maximum length. A unique constraint prevents duplicate entry of social security numbers into an EMPLOYEE table. A data consistency rule may state that for any delete of a student record, all corresponding enrollment and grade records are deleted; this is done with a referential integrity foreign key constraint and the ON DELETE CASCADE keyword.

Other business rules may not be as easily enforceable with any of Oracle's declarative constraints. For instance, your rule states that a student cannot enroll after a class has already started. To enforce this rule you have to check that the value in the ENROLL_DATE column of the ENROLLMENT table contains a value less than or equal to the value in the START_DATE TIME column of the SECTION table for the student's enrolled section. Database triggers enforce such rules and fire on the INSERT, UPDATE, or DELETE operation of a specific table and check other tables to see if the values satisfy the business rule criteria. If not, the operation will fail and the statement will be rejected.

WHAT IS A DATABASE TRIGGER?

Database triggers are PL/SQL programs associated with a table, view, system or database event. The following trigger is used to audit data modification. The trigger fires before the UPDATE of each row on the STUDENT table and it automatically updates the MODIFIED_DATE column with the SYSDATE function, filling in the current date and time whenever any update in the table takes place. This database trigger is written in Oracle's PL/SQL language and you will learn more about the language and triggers in general in the *Oracle PL/SQL by Example* by Benjamin Rosenzweig and Elena Silvestrova. Without going into great depth about the language, you see the trigger has the name STUDENT_TRG_BUR, and it fires BEFORE UPDATE of an individual row in the STUDENT table. The BEFORE keyword indicates that the trigger can access the new value before it is applied and can change the value with the :NEW.column name correlation value. The value in the MODIFIED_DATE column is changed upon the UPDATE of the affected rows to the current date and time as indicated by the SYSDATE function.

```
CREATE OR REPLACE TRIGGER student_trg_bur BEFORE UPDATE ON STUDENT
FOR EACH ROW
BEGIN
  :new.modified_date:=SYSDATE;
END;
/
```

Triggers can also enforce referential integrity constraints instead of applying a foreign key constraint. However, it is preferable to use Oracle's built-in declarative constraints, such as the foreign key constraint, to enforce these rules. Constraints are easier to maintain, simpler, and faster than duplicating identical functionality in a trigger.

WHERE TO ENFORCE BUSINESS RULES?

Business rules can be enforced either on the client side through the front-end program or on the database server. Alternatively, the business logic can also reside on a third tier, perhaps an application server. At times you may see that some rules are enforced in multiple places. The decision often depends on a number of factors: Rules imposed across all applications are often done on the database server, so the need to program and enforce this rule consistently in various programs may be unnecessary.

On the other hand, certain data validation needs to be performed in the front-end program. For example, if your business rule states that a salary must be larger than zero and not null, you may perform this validation within the data entry screen. If the rule is violated, the user receives a friendly error message to correct the data entry. Otherwise, it is annoying to the user to enter the data only to find out the server rejected the entry. If the salary can be updated by programs other than the front-end screen, you may consider enforcing the rules on both the client front-end program and the server. Be sure to keep the rules consistent throughout.

There are many options to keep in mind regarding the placement of business rules when you are designing applications and database systems, including considerations about user-friendliness, data integrity, consistency, future maintenance, and elimination of duplicate efforts on both the front end and the back end.

Data validation is key to any successful database operation, and finding the right balance requires a thorough understanding of many aspects of a system. Ignorance of data validation leads to invalid data, data inconsistencies, formatting problems, programming and processing errors, as well as misinterpretation of data.

CREATING TABLES BASED ON OTHER TABLES

Another method of creating a table is to base it on another table or tables using a query construct. You can choose to include the data or not. The following example creates a table called JAN_03_ENROLLMENT based on the January 2003 enrollment rows in the ENROLLMENT table.

```
CREATE TABLE jan_03_enrollment AS
SELECT *
  FROM enrollment
 WHERE enroll_date >= TO_DATE('01/01/2003',
        'MM/DD/YYYY')
    AND enroll_date <  TO_DATE('02/01/2003',
        'MM/DD/YYYY')
Table created.
```

The database feedback `Table created` confirms the JAN_03_ENROLLMENT table is successfully created. Notice the columns and their datatypes when you DESCRIBE the new table.

```
SQL> DESC jan_03_enrollment
 Name                        Null?     Type
 ----------------------      --------  --------------
 STUDENT_ID                  NOT NULL  NUMBER(8)
 SECTION_ID                  NOT NULL  NUMBER(8)
 ENROLL_DATE                 NOT NULL  DATE
 FINAL_GRADE                           NUMBER(3)
 CREATED_BY                  NOT NULL  VARCHAR2(30)
 CREATED_DATE                NOT NULL  DATE
 MODIFIED_BY                 NOT NULL  VARCHAR2(30)
 MODIFIED_DATE               NOT NULL  DATE
```

The new table has the same columns, datatypes, and lengths as the ENROLL-MENT table on which it is based. A SELECT statement on the new table confirms that the inserted data is equal to the condition listed in the WHERE clause.

```
SELECT student_id, section_id, enroll_date
  FROM jan_03_enrollment
STUDENT_ID SECTION_ID ENROLL_DA
---------- ---------- ----------
       102         89 30-JAN-03
       102         86 30-JAN-03
...
       109        101 30-JAN-03
       109         99 30-JAN-03

11 rows selected.
```

You can use the same syntax to create a table without data. Instead of the WHERE clause restricting specific rows from the ENROLLMENT table, here no rows are returned. The ROWNUM pseudocolumn indicates the order in which Oracle selects a row from a table or set of tables. The first selected row has a ROWNUM of 1, the second has a 2, and so on. Because the query asks for less than one row, the statement subsequently creates an empty table.

```
CREATE TABLE jan_03_enrollment AS
SELECT *
  FROM enrollment
 WHERE rownum < 1
```

Alternatively, you can also write the statement with a query that never evaluates to true, such as in the next example. However, this takes more time than the previously issued statement with the ROWNUM.

```
CREATE TABLE jan_03_enrollment AS
SELECT *
  FROM enrollment
 WHERE 1 = 2
```

Tables created with this construct do not inherit the primary key, foreign keys, constraints, indexes, column default values, or any other objects associated with the base table except the NOT NULL constraints, which receive a system-generated name starting with the letters SYS_.

If a SELECT statement in a CREATE TABLE statement joins two tables or more, it is best not to use the asterisk wildcard in the SELECT list. The tables being joined may contain columns with the same name, resulting in an error message when Oracle attempts to create two columns with the same name in one table.

If you want to create a table based on an existing table and/or change the new table's table or column definitions somewhat, you can extract the DDL for the existing table. This allows you to modify the DDL to create the new table. You will learn more about this in Chapter 13, "The Data Dictionary and Advanced SQL*Plus Commands."

RENAMING TABLES

Tables can be renamed with the RENAME command. The syntax of the command is as follows:

```
RENAME oldname TO newname
```

You can use the RENAME command not only to rename tables but also views and synonyms, these object types are discussed in the following chapters.

The next statement renames the JAN_03_ENROLLMENT table to JAN_03.

```
RENAME jan_03_enrollment TO jan_03
```
Table renamed.

Alternatively, you can use the ALTER TABLE command, which will be discussed in Lab 11.2.

```
ALTER TABLE jan_03_enrollment RENAME TO jan_03
```

Constraint names and dependent database objects, such as indexes and triggers, are not renamed when the table name is changed. Any granted privileges on the table to other users remain intact. Dependent objects such as views become invalid and need to be recompiled.

DROPPING TABLES

Tables can be dropped when they are no longer needed, using the DROP TABLE command. The syntax is:

```
DROP TABLE tablename [CASCADE CONSTRAINTS] [PURGE]
```

When you drop a table, the table as well as its data is removed along with any indexes, triggers and constraints.

```
DROP TABLE jan_03
Table dropped.
```

In Oracle 10*g* the table is moved into a recycle bin from which it can be recovered; this is also referred to as *flashback drop*. Prior versions permanently removed the table and reclaimed the space from the database. If do not want to place the table in the recycle bin, use the new PURGE syntax option.

Other tables may be dependent on the dropped table as a domain for a foreign key reference. For example, if you drop the ZIPCODE table, an Oracle error message occurs because there are other tables with a foreign key referencing the ZIP column of the ZIPCODE table. One solution is to disable or drop the individual foreign key constraints with individual ALTER TABLE commands on these dependent tables, which you will learn in Lab 11.2. Another is to let Oracle drop the foreign key constraints with the CASCADE CONSTRAINTS option. Caution: Do not actually execute the following statement unless you are prepared to reload the data from the ZIPCODE table and add the foreign key constraints on the STUDENT and INSTRUCTOR tables.

```
DROP TABLE zipcode CASCADE CONSTRAINTS
```

Database objects that depend on the table, such as a view referencing the table, synonyms, or PL/SQL packages, procedures, and functions, become invalid. To find out which objects reference a table, query the data dictionary view ALL_DEPENDENCIES or USER_DEPENDENCIES. If any rights on the table were granted to other users, such as the privileges to SELECT, INSERT, UPDATE, or DELETE from the table, they are removed. If you re-create the table with the same name and want other users to continue having these privileges, you will need to reissue the grants (see Chapter 14, "Security.")

FLASHBACK A TABLE

You have learned about some of the capabilities of the FLASHBACK TABLE command in Chapter 10, "Insert, Update, and Delete." This new Oracle 10*g* FLASHBACK TABLE command allows you to restore a dropped table from the recycle bin. The syntax of the FLASHBACK TABLE command is repeated once more:

```
FLASHBACK TABLE table name [, tablename...] TO
{{SCN|TIMESTAMP} expr [ENABLE|DISABLE TRIGGERS]|
  BEFORE DROP [RENAME TO newtablename]}
```

The following statements show how the table JAN_03 is dropped and subsequently restored.

```
DROP TABLE jan_03
Table dropped.
```

Data associated with the dropped table is stored in the recycle bin. You can query the USER_RECYCLEBIN data dictionary table or its synonym RECYCLEBIN.

```
SELECT object_name, original_name, type
  FROM user_recyclebin
OBJECT_NAME              ORIGINAL_NAME    TYPE
---------------------    ---------------  ---------
RB$$43144$TABLE$0        JAN_03           TABLE

1 row selected.
```

The following command restores the dropped table. You can refer to the table by either the original name or the system-generated recycle bin name.

```
FLASHBACK TABLE jan_03 TO BEFORE DROP
Flashback complete.
```

If any triggers, constraints or indexes are associated with the table, they are restored as well, except for bitmap join indexes and referential integrity constraints to other tables. Note that all these objects will have their recycle bin names, not the original name. Before you issue the FLASHBACK TABLE command, make a note of the names, so you can rename them back to their original names.

Instead of querying the recycle bin with a SELECT statement, you can display some of the columns of the RECYLEBIN data dictionary with the SQL*Plus SHOW RECYCLEBIN command.

```
SQL> SHOW RECYCLEBIN
ORIGINAL NAME   UNDROP NAME          OBJECT TYPE   DROP TIME
-------------   -------------------  ------------  --------------------
JAN_03          RB$$43144$TABLE$0    TABLE         2003-08-03:17:28:46
```

PURGING THE RECYCLE BIN

You can purge an individual table, index, or the entire recycle bin with the PURGE command. The syntax is as follows:

```
PURGE {{TABLE|INDEX} recyclebin_objectname|
    RECYCLEBIN|
    DBA_RECYCLEBIN|
    TABLESPACE tablespacename [USER user]}
```

The next command reclaims all the space in the user's recycle bin.

```
PURGE RECYCLEBIN
Recyclebin purged.
```

The DBA has the additional option to reclaim all objects from the system-wide DBA_RECYCLEBIN or may use the TABLESPACE clause of the PURGE command to reclaim space in a specific tablespace for a specific user account. You will learn more about tablespaces shortly.

TRUNCATE TABLE VERSUS DROP TABLE

The TRUNCATE TABLE command, discussed in Chapter 10, "Insert, Update, and Delete," removes all data from the table; however, the structure of table remains intact as do any triggers and grants. Like the DROP TABLE command, it does not generate any rollback information and does not fire any triggers, should they exist on the table. The TRUNCATE statement is a DDL command and implicitly issues a COMMIT. By default the TRUNCATE TABLE command deallocates all of the table's storage except for the initial extent(s); you can retain all the existing storage extents with the REUSE STORAGE clause.

```
TRUNCATE TABLE grade REUSE STORAGE
```

STORAGE CLAUSE

A CREATE TABLE statement may have an optional storage clause specifying space definition attributes. Each table allocates an initial extent that specifies how much diskspace is reserved for the table at the time of creation. After the table runs out of the initial extent, Oracle automatically allocates additional space based on the storage parameters of the NEXT extent parameter.

The following statement creates a table called CTX_BOOKMARK with a storage clause specifying an initial size of 5 megabytes on the tablespace called USERS. Once the table is out of the allocated space, each subsequent extent allotted is one additional megabyte in size as indicated with the NEXT parameter.

```
CREATE TABLE ctx_bookmark
  (bookmark_id    NUMBER,
   container_id   NUMBER,
   bookmark_tx    VARCHAR2(300) NULL,
   modified_date  DATE)
    TABLESPACE users
      STORAGE (INITIAL 5M NEXT 1M)
      PCTFREE 20
```

A tablespace consists of one or more physical data files. For performance reasons, tables and indexes are usually stored in separate tablespaces located on different physical disk drives. To find out which tablespaces are available to you query the data dictionary view USER_TABLESPACES.

If no specific storage parameters are defined, the default storage parameters of the tablespace apply. Statements with a missing tablespace name create the data on the default tablespace assigned when the user was created and listed in the USER_USERS data dictionary view. If a user account does not have any rights to create any table objects, or no rights on certain tablespaces, these rights must be granted to the user first. You will learn more about granting access to tablespaces in Chapter 14, "Security."

ESTIMATING THE TABLE SIZE

Estimating the size of a table is useful to reduce the amount of wasted space. When you create a table, you can pre-allocate space with the INITIAL syntax parameter and plan for any subsequent expansion with the NEXT parameter option. While determining how much space will actually be consumed by the table is an inexact science; you can estimate how much initial space to allocate. You determine a rough size by entering sample data in the table and then computing statistics with one of the DBMS_STATS procedures (discussed in Chapter 17, "SQL Optimization"). The procedures will update the data dictionary information with statistics about the table including the average row length in bytes (AVG_ROW_LEN column in the USER_TABLES data dictionary view). Multiply this figure by the number of rows you expect in the table plus about 10 to 15 percent for overhead. Increase the number by how much free space you want to leave in each data block for updates that increase the size of the rows; this figure is determined as a percentage with the PCTFREE ("percent free") parameter in the storage clause.

```
avg_row_len in bytes * number of rows * (1 + PCTFREE/100) * 1.15
```

STORAGE CLAUSE   Next, you see the most frequently used options of the storage clause. The PCTUSED parameter determines when a block becomes available again for inserts after its used space falls below the PCTUSED integer.

```
[TABLESPACE tablespacename]
[PCTFREE integer]
[PCTUSED integer]
[COMPRESS|NOCOMPRESS]
[STORAGE
   ([INITIAL integer [K|M]]
   [NEXT integer [K|M]])]
```

To determine the total allocated space of an existing table, you query the BYTES column in the data dictionary views USER_SEGMENTS or DBA_SEGMENTS.

 Please note that the SQL command syntax in this book highlights the most relevant syntax options. Oracle's SQL commands often include a myriad of different options, some of which are rarely used and

therefore not included here. If you need to look up the complete syntax in the Oracle documentation, please refer to Appendix G, "Navigating through the Oracle Documentation."

PARTITIONING OF TABLES

Partitioning a table essentially means splitting a table into smaller pieces. The individual partitions often are stored in different tablespaces. Very large tables become more manageable for database administration tasks when they are stored on different partitions. Partitioning can also improve performance because I/O can be balanced. The partitioning can be accomplished in many different ways and Oracle offers a variety of syntax options. For example, you can place sales data by year in individual partitions. There is no need to change any SQL statements for DML operations because the partitioning is completely transparent. If you want to access an individual partition specifically with a DML statement, Oracle provides syntax to do so. You most often use partitioning if the tables are very large, such as tables in the gigabyte range or tables containing millions of rows.

DATA COMPRESSION

Oracle allows data compression to save storage space; this can be desirable for large database tables in data warehouses where very few updates and deletes take place.

ORACLE'S OTHER TABLE TYPES

The vast majority of data is stored in an "ordinary" Oracle table. The following paragraphs list other table types for completeness only; a detailed discussion of these table types goes beyond the scope of this book. The other Oracle table types available are temporary tables, index-organized tables, and external tables. A brief overview of their capabilities follows. Additionally, Oracle allows object-oriented capabilities with tables; in practice, object-oriented database table features are only slowly gaining acceptance.

TEMPORARY TABLES

When a query becomes too complicated, you can resolve it by writing part of the data to a temporary table before continuing with the main query. Oracle allows two types of temporary tables: session-specific or transaction-specific temporary tables. The data in the temporary table is visible to multiple sessions or transactions, but only with respect to the data created by each session or transaction. Once the session or transaction is complete, the data is deleted.

CREATING TEMPORARY TABLES   The table is session-specific when created with the ON COMMIT PRESERVE ROWS keywords and transaction-specific when created with the ON COMMIT DELETE ROWS keywords.

The following statement creates a session-specific temporary table that will retain its value until the session ends, not when a transaction ends because of an issued COMMIT or ROLLBACK command.

```
CREATE GLOBAL TEMPORARY TABLE s_num_rows
   (student_id              NUMBER,
    last_name               VARCHAR2(25),
    num_classes_enrolled NUMBER)
   ON COMMIT PRESERVE ROWS
```

You enter values into the table with an INSERT statement.

```
INSERT INTO s_num_rows
VALUES (123, 'Hesse', 5)
```

The next temporary table is transaction-specific, as you see from the ON COMMIT DELETE ROWS keywords. It uses the SELECT command to populate rows to the table.

```
CREATE GLOBAL TEMPORARY TABLE t_grade
   ON COMMIT DELETE ROWS AS
   SELECT student_id, AVG(numeric_grade) AS avg_grade
     FROM grade
    WHERE student_id IN (SELECT student_id
                           FROM enrollment
                          WHERE final grade IS NOT NULL)
   GROUP BY student_id
```

Temporary tables behave much like regular tables whereby you can add indexes, triggers, and some types of constraints, but certain restrictions apply; for example, no referential integrity constraints are allowed.

```
SQL> DESCR t_grade
 Name                        Null?     Type
 ------------------------    --------  ---------
 STUDENT_ID                  NOT NULL  NUMBER(8)
 AVG_GRADE                             NUMBER
```

When are temporary tables useful? Use temporary tables in cases where it simplifies the query logic and the query is infrequently executed. Be sure to keep in mind that this may not be the most efficient way to execute the query, but as with all queries, only testing against a representative data set will determine if this temporary table solves your complicated query dilemma.

 Data in temporary tables is not stored permanently and only persists during a session or transaction; however, the structure of the temporary table exists until explicitly dropped with a DROP TABLE command.

INDEX-ORGANIZED TABLES

When the primary key of a table comprises most or all of the columns in a table, you may want to consider storing the data in an index-organized table. An index-organized table is useful for frequently used lookup tables that hold currencies, state abbreviations, or stock prices with their respective dates. This type of table executes queries quickly that are looking for the primary key value. Queries do not require the lookup of a value in the index first, and then the corresponding retrieval of the row in the table because all the data is stored only in the index. You cannot disable or drop the primary key of an index-organized table.

```
CREATE TABLE states
   (state_code     VARCHAR2(2),
    state_tx       VARChAR2(200),
   CONSTRAINT state_pk PRIMARY KEY (state_code))
   ORGANIZATION INDEX
```

EXTERNAL TABLES

With the help of external tables, Oracle allows read access to data stored outside the database, such as legacy systems. SELECT statements are issued against external tables, much like any other table. You cannot insert into or update and delete from an external table, nor can you build an index on an external table.

To define an external table, you describe the individual columns with Oracle datatypes and how to map to these columns. A data access driver and external table layer perform the necessary transformation. Because external data remains stored outside the database, no backup or recovery capabilities within Oracle are performed. External tables are useful to load data into the database, but their setup requires the help of a DBA and some knowledge of Oracle's SQL*Loader bulk-load utility is useful.

Here is a simple example of a flat ASCII example file that is located on the one of the directories of the Oracle database server. Such a file may have data such as the following where the values are separated by commas.

```
102,Crocitto,Fred
103,Landry,J.
104,Enison,Laetia
105,Moskowitz,Angel
106,Olvsade,Judith
107,Mierzwa,Catherine
108,Sethi,Judy
109,Walter,Larry
```

Then you create a ORACLE DIRECTORY entry so the database knows where to find the file on an accessible directory and drive. If you use the Windows operating system, you may choose to specify a directory such as the C:\GUEST as the directory, or wherever your file is located.

```
CREATE DIRECTORY dir_guest AS 'C:\GUEST'
Directory created.
```

You must make sure the Oracle database has operating system read and write access to the operating system directory; otherwise, Oracle cannot load the data! To create an ORACLE DIRECTORY entry within the Oracle database, you must have the DBA privilege or the CREATE ANY DIRECTORY system privilege. Logon as a user with DBA rights or the SYSTEM account then issue the following command: GRANT CREATE ANY DIRECTORY TO student.

You create the external table based on the contents of the flat file with the CREATE TABLE command. The name of the table is STUDENT_EXTERNAL with three columns: STUDENT_ID, LAST_NAME, and FIRST_NAME. The keywords ORGANIZATION EXTERNAL identify that this table is located outside the Oracle database. The TYPE indicates the driver used to read the data. The DEFAULT DIRECTORY identifies the directory where the file is located. The structure of the flat file is defined by the individual field names that are to be read as well as how these individual fields are separated from each other. In this example a comma separates the fields. Additionally, you see the LOCATION keyword indicating the name of the file. This temp.lst file must be located in the directory defined as DIR_GUEST, which maps to the server's C:\GUEST directory.

```
CREATE TABLE student_external
  (student_id NUMBER(3),
   last_name VARCHAR2(25),
   first_name VARCHAR2(25))
  ORGANIZATION EXTERNAL
  (TYPE oracle_loader
   DEFAULT DIRECTORY dir_guest
   ACCESS PARAMETERS
   (FIELDS TERMINATED BY ','
    (student_id, last_name, first_name))
   LOCATION ('temp.lst'))
```

Table created.

There are different types of files; this example shows a comma-separated value file (CSV). Some files enclose the text fields in double quotes, others have fixed lengths where the starting and ending position of each column is predetermined.

After you successfully created the table and placed the temp.lst file in the appropriate directory, you can retrieve data from the table.

```
SELECT *
  FROM student_external
STUDENT_ID LAST_NAME                    FIRST_NAME
---------- -------------------------    ----------------
       102 Crocitto                     Fred
       103 Landry                       J.
       104 Enison                       Laetia
       105 Moskowitz                    Angel
       106 Olvsade                      Judith
       107 Mierzwa                      Catherine
       108 Sethi                        Judy
       109 Walter                       Larry

8 rows selected.
```

Although you have learned about the different Oracle table types, you must know that most of the time you will deal with ordinary Oracle tables and the aforementioned table types currently represent the exception to the norm.

LAB 11.1 EXERCISES

11.1.1 CREATE AND DROP TABLES

a) Explain the error(s) in the following CREATE TABLE statement, if any. If there are errors, rewrite the statement correctly.

```
CREATE TABLE student candidate
   (name      VARCHAR2(25)
    address   VARCHAR2(20)
    city      VARCHAR2
    zip       NUMBER)
```

b) Write and execute a CREATE TABLE statement to create an empty table called NEW_STUDENT containing the following columns: first name, last name, the description of the first course the student takes, and the date the student registered in the program. Determine the datatype and length necessary for each column based on the tables in the STUDENT schema. DESCRIBE the table when you have finished.

c) Execute the following CREATE TABLE statement and explain the result.

```
CREATE TABLE school_program AS
SELECT last_name||', '||first_name name
   FROM student
UNION
SELECT last_name||', '||first_name
   FROM instructor
```

d) Rename the SCHOOL_PROGRAM table you created in Exercise c to a table called SCHOOL_PROGRAM2. Then drop both the SCHOOL_PROGRAM and SCHOOL_PROGRAM2 tables and explain your observations.

11.1.2 CREATE CONSTRAINTS

a) Execute the following SQL statements to create an empty table called COURSE2 and insert two rows into COURSE2, respectively. What do you observe about the values of the COURSE_NO column in the COURSE2 table?

```
CREATE TABLE course2 AS
SELECT *
   FROM course
   WHERE 1 = 2
Table created.

INSERT INTO course2
   (course_no, description, cost, prerequisite,
   created_by, created_date, modified_by, modified_date)
VALUES
   (999, 'Teaching SQL - Part 1', 1495, NULL,
   'AMORRISON', SYSDATE, 'AMORRISON', SYSDATE)
1 row created.

INSERT INTO course2
   (course_no, description, cost, prerequisite,
   created_by, created_date, modified_by, modified_date)
VALUES
   (999, 'Teaching SQL - Part 2', 1495, NULL,
   'AMORRISON', SYSDATE, 'AMORRISON', SYSDATE)
1 row created.
```

b) Identify the constraints in the following CREATE TABLE statement and explain their purpose.

```
CREATE TABLE extinct_animal
   (animal_id      NUMBER,
   species_id      NUMBER,
   name            VARCHAR2(30) NOT NULL,
```

```
native_country  VARCHAR2(20)
   CONSTRAINT extinct_animal_country_fk
   REFERENCES country(country_name),
remaining       NUMBER(2,0),
CONSTRAINT extinct_animal_pk PRIMARY KEY(animal_id,
   species_id),
CONSTRAINT extinct_animal_remaining_ck
   CHECK (remaining BETWEEN 0 and 10))
```

c) Rewrite and execute the following CREATE TABLE statement to give the primary key and the foreign key constraints a name.

```
CREATE TABLE former_student
  (studid    NUMBER(8) PRIMARY KEY,
   first_nm  VARCHAR2(25),
   last_nm   VARCHAR2(25),
   enrolled  VARCHAR2(1) DEFAULT 'N',
   zip       VARCHAR2(5) REFERENCES zipcode(zip))
```

d) Rewrite the solution to Exercise c to add a UNIQUE constraint on the FIRST_NM and LAST_NM columns.

LAB 11.1 EXERCISE ANSWERS

11.1.1 ANSWERS

a) Explain the error(s) in the following CREATE TABLE statement, if any. If there are errors, rewrite the statement correctly.

```
CREATE TABLE student candidate
  (name      VARCHAR2(25)
   address   VARCHAR2(20)
   city      VARCHAR2
   zip       NUMBER)
```

Answer: The statement will not execute, as there are three errors: One is that the table name contains spaces. Another is that the length of the CITY column is not specified, and last, commas are required to separate the column definitions.

```
CREATE TABLE student_candidate
  (name      VARCHAR2(25),
   address   VARCHAR2(20),
   city      VARCHAR2(15),
   zip       NUMBER)
```

b) Write and execute a CREATE TABLE statement to create an empty table called NEW_STUDENT containing the following columns: first name, last name, the description of the first course the student takes, and the date the student registered in the program. Determine the datatype and length necessary for each column based on the tables in the STUDENT schema. DESCRIBE the table when you have finished.

Answer: The table contains the four columns FIRST_NAME, LAST_NAME, DESCRIPTION, and REGISTRATION_DATE. The first three are of datatype VARCHAR2 and REGISTRATION_DATE is of datatype DATE.

```
CREATE TABLE new_student
   (first_name             VARCHAR2(25),
    last_name              VARCHAR2(25),
    description            VARCHAR2(50),
    registration date      DATE)
```

```
SQL> DESC new_student
```

Name	Null?	Type
FIRST_NAME		VARCHAR2(25)
LAST_NAME		VARCHAR2(25)
DESCRIPTION		VARCHAR2(50)
REGISTRATION_DATE		DATE

DOCUMENTING THE TABLES AND COLUMNS

When you create tables and columns, you can add comments to them thereby documenting their purposes. This is accomplished with the COMMENT statement. These comments are stored in the data dictionary for reporting and self-documentation purposes. If you want to view the comments, you can query the involved data dictionary views ALL_COL_COMMENTS and ALL_TAB_COMMENTS.

Here is an example of how to create a *table comment* on the NEW_STUDENT table. The comment is enclosed in a single quote.

```
COMMENT ON TABLE new_student IS 'Table holding student
information used for exercises'
Comment created.
```

Next is an example of a *column comment* for the FIRST_NAME column on the NEW_STUDENT table. Notice two individual quotes are necessary to represent a single quote.

```
COMMENT ON COLUMN new_student.first_name is 'The
student''s first name.'
Comment created.
```

c) Execute the following CREATE TABLE statement and explain the result.

```
CREATE TABLE school_program AS
SELECT last_name||', '||first_name name
  FROM student
UNION
SELECT last_name||', '||first_name
  FROM instructor
```

Answer: The statement creates a table called SCHOOL_PROGRAM based on a query of two other tables combining student and instructor names. The first and last names are concatenated into one column.

```
SQL> DESC school_program
 Name                                     Null?    Type
 ------------------------------ -------- ------------
 NAME                                              VARCHAR2(52)
```

Notice the length of the name column in the new table: It is long enough to accommodate the combined length of first and last names, plus a comma and a space.

d) Rename the SCHOOL_PROGRAM table you created in Exercise c to a table called SCHOOL_PROGRAM2. Then drop both the SCHOOL_PROGRAM and SCHOOL_PROGRAM2 tables and explain your observations.

Answer: The RENAME and DROP TABLE commands are used. The SCHOOL_PRO-GRAM table no longer exists because it is renamed to SCHOOL_PROGRAM2, so it cannot be dropped.

```
RENAME school_program TO school_program2
Table renamed.

DROP TABLE school_program
DROP TABLE school_program
           *
ERROR at line 1:
ORA-00942: table or view does not exist

DROP TABLE school_program2
Table dropped.
```

11.1.2 ANSWERS

a) Execute the following SQL statements to create an empty table called COURSE2 and insert two rows into COURSE2, respectively. What do you observe about the values of the COURSE_NO column in the COURSE2 table?

```
CREATE TABLE course2 AS
SELECT *
  FROM course
 WHERE 1 = 2
```
Table created.

```
INSERT INTO course2
   (course_no, description, cost, prerequisite,
    created_by, created_date, modified_by, modified_date)
VALUES
   (999, 'Teaching SQL - Part 1', 1495, NULL,
    'AMORRISON', SYSDATE, 'AMORRISON', SYSDATE)
```
1 row created.

```
INSERT INTO course2
   (course_no, description, cost, prerequisite,
    created_by, created_date, modified_by, modified_date)
VALUES
   (999, 'Teaching SQL - Part 2', 1495, NULL,
    'AMORRISON', SYSDATE, 'AMORRISON', SYSDATE)
```
1 row created.

Answer: The primary key constraint is not preserved.

When a table is created from another table, constraints are not automatically preserved in the new table, except for the NOT NULL constraint. The COURSE_NO column is the primary key in the COURSE table and, therefore, prevents duplicate values. But, when the COURSE2 table is created from the COURSE table, a primary key constraint is not created so the COURSE_NO column in the COURSE2 table allows duplicate values to be inserted.

After creating a table based on another, you can add constraints with the ALTER TABLE command discussed in Lab 11.2.

b) Identify the constraints in the following CREATE TABLE statement and explain their purpose.

```
CREATE TABLE extinct_animal
   (animal_id       NUMBER,
    species_id      NUMBER,
    name            VARCHAR2(30) NOT NULL,
    native_country  VARCHAR2(20)
       CONSTRAINT extinct_animal_country_fk
       REFERENCES country(country_name),
    remaining       NUMBER(2,0),
    CONSTRAINT extinct_animal_pk PRIMARY KEY(animal_id,
       species_id),
    CONSTRAINT extinct_animal_remaining_ck
       CHECK (remaining BETWEEN 0 AND 10))
```

Answer: The first constraint in the EXTINCT_ANIMAL table is a NOT NULL constraint on the NAME column and because it is not named, it receives a system-generated name. The NATIVE_COUNTRY column is a constraint with a foreign key to values from the COUNTRY_NAME column in a table called COUNTRY, which must exist before the command is successful.

The concatenated PRIMARY KEY constraint called EXTINCT_ANIMAL_PK consists of the ANIMAL_ID and SPECIES_ID columns. When a primary key on a table consists of more than one column, the constraint must be written as a table-level constraint on a separate line of the CREATE TABLE statement. The CHECK constraint on the column called EXTINCT_ANIMAL_REMAINING_CK checks whether a number inserted or updated is between the values 0 and 10 inclusively.

A NOT NULL constraint on the ANIMAL_ID and SPECIES_ID columns is not required because the columns are defined as the primary key.

c) Rewrite and execute the following CREATE TABLE statement to give the primary key and the foreign key constraints a name.

```
CREATE TABLE former_student
    (studid     NUMBER(8) PRIMARY KEY,
     first_nm      VARCHAR2(25),
     last_nm       VARCHAR2(25),
     enrolled   VARCHAR2(1) DEFAULT 'N',
     zip        VARCHAR2(5) REFERENCES zipcode(zip))
```

Answer: The constraint definitions are moved to the end of the CREATE TABLE statement where they are created with specific names.

```
CREATE TABLE former_student
    (studid     NUMBER(8),
     first_nm   VARCHAR2(25),
     last_nm    VARCHAR2(25),
     enrolled   VARCHAR2(1) DEFAULT 'N',
     zip        VARCHAR2(5),
     CONSTRAINT former_student_pk PRIMARY KEY(studid),
     CONSTRAINT former_student_zipcode_fk FOREIGN KEY(zip)
        REFERENCES zipcode(zip))
```

Alternatively, you can also use the column-level constraints. Your solution may look similar to this statement:

```
CREATE TABLE former_student
    (studid     NUMBER(8) CONSTRAINT former_student_pk PRIMARY KEY,
     first_nm  VARCHAR2(25),
     last_nm   VARCHAR2(25),
```

```
enrolled  VARCHAR2(1) DEFAULT 'N',
zip          VARCHAR2(5) CONSTRAINT former_student_zipcode_fk
                 REFERENCES zipcode(zip))
```

When a constraint is not named and an error occurs, you will receive a system-generated constraint error name. Here is such an example.

```
INSERT INTO former_student
   (studid, first_nm, last_nm, enrolled, zip)
VALUES
   (101, 'Alex', 'Morrison', NULL, '10005')
1 row created.

INSERT INTO former_student
   (studid, first_nm, last_nm, enrolled, zip)
VALUES
   (101, 'Alex', 'Morrison', NULL, '11717')
INSERT INTO former_student
             *
ERROR at line 1:
ORA-00001: unique constraint (STUDENT.SYS_C001293) violated
```

From the error message, it is impossible to figure out which column(s) caused the error; you can only determine that the constraint is in the STUDENT schema. You need to look up the name of the constraint in the Oracle data dictionary views USER_CONSTRAINTS or ALL_CONSTRAINTS to determine the reason for the error. The system-generated name is not informative; therefore, always name your constraints.

d) Rewrite the solution to Exercise c to add a UNIQUE constraint on the FIRST_NM and LAST_NM columns.

Answer: The constraint is added to the end of the CREATE TABLE statement with a specific name.

```
CREATE TABLE former_student
   (studid    NUMBER(8),
    first_nm  VARCHAR2(25),
    last_nm   VARCHAR2(25),
    enrolled  VARCHAR2(1) DEFAULT 'N',
    zip       VARCHAR2(5),
    CONSTRAINT former_student_pk PRIMARY KEY(studid),
    CONSTRAINT former_student_zipcode_fk FOREIGN KEY(zip)
       REFERENCES zipcode(zip),
    CONSTRAINT former_student_uk UNIQUE(first_nm, last_nm))
```

A UNIQUE constraint prevents duplicate values from being inserted into a column. It is different from a PRIMARY KEY constraint because a UNIQUE constraint allows NULL values.

LAB 11.1 SELF-REVIEW QUESTIONS

In order to test your progress, you should be able to answer the following questions.

1) The primary key of the following CREATE TABLE statement is a concatenated primary key.

```
CREATE TABLE class_roster
  (class_id          NUMBER(3),
   class_name        VARCHAR2(20) UNIQUE,
   first_class       DATE NOT NULL,
   num_of_students   NUMBER(3),
   CONSTRAINT class_roster_pk
    PRIMARY KEY(class_id, class_name))
```

a) _____ True
b) _____ False

2) It is possible to create one table from three different tables in a single CREATE TABLE statement.

a) _____ True
b) _____ False

3) The CASCADE CONSTRAINTS keywords in a DROP TABLE statement drop all referencing child tables.

a) _____ True
b) _____ False

4) Every column of a table can have one or more constraints.

a) _____ True
b) _____ False

5) You cannot create a table from another table if it has no rows.

a) _____ True
b) _____ False

6) A CREATE TABLE statement automatically commits all previously issued DML statements.

a) _____ True
b) _____ False

7) A foreign key must match a primary key or unique key.

a) _____ True
b) _____ False

8) Primary key values should always be subject to frequent change.

a) _____ True
b) _____ False

9) The STORAGE clause on a CREATE TABLE statement can specify how much space to allocate.

a) _____ True
b) _____ False

10) The datatype definitions of NUMBER(10) and NUMBER(10,0) are equivalent.

a) _____ True
b) _____ False

11) The maximum value for a column defined as NUMBER(3,2) is 999.

a) _____ True
b) _____ False

Answers appear in Appendix A, Section 11.1.

LAB 11.2

ALTERING TABLES AND MANIPULATING CONSTRAINTS

LAB OBJECTIVES

After this lab, you will be able to:
✔ Alter Tables and Manipulate Constraints

Once a table is created, you sometimes find you must change its characteristics. The ALTER TABLE command, in conjunction with the ADD, DROP, MODIFY, and RENAME clauses, allows you to do this. You can add or delete a column; change the length, datatype, or default value of a column; or add, drop, enable, disable or rename a table's integrity constraints.

Following is the general syntax for the ALTER TABLE command: You will see examples of these many options throughout this lab and in the following exercises.

```
ALTER TABLE tablename
  [ADD [(columnname datatype[DEFAULT expr]
      [column_constraint]
      [, columnname datatype[DEFAULT expr]
      [column_constraint]]...)]
      [, table_constraint [, table_constraint...]]
  [MODIFY [(columnname datatype [DEFAULT expr]
      [column_constraint]
  [MODIFY CONSTRAINT constraint_name
      [ENABLE|DISABLE] [NOVALIDATE|VALIDATE]]
  [DROP CONSTRAINT constraint_name|
      PRIMARY KEY|
      UNIQUE (columnname[,columnname...])
        [CASCADE]
```

```
[DISABLE|ENABLE [VALIDATE|NOVALIDATE]
   CONSTRAINT constraint_name|
    PRIMARY KEY|
    UNIQUE (columnname[,columnname]...)
    [USING INDEX indexname [storage_clause]]
    [CASCADE] [{KEEP|DROP}INDEX]]
[RENAME CONSTRAINT constraint_name TO new_constraint_name
[DROP (columnname)|DROP COLUMN (columnname[,columnname...])]
[SET UNUSED COLUMN columnname|SET UNUSED
   (columnname[,columnname...])]
[DROP UNUSED COLUMNS]
[RENAME COLUMN columnname TO newcolumnname]
[RENAME TO newtablename]
[storage_clause]
```

ADDING COLUMNS

This is a list of the columns of the TOY table created at the beginning of Lab 11.1.

```
SQL> DESC toy
Name                                    Null?      Type
--------------------------------------  ---------  ------------
TOY_ID                                             NUMBER(10)
DESCRIPTION                             NOT NULL   VARCHAR2(15)
LAST_PURCHASE_DATE                                 DATE
REMAINING_QUANTITY                                 NUMBER(6)
```

The following statement alters the TOY table to add a new column called MAN-UFACTURER.

```
ALTER TABLE toy
   ADD (manufacturer VARCHAR2(30) NOT NULL)
Table altered.
```

The `Table altered` command indicates the successful completion of the operation. When the column is added, it is defined as VARCHAR2(30). The column also has a NOT NULL constraint. When you issue another DESCRIBE command, you see the new column.

```
SQL> DESC toy
Name                                    Null?      Type
--------------------------------------  ---------  ------------
TOY_ID                                             NUMBER(10)
DESCRIPTION                             NOT NULL   VARCHAR2(15)
LAST_PURCHASE_DATE                                 DATE
REMAINING_QUANTITY                                 NUMBER(6)
MANUFACTURER                            NOT NULL   VARCHAR2(30)
```

Alternatively, you can add the column and name the constraint as in the following example.

```
ALTER TABLE TOY
   ADD (manufacturer VARCHAR2(30)
      CONSTRAINT toy_manufacturer_nn NOT NULL)
```

 You can only add a column together with a NOT NULL constraint if the table contains no data. Otherwise, add the column first without the NOT NULL constraint, then update the column with data and change the column definition to a NOT NULL constraint with the MODIFY clause of the ALTER TABLE statement.

DROPPING COLUMNS

Columns can also be dropped from a table with the ALTER TABLE command using the DROP clause. The following statement drops the LAST_PURCHASE_DATE column from the TOY table.

```
ALTER TABLE toy
   DROP (last_purchase_date)
```
Table altered.

If you want to drop multiple columns, separate the columns with commas.

```
ALTER TABLE toy
   DROP (manufacturer, remaining_quantity)
```
Table altered.

Instead of dropping a column, you can mark it as unused with the SET UNUSED clause of the ALTER TABLE statement.

```
ALTER TABLE toy
   SET UNUSED (last_purchase_date)
```
Table altered.

Setting the column as unused is useful if you want to make the column no longer visible but do not want to physically remove it yet. When you issue a subsequent ALTER TABLE with the DROP COLUMN clause, or the ALTER TABLE command with the DROP UNUSED COLUMNS clause, Oracle physically removes the column from the database.

```
ALTER TABLE toy
   DROP UNUSED COLUMNS
```
Table altered.

Changing a column to unused instead of dropping it is quicker, because it does not demand a lot of system resources. When the system is less busy, you can then physically remove the column.

RENAMING COLUMNS

You can rename an individual column with the following command:

```
ALTER TABLE toy RENAME COLUMN description TO
    description_tx
```

Keep in mind that any dependent objects that reference this column become invalid.

MODIFYING COLUMNS

You modify the datatype, length, and column default of existing columns with the ALTER TABLE statement. There are a number of restrictions, as you see in the lab exercises.

The following statement changes the length of the DESCRIPTION column from 15 to 25 characters.

```
ALTER TABLE toy
    MODIFY (description VARCHAR2(25))
Table altered.
```

The next statement modifies the datatype of the REMAINING_QUANTITY column from NUMBER to VARCHAR2 and makes the column NOT NULL simultaneously. This statement executes successfully because the table contains no data.

```
ALTER TABLE toy
    MODIFY (remaining_quantity VARCHAR2(6) NOT NULL)
Table altered.
```

You can also execute the statements individually.

```
ALTER TABLE toy
    MODIFY (remaining_quantity VARCHAR2(6))
Table altered.

ALTER TABLE toy
    MODIFY (remaining_quantity NOT NULL)
Table altered.
```

If you want to give the NOT NULL constraint a name, you use this command. Instead of the system-generated SYS_ name, the constraint's name will be REMAIN_QT_NN.

```
ALTER TABLE toy
  MODIFY (remaining_quantity
  CONSTRAINT remain_qt_nn NOT NULL)
Table altered.
```

Any changes to the structure of a table will invalidate other dependent database objects, such as views, triggers, and stored PL/SQL objects. The next time they are accessed, Oracle will attempt to compile or revalidate them. You can find the list of invalid objects in the ALL_OBJECTS or ALL_OBJECTS data dictionary view. Before making any changes you can find out which objects are dependent on the table by querying the USER_DEPENDENCIES or ALL_DEPENDENCIES data dictionary news.

ADDING, DROPPING, DISABLING, AND ENABLING CONSTRAINTS

ADDING CONSTRAINTS

Any of the constraints you learned in Lab 11.1 can be added to a table with the ALTER TABLE...ADD command. When the TOY table was created, no primary key was specified. The following statement alters the TOY table to add a primary key constraint based on the TOY_ID column.

```
ALTER TABLE toy
  ADD PRIMARY KEY(toy_id)
Table altered.
```

The same statement can be rewritten with a constraint name and a storage clause for the index as well as the tablespace on which the index is to be stored.

```
ALTER TABLE toy
  ADD CONSTRAINT toy_pk PRIMARY KEY(toy_id)
  USING INDEX TABLESPACE store_idx
  STORAGE (INITIAL 1M NEXT 500 K)
Table altered.
```

For performance reasons, you typically separate indexes and data by storing them on separate tablespaces on different physical devices. The index is created in a tablespace called STORE_IDX. Other characteristics of a table, such as its storage parameters and size, can also be specified with the ALTER TABLE command. In the previous example, one megabyte of space is allocated, regardless of whether any rows exist. After this space is used, each subsequent amount of space allocated is 500 kilobytes in size.

The following statement is an example of a SQL statement that creates the concatenated primary key constraint for the GRADE table consisting of four columns. Additionally, the space allocation and tablespace for the automatically associated unique index is located on the INDX tablespace, and 100 kilobytes are used for the initial extent.

LAB
11.2

```
ALTER TABLE grade
   ADD CONSTRAINT gr_pk PRIMARY KEY
   (student_id, section_id, grade_type_code,
   grade_code_occurrence)
   USING INDEX TABLESPACE indx
   STORAGE (INITIAL 100K NEXT 100K)
```

FOREIGN KEY   The following statement illustrates the creation of the two-column foreign key constraint on the GRADE table referencing the concatenated primary key columns of the ENROLLMENT table.

```
ALTER TABLE grade
   ADD CONSTRAINT gr_enr_fk FOREIGN KEY
   (student_id, section_id)
   REFERENCES enrollment (student_id, section_id)
```

SELF-REFERENCING FOREIGN KEY   The COURSE table has a recursive relationship; the PREREQUISITE column refers back to the COURSE_NO column. It checks to see if the values in the PREREQUISITE column are in fact valid COURSE_NO values. The following SQL statement shows the foreign key constraint command used to create the self-referencing constraint on the COURSE table.

```
ALTER TABLE course
   ADD CONSTRAINT crse_crse_fk FOREIGN KEY (prerequisite)
   REFERENCES course (course_no)
```

If you are loading large amounts of data, you may want to consider temporarily disabling this constraint unless you can be sure that the sequence in which the data is inserted into the table is correct. The correct order requires any courses that are prerequisites for other courses to be entered first.

UNIQUE INDEX   The next example shows how the ALTER TABLE command on the SECTION table creates the unique index on the SECTION_NO and COURSE_NO columns. Because unique constraints automatically create an associated index, you want to place the index on a separate tablespace. Following is the syntax to place the index on the INDX tablespace, and the command also defines the initial and each subsequent extent.

```
ALTER TABLE section
   ADD CONSTRAINT sect_sect2_uk
       UNIQUE (section_no, course_no)
   USING INDEX TABLESPACE indx
   STORAGE
   (INITIAL 120K NEXT 120K)
```

CHECK CONSTRAINTS   The following statement adds a check constraint to the ZIP-CODE table. It verifies that the entries in the ZIP primary key column are exactly five characters long and only numbers, not letters or special characters. The TRANSLATE function converts each entered digit into a 9 and then checks to see if the format equals to 99999. Any nonnumeric digits are not translated; therefore, the result of the TRANSLATE is unequal to 99999 and the value is rejected.

```
ALTER TABLE zipcode
   ADD CONSTRAINT zipcode_zip_ck
   CHECK (TRANSLATE(zip, '1234567890',
                         '9999999999') = '99999')
```

Alternatively, you could come up with the following check constraint, but it has one drawback. A value such as '123.4' does not raise an error when the TO_NUMBER conversion function is applied. The LENGTH function is also fine because this is a string with a five-character length. There are many ways to handle checking of data validity. In Oracle 10*g* you can also use a regular expression, which offers even more flexibility and you will see some examples how they can be applied shortly.

```
ALTER TABLE zipcode
   ADD CONSTRAINT zipcode_zip_ck
   CHECK (TO_NUMBER(zip)>0 AND LENGTH(zip)= 5)
```

This check constraint is applied to the SALUTATION column of the INSTRUCTOR table.

```
ALTER TABLE instructor
   ADD CONSTRAINT instructor_salutation_ck
   CHECK (salutation IN ('Dr', 'Hon', 'Mr', 'Ms', 'Rev')
         OR salutation IS NULL)
```

With the implementation of floating-point numbers in Oracle 10*g*, additional floating-point constraints are available for the BINARY_FLOAT and BINARY_DOUBLE datatypes. These new constraint types allow for checking for NAN (not a Number) and infinity.

```
CREATE TABLE float_constraint
   (col_1 BINARY_FLOAT,
    col_2 BINARY_DOUBLE)

ALTER TABLE float_constraint
   ADD CONSTRAINT col_1_ck_nan
   CHECK(col_1 IS NOT NAN)
```

```
ALTER TABLE float_constraint
  ADD CONSTRAINT col_2_ck_inf
  CHECK(col_2 IS NOT INFINITE)
```

DROPPING CONSTRAINTS

When a constraint is no longer needed, you drop it with the ALTER TABLE command and the DROP clause. The next statement drops a constraint by explicitly specifying the constraint name.

```
ALTER TABLE toy
  DROP CONSTRAINT toy_pk
```
Table altered.

Alternatively, you can drop a primary key constraint with the following statement.

```
ALTER TABLE toy
  DROP PRIMARY KEY
```

If there is a unique constraint, you either issue the command with the constraint name or use a statement similar to this:

```
ALTER TABLE toy
  DROP UNIQUE (description)
```

RENAMING CONSTRAINTS

You can rename a constraint name with the following command:

```
ALTER TABLE section RENAME CONSTRAINT sect_crse_fk TO scct_fk_crse
```

You may want to use the RENAME CONSTRAINT command to rename any system-generated constraint name to a more descriptive name.

DISABLING AND ENABLING CONSTRAINTS

Constraints are enabled or disabled as necessary with the ALTER TABLE command. By default, when a constraint is created, it is enabled, unless you explicitly disable it. You may want to disable constraints when updating massive volumes of data or inserting large amounts of data at once to decrease overall time for these operations. Once the data manipulation is performed, you re-enable the constraint.

The following statement disables an existing primary key constraint named TOY_PK on the TOY table.

```
ALTER TABLE toy
   DISABLE CONSTRAINT toy_pk
```
Table altered.

Note, when a primary key or unique constraint is disabled, by default any associated index is dropped. When the constraint is re-enabled, a unique index is recreated.

Alternatively, you can preserve the index of a unique or primary key, if you specify the KEEP INDEX clause of the ALTER TABLE statement, as you see in the next statement.

```
ALTER TABLE toy
   DISABLE CONSTRAINT toy_pk KEEP INDEX
```

Naming constraints helps when you want to disable or enable them. Once data changes are completed, you can enable the primary key with the following statement.

```
ALTER TABLE toy
   ENABLE PRIMARY KEY
```
Table altered.

This statement explicitly specifies the constraint name and creates the index on a specified table space with the listed storage parameters.

```
ALTER TABLE toy
   ENABLE CONSTRAINT toy_pk
   USING INDEX TABLESPACE store_idx
   STORAGE (INITIAL 1 M
            NEXT 500 K)
```
Table altered.

 To find out the name of a constraint and its status (enabled or disabled), query the data dictionary views USER_CONSTRAINTS and USER_CONS_COLUMNS.

If an index does not exist for the constraint and you don't specify the tablespace name when you enable the constraint, the index will be stored on your default tablespace with the default storage size parameters. The storage clause on constraints is only relevant with primary and unique constraints because they create indexes.

The following statement disables the foreign key constraint between the COURSE and the SECTION tables.

```
ALTER TABLE section
  DISABLE CONSTRAINT sect_crse_fk
Table altered.
```

If you want to disable multiple constraints, you can issue multiple statements or issue them in one ALTER TABLE statement. Note that the individual DISABLE clauses are not separated by commas.

```
ALTER TABLE section
  DISABLE CONSTRAINT sect_crse_fk
  DISABLE CONSTRAINT sect_inst_fk
```

NOVALIDATE OPTION   As part of the ENABLE clause of the ALTER TABLE statement, Oracle also provides a NOVALIDATE option, allowing only subsequent DML operations on the table to comply with the constraint; existing data can violate the constraint.

DETERMINE WHICH ROWS VIOLATE CONSTRAINTS

Unless the NOVALIDATE option is used, when a constraint is re-enabled, Oracle checks to see if all the rows satisfy the condition of the constraint. If some rows violate the constraint, the statement fails and Oracle issues an error message. The constraint cannot be enabled unless all exceptions are fixed or the offending rows are deleted.

FOREIGN KEY CONSTRAINT VIOLATIONS

For example, if a row with a new course number was added to the SECTION table but the COURSE table has no such COURSE_NO, the foreign key constraint cannot be enabled as indicated by the error message.

```
ALTER TABLE section
  ENABLE CONSTRAINT sect_crse_fk
ALTER TABLE section
*
ERROR at line 1:
ORA-02298: cannot validate (STUDENT.SECT_CRSE_FK) - parent keys not found
```

There are a variety of ways to determine the offending rows. For example, you can issue the following statement to display the rows:

```
SELECT course_no
  FROM section
 MINUS
```

```
SELECT course_no
  FROM course
```

PRIMARY KEY CONSTRAINT VIOLATIONS

To determine which rows violate the primary key constraint, you can group by the primary key column and query for duplicates with the HAVING clause as you see in the following SQL command:

```
SELECT section_id, COUNT(*)
  FROM section
 GROUP BY section_id
HAVING COUNT(*) > 1
```

A subsequent DELETE operation of the duplicate rows may look like this:

```
DELETE
  FROM section
 WHERE ROWID IN (SELECT MAX(ROWID)
                   FROM section
                  GROUP BY section_id
                 HAVING COUNT(*) > 1)
```

The subquery identifies the duplicate SECTION_ID column values. The SELECT of the subquery retrieves the largest value of the ROWID pseudocolumn. Each Oracle table has a pseudocolumn called ROWID, which is not visible when describing the table or with a SELECT * statement. The ROWID is unique for every row, and this subquery statement picks the largest ROWID value using the MAX function. The rows with these duplicate SECTION_ID values will be deleted. (Make sure that the non-primary key column values are identical, so you don't inadvertently delete rows that you want to keep.)

The Whole Truth

Another way to identify constraint violations: Oracle allows you to record all the rows violating a constraint in a table called EXCEPTIONS and you can create the table with the Oracle script utlexcpt.sql found in the %ORACLE_HOME%\rdbms\admin directory. You can then use the ALTER TABLE tablename ENABLE CONSTRAINT constraint_name EXCEPTIONS INTO exceptions syntax to place the violating rows into the EXCEPTIONS table.

WRITING COMPLEX CHECK CONSTRAINTS

You have seen a number of check constraint examples that validate data against simple logic. Sometimes a seemingly straightforward requirement can turn into a fairly complex check constraint. For example, imagine you need to add validation to the PHONE column of the STUDENT table that ensures that the entered number fits the (###) ###-#### format. You can perform this validation with the TRANSLATE function (discussed in Lab 3.1) as you see in the following statement.

```
ALTER TABLE student
   ADD CONSTRAINT student_phone_ck CHECK
      (TRANSLATE(phone,
       '012345678',
       '999999999') = '999-999-9999')
```

The TRANSLATE function determines if any of the characters listed in the PHONE column are listed in the IF parameter of the function '012345678'. When true, it translates them to the corresponding THEN input characters, which in our case is always '9'. Any character not listed is not translated and retained as the original character. If the result of the TRANSLATE function equals to the pattern '999-999-9999', the value passes the check constraint.

If you want to include phone numbers without area codes, or allow an optional period or space instead of the hyphen as a separation character, your check constraint quickly becomes complex, as you need to cover all the various combinations with OR conditions. You may even end up writing a trigger to make the logic more transparent.

Oracle 10*g* includes regular expressions capabilities in the SQL language. A regular expression is a pattern matching language found in many programming languages. While regular expressions look fairly complex initially, you will appreciate their power and flexibility once you understand the meaning of the metacharacters that make up the regular expression. The next example duplicates the identical functionality of the TRANSLATE function to illustrate the meaning of some of the metacharacters.

```
ALTER TABLE student
   ADD CONSTRAINT student_phone_ck CHECK
      (REGEXP_LIKE(phone,
       '^[[:digit:]]{3}-[[:digit:]]{3}-[[:digit:]]{4}$'))
```

The REGEXP_LIKE operator is similar to the LIKE operator because it checks if a pattern is found. The first metacharacter '^' indicates that there may not be any characters before the pattern, just like the '$' at the end of the regular expression directs that there may not be no extra characters at the end of the line. The [[:digit:]] character class and list specify that only a digit is allowed. The digit class is repeated three times as indicated with the {3} repetition operator. This part of the regular expression represents the areacode. The pattern continues with a hyphen, followed by another three digits, a hyphen, and last, another four digits.

If characters other than a hyphen are valid in your phone number format, you can modify the regular expression by including those characters inside a character list enclosed by square brackets '[ ]'. In this instance, spaces, periods, and dashes are allowed, or consecutive numbers without any separator. The character list now reads as [-.]? with the '?' metacharacter indicating that 0 or 1 repetition of this class list is allowed.

```
ALTER TABLE student
  ADD CONSTRAINT student_phone_ck CHECK
    (REGEXP_LIKE(phone,
    '^[[:digit:]]{3}[-. ]?[[:digit:]]{3}[-. ]?[[:digit:]]{4}$'))
```

You can take the regular expression functionality another step further and add validation for phone extension numbers, area codes beginning only with numbers 2 through 9, optional area code parentheses, and alphanumeric formats such as 800-REGEXPR. In Chapter 15, "Regular Expressions and Hierarchical Queries," you will learn more about the many other metacharacters to help you validate pattern such as zipcodes, e-mail addresses, or URLs.

RESTRICTIONS ON CHECK CONSTRAINTS

Check constraints impose a few restrictions you should be aware of. Your check constraint may not refer to a column in another table; only columns within the same table are allowed. You may not use subqueries or scalar subquery expressions. References to nondeterministic functions such as SYSDATE, USER, CURRENT_TIMESTAMP are not allowed because they may return different results each time they are called. (Note: You can use them for default values.) The pseudocolumns CURRVAL, NEXTVAL, LEVEL and ROWNUM are also not permitted.

You can overcome these restrictions by writing triggers using the PL/SQL language. For example, you can write a trigger to reference columns in other tables to validate data, call the SYSDATE function to fill in the current date and time into the LASTMOD_DT column, or to automatically create primary key column values that reference the NEXTVAL pseudocolumn of a sequence. At the beginning of this chapter, one trigger example illustrated the use of the SYSDATE function; you will see another PL/SQL trigger example referencing a sequence in Chapter 12, "Views, Indexes, and Sequences."

DML AND DDL OPERATIONS

When a DML operation, such as an insert, update, or delete command, is not yet committed, a lock is placed on the affected rows. Because a DDL command requires exclusive access to the table or index, another session cannot issue such a command unless the locks are released. This is just one of the many reasons why data structure changes are performed during times when users are not accessing the system.

Figure 11.1 illustrates such as scenario where a session issuing an ALTER TABLE command is conflicting with another session holding a lock due to an uncommitted update on the same table. The resulting error message indicates that the session issuing the DDL command cannot obtain the exclusive lock of the entire table and must wait until the other session issues a COMMIT or ROLLBACK.

TIME	SESSION #1	SESSION #2

T1	`UPDATE instructor`
	`    SET first_name = 'John'`
	`  WHERE instructor_id = 109`
	1 row updated.	

T2		`ALTER TABLE instructor`
		`    ADD (test_col NUMBER)`
		ALTER TABLE instructor
		ORA-00054: resource busy and
		`      acquire with NOWAIT specified`

Figure 11.1 ■ The effect of DDL and DML commands on the same table.

ONLINE TABLE DEFINITION

As the previous example illustrated, Oracle will only execute your DDL command if there are no sessions holding any locks. As the demand for 24/7 database availability has significantly increased, Oracle has put functionality into place that allows you to perform DDL tasks that alter the table while users are performing data manipulation on the tables. This is accomplished with a set of PL/SQL procedures within the DBMS_REDEFINITION package that copies the data to an interim table and keeps track of the changes until the new table with the desired characteristics is ready to be used.

ORACLE ENTERPRISE MANAGER (OEM)

Many of the tasks listed in this chapter can be performed by using a graphical user interface (GUI) instead of a SQL command. Oracle's Enterprise Manager along with many other third-party tools allow you to create tables and execute alterations on tables by clicking buttons and selecting from menus. You can view the respective SQL statement that will be executed before completing the task.

Figure 11.2 displays the table edit screen of OEM's Web version. Here you can delete columns, add new columns, or change the definitions of existing columns. This particular screen shows the columns of the COURSE table. To login to OEM's Web version use the URL in the format of http://machine_name:5500/em.

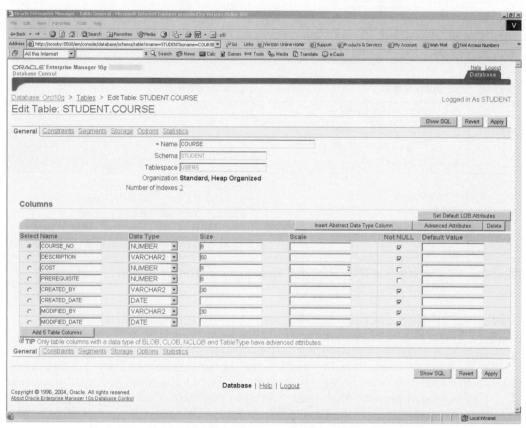

Figure 11.2 ■ **Performing a table alteration using Oracle Enterprise Manager.**

Using a GUI can simplify database administration tasks because you don't need to remember the exact syntax. It also provides you with easy to view listings of database objects together with available command and syntax choices. While working with an interface has many advantages, it nevertheless requires you to know the effects of your actions.

LAB 11.2 EXERCISES

11.2.1 ALTER TABLES AND MANIPULATE CONSTRAINTS

a) Alter the table called NEW_STUDENT you created in Exercise 11.1.1 b to add four columns called PHONE, NUM_COURSES with datatype and length NUMBER(3), CREATED_BY, and CREATED_DATE. Determine the other column datatypes and lengths based on the STUDENT table. The PHONE, NUM_COURSES, and CREATED_BY columns should allow null values with the CREATED_BY column defaulting to the user's login name. The CREATED_DATE column should not allow null values and default to today's date. DESCRIBE the table when you have finished.

b) Execute the following INSERT statement to insert a row into the NEW_STUDENT table. Then alter the table to change the PHONE column from NULL to NOT NULL. What do you observe?

```
INSERT INTO new_student
   (first_name, last_name, description, registration_date)
VALUES
   ('Joe', 'Fisher', 'Intro to Linux', SYSDATE)
```

c) Alter the NEW_STUDENT table to change the REGISTRATION_DATE column from DATE datatype to VARCHAR2 datatype. What do you observe?

d) Alter the NEW_STUDENT table to create a primary key consisting of the FIRST_NAME and LAST_NAME columns.

e) Alter the NEW_STUDENT table to change the length of the LAST_NAME column from 25 to 2. What do you observe?

f) Disable the primary key constraint on the NEW_STUDENT table and write an INSERT statement with the value "Joe Fisher" for the first and last name to prove it is successful. Then enable the constraint again and describe the result.

g) Add the column STUDY_DURATION of datatype INTERVAL YEAR TO MONTH and the column ALUMNI_JOIN_DATE with a datatype of TIMESTAMP WITH TIME ZONE and a six-digit precision to the NEW_STUDENT table.

h) Drop the foreign key constraint FORMER_STUDENT_ ZIPCODE_FK on the FORMER_STUDENT table and change it to an ON DELETE SET NULL foreign key constraint. Test the behavior by inserting a new zip code in the ZIPCODE table and creating a new student row with this new zip code, and then deleting the same zip code from the ZIPCODE table. Query the FORMER_STUDENT table to see the effect.

i) Drop all the tables created throughout the labs. The table names are: STUDENT_CANDIDATE, NEW_STUDENT, COURSE2, EXTINCT_ANIMAL, and FORMER_STUDENT.

LAB 11.2 EXERCISE ANSWERS

11.2.1 ANSWERS

a) Alter the table called NEW_STUDENT you created in Exercise 11.1.1 b to add four columns called PHONE, NUM_COURSES with datatype and length NUMBER(3), CREATED_BY, and CREATED_DATE. Determine the other column datatypes and lengths based on the STUDENT table. The PHONE, NUM_COURSES, and CREATED_BY columns should allow null values with the CREATED_BY column defaulting to the user's login name. The CREATED_DATE column should not allow null values and default to today's date. DESCRIBE the table when you have finished.

Answer: The four columns are added with a single ALTER TABLE...ADD command, separated by commas. The CREATED_BY column has a DEFAULT clause to default the column to the value of the user's login name; the CREATED_DATE column contains a NOT NULL constraint and defaults the column to the value SYSDATE.

```
ALTER TABLE new_student
  ADD (phone VARCHAR2(15),
       num_courses NUMBER(3),
       created_by VARCHAR2(30) DEFAULT USER,
       created_date DATE DEFAULT SYSDATE NOT NULL)
Table altered.

SQL> DESC new_student
 Name                             Null?     Type
 -------------------------------- --------- -----------
 FIRST_NAME                                 VARCHAR2(25)
 LAST_NAME                                  VARCHAR2(25)
 DESCRIPTION                                VARCHAR2(50)
 REGISTRATION_DATE                          DATE
 PHONE                                      VARCHAR2(15)
 NUM_COURSES                                NUMBER(3)
 CREATED_BY                                 VARCHAR2(30)
 CREATED_DATE                     NOT NULL  DATE
```

A column or columns can be added to a table regardless of whether the table contains data. However, you cannot add columns with a NOT NULL constraint if the column contains NULL values. Therefore, you must first add the column with the NULL constraint, update the column with values, then alter the table to modify the column to add the NOT NULL constraint.

SETTING COLUMNS TO THE DEFAULT VALUES

How do default values behave when you insert data into the column? The CREATED_DATE column has a default value of SYSDATE. If you want this default value to appear in an INSERT statement, you can either not list the column on the INSERT statement or explicitly state the DEFAULT keyword. The CREATED_DATE column is explicitly specified and the DEFAULT keyword is used. It places the current date and time into the column. The CREATED_BY default returns the value of the USER function, which is the name of the user currently logged in. Because it's not listed in the following INSERT statement, this default value is used.

```
INSERT INTO new_student
   (first_name, last_name, description, created_date)
VALUES
   ('Julian', 'Soehner', 'Test#1', DEFAULT)

SELECT description, created_by, created_date
   FROM new_student
DESCRIPTION       CREATED_BY                    CREATED_D
---------------   -----------------------------  ---------
Test#1            STUDENT                       18-MAY-02

1 row selected.


ROLLBACK
Rollback complete.
```

MODIFYING OR REMOVING COLUMN DEFAULT VALUES

A column with a DEFAULT option can also be changed to another default value or the default value can be removed. The next example removes the default value for the CREATED_BY column and changes the value for CREATED_DATE column to '01-JAN-2003'.

```
ALTER TABLE new_student
   MODIFY (created_by VARCHAR2(30) DEFAULT NULL,
           created_date DATE DEFAULT TO_DATE('01-Jan-2003'))
Table altered.
```

Note that DDL commands such as this ALTER TABLE command cannot be rolled back, and they COMMIT any previously issued DML statements.

An update of a column to reset its present value to the default value using the DEFAULT keyword would look like this:

```
UPDATE new_student
   SET created_date = DEFAULT
 WHERE description = 'Test#1'
```

The result now shows the CREATED_DATE column with the 01-Jan-2003 value.

```
SELECT description, created_date
  FROM new_student
DESCRIPTION      CREATED_D
---------------  ---------
Test#1           01-JAN-03

1 row selected.
```

b) Execute the following INSERT statement to insert a row into the NEW_STU-DENT table. Then alter the table to change the PHONE column from NULL to NOT NULL. What do you observe?

```
INSERT INTO new_student
   (first_name, last_name, description, registration_date)
VALUES
   ('Joe', 'Fisher', 'Intro to Linux', SYSDATE)
```

Answer: The column cannot be modified to have a NOT NULL constraint because there is already a row in the table containing a NULL value in the column.

```
ALTER TABLE new_student
  MODIFY (phone NOT NULL)
MODIFY (phone NOT NULL)
       *
ERROR at line 2:
ORA-02296: cannot enable (STUDENT.) - null values found
```

You cannot modify an existing column to NOT NULL if it contains NULL values. You must first add data to the column and then modify the column to add the constraint.

```
UPDATE new_student
   SET phone = '917-555-1212'
```

```
ALTER TABLE new_student
   MODIFY (phone NOT NULL)
```
Table altered.

```
SQL> DESC new_student
```

Name	Null?	Type
FIRST_NAME		VARCHAR2(25)
LAST_NAME		VARCHAR2(25)
DESCRIPTION		VARCHAR2(50)
REGISTRATION_DATE		DATE
PHONE	NOT NULL	VARCHAR2(15)
NUM_COURSES		NUMBER(3)
CREATED_BY	NOT NULL	VARCHAR2(30)
CREATED_DATE	NOT NULL	DATE

The column can also be changed back to NULL with the following statement.

```
ALTER TABLE new_student
   MODIFY (phone NULL)
```
Table altered.

```
SQL> DESC new_student
```

Name	Null?	Type
FIRST_NAME		VARCHAR2(25)
LAST_NAME		VARCHAR2(25)
DESCRIPTION		VARCHAR2(50)
REGISTRATION_DATE		DATE
PHONE		VARCHAR2(15)
NUM_COURSES		NUMBER(3)
CREATED_BY	NOT NULL	VARCHAR2(30)
CREATED_DATE	NOT NULL	DATE

DEFINING A COLUMN AS NULL VERSUS NOT NULL

Deciding if a column should be NOT NULL or NULL leads into a discussion of nulls in general. A column allowing null values is subject to different interpretations. If you find a null value in a column it may mean many things: Perhaps the value is simply unknown, unspecified (user didn't pick any of the available choices), or perhaps not applicable. An encoded value can help distinguish between these differences.

Suppose you have a table holding client data containing a GENDER column. There simply aren't just two genders—male and female. What if your client is not an individual, but a corporation? Do you enter a null value and does a null value mean not applicable? What if the gender is unknown? You can come up with a lot of different other scenarios for a seemingly simple GENDER column.

Therefore, database designers use consistent values throughout to ensure that null values are interpreted correctly. For example, you can enter a value of "?" for unknown, a "N/A" for not applicable, "OTH" for other, or create a default value for unspecified.

Writing queries against data that contains null values poses another challenge. Unless you specifically use the IS NULL operator (or the NVL or COALESCE function) on a column, null values are ignored. You must always keep the possibility of null values in mind when dealing with data. Furthermore, if you apply a function to an indexed column or query using the IS NULL or IS NOT NULL operator, the query won't be able to take advantage of the index. Nulls can also have positive effects. An example of this is an order status flag column on your order table indicating if the order needs processing. If you enter a "YES" it indicates the order is incomplete; if you enter a "NO" it indicates that the order is processed. If instead you only allow "YES" or a null value, you can actually improve the performances of queries looking for orders to be processed, because you can build an index on this status flag column and only nonnull entries are stored in the index, which is rather small because there are few entries. Values are then retrieved quickly.

c) Alter the NEW_STUDENT table to change the REGISTRATION_DATE column from DATE datatype to VARCHAR2 datatype. What do you observe?

Answer: A column's datatype cannot be changed when there is data in the column.

```
ALTER TABLE new_student
  MODIFY (registration_date VARCHAR2(12))
MODIFY (registration_date VARCHAR2(12))
       *
ERROR at line 2:
ORA-01439: column to be modified must be empty to change
datatype
```

CHANGING A COLUMN'S DATATYPE

It is possible to change a column's datatype under two sets of circumstances. The first is when changing from one datatype to a compatible datatype, such as VARCHAR2 to CHAR. The next statement changes the REGISTRATION_DATE column from the DATE datatype to the compatible TIMESTAMP datatype. You can't change from a TIMESTAMP back to a DATE datatype unless the column is null.

```
ALTER TABLE new_student
  MODIFY (registration_date TIMESTAMP(3))
Table altered.
```

The second circumstance is when the column is empty, as in the following example. This statement sets the column to null to facilitate the change to a completely different datatype.

```
UPDATE new_student
   SET registration_date = NULL
1 row updated.

ALTER TABLE new_student
   MODIFY (registration_date VARCHAR2(12))
Table altered.
```

d) Alter the NEW_STUDENT table to create a primary key consisting of the FIRST_NAME and LAST_NAME columns.

Answer: The NEW_STUDENT table is altered to add a PRIMARY KEY constraint consisting of the two columns, separated by a comma inside the parentheses.

```
ALTER TABLE new_student
   ADD CONSTRAINT new_student_pk
      PRIMARY KEY(first_name, last_name)
Table altered.
```

The ADD PRIMARY KEY keywords are used to add the primary key constraint. (Actually, the choice of this primary key is not a very good one, aside from students having the same name, because a name entered in all uppercase is considered different than a name entered in mixed case.)

e) Alter the NEW_STUDENT table to change the length of the LAST_NAME column from 25 to 2. What do you observe?

Answer: The length of a column cannot be decreased when the values in the column are larger than the new column width.

```
ALTER TABLE new_student
   MODIFY (last_name VARCHAR2(2))
MODIFY (last_name VARCHAR2(2))
        *
ERROR at line 2:
ORA-01441: cannot decrease column length because some
value is too big
```

INCREASING AND DECREASING THE COLUMN WIDTH

For columns containing data, the length of the column can always be increased, as in the following example, but not decreased if existing data is larger than the new column width.

```
ALTER TABLE new_student
   MODIFY (last_name VARCHAR2(30))
Table altered.
```

f) Disable the primary key constraint on the NEW_STUDENT table and write an INSERT statement with the value "Joe Fisher" for the first and last name to prove it is successful. Then enable the constraint again and describe the result.

Answer: The value "Joe Fisher" exists twice in the FIRST_NAME and LAST_NAME columns, respectively, so the primary key constraint cannot be enabled on the table.

```
ALTER TABLE new_student
  DISABLE PRIMARY KEY
Table altered.

INSERT INTO new_student
   (first_name, last_name, phone, created_by, created_date)
VALUES
   ('Joe', 'Fisher', '718-555-1212', USER, SYSDATE)
1 row created.

ALTER TABLE new_student
  ENABLE PRIMARY KEY
ALTER TABLE new_student
*
ERROR at line 1:
ORA-02437: cannot enable (STUDENT.SYS_C001265) - primary
key violated
```

It is dangerous to disable a table's primary key because the integrity of the data may be violated. The only time you may want to disable constraints is when you are performing large data loads. Otherwise, if the constraints are enabled, each row must be evaluated to ensure it does not violate any of the constraints, thus slowing down the data-loading process. Therefore, for large data loads or updates, it's best to disable constraints temporarily, load the data, and re-enable the constraints. (Note you may want to keep some constraints enabled if they are associated with indexes that are used as part of an UPDATE's WHERE clause. This may decrease the data retrieval time of the to be updated rows.)

In Chapter 13, "The Data Dictionary and Advanced SQL*Plus Commands," you will learn how to write statements to enable or disable multiple constraints by creating a SQL statement that generates other SQL statements. The chapter also teaches you how to query the Oracle Data Dictionary for existing constraints and their respective status, such as enabled or disabled.

g) Add the column STUDY_DURATION of datatype INTERVAL YEAR TO MONTH and the column ALUMNI_JOIN_DATE with a datatype of TIMESTAMP WITH TIME ZONE and a six-digit precision to the NEW_STUDENT table.

Answer: The ALTER TABLE statement adds both columns simultaneously. The six-digit fractional seconds are the default for the TIMESTAMP WITH TIME ZONE datatype and do not need to be specified explicitly.

```
ALTER TABLE new_student
   ADD (study_months INTERVAL YEAR TO MONTH,
        alumni_join_date TIMESTAMP (6) WITH TIME ZONE)
```
Table altered.

h) Drop the foreign key constraint FORMER_STUDENT_ZIPCODE_FK on the FORMER_STUDENT table and change it to an ON DELETE SET NULL foreign key constraint. Test the behavior by inserting a new zip code in the ZIPCODE table and creating a new student row with this new zip code, and then deleting the same zip code from the ZIPCODE table. Query the FORMER_STUDENT table to see the effect.

**LAB
11.2**

Answer: The DROP CONSTRAINT clause removes the constraint and you can then add the foreign key with the ON DELETE SET NULL constraint instead.

```
ALTER TABLE former_student
   DROP CONSTRAINT former_student_zipcode_fk
```
Table altered.

```
ALTER TABLE former_student
   ADD CONSTRAINT former_student_zipcode_fk
      FOREIGN KEY(zip)
      REFERENCES zipcode (ZIP) ON DELETE SET NULL
```
Table altered.

Insert a new zip code into the ZIPCODE table with the value of 90210.

```
INSERT INTO zipcode
   (zip, city, state, created_by,
    created_date, modified_by, modified_date)
VALUES
   ('90210','Hollywood', 'CA', 'Alice',
    sysdate, 'Alice', sysdate);
```
1 row created.

To demonstrate the functionality, insert a zip code into the FORMER_STUDENT table.

```
INSERT INTO former_student
   (studid, first_nm, last_nm, enrolled, zip)
VALUES
   (109, 'Alice', 'Rischert', 3, '90210')
```
1 row created.

Now delete the zip code 90210 from the ZIPCODE table.

```
DELETE FROM zipcode
 WHERE zip = '90210'
1 row deleted.
```

A query against the FORMER_STUDENT table reveals the effect; the column ZIP is updated to a null value. Note that the ZIP column must permit entry of null values.

```
SELECT studid, zip
  FROM former_student
 WHERE studid = 109
    STUDID ZIP
---------- -----
       109

1 row selected.
```

If you attempt to delete a row that exists not just in the NEW_STUDENT table, but perhaps also in the STUDENT or INSTRUCTOR table, such as the value 10025, you will be prevented from the DELETE operation because these other tables are referencing the ZIPCODE with a DELETE restrict. In this case, it indicates that the INSTRUCTOR table is referencing this value as well and that orphan rows are not allowed.

```
DELETE FROM zipcode
 WHERE zip = '10025'
DELETE FROM zipcode
*
ERROR at line 1:
ORA-02292: integrity constraint (STUDENT.INST_ZIP_FK)
violated - child record found
```

Note, if your schema name is not STUDENT, but a different account name, the constraint name error will be prefixed with the respective name.

The other foreign key alternatives to the ON DELETE SET NULL options are the two statements listed next. The first would add the DELETE RESTRICT default instead, and the second shows the ON DELETE CASCADE constraint alternative.

```
ALTER TABLE former_student
  ADD CONSTRAINT former_student_zipcode_fk
      FOREIGN KEY(zip)
      REFERENCES zipcode (ZIP)

ALTER TABLE former_student
  ADD CONSTRAINT former_student_zipcode_fk
      FOREIGN KEY(zip)
      REFERENCES zipcode (ZIP) ON DELETE CASCADE
```

The foreign key constraint also enforces the relationship between the tables with respect to inserts and updates. Only values found in the parent table are allowed. Null values are allowed if the foreign key column is defined as NULL.

i) Drop all the tables created throughout the labs. The table names are: STU-DENT_CANDIDATE, NEW_STUDENT, COURSE2, EXTINCT_ANIMAL, and FORMER_STUDENT.

Answer: Use the DROP TABLE command to remove the tables from the schema.

```
DROP TABLE student_candidate
Table dropped.

DROP TABLE new_student
Table dropped.

DROP TABLE course2
Table dropped.

DROP TABLE extinct_animal
Table dropped.

DROP TABLE former_student
Table dropped.
```

LAB 11.2 SELF-REVIEW QUESTIONS

In order to test your progress, you should be able to answer the following questions.

1) The following ALTER TABLE statement contains an error.

```
ALTER TABLE new_student
   DROP CONSTRAINT PRIMARY_KEY
```

a) _____ True
b) _____ False

2) The ADD and MODIFY keywords can be used interchangeably in an ALTER TABLE statement.

a) _____ True
b) _____ False

3) You can add a NOT NULL constraint to a column providing all the rows of the column contain data.

a) _____ True
b) _____ False

4) A constraint must have a name in order for it to be disabled.

    a) _____ True

    b) _____ False

5) A column's datatype can be changed only when the column contains no data.

    a) _____ True

    b) _____ False

Answers appear in Appendix A, Section 11.2.

CHAPTER 11

TEST YOUR THINKING

The projects in this section are meant to have you utilize all of the skills that you have acquired throughout this chapter. The answers to these projects can be found at the companion Web site to this book, located at: *http://authors.phptr.com/rischert3e*. Visit the Web site periodically to share and discuss your answers.

1) Create a table called TEMP_STUDENT with the following columns and constraints: a column STUDID for student ID that is NOT NULL and is the primary key, a column FIRST_NAME for student first name, a column LAST_NAME for student last name, a column ZIP that is a foreign key to the ZIP column in the ZIPCODE table, and a column REGISTRATION_DATE that is NOT NULL and has a CHECK constraint to restrict the registration date to dates after January 1, 2000.

2) Write an INSERT statement violating one of the constraints for the TEMP_STUDENT table you just created. Write another INSERT statement that succeeds when executed and commit your work.

3) Alter the TEMP_STUDENT table to add two more columns called EMPLOYER and EMPLOYER_ZIP. The EMPLOYER_ZIP column should have a foreign key constraint referencing the ZIP column of the ZIPCODE table. Update the EMPLOYER column and alter the table once again to make the employer column NOT NULL. Drop the TEMP_STUDENT table once you are done with the exercise.

VIEWS, INDEXES, AND SEQUENCES

This chapter covers three different yet very important database objects: views, indexes, and sequences.

Views are significant in a database because they provide row-level and column-level security to the data. They allow you to look at the data differently and/or display only specific information to the user. Views are also useful to simplify the writing of queries for end users because they can hide the complexities of joins and conditional statements.

Indexes are required for good performance of any database. A well-thought-out indexing strategy entails the careful placement of indexes on relevant columns. You will gain an understanding about the advantages and trade-offs when using indexes on tables.

Sequences generate unique values and are used mainly for creating primary key values. You will learn how to create and use sequences.

L A B   1 2 . 1

CREATING AND MODIFYING VIEWS

L A B   O B J E C T I V E S

After this lab, you will be able to:

✔ Create, Alter, and Drop Views
✔ Understand the Data Manipulation Rules for Views

The view is a virtual table consisting of columns and rows, but it is only the SELECT statement that is stored, not a physical table with data. A view's SELECT query may reference one or multiple tables. These tables are called *base tables*. The base tables are typically actual tables or other views.

PURPOSE OF VIEWS

Views simplify the writing of queries. You can query a single view instead of writing a complicated SQL statement joining many tables. The complexity of the underlying SQL statement is hidden from the user and contained only in the view.

Views are useful for security reasons because they can hide data. The data retrieved from the view can show only certain columns by listing those columns in the SELECT list of the query. You can also restrict the view to display specific rows with the WHERE clause of the query.

In a view you can give a column a different name from the one in the base table. Views may be used to isolate an application from a change in the definition of the base tables. Suppose a program refers to a column and now the column is renamed. Rather than changing the program, the view can continue to refer to the data with the old column name.

A view looks just like any other table, you may describe and query the view and also issue INSERT, UPDATE, and DELETE statements to a certain extent as you will see when performing the exercises in this lab.

CREATING A VIEW

The simplified syntax for creating a view is as follows:

```
CREATE [OR REPLACE] [FORCE|NOFORCE] VIEW viewname
[(column_alias[, column_alias]...)]
AS query
[WITH CHECK OPTION|WITH READ ONLY [CONSTRAINT constraintname]]
```

The next statements create a view called COURSE_NO_COST and describe the new view.

```
CREATE OR REPLACE VIEW course_no_cost AS
SELECT course_no, description, prerequisite
  FROM course
View created.
```

```
SQL> DESC course_no_cost
```

Name	Null?	Type
COURSE_NO	NOT NULL	NUMBER(8)
DESCRIPTION	NOT NULL	VARCHAR2(50)
PREREQUISITE		NUMBER(8)

The COURSE_NO_COST view hides a number of columns that exist in the COURSE table. You do not see the COST column or the CREATED_DATE, CRE-ATED_BY, MODIFIED_DATE, and MODIFIED_BY columns. The main purpose of this view is security. You can grant access just to the view COURSE_NO_COST instead of to the COURSE table itself. For more information on granting access privileges to database objects, see Chapter 14, "Security."

USING COLUMN ALIASES

The following statement demonstrates a view with column names different from the column names in the base tables. Here the view named STUD_ENROLL shows a listing of the STUDENT_ID, the last name of the student in capital letters, and the number of classes the student is enrolled in. The column STUDENT_ID from the STUDENT table is renamed in the view to STUD_ID using a column alias. When a column contains an expression such as a function, a column alias is required. The two expressions in the STUD_ENROLL view, namely the student last name in caps and the count of classes enrolled, are therefore aliased.

```
CREATE OR REPLACE VIEW stud_enroll AS
SELECT s.student_id stud_id,
       UPPER(s.last_name) last_name,
       COUNT(*) num_enrolled
  FROM student s, enrollment e
 WHERE s.student_id = e.student_id
 GROUP BY s.student_id, UPPER(s.last_name)
```

The OR REPLACE keywords are useful in case the view already exists. It allows you to replace the view with a different SELECT statement without having to drop the view first. This also means you do not have to regrant privileges to the view; the rights to the view are retained by those who have already been granted access privileges.

The next example shows an alternate SQL statement for naming columns in a view, whereby the view's columns are listed in parentheses after the view name.

```
CREATE OR REPLACE VIEW stud_enroll
       (stud_id, last_name, num_enrolled) AS
SELECT s.student_id,
       UPPER(s.last_name),
       COUNT(*)
  FROM student s, enrollment e
 WHERE s.student_id = e.student_id
 GROUP BY s.student_id, UPPER(s.last_name)
```

ALTERING A VIEW

You use the ALTER VIEW command to recompile an invalid view after altering one of the base tables to ensure that the view continues to be valid. The syntax of the ALTER VIEW statement is:

```
ALTER VIEW viewname COMPILE
```

The ALTER VIEW command allows for additional syntax options not mentioned. These options let you create primary or unique constraints on views. However, these constraints are not enforced, do not maintain data integrity, and an index is never built, because they can only be created in DISABLE NOVALIDATE mode. These constraint types are primarily useful with *materialized views,* a popular data warehousing feature that allows you to physically store pre-aggregated results and/or joins for speedy access. Unlike the views discussed in this chapter, materialized views result in physical data stored in tables.

RENAMING A VIEW

The RENAME command allows you to change the name of a view.

```
RENAME stud_enroll TO stud_enroll2
```

All underlying constraints and granted privileges remain intact. However, any objects that use this view (perhaps another view or a PL/SQL procedure, package, or function) become invalid and need to be compiled.

DROPPING A VIEW

To drop a view you use the DROP VIEW command. The next statement drops the STUD_ENROLL2 view.

```
DROP VIEW stud_enroll2
View dropped.
```

LAB 12.1 EXERCISES

12.1.1 CREATE, ALTER, AND DROP VIEWS

a) Create a view called LONG_DISTANCE_STUDENT with all the columns in the STUDENT table plus the CITY and STATE columns from the ZIPCODE table. Exclude students from New York, New Jersey, and Connecticut.

b) Create a view named CHEAP_COURSE showing all columns of the COURSE table where the course cost is 1095 or less.

c) Issue the following INSERT statement. What do you observe when you query the CHEAP_COURSE view?

```
INSERT INTO cheap_course
  (course_no, description, cost,
  created_by, created_date, modified_by,
  modified_date)
VALUES
  (900, 'Expensive', 2000,
  'ME', SYSDATE, 'ME', SYSDATE)
```

d) Drop the views named LONG_DISTANCE_STUDENT and CHEAP_COURSE.

e) Using the following statement, create a table called TEST_TAB and build a view over it. Then, add a column to the table and

DESCRIBE the view. What do you observe? Drop the table and view after you complete the exercise.

```
CREATE TABLE test_tab
  (col1 NUMBER)
```

12.1.2 UNDERSTAND THE DATA MANIPULATION RULES FOR VIEWS

a) Create a view called BUSY_STUDENT based on the following query. Update the number of enrollments for STUDENT_ID 124 to five through the BUSY_STUDENT view. Record your observation.

```
SELECT student_id, COUNT(*)
  FROM enrollment
 GROUP BY student_id
HAVING COUNT(*) > 2
```

b) Create a view listing the addresses of students. Include the columns STUDENT_ID, FIRST_NAME, LAST_NAME, STREET_ADDRESS, CITY, STATE, and ZIP. Using the view, update the last name of STUDENT_ID 237 from Frost to O'Brien. Then, update the state for the student from NJ to CT. What do you notice for the statements you issue?

LAB 12.1 EXERCISE ANSWERS

12.1.1 ANSWERS

a) Create a view called LONG_DISTANCE_STUDENT with all the columns in the STUDENT table plus the CITY and STATE columns from the ZIPCODE table. Exclude students from New York, New Jersey, and Connecticut.

Answer: To select all columns from the STUDENT table, use the wildcard symbol. For the columns CITY and STATE in the view, join to the ZIPCODE table. With this view definition you see only records where the state is not equal to New York, Connecticut, or New Jersey.

```
CREATE OR REPLACE VIEW long_distance_student AS
SELECT s.*, z.city, z.state
  FROM student s, zipcode z
 WHERE s.zip = z.zip
   AND state NOT IN ('NJ','NY','CT')
View created.
```

You can issue a query against the view or DESCRIBE the view. As you observe, you can restrict the columns and/or the rows of the view.

```
SELECT state, first_name, last_name
  FROM long_distance_student
ST FIRST_NAME          LAST_NAME
-------------------- -----------
MA James E.            Norman
MA George              Kocka
...
OH Phil                Gilloon
MI Roger               Snow

10 rows selected.
```

You might want to validate the view by querying for students living in New Jersey.

```
SELECT *
  FROM long_distance_student
 WHERE state = 'NJ'

no rows selected
```

As you see, there are none because the view's defining query excludes these records.

b) Create a view named CHEAP_COURSE showing all columns of the COURSE table where the course cost is 1095 or less.

Answer: The view restricts the rows to courses with a cost of 1095 or less.

```
CREATE OR REPLACE VIEW cheap_course AS
SELECT *
  FROM course
 WHERE cost <= 1095
```

c) Issue the following INSERT statement. What do you observe when you query the CHEAP_COURSE view?

```
INSERT INTO cheap_course
  (course_no, description, cost,
   created_by, created_date, modified_by,
   modified_date)
VALUES
  (900, 'Expensive', 2000,
   'ME', SYSDATE, 'ME', SYSDATE)
```

Answer: You can insert records through the view, violating the view's defining query condition.

A cost of 2000 is successfully inserted into the COURSE table through the view, even though this is higher than 1095, which is the defining condition of the view.

You can query the CHEAP_VIEW to see if the record is there. The course was successfully inserted in the underlying COURSE base table, but it does not satisfy the view's definition and is not displayed.

```
SELECT course_no, cost
  FROM cheap_course
COURSE_NO      COST
---------  ---------
      135       1095
      230       1095
      240       1095

3 rows selected.
```

A view's WHERE clause works for any query, but not for DML statements. The course number 900 is not visible through the CHEAP_COURSE view, but insert, update, or delete operations are permitted despite the conflicting WHERE condition. To change this security-defying behavior, create the view with the WITH CHECK OPTION constraint. But first undo the INSERT statement with the ROLLBACK command, because any subsequent DDL command, such as the creation of a view, automatically commits the record.

```
ROLLBACK
Rollback complete.

CREATE OR REPLACE VIEW cheap_course AS
SELECT *
  FROM course
 WHERE cost <= 1095
WITH CHECK OPTION CONSTRAINT check_cost
View created.
```

It is a good habit to name constraints. You understand the benefit of well-named constraints when you query the Oracle data dictionary or when you violate constraints with data manipulation statements.

The following error message appears when inserts, updates, and deletes issued against a view violate the view's defining query. The previous INSERT statement would now be rejected with the following error message.

ORA-01402: view WITH CHECK OPTION where-clause violation

What happens if you attempt to insert a record with a value of NULL for the course cost? Again, Oracle rejects the row because the condition is not satisfied. The NULL value is not less than or equal to 1095.

VIEW CONSTRAINTS

You can enforce constraints in a variety of ways: The underlying base tables automatically ensure data integrity or you can use the WITH CHECK OPTION. You can also avoid any data manipulation on the view through the READ ONLY option. The following statement creates a read-only view named COURSE_V.

```
CREATE OR REPLACE VIEW course_v AS
SELECT course_no, description,
       created_by, created_date,
       modified_by, modified_date
  FROM course
  WITH READ ONLY CONSTRAINT course_v_read_check
View created.
```

d) Drop the views named LONG_DISTANCE_STUDENT and CHEAP_COURSE.

Answer: Just like other operations on data objects, the DROP keyword removes a database object from the database.

```
DROP VIEW long_distance_student
View dropped.

DROP VIEW cheap_course
View dropped.
```

 Remember, any DDL operation, such as the creation of a view, cannot be rolled back, and any prior DML operations, such as inserts, updates, and deletes, are automatically committed.

e) Using the following statement, create a table called TEST_TAB and build a view over it. Then, add a column to the table and DESCRIBE the view. What do you observe? Drop the table and view after you complete the exercise.

```
CREATE TABLE test_tab
  (col1 NUMBER)
```

Answer: The view does not show the newly added column.

```
CREATE OR REPLACE VIEW test_tab_view AS
SELECT *
  FROM test_tab
View created.
```

After the table creation, the view is created. Here, the name TEST_TAB_VIEW is used. Then add an additional column to the TEST_TAB table; here it is named col2.

```
ALTER TABLE test_tab
  ADD (col2 NUMBER)
Table altered.
```

A subsequently issued DESCRIBE of the view reveals an interesting fact.

```
SQL> DESC test_tab_view
 Name                                      Null?    Type
 ----------------------------------------- -------- ------
 COL1                                                NUMBER
```

Where is the new column that was added? Whenever a view is created with the wildcard (*) character, Oracle stores the individual column names in the definition of the view. A query against the data dictionary table USER_VIEWS shows how Oracle stores the view's definition at the time of the view creation; as you can see only the COL1 column is defined. Note, the column is also listed with enclosed quotation marks, just in case of mixed case column names.

```
SELECT text
  FROM user_views
 WHERE view_name = 'TEST_TAB_VIEW'
TEXT
------------------------------------------
SELECT "COL1"
  FROM test_tab

1 row selected.
```

Altering the table by adding or dropping columns invalidates the view. In this case, the view is automatically recompiled the next time you access the view. You need to reissue the creation of the view statement for the view to include the new column.

```
CREATE OR REPLACE VIEW test_tab_view AS
SELECT *
  FROM test_tab
View created.
```

Now, when a DESCRIBE is issued on the view, the new column is included.

```
SQL> DESC test_tab_view
 Name                                      Null?    Type
 ----------------------------------------- -------- ------
 COL1                                                NUMBER
 COL2                                                NUMBER
```

COMPILE A VIEW

You can use the ALTER VIEW command to define, modify, or drop view constraints. Also the command ALTER VIEW viewname COMPILE command explicitly compiles the view to make sure it is valid. The following command compiles the view successfully:

```
ALTER VIEW test_tab_view COMPILE
View altered.
```

Drop the no-longer-needed table and notice the effect on the view.

```
DROP TABLE test_tab
Table dropped.
```

```
ALTER VIEW test_tab_view COMPILE
Warning: View altered with compilation errors.
```

REFERENCING AN INVALID VIEW

When you access an invalid view, Oracle returns an error message to the user indicating that the view exists. However, it is currently invalid because the underlying objects were altered or dropped. Any subsequent attempt to access the view or to compile it returns an error.

```
SELECT *
  FROM test_tab_view
ERROR at line 2:
ORA-04063: view "STUDENT.TEST_TAB_VIEW" has errors
```

Drop the view to restore the STUDENT schema to its previous state.

```
DROP VIEW test_tab_view
View dropped.
```

FORCING THE CREATION OF A VIEW

If the view's base tables do not exist or the creator of the view doesn't have privileges to access the view, the creation of the view will fail. The next example shows the creation of the view named TEST based on a nonexistent SALES table.

```
CREATE VIEW test AS
SELECT *
  FROM sales
ERROR at line 3:
ORA-00942: table or view does not exist
```

If you want to create the view despite its being invalid you can create it with the FORCE option; the default on the CREATE VIEW syntax is NOFORCE. This FORCE option is useful if you need to create the view and you add the referenced table later or you expect to obtain the necessary privileges to the referenced object shortly.

```
CREATE FORCE VIEW test AS
SELECT *
  FROM sales
Warning: View created with compilation errors.
```

The view, though invalid, now exists in the database.

12.1.2 ANSWERS

a) Create a view called BUSY_STUDENT based on the following query. Update the number of enrollments for STUDENT_ID 124 to five through the BUSY_STUDENT view. Record your observation.

```
SELECT student_id, COUNT(*)
  FROM enrollment
 GROUP BY student_id
HAVING COUNT(*) > 2
```

Answer: The UPDATE operation fails. Data manipulation operations on a view impose a number of restrictions.

To create the view, you need to give the COUNT(*) expression a column alias; otherwise, this error occurs:

```
ERROR at line 2:
ORA-00998: must name this expression with a column alias

CREATE OR REPLACE VIEW busy_student AS
SELECT student_id, COUNT(*) enroll_num
  FROM enrollment
 GROUP BY student_id
HAVING COUNT(*) > 2
View created.
```

You can now attempt to update the ENROLLMENT table using the view with the following UPDATE statement.

```
UPDATE busy_student
   SET enroll_num = 5
 WHERE student_id = 124
ORA-01732: data manipulation operation not legal on this view
```

DATA MANIPULATION RULES ON VIEWS

For a view to be updatable, it needs to conform to a number of rules: The view may not contain:

> An expression (e.g., TO_DATE(enroll_date))
>
> A aggregate function
>
> A set operator such as UNION, UNION ALL, INTERSECT, MINUS
>
> The DISTINCT keyword
>
> The GROUP BY clause
>
> The ORDER BY clause

Special rules apply to views containing join conditions, as you see in the next exercise.

b) Create a view listing the addresses of students. Include the columns STUDENT_ID, FIRST_NAME, LAST_NAME, STREET_ADDRESS, CITY, STATE, and ZIP. Using the view, update the last name of STUDENT_ID 237 from Frost to O'Brien. Then, update the state for the student from NJ to CT. What do you notice for the statements you issue?

Answer: Not all updates to views containing joins are allowed. The update of the last name is successful, but not the update of the STATE column.

```
CREATE OR REPLACE VIEW student_address AS
SELECT student_id, first_name, last_name,
       street_address, city, state, s.zip szip,
       z.zip zzip
  FROM student s, zipcode z
 WHERE s.zip=z.zip
View created.
```

Now update the last name to O'Brien with the following statement. To indicate a single quote, prefix the single quote with another single quote.

```
UPDATE student_address
   SET last_name = 'O''Brien'
 WHERE student_id = 237
1 row updated.
```

Because the test was successful, rollback the UPDATE to retain the current data in the table.

```
ROLLBACK
Rollback complete.
```

As you can see, you are able to update the data in the underlying base table STU-DENT. Now update the column STATE in the base table ZIPCODE through the STUDENT_ADDRESS view.

```
UPDATE student_address
   SET state = 'CT'
 WHERE student_id = 237
ORA-01779: cannot modify a column which maps to a nonkey-
preserved table
```

JOIN VIEWS AND DATA MANIPULATION

The understanding of a key-preserved table is essential to understanding the restrictions on join views. A table is considered key-preserved if every key of the table can also be a key of the result of the join. In this case, the STUDENT table is the key-preserved or child table.

For a join view to be updatable, the DML operation may affect only the key-preserved table (also known as the child base table) and the child's primary key must be included in the view's definition. In this case, the child table is the STU-DENT table and the primary key is the STUDENT_ID.

If you are in doubt regarding which table is the key-preserved table, query the Oracle data dictionary table USER_UPDATABLE_COLUMNS. The result shows you which columns are updatable. Also, note the STUDENT table's ZIP column is updatable, but not the ZIP column from the ZIPCODE table. Only the STUDENT table's ZIP column (aliased as SZIP) is considered key-preserved.

```
SELECT column_name, updatable
  FROM user_updatable_columns
 WHERE table_name = 'STUDENT_ADDRESS'
```

COLUMN_NAME	UPD
STUDENT_ID	YES
FIRST_NAME	YES
LAST_NAME	YES
STREET_ADDRESS	YES
CITY	NO
STATE	NO
SZIP	YES
ZZIP	NO

```
8 rows selected.
```

The data dictionary is covered in greater detail in Chapter 13, "The Data Dictionary and Advanced SQL*Plus Commands." If you need to manipulate key-preserved data through a view, you overcome this limitation with an INSTEAD OF trigger. This type of trigger works only against views and allows you to manipulate data based on the code within the trigger. The INSTEAD OF trigger fires in place of your issued INSERT, UPDATE, or DELETE command. For example, if you execute an INSERT command against the view, the statement may actually perform an UPDATE instead. The view's associated INSTEAD OF trigger code can perform any type of data manipulation against one or multiple tables. These powerful INSTEAD OF triggers are created using the Oracle PL/SQL language and covered in great detail in *Oracle PL/SQL by Example* by Benjamin Rosenzweig and Elena Silvestrova (Prentice Hall, 2004).

LAB 12.1

LAB 12.1 SELF-REVIEW QUESTIONS

In order to test your progress, you should be able to answer the following questions.

1) Views are useful for security, for simplifying the writing of queries, and for hiding data complexity.

a) _____ True
b) _____ False

2) Under what circumstances can views become invalid? Check all that apply.

a) _____ The datatype of a column changes.
b) _____ The underlying table(s) are dropped.
c) _____ Views never become invalid, they automatically recompile.

3) Identify the error in the following view definition.

```
CREATE OR REPLACE VIEW my_student
       (studid, slname, szip) AS
SELECT student_id, last_name, zip
  FROM student
 WHERE student_id BETWEEN 100 AND 200
```

a) _____ Line 1
b) _____ Line 2
c) _____ Line 4
d) _____ Line 1, 2, 4
e) _____ No error

4) An UPDATE to the STATE column in the ZIPCODE table is permitted using the following view.

```
CREATE OR REPLACE VIEW my_zipcode AS
SELECT zip, city, state, created_by,
       created_date, modified_by,
```

```
        TO_CHAR(modified_date, 'DD-MON-YYYY') modified_date
FROM zipcode
```

a) _____ True
b) _____ False

5) Views provide security by restricting access to specific rows and/or columns of a table.

a) _____ True
b) _____ False

6) A column in a view may have a different name than in the base table.

a) _____ True
b) _____ False

Answers appear in Appendix A, Section 12.1.

LAB 12.2

INDEXES

LAB OBJECTIVES

After this lab, you will be able to:
- ✔ Create B-Tree Indexes
- ✔ Understand When Indexes Are Useful

To achieve good performance for data retrieval and data manipulation statements, you need to understand Oracle's use of indexes. Just like the index in the back of a book, Oracle uses indexes to look up data quickly. If the appropriate index does not exist on a table, Oracle needs to examine every row. This is called a *full table scan*.

If the index speeds up query time, you may wonder why not just index every column in the table? When you retrieve a large number of rows in a table, it may be more efficient to read the entire table rather than look up the values from the index. It also takes a significant amount of time and storage space to build and maintain an index. For each DML statement that changes a value in an indexed column, the index needs to be maintained.

THE B-TREE INDEX

In this book, you will perform exercises centered on Oracle's most popular index storage structure—the B-tree index. The merits and uses of another type of index, the bitmapped index, will be discussed briefly at the end of the lab; this type of index can only be created in Oracle's Enterprise Server Edition.

The B-tree (balanced tree) index is by far the most common type of index. It provides excellent performance in circumstances where there are many distinct values on a column or columns. If you have several low-selectivity columns, you can also consider combining them into one *composite index*, also called a *concatenated index*. B-tree indexes are best for exact match and range searches against both small and very large tables.

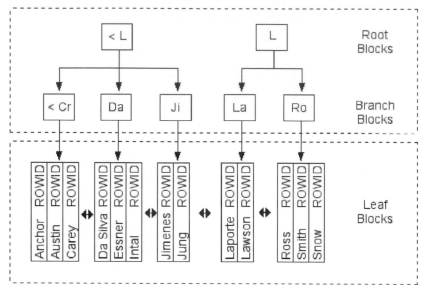

Figure 12.1 ■ B-tree Index.

Figure 12.1 illustrates the structure of a B-tree index. It looks like an inverted tree and consists of two types of blocks: *Root/branch blocks* and *leaf blocks*. Root or branch blocks are used for storing the key together with a pointer to the child block containing the key; leaf blocks store the key values along with the ROWID, which is the physical storage location for the data in the table.

STEPS PERFORMED TO SEARCH FOR VALUES IN A B-TREE INDEX

The first step is to start with the root block of the index. The searched value is compared with the root block keys. For example, if you are looking for the student with the last name of Essner, you must go down the root block of <L. This block points to the next leaf blocks, which are greater than Da and less than Ji; going down on this leaf block, you find the value Essner and the associated ROWID, the physical address of the row. A leaf block also contains links to the next and previous leaf blocks, which allow scanning the index for ranges.

THE ROWID PSEUDOCOLUMN

Every row in the database has a unique address called the ROWID. The address determines exactly where the row is located. Indexes store the ROWID to retrieve rows quickly. The ROWID consists of several components: the data object number, the number of the data block, the number of rows within the data block, and the data file number. The data block and the data file define the physical storage characteristics of data within the individual Oracle database.

```
SELECT ROWID, student_id, last_name
  FROM student
 WHERE student_id = 123
ROWID                STUDENT_ID LAST_NAME
------------------   --------------------
AAADA1AABAAARAIAAD          123 Radicola

1 row selected.
```

 A ROWID is always unique. It is the fastest way to access a row.

You can use the ROWID in UPDATE statements to directly access the row, rather than searching the index. For example, because the ROWID of the student named Radicola is already selected as part of the query, a subsequent update to the name of the student can find the row in the table immediately without having to scan the entire table or use an index.

```
UPDATE student
   SET last_name = 'Radicolament'
 WHERE student_id = 123
   AND ROWID = 'AAADA1AABAAARAIAAD'
   AND last_name = 'Radicola'
```

You cannot update the ROWID, but the ROWID may change if you first delete the row and then reinsert the row since it may now be placed in another physical location. Never use the ROWID as a table's primary key because it is subject to change.

As you learned in Chapter 10, "Insert, Update, and Delete," it is always good practice to include the old values in the WHERE clause of the UPDATE to ensure that another session or user has not changed the name in the meantime.

A pseudocolumn is not an actual column, but it acts like one. One of the pseudocolumns you have already used is the ROWNUM, which restricts the number of rows a query returns. You will learn about other Oracle pseudocolumns, namely NEXTVAL and CURRVAL, shortly.

CREATE AN INDEX

You create an index using the following general syntax:

```
CREATE [UNIQUE|BITMAPPED] INDEX indexname
  ON tablename
  (column|col_expression [,column|col_expression]...)
  [PCTFREE integer]
```

```
[TABLESPACE tablespacename|DEFAULT]
[STORAGE ([INITIAL integer [K|M]]
          [NEXT integer [K|M]]])]
[ONLINE]
```

The following statement creates an index named SECT_LOCATION_I on the LOCATION column of the SECTION table.

```
CREATE INDEX sect_location_i
  ON section(location)
```
Index created.

A subsequent query to find all the classes held in LOCATION L206 can take advantage of this index. Oracle looks up the value in the index. This retrieves the row faster than reading every row, particularly if the table has many records.

```
SELECT course_no, section_no, start_date_time, location
  FROM section
 WHERE location = 'L206'
```
COURSE_NO SECTION_NO START_DAT LOCATION
```
--------- ---------- --------- --------
      120          2 24-JUL-03 L206
```

1 row selected.

COMPOSITE INDEXES

Sometimes it is useful to build indexes based on multiple columns; this type of index is called a *composite index* or *concatenated index*. For example, you can create a composite index on two columns with a low selectivity (i.e., not many distinct values). The combination of these low selectivity values makes the composite index more selective. If you compare the query access time of a composite index to that of two individual single-column indexes, the composite index offers better performance.

The next statement creates a composite index on the columns DESCRIPTION and COST. The first column of the index, also called the leading edge of the index, is the DESCRIPTION column; the second column of the index is the COST column.

```
CREATE INDEX course_description_cost_i
  ON course (description, cost)
```

Columns that are used together frequently in a WHERE clause and combined with the AND logical operator are often good candidates for a composite index, particularly if their combined selectivity is high. The order of the individual columns in the index can affect query performance. Choose the column you use most frequently in the WHERE clause first. If both columns are accessed with equal frequency, then choose the column with the highest selectivity. In this example, the COST column has very few distinct values and is therefore considered a low-selectivity column; access against an index with a low-selectivity column as the leading edge requires more index blocks reads and is therefore less desirable.

There are some caveats about composite indexes you must know about when writing queries. When executed in Oracle versions prior to 9*i*, a query such as the following using the COST column in the WHERE clause cannot use the COURSE_DESCRIPTION_COST_I index, because it's not the leading edge of the index. However, Oracle can use a technique called *skip scan*, which may use the index nonetheless. As you work your way through this lab, you will learn more about this feature.

```
SELECT course_no, description, cost
  FROM course
 WHERE cost = 1095
```

To find out what columns of a table are indexed and the order of the columns in an index, you can query the data dictionary views USER_INDEXES and USER_IND_COLUMNS.

NULLS AND INDEXES

NULL values are not stored in a B-tree index, unless it is a composite index where at least the first column of the index contains a value. The following query does not make use of the single-column index on the FIRST_NAME column.

```
SELECT student_id, first_name
  FROM student
 WHERE first_name IS NULL
```

FUNCTIONS AND INDEXES

Even when you create an index on one or multiple columns of a table, Oracle may not be able to use it. In the next scenario assume that the LAST_NAME column of the STUDENT table is indexed. The following SQL query applies the UPPER function on the LAST_NAME column. You may use this WHERE clause expression if you don't know how the last name is stored in the column—it may be stored with the first initial in uppercase, all uppercase, or perhaps in mixed case. This query will not take advantage of the index because the column is modified by a function.

```
SELECT student_id, last name, first_name
  FROM student
 WHERE UPPER(last_name) = 'SMITH'
```

You can avoid this behavior by creating a function-based index instead, as in the following example. This allows for case-insensitive searches on the LAST_NAME column.

```
CREATE INDEX stud_last_name_i
    ON student(UPPER(last_name))
```

INDEXES AND TABLESPACES

To optimize performance, it is important that you separate indexes from data by placing them in separate tablespaces residing on different physical devices. This significantly improves the performance of your queries. Use the following statement to create an index named SECT_LOCATION_I on a tablespace called INDEX_TX with an initial size of 500 kilobytes and 100 kilobytes in size for each subsequent extent.

```
CREATE INDEX sect_location_i
    ON section(location)
    TABLESPACE index_tx
    STORAGE (INITIAL 500K NEXT 100K)
```

The storage clause of indexes is similar to the storage clause discussed in Chapter 11, "Create, Alter, and Drop Tables."; however, the PCTUSED parameter is not applicable for indexes. If you want to see a list of tablespaces accessible to you, query the data dictionary view USER_TABLESPACES.

UNIQUE INDEX VERSUS UNIQUE CONSTRAINT

At times you may want to enforce a unique combination of the values in a table (e.g., the COURSE_NO and SECTION_NO columns of the SECTION table). You can create a unique constraint on the table that automatically creates a unique index:

```
ALTER TABLE section
    ADD CONSTRAINT sect_sect2_uk UNIQUE
    (section_no, course_no)
    USING INDEX
    TABLESPACE index_tx
    STORAGE (INITIAL 12K NEXT 12K)
```

Or you can use the CREATE UNIQUE INDEX command:

```
CREATE UNIQUE INDEX section_sect_course_no_i
    ON section (section_no, course_no)
    TABLESPACE index_tx
    STORAGE (INITIAL 12K NEXT 12K)
```

Oracle prefers if you use the unique constraint syntax for future compatibility.

CREATING AN INDEX ASSOCIATED WITH A CONSTRAINT

When creating a primary key constraint or a unique constraint, Oracle creates the index automatically unless a suitable index already exists. In Chapter 11, "Create, Alter, and Drop Tables," you learned about various syntax options you can use.

The index NEW_TERM_PK is created as part of the CREATE TABLE statement and is associated with the primary key constraint.

```
CREATE TABLE new_term
   (term_no NUMBER(8) NOT NULL PRIMARY KEY USING INDEX
      (CREATE INDEX new_term_pk ON new_term(term_no)
         STORAGE (INITIAL 100 K NEXT 100K)),
   season_tx VARCHAR2(20),
   sequence_no NUMBER(3))
```

The advantage of using this syntax is that you can create an index in the same statement of the CREATE TABLE command whereby you have control over the storage characteristics of the index. It doesn't require two separate statements: a CREATE TABLE statement and an ALTER TABLE statement that adds the constraint and the index plus storage clause.

If you already have an existing index and you want to associate a constraint with it you can use a statement similar to the following. It assumes an existing index called SEMESTER_SEMESTER_ID_I based on the SEMESTER_ID column.

```
ALTER TABLE semester
   ADD CONSTRAINT semester_pk PRIMARY KEY (semester_id)
   USING INDEX semester_semester_id_i
```

The next statement shows an example of a unique constraint that is associated with a unique index.

```
CREATE TABLE semester
   (semester_id NUMBER(8),
   semester_name VARCHAR2(8) NOT NULL,
   year_no   NUMBER(4) NOT NULL,
   CONSTRAINT semester_uk UNIQUE (semester_name, year_no)
   USING INDEX
   (CREATE UNIQUE INDEX semester_sem_yr_uk
      ON semester(semester_name, year_no)))
```

 These syntax alternatives are advantageous when you drop or disable the primary key or unique constraint, as the index will continue to exist. This saves time, particularly on large tables where it may take

> *many hours to recreate the index. Note in Oracle 10g you can preserve the index of a unique or primary key, if you specify the KEEP INDEX clause in an ALTER TABLE statement.*

**LAB
12.2**

INDEXES AND FOREIGN KEYS

You should almost always index foreign keys because they are frequently used in joins. Additionally, if you intend to delete or update unique or primary keys on the parent table, you should index the foreign keys to improve the locking of child records. Foreign keys that are not indexed require locks to be placed on the entire child table when a parent row is deleted or the primary or unique keys of the parent table are updated. This prevents any inserts, updates, and deletes on the entire child table until the row is committed or rolled back. The advantage of an index on the foreign key column is that the locks are placed on the affected indexed child rows instead, thus not locking up the entire child table. This is more efficient and allows data manipulation of child rows *not* affected by the updates and deletes of the parent table.

This key issue has caused headaches for many unwitting programmers who spent days reviewing their code for performance improvements. The lack of a foreign index key frequently turns out to be the culprit for the slow performance of updates.

DROP AN INDEX

To drop an index, use the DROP INDEX command. You might drop an index if queries in your applications do not utilize the index. You find out which indexes are used by querying the V$OBJECT_USAGE data dictionary view.

```
DROP INDEX sect_location_i
Index dropped.
```

 When you drop a table, all associated indexes are dropped automatically.

BITMAPPED INDEX

The bitmapped index is another type of index supported by Oracle. This index is typically used in a data warehouse where the primary goal is the querying and analyzing of data with bulk data loads occurring at certain intervals. Bitmapped indexes are not suitable for tables with heavy data manipulation activity by many users because any such changes on this type of index may significantly slow down the transactions. A bitmapped index is typically used on columns with a very low selectivity—that is, columns with very few distinct values. For example, a column like GENDER, with four distinct values of female, male, unknown, and not applicable (in case of a legal entity such as a corporation) has a very low selectivity.

A low selectivity is expressed as the number of distinct values as a total against all the rows in the database. For example, if you had 9,000 distinct values in a table with one million rows, it would be considered a low-selectivity column. In this scenario, the number of distinct values represents less than 1% of the entire rows in the table and this column may be a good candidate for a bitmapped index.

Figure 12.2 illustrates the concept of a bitmapped index. The example is a hypothetical CUSTOMER table with a bitmapped index on the GENDER column. The bitmapped index translates the distinct values for the GENDER column of individual customers. In this simplified example, the customer with the IDs of 1 and 2 has the GENDER = F, which makes the bit turned on to 1. The other values such as GENDER = M, GENDER = N/A, and GENDER = UNKNOWN have a 0, indicating that these values are not true for the row. The next customer with the ID of 3 has the 1 bit turned on GENDER = M, the other values are zero.

CUSTOMER Table

ID	FIRST_NAME	LAST_NAME	GENDER
1	Mary	Jones	F
2	Carol	Smith	F
3	Fred	Olson	M
4		ABC, Inc.	N/A
...	...	...	...

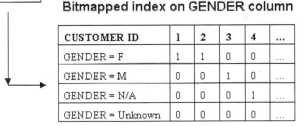

Bitmapped index on GENDER column

CUSTOMER ID	1	2	3	4	...
GENDER = F	1	1	0	0	...
GENDER = M	0	0	1	0	...
GENDER = N/A	0	0	0	1	...
GENDER = Unknown	0	0	0	0	...

Figure 12.2 ■ A bitmapped index.

The next statement creates a bitmapped index on the GENDER column of a CUSTOMER table.

```
CREATE BITMAP INDEX customer_bm_gender_i
    ON customer(gender)
```

If you have multiple bitmapped indexes, such as one for GENDER, MARITAL STATUS, and ZIP, and you need to retrieve rows based on certain AND and OR conditions, then bitmapped indexes perform very fast. They quickly compare and merge the bit settings of these conditions and are therefore highly effective for large tables. Bitmapped indexes require less storage space than traditional B-tree indexes, but they do not perform as well for less than or greater than comparisons. Note that bitmapped indexes are only available with Oracle's Enterprise Edition.

BITMAP JOIN INDEX

The bitmap join index is another type of index that reduces the amount of data to be joined during a query. Essentially, it precomputes the join and stored the result in a bitmap; this type of index is useful in data warehousing environments. The next statement shows the creation of such an index.

```
CREATE BITMAP INDEX enroll_bmj_student_i
    ON enrollment(e.student_id)
  FROM enrollment e, student s
 WHERE e.student_id = s.student_id
Index created.
```

GUIDELINES WHEN TO INDEX

You want to consider indexing columns frequently used in the WHERE clause of SQL statements and foreign key columns. Note that Oracle automatically creates a unique index to enforce the primary key constraint and the unique constraint. Here are some general guidelines for when an index is typically useful:

1. Frequently accessed columns containing highly selective data for B-tree indexes.
2. Columns frequently accessed with a small range of values for bitmapped indexes.
3. Columns frequently accessed with many null values, but the query is looking for the NOT NULL values.
4. Frequent queries against large tables retrieving less than 5 to 15 percent of the rows. The percentage may vary depending on a number of factors, including the size of the table.

Building an index is often useless if:

1. The table is small, but you should nevertheless create unique and primary constraints to enforce business rules.
2. The query retrieves more than 5 to 15 percent of the rows.
3. The indexed column is part of an expression: Consider creating a function-based index instead.

In Chapter 17, "SQL Optimization," you learn to verify that SQL statements issued actually use an index.

Although adding indexes may improve performance of certain queries, you must realize that Oracle may use this new index for other queries that previously used a different index. This rarely has an adverse effect, but you must nevertheless make certain that your overall application performance does not suffer because of this change. Keep in mind that adding indexes may increase the time required for data manipulation operations, such as INSERT, UPDATE, and DELETE. If you primarily query the table, then creating the index may offset the disadvantage of additional time required for DML statements.

ALTERING AN INDEX

There are a number of syntax options that let you change various characteristics of an index such as renaming or rebuilding the index or altering the storage clause. Here are some of the general syntax options:

```
ALTER INDEX indexname
   [STORAGE ([NEXT integer [K|M]]])]
   [REBUILD [ONLINE]
[RENAME TO newindexname]
```

The next SQL statement shows the rebuild of an index. Periodically, you need to rebuild indexes to compact the data and balance the index tree. This is particularly important after data is subject to a large number of DML changes and the rebuild operation will improve the performance of the queries. Oracle provides the index rebuild option. It is faster to rebuild the index than to drop and recreate the index; furthermore, the index continues to be available for queries while the rebuild operation is in progress.

```
ALTER INDEX stu_zip_fk_i REBUILD
```
Index altered.

Because a DDL command requires exclusive access to the table or index, other sessions issuing any DML commands are preventing such changes. Therefore, data structure changes are usually performed during times when users are not accessing the system. However, you can create or rebuild indexes with the ONLINE option while users are performing DML commands.

```
ALTER INDEX stu_zip_fk_i REBUILD ONLINE
```

LOADING LARGE AMOUNTS OF DATA

When you insert or update large amounts of data, you may want to consider dropping certain indexes not used for the DML operation's WHERE clause to improve performance. After the operation is complete, recreate the appropriate indexes.

LAB 12.2 EXERCISES

12.2.1 CREATE B-TREE INDEXES

a) Create an index on the PHONE column of the STUDENT table. Drop the index after you successfully create it to return the STUDENT schema to its original state.

b) Create a composite index on the first and last name columns of the STUDENT table. Drop the index when you have finished.

c) Create an index on the DESCRIPTION column of the COURSE table. Note that queries against the table often use the UPPER function. Drop the index after you successfully create it.

d) Execute the following SQL statements. Explain the reason for the error.

```
CREATE TABLE test (col1 NUMBER)
CREATE INDEX test_col1_i ON test(col1)
DROP TABLE test
DROP INDEX test_col1_i
```

12.2.2 UNDERSTAND WHEN INDEXES ARE USEFUL

a) Would you create a B-tree index on a frequently accessed column with few distinct values? Explain.

b) List the advantages and disadvantages of indexes on performance.

c) Assume an index exists on the column ENROLL_DATE in the ENROLLMENT table. Change the following query so it uses the index.

```
SELECT student_id, section_id,
       TO_CHAR(enroll_date,'DD-MON-YYYY')
  FROM enrollment
 WHERE TO_CHAR(enroll_date,'DD-MON-YYYY') = '12-MAR-2003'
```

LAB 12.2 EXERCISE ANSWERS

12.2.1 ANSWERS

a) Create an index on the PHONE column of the STUDENT table. Drop the index after you successfully create it to return the STUDENT schema to its original state.

Answer: To create the index on the table, issue a CREATE INDEX statement.

```
CREATE INDEX stu_phone_i
   ON student(phone)
Index created.
```

Include the name of the table and the indexed column(s) in the index name; this allows you to identify the indexed columns in a particular table without querying the data dictionary views USER_INDEXES and USER_IND_COLUMNS. But remember, no database object's name, such as an index, may be longer than 30 characters.

To drop the index, simply issue the DROP INDEX command.

```
DROP INDEX stu_phone_i
Index dropped.
```

b) Create a composite index on the first and last name columns of the STUDENT table. Drop the index when you have finished.

Answer: There are two possible solutions for creating a composite index using the first and last name columns.

A composite or concatenated index is an index that consists of more than one column. Depending on how you access the table, you need to order the columns in the index accordingly.

To determine the best column order in the index, determine the selectivity of each column. That means determining how many distinct values each column has. You also need to determine what types of queries to write against the table. All this information helps you choose the best column order for the index.

SOLUTION 1:

The index is created in the order first_name, last_name.

```
CREATE INDEX stu_first_last_name_i
   ON student(first_name, last_name)
```

This index is used in a SQL statement only if you refer in the WHERE clause to either both columns or the FIRST_NAME column. Oracle can access the index only if the WHERE clause lists the leading column of the index. The leading column, also called the leading edge, of the aforementioned index is the FIRST_NAME column. If the WHERE clause of a SQL statement lists only the LAST_NAME column, the SQL statement cannot access the index. For example, the next two WHERE clauses do not use the index.

```
WHERE last_name = 'Smith'
WHERE last_name LIKE 'Sm%'
```

SOLUTION 2:

The index is created in the order LAST_NAME, FIRST_NAME. The LAST_NAME column is the leading column of the index.

```
CREATE INDEX stu_last_first_name_i
   ON student(last_name, first_name)
```

This index is used in a SQL statement if you query both columns or only the LAST_NAME column. If a WHERE clause in a SQL statement lists only the FIRST_NAME column, Oracle does not use the index because it is not the leading column of the index.

COMPOSITE INDEXES VERSUS INDIVIDUAL INDEXES

An alternative to the composite index is to create two separate indexes: one for the FIRST_NAME and one for the LAST_NAME column.

```
CREATE INDEX stu_first_name_i
   ON student(first_name)
Index created.


CREATE INDEX stu_last_name_i
   ON student(last_name)
Index created.
```

A SQL statement with one of the columns in the WHERE clause uses the appropriate index. In the case where both columns are used in the WHERE clause, Oracle typically merges the two indexes together to retrieve the rows. You may wonder, why, then, have concatenated indexes at all? A composite index outperforms individual column indexes, provided all the columns are referenced in the WHERE clause.

 A feature called skip scan allows the skipping of the leading edge of an index. During a skip scan, the B-tree index is probed for the distinct values of the leading edge column; ideally this column has few distinct values. The skip scan feature allows queries that previously had to read the entire table to use the composite index instead. A second benefit of the skip scan feature is the reduced need for indexes; fewer indexes require less storage space and therefore result in better performance of DML statements. Note that skip scan is not supported for bitmapped and function-based indexes.

The database designer, together with the application developer, decides how to structure the indexes to make them most useful, based on the SQL statements issued. Make sure to verify that Oracle actually uses the index; you can do this with the help of an explain plan, which is covered in Chapter 17, "SQL Optimization."

■ *FOR EXAMPLE*

Assume that on a given table you create a composite index on columns A, B, and C in this order. To make use of the index, specify in the WHERE clause either column A; columns A and B; columns A, B, and C; or columns A and C. Queries listing column C only, or B only, or B and C only do not use the index because they are not leading edge columns.

To determine the best order, again think about the types of queries issued and the selectivity of each column. The following three indexes cover all the query possibilities. This solution requires with the least amount of storage and offers the best overall performance.

```
CREATE INDEX test_table_a_b_c ON test_table(a, b, c)
CREATE INDEX test_table_b_c ON test_table(b, c)
CREATE INDEX test_table_c ON test_table(c)
```

Your queries may take advantage of the skip scan, and you may not need to build as many indexes. You must test your statements carefully to ensure adequate performance.

c) Create an index on the DESCRIPTION column of the COURSE table. Note that queries against the table often use the UPPER function. Drop the index after you successfully create it.

Answer: A function-based index is created on the DESCRIPTION column.

```
CREATE INDEX crse_description_i
  ON course(UPPER(description))
```

A function-based index stores the indexed values and uses the index based on the following SELECT statement, which retrieves the course number for the course called Hands-On Windows. If you don't know in what case the description was entered into the COURSE table, you may want to apply the UPPER function to the column.

```
SELECT course_no, description
  FROM course
 WHERE UPPER(description) = 'HANDS-ON WINDOWS'
```

Any query that modifies a column with a function in the WHERE clause does not make use of an index unless you create a function-based index.

An index like the following cannot be used for the previously issued SQL statement.

```
CREATE INDEX crse_description_i
  ON course(description)
```

To restore the schema to its previous state, drop the index.

```
DROP INDEX crse_description_i
```
Index dropped.

d) Execute the following SQL statements. Explain the reason for the error.

```
CREATE TABLE test (col1 NUMBER)
CREATE INDEX test_col1_i ON test(col1)
DROP TABLE test
DROP INDEX test_col1_i
```

Answer: Dropping a table automatically drops any associated index. There is no need to drop the index separately.

```
DROP INDEX test_col1_i
               *
```
ERROR at line 1:
ORA-01418: specified index does not exist

12.2.2 ANSWERS

a) Would you create a B-tree index on a frequently accessed column with few distinct values? Explain.

Answer: It may be advantageous to create a B-tree index even on a low-selectivity column.

Assume you have an EMPLOYEE table with a column named GENDER that you consider indexing. Also assume that 90 percent of your employees are male and 10 percent are female. You frequently query for female employees. In this case, the index is helpful and improves the performance of your query. A query for male employees will probably perform a full tablescan because this is more efficient than looking up all the values in the index; the Oracle optimizer (discussed in Chapter 17, "SQL Optimization") makes the decision regarding the best access path.

b) List the advantages and disadvantages of indexes on performance.

Answer: Advantages: Adding an index on a table increases the performance of SQL statements using the indexed column(s) in the WHERE clause. This assumes that only a small percentage of the rows are accessed. Should you access many rows in the table, accessing the entire table via a full table scan probably yields better performance. Indexes on the foreign key columns also improve locking. Disadvantages: Adding indexes may increase the time required for insert, update, and delete operations because the index needs to be updated. Indexes also require additional disk space.

c) Assume an index exists on the column ENROLL_DATE in the ENROLLMENT table. Change the following query so it uses the index.

```
SELECT student_id, section_id,
       TO_CHAR(enroll_date,'DD-MON-YYYY')
  FROM enrollment
 WHERE TO_CHAR(enroll_date,'DD-MON-YYYY') = '12-MAR-2003'
```

Answer: When you modify an indexed column with a function, such as the function TO_CHAR in the WHERE clause, the SQL statement is not able to access the index. The exception is when you create a function-based index on the column.

In this case you do not need a function-based index. The SQL statement is changed so it does not modify the indexed column with a function. Refer to Chapter 4, "Date and Conversion Functions," about the dangers of using TO_CHAR with a DATE column in the WHERE clause.

```
SELECT student_id, section_id,
       TO_CHAR(enroll_date,'DD-MON-YYYY')
  FROM enrollment
 WHERE enroll_date = TO_DATE('12-MAR-2003','DD-MON-YYYY')
```

LAB 12.2 SELF-REVIEW QUESTIONS

In order to test your progress, you should be able to answer the following questions.

1) For the following query, choose which index(es), if any, probably yield the best performance.

```
SELECT student_id, last_name, employer, phone
  FROM student
 WHERE employer = 'FGIC'
   AND phone = '201-555-5555'
```

a) _____ Index on employer
b) _____ Index on phone
c) _____ Index in the order employer, phone
d) _____ Index in the order phone, employer
e) _____ No index

2) You should always index as many columns as possible.

a) _____ True
b) _____ False

3) Frequently queried columns and foreign keys should almost always be indexed.

a) _____ True
b) _____ False

4) The ROWID is the fastest way to access a row.

    a) _____ True
    b) _____ False

5) The following query uses the single-column B-tree index on the ZIP column of the INSTRUCTOR table.

```
SELECT instructor_id, last_name, first_name, zip
  FROM instructor
 WHERE zip IS NULL
```

    a) _____ True
    b) _____ False

6) The following SQL statement benefits from an index on the column INSTRUCTOR_ID.

```
UPDATE instructor
   SET phone = '212-555-1212'
 WHERE instructor_id = 123
```

    a) _____ True
    b) _____ False

Answers appear in Appendix A, Section 12.2.

LAB 12.3

SEQUENCES

LAB OBJECTIVES

After this lab, you will be able to:
✔ Create and Use Sequences

Sequences are Oracle database objects allowing you to generate unique integers. Recall the STUDENT table with the primary key column STUDENT_ID. The value of STUDENT_ID is a *surrogate key* or *artificial key* generated from a sequence. This key is useful to the system but usually has no meaning for the user, is not subject to changes, and is never NULL.

Assume a student is uniquely identified by the first name, last name, and address. These columns are called the alternate key. If you choose these columns as the primary key, imagine a scenario where a student's name or address changes. This requires a large amount of updates in many tables because all the foreign key columns need to be changed, involving a lot of customized programming. Instead, a surrogate key column is created and populated by a sequence. This surrogate key is not subject to change and the users rarely see this column.

Sequences assure that no user gets the same value from the sequence, thus guaranteeing unique values for primary keys. Sequences are typically incremented by 1, but other increments can be specified. You can also start sequences at a specific number.

Because you still need to enforce your users' business rule and prevent duplicate student entries, consider creating a unique constraint on the alternate key.

CREATE A SEQUENCE

The syntax for creating sequences is as follows:

```
CREATE SEQUENCE sequencename
  [INCREMENT BY integer]
```

```
[START WITH integer]
[CACHE integer|NOCACHE]
[MAXVALUE integer|NOMAXVALUE]
[MINVALUE integer|NOMINVALUE]
[CYCLE|NOCYCLE]
[ORDER|NOORDER]
```

To create a sequence named STUDENT_ID_SEQ_NEW, issue the CREATE SEQUENCE command.

```
CREATE SEQUENCE student_id_seq_new START WITH 1 NOCACHE
Sequence created.
```

Basing the name of the sequence on the name of the column for which you want to use it is helpful for identification, but it does not associate the sequence with a particular column or table. The START WITH clause starts the sequence with the number 1. The NOCACHE keyword indicates the sequence numbers should not be kept in memory, so that when the system shuts down you will not lose any cached numbers. However, losing numbers is not a reason for concern because there are many more available from the sequence. It is useful to leave the sequence numbers in the cache only if you access the sequence frequently. If you don't specify a CACHE choice, by default the first 20 numbers are cached. The MAXVALUE and MINVALUE parameters determine the minimum and maximum range values of the sequence; the defaults are NOMAXVALUE and NOMINVALUE. The ORDER option, which is the default, assures that the sequence numbers are generated in order of request. The CYCLE parameter will recycle the numbers after it reaches the maximum or minimum value depending if it's an ascending or descending sequence; it will restart at the minimum and maximum values respectively. The default value is NOCYCLE.

USING SEQUENCE NUMBERS

To increment the sequence and display the unique number, use the NEXTVAL pseudocolumn. The following SQL statement takes the next value from the sequence. Because the sequence was just created and starts with the number 1, it takes the number 1 as the first available value.

```
SELECT student_id_seq_new.NEXTVAL
  FROM dual
  NEXTVAL
---------
        1

1 row selected.
```

Typically, you use NEXTVAL in INSERT and UPDATE statements. To display the current value of the sequence after it is incremented, use the CURRVAL pseudocolumn.

ALTERING A SEQUENCE

The ALTER SEQUENCE command allows you to change the properties of a sequence, such as the increment value, min and max values, and cache option. The syntax of the ALTER SEQUENCE command is listed as follows:

```
ALTER SEQUENCE sequencename
    [INCREMENT BY integer]
    [MAXVALUE integer|NOMAXVALUE]
    [MINVALUE integer|NOMINVALUE]
    [CACHE integer|NOCACHE]
    [CYCLE|NOCYCLE]
    [ORDER|NOORDER]
```

**LAB
12.3**

 To restart sequence numbers at a lower number, you must drop and recreate the sequence. Any GRANTs to other users of the sequence must be reissued. For more on the GRANT command see Chapter 14, "Security."

RENAME A SEQUENCE

You can rename a sequence with the RENAME command.

```
RENAME student_id_seq_new TO student_id_seq_newname
```

USAGE OF SEQUENCE VALUES

The NEXTVAL and CURRVAL pseudocolumns can be used in the following SQL constructs:

VALUES clause of an INSERT statement

SET clause of an UPDATE STATEMENT

SELECT list (unless it is part of a subquery, view, or materialized view)

SELECT list of a subquery in an INSERT statement

Sequence values are not allowed in these statements:

Subquery of a SELECT, UPDATE, or DELETE statement

SELECT statement containing DISTINCT, GROUP BY, ORDER BY, UNION, UNION ALL, INTERSECT or MINUS

WHERE clause of a SELECT statement

DEFAULT clause of a column in a CREATE or ALTER TABLE statement

CHECK constraint

LAB 12.3 EXERCISES

12.3.1 CREATE AND USE SEQUENCES

a) Describe the effects of the following SQL statement on the sequence SECTION_ID_SEQ.

```
INSERT INTO section
   (section_id, course_no, section_no,
   start_date_time, location,
   instructor_id, capacity, created_by,
   created_date, modified_by, modified_date)
VALUES
   (section_id_seq.NEXTVAL, 122, 6,
   TO_DATE('15-MAY-2003', 'DD-MON-YYYY'), 'R305',
   106, 10, 'ARISCHERT',
   SYSDATE, 'ARISCHERT', SYSDATE)
```

b) Write a SQL statement to increment the sequence STUDENT_ID_ SEQ_NEW with NEXTVAL and then issue a ROLLBACK command. Determine the effect on the sequence number.

c) Drop the sequence STUDENT_ID_SEQ_NEW.

LAB 12.3 EXERCISE ANSWERS

12.3.1 ANSWERS

a) Describe the effects of the following SQL statement on the sequence SECTION_ID_SEQ.

```
INSERT INTO section
   (section_id, course_no, section_no,
   start_date_time, location,
   instructor_id, capacity, created_by,
   created_date, modified_by, modified_date)
VALUES
   (section_id_seq.NEXTVAL, 122, 5,
   TO_DATE('15-MAY-2003', 'DD-MON-YYYY'), 'R305',
   106, 10, 'ARISCHERT',
   SYSDATE, 'ARISCHERT', SYSDATE)
```

Answer: The sequence is accessible from within an INSERT statement. The sequence is incremented with the next value and this value is inserted in the table.

AUTOMATING SEQUENCE NUMER CREATION WITH TRIGGERS

You can automatically increment the sequence and insert the primary key value whenever you insert a new row in a table. This can be accomplished if you write a trigger. Following is the code for a trigger associated with the SECTION table. The trigger fires upon INSERT to the SECTION table. It checks to see if a a value for the SECTION_ID column is supplied as part of the INSERT statement. If not, it retrieves the value from the SECTION_ID_SEQ sequence and holds the value in the correlation variable :new.SECTION_ID. This value is then inserted into the SECTION_ID column.

```
CREATE OR REPLACE TRIGGER section_trg_bir
BEFORE INSERT ON section
FOR EACH ROW
BEGIN
  IF :new.SECTION_ID IS NULL THEN
     SELECT section_id_seq.NEXTVAL
       INTO :new.SECTION_ID
       FROM DUAL;
   END IF;
END;
/
```

The next command shows the primary key column SECTION_ID not listed as part of the INSERT statement. The command is successful; it does not return an error message indicating that the NOT NULL and primary key column SECTION_ID is missing.

```
INSERT INTO section
  (course_no, section_no, instructor_id, created_by, created_date,
   modified_by, modified_date)
VALUES
  (20, 99, 109, 'Alice', SYSDATE,
   'Alice', SYSDATE)
```
1 row created.

A subsequent SELECT statement queries the newly inserted row and displays the automatically created SECTION_ID value.

```
SELECT section_id, course_no, section_no, created_date
  FROM section
 WHERE course_no = 20
   AND section_no = 99
```

SECTION_ID	COURSE_NO	SECTION_NO	CREATED_D
161	20	99	12-SEP-03

1 row selected.

For more information on triggers and the PL/SQL language, please refer to *Oracle PL/SQL by Example* by Benjamin Rosenzweig and Elena Silvestrova or the *Oracle Application Developer's Guide—Fundamentals* manual.

b) Write a SQL statement to increment the sequence STUDENT_ID_SEQ_NEW with NEXTVAL and then issue a ROLLBACK command. Determine the effect on the sequence number.

Answer: Once a sequence is incremented, the ROLLBACK command does not restore the number.

If you haven't already done so, create the sequence with the CREATE SEQUENCE student_id_seq_new command. Then retrieve the next number from the sequence.

```
SELECT student_id_seq_new.NEXTVAL
  FROM dual
  NEXTVAL
---------
        2

1 row selected.


ROLLBACK
Rollback complete.

SELECT student_id_seq_new.NEXTVAL
  FROM dual
  NEXTVAL
---------
        3

1 row selected.
```

If there are any gaps in the primary key sequence numbers it really doesn't matter because the numbers have no meaning to the user and there are many more numbers available from the sequence. One of the unique properties of sequences is that no two users receive the same number.

You can see information about the sequence in the USER_SEQUENCES data dictionary view. Here the LAST_NUMBER column indicates the last used number of the sequence.

```
SELECT sequence_name, last_number, cache_size
  FROM user_sequences
 WHERE sequence_name = 'STUDENT_ID_SEQ_NEW'
SEQUENCE_NAME                         LAST_NUMBER CACHE_SIZE
------------------------------------- ----------- ----------
STUDENT_ID_SEQ_NEW                              3          0

1 row selected.
```

The current number of the sequence may be obtained using CURRVAL providing the sequence was incremented by the user's session.

```
SELECT student_id_seq_new.CURRVAL
  FROM dual
  CURRVAL
----------
        3

1 row selected.
```

c) Drop the sequence STUDENT_ID_SEQ_NEW.

Answer: Just as with other database objects, you use the DROP command to drop a sequence.

```
DROP SEQUENCE student_id_seq_new
Sequence dropped.
```

LAB 12.3 SELF-REVIEW QUESTIONS

In order to test your progress, you should be able to answer the following questions.

1) Sequences are useful for generating unique values.

    a) _____ True
    b) _____ False

2) A student's social security number is a good choice for a primary key value instead of a sequence.

    a) _____ True
    b) _____ False

3) The default increment of a sequence is 1.

    a) _____ True
    b) _____ False

4) When you drop a table, the associated sequence is also dropped.

    a) _____ True
    b) _____ False

5) The following statement creates a sequence named EMPLOYEE_ID_SEQ, which starts at the number 1000.

```
CREATE SEQUENCE employee_id_seq START WITH 1000
```

    a) _____ True
    b) _____ False

Answers appear in Appendix A, Section 12.3.

LAB
12.3

CHAPTER 12

TEST YOUR THINKING

 The projects in this section are meant to have you utilize all of the skills that you have acquired throughout this chapter. The answers to these projects can be found at the companion Web site to this book, located at: *http://authors.phptr. com/rischert3e*. Visit the Web site periodically to share and discuss your answers.

1) Who can update the SALARY column through the MY_EMPLOYEE view? Hint: The USER function returns the name of the currently logged in user.

```
CREATE OR REPLACE VIEW my_employee AS
SELECT employee id, employee_name, salary, manager
  FROM employee
 WHERE manager = USER
   WITH CHECK OPTION CONSTRAINT my_employee_ck_manager
```

2) Which columns in a table should you consider indexing?

3) Explain the purpose of the following Oracle SQL command.

```
ALTER INDEX crse_crse_fk_i REBUILD
```

4) Are null values stored in an index? Explain.

THE DATA DICTIONARY AND ADVANCED SQL*PLUS COMMANDS

The Oracle data dictionary is a set of tables and views that contains data about the database; it is also sometimes referred to as the *catalog*. The data dictionary is used internally by Oracle for many purposes; for instance, to determine if a SQL statement contains valid column and table names or to determine the privileges of an individual user. You will find it useful to query the data dictionary because it contains a wealth of information about the database.

You have learned writing SQL scripts in Chapter 2, "SQL: The Basics." This lab will expand your knowledge of SQL*Plus and its capabilities as a SQL execution environment. In many situations, you can simplify the writing of SQL statements and the administration of the database by writing SQL scripts that execute other SQL statements.

LAB 13.1

THE ORACLE DATA DICTIONARY VIEWS

LAB OBJECTIVES

After this lab, you will be able to:
✔ Query the Data Dictionary

The data dictionary has two distinct sets of views: the *static* data dictionary views and the *dynamic* data dictionary views, also referred to as *dynamic performance views* or as *V$TABLES* (V-Dollar tables).

THE STATIC DATA DICTIONARY VIEWS

The static data dictionary stores details about database objects, such as tables, indexes, and views. It also lists information about referential integrity constraints and indexed columns. Whenever a new object is added or an object is changed, data about the object is recorded in the data dictionary.

Most of the static dictionary views begin with the prefix USER_, ALL_, or DBA_. The USER_ views show information belonging to the user querying the data dictionary. For example, when you login as STUDENT, the views beginning with the USER_ prefix show all the objects belonging to the STUDENT schema.

The ALL_ views show the same information, plus any information granted to the STUDENT user by another user, and public objects. You learn how to grant and receive access rights in Chapter 14, "Security." The DBA_ views show all objects in the entire database, but you need DBA privileges or the SELECT ANY DICTIONARY privilege to be able to query these views.

Table 13.1 ■ Overview of Oracle Data Dictionary Views

Prefix	Purpose
USER_	Objects belonging to the user querying
ALL_	Objects belonging to the user and objects accessible to the user
DBA_	All objects in the entire database, accessible only to users with DBA or SELECT ANY DICTIONARY privileges
V$	Dynamic performance views, accessible only to users with DBA privileges or the SELECT ANY DICTIONARY privileges

THE DYNAMIC DATA DICTIONARY VIEWS

The dynamic views begin with V$ and are typically used by the DBA to monitor the system. They are called dynamic because they are continuously updated by the database but never by the user. Table 13.1 shows the different types of data dictionary views.

THE DICTIONARY

The collection of static and dynamic data dictionary tables and views, along with a description of each, is listed in the view called DICTIONARY, also known by the synonym DICT. A synonym is another name for a database object; instead of using DICTIONARY, you can refer to its shorter synonym DICT. You learn about synonyms and their use in Chapter 14, "Security." You can examine the columns of the DICT view by issuing the SQL*Plus DESCRIBE command.

```
SQL> DESC dict
Name                        Null?      Type
--------------------        --------   --------------
TABLE_NAME                             VARCHAR2(30)
COMMENTS                               VARCHAR2(4000)
```

The column TABLE_NAME contains the name of the individual data dictionary view accessible to you, together with a brief description in the COMMENTS column.

For example, to find information about sequences in the database, you can query the DICT view. The column TABLE_NAME stores the names of the data dictionary views in uppercase. The following query results in all data dictionary views with the letters SEQ in their name.

```
SELECT table_name, comments
  FROM dict
 WHERE table_name LIKE '%SEQ%'
```

```
TABLE_NAME          COMMENTS
---------------     ------------------------------------------------
ALL_SEQUENCES       Description of SEQUENCEs accessible to the user
DBA_SEQUENCES       Description of all SEQUENCEs in the database
USER_SEQUENCES      Description of the user's own SEQUENCEs
SEQ                 Synonym for USER_SEQUENCES
```

4 rows selected.

Four different data dictionary views contain information about sequences. Note that if you do not have DBA access or the SELECT ANY DICTIONARY privileges, you may not see the DBA_SEQUENCES view. To display the columns of the SEQ view, issue the DESCRIBE command at the SQL*Plus prompt.

```
SQL> DESC SEQ
 Name                                Null?     Type
 ----------------------------------- --------- ---------
 SEQUENCE_NAME                       NOT NULL  VARCHAR2(30)
 MIN_VALUE                                     NUMBER
 MAX_VALUE                                     NUMBER
 INCREMENT_BY                        NOT NULL  NUMBER
 CYCLE_FLAG                                    VARCHAR2(1)
 ORDER_FLAG                                    VARCHAR2(1)
 CACHE_SIZE                          NOT NULL  NUMBER
 LAST_NUMBER                         NOT NULL  NUMBER
```

To find out which individual sequences are in the STUDENT schema, query the view.

```
SELECT sequence_name
  FROM seq
SEQUENCE_NAME
-------------------------------
COURSE_NO_SEQ
INSTRUCTOR_ID_SEQ
SECTION_ID_SEQ
STUDENT_ID_SEQ

4 rows selected.
```

If you are unclear about the meaning of the different columns in the SEQ view, query yet another view named DICT_COLUMNS. It describes each column.

```
SELECT column_name, comments
  FROM dict_columns
 WHERE table_name = 'USER_SEQUENCES'
```

```
COLUMN_NAME        COMMENTS
---------------    ------------------------------------
SEQUENCE_NAME      SEQUENCE name
MIN_VALUE          Minimum value of the sequence
...
CACHE_SIZE         Number of sequence numbers to cache
LAST_NUMBER        Last sequence number written to disk

8 rows selected.
```

*If you have performed most of the exercises in the previous chapters,
your results will differ from the results shown in the outputs of this
chapter as you have added new objects and altered existing objects
in the STUDENT schema. To bring back the STUDENT schema to its
original state, run the rebuildStudent.sql script at the SQL*Plus
prompt. For example:* `SQL>@c:\guest\schemasetup\
rebuildStudent.sql`. *This script drops the STUDENT database-
related tables, recreates the tables, and reloads the data.
If you added the supplemental tables mentioned in the previous
chapters, you can drop them with the sql_book_drop_extra_
tables.sql script. This script will not recreate them. To run the script
execute this command at the SQL*Plus prompt:* `SQL>@:c:\guest\
schemasetup\sql_book_drop_extra_tables.sql`. *Both
SQL*Plus commands assume that you are running the Windows
environment and your scripts are stored in the c:\guest\schemasetup
directory. If you are using iSQL*Plus, refer to Chapter 2, "SQL: The
Basics," about loading the file and executing the script.*

RETRIEVING DDL ABOUT SCHEMA OBJECTS

Oracle supplies a PL/SQL package called DBMS_METADATA that allows you to
retrieve metadata, also called database object definitions or data about data. You
can use this information to retrieve the definition of an object or to recreate the
object without querying of the dictionary and constructing the statement from
the data dictionary. For example, to retrieve the DDL to create the COURSE table,
you use the GET_DLL function, which is one of the functions of the package. The
parameters of this function are the object type, the name of the object, followed
by the optional schema name.

```
SET LONG 999999
SET PAGESIZE 0
SELECT DBMS_METADATA.GET_DDL('TABLE', 'COURSE', 'STUDENT')
  FROM dual
```

```
CREATE TABLE "STUDENT"."COURSE"
   (    "COURSE_NO" NUMBER(8,0) CONSTRAINT
          "CRSE_COURSE_NO_NNULL" NOT NULL ENABLE,
        "DESCRIPTION" VARCHAR2(50) CONSTRAINT
          "CRSE_DESCRIPTION_NNULL" NOT NULL ENABLE,
        "COST" NUMBER(9,2),
        "PREREQUISITE" NUMBER(8,0),
        "CREATED_BY" VARCHAR2(30) CONSTRAINT
          "CRSE_CREATED_BY_NNULL" NOT NULL ENABLE,
        "CREATED_DATE" DATE CONSTRAINT
          "CRSE_CREATED_DATE_NNULL" NOT NULL ENABLE,
        "MODIFIED_BY" VARCHAR2(30) CONSTRAINT
          "CRSE_MODIFIED_BY_NNULL" NOT NULL ENABLE,
        "MODIFIED_DATE" DATE CONSTRAINT
          "CRSE_MODIFIED_DATE_NNULL" NOT NULL ENABLE,
        CONSTRAINT "CRSE_PK" PRIMARY KEY ("COURSE_NO")
 USING INDEX PCTFREE 10 INITRANS 2 MAXTRANS 255 COMPUTE STATISTICS
...
   ) PCTFREE 10 PCTUSED 40 INITRANS 1 MAXTRANS 255 NOCOMPRESS LOGGING
 STORAGE(INITIAL 65536 NEXT 1048576 MINEXTENTS 1 MAXEXTENTS 2147483645
 PCTINCREASE 0 FREELISTS 1 FREELIST GROUPS 1 BUFFER_POOL DEFAULT)
```

The output shows the DDL necessary to exactly replicate the COURSE table including all the storage parameters. The result includes the identifiers such as the schema, table, column names, and so on in double quotes. This ensures that the case of these identifiers stays exactly as indicated. By default all identifiers are stored in uppercase unless you specifically surround an identifier with double quotes to allow for mixed or lowercase characters.

The SET LONG SQL*Plus command is needed as the function call returns the DDL in a LONG datatype and truncates by default after the first 80 characters. Setting it to a larger number will display the entire DDL. The second setting SET PAGE-SIZE 0 suppresses the column headings. Note that these settings are then stored for the duration of your SQL*Plus session. When you exit SQL*Plus, they revert to the default values, unless you include them in your login.sql or glogin.sql file (see the companion Web site on modifying these files).

If you don't want to include the storage parameter in the metadata result, you can execute the following statement. It will be effective for any subsequently issued statements. The BEGIN and END commands indicate the start and end of a PL/SQL block and require the forward slash to execute. You cannot call the SESSION_TRANSFORM procedure from a SELECT statement because it is a procedure. Instead you must enclose the statement within a PL/SQL block.

```
BEGIN
  DBMS_METADATA.SET_TRANSFORM_PARAM(
    DBMS_METADATA.SESSION_TRANSFORM, 'STORAGE', false);
END;
/
```

The next statement shows the execution of the DBMS_METADATA.GET_DLL function; This time it is with a table other than DUAL. In this instance, the columns of the query supply the appropriate parameter values. Specifically, this query will return the metadata for all the sequences owned by the current user. It passes as the parameter the character literal 'SEQUENCE' as the object type and the name of the sequence from the column SEQUENCE_NAME in the data dictionary USER_SEQUENCES. The third parameter is missing and therefore assumed to be the default schema name.

```
SELECT DBMS_METADATA.GET_DLL('SEQUENCE',sequence_name)
  FROM user_sequences
CREATE SEQUENCE   "STUDENT"."INSTRUCTOR_ID_SEQ"
   MINVALUE 1 MAXVALUE 1.0000000000000E+27
    INCREMENT BY 1 START WITH 141 NOCACHE   NOORDER   NOCYCLE
CREATE SEQUENCE   "STUDENT"."SECTION_ID_SEQ"
   MINVALUE 1 MAXVALUE 1.0000000000000E+27
    INCREMENT BY 1 START WITH 158 NOCACHE   NOORDER   NOCYCLE
CREATE SEQUENCE   "STUDENT"."STUDENT_ID_SEQ"
   MINVALUE 1 MAXVALUE 1.0000000000000E+27
    INCREMENT BY 1 START WITH 404 NOCACHE   NOORDER   NOCYCLE
CREATE SEQUENCE   "STUDENT"."COURSE_NO_SEQ"
   MINVALUE 1 MAXVALUE 1.0000000000000E+27
    INCREMENT BY 1 START WITH 452 NOCACHE   NOORDER   NOCYCLE
```

You can use just about any of the object types to retrieve the DDL. Table 13.2 lists a few examples of parameter calls for frequently used object types.

To save the output of your result so you may edit it later, you can use the SPOOL command. This SQL*Plus command captures all the output in a file. You will learn more about the SPOOL command and other useful SQL*Plus commands in the next lab.

Table 13.2 ■ Metadata Extraction Examples

Object	Function Call
Table	DBMS_METADATA.GET_DDL('TABLE', 'COURSE', 'STUDENT')
Index	DBMS_METADATA.GET_DDL('INDEX', 'ENR_SECT_FK_I', 'STUDENT')
View	DBMS_METADATA.GET_DDL('VIEW','MY_VIEW', 'STUDENT')
Sequence	DBMS_METADATA.GET_DDL('SEQUENCE','STUDENT_ID_SEQ', 'STUDENT')

LAB 13.1 EXERCISES

13.1.1 QUERY THE DATA DICTIONARY

a) Execute the following SQL statement. Describe the result of the query and name the different object types.

```
SELECT object_name, object_type
  FROM user_objects
```

b) Based on the USER_OBJECTS view, what information is stored in the columns CREATED, LAST_DDL_TIME, and STATUS?

c) Name the data dictionary view listing tables only in the STUDENT schema.

d) Query the data dictionary view USER_TAB_COLUMNS for the GRADE table and describe the information found in the columns DATA_TYPE, DATA_LENGTH, NULLABLE, and DATA_DEFAULT.

e) Show a list of all indexes and their columns for the ENROLLMENT table.

f) Display a list of all the sequences in the STUDENT schema and the current value of each.

g) Execute the following two SQL statements. The first statement creates a view, and the second queries the data dictionary view called USER_VIEWS. What information is stored in the TEXT column of USER_VIEWS? Drop the view afterward.

```
CREATE OR REPLACE VIEW my_test AS
SELECT first_name, instructor_id
  FROM instructor

SELECT view_name, text
  FROM user_views
 WHERE view_name = 'MY_TEST'
```

h) Execute the following query. What do you observe?

```
SELECT constraint_name, table_name, constraint_type
  FROM user_constraints
```

i) What columns are listed in the data dictionary view USER_CONS_COLUMNS?

j) Execute the following SQL statement. Describe the result.

```
SELECT username
  FROM all_users
```

k) Execute the following query. What do you observe about the result?

```
SELECT segment_name, segment_type, bytes/1024
  FROM user_segments
 WHERE segment_name = 'ZIPCODE'
   AND segment_type = 'TABLE'
```

LAB 13.1 EXERCISE ANSWERS

13.1.1 ANSWERS

a) Execute the following SQL statement. Describe the result of the query and name the different object types.

```
SELECT object_name, object_type
  FROM user_objects
```

Answer: The query returns a list of all the objects owned by the current user. The object types listed are table, sequence, and index.

```
OBJECT_NAME                          OBJECT_TYPE
------------------------------       -----------
COURSE                               TABLE
...
COURSE_NO_SEQ                        SEQUENCE
...
ZIP_PK                               INDEX

36 rows selected.
```

Depending on the objects created in your individual schema, you see different results. Most likely, you see a list of tables, indexes, and sequences, but the list can also include views, procedures, packages, functions, synonyms, triggers, and other object types.

The ALL_OBJECTS view is different from the USER_OBJECTS view because it includes an additional column called OWNER and lists all the objects accessible to the user. It identifies the name of the schema in which the object is stored. The USER_OBJECTS view shows only those objects in the user's own schema.

The columns OWNER and OBJECT_NAME represent the unique identifier of the ALL_OBJECTS data dictionary view. There can be objects with the same name in other schemas, but within a schema, the object name has to be unique.

b) Based on the USER_OBJECTS view, what information is stored in the columns CREATED, LAST_DDL_TIME, and STATUS?

Answer: The CREATED column shows the creation date of an object. The LAST_DDL_TIME column indicates when an object was last modified via a DDL command, such as when a column was added to a table or a view was recompiled. The STATUS column indicates whether an object is valid or invalid.

The resulting output may vary depending on the objects in your schema.

```
SELECT object_name, created, last_ddl_time, status
  FROM user_objects
OBJECT_NAME              CREATED    LAST_DDL_ STATU
----------------------   ---------- --------- -----
COURSE                   14-AUG-03 23-OCT-03 VALID
...
ZIP_PK                   14-AUG-03 14-AUG-03 VALID

36 rows selected.
```

A view may become invalid if the underlying table is modified or dropped. Other objects, such as PL/SQL procedures, packages, or functions, may become invalid if dependent objects are modified, and they subsequently need to be recompiled.

If you are unclear about the meaning of a particular column, refer to the DICT_COLUMNS view for information.

```
SELECT column_name, comments
  FROM dict_columns
 WHERE table_name = 'USER_OBJECTS'
   AND column_name IN ('STATUS', 'LAST_DDL_TIME',
                       'CREATED')
COLUMN_NAME         COMMENTS
------------------  --------------------------------------------
CREATED             Timestamp for the creation of the object
LAST_DDL_TIME       Timestamp for the last DDL change (including
                    GRANT and REVOKE) to the object
STATUS              Status of the object

3 rows selected.
```

c) Name the data dictionary view listing tables only in the STUDENT schema.

Answer: The view is USER_TABLES. You can find out which data dictionary table contains this information by querying the DICT view.

```
SELECT table_name
  FROM user_tables
TABLE_NAME
------------------
COURSE
...
ZIPCODE

10 rows selected.
```

d) Query the data dictionary view USER_TAB_COLUMNS for the GRADE table and describe the information found in the columns DATA_TYPE, DATA_LENGTH, NULLABLE, and DATA_DEFAULT.

Answer: The column DATA_TYPE shows the datatype of the column, DATA_LENGTH displays the length of the column in bytes, and there is either a 'Y' or 'N' in the column NULLABLE indicating whether NULL values are allowed in the column. The column DATA_DEFAULT represents the default value for the column, if any.

```
SELECT table_name, column_name, data_type, data_length,
       nullable, data_default
  FROM user_tab_columns
 WHERE table_name = 'GRADE'
```

TABLE_NA	COLUMN_NAME	DATA_TYP	DATA_LENGTH	N	DATA_
GRADE	STUDENT_ID	NUMBER	22	N	
...					
GRADE	NUMERIC_GRADE	NUMBER	22	N	0
...					
GRADE	MODIFIED_BY	VARCHAR2	30	N	
GRADE	MODIFIED_DATE	DATE	7	N	

```
10 rows selected.
```

Note the zero value in the last column named DATA_DEFAULT. This means the column called NUMERIC_GRADE has a column default value of zero. This value is inserted into a table's row if the NUMERIC_GRADE column is not specified during an INSERT operation. For example, the following INSERT statement does not list the NUMERIC_GRADE column and, therefore, the NUMERIC_GRADE column is zero; alternatively, you can use the DEFAULT keyword discussed in Chapter 10, "Insert, Update, and Delete."

```
INSERT INTO GRADE
  (student_id, section_id, grade_type_code,
   grade_code_occurrence,
   created_by, created_date,
   modified_by, modified_date)
```

```
VALUES
  (102,89, 'FI',
   2,
   'ARISCHERT', SYSDATE,
   'ARISCHERT', SYSDATE)
1 row created.
```

e) Show a list of all indexes and their columns for the ENROLLMENT table.

Answer: The data dictionary view USER_IND_COLUMNS lists the desired result.

```
SELECT index_name, table_name, column_name,
       column_position
  FROM user_ind_columns
 WHERE table_name = 'ENROLLMENT'
 ORDER BY 1, 4
INDEX_NAME        TABLE_NAME  COLUMN_NAM  COLUMN_POSITION
---------------   ----------  ----------  ---------------
ENR_SECT_FK_I     ENROLLMENT  SECTION_ID                1
ENR_PK            ENROLLMENT  STUDENT_ID                1
ENR_PK            ENROLLMENT  SECTION_ID                2

3 rows selected.
```

The ENROLLMENT table has two indexes: ENR_SECT_FK_I and ENR_PK. The first index consists of the column SECTION_ID. The second index, a unique index created by the primary key constraint, has the columns STUDENT_ID and SECTION_ID in that order. The COLUMN_POSITION shows the order of the columns within the index.

If you want to show just the indexes, you can query USER_INDEXES. This view also indicates if an index is unique. Details about function-based indexes are listed in the USER_IND_EXPRESSIONS view.

f) Display a list of all the sequences in the STUDENT schema and the current value of each.

Answer: The USER_SEQUENCES data dictionary view shows the sequence name and the current value of the sequence.

The resulting output may vary depending on the sequences in your schema.

```
SELECT sequence_name, last_number
  FROM user_sequences
SEQUENCE_NAME                          LAST_NUMBER
-----------------------------------    -----------
COURSE_NO_SEQ                                  451
INSTRUCTOR_ID_SEQ                              111
```

```
SECTION_ID_SEQ                          157
STUDENT_ID_SEQ                          400

4 rows selected.
```

g) Execute the following two SQL statements. The first statement creates a view, and the second queries the data dictionary view called USER_VIEWS. What information is stored in the TEXT column of USER_VIEWS? Drop the view afterward.

```
CREATE OR REPLACE VIEW my_test AS
SELECT first_name, instructor_id
  FROM instructor

SELECT view_name, text
  FROM user_views
 WHERE view_name = 'MY_TEST'
```

Answer: The TEXT column of the USER_VIEWS data dictionary view stores the view's defining SQL statement.

```
VIEW_NAME   TEXT
---------- -------------------------------
MY_TEST     SELECT first_name, instructor_id
              FROM instructor

1 row selected.
```

From Chapter 12, "Views, Indexes, and Sequences," recall the definition of a view as a stored query. The query is stored in the column named TEXT of USER_VIEWS.

 The TEXT column in the USER_VIEWS data dictionary is of the LONG datatype. By default SQL*Plus does not display more than 80 characters of a LONG. You can increase this length with the SQL*Plus SET LONG command and wrap whole words using the SQL*Plus FORMAT COLUMN command with the WORD_WRAPPED option.

OBJECT DEPENDENCIES

Some objects, such as a view, synonym, procedure, function, or package, depend on other objects. For example, the view MY_TEST depends on the INSTRUCTOR table. You can find out about these dependencies in the USER_DEPENDENCIES view. The query shows that this object is a view and that it references the INSTRUCTOR table. While this is easy to determine with a simple view, some objects are more complicated and querying this view helps identify the effect of any potential change.

```
SELECT name, type, referenced_name
  FROM user_dependencies
 WHERE name = 'MY_TEST'
NAME          TYPE           REFERENCED_NAME
----------    ------------   --------------------
MY_TEST       VIEW           INSTRUCTOR

1 row selected.
```

The MY_TEST view is dropped with the DROP VIEW command.

```
DROP VIEW my_test
View dropped.
```

h) Execute the following query. What do you observe?

```
SELECT constraint_name, table_name, constraint_type
  FROM user_constraints
```

Answer: The output shows the constraints on the various tables. The foreign key constraint is listed as constraint type R (Referential Integrity constraint), the NOT NULL and check constraints are shown as constraint type C, and the primary key constraints are displayed as constraint type P. The SECTION table has a unique constraint listed as constraint type U.

```
CONSTRAINT_NAME                    TABLE_NAME  C
-------------------------------    ----------  -
CRSE_CRSE_FK                       COURSE      R
...
SYS_C001441                        GRADE       C
ENR_STU_FK                         ENROLLMENT  R
...
SECT_SECT2_UK                      SECTION     U
...
ZIP_PK                             ZIPCODE     P
...
ZIP_MODIFIED_BY_NNULL              ZIPCODE     C

94 rows selected.
```

Note any constraint not explicitly named receives a system-assigned name, such as the constraint called SYS_C001441.

The USER_CONSTRAINTS view contains additional useful columns, particularly for referential integrity constraints.

For example, query the view for the foreign key constraint called ENR_STU_FK. The result shows the name of the primary key constraint. This constraint is referenced by the foreign key.

```
SELECT r_owner, r_constraint_name, delete_rule
  FROM user_constraints
 WHERE constraint_name = 'ENR_STU_FK'
R_OWNER      R_CONSTRAINT_NAME              DELETE_RU
----------   -----------------------------  ---------
STUDENT      STU_PK                         NO ACTION

1 row selected.
```

You'll notice from the result that the delete rule on the ENR_STU_FK constraint specifies NO ACTION, which means any delete of a student row (parent record) is restricted if dependent enrollment rows (child records with the same STU DENT_ID) exist. This is in contrast to a CASCADE, which means if a parent record is deleted the children are automatically deleted. If the referential integrity constraint is on delete set null, you would see the value SET NULL in the DELETE_RULE column.

The referential integrity constraints avoid the creation of orphan rows, meaning enrollment records without corresponding students. Also, the parent table may not be dropped unless the foreign key constraint is dropped. To disable constraints use the ALTER TABLE command. Alternatively, the parent table may be dropped using the DROP TABLE command with the CASCADE CONSTRAINTS clause, automatically dropping the foreign key constraints.

OTHER CONSTRAINT TYPES

In addition to the constraint types mentioned, Table 13.3 shows additional constraint types, they are the view constraint with check option (V) and the view constraint with the read-only option (O).

Table 13.3 ■ Constraint Types

Constraint Type	Description
R	Referential Integrity Constraint
C	Check Constraint including Not Null Constraint
P	Primary Key Constraint
U	Unique Constraint
V	View Constraint with Check Option
O	View Constraint with Read-Only Option

DISTINGUISH NOT NULL CONSTRAINTS FROM CHECK CONSTRAINTS

The NOT NULL constraint is listed as a check constraint and you can distinguish this type from other user-defined check constraints by looking at the SEARCH_CONDITION column. The next query shows the constraints of the GRADE_TYPE table. For example, the NOT NULL constraint called GRTYP_DESCRIPTION_NNULL on the DESCRIPTION column lists the NOT NULL column with the column name in quotes (in case of case-sensitive column names) together with the words IS NOT NULL. By comparison the GRTYP_GRADE_TYPE_CODE_LENGTH constraint checks for the length of the GRADE_TYPE_CODE column to be exactly 2.

```
SELECT constraint_name, search_condition
  FROM user_constraints
 WHERE constraint_type = 'C'
   AND table_name = 'GRADE_TYPE'
CONSTRAINT_NAME                  SEARCH_CONDITION
-----------------------------    ------------------------------
GRTYP_DESCRIPTION_NNULL          "DESCRIPTION" IS NOT NULL
...
GRTYP_GRADE_TYPE_CODE_LENGTH     LENGTH(grade_type_code)=2

7 rows selected.
```

i) What columns are listed in the data dictionary view USER_CONS_COLUMNS?

Answer: The columns are OWNER, CONSTRAINT_NAME, TABLE_NAME, COLUMN_NAME, and POSITION.

This data dictionary view shows which columns are referenced in a constraint. A query against the view illustrates this on the example of the primary key constraint ENR_PK, which consists of the two columns STUDENT_ID and SECTION_ID.

```
SELECT constraint_name, column_name, position
  FROM user_cons_columns
 WHERE constraint_name = 'ENR_PK'
CONSTRAINT_NAME        COLUMN_NAME            POSITION
--------------------   --------------------   ----------
ENR_PK                 STUDENT_ID                    1
ENR_PK                 SECTION_ID                    2

2 rows selected.
```

j) Execute the following SQL statement. Describe the result.

```
SELECT username
  FROM all_users
```

Answer: It shows a list of all the users in the database.

The resulting output may vary, depending on your database.

```
USERNAME
--------------------------
SYS
SYSTEM
...
SCOTT
...
STUDENT

15 rows selected.
```

Note that there are two users named SYS and SYSTEM. The SYS user is the owner of the Oracle data dictionary. Never log in as this "super user" unless you are an experienced Oracle DBA or are instructed by Oracle to do so. Otherwise, you may inadvertently perform actions that could adversely affect the database. The SYSTEM user has DBA privileges, but does not own the data dictionary. You will learn more about these two user accounts in the next chapter.

Another useful view is the USER_USERS view. Following is a query displaying information about the current user or schema. It shows your login name and the name of the default tablespace on which any tables or indexes you create are stored, unless you explicitly specify another tablespace. It also shows when your account was created.

```
SELECT username, default_tablespace, created
  FROM user_users
```

USERNAME	DEFAULT_TABLESPACE	CREATED
STUDENT	USERS	04-MAY-02

```
1 row selected.
```

k) Execute the following query. What do you observe about the result?

```
SELECT segment_name, segment_type, bytes/1024
  FROM user_segments
 WHERE segment_name = 'ZIPCODE'
   AND segment_type = 'TABLE'
```

Answer: The query displays the size of the ZIPCODE table.

SEGMENT_NA	SEGMENT_TYPE	BYTES/1024
ZIPCODE	TABLE	64

```
1 row selected.
```

The most common segment types are tables and indexes. The USER_SEGMENT view shows the storage in bytes for a particular segment. Dividing the bytes by 1024 displays the size in kilobytes (KB). Note, your actual number of bytes may vary from the figure listed here depending on the storage parameter chosen for the default tablespace in your individual user account.

To see a listing of the different available tablespaces, you query the USER_TABLE-SPACES or DBA_TABLESPACES view. It may yield a result similar to the following.

```
SELECT tablespace_name
  FROM user_tablespaces
 ORDER BY tablespace_name
TABLESPACE_NAME
------------------------------
INDX
SYSTEM
TEMP
USERS

4 rows selected.
```

To find out how much space is available in total on each of the tablespaces you write a SQL statement against the view USER_FREE_SPACE. The result shows you the available megabytes (MB) for each tablespace. You learn more about table-space and space management topics in the *Oracle Database Administrator's Guide*.

```
SELECT tablespace_name, SUM(bytes)/1024/1024
  FROM user_free_space
 GROUP BY tablespace_name
TABLESPACE_NAME                    SUM(BYTES)/1024/1024
------------------------------     --------------------
INDX                                            24.8125
SYSTEM                                       14.6796875
USERS                                           82.8125

3 rows selected.
```

LAB 13.1 SELF-REVIEW QUESTIONS

In order to test your progress, you should be able to answer the following questions.

1) The data dictionary contains data about the database.

    a) _____ True
    b) _____ False

2) The data dictionary view USER_OBJECTS stores information about tables, indexes, and sequences.

    a) _____ True
    b) _____ False

3) The dynamic data dictionary is updated only by the Oracle database.

    a) _____ True
    b) _____ False

4) The ALL_TABLES data dictionary view shows all the tables in the entire database.

    a) _____ True
    b) _____ False

5) The OBJ view is a public synonym for the USER_OBJECTS view.

    a) _____ True
    b) _____ False

Answers appear in Appendix A, Section 13.1.

LAB 13.2

ADVANCED SQL*PLUS COMMANDS

LAB OBJECTIVES

After this lab, you will be able to:
✔ Write Interactive SQL Statements
✔ Use Advanced Scripting Capabilities in SQL*Plus

So far, you have executed many SQL statements in the SQL*Plus environment. In this lab, you learn how to write SQL statements that allow user input and create or execute other SQL statements. This will give you a deeper understanding of the SQL*Plus capabilities.

SQL*PLUS SUBSTITUTION VARIABLES

You probably find yourself executing the same command over and over again, sometimes just with slight modifications. Instead of editing the SQL statement each time, you can substitute part of the SQL statement with a variable. When the statement is executed, you supply the appropriate value for the variable.

For example, the variable in the following statement is named v_course_no. You identify a variable by prefixing an arbitrary variable name with an ampersand (&) symbol. When you execute the statement, SQL*Plus prompts you for a value and the supplied value is assigned to the variable.

```
SELECT course_no, description
   FROM course
  WHERE course_no = &v_course_no
```

The prompt you see in *i*SQL*Plus looks similar to Figure 13.1.

Figure 13.1 ■ Substitution variables prompt in *i*SQL*Plus.

If you use SQL*Plus your prompt looks like this:

```
Enter value for v_course_no:
```

Once you enter the value of 240 and press Enter or the Continue button, SQL*Plus will assign the variable v_course_no the value of 240, which then subsequently executes the statement and displays the result similar to the result you see in Figure 13.2 if you use *i*SQL*Plus.

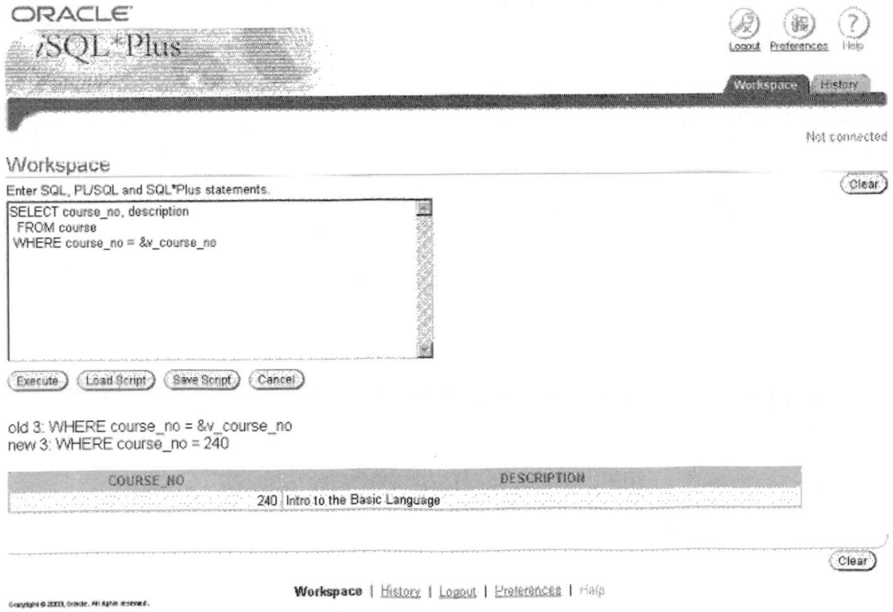

Figure 13.2 ■ Result in *i*SQL*Plus.

If you use SQL*Plus, you will see a result much like the following:

```
SQL> SELECT course_no, description
  2    FROM course
  3   WHERE course_no = &v_course_no
  4   /
Enter value for v_course_no: 240
old    3:   WHERE course_no = &v_course_no
new    3:   WHERE course_no = 240

 COURSE_NO DESCRIPTION
---------- ---------------------------------------
       240 Intro to the Basic Language

1 row selected.
```

The text displayed after the substitution variable prompt shows the value before (old) and after the substitution of the value (new). The number 3 indicates that the substitution variable is found on line 3 of the SQL statement. You can change this default behavior with the SET VERIFY OFF SQL*Plus command that will no longer display the old and new values.

If you want to re-execute the statement in the buffer, use the forward slash (/) and you are prompted for a value for the v_course_no substitution variable each time.

You can use a substitution variable in any SQL statement executed within the SQL*Plus environment. The next statement shows you an example of a query against the USER_OBJECTS data dictionary view. This SQL statement determines if the name of a particular database object is valid and its object type. Instead of repeatedly editing the same statement, use a variable to substitute the value of the object name. Because the datatype of the OBJECT_NAME column and the variable name must agree, the variable name is enclosed in single quotation marks.

```
SELECT object_name, object_type, status
  FROM obj
 WHERE object_name LIKE UPPER('&v_object_name')
Enter value for v_object_name: student
old    3:   WHERE object_name LIKE UPPER('&v_object_name')
new    3:   WHERE object_name LIKE UPPER('student')

OBJECT_NAME                     OBJECT_TYPE        STATUS
------------------------------- ------------------ ------
STUDENT                         TABLE              VALID

1 row selected.
```

You can save the file so you may re-execute it at a later time. Substitution variables are not limited to the WHERE clause of a statement. You can also use them in the ORDER BY clause, the FROM clause to substitute a table name, as an individual column expression, or even substitute an entire WHERE clause.

SUPPRESSING THE USE OF SUBSTITUTION VARIABLES

There are times in SQL*Plus when you do not want the ampersand to be an indicator that a substitution variable follows, but a literal ampersand instead. The following example illustrates this scenario.

```
UPDATE student
   SET employer = 'Soehner & Peter'
 WHERE student_id = 135
Enter value for peter:
```

SQL*Plus thinks you want to use a substitution parameter rather than the literal ampersand. To remedy this, use the SET DEFINE command to turn the use of substitution parameters on or off.

```
SET DEFINE OFF
UPDATE student
   SET employer = 'Soehner & Peter'
 WHERE student_id - 135
1 row updated.
SET DEFINE ON
```

Last, issue a ROLLBACK command to undo the change of employer and set it back to the original value.

```
ROLLBACK
Rollback complete.
```

PREDEFINED SQL*PLUS VARIABLES

Oracle has a number of already predefined system variables, which are listed in the following output. These variables are can be referenced during your SQL*Plus session or during the execution of a script. The following DEFINE command shows all the system variables available in Oracle 10*g*.

```
SQL> DEFINE
DEFINE _DATE            = "27-MAR-04" (CHAR)
DEFINE _CONNECT_IDENTIFIER = "orcl" (CHAR)
DEFINE _USER            = "STUDENT" (CHAR)
DEFINE _PRIVILEGE       = "" (CHAR)
DEFINE _SQLPLUS_RELEASE = "1001000200" (CHAR)
DEFINE _EDITOR          = "Notepad" (CHAR)
```

```
DEFINE _O_VERSION        = "Oracle10g Enterprise Edition
                           Release 10.1.0.2.0 - Production
   With the Partitioning, OLAP and Data Mining options" (CHAR)
DEFINE _O_RELEASE        = "1001000200" (CHAR)
```

These predefined variables are also useful, if you want to change your SQL*Plus prompt from the default SQL> prompt. For example, if you wish to always see to which user account and instance you are connected to, you can change the default prompt with the SET SQLPROMPT command and the _USER and _CONNECT_IDENTIFIER system variables. In the following example, the prompt will display the current user followed by the @ symbol, the instance name, and the > symbol.

```
SQL> SET SQLPROMPT _USER'@'_CONNECT_IDENTIFIER>
STUDENT@orcl>
```

If you change login during your SQL*Plus session to a different user account, the login automatically reflects the new value. In Chapter 14, you will learn about changing login accounts and the CONNECT command. If you would like to always keep certain SQL*Plus settings in effect, you can place those commands into the login.sql or glogin.sql file. Refer to the companion Web site for more information on this file.

GENERATE DYNAMIC SQL

Dynamic SQL allows you to execute SQL commands built at runtime. Dynamic SQL is often executed in Oracle's PL/SQL language, but can also be generated and executed in SQL*Plus using SQL*Plus scripts. These scripts are often referred to as *SQL to generate SQL scripts* or *master/slave scripts*.

 Please note that there are a number of SQL*Plus commands not supported in the iSQL*Plus release. They include the SPOOL, SET TERMOUT, and HOST commands, among others. Some of these commands are simply not applicable in the Web environment or pose a security and authentication concern for the middle-tier application server. For a complete list, see Appendix C, "SQL*Plus Command Reference." Attempting to use any of the unsupported commands or command options raises an SP2-0850 error message. To complete this portion of the lab and the accompanying exercises, please use the client-server SQL*Plus software instead of the Web-based iSQL*Plus version.

Using SQL*Plus you can automatically generate SQL statements and spool them to a file for use.

For example, you made some database changes to tables, causing other database objects, such as views, to become invalid. To compile the views, you can repeatedly type the ALTER VIEW command for each invalid view, or you can wait for the user to access the views and let Oracle compile them. However, it is best to compile them after the table changes to make sure there are no errors. This is achieved by writing a script to generate the ALTER VIEW statement for each invalid view. The following SQL statement generates the dynamic SQL.

**LAB
13.2**

```
SELECT 'ALTER VIEW '|| object_name || ' COMPILE;'
   FROM user_objects
  WHERE object_type = 'VIEW'
    AND status <> 'VALID'
```

If you have any invalid views, your result may look like this:

```
'ALTERVIEW'||OBJECT_NAME||'COMPILE;'
-------------------------------------
ALTER VIEW CAPACITY_V COMPILE;
ALTER VIEW CT_STUDENT_V COMPILE;
ALTER VIEW NJ_STUDENT_V COMPILE;
ALTER VIEW NY_STUDENT_V COMPILE;

4 rows selected.
```

The text literal 'ALTER VIEW' is concatenated with the view name and then with the text literal 'COMPILE;'. You can spool the result into a file using the SPOOL command and execute the file to compile all the invalid views.

LAB 13.2 EXERCISES

13.2.1 WRITE INTERACTIVE SQL STATEMENTS

a) Execute the following statements. What result do you see when you substitute the variable with the value ENR_PK?

```
COL column_name FORMAT A20
COL owner FORMAT A10
COL constraint_name HEADING 'Constraint|Name' FORMAT A20
UNDEFINE vname
SELECT t.constraint_type, c.column_name,
       t.constraint_name, t.owner
  FROM all_constraints t, all_cons_columns c
 WHERE t.owner = c.owner
   AND t.constraint_name = c.constraint_name
   AND t.constraint_name LIKE UPPER('%&vname%')
 ORDER BY position
```

b) Execute the SQL*Plus command SET VERIFY OFF. Re-execute the SQL statement from exercise a by entering the forward slash. What do you observe?

c) Enter the following SQL statement into a text file named s_query.sql. Don't forget to end the statement with a semicolon or a forward slash on a separate line. Save the file and execute it at the SQL*Plus prompt with the command @s_query 252. What result do you see?

```
SELECT last_name, student_id
  FROM student
 WHERE student_id = &1
```

d) Execute the following SQL*Plus commands and the SQL statement that determines the maximum and minimum value of a column in a table. When prompted for the value of the vcol variable, enter the value cost; for the vtable variable, enter course. Describe your observation about the SQL*Plus prompts.

```
UNDEFINE vcol
UNDEFINE vtable
SET VERIFY OFF
SELECT MIN(&vcol), MAX(&vcol)
  FROM &vtable
```

e) Enter all the following commands in a file named maxval.sql, then execute the script. For the column name supply the value capacity and for the table name enter the value section. What do you observe?

```
PROMPT Determine the maximum and minimum value of a column
ACCEPT vcol CHAR PROMPT 'Enter the column name: '
ACCEPT vtable CHAR PROMPT 'Enter the corresponding table name: '
SET VERIFY OFF
SELECT MIN(&vcol), MAX(&vcol)
  FROM &vtable
```

13.2.2 USE ADVANCED SCRIPTION CAPABILITIES IN SQL*PLUS

The following SQL statement disables the foreign key constraint on the ZIP column of the STUDENT table.

```
ALTER TABLE student DISABLE CONSTRAINT stu_zip_fk
```

Disabling the constraint allows child values to be entered where no corresponding parent exists. This means you can insert or update a zipcode in the STUDENT table that does not have a corresponding value in the ZIPCODE table. There are times when you want to disable constraints temporarily, such as when you must bulk load data or update large quantities of data quickly. Afterward you enable the constraints again. The following exercises show you how to disable and enable constraints using a dynamic SQL script.

a) Execute the following SQL statement to generate other SQL statements. What do you observe?

```
SELECT 'ALTER TABLE ' || table_name
  FROM user_constraints
 WHERE constraint_type = 'R'
```

b) Expand the SQL statement in exercise a by adding the constraint name dynamically. The resulting output should look like this:

```
ALTER TABLE COURSE DISABLE CONSTRAINT CRSE_CRSE_FK;
...
ALTER TABLE SECTION DISABLE CONSTRAINT SECT_CRSE_FK;
ALTER TABLE SECTION DISABLE CONSTRAINT SECT_INST_FK;
ALTER TABLE STUDENT DISABLE CONSTRAINT STU_ZIP_FK;

11 rows selected.
```

c) Save the SQL statement in exercise b to a file named disable_fk.sql. Add the following SQL*Plus statements at the beginning of the file. Note that the double dashes represent single-line comments.

```
-- File Name: disable_fk.sql
-- Purpose: Disable Foreign Key constraints.
-- Created Date: Place current date here
-- Author: Put your name here
SET PAGESIZE 0
SET LINESIZE 80
SET FEEDBACK OFF
SET TERM OFF
SPOOL disable_fk.out
```

Add a semicolon at the end of the SQL statement and the following SQL*Plus commands afterward.

```
SPOOL OFF
SET PAGESIZE 20
SET LINESIZE 100
```

```
SET FEEDBACK ON
SET TERM ON
```

Save the file and run the disable_fk.sql file at the SQL*Plus prompt with the @ command. Describe the output from the spooled file named disable_fk.out.

d) Write a dynamic SQL script performing the opposite operation, which is enabling the foreign key constraints. Name the file enable_fk.sql.

e) Explain each line in the following SQL script and then describe the purpose of the script in one sentence.

```
01 /*
02 ---------------------------------------------------
03 File name:   rows.sql
04 Purpose:
05 Created by:  H. Ashley on January 7, 2000
06 Modified by: A. Christa on September 29, 2001
07 ---------------------------------------------------
08 */
09 SET TERM OFF
10 SET PAGESIZE 0
11 SET FEEDBACK OFF
12 SPOOL temp
13 SELECT 'SELECT ' || '''' || table_name || '''' ||
14        ', COUNT(*) '||CHR(10) ||
15        ' FROM '|| LOWER(table_name) || ';'
16   FROM user_tables;
17 SPOOL OFF
18 SET FEEDBACK 1
19 SET PAGESIZE 20
20 SET TERM ON
21 @temp.lst
22 HOST DEL temp.lst
```

f) Enter the following commands in a file called ascii_test.sql and run the file. Describe the result of the ascii_test.out file.

```
-- File Name: ascii_test.sql
SET TRIMSPOOL ON
SET PAGESIZE 0
SET LINESIZE 100
SET FEEDBACK OFF
PROMPT Enter the starting and ending course numbers
ACCEPT v_start_course_no CHAR PROMPT 'Enter starting course number: '
ACCEPT v_end_course_no CHAR PROMPT 'Enter ending course number: '
SET TERM OFF
SPOOL ascii_test.out
```

```
SELECT course_no||','''||description||''','||
       Cost||','''||modified_date||''''
  FROM course
 WHERE course_no BETWEEN &v_start_course_no
       AND &v_end_course_no;
SPOOL OFF
SET PAGESIZE 20
SET LINESIZE 80
SET FEEDBACK ON
SET TERM ON
SET TRIMSPOOL OFF
```

g) Explain the result of the following script.

```
--File: dump_file.sql
SET TRIMSPOOL ON
SET PAGESIZE 0
SET LINESIZE 100
SET FEEDBACK OFF
SPOOL dump_file.out
SELECT 'INSERT INTO STUDENT_TEST VALUES
('|| student_id||','''||last_name||
 ''','''||first_name||''');'
 FROM student;
SPOOL OFF
SET PAGESIZE 20
SET LINESIZE 80
SET FEEDBACK ON
SET TERM ON
SET TRIMSPOOL OFF
```

h) Imagine a scenario in which you would execute a script like the following.

```
--File: re_create_seq.sql
SET PAGESIZE 0
SET LINESIZE 100
SET FEEDBACK OFF
SPOOL re_create_seq.out
SELECT 'CREATE SEQUENCE '||sequence_name||
       ' START WITH '||last_number||CHR(10)||
       ' INCREMENT BY '||increment_by ||
       DECODE(cache_size, 0, ' NOCACHE',
       ' CACHE  '||cache_size)||';'
  FROM seq;
SPOOL OFF
SET PAGESIZE 20
SET LINESIZE 80
SET FEEDBACK ON
SET TERM ON
```

LAB 13.2 EXERCISE ANSWERS

13.2.1 ANSWERS

a) Execute the following statements. What result do you see when you substitute the variable with the value ENR_PK?

```
COL column_name FORMAT A20
COL owner FORMAT A10
COL constraint_name HEADING 'Constraint|Name' FORMAT A20
UNDEFINE vname
SELECT t.constraint_type, c.column_name,
       t.constraint_name, t.owner
  FROM all_constraints t, all_cons_columns c
 WHERE t.owner = c.owner
   AND t.constraint_name = c.constraint_name
   AND t.constraint_name LIKE UPPER('%&vname%')
 ORDER BY position
```

Answer: The old and new substitution values for the vname variable are displayed. After the value is entered, the SQL statement displays constraints with a similar name.

The number 6, after the old and new values, represents the line number where the substitution variable is located within the SQL statement.

```
Enter value for vname: enr_pk
old  6:     AND t.constraint_name LIKE UPPER('%&vname%')
new  6:     AND t.constraint_name LIKE UPPER('%enr_pk%')

                       Constraint
C COLUMN_NAME          Name                 OWNER
- -------------------- -------------------- --------
P STUDENT_ID           ENR_PK               STUDENT
P SECTION_ID           ENR_PK               STUDENT

2 rows selected.
```

The result includes the constraint type; in this example it is the primary key constraint. Additionally, you see the individual primary key columns STUDENT_ID and SECTION_ID. Also, note the substitution value can be entered in either lowercase or uppercase; the UPPER function in the SQL statement converts it into uppercase.

The query that provides this result joins the table constraints (ALL_CONSTRAINTS) and column constraints (ALL_CONS_COLUMNS) via the OWNER and CONSTRAINT_NAME columns. These two columns represent the unique identifier of the ALL_CONSTRAINTS view. Although a view cannot have a primary key or unique constraint, the view's underlying data dictionary tables have these columns as a unique identifier.

The UNDEFINE command deletes any previous reference to the vname SQL*Plus variable. A variable is typically defined when you explicitly use the DEFINE command, the ampersand (&), the double ampersand (&&), or the ACCEPT command. You learn about the double ampersand and the ACCEPT command shortly. The value of the variable is retained until you UNDEFINE the variable, use the variable with a single ampersand, use the variable with the ACCEPT command, or exit SQL*Plus. To show the current value of a defined variable issue DEFINE followed by the variable name. For a list of all defined variables, simply type DEFINE.

The SQL*Plus FORMAT command shows the use of the COL HEADING command. The vertical pipe permits splitting of a column name across multiple lines.

b) Execute the SQL*Plus command `SET VERIFY OFF`. Re-execute the SQL statement from exercise a by entering the forward slash. What do you observe?

Answer: The VERIFY command suppresses the listing of the OLD and NEW substitution values.

Reset it back to its SQL*Plus default with the SET VERIFY ON command.

c) Enter the following SQL statement into a text file named s_query.sql. Don't forget to end the statement with a semicolon or a forward slash on a separate line. Save the file and execute it at the SQL*Plus prompt with the command `@s_query 252`. What result do you see?

```
SELECT last_name, student_id
  FROM student
 WHERE student_id = &1
```

Answer: The result displays the last name of the student with the STUDENT_ID of 252.

```
old    3:   WHERE student_id = &1
new    3:   WHERE student_id = 252


LAST_NAME                       STUDENT_ID
--------------------------   -----------
Barogh                              252


1 row selected.
```

You can pass parameters (arguments) when running a script file in SQL*Plus. This works only if your substitution variable is a numeral. The &1 parameter is substituted with the first parameter passed (in this example with the value 252). If you include another parameter, such as &2, you can pass a second argument, and so on.

d) Execute the following SQL*Plus commands and the SQL statement that determines the maximum and minimum value of a column in a table. When prompted for the value of the vcol variable, enter the value `cost`; for the vtable variable, enter `course`. Describe your observation about the SQL*Plus prompts.

```
UNDEFINE vcol
UNDEFINE vtable
SET VERIFY OFF
SELECT MIN(&vcol), MAX(&vcol)
   FROM &vtable
```

Answer: When a variable with the same name occurs multiple times, SQL*Plus prompts you for each one.

```
Enter value for vcol: cost
Enter value for vcol: cost
Enter value for vtable: course

MIN(COST) MAX(COST)
--------- ---------
     1095      1595

1 row selected.
```

To avoid being reprompted, define the variable with a double ampersand (&&).

```
UNDEFINE vcol
UNDEFINE vtable
SET VERIFY OFF
SELECT MIN(&&vcol), MAX(&&vcol)
   FROM &vtable
Enter value for vcol: cost
Enter value for vtable: course

MIN(COST) MAX(COST)
--------- ---------
     1095      1595

1 row selected.
```

Note that, until you exit SQL*Plus, the && variable is defined with the entered value, so any subsequent execution of the statement has the value for the variable vcol already defined without reprompting. Observe the effect of yet another execution. Only the prompt for the table name will appear because the vtable variable has only one & symbol. When the value `section` is now entered for a table name, this leads to an error because the value `cost` was retained for the v_col variables. The COST column is not a valid column name for the SECTION table.

```
Enter value for vtable: section
SELECT MIN(cost), MAX(cost)
                        *
ERROR at line 1:
ORA-00904: "COST": invalid identifier
```

It can also be confusing to use the && if you forget you defined the variable because you are not prompted again. Undefine the vcol variable and rerun the statement.

```
UNDEFINE vcol
/
Enter value for vcol: capacity
Enter value for vtable: section

MIN(CAPACITY) MAX(CAPACITY)
------------- -------------
          10            25

1 row selected.
```

 To display the values defined and their associated values, use the DEFINE command.

e) Enter all the following commands in a file named maxval.sql, then execute the script. For the column name supply the value `capacity` and for the table name enter the value `section`. What do you observe?

```
PROMPT Determine the maximum and minimum value of a column
ACCEPT vcol CHAR PROMPT 'Enter the column name: '
ACCEPT vtable CHAR PROMPT 'Enter the corresponding table name: '
SET VERIFY OFF
SELECT MIN(&vcol), MAX(&vcol)
  FROM &vtable
```

Answer: The PROMPT and ACCEPT commands allow for user-friendly inputs and prompts.

```
@maxval
Determine the maximum and minimum value of a column
Enter the column name: capacity
Enter the corresponding table name: section

MIN(CAPACITY) MAX(CAPACITY)
------------- -------------
          10            25

1 row selected.
```

Notice the ACCEPT SQL*Plus command defines a variable that can then be referenced with the ampersand symbol and permits prompting for the values. The SQL*Plus ACCEPT command allows for datatype checking of the entered value.

13.2.2 ANSWERS

a) Execute the following SQL statement to generate other SQL statements. What do you observe?

```
SELECT 'ALTER TABLE ' || table_name
  FROM user_constraints
 WHERE constraint_type = 'R'
```

Answer: The statement generates a list of all the tables with foreign key constraints together with a literal "ALTER TABLE".

```
'ALTERTABLE'||TABLE_NAME
-----------------------------------
ALTER TABLE COURSE
...
ALTER TABLE SECTION
ALTER TABLE SECTION
ALTER TABLE STUDENT

11 rows selected.
```

Note there are multiple rows with the same table name because a table may have multiple foreign keys.

b) Expand the SQL statement in exercise a by adding the constraint name dynamically. The resulting output should look like this:

```
ALTER TABLE COURSE DISABLE CONSTRAINT CRSE_CRSE_FK;
...
ALTER TABLE SECTION DISABLE CONSTRAINT SECT_CRSE_FK;
ALTER TABLE SECTION DISABLE CONSTRAINT SECT_INST_FK;
ALTER TABLE STUDENT DISABLE CONSTRAINT STU_ZIP_FK;

11 rows selected.
```

Answer: The disable clause is added to the statement by concatenating the text literal 'DISABLE CONSTRAINT' with the constraint name and then with another text literal containing the semicolon.

```
SELECT 'ALTER TABLE ' || table_name ||
       ' DISABLE CONSTRAINT '|| constraint_name||';'
  FROM user_constraints
 WHERE constraint_type = 'R'
```

```
'ALTERTABLE'||TABLE_NAME||'DISABLECONSTRAINT'||CONSTRAIN
--------------------------------------------------------
ALTER TABLE COURSE DISABLE CONSTRAINT CRSE_CRSE_FK;
...
ALTER TABLE SECTION DISABLE CONSTRAINT SECT_CRSE_FK;
ALTER TABLE SECTION DISABLE CONSTRAINT SECT_INST_FK;
ALTER TABLE STUDENT DISABLE CONSTRAINT STU_ZIP_FK;

11 rows selected.
```

c) Save the SQL statement in exercise b to a file named disable_fk.sql. Add the following SQL*Plus statements at the beginning of the file. Note that the double dashes represent single-line comments.

```
-- File Name: disable_fk.sql
-- Purpose: Disable Foreign Key constraints.
-- Created Date: Place current date here
-- Author: Put your name here
SET PAGESIZE 0
SET LINESIZE 80
SET FEEDBACK OFF
SET TERM OFF
SPOOL disable_fk.out
```

Add a semicolon at the end of the SQL statement and the following SQL*Plus commands afterward.

```
SPOOL OFF
SET PAGESIZE 20
SET LINESIZE 100
SET FEEDBACK ON
SET TERM ON
```

Save the file and run the disable_fk.sql file at the SQL*Plus prompt with the @ command. Describe the output from the spooled file named disable_fk.out.

Answer: The spooled file contains a list of all SQL statements necessary to disable the foreign constraints.

After editing the file, the disable_fk.sql script should look similar to the following:

```
-- File Name: disable_fk.sql
-- Purpose: Disable Foreign Key constraints.
-- Created Date: Place current date here
-- Author: Put your name here
SET PAGESIZE 0
SET LINESIZE 80
SET FEEDBACK OFF
```

**LAB
13.2**

```
SET TERM OFF
SPOOL disable_fk.out
SELECT 'ALTER TABLE ' || table_name || CHR(10)||
  '          DISABLE CONSTRAINT '|| constraint_name||';'
  FROM user_constraints
  WHERE constraint_type = 'R';
SPOOL OFF
SET PAGESIZE 20
SET LINESIZE 100
SET FEEDBACK ON
SET TERM ON
```

Executing the script disable_fk.sql with the @ command results in the disable_fk.out file, which looks like the following:

```
ALTER TABLE COURSE
      DISABLE CONSTRAINT CRSE_CRSE_FK;
...
ALTER TABLE STUDENT
      DISABLE CONSTRAINT STU_ZIP_FK;
```

You can now execute the commands in the file by typing `@disable_fk.out` at the SQL*Plus prompt. You need to specify the extension here because the file does not have the default .SQL extension.

Note the SQL statement contains the function CHR(10). This column function automatically returns a new line in the result.

COMMON SQL*PLUS COMMANDS IN SQL*PLUS SCRIPTS

The SQL*Plus commands before and after the SQL statement in the script change the settings of the SQL*Plus environment.

The SPOOL command, together with a filename, spools any subsequently issued SQL*Plus or SQL command to a file named disable_fk.out. If you don't add an extension, the default extension is .LST. The following command creates a file named temp.lst. If a file with the same name already exists, it is overwritten without warning, unless you use the new Oracle 10*g* CREATE syntax option. You can also optionally append a file with the APPEND syntax option.

```
SPOOL temp CREATE
```

To show the file name you're currently spooling to, use the SPOOL command.

```
SPOOL
currently spooling to temp.lst
```

To end the spooling and close the file, enter this command:

```
SPOOL OFF
```

Just as with other file names, you can add a path to store the file in a directory other than your default directory. To learn how to change your default directory, see Chapter 2, "SQL: The Basics."

The PAGESIZE 0 command suppresses the column headings.

The FEEDBACK command returns the number of records returned by a query. Because you don't want to see this in the resulting file you subsequently execute, issue either the command SET FEEDBACK 0 or the command SET FEEDBACK OFF.

The SET TERMOUT OFF or SET TERM OFF command controls the display of output generated by the commands. The OFF setting suppresses the output from the screen only when the command is executed from a script file.

The SET LINESIZE command determines the total number of characters SQL*Plus displays in one line before beginning a new line. Setting it to 80 makes it easy to read the spooled output in a text editor.

You want to reset all the SQL*Plus environmental variables to their previous settings. To see the current settings of all environmental variables, use the SHOW ALL command at the SQL*Plus prompt.

DOCUMENTING YOUR SCRIPT

You can document your scripts by using comments. You begin a single-line comment with two hyphens (--). A multiline comment begins with a slash and an asterisk (/*) and ends with an asterisk and a slash (*/). In SQL*Plus scripts, you can also use the REMARK (REM) command.

```
/* This is a multi-line
comment */
-- A single-line comment, it ends with a line break.
REM Another single-line comment, only used in SQL*Plus.
```

d) Write a dynamic SQL script performing the opposite operation, which is enabling the foreign key constraints. Name the file enable_fk.sql.

Answer: The spooled file contains a list of all SQL statements necessary to enable the foreign key constraints.

```
-- File Name: enable_fk.sql
-- Purpose: Enable Foreign Key constraints.
-- Created Date: Place current date here
-- Author: Put your name here
```

```
SET PAGESIZE 0
SET LINESIZE 80
SET FEEDBACK OFF
SET TERM OFF
SPOOL enable_fk.out
SELECT 'ALTER TABLE ' || table_name || CHR(10)||
       '          ENABLE CONSTRAINT '|| constraint_name||';'
  FROM user_constraints
 WHERE constraint_type = 'R';
SPOOL OFF
SET PAGESIZE 20
SET LINESIZE 80
SET FEEDBACK ON
SET TERM ON
```

e) Explain each line in the following SQL script and then describe the purpose of the script in one sentence.

```
01 /*
02 ----------------------------------------------------
03 File name:   rows.sql
04 Purpose:
05 Created by:  H. Ashley on January 7, 2000
06 Modified by: A. Christa on September 29, 2001
07 ----------------------------------------------------
08 */
09 SET TERM OFF
10 SET PAGESIZE 0
11 SET FEEDBACK OFF
12 SPOOL temp
13 SELECT 'SELECT ' || '''' || table_name || '''' ||
14        ', COUNT(*) '||CHR(10) ||
15        '  FROM '|| LOWER(table_name) || ';'
16   FROM user_tables;
17 SPOOL OFF
18 SET FEEDBACK 1
19 SET PAGESIZE 20
20 SET TERM ON
21 @temp.lst
22 HOST DEL temp.lst
```

Answer: The purpose of the script is to display a list of all user-accessible tables, together with a row count for each.

The script dynamically generates these statements and spools them to the resulting temp.lst file as follows.

```
SELECT 'course', COUNT(*)
  FROM course;
...
SELECT 'zipcode', COUNT(*)
  FROM zipcode;
```

The temp.lst file is then executed with the @temp.lst command and a count of all rows for each table is displayed.

```
'STUDEN  COUNT(*)
-------  ---------
student       268


1 row selected.
...
'ZIPCOD  COUNT(*)
-------  ---------
zipcode       227


1 row selected.
```

Lines 1 through 8 show a multiline comment; the comment starts with a /* and ends with */. Line 9 listing the command SET TERM OFF turns the output to the screen off. Line 10 sets the PAGESIZE to zero, line 11 avoids any FEEDBACK, and line 12 spools the result of all subsequent statements to the temp.lst file in the current directory. Line 13 shows an example of the literal SELECT concatenated with four single quotes. The four single quotes result in a single quote in the spooled file and the table name shows between the single quotes.

USING QUOTES IN SQL

As you see in many SQL statements, a single quote is used to enclose a text literal.

```
SELECT last_name
  FROM student
 WHERE last_name = 'Smith'
```

If you want to query, insert, update, or delete a value containing a single quote, prefix the quote with another quote.

```
SELECT last_name
  FROM student
 WHERE last_name = 'O''Neil'
```

To replicate a single quote in a dynamic SQL script, you need four quotes: two individual quotes to represent a single quote and two quotes to surround this text literal.

From Chapter 10, "Insert, Update, and Delete", you already learned that in Oracle 10*g*, you can also use an alternate quoting mechanism, which is indicated with the letter q or Q.

Line 14 displays the COUNT function to count rows. The CHR(10) function results in a new line in the spooled file. The resulting concatenation is then further combined with the literal FROM in line 15 together with the table name in lowercase and a semicolon.

Line 16 shows the query is issued against the USER_TABLES data dictionary view. Line 17 ends the spooling to the file. Lines 18, 19, and 20 reset the SQL*Plus settings to their defaults. Line 21 runs the spooled temp.lst file. Line 22 uses the HOST command to execute the operating system DEL (Delete) command to delete the temp.lst file. Instead of the HOST command, you can also use a $ (Windows and VMS operating systems) or a ! (Unix operating system). Note the delete command is unnecessary because the file is overwritten the next time you run the script. But it demonstrates the use of a Windows operating system command within SQL*Plus.

 *Frequently used SQL*Plus commands and their syntax options are listed in Appendix C, "SQL*Plus Command Reference."*

f) Enter the following commands in a file called ascii_test.sql and run the file. Describe the result of the ascii_test.out file.

```
-- File Name: ascii_test.sql
SET TRIMSPOOL ON
SET PAGESIZE 0
SET LINESIZE 100
SET FEEDBACK OFF
SET VERIFY OFF
PROMPT Enter the starting and ending course numbers
ACCEPT v_start_course_no CHAR PROMPT 'Enter starting course number: '
ACCEPT v_end_course_no CHAR PROMPT 'Enter ending course number: '
SET TERM OFF
SPOOL ascii_test.out
SELECT course_no||','''||description||''','||
       cost||','''||modified_date||''''
  FROM course
 WHERE course_no BETWEEN &v_start_course_no
       AND &v_end_course_no;
SPOOL OFF
SET PAGESIZE 20
SET LINESIZE 80
SET FEEDBACK ON
SET TERM ON
SET VERIFY ON
SET TRIMSPOOL OFF
```

Answer: The result is a comma-separated ASCII file or a flat file. You can use files of this nature to load data into other systems that accept comma-separated ASCII files. If you need to create fixed-width ASCII files, use the LPAD commands to pad values. The TRIMSPOOL command removes any trailing blanks starting at the end of the line.

The script prompts the user to enter starting and ending course number values, which in turn select only certain course numbers and their respective descriptions, costs, and last modification dates. Commas separate the column value and single quotes surround text and DATE information.

The output result of the file looks like this when the user enters a starting course number of 120 and an ending course number of 150.

```
120,'Intro to Java Programming',1195,'05-APR-03'
122,'Intermediate Java Programming',1195,'05-APR-03'
124,'Advanced Java Programming',1195,'05-APR-03'
125,'JDeveloper',1195,'05-APR-03'
130,'Intro to Unix',1195,'05-APR-03'
132,'Basics of Unix Admin',1195,'05-APR-03'
134,'Advanced Unix Admin',1195,'05-APR-03'
135,'Unix Tips and Techniques',1095,'05-APR-03'
140,'Structured Analysis',1195,'05-APR-03'
142,'Project Management',1195,'05-APR-03'
144,'Database Design',1195,'05-APR-03'
145,'Internet Protocols',1195,'05-APR-03'
146,'Java for C/C++ Programmers',1195,'05-APR-03'
147,'GUI Programming',1195,'05-APR-03'
```

g) Explain the result of the following script.

```
--File: dump_file.sql
SET TRIMSPOOL ON
SET PAGESIZE 0
SET LINESIZE 100
SET FEEDBACK OFF
SPOOL dump_file.out
SELECT 'INSERT INTO student_test VALUES
('|| student_id||','''||last_name||
''','''||first_name||''');'
  FROM student;
SPOOL OFF
SET PAGESIZE 20
SET LINESIZE 80
SET FEEDBACK ON
SET TRIMSPOOL OFF
SET TERM ON
```

Answer: This script produces INSERT statements for a table called STUDENT_TEST with values from the STUDENT_ID, LAST_NAME, and FIRST_NAME columns of the STUDENT table.

The result in the created file named dump_file.out will look similar to this result. You can then use the dump_file.out and run it to insert the values into the STUDENT_TEST table.

```
INSERT INTO student_test VALUES
(102,'Crocitto','Fred');
INSERT INTO student_test VALUES
(103,'Landry','J.');
...
INSERT INTO student_test VALUES
(397,'Lloyd','Margaret');
INSERT INTO student_test VALUES
(399,'Abdou','Jerry');
```

h) Imagine a scenario in which you would execute a script like the following.

```
--File: re_create_seq.sql
SET PAGESIZE 0
SET LINESIZE 100
SET FEEDBACK OFF
SPOOL re_create_seq.out
SELECT 'CREATE SEQUENCE '||sequence_name||
       ' START WITH '||last_number||CHR(10)||
       ' INCREMENT BY '||increment_by ||
       DECODE(cache_size, 0, ' NOCACHE',
       ' CACHE'||cache_size)||';'
  FROM seq;
SPOOL OFF
SET PAGESIZE 20
SET LINESIZE 80
SET FEEDBACK ON
SET TERM ON
```

Answer: There are times when you need to recreate certain database objects; perhaps you need to replicate the same setup in another database or to make changes to database objects without creating the scripts from scratch. You can also use the DBMS_METADATA package to retrieve DDL for data dictionary objects.

```
CREATE SEQUENCE COURSE_NO_SEQ START WITH 454
  INCREMENT BY 1 NOCACHE;
...
CREATE SEQUENCE STUDENT_ID_SEQ START WITH 401
  INCREMENT BY 1 NOCACHE;
```

LAB 13.2 SELF-REVIEW QUESTIONS

In order to test your progress, you should be able to answer the following questions.

1) The following statements are SQL*Plus commands, not SQL commands.

```
SET FEEDBACK ON
SET HEADING ON
COL student FORMAT A20
START
DEFINE v_stud_id
```

   a) _____ True
   b) _____ False

2) What is the result of the following SELECT statement?

```
SELECT 'HELLO ' || CHR(10) || 'THERE'
   FROM dual
```

   a) _____ HELLO THERE
   b) _____ HELLO
                 THERE
   c) _____ Invalid query

3) Dynamic SQL scripts are useful for generating SQL statements.

   a) _____ True
   b) _____ False

4) The $ command and the HOST command are equivalent in SQL*Plus.

   a) _____ True
   b) _____ False

5) The following SELECT statement returns a single quote.

```
SELECT ''''
   FROM dual
```

   a) _____ True
   b) _____ False

6) Dynamic SQL scripts avoid repetitive coding.

    a) _____   True

    b) _____   False

Answers appear in Appendix A, Section 13.2.

CHAPTER 13

TEST YOUR THINKING

The projects in this section are meant to have you utilize all of the skills that you have acquired throughout this chapter. The answers to these projects can be found at the companion Web site to this book, located at: *http://authors.phptr.com/rischert3e*. Visit the Web site periodically to share and discuss your answers.

1) Formulate the question that is answered by the following query.

```
SELECT table_name, column_name, comments
  FROM user_col_comments
```

2) Describe the differences between the views USER_USERS, ALL_USERS, and DBA_USERS.

3) Name the underlying data dictionary views for the public synonyms TABS and COLS.

4) Write a dynamic SQL script to drop all views in the STUDENT schema. If there are no views, create some to test your script.

SECURITY

Oracle protects the data in the database by implementing security via users, roles, and privileges. The SQL language commands used to accomplish these security tasks are known as data control language (DCL) commands.

Oracle provides several different ways to enforce access control to ensure that only authorized users can login to the database. You want to avoid situations whereby a user can accidentally drop an important table or sidestep security rules. Every database user has certain *system privileges* that determine the type of actions a user can perform, such as create tables, drop views, or create other users.

Object privileges avoid any wrongful data modifications to individual tables or columns. The owner of the database objects can assign these object privileges which control exactly who can access what objects and to what extent.

System and object privileges can be grouped together into a *role*. Setting up the correct security for database users is a task performed by a DBA. It is vital that the database is properly protected against any wrongful actions and unauthorized access.

LAB 14.1

USERS, PRIVILEGES, ROLES, AND SYNONYMS

LAB OBJECTIVES

After this lab, you will be able to:
✔ Create Users and Grant and Revoke Privileges
✔ Create and Use Synonyms
✔ Create User-Defined Roles

WHAT IS A SCHEMA?

A *schema* is a collection of objects (e.g., tables, views, indexes, sequences, triggers, synonyms). Each schema is owned by a single user account with the same name; in fact, the two terms are often used interchangeably.

You can list the types of objects in the STUDENT schema by querying the USER_OBJECTS data dictionary view.

```
SELECT DISTINCT object_type
  FROM user_objects
OBJECT_TYPE
------------------
INDEX
SEQUENCE
...
VIEW

5 rows selected.
```

To see all the different types of objects available for the user accessing the database, query the ALL_OBJECTS view. The result set on your database may vary from this result, as various users may have different object types and different privileges.

```
SELECT DISTINCT object_type
  FROM all_objects
OBJECT_TYPE
------------------
...
INDEX
...
PACKAGE
PACKAGE BODY
PROCEDURE
SEQUENCE
SYNONYM
TABLE
TABLE PARTITION
TRIGGER
...

25 rows selected.
```

SPECIAL USERS. SYSTEM AND SYS

When an Oracle database is created it comes with a number of default accounts. Two extremely important accounts are SYS and SYSTEM.

The SYS account is the most privileged user. It owns the data dictionary. Do not drop any of the objects of the SYS schema because you will endanger the critical operation of the Oracle database.

The SYSTEM account is automatically granted the DBA role. This role includes all the database administration privileges, except for the startup and shutdown privilege of the database. The SYSTEM account is typically used to create regular user accounts or accounts with the DBA role.

Oracle suggests that you create an administrative type of account after the creation of the database with the DBA role. This account is used to perform daily administrative tasks and avoids the use of the SYS and SYSTEM accounts.

CREATING USERS

To log into the Oracle database, a user must have a user name, a password, and certain system privileges. A user name is created with the CREATE USER command. Following is the syntax:

```
CREATE USER user IDENTIFIED
    {BY password [REPLACE oldPassword]
     |EXTERNALLY|GLOBALLY AS 'external name'}
[{DEFAULT TABLESPACE tablespace |
 TEMPORARY TABLESPACE {tablespace|tablespace_group}|
 QUOTA {integer[K|M] | UNLIMITED} ON tablespace
    [[QUOTA {integer[K|M] | UNLIMITED} ON tablespace]...]|
 PROFILE profile |
 PASSWORD EXPIRE |
 ACCOUNT {LOCK|UNLOCK}
    }]
```

To create a new user, first login as a user that has DBA privileges or as the user SYSTEM. The creation of user accounts is a task a database administrator performs. The following statement creates a new user called MUSIC with a password of LISTEN.

```
CREATE USER music IDENTIFIED BY listen
   DEFAULT TABLESPACE users
   TEMPORARY TABLESPACE temp
   QUOTA 15 M ON users
User created.
```

The User created message indicates the successful creation of the user. The keywords DEFAULT TABLESPACE indicate where any of the user's objects are stored. Here the tablespace is called USERS. The TEMPORARY TABLESPACE keywords allow you to determine where any sorting of data that cannot be performed in memory is temporarily stored.

In preparation for creating users in your database, you must find out what tablespaces exist in your Oracle database. Query the USER_TABLESPACES or DBA_TABLESPACES data dictionary views with the following query:

```
SELECT tablespace_name
  FROM dba_tablespaces
 ORDER BY tablespace_name
```

You can also refer to the readme.txt file on the companion Web site located at: *http://authors.phptr.com/rischert3e* for an example of how the STUDENT user was created.

After you assign a default tablespace to the user, this does not mean that the user can actually store objects in this tablespace. The QUOTA 15 M ON users clause allows the MUSIC user to use up to 15 megabytes on the USERS tablespace.

If you do not specify a default tablespace or temporary tablespace clause, the default tablespace and temporary tablespace will default to the SYSTEM tablespace. It is never good practice to use the SYSTEM tablespace as the default or temporary tablespace because the SYSTEM tablespace should only contain the data dictionary and other internal Oracle system-related objects. If you run out of space on this SYSTEM tablespace, it will bring the system to a complete halt.

In Oracle 10g, you can specify a default temporary tablespace at the time of database creation or later on through an ALTER DATABASE command. This avoids the use of the SYSTEM tablespace in case the default and/or temporary tablespace for a user was not setup.

CHANGING THE PASSWORD
AND ALTERING THE USER SETTINGS

When a individual user's account settings need to change, such as the password or the default tablespace, the user can be altered. The syntax of the ALTER USER command is as follows:

```
ALTER USER {user [IDENTIFIED
    {BY password [REPLACE oldPassword]|
     EXTERNALLY|GLOBALLY AS 'external name'}
    DEFAULT TABLESPACE tablespace |
    TEMPORARY TABLESPACE {tablespace|tablespace_group} |
    QUOTA {integer [K|M] | UNLIMITED} ON tablespace
      [[QUOTA {integer [K|M] | UNLIMITED} ON tablespace]...]|
    PROFILE profile |
    DEFAULT ROLE
      {role [,role]...|ALL[EXCEPT role [,role]...]|NONE}|
    PASSWORD EXPIRE |
    ACCOUNT {LOCK|UNLOCK}
    }}
```

The following statement changes MUSIC's password from LISTEN to TONE and changes the default tablespace from USERS to USER_DATA.

```
ALTER USER music IDENTIFIED BY tone
   DEFAULT TABLESPACE USER_DATA
User altered.
```

CHANGING THE PASSWORD WITHIN SQL*PLUS OR iSQL*PLUS

If you are using SQL*Plus for Windows or *i*SQL*Plus, you don't have to enter the ALTER USER command to change your password.

If you are using *i*SQL*Plus, click on Preferences to display the Change Password screen and enter the new and old passwords. Remember to click the Apply button when you are done.

If you are using SQL*Plus for Windows, type the SQL*Plus PASSWORD command at the SQL> prompt. This will bring up a dialog box that prompts you to enter the old and new passwords.

OPERATING SYSTEM AUTHENTICATION

Instead of using Oracle's logon name, a user can be authenticated through the operating system account; this is done via the IDENTIFIED BY EXTERNALLY password option. Operating system authentication is offered on some platforms (e.g., Unix and Windows) and a user name and password does not need to be entered when connecting to SQL*Plus. Furthermore, the operating system controls password modifications and expirations. You can find out more about this topic in the *Oracle Platform Guide* for your respective operating system.

LOCKED ACCOUNTS

Oracle creates a number of default user accounts as part of the database installation process that may be locked. You can use the ALTER USER command with the ACCOUNT LOCK option to unlock those accounts if they need to be used by your user community.

As you have noticed, Oracle has a large number of syntax options as part of the ALTER USER command. You will explore these different options throughout this lab.

DROPPING USERS

A user is dropped with the following command.

```
DROP USER music
User dropped.
```

The DROP USER command drops the user if the user does not own any objects. This is the syntax for the DROP USER command:

```
DROP USER user [CASCADE]
```

If you want to also drop the objects owned by the user, execute the DROP USER command with the CASCADE keyword:

```
DROP USER music CASCADE
```

 If the objects and their data need to be preserved, be sure to first back up the data using the Oracle Data Pump Export utility program or any other reliable method.

LOGIN AND LOGOUT OF SQL*PLUS

Instead of exiting *i*SQL*Plus or SQL*Plus and starting another session under a different login name, you can login with the CONNECT command at the SQL*Plus prompt. The CONNECT command can be abbreviated to CONN, followed by the user ID, a forward slash, and the password:

```
SQL> CONN system/manager
Connected.
```

Following is the syntax for the CONNECT command.

```
CONN[ECT] username/password[@connect_identifier] [AS
{SYSOPER|SYSDBA}]
```

Or:

```
CONN[ECT] /[@connect_identifier] AS {SYSOPER|SYSDBA}
```

If you do not supply the password, you will be prompted to enter it as you see in the next example. This may be useful if you do not want to display the password on the screen. Note that if you are using *i*SQL*Plus, you must always supply the username and password; *i*SQL*Plus cannot prompt you for these values.

```
SQL> CONN system
Enter password: ******
Connected.
```

The next example shows how you include the host string identifying the name of the database you want to connect if you are connecting to a database other than

LAB 14.1

the default or local database. In this case the remote database name is called ITCHY and is referenced with the @ symbol.

```
CONN system/manager@itchy
```

The second set of syntax options shows the forward slash (/) instead of the user-name and password. This allows a logon with the operating system account. Later in the chapter you will learn about the /NOLOG option, SYSOPER, and SYSDBA privileges.

When you connect as another user while you are running a SQL*Plus session, you are no longer logged in as the previous user. If you prefer, you can just start a new SQL*Plus session to keep both sessions connected.

 *If during your session, you are unsure to which login account you are connected to, issue the SHOW USER command, or simply change your SQLPROMPT from SQL> to the current user account with the SET SQLPROMPT _USER> command. The SQLPROMPT command is discussed in Chapter 13, "The Data Dictionary and Advanced SQL*PLUS commands."*

WHAT ARE PRIVILEGES?

A privilege is a right to execute a particular type of SQL statement. There are two types of privileges: system privileges and object privileges. An example of a system privilege is the right to create a table or an index. A particular object privilege allows you to access an individual object, such as the privilege to SELECT from the INSTRUCTOR table, to DELETE from the ZIPCODE table, or to SELECT a number from a specific sequence.

SYSTEM PRIVILEGES

To establish a connection to the database, the user must be granted certain system privileges. These privileges are granted either individually or in the form of roles. A role is a collection of privileges.

Although the user MUSIC is created, the user cannot start a SQL*Plus session, as you see from the following error message. The user lacks the CREATE SESSION system privilege to login to the database.

```
CONN music/tone
ERROR: ORA-01045: user MUSIC lacks CREATE SESSION
privilege; logon denied
```

Table 14.1 ■ Examples of System Privileges

	System Privilege Name
Session	CREATE SESSION
	ALTER SESSION
Table	CREATE TABLE
	CREATE ANY TABLE
	ALTER ANY TABLE
	DROP ANY TABLE
	SELECT ANY TABLE
	UPDATE ANY TABLE
	DELETE ANY TABLE
	FLASHBACK ANY TABLE
Index	CREATE ANY INDEX
	ALTER ANY INDEX
	DROP ANY INDEX
Sequence	CREATE SEQUENCE
	CREATE ANY SEQUENCE
	ALTER ANY SEQUENCE
	DROP ANY SEQUENCE
View	CREATE VIEW
	CREATE ANY VIEW
	DROP ANY VIEW

Table 14.1 lists a few examples of individual system privileges that can be granted to a user.

For example, if you have the CREATE TABLE privilege, you may create tables in your schema; if you have the CREATE ANY TABLE privilege, you may create tables in another user's schema. The CREATE TABLE privilege includes the CREATE INDEX privilege, but before you are allowed to create these objects you must make sure you have been granted a quota on the individual tablespace on which you would like to place the object. In Oracle versions prior to 10*g*, the SELECT ANY TABLE privilege gave access to all tables, including the data dictionary views. Now the SELECT ANY TABLE no longer permits data dictionary access; instead, a new object privilege called SELECT ANY DICTIONARY privileges provides SELECT rights on the data dictionary views.

OBJECT PRIVILEGES

Object privileges are granted for a particular object (i.e., table, view, sequence). Examples of object privileges are listed in Table 14.2.

Table 14.2 ■ Examples of Commonly Used Object Privileges

Object Type	Privilege	Purpose
TABLE	SELECT	The right to query from an individual table.
	INSERT	The right to add new rows into an individual table
	UPDATE	The right to change rows in an individual table. You can optionally specify to allow UPDATE rights only on individual columns.
	DELETE	The right to remove rows from an individual table.
	REFERENCES	The right to reference a table in a foreign key constraint.
	ALTER	The right to change table and column definitions.
	INDEX	The right to create indexes on the individual table.
	FLASHBACK	The right to flashback a table.
	ALL	All possible object privileges on a table.
SEQUENCE	SELECT	Increment values from a sequence and retrieve current values.
	ALTER	Change the sequence definition.
PL/SQL Stored Objects	EXECUTE	Execute any stored procedure, function, or package.

THE GRANT COMMAND

A system privilege or an object privilege is given to a user with the GRANT command. Privileges can be granted individually or through a role.

The syntax to grant system privileges is as follows:

```
GRANT {system_privilege|role|ALL PRIVILEGES}
   [,{system_privilege|role|ALL PRIVILEGES}]...
TO {user|role|PUBLIC}[,{user|role|PUBLIC}]...
[WITH ADMIN OPTION]
```

The following statement grants the CREATE SESSION system privilege to the MUSIC user. This allows the MUSIC user to establish a session to the database.

```
GRANT CREATE SESSION TO music
```

Object privileges grant certain privileges on specific objects such as tables, views, or sequences. You grant object privileges to other users when you want them to have access to objects you created. You can also grant users access to objects you do not own if the object's owner gave you permission to extend rights to others.

The following lists the general syntax for granting object privileges:

```
GRANT {object_privilege|ALL [PRIVILEGES]}
      [(column[,column]... )]
   [,{object_privilege|ALL [PRIVILEGES]}
      [(column[,column]... )]]...
ON objectname
TO {user|role|PUBLIC}[,{user|role|PUBLIC}]...
[WITH GRANT OPTION]
```

For example, the following statement connects as the STUDENT user account and grants the SELECT privilege on the COURSE table to the new user MUSIC.

```
CONN student/learn
Connected.


GRANT SELECT ON course TO music
Grant succeeded.
```

In this case, the STUDENT user is the grantor and MUSIC is the grantee, the recipient of the privileges. Now the MUSIC user can query the COURSE table.

In addition to SELECT, other object privileges can be granted on a table, such as INSERT, UPDATE, DELETE, ALTER, INDEX, and REFERENCES (see Table 14.2). The ALTER privilege allows another user to change table definitions with the ALTER table command, the INDEX privilege allows the creation of indexes on the table, and the REFERENCES privilege allows the table to be referenced with a foreign key constraint. You can also grant all object privileges at once with the GRANT ALL command.

Object privileges can be assigned to other database objects such as sequences, packages, procedures, and functions. SELECT and ALTER privileges can be granted on sequences. Packages, procedures, and functions require the EXECUTE privilege if other users want to run these stored programs.

If an object, such as a table, is dropped and then re-created, the grants need to be reissued. This is not the case if the object is replaced with the CREATE OR REPLACE keywords available for views and stored programs.

GRANTING PRIVILEGES ON COLUMNS

You can grant UPDATE and REFERENCES privileges on individual columns on a table. For example, to grant UPDATE on the columns COST and DESCRIPTION of the COURSE table, execute the following command.

```
GRANT UPDATE (cost, description) ON course TO music
Grant succeeded.
```

ROLES

Roles are several privileges collected under one role name; this aids in administration of multiple privileges to users. Oracle includes predefined roles—three popular ones that contain a number of different system privileges are CONNECT, RESOURCE, and DBA.

The CONNECT role includes the CREATE SESSION system privilege that allows a user to start a SQL*Plus session, as well as create views, tables, and sequences among other operations. The RESOURCE role allows the user to create tables and indexes on any tablespace and to create PL/SQL stored objects (packages, procedures, functions). The DBA role includes all system privileges. This role is usually granted only to a user who performs database administration tasks. Table 14.3 lists the system privileges associated with each role. You also can query the DBA_SYS_PRIVS data dictionary view to list the individual system privileges for each role as this may change in future versions.

Table 14.3 ■ The CONNECT, RESOURCE, and DBA Roles

Role	Purpose
CONNECT	This role encompasses the following system privileges: CREATE SESSION, CREATE TABLE, CREATE VIEW, CREATE SYNONYM, CREATE SEQUENCE, ALTER SESSION, CREATE CLUSTER, CREATE DATABASE LINK
RESOURCE	This role includes these system privileges: CREATE TABLE, CREATE SEQUENCE, CREATE TRIGGER, CREATE PROCEDURE, CREATE CLUSTER, CREATE INDEXTYPE, CREATE OPERATOR, CREATE TYPE
DBA	This role includes all system privileges and allows them to be granted WITH ADMIN OPTION.

When a user is granted a role, the user acquires all the privileges defined within the role. The following statement uses the two predefined Oracle roles, CONNECT and RESOURCE, to grant a number of system privileges to the new user.

```
GRANT CONNECT, RESOURCE TO music
Grant succeeded.
```

ABILITY TO EXTEND THE PRIVILEGES TO OTHERS

To extend an object privilege to another user, you must be the owner of the object or have received the privilege to pass it on to others through the WITH GRANT OPTION. You may also pass on the privilege, if you have been granted the GRANT

ANY OBJECT system privilege. The following SQL statement grants all object privileges on the COURSE table to the MUSIC user. It also passes on to the MUSIC user the ability to grant these privileges to yet other users using the WITH GRANT OPTION. Here, MUSIC is the grantee, but can become a grantor if the privilege is passed on to another user.

```
GRANT ALL ON course TO music WITH GRANT OPTION
Grant succeeded.
```

To allow users to pass on system privileges to other users, you must have been granted the system privilege with the WITH ADMIN OPTION or have been granted the GRANT ANY PRIVILEGE system privilege. For example, after execution of the following statement, the user MUSIC will be able to grant the CREATE SESSION system privilege to other users:

```
GRANT CREATE SESSION TO music WITH ADMIN OPTION
Grant succeeded.
```

If you want other users to pass on a role to others, you must have either created the role, have been granted the role through the WITH ADMIN OPTION, or been granted the GRANT ANY ROLE system privilege.

You can see which system privileges you received through a role by querying the Oracle data dictionary view ROLE_SYS_PRIVS. For granted system privileges, query the data dictionary views USER_SYS_PRIVS or DBA_SYS_PRIVS. Table 14.4 lists a number of data dictionary views you may find useful when trying to determine individual object privileges, system privileges, and roles.

Table 14.4 ■ Useful Data Dictionary Views

Data Dictionary View	Purpose
SESSION_PRIVS	All current system privileges available to an individual user
USER_SYS_PRIVS	System privileges granted to the user
ROLE_SYS_PRIVS	System privileges received through a role
ROLE_TAB_PRIVS	Object privileges received through a role
USER_TAB_PRIVS	Object grants
USER_COL_PRIVS	Individual column grants
USER_TAB_PRIVS_RECD	Object privileges received by the user
USER_TAB_PRIVS_MADE	Object privileges made by the user

THE REVOKE COMMAND

Privileges can be taken away with the REVOKE command. Use this syntax to revoke system privileges.

```
REVOKE {system_privilege|role|ALL PRIVILEGES}
   [,{system_privilege|role|ALL PRIVILEGES}]...
FROM {user|role|PUBLIC}[,{user|rolc|PUBLIC}]...
```

The next example shows how the RESOURCE role is revoked from the user named MUSIC.

```
REVOKE RESOURCE FROM music
Revoke succeeded.
```

Object privileges can also be revoked, as in the following statement.

```
REVOKE UPDATE ON course FROM music
Revoke succeeded.
```

The syntax for revoking object privileges is listed here:

```
REVOKE {object_privilege|ALL [PRIVILEGES]}
   [( column[,column]... )]
   [,{object_privilege|ALL [PRIVILEGES]}
   [(column[,column]...)]]...
ON objectname
FROM {user|role|PUBLIC}[,{user|role|PUBLIC}]...
[CASCADE CONSTRAINTS]
```

The CASCADE CONSTRAINTS clause is only needed if you revoke the REFER-ENCES or ALL privileges. The REFERENCES privilege allows you to create a referential integrity constraint based on another user's object. The CASCADE CON-STRAINT options will drop any defined referential constraints when you revoke the REFERENCES privilege.

Object privileges granted using the WITH GRANT OPTION are revoked if the grantor's object privilege is revoked. For example, assume USER1 is granted SELECT privilege on the COURSE table using the WITH GRANT OPTION and grants the same privilege to USER2. If the SELECT privilege is revoked from USER1, then the revoke cascades to USER2.

Revoking object privileges cascades the REVOKE to other users. However, revoking system privileges does not have a cascading effect.

REFERRING TO OBJECTS IN OTHER SCHEMAS

The MUSIC user still has the SELECT privilege on the COURSE table issued earlier. Observe what occurs when you connect as the MUSIC user and attempt to query the table.

```
CONN music/tone
Connected.

SELECT description
  FROM course
  FROM course
      *
ERROR at line 2:
ORA-00942: table or view does not exist
```

Even though the user MUSIC is allowed to query the COURSE table, MUSIC does not own the COURSE table and must qualify the name of the schema where the object exists. Because the COURSE table exists in the STUDENT schema, you prefix the table name with the schema name.

```
SELECT description
  FROM student.course
DESCRIPTION
---------------------------
DP Overview
Intro to Computers
...
JDeveloper Techniques
DB Programming in Java

30 rows selected.
```

The COURSE table is now qualified with the name of the user who owns the COURSE table, namely STUDENT. When any query, DML, or DDL statement is issued in Oracle, the database assumes the object being referenced is in the user's own schema unless it is otherwise qualified.

PRIVATE SYNONYMS

Instead of qualifying the name of an object with the object owner's name, a synonym can be used. A synonym is a way to alias an object with another name. You can create private and public synonyms. A private synonym is a synonym in a user's schema; public synonyms are visible to everyone.

The syntax for creating synonyms is as follows:

```
CREATE [PUBLIC] SYNONYM [schema.]synonymname
   FOR [schema.]objectname[@dblink]
```

The next CREATE SYNONYM command creates a private synonym called COURSE in the MUSIC schema for the COURSE table located in the STUDENT schema.

```
CREATE SYNONYM course FOR student.course
```
Synonym created.

If you are not logged in as the MUSIC user, but as a user who has rights to create synonyms in another user's schema, such as a DBA, you must prefix the synonym's name with the schema name in which the synonym should be created.

```
CREATE SYNONYM music.course FOR student.course
```

After the synonym is successfully created in the MUSIC schema, you can select from the COURSE table without prefixing the table with the schema name.

```
SELECT description
   FROM course
```
DESCRIPTION

DP Overview
Intro to Computers
...
JDeveloper Techniques
DB Programming in Java

30 rows selected.

The SELECT statement is resolved by looking at the synonym COURSE, which points to the COURSE table located in the STUDENT schema.

Whenever any statement is executed, Oracle looks in the current schema for the object. If there is no object of that name in the current schema, Oracle checks for a public synonym of that name.

When you create a synonym, the validity of the underlying object is not checked; that is, you can create a synonym without the object existing. The synonym will be created without error, but will get an error message if you attempt to access the synonym. The next synonym called SYN_TEST is based on a nonexisting TEST_ME object, which could be a view, table, another synonym, or another type of Oracle object.

```
CREATE SYNONYM syn_test FOR test_me
```
Synonym created.

The access of the synonym results in this message:

```
SQL>SELECT *
  2    FROM test_me;
  FROM test_me
       *
ERROR at line 2:
ORA-00942: table or view does not exist
```

PUBLIC SYNONYMS

All synonyms are private unless the keyword PUBLIC is specified. Public synonyms are visible to all users of the database. However, this does not automatically grant any object privileges to the underlying objects. Grants still need to be issued to either individual users or to PUBLIC by referring to either the public synonym or the underlying object. For the user MUSIC, the following statements create a table, create a public synonym for the table, and grant the SELECT privilege on the table to the user STUDENT.

```
CREATE TABLE instrument
  (instrument_id  NUMBER(10),
   description     VARCHAR2(25))
Table created.

CREATE PUBLIC SYNONYM instrument FOR instrument
Synonym created.

GRANT SELECT ON instrument TO student
Grant succeeded.
```

Now the user STUDENT can perform queries against the public synonym or table INSTRUMENT located in the MUSIC schema. The user STUDENT, or for that matter any other user, does not need to prefix the INSTRUMENT table with the owner. However, users other than the user STUDENT do not have access to the table. If you want every user in the database system to have SELECT privileges, you can grant the SELECT privilege to PUBLIC:

```
GRANT SELECT ON instrument TO PUBLIC
```

 The ability to create public synonyms is typically granted to users with DBA privileges. To complete the exercises in this chapter for public synonyms, have your database administrator grant the user STUDENT this privilege or login as SYSTEM and grant the system privilege CREATE PUBLIC SYNONYM with the following statement:
```
GRANT CREATE PUBLIC SYNONYM TO student.
```

DROP AND RENAME SYNONYMS

Synonyms are dropped with the DROP SYNONYM command. The next commands drop the COURSE synonym and the public INSTRUMENT synonym.

```
DROP SYNONYM course
```
Synonym dropped.

```
DROP PUBLIC SYNONYM instrument
```
Synonym dropped.

Should a synonym already exist and you want to change the definition, you can use the CREATE OR REPLACE SYNONYM command, instead of dropping and re-creating a synonym.

```
CREATE OR REPLACE PUBLIC SYNONYM instrument FOR guitar
```

The RENAME command renames a synonym to a new name.

```
RENAME instrument TO instrument2
```

RESOLVING SCHEMA REFERENCES

Suppose your schema contains a public synonym INSTRUMENT referring to a table in another user's schema and a table named INSTRUMENT in your own schema. When you issue a query against INSTRUMENT, Oracle resolves the schema reference by referring to the object in your own schema first. If such an object does not exist, it refers to the public synonym.

USER-DEFINED ROLES

In addition to Oracle's predefined system privilege roles (e.g., CONNECT, RESOURCE, DBA), user-defined roles can be created to customize a grouping of system and/or object privileges. There may be different types of users for a given system. Sometimes, there are users who only view data, so those users only need SELECT privileges. There are other users who maintain the data, so they typically need a combination of SELECT, INSERT, UPDATE, and DELETE privileges on certain tables and columns. Perhaps a group of programmers need to privileges to create procedures, functions, and packages.

The syntax to create a role is as follows:

```
CREATE ROLE rolename
```

The following statement creates a role named READ_DATA_ONLY for users who only need to query the data in the STUDENT schema.

```
CREATE ROLE read_data_only
```
Role created.

The role still does not have any privileges associated with it. The following SELECT statement generates other statements, granting SELECT privileges on all of the STUDENT schema's tables to the new role READ_DATA_ONLY.

```
SELECT 'GRANT SELECT ON '||table_name||
       ' TO read_data_only;'
  FROM user_tables
```

When the statement is executed from a script that in turn executes each resulting statement, the individual commands issued look similar to the following. If you are unsure how dynamic SQL scripts work, refer to Chapter 13, "The Data Dictionary and Advanced SQL*Plus Commands."

```
GRANT SELECT ON COURSE TO read_data_only;
...
GRANT SELECT ON STUDENT TO read_data_only;
GRANT SELECT ON ZIPCODE TO read_data_only;
```

With these individually executed statements, the role READ_DATA_ONLY obtains a collection of privileges. The next step is to grant the READ_DATA_ONLY role to users so these users have the privileges defined by the role. The following statement grants every user in the database this role by granting the READ_DATA_ONLY role to PUBLIC.

```
GRANT read_data_only TO PUBLIC
```
Grant succeeded.

Now all users of the database have SELECT privileges on all of the STUDENT schema's tables. All privileges defined by the role can be revoked in a single statement, as in the following.

```
REVOKE read_data_only FROM PUBLIC
```
Revoke succeeded.

If you want none of the users to have the SELECT privilege to the COURSE table any more, you can revoke this privilege from the individual role only, and all users that have been granted this role will no longer have access to the table. You see that this makes the management of privileges fairly easy. If you want to grant the READ_DATA_ONLY role only to individual users, such as the MUSIC user instead of PUBLIC, you can issue a statement such as this:

```
GRANT read_data_only TO MUSIC
```

Roles can be granted with the WITH ADMIN option. It allows the user to pass these privileges on to others.

The data dictionary views shown in Table 14.5 list information about roles.

Table 14.5 ■ Data Dictionary Views Related to Roles

Data Dictionary View	Purpose
DBA_ROLES	All roles in the database
USER_ROLE_PRIVS	Roles granted to current user
DBA_ROLE_PRIVS	Shows roles granted to users and other roles
ROLE_ROLE_PRIVS	Roles granted to roles
ROLE_SYS_PRIVS	System privileges granted to roles
DBA_SYS_PRIVS	System privileges granted to roles and users
ROLE_TAB_PRIVS	Object privileges granted to roles
SESSION_ROLES	Roles a user has currently enabled

The ability to create roles may be performed only by users with DBA privileges or by individual users granted the CREATE ROLE privilege. To complete the exercises in this chapter for user-defined roles, have your DBA grant this privilege to the STUDENT user or login as SYSTEM and grant this system privilege by executing the following statement: GRANT CREATE ROLE TO student.

Roles are dropped with the DROP ROLE command.

```
DROP ROLE read_data_only
Role dropped.
```

PROFILE

A profile is a name for identifying specific resource limits or password features. A user account is always associated with a profile. If at the creation of an account a profile is not specified, the default profile is used. With a profile you can enforce features such as password expiration settings, maximum idle times (maximum time without any activity for a session), or the maximum number of concurrent sessions.

There are many different profile options; the following syntax lists the most commonly used options:

```
CREATE PROFILE profilename LIMIT
{{SESSIONS_PER_USER|
  CPU_PER_SESSION|
  CPU_PER_CALL|
  CONNECT_TIME|
  IDLE_TIME}
   {integer|UNLIMITED|DEFAULT}}|
{{FAILED_LOGIN_ATTEMPTS|
  PASSWORD_LIFE_TIME|
  PASSWORD_REUSE_TIME|
  PASSWORD_REUSE_MAX|
  PASSWORD_LOCK_TIME|
  PASSWORD_GRACE_TIME}
   {expression|UNLIMITED|DEFAULT}}
```

The next statement creates a profile named MEDIUM_SECURITY. The effect of this profile is that the password expires after 30 days. If the user logs in with the wrong password, the account is locked after three failed attempts. The password will be locked for one hour (1/24th of a day) unless the DBA unlocks it with the ALTER USER user_name ACCOUNT UNLOCK command. The maximum number of concurrent sessions a user may have is 3 and the inactivity time, excluding long-running queries, is 15 minutes.

```
CREATE PROFILE medium_security
  LIMIT
  PASSWORD_LIFE_TIME 30
  FAILED_LOGIN_ATTEMPTS 3
  PASSWORD_LOCK_TIME 1/24
  SESSIONS_PER_USER 3
  IDLE_TIME 15
Profile created.
```

When the password expires after the 30 days, the user will be prompted in SQL*Plus to change the password and can only login if the change is successful.

You assign a profile to an individual user with the ALTER USER command. The user's resource and password restrictions and are then limited within the definition of the profile.

```
ALTER USER music
  PROFILE medium_security
User altered.
```

Profiles can be changed with the ALTER PROFILE command and removed with the DROP PROFILE statement. If you drop a profile, any assigned users associated with this profile will automatically be assigned the DEFAULT profile. You can see information about profiles in the data dictionary views DBA_PROFILES and

DBA_USERS. These views are only available if you have the right to see DBA_ views.

The Whole Truth

You can implement stored PL/SQL procedures to encapsulate the security access and business rules to certain transactions. For example, you can create a PL/SQL procedure to update individual employee salaries only during certain hours and within a certain percentage increase range. This avoids granting UPDATE rights on the SALARY column of the EMPLOYEE table; instead, you grant the users the right to execute the procedure through which all salary updates must be performed. All the security and logic is enforced and encapsulated within the procedure. For even finer grained access control, Oracle provides a feature called the *virtual private database* (VPD) also referred to as *Fine Grained Access Control* (FGAC); it allows very sophisticated control over many aspects of data manipulation and data access.

SECURITY IMPLEMENTATION

In live production environments users typically never log on as the owner of the tables they access. Imagine the scenario whereby an application user knows the password of the STUDENT account. If the user logs in as the owner of the objects using SQL*Plus, he or she has the ability to drop tables, update any of the data, or drop any of the indexes in the schema. Needless to say, this situation is a disaster waiting to happen. Therefore, a responsible and cautious DBA creates one user account that receives grants for the objects. For example, the DBA may create a STUDENT_USER account to which the application users have access instead. This account is granted SELECT, INSERT, UPDATE, and DELETE privileges on the various tables. The DBA creates synonyms (private or public) so the STUDENT_USER's queries do not need the owner prefix. This STUDENT_USER account cannot drop individual tables or alter them because the account is not the owner of the table, and the DBA does not grant the system privileges such as the DROP ANY TABLE or ALTER ANY TABLE privilege. There are many ways to implement security and additional fine-grained security will probably be accomplished through the individual application that restrict users to specific screens. Each individual security implementation will depend on the unique requirements of an application. Oracle provides a variety of ways to control user access including administration through granting of various privileges and administration through roles or different user accounts.

CONNECTING WITH SPECIAL
PRIVILEGES: SYSOPER AND SYSDBA

Oracle allows special privileged modes of connection to the database. They are called SYSOPER and SYSDBA. The SYSOPER privilege allows startup and shutdown operations and other basic operational tasks such as backups, but does not allow the user to look at the user data. The SYSDBA privilege allows you to perform startup and shutdown of the database and to effectively connect as the most privileged user, which is the SYS user account.

You connect with your user schema name and append AS SYSOPER or AS SYSDBA. For example, to connect in SQL*Plus (not *i*SQL*Plus), you can issue the following CONNECT command if the MUSIC user has been granted the SYSDBA privilege.

```
CONNECT music AS SYSDBA
```

The user MUSIC is now in a privileged mode of connection that allows the startup or shutdown the database with the STARTUP and SHUTDOWN commands.

When connected as SYSDBA or SYSOPER, you are not connected with the schema associated with your username. But rather, if you connect as SYSOPER, you connect as the owner PUBLIC, and for SYSDBA as the owner SYS, which is the most highly privileged user and owns the data dictionary.

STARTING UP AND SHUTTING DOWN A DATABASE

The next statements show how to shut down a database with the SHUTDOWN command.

```
SQL> CONN system AS SYSDBA
Enter password: *****
Connected.

SQL> SHUTDOWN
Database closed.
Database dismounted.
ORACLE instance shut down.
```

To start up the database, you use the STARTUP command.

```
SQL> CONN system AS SYSDBA
Enter password: *****
Connected.

SQL> STARTUP
ORACLE instance started.
```

```
Total System Global Area    192937984 bytes
Fixed Size                      769488 bytes
Variable Size               143573552 bytes
Database Buffers             25165824 bytes
Redo Buffers                 23429120 bytes
Database mounted.
Database opened.
```

THE NOLOG ARGUMENT

You may also use the SQL*Plus NOLOG argument to obtain the SQL*Plus prompt but not yet login to the database. This is useful if you want to connect as SYSDBA or SYSOPER to perform database administration tasks such the STARTUP or SHUT-DOWN of the database. Figure 14.1 shows how to enter the NOLOG option at the SQL*Plus for Windows log on dialog box.

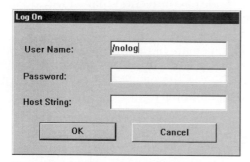

Figure 14.1 ■ The NOLOG argument.

Note, you cannot connect as SYSDBA or SYSOPER using *i*SQL*Plus. Instead you must use *i*SQL*Plus DBA, which has special security and authentication requirements. You use a URL in the format http://machine_name.domain:port/isqlplus/dba. Furthermore, your name must be added to an authentication file to allow access.

LAB 14.1 EXERCISES

14.1.1 CREATE USERS AND GRANT AND REVOKE PRIVILEGES

a) Login to SQL*Plus as SYSTEM/MANAGER (or any other account that allows you to create a new user) and create a user called TEACHER with a password of SUBJECT, with the appropriate default and temporary tablespaces for your database. Using Oracle's predefined roles, grant enough privileges to the new user to start a SQL*Plus session, create a table, and create a view. Login to SQL*Plus as the new user and create a table called ACCOUNT with these three columns: ACCOUNT_NUM as the primary key column and the columns ACCOUNT_TYPE and ACCOUNT_STATUS. Determine appropriate datatypes for the columns. Insert a row with the values 1001, Checking, and Active, respectively. Create a view based on the ACCOUNT table called ACCOUNT_STATUS with the ACCOUNT_NUM and STATUS columns.

b) While logged in as the new user TEACHER created in exercise a, execute the following SELECT statements against the data dictionary views. What do these views tell you about the new user?

```
SELECT username, granted_role, admin_option
  FROM user_role_privs
```

```
SELECT *
  FROM session_privs
```

c) While logged in as the user TEACHER, grant the SELECT privilege for the ACCOUNT table to the STUDENT user and allow the STUDENT user to grant the same privilege to another user. Then login as the STUDENT user and execute the following three statements. What do you observe?

```
SELECT *
  FROM teacher.account
```

```
INSERT INTO teacher.account
  (account_num, type, status)
VALUES
  (1002, 'Savings', 'Active')
```

```
SELECT *
  FROM teacher.account_status
```

d) Connect as SYSTEM/MANAGER and change the password for the user TEACHER from SUBJECT to CLASS. Login as TEACHER and revoke the SELECT privileges from STUDENT on the ACCOUNT table.

e) Execute the following query as the TEACHER user. What purpose do you think this data dictionary view serves?

```
SELECT username, default_tablespace, temporary_tablespace
  FROM user_users
```

14.1.2 CREATE AND USE SYNONYMS

a) While logged in as the STUDENT user, create a private synonym called COURSE for the COURSE table. Describe your observations.

b) Explain the result of the following SELECT statement.

```
SELECT 'CREATE PUBLIC SYNONYM '||table_name||
       ' FOR '||table_name||';'
  FROM user_tables
```

14.1.3 CREATE USER-DEFINED ROLES

a) While logged in as the STUDENT user, create a role called STUDENT_ADMIN. Grant INSERT and UPDATE privileges on the COURSE table to the role. Then grant the role to TEACHER.

b) Execute the following SELECT statement and describe the result.

```
SELECT *
  FROM user_tab_privs_made
```

LAB 14.1 EXERCISE ANSWERS

14.1.1 ANSWERS

The text `<default_tablespace>` and `<temporary_tablespace>` in the following exercise solutions is where the name of the appropriate tablespaces in your database should appear in your answers.

a) Login to SQL*Plus as SYSTEM/MANAGER (or any other account that allows you to create a new user) and create a user called TEACHER with a password of SUBJECT, with the appropriate default and temporary tablespaces for your database. Using Oracle's predefined roles, grant enough privileges to the new user to start a SQL*Plus session, create a table, and create a view. Login to SQL*Plus as the new user and create a table called ACCOUNT with these three columns: ACCOUNT_NUM as the primary key column and the columns ACCOUNT_TYPE and ACCOUNT_STATUS. Determine appropriate datatypes for the columns. Insert a row with the values 1001, Checking, and Active, respectively. Create a view based on the account table called ACCOUNT_STATUS with the ACCOUNT_NUM and STATUS columns.

Answer: The CONNECT command is used to connect as the SYSTEM user. The CREATE USER command and the GRANT commands create the new user and grant system privileges to the user. The CONNECT command is used again to connect as the

*new user and the CREATE TABLE and CREATE OR REPLACE VIEW commands create
two new objects for the new user.*

```
CONN system/manager
Connected.

CREATE USER teacher IDENTIFIED BY subject
   DEFAULT TABLESPACE <default_tablespace>
   TEMPORARY TABLESPACE <temporary_tablespace>
User created.

GRANT CONNECT, RESOURCE TO teacher
Grant succeeded.

CONN teacher/subject
Connected.

CREATE TABLE account
   (account_num  NUMBER(15),
    type         VARCHAR(10),
    status       VARCHAR(6),
    CONSTRAINT account_pk PRIMARY KEY(account_num))
Table created.

INSERT INTO account
   (account_num, type, status)
VALUES
   (1001, 'Checking', 'Active')
1 row created.

CREATE OR REPLACE VIEW account_status AS
SELECT account_num, status
   FROM account
View created.
```

Note that a COMMIT command does not need to be issued after the INSERT statement, because the DDL command CREATE OR REPLACE VIEW implicitly issues a COMMIT.

b) While logged in as the new user TEACHER created in exercise a, execute the following SELECT statements against the data dictionary views. What do these views tell you about the new user?

```
SELECT username, granted_role, admin_option
   FROM user_role_privs

SELECT *
   FROM session_privs
```

Answer: The query against the USER_ROLE_PRIVS view lists what Oracle roles the user TEACHER has been granted and whether the user has been granted the administration option on those roles. The query against the SESSION_PRIVS view shows the privileges currently available to the user TEACHER.

```
SELECT username, granted_role, admin_option
  FROM user_role_privs
```

USERNAME	GRANTED_ROLE	ADM
TEACHER	CONNECT	NO
TEACHER	RESOURCE	NO

2 rows selected.

```
SELECT *
  FROM session_privs
```

PRIVILEGE
```
----------------------------------------
```
**CREATE SESSION
ALTER SESSION
UNLIMITED TABLESPACE
...
CREATE SEQUENCE**

14 rows selected.

The user TEACHER, or grantee, can grant the same system privileges to another user, becoming the grantor and enabling the TEACHER account to grant these same privileges to another user if the following statement is issued by the SYSTEM account instead.

```
GRANT CONNECT, RESOURCE TO teacher WITH ADMIN OPTION
```
Grant succeeded.

If you were to subsequently re-execute the query against the USER_ROLE_PRIVS view, you would see 'YES' in the ADMIN_OPTION column.

```
SELECT username, granted_role, admin_option
  FROM user_role_privs
```

USERNAME	GRANTED_ROLE	ADM
TEACHER	CONNECT	YES
TEACHER	RESOURCE	YES

2 rows selected.

These privileges are sufficient to create tables, views, and other objects, but not user accounts. The ability to create users must be granted individually or via the

DBA role to the TEACHER user if you choose to do so. The following grant would
need to be issued by the SYSTEM user:

```
GRANT CREATE USER TO teacher
Grant succeeded.
```

c) While logged in as the user TEACHER, grant the SELECT privilege for the
ACCOUNT table to the STUDENT user and allow the STUDENT user to
grant the same privilege to another user. Then login as the STUDENT user and
execute the following three statements. What do you observe?

```
SELECT *
  FROM teacher.account

INSERT INTO teacher.account
  (account_num, type, status)
VALUES
  (1002, 'Savings', 'Active')

SELECT *
  FROM teacher.account_status
```

Answer: Some of the statements result in errors due to insufficient privileges.

While logged on as the TEACHER user, issue the GRANT SELECT command on the
ACCOUNT table. The WITH GRANT option allows the STUDENT user to pass this
privilege on to others.

```
CONN teacher/subject
Connected.

GRANT SELECT ON account TO student WITH GRANT OPTION
Grant succeeded.
```

The first statement queries the ACCOUNT table in the TEACHER schema without
any problems. The SELECT privilege on the ACCOUNT table was granted. The
table name must be prefixed with the schema name.

```
CONN student/learn
Connected.

SELECT *
  FROM teacher.account
ACCOUNT_NUM TYPE        STATUS
----------- ----------- ------
       1001 Checking    Active

1 row selected.
```

The second statement attempts to insert a row into the ACCOUNT table. However, the STUDENT user does not have the privilege to perform this action. No INSERT grant on the table was issued to the STUDENT user; therefore, this leads to the insufficient privileges error.

```
INSERT INTO teacher.account
   (account_num, type, status)
VALUES
   (1002, 'Savings', 'Active')
INSERT INTO teacher.account
              *
ERROR at line 1:
ORA-01031: insufficient privileges
```

The last statement queries the ACCOUNT_STATUS view of the TEACHER schema, but the STUDENT user has not been granted SELECT privileges on the view.

```
SELECT *
  FROM teacher.account_status
  FROM teacher.account_status
           *
ERROR at line 2:
ORA-00942: table or view does not exist
```

d) Connect as SYSTEM/MANAGER and change the password for the user TEACHER from SUBJECT to CLASS. Login as TEACHER and revoke the SELECT privileges from STUDENT on the ACCOUNT table.

Answer: The ALTER USER command is used to change the password from SUBJECT to CLASS. The REVOKE command revokes the SELECT privilege on the ACCOUNT table from the STUDENT user.

```
CONN system/manager
Connected.

ALTER USER teacher identified by class
User altered.

CONN teacher/class
Connected.

REVOKE SELECT ON account FROM student
Revoke succeeded.
```

e) Execute the following query as the TEACHER user. What purpose do you think this data dictionary view serves?

```
SELECT username, default_tablespace, temporary_tablespace
  FROM user_users
```

Answer: It shows the current user's default and temporary tablespace.

USERNAME	DEFAULT_TABLESPACE	TEMPORARY_TABLESPACE
TEACHER	USERS	TEMP

1 row selected.

If the user has any tablespace quotas assigned you can issue this query to determine the quota for each tablespace. Your result may obviously differ from the output listed here.

```
SELECT tablespace_name, bytes/1024/1024 "MB"
  FROM user_ts_quotas
```

TABLESPACE_NAME	MB
SYSTEM	.95703125
USERS	13.8125
INDX	.125

3 rows selected.

Quotas are assigned with the ALTER USER command such as one of the following statements. The first assigns 100 megabytes of space on the USERS tablespace to the TEACHER user. Alternatively, the second statement assigns unlimited use of the tablespace USERS to the TEACHER account.

```
ALTER USER teacher QUOTA 100 M ON users
ALTER USER teacher QUOTA UNLIMITED ON users
```

A user must have a quota for the tablespace or have been granted the UNLIMITED TABLESPACE system privilege (e.g., through the RESOURCE role) to be able to create indexes and tables.

14.1.2 ANSWERS

a) While logged in as the STUDENT user, create a private synonym called COURSE for the COURSE table. Describe your observations.

Answer: Two objects with the same name cannot exist in the same schema.

```
CREATE SYNONYM course FOR course
CREATE SYNONYM course FOR course
*
ERROR at line 1:
ORA-01471: cannot create a synonym with same name as object
```

It is not necessary to create private synonyms for objects you already own. However, it is possible to do so but the synonym must have a different name from the underlying object. Within one schema, all object names must be unique, regardless of the type of object. You may create a public synonym called COURSE, which is then available to all schemas.

 Public synonyms are not owned by the user who creates them, so there is no conflict between the public synonym name and the name of the object on which it is based.

b) Explain the result of the following SELECT statement.

```
SELECT 'CREATE PUBLIC SYNONYM '||table_name||
       ' FOR '||table_name||';'
  FROM user_tables
```

Answer: The SELECT statement generates other SELECT statements dynamically. Each statement generated creates a public synonym for each table owned by the current user.

When you create public synonyms for other users to see your objects, you typically do it for many objects in your schema. Using a SELECT statement to generate other statements is the fastest way to do this.

14.1.3 ANSWERS

a) While logged in as the STUDENT user, create a role called STUDENT_ADMIN. Grant INSERT and UPDATE privileges on the COURSE table to the role. Then grant the role to TEACHER.

Answer: First, the CREATE ROLE command is used to create the role. Then a GRANT command is used to grant INSERT and UPDATE privileges, separated by commas, to the role. Then another GRANT statement grants the role to the user TEACHER.

```
CREATE ROLE student_admin
Role created.

GRANT INSERT, UPDATE ON course TO student_admin
Grant succeeded.

GRANT student_admin TO TEACHER
Grant succeeded.
```

The WITH ADMIN OPTION can be used to pass on the ability to grant the privileges being granted. The following statement is the same as the previous GRANT statement, but also gives the ability to the TEACHER user to pass on the privileges being granted.

```
GRANT student_admin TO teacher WITH ADMIN OPTION
Grant succeeded.
```

Now the user TEACHER can pass the same set of privileges on to other users.

b) Execute the following SELECT statement and describe the result.

```
SELECT *
    FROM user_tab_privs_made
```

Answer: The result shows the details of all grants made on tables by the STUDENT user: the recipient of the grant (the grantee); the table on which the grant was based; the grantor, or the user who granted the privilege; the privilege granted on the table; and whether the privilege is grantable to other users.

The results vary depending on the privileges you have granted, and have been granted by other users.

GRANTEE	TABLE_NAME	GRANTOR	PRIVILEGE	GRA
STUDENT_ADMIN	COURSE	STUDENT	INSERT	NO
STUDENT_ADMIN	COURSE	STUDENT	UPDATE	NO

```
2 rows selected.
```

You can see that the STUDENT_ADMIN role is the grantee of INSERT and UPDATE privileges on the COURSE table, and the STUDENT user is the grantor.

The DICT data dictionary view can be queried to list several other data dictionary views containing information about the roles created and privileges granted in a system.

LAB 14.1 SELF-REVIEW QUESTIONS

In order to test your progress, you should be able to answer the following questions.

1) A user's objects must be dropped in a separate statement before the user can be dropped.

    a) _____ True
    b) _____ False

2) The SQL*Plus CONNECT command is not the same as the CONNECT role.

   a) _____ True
   b) _____ False

3) The following statement contains an error.

   ```
   REVOKE resource, SELECT ON course FROM music
   ```

   a) _____ True
   b) _____ False

4) System privileges cannot be granted through a role.

   a) _____ True
   b) _____ False

5) Dropping a role drops the underlying object the role's privileges are based on.

   a) _____ True
   b) _____ False

6) Grants can be given to users, roles, or public.

   a) _____ True
   b) _____ False

7) DCL commands require that you execute the COMMIT command to make the change permanent.

   a) _____ True
   b) _____ False

Answers appear in Appendix A, Section 14.1.

CHAPTER 14

TEST YOUR THINKING

The projects in this section are meant to have you utilize all of the skills that you have acquired throughout this chapter. The answers to these projects can be found at the companion Web site to this book, located at: *http://authors.phptr.com/rischert3e*. Visit the Web site periodically to share and discuss your answers.

To complete the following exercises, create a new user called SCHOOL with the password PROGRAM and grant CONNECT and RESOURCE privileges to it. Then logon as the STUDENT user.

1) Create two roles: one called REGISTRAR the other called INSTRUCTOR.

2) Create a view called CURRENT_REGS reflecting all students that registered on January 25, 2003. Grant the SELECT privilege on the new view to the REGISTRAR role.

3) Create a view called ROSTER, reflecting all students taught by the instructor Marilyn Frantzen. Grant the SELECT privilege on the new view to the INSTRUCTOR role.

4) Grant the REGISTRAR and INSTRUCTOR roles to the new user called SCHOOL.

5) Start a SQL*Plus session as the user SCHOOL and select from the two previously created views.

REGULAR EXPRESSIONS AND HIERARCHICAL QUERIES

Regular expression functionality is new to Oracle 10*g*. In the previous chapters you have seen a few examples of its usage; this lab expands your knowledge of regular expressions so you can fully harness its potential. If you are not already familiar with regular expressions, you will learn about the essential metacharacters. If you are familiar with this topic, you will gain an understanding of how regular expressions are implemented within the context of the Oracle database.

Hierarchical Queries are discussed in Lab 15.2. You will learn how to use the CONNECT BY clause and the PRIOR operators to graphically display a hierarchy and reveal the relationship of records within a table.

LAB 15.1

REGULAR
EXPRESSIONS

LAB OBJECTIVES

After this lab, you will be able to:
✔ Use Regular Expression Functionality within the Oracle
  Database

WHAT IS A REGULAR EXPRESSION?

A regular expression is a notation for describing textual patterns. It consists of one or more literals and/or *metacharacters* that specify algorithms to perform complex text searches and modifications. A simple regular expression can consist only of character literals such as the regular expression 'hat'. You read it as the letter 'h' followed by the letters 'a' and 't'. It will match character strings such as 'hat', 'Manhattan', or 'chatter'. One of the metacharacters is the match any character (.). The regular expression 'h.t' matches strings such as 'hot', 'hat', or 'shutter'.

PRACTICAL USES OF REGULAR EXPRESSIONS

Data validation, identification of duplicate word occurrences, detection of extraneous white spaces, and parsing of strings are just some of the uses of regular expressions. You can take advantage of a regular expression to determine valid formats of phone numbers, zip codes, social security numbers, IP addresses, file and path names, and so on. Furthermore, you can locate patterns such as HTML tags, email addresses, numbers, dates, or anything that fits any pattern within any textual data and also replace them with another pattern.

REGULAR EXPRESSIONS AND THE ORACLE DATABASE

You find regular expressions in many programming languages, most notably in Perl and the UNIX grep, egrep, awk, and sed utilities. Finally, its power and flexibility are available within the 10*g* Oracle database through the use of the Oracle SQL operator REGEXP_LIKE, and the REGEXP_INSTR, REGEXP_REPLACE, and REGEXP_SUBSTR functions. The operator and functions work much like the familiar LIKE operator and the INSTR, REPLACE, and SUBSTR functions. In any SQL statement where you can use the LIKE operator or these functions, you can take advantage of regular expressions.

From Chapter 11, "Create, Alter, and Drop Tables," you may recall examples that demonstrated regular expressions in column check constraints to enforce data validation rules. You can also use regular expressions in a query to find a particular pattern, determine the starting position of a pattern, extract the substring of the pattern, or replace a pattern with another pattern.

Oracle supports POSIX ERE (Portable Operating System Interface Extended Regular Expressions)-compliant regular expressions. Learning the syntax of the regular expression language is useful because you can extend this knowledge to many other software products and languages.

Before using the regular expression functionality, you need to understand the meaning of the metacharacters. After this brief introduction, you will see how to apply the new Oracle operator and functions within the Oracle database.

THE MATCH ANY AND ANCHORING METACHARACTERS

The period (.) matches any character (except newline) in a regular expression (see Table 15.1). For example, the regular expression 'x.z' matches a string containing the letter 'x', followed by any other single character (except newline), followed by the letter 'z'. The strings 'xpz', 'xxyzd', and 'xyz' contain this pattern.

Table 15.1 ■ Match Any Character

Metacharacter	Description
. Match-any-character	Match any single character except a newline.

If you want to exactly match a three-character string in which the line begins with 'x' and ends with 'z', you must anchor the regular expression to the start and end of the regular expression pattern. The caret (^) metacharacter indicates the start of a line, and the dollar symbol ($) designates the end of the line (see Table 15.2). Therefore, the regular expression '^x.z$' matches the strings 'xaz', 'xoz', or 'xyz'. To contrast this approach with the familiar pattern matching available with the LIKE operator, you can express such a pattern as 'x_z', where the underscore (_) is the one-character wildcard.

Table 15.2 ■ Anchoring Metacharacters

Meta-character	Description
^	Anchors the expression to the start of the line.
$	Anchors the expression to the end of a line.

EXPLORING QUANTIFIERS

Because an individual character in a regular expression matches just once, you need to specify multiple occurrences of a character with a *quantifier,* also called a *repetition operator.* If you want a match that starts with the letter 'x' and ends with the letter 'z' and has one or multiple characters in between, your regular expression looks like this—'^x.*z$'. The '*' metacharacter repeats the preceding match any metacharacter (.) zero, one, or more times. The equivalent pattern with the LIKE operator is 'x%z', with the percent (%) indicating zero, one, or multiple occurrences of any character. Valid matches for the pattern are 'xz', 'xyyyyz', 'xyz', and 'xkkkkkz'. When you review Table 15.3, you will notice that these repetition choices allow more options than the existing LIKE wildcard characters.

Table 15.3 ■ Quantifier Operators

Quantifier	Description	Example
*	Match 0 or more times	'ca*t' matches 'ct', 'cat', 'caat', 'caaat', and so on.
?	Match 0 or 1 time	'ca?t' matches 'ct' or 'cat'.
+	Match 1 or more times	'ca+t' matches 'cat', 'caat', and so on. 'ct' is not a valid match.
{m}	Match exactly m times	'ca{3}t' matches 'caaat'.
{m,}	Match m or more times	'ca{3,}t' matches 'caaat', 'caaaat', and so on.
{m, n}	Match at least m times, but no more than n times	'ca{3,5}t' matches 'caaat', 'caaaat', and 'caaaaat'.

THE POSIX CHARACTER CLASSES

The POSIX character classes allow you to specify what type of character you are looking for; they are shown in Table 15.4. You must specify the class name in lowercase, otherwise the POSIX character class is invalid.

Table 15.4 ■ Predefined POSIX Character Classes

Character Class	Description
[:alpha:]	Alphabetic characters
[:lower:]	Lowercase alphabetic characters
[:upper:]	Uppercase alphabetic characters
[:digit:]	Numeric digits
[:alnum:]	Alphanumeric characters
[:space:]	Space characters (nonprinting) such as carriage return, newline, vertical tab, and form feed.
[:punct:]	Punctuation characters
[:cntrl:]	Control characters (nonprinting)
[:print:]	Printable characters

For example, a regular expression such as '[[:digit:]]{5}' shows the POSIX character class "digit" delimited by colons and square brackets. The second set of brackets (as in "[[:digit:]]") encloses a character class list and is required because POSIX character classes may only be used to construct a character list. The '{5}' is a quantifier; it specifies the exact five repetitions of the digit character class.

CHARACTER LISTS

In addition to the predefined POSIX character classes, you can create your own character classes or lists. The square bracket '[ ]' symbol indicates a character list where any of the characters can be matched. With the '-' hyphen, you define a range between the starting and ending point. For example, the regular expression [0-5] includes characters with digits from 0–5. Multiple ranges such as [a-zA-Z] include the upper and lowercase characters. Ranges must be in order; a range such as [z-a] is not valid. If you want to include all characters a-z, you may still want to consider using the [:lower:] POSIX character class because the POSIX standard supports multilingual environment.

When characters are not in a range, they can be placed in any order such as [5738]; this expression would find any string that contains a 5, 7, 3, or 8.

A hyphen placed as the first character of a list, indicates the literal hyphen and not a range, i.e. [-abc]. Within a character class most metacharacters are treated as the character literals rather than as special metacharacter operators. The special cases are the hyphen, caret, and the backslash. You will see some examples shortly that illustrate their use and to help you understand when a metacharacter should be the literal character instead.

NEGATION OF CHARACTER LISTS

Some metacharacters have different meanings depending on their position within the regular expression. You already learned about the '^' start of line metacharacter. Its second meaning is the negation metacharacter; it negates a character list if it is the first character in the character list. For example, '[^58]' will match any character except for '5' or '8'. The strings '0', '395', 'abc', or '5890' are valid matches, because all or some characters are "not 5 or 8;" however, '58', '85', or '585' are not matches.

Table 15.5 contains an overview of the character list metacharacters.

Table 15.5 ■ Character List Metacharacters

Metacharacter	Description
[^] Negated character list	If this metacharacter is the first character in the character list, it negates the list. Otherwise it's the literal '^'. ('^' can also mean the beginning of a line outside the bracketed expression as described in the "The Match Any and Anchoring Metacharacters" section.)
[char] Matching character list	Indicates a character list. Most metacharacters inside a character list are interpreted as literals, with the exception of '^' and '-'.
- Range	Represents characters in a range. To match the literal hyphen and not a range, it must be the first character inside the character list such as '[-a-z]'.
[: :] Character class	The predefined POSIX standard character classes include linguistic ranges for the current locale.
[.char.] Collating sequence	Indicates a POSIX collation element useful for foreign language support.
[=char=] Character equivalence class.	POSIX character equivalence class lets you search for characters in the current locale that are equivalent. This can be useful for ignoring accents and case in foreign languages.

SUBEXPRESSIONS AND ALTERNATE MATCHES

A subexpression is a part of a regular expression and enclosed with a set of parentheses. A subexpression can be repeated a certain number of times. The regular expression 'ba(na)*split' allows 0 or more repetitions of the subexpression 'na' for matches such as 'basplit', 'banasplit', 'bananasplit', 'banananasplit'.

Parentheses are also used for alternation with the vertical bar '|' symbol separating the alternates. The regular expression 't(a|e|i)n' allows three possible choices between the letters 't' and 'n'. Valid results include words such as 'tan', 'ten', 'tin', and Pakistan, but not 'teen', 'mountain', or 'tune'. Alternatively, an character list like 't[aei]n' yields the identical result. Table 15.6 describes the use of these metacharacters.

Table 15.6 ■ Alternate Matching and Grouping of Expressions

Metacharacter		Description
|	Alternation	Separates alternates, usually used with grouping operator ( ).
( )	Group	Group subexpressions into a unit for alternations, for quantifiers, or for backreferencing (see section on "Backreference" later).

THE REGEXP_LIKE OPERATOR

Now that you are familiar with the most important metacharacters, you can use the REGEXP_LIKE operator to see how the regular expression functionality is applied within the Oracle database. The following SQL query's WHERE clause shows the REGEXP_LIKE operator, which searches the ZIP column for a pattern that satisfies the regular expression [^[:digit:]]. It will retrieve those rows in the ZIPCODE_EXAMPLE table for which the ZIP column values contain any character that is not a numeric digit.

```
SELECT zip
  FROM zipcode_example
 WHERE REGEXP_LIKE(zip, '[^[:digit:]]')
ZIP
-----
ab123
123xy
007ab
abcxy

4 rows selected.
```

This regular expression consists only of metacharacters—more specifically the POSIX character class digit delimited by colons and square brackets. The second set of brackets (as in [^[:digit:]]) encloses a character class list. As previously mentioned, this is required because you can use POSIX character classes only for constructing a character list. (Note: The ZIPCODE_EXAMPLE table exists in your schema only if you downloaded and installed the additional script available from the companion Web site located at http://authors.phptr.com/rischert3e.)

Following is the syntax of the REGEXP_LIKE operator.

```
REGEXP_LIKE(source_string, pattern
   [, match_parameter])
```

The SOURCE_string supports character datatypes. The PATTERN parameter is another name for the regular expression. The MATCH_PARAMETER allows optional parameters such as handling the newline character, retaining multiline formatting, and providing control over case-sensitivity. You will see some examples of this parameter later in the lab.

THE REGEXP_SUBSTR FUNCTION

The REGEXP_SUBSTR function returns the substring that matches the pattern and the syntax is as follows:

```
REGEXP_SUBSTR(source_string, pattern
   [, position [, occurrence
   [, match_parameter]]])
```

The POSITION parameter indicates the starting position for the search, which defaults to 1, the beginning of the string. The default value for the OCCURRENCE parameter is 1, looking for the first occurrence of the pattern.

The following query uses the new REGEXP_SUBSTR function to find and return the five-digit zip code pattern within a string. The pattern requires five consecutive digits anchored to the end of the line as indicated with the $ metacharacter, otherwise you will get the house number 12345 instead.

```
SELECT REGEXP_SUBSTR('Joe Smith, 12345 Berry Lane, Orta, CA 91234',
       '[[:digit:]]{5}$')
       AS substr
  FROM dual
SUBST
-----
91234

1 row selected.
```

THE REGEXP_INSTR FUNCTION

This function works somewhat like the familiar INSTR function; however, it looks for a pattern rather than a specific string.

The next example uses the function to determine the starting position of the five-digit zip code pattern within a string.

```
SELECT REGEXP_INSTR('NY 10032 USA',
       '[[:digit:]]{5}')
       AS rx_instr
  FROM dual
  RX_INSTR
----------
         4

1 row selected.
```

You can indicate the starting position of the search and which occurrence of the pattern you want to find, both of which default to 1. The default value for the RETURN_OPTION parameter is 0 and returns the starting position of the match. Alternatively, a return option parameter value of 1 indicates the starting position of the next character following the match. The syntax of the REGEXP_INSTR function is as follows:

```
REGEXP_INSTR(source_string, pattern
[, startposition [, occurrence [, return_option
[, match_parameter]]]])
```

THE REGEXP_REPLACE FUNCTION

You learned about the REPLACE function in Chapter 3, "Character, Number, and Miscellaneous Functions." It substitutes one string with another string. Assume your data has extraneous spaces in the text and you would like to replace them with a single space. If you use the REPLACE function, you have to list exactly how many spaces you want to replace. However, the number of extraneous spaces may not be the same everywhere in the text.

The next example has three spaces between 'Joe' and 'Smith'. The function's parameter specifies that two spaces are replaced with one space. In this case, the result leaves an extra space between 'Joe' and 'Smith'.

```
SELECT REPLACE('Joe   Smith',' ', ' ')
       AS replace
  FROM dual
REPLACE
----------
Joe  Smith

1 row selected.
```

The REGEXP_REPLACE function takes the substitution a step further; it replaces the matching pattern with a specified regular expression allowing complex search and replace operations. The following query replaces any two or more spaces '{2,}' with a single space. The '( )' subexpression contains a single space, which can be repeated two or more times. As you see from the result, only one space exists between the 'Joe' and 'Smith'.

```
SELECT REGEXP_REPLACE('Joe    Smith',
       '( ){2,}', ' ')
       AS RX_REPLACE
  FROM dual
RX_REPLAC
---------
Joe Smith

1 row selected.
```

The syntax of the REGEXP_REPLACE function is as follows:

```
REGEXP_REPLACE(source_string, pattern
  [, replace_string [, position [,occurrence, [match_parameter]]]])
```

By default the start position is 1 and the OCCURRENCE parameter defaults to 0, which indicates that all matches are replaced.

EXPLORING THE MATCH PARAMETER OPTION

The REGEXP_LIKE operator and all regular expression functions contain an optional MATCH_PARAMETER. It allows matching for case, ignoring newlines, and matching across multiple lines.

CASE-SENSITIVE MATCHES

The next example shows how to ignore the case. The 'i' value in the match parameter performs a case-insensitive search and the 'c' parameter makes it case-sensitive. The default is case-sensitive. The query searches all student rows where the first name matches the pattern 'ta', regardless of case. The result includes the name 'Tamara' in the result.

```
SELECT first_name
  FROM student
 WHERE REGEXP_LIKE(first_name, 'ta', 'i')
FIRST_NAME
-------------------------
Julita
Tamara
```

```
Benita
Rita
Sengita

5 rows selected.
```

MATCHING A PATTERN THAT CROSSES MULTIPLE LINES

Recall that the match any character '.' matches all characters except newline. Sometimes you may need to search for a pattern that stretches across multiple lines. The 'n' match parameter allows you to include the newline character as part of the match any character. The following SQL statement shows a three-line source string; the desired substring of the pattern is 'cat.*dog'.

```
SELECT REGEXP_SUBSTR('My cat could have
followed the dog almost
immediately.', 'cat.*dog', 1, 1, 'n')
  FROM dual
REGEXP_SUBSTR('MYCAT
-------------------
cat could have
followed the dog

1 row selected.
```

The displayed output shows the substring that contains this pattern. The REG-EXP_SUBSTR function lists the starting position of the search as 1, followed by the first occurrence, and last the 'n' match parameter option. If the 'n' option is omitted, the substring containing the pattern is not displayed.

TREATING A STRING AS A MULTILINE SOURCE

The multiline mode, 'm,' effectively retains the source string as multiple logical lines and therefore allows the matching of the start and end of line metacharacters. The next example shows a three-line string and determines the position of the pattern '^cat'. As indicated with the '^' metacharacter, the desired pattern is at the start of the line. The result shows that this pattern is found at position 49 of the string.

```
SELECT REGEXP_INSTR('My cat
followed the dog who followed another
cat.',
'^cat', 1,1,1,'m') AS cat_search
  FROM dual
CAT_SEARCH
----------
        49

1 row selected.
```

Table 15.7 ▪ Match Parameter Choices

Parameter	Description
i	Match case-insensitive.
c	Match case-sensitive, the default.
n	A match for any character (.) in the pattern allows your search to include the newline character.
m	The source string is retained as multiple lines and the anchoring metacharacters (^ and $) are respected as the start and end of each line.

COMBINING MATCH PARAMETERS

You can also combine match parameters. For example, 'in' makes the result case insensitive and includes the newline character. However, an 'ic' parameter is contradictory and will default to case-sensitive matching. Table 15.7 contains an overview of the match parameter options.

BACKREFERENCES

A useful feature of regular expression is the ability is to store subexpressions for later reuse; this is also referred to as *backreferencing*. This functionality allows sophisticated replace capabilities such as swapping patterns in new positions or determining repeated word or letter occurrences. The matched part of the pattern is stored in a temporary buffer. The buffer is numbered from left to right and accessed with the '\digit' notation whereby *digit* is a number between 1 through 9 and matches the digit-th subexpression as indicated by a set of a set of parentheses.

The next example shows the name 'Ellen Hildi Smith' transformed to 'Smith, Ellen Hildi'.

```
SELECT REGEXP_REPLACE(
       'Ellen Hildi Smith',
       '(.*) (.*) (.*)', '\3, \1 \2')
  FROM dual
REGEXP_REPLACE('EL
------------------
Smith, Ellen Hildi

1 row selected.
```

The query lists three individual subexpressions enclosed by the parentheses. Each individual subexpression consists of a match any metacharacter ('.') followed by the '*' metacharacter, indicating that the match any character must be matched 0 or more times. A space separates each subexpression and must be matched as well. In this case, the parentheses effectively create subexpressions that capture the values and can be referenced with '\digit'. The first subexpression is assigned \1, the second \2, and so on. These stored values are then backreferenced in the function as '\3, \1 \2', which effectively transform the string to the desired order and separate the third subexpression from the first with a comma.

Backreferences are also valuable for finding duplicate words like in the following query, which looks for one or more alphanumeric characters followed by one or more spaces, followed by the same value found in the first subexpression. The result of the REGEXP_SUBSTR function shows the duplicated word 'is'.

```
SELECT REGEXP_SUBSTR(
       'There is is a speed limit!',
       '([[:alnum:]]+)([[:space:]]+)\1') AS substr
  FROM dual
SUBST
-----
is is


1 row selected.
```

WORD BOUNDARIES

At times you may want to match entire words, not just individual characters within a word or string. This is useful if you need to enclose certain words with HTML tags or simply replace whole words. As mentioned previously, the regular expression 'cat' matches 'cat', 'caterpillar' or 'location'. The following regular expression query will replace the word 'cat' within the string 'The cat sat on the roof', with the word 'mouse'. If the input string is changed, to something like 'location is everything' or 'caterpillar', the replacement will not occur.

```
SELECT REGEXP_REPLACE('The cat sat on the roof',
       '(^|[^[:alpha:]])cat($|[^[:alpha:]])', ' mouse ')
  FROM dual
REGEXP_REPLACE('THECATSAT
-------------------------
The mouse sat on the roof


1 row selected.
```

The pattern 'cat' starts with either a beginning of the line character (^) or a non-alpha character ([^[:alpha:]]) and the two choices are separated by the alternation metacharacter (|). The non-alpha character is anything but a letter and therefore includes punctuation, spaces, commas, and so on. Then the letters cat can be followed by either the end of the line character or another non-alpha character.

THE BACKSLASH CHARACTER

The backslash '\' has various meanings in the regular expression. You have already learned to apply it to backreference expressions; it is also used as the escape character. For example, if you want to search for the '*' as a literal rather than use it as a metacharacter, you precede it with the backslash escape character. The expression will read '*' and the '\' indicates that '*' is not the repetition operator, but a literal '*'. Table 15.8 summarizes the escape and backreference metacharacters together with some examples.

Table 15.8 ■ The Escape and Backreference Metacharacters

Metacharacter		Description	Example
\char	Backslash	The backslash indicates the escape character. The character following the escape character is matched as a literal rather than a metacharacter.	'abc*def' matches the string 'abc*def', because '*' is meant as the literal '*' rather than the repetition operator.
			When used within a character list, the literal '\' does not need to be escaped. For example, the regular expression '[\abc]' matches the literal '\'. In that case, you do not need to escape the backslash.
\digit	Backslash	The backslash with a digit between 1 and 9 matches the preceding digit-th parenthesized subexpression.	The regular expression '(abc)\1' checks for adjacent occurrences of the parenthesized subexpression 'abc'.

Note that many metacharacters do not need to be escaped when within a character list. For example, [.] indicates the literal period and requires a backslash escape character.

APPLYING REGULAR EXPRESSIONS IN DATA VALIDATION

Regular expressions are useful not only in queries, but also for data validation. The next statement applies a column check constraint to the LAST_NAME column of the STUDENT table. This regular expression will perform very basic validation.

```
ALTER TABLE student
  ADD CONSTRAINT stud_last_name_ck CHECK
  (REGEXP_LIKE(last_name, '^[-[:alpha:] .,()'']*$'))
```

Allowed are only alphabetical characters (lower or uppercase), spaces, hyphens, periods, commas, quotes, and parentheses. The brackets effectively create a character list encompassing these characters and the POSIX class [:alpha:]. The characters within the character list can appear in any order within the pattern. The '-' hyphen is the first character in the list and therefore indicates the literal hyphen. Names that pass the column validation include Miller-Johnson or Smith Woldo. There are two single quotation marks in the character list; they allow the single quote character to appear. For example, a name such as O'Connor is a valid pattern. The '*' metacharacter follows the character list thus allowing zero to many repetitions. The regular expression begins and ends with the anchoring characters '^' and '$' to avoid any other characters before or after the pattern.

UNDERSTANDING MATCHING MECHANICS

When you are searching for patterns within text, you may come across instances whereby the pattern can be found multiple times. The next example illustrates this scenario. The letters 'is' occur multiple times in the string 'This is an isolated issue'. The REGEXP_INSTR returns the first occurrence of the pattern the first position of the string (the default), which displays the starting position of the pattern as 3 and the character following the end of the pattern as 5. You can specify any subsequent occurrence with the appropriate occurrence parameter. If you need to find all occurrences, you may want to consider writing a small PL/SQL program to perform a loop to retrieve them.

```
SELECT REGEXP_INSTR('This is an isolated issue',
       'is', 1, 1, 0) AS start_pos,
       REGEXP_INSTR('This is an isolated issue',
       'is', 1, 1, 1) AS after_end
  FROM dual
  START_POS  AFTER_END
---------- ----------
         3          5

1 row selected.
```

The next example shows that when quantifiers are involved, Oracle's regular expressions are *greedy*. That means that the regular expression engine tries to find the longest possible match. This pattern begins with an optional spaces, followed by the letters 'is' and followed by optional characters.

```
SELECT REGEXP_SUBSTR('This is an isolated issue',
       '[[:space:]]*is.*')
  FROM dual
REGEXP_SUBSTR('THISISAN
----------------------
is is an isolated issue

1 row selected.
```

COMPARING REGULAR EXPRESSIONS
TO EXISTING FUNCTIONALITY

Regular expressions have several advantages over the familiar LIKE operator and INSTR, SUBSTR, and REPLACE functions. These traditional SQL functions have no facility for matching patterns. Only the LIKE operator performs matching of characters, through the use of the % and _ wildcards, but LIKE does not support repetitions of expressions, complex alternations, ranges of characters, characters lists, POSIX character classes, and so on. Furthermore, the new regular expression functions allow detection of duplicate word occurrences and swapping of patterns. Table 15.9 contrasts and highlights the capabilities of regular expressions versus the traditional SQL operator and functions.

Table 15.9 ■ Regular Expression Pattern Matching versus Existing Functionality

REGEXP	LIKE and SQL Functions
Complex pattern matching with repetitions, character classes, negation, alternations, and so on.	Simple pattern matching for LIKE operator with '%' and '_' indicating single or multiple characters, but does not support character classes, ranges and repetitions. The INSTR, SUBSTR, and REPLACE functions do not have any pattern matching capabilities.
Backreference capabilities allow sophisticated replace functionality.	Very basic replace functionality.
Not supported in versions prior to 10*g*.	All Oracle versions.
Choices of expression patterns are easily formulated with the alternation operator.	Alternations must be formulated with OR conditions which can easily become very complex.
Sensitive to language, territory, sort order, and character set.	No support for various locales unless specifically coded within the criteria of the query.

WHY SHOULD YOU USE REGULAR EXPRESSIONS?

Regular expressions are very powerful because they help solve complex problems. Some of the functionality in the regular expressions is very difficult to duplicate using traditional SQL functions. Once you learn the basic building blocks of this somewhat cryptic language, you will see that regular expressions become an indispensable part of your toolkit not only in the context of the SQL language but also with other programming languages. While trial and error are often necessary to get your individual pattern right, the elegance and power of the regular expressions are indisputable.

REGULAR EXPRESSION RESOURCES

This lab illustrates a number of regular expression patterns; you may find yourself trying to come up with your own pattern to validate an email address, URL, or credit card number. Writing a regular expression that covers all the different pattern options is not a trivial task, and it helps to review similar patterns to see if they fit your individual validation requirements. You can find a number of regular expression patterns on the Web. Some of these patterns may not be in POSIX standard format and you will need to modify them accordingly. You can also visit the companion Web site to this book located at http://authors.phptr .com/rischert3e to find commonly used patterns and to locate links to useful regular expression related Web sites.

LAB 15.1 EXERCISES

15.1.1 USE REGULAR EXPRESSION FUNCTIONALITY WITHIN THE ORACLE DATABASE

a) Write a regular expression column constraint against the FIRST_NAME column of the STUDENT table that ensures that the first name starts with an uppercase character. The subsequent characters allowed are alphabetical letters, spaces, hyphens, quotes, and periods.

b) Describe the difference between the following two regular expressions and the corresponding result.

```
SELECT zip,
       REGEXP_INSTR(zip, '[[:digit:]]{5}') exp1,
       REGEXP_INSTR(zip, '[[:digit:]{5}]') exp2
  FROM zipcode_example
ZIP         EXP1        EXP2
-----    ----------  ----------
ab123         0           3
007ab         0           1
```

123xy	0	1
abcxy	0	0
10025	1	1

5 rows selected.

c) The following SQL statement creates a table called DOC_LOCA-TION and adds a regular expression column check constraint to the FILE_NAME column. List examples of different file names that will pass the validation.

```
CREATE TABLE doc_location
   (doc_id NUMBER,
    file_name VARCHAR2(200) CONSTRAINT doc_loc_file_name_ck
    CHECK (REGEXP_LIKE(file_name,
     '^([a-zA-Z]:|[\])[\]([^\]+[\])*[^?*;"<>|\/]+\.[a-zA-Z]{1,3}$')))
```

d) Explain the regular expression metacharacters used in the following SQL statement and their effect on the resulting output.

```
SELECT REGEXP_SUBSTR('first field, second field   , third field',
      ', [^,]*,')
   FROM dual
REGEXP_SUBSTR('FIR
------------------
, second field   ,
```

1 row selected.

e) Explain what the following statement accomplishes.

```
CREATE TABLE zipcode_regexp_test
   (zip VARCHAR2(5) CONSTRAINT zipcode_example_ck
     CHECK(REGEXP_LIKE(zip,
      '[[:digit:]]{5}(-[[:digit:]]{4})?$')))
```

f) Describe the result of the following query:

```
SELECT REGEXP_INSTR('Hello', 'x?'),
       REGEXP_INSTR('Hello', 'xy?')
   FROM dual
```

g) Describe the individual components of the next regular expression check constraint.

```
ALTER TABLE instructor
   ADD CONSTRAINT inst_phone_ck CHECK
   (REGEXP_LIKE(phone,
  '^(\([[:digit:]]{3}\)|[[:digit:]]{3})[- ]?[[:digit:]]{3}[- ]?[[:digit:]]{4}$'))
```

LAB 15.1 EXERCISE ANSWERS

15.1.1 ANSWERS

a) Write a regular expression column constraint against the FIRST_NAME column of the STUDENT table that ensures that the first name starts with an upper-case character. The subsequent characters allowed are alphabetical letters, spaces, hyphens, quotes, and periods.

Answer: The individual components of the regular expression are listed in Table 15.10.

```
ALTER TABLE student
  ADD CONSTRAINT stud_first_name_ck CHECK
  (REGEXP_LIKE(first_name, '^[[:upper:]]{1}[-[:alpha:] .'']*$'))
```

Table 15.10 ■ First Name Regular Expression Example

Metacharacter	Description
^	Start of line metacharacter anchors the pattern to the beginning of the line and therefore does not permit leading characters before the pattern.
[	Start of class list.
[:upper:]	Uppercase alphabetic POSIX character class.
]	End of class list.
{1}	Exactly one repetition of the uppercase alphabetical character class list.
[	Start of another character list.
-	A hyphen; this does not indicate range because it is at the beginning of the character list.
[:alpha:]	POSIX alphabetical character class.
	Blank space.
.	The period, not the match any character.
''	The two individual quotes indicate a single quote.
]	End of the second character list.
*	Zero to many repetitions of the character list.
$	The end of line metacharacter anchors the pattern to the end of the line and therefore does not permit any other characters following the pattern.

This solution looks for allowable characters. You can approach a regular expression validation by defining which characters to exclude with the '^' negation character at the beginning of the character list or by using the NOT REGEXP_LIKE operator. As always, there are a number of ways to solve the problem depending on the individual requirements and circumstances. Careful testing for various ranges of values and scenarios ensures that the regular expression satisfies the desired validation rules.

b) Describe the difference between the following two regular expressions and the corresponding result.

```
SELECT zip,
       REGEXP_INSTR(zip, '[[:digit:]]{5}') exp1,
       REGEXP_INSTR(zip, '[[:digit:]{5}]') exp2
  FROM zipcode_example
```

ZIP	EXP1	EXP2
ab123	0	3
007ab	0	1
123xy	0	1
abcxy	0	0
10025	1	1

5 rows selected.

Answer: The difference between the two regular expressions is the location of the repetition operator. The first regular expression requires exactly five occurrences of the POSIX digit class. The result shows the starting position of those rows that match the pattern. A row such as 'ab123' does not have five consecutive numbers, therefore the result of the REGEXP_INSTR returns 0. In the second regular expression the position of the repetition operator '{5}' was purposely misplaced within the character list and as a result, the regular expressions requires the occurrence of either a digit or the opening and closing braces ({}). Therefore, the zip value of 'ab123' fulfils this requirement at starting position 3.

c) The following SQL statement creates a table called DOC_LOCATION and adds a regular expression column check constraint to the FILE_NAME column. List examples of different file names that will pass the validation.

```
CREATE TABLE doc_location
   (doc_id NUMBER,
    file_name VARCHAR2(200) CONSTRAINT doc_loc_file_name_ck
    CHECK (REGEXP_LIKE(file_name,
    '^([a-zA-Z]:|[\])[\]([^\]+[\])*[^?*;"<>|\/]+\.[a-zA-Z]{1,3}$')))
```

Answer: Valid file names include c:\filename.txt, c:\mydir\filename.d, c:\myfile\mydir\ filename.sql, \\myserver\mydir\filename.doc.

The regular expression checks for these valid Windows files name and directory conventions. The pattern begins with either a drive letter followed by a colon and a backslash or begins with double backslash, which indicates the server name. This is possibly followed by subdirectory names. The subsequent file name ends with a one-, two-, or three-letter extension. Table 15.11 shows the individual components of the regular expression broken down by drive/machine name, directory, file name, and extension.

Table 15.11 ■ File Name Validation

Metacharacter(s)	Description
^	No leading characters are permitted prior to the start of the pattern.
([a-zA-Z]:|[\\])	This subexpression allows either a drive letter followed by a colon or a machine name as indicated with the backslash (machine names start with two backslashes as you see later). The choices are separated by the '|' alternation operator. The backslash character is enclosed within the character list because it is not meant as the escape character or as a backreference. Valid patterns can start as "c:" or "\".
[\\]	The backslash is again a literal backslash; a valid start of the pattern may now look like "c:\" or "\\".
([^\\]+[\\])*	The next subexpression allows 0, 1 or multiple repetitions. This subexpression builds the machine name and/or the directory name(s). It starts with one or many characters as indicated by the '+' quantities but the first character cannot be a backslash character. It is ended by a backslash. Effectively, a valid pattern so far can read as "c:\", "c:\mydir\", "c:\mydir\mydir2\", "\\myserver\", or "\\myserver\mydir\".
[^?*;"<>|\/]+	This part of the regular expression validates the file name. A file name can consist of one or more characters, hence the "+", but may not contain any of the characters listed in the character lists as indicated with the '^' negation character. The start of a valid pattern may read like "c:\filename", "c:\mydir\filename", "c:\mydir\mydir2\filename", "\\myserver\filename", or "\\myserver\mydir\filename".
\.[a-zA-Z]{1,3}	The file name is followed by a period. Here the period must be escaped otherwise it indicates the match any character. The period is followed by an alphabetical one-, two-, or three-letter extension.
$	The end of line metacharacter ends the regular expression and ensures no other characters are permitted.

Compared to the other regular expressions you have seen, this regular expression is faily long. If you try out the statement, be sure that the regular expression fits in one line. Otherwise, the end of line character is part of the regular expression and you will not get the desired result.

Please note that chosen regular expression permits valid Windows file names but does not include all allowable variations.

d) Explain the regular expression metacharacters used in the following SQL statement and their effect on the resulting output.

```
SELECT REGEXP_SUBSTR('first field, second field   , third field',
      ', [^,]*,')
   FROM dual
REGEXP_SUBSTR('FIR
------------------
, second field    ,

1 row selected.
```

> *Answer: The REGEXP_SUBSTR function extracts part of a string that matches the pattern ', [^,]*,'. The function looks for a comma followed by a space, then zero or more characters that are not commas, and then another comma.*

As you see from this example, you can use regular expression to extract values from a comma-separated string. The occurrence parameter of the function lets you pick the appropriate values. The pattern must be modified if you look for the first or last value in the string.

e) Explain what the following statement accomplishes.

```
CREATE TABLE zipcode_regexp_test
   (zip VARCHAR2(5) CONSTRAINT zipcode_example_ck
     CHECK(REGEXP_LIKE(zip,
      '[[:digit:]]{5}(-[[:digit:]]{4})?$')))
```

> *Answer: The statement creates a table named ZIPCODE_REGEXP_TEST with a column called ZIP. The constraint checks if the entered value in the ZIP column is either in a 5-digit zip code or the 5-digit + 4 zip code format.*

In this example, the parenthesized subexpression (-[[:digit:]]{4}) is repeated zero or one times, as indicated by the ? repetition operator. The various components of this regular expression example are explained in Table 15.12.

Table 15.12 ■ Explanation of 5-digit + 4 Zip Code Expression

Metacharacter(s)	Description
^	Start of line anchoring metacharacter.
[	Start of character list.
[:digit:]	POSIX numeric digit class.
]	End of character list.
{5}	Repeat exactly five occurrences of the character list.
(	Start of subexpression.
-	A literal hyphen, because it is not a range metacharacter inside a character list.
[	Start of character list.
[:digit:]	POSIX [:digit:] class.
]	End of character list.
{4}	Repeat exactly four occurrences of the character list.
)	Closing parenthesis, to end the subexpression.
?	The ? quantifier matches the grouped subexpression 0 or 1 time thus making the 4-digit code optional.
$	Anchoring metacharacter, to indicate the end of the line.

f) Describe the result of the following query:

```
SELECT REGEXP_INSTR('Hello', 'x?'),
       REGEXP_INSTR('Hello', 'xy?')
  FROM dual
```

Answer: The REGEXP_INSTR function returns a starting position of 1 even though the pattern 'x?' cannot be found anywhere in the string 'Hello'. The second function call looks for the pattern 'xy?' and the function returns a 0, because the required letter 'x' followed by an optional letter 'y' doesn't exist in the source string.

```
SELECT REGEXP_INSTR('Hello', 'x?'),
       REGEXP_INSTR('Hello', 'xy?')
  FROM dual
REGEXP_INSTR('HELLO','X?')  REGEXP_INSTR('HELLO','XY?')
--------------------------  --------------------------
                         1                           0

1 row selected.
```

The first function returns a result of 1, which indicates the pattern exists at the first position of the source string. However, 'x?' is optional, so it can match an empty string and it does so in the example.

You will notice that passing the return option parameter value of 0 (beginning of the string) and 1 (character after the end of the string) returns again the same result, indicating that it matches an empty string.

```
SELECT REGEXP_INSTR('Hello', 'x?',1,1,0)
       AS start_pos,
       REGEXP_INSTR('Hello', 'x?',1,1,1)
       AS after_end
  FROM dual
  START_POS   AFTER_END
---------- ----------
         1           1
```

1 row selected.

The next query matches an empty string much like the previous 'x?' pattern, because the set of parenthesis around the enclosed 'xy' make both letters optional.

```
SELECT REGEXP_INSTR('Hello', '(xy)?', 1, 1, 0)
       AS start_pos,
       REGEXP_INSTR('Hello', '(xy)?', 1, 1, 1)
       AS after_end
  FROM dual
  START_POS   AFTER_END
---------- ----------
         1           1
```

1 row selected.

g) Describe the individual components of the next regular expression check constraint.

```
ALTER TABLE instructor
  ADD CONSTRAINT inst_phone_ck CHECK
  (REGEXP_LIKE(phone,
'^(\([[:digit:]]{3}\)|[[:digit:]]{3})[- ]?[[:digit:]]{3}[- ]?[[:digit:]]{4}$'))
```

Answer: The check constraint validates the entries in the PHONE column of the INSTRUCTOR table. The phone number must follow specific patterns such as a ###-#######, ### #######, (###) ###-#### and so on. The individual components are listed in Table 15.13.

Table 15.13 ■ A Simple Phone Number Regular Expression Example

Metacharacter(s)	Description
^	Start of line metacharacter doesn't permit leading characters before the regular expression.
(	Start of subexpression, which allows two choices for area code validation: Either a three-digit number enclosed by parentheses or a three-digit number without parentheses.
\(	The backslash escape character indicates that the following open parenthesis character represents a literal rather than a metacharacter.
[[:digit:]]{3}	The following numbers of the area code can be any three digits.
\)	Escape character indicates that the following character is not a metacharacter; in this case it is the closing parentheses for the area code.
|	The alternation metacharacter specifies the end of the first choice, which is the area code enclosed by parentheses, and the start of the next area code choice which does not require the area code enclosed by parentheses.
[[:digit:]]{3}	Three required digits.
)	End of the subexpression alternation.
[-]?	The area code follows an optional character consisting either of a hyphen or a space.
[[:digit:]]{3}	These are the first three digits of the phone number following the area code.
[-]?	The first three digits of the phone number are separated by either an optional hyphen or space.
[[:digit:]]{4}	The last four digits of the phone number.
$	End of line metacharacter ends the regular expression and ensures no other characters are permitted.

You can expand this phone number example to include different formatting separators, such as optional extension formats or even the entry of letters, such as 800-DON-OTCAL. Perhaps you want to validate that the first digit of an area code or phone number may not begin with a 0 or 1. As you can see, validating a seemingly simple phone number can involve complex alternations, logic, and an arsenal of metacharacter. If you want to include foreign phone numbers in your validation, then the regular expression becomes even more involved.

You may consider simplifying the validation altogether by only allowing ten numbers in the phone column. The appropriate display of the data to the desired format can be accomplished through a view, or a SELECT statement.

Another way to approach phone number validation is to separate the entire phone number into different components such as area code, first three digits of the number, and remaining four digits.

LAB 15.1 SELF-REVIEW QUESTIONS

In order to test your progress, you should be able to answer the following questions.

1) The following query is valid.

```
SELECT REGEXP_LIKE('10025', '[[:digit:]]')
   FROM dual
```

a) _____ True
b) _____ False

2) Choose all the valid values for the regular expressions 'hat{4,1}'.

a) _____ hat
b) _____ haaat
c) _____ hatttt
d) _____ hathathat
e) _____ Invalid regular expression

3) Based on the next query, which value will be shown in the resulting output?

```
SELECT REGEXP_REPLACE('ABC10025', '[^[:digit:]]{1,5}$', '@')
   FROM dual
```

a) _____ @@@@@
b) _____ ABC10025
c) _____ @@@10025
d) _____ ABC@@@@@
e) _____ Invalid regular expression

4) The following two regular expressions are equivalent:

```
([[:space:]]|[[:punct:]])+
```

```
[[:space:][:punct:]]+
```

a) _____ True
b) _____ False

5) The following query is invalid.

```
SELECT REGEXP_SUBSTR('ABC10025', '[[:ALPHA:]]')
  FROM dual
```

a) _____ True
b) _____ False

6) Based on the following regular expression, the value of 'CD' will be returned.

```
SELECT REGEXP_SUBSTR('abCDefgH', '[[:upper:]]+')
  FROM dual
```

a) _____ True
b) _____ False

7) The following two regular expressions are equivalent:

```
^[[:digit:]]{5}$

^[0-9]{5}$
```

a) _____ True
b) _____ False

Quiz answers appear in Appendix A, Section 15.1

LAB 15.2

HIERARCHICAL QUERIES

LAB OBJECTIVES

After this lab, you will be able to:
- ✔ Restrict the Result Set in Hierarchical Queries
- ✔ Move Up and Down the Hierarchy Tree

A recursive relationship, also called a self-referencing relationship, exists on the COURSE table in the STUDENT schema (see Figure 15.1). This recursive relationship is between the columns COURSE_NO and PREREQUISITE. It is just like any other parent–child table relationship, except the relationship is with itself.

COURSE

COURSE_NO (PK)	NUMBER(8,0)	NOT NULL
DESCRIPTION	VARCHAR2(50)	NOT NULL
COST	NUMBER(9,2)	NULL
PREREQUISITE (FK)	NUMBER(8,0)	NULL
CREATED_BY	VARCHAR2(30)	NOT NULL
CREATED_DATE	DATE	NOT NULL
MODIFIED_BY	VARCHAR2(30)	NOT NULL
MODIFIED_DATE	DATE	NOT NULL

CRSE_CRSE_FK

Figure 15.1 ■ **The self-referencing relationship of the COURSE table.**

The PREREQUISITE column is a foreign key referencing its own table's primary key. Only valid course numbers can be entered as prerequisites. Any attempt to insert or update the PREREQUISITE column to a value for which no COURSE_NO exists is rejected. A course can have zero or one prerequisite. For a course to be considered a prerequisite, it must appear at least once in the PREREQUISITE column.

This relationship between the parent and child can be depicted in a query result as a hierarchy or tree, using Oracle's CONNECT BY clause and the PRIOR operator. The following result visually displays the relationship of the courses that have the course number 310, Operating Systems, as their prerequisite.

```
310  Operating Systems
   130   Intro to Unix
      132   Basics of Unix Admin
         134   Advanced Unix Admin
            135   Unix Tips and Techniques
      330   Network Administration
   145   Internet Protocols
```

Reading from the outside in, the student first needs to take Operating Systems and then decide on either Intro to Unix or Internet Protocols. If the student completes the Intro to Unix course, he or she may choose between the Basics of Unix Admin class and the Network Administration class. If the student completes the Basics of Unix Admin, he or she may enroll in Advanced Unix Admin. After completion of this course, the student may enroll in Unix Tips and Techniques.

You can also travel the hierarchy in the reverse direction. If a student wants to take course number 134, Advanced Unix Administration, you can determine the required prerequisite courses until you reach the first course required.

In the business world, you may often encounter hierarchical relationships, such as the relationship between a manager and employees. Every employee may have at most one manager (parent) and to be a manager (parent) one must manage one or multiple employees (children). The root of the tree is the company's president; the president does not have a parent and, therefore, shows a NULL value in the parent column.

THE CONNECT BY CLAUSE AND THE PRIOR OPERATOR

To accomplish the hierarchical display, you need to construct a query with the CONNECT BY clause and the PRIOR operator. You identify the relationship between the parent and the child by placing the PRIOR operator before the parent column. To find the children of a parent, Oracle evaluates the expression qualified by the PRIOR operator for the parent row. Rows for which the condition is true are the children of the parent. With the following CONNECT BY clause, you can see the order of courses and the sequence in which they need to be taken.

```
CONNECT BY PRIOR course_no = prerequisite
```

The COURSE_NO column is the parent and the PREREQUISITE column is the child. The PRIOR operator is placed in front of the parent column COURSE_NO. Depending on which column you prefix with the PRIOR operator, you can change the direction of the hierarchy.

The CONNECT BY condition can contain additional conditions to filter the rows and eliminate branches from the hierarchy tree, but cannot contain a subquery or scalar subquery expression.

THE START WITH CLAUSE

The START WITH clause determines the root rows of the hierarchy. The records for which the START WITH clause is true are first selected. All children are retrieved from these records going forward. Without this clause, Oracle uses all rows in the table as root rows.

The following query selects the parent course number 310, its child rows, and for each child its respective descendents. The LPAD function, together with the LEVEL pseudocolumn, accomplishes the indentation.

```
SELECT LPAD(' ', 3*(LEVEL-1)) ||course_no
       || ' ' ||description
  FROM course
 START WITH course_no = 310
CONNECT BY PRIOR course_no = prerequisite
LPAD('',3*(LEVEL-1))||COURSE_NO||''||DESCRIPTION
-------------------------------------------------
310  Operating Systems
   130  Intro to Unix
      132  Basics of Unix Admin
         134  Advanced Unix Admin
            135  Unix Tips and Techniques
      330  Network Administration
   145  Internet Protocols

7 rows selected.
```

Following is the syntax of the CONNECT BY clause:

```
[START WITH condition]
CONNECT BY [NOCYCLE] condition
```

The optional NOCYCLE parameter allows the query to continue even if a loop exists in the hierarchy. You will see some examples of loops later in the exercises.

UNDERSTANDING LEVEL AND LPAD

The pseudocolumn LEVEL returns the number 1 for the root of the hierarchy, 2 for the child, 3 for the grandchild, and so on. The LPAD function allows you to visualize the hierarchy by indenting it with spaces. The length of the padded characters is calculated with the LEVEL function.

In Chapter 9, "Complex Joins," you learned about self-joins. You may wonder how they compare to the hierarchical query. There are some fundamental differences: Only the hierarchical query with the CONNECT BY clause allows you to visually display the hierarchy; the self-join shows you the prerequisite in a vertical fashion only.

HIERARCHY PATH

You can show the path of a value from the root to the last node of the branch for any of the rows using the SYS_CONNECT_BY_PATH function. The following query example displays the hierarchy path and each course number is separated by a forward slash.

```
SELECT LPAD(' ', 1*(LEVEL-1))
       ||SYS_CONNECT_BY_PATH(course_no, '/') AS "Path" ,
       description
  FROM course
 START WITH course_no = 310
 CONNECT BY PRIOR course_no = prerequisite
Path                        DESCRIPTION
--------------------------  -------------------------
/310                        Operating Systems
 /310/130                   Intro to Unix
  /310/130/132              Basics of Unix Admin
   /310/130/132/134         Advanced Unix Admin
    /310/130/132/134/135    Unix Tips and Techniques
  /310/130/330              Network Administration
 /310/145                   Internet Protocols

7 rows selected.
```

The SYS_CONNECT_BY_PATH function is only valid for a hierarchical query and its syntax is as follows:

```
SYS_CONNECT_BY_PATH (column, char)
```

PRUNING THE HIERARCHY TREE

A hierarchy can be described as a tree; if you want to remove specific rows from the result, you can use either the WHERE clause to eliminate individual rows or the CONNECT BY clause to eliminate branches.

The effect of the WHERE clause on the rest of the hierarchy is graphically depicted in Figure 15.2. It effectively eliminates individual rows from the hierarchy.

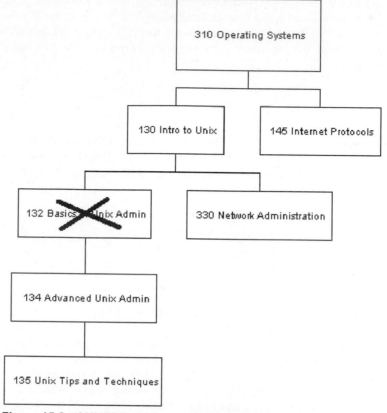

Figure 15.2 ■ WHERE clause to eliminate rows.

Only those rows that satisfy the CONDITION of the WHERE clause are included in the result. The following SQL statement shows the WHERE clause that eliminates the specific row. Notice that the child rows of the eliminated course are listed.

```
SELECT LPAD(' ', 3*(LEVEL-1)) ||course_no
       || ' ' ||description AS hierarchy
  FROM course
 WHERE course_no <> 132
 START WITH course_no = 310
CONNECT BY PRIOR course_no = prerequisite
HIERARCHY
-------------------------------------------
310   Operating Systems
    130   Intro to Unix
         134   Advanced Unix Admin
              135   Unix Tips and Techniques
      330   Network Administration
    145   Internet Protocols

6 rows selected.
```

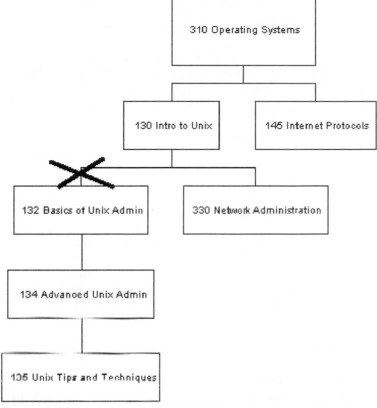

Figure 15.3 ■ Use of the CONNECT BY clause to eliminate the entire branch.

Figure 15.3 displays the scenario when the condition is moved to the CONNECT BY clause causing the removal of a branch of the tree.

The condition is part of the CONNECT BY clause and when you examine the result you find that COURSE_NO 132 and its respective descendants are eliminated.

```
SELECT LPAD(' ', 3*(LEVEL-1)) ||course_no
       || ' ' ||description AS hierarchy
  FROM course
 START WITH course_no = 310
CONNECT BY PRIOR course_no = prerequisite
   AND course_no <> '132'
HIERARCHY
----------------------------------

310  Operating Systems
   130  Intro to Unix
      330  Network Administration
   145  Internet Protocols

4 rows selected.
```

ACCESSING ROOT ROW DATA WITH THE CONNECT_BY_ROOT OPERATOR

Oracle 10*g* introduced the CONNECT_BY_ROOT operator; it returns column data from the root row. The next SQL statement displays the course number of the root row in the column labeled ROOT. Note that the CONNECT_BY_ROOT operator is invalid in the START WITH and the CONNECT BY clauses.

```
SELECT description, course_no,
       CONNECT_BY_ROOT course_no AS root,
       LPAD(' ', 1*(LEVEL-1))
       ||SYS_CONNECT_BY_PATH(course_no, '/') AS "Path"
  FROM course
 START WITH course_no IN (310, 130)
CONNECT BY PRIOR course_no = prerequisite
```

DESCRIPTION	COURSE_NO	ROOT	Path
Intro to Unix	130	130	/130
Basics of Unix Admin	132	130	/130/132
Advanced Unix Admin	134	130	/130/132/134
Unix Tips and Techniques	135	130	/130/132/134/135
Network Administration	330	130	/130/330
Operating Systems	310	310	/310
Intro to Unix	130	310	/310/130
Basics of Unix Admin	132	310	/310/130/132
Advanced Unix Admin	134	310	/310/130/132/134
Unix Tips and Techniques	135	310	/310/130/132/134/135
Network Administration	330	310	/310/130/330
Internet Protocols	145	310	/310/145

```
12 rows selected.
```

THE CONNECT_BY_ISLEAF PSEUDOCOLUMN

The CONNECT_BY_ISLEAF is a new 10*g* pseudocolumn that displays the value 1 if the row is the last child, also referred to as the leaf, of the hierarchy tree as defined with the CONNECT BY clause. The output of the following query displays for course numbers 135, 350 and 145 the value 1 in the LEAF column; the others show zero as they are either root or branch nodes.

```
SELECT course_no, LPAD(' ', 1*(LEVEL-1))
       ||SYS_CONNECT_BY_PATH(course_no, '/') AS "Path",
       LEVEL, CONNECT_BY_ISLEAF AS leaf
```

```
   FROM course
 START WITH course_no = 310
 CONNECT BY PRIOR course_no = prerequisite
```

COURSE_NO	Path	LEVEL	LEAF
310	/310	1	0
130	/310/130	2	0
132	/310/130/132	3	0
134	/310/130/132/134	4	0
135	/310/130/132/134/135	5	1
330	/310/130/330	3	1
145	/310/145	2	1

7 rows selected.

JOINING TABLES

Prior to Oracle 9*i*, joins in hierarchical queries were not allowed. To achieve somewhat similar results, you had to write inline views or use custom-written PL/SQL functions to display any columns from related tables. The effect of a join in a hierarchical query is shown below. The query joins the COURSE and SECTION tables and includes the SECTION_ID column in the result.

The join uses the common COURSE_NO column. The root rows are chosen via the START WITH clause. Here only those root rows with a COURSE_NO of 310 are selected as the root rows on which the hierarchy will be based. From the root row, the children, grandchildren, and any further descendants are determined.

As a result, you will notice a large number of rows because some courses have multiple sections. For example, COURSE_NO 132, Basics of Unix Admin, has two sections: They are SECTION_ID 139 and 138. For each section the hierarchy is listed with the respective child sections. The individual child sections then show their child rows and so on.

```
    SELECT LPAD(' ', 3*(LEVEL-1)) || c.course_no||' '||
           description AS hierarchy, s.section_id
      FROM course c, section s
     WHERE c.course_no = s.course_no
     START WITH c.course_no = 310
 CONNECT BY PRIOR c.course_no = prerequisite
```

HIERARCHY	SECTION_ID
310 Operating Systems	103
130 Intro to Unix	107
330 Network Administration	104
132 Basics of Unix Admin	139

```
          134 Advanced Unix Admin                110
              135 Unix Tips and Techniques       112
              135 Unix Tips and Techniques       115
              135 Unix Tips and Techniques       114
              135 Unix Tips and Techniques       113
          134 Advanced Unix Admin                111
              135 Unix Tips and Techniques       112
              135 Unix Tips and Techniques       115
              135 Unix Tips and Techniques       114
              135 Unix Tips and Techniques       113
          134 Advanced Unix Admin                140
              135 Unix Tips and Techniques       112
              135 Unix Tips and Techniques       115
              135 Unix Tips and Techniques       114
              135 Unix Tips and Techniques       113
     132 Basics of Unix Admin                    138
          134 Advanced Unix Admin                110
              135 Unix Tips and Techniques       112
              135 Unix Tips and Techniques       115
   ...
   139 rows selected.
```

SORTING

The following query lists all the courses that require COURSE_NO 20 as a prerequisite. Examine the order of the rows with COURSE_NO 100, 140, 142, 147, and 204 in the next result. These five rows share the same hierarchy level (and the same parent PREREQUISITE value). The order within a hierarchy level is rather arbitrary.

```
SELECT LEVEL, LPAD(' ', 2*(LEVEL-1)) || c.course_no
       AS course_no,
       description, prerequisite AS pre
  FROM course c
 START WITH c.course_no = 20
CONNECT BY PRIOR c.course_no = prerequisite
```

LEVEL	COURSE_NO	DESCRIPTION	PRE
1	20	Intro to Computers	
2	100	Hands-On Windows	20
2	140	Structured Analysis	20
3	25	Intro to Programming	140
4	240	Intro to the Basic Language	25
4	420	Database System Principles	25
5	144	Database Design	420
2	142	Project Management	20
2	147	GUI Programming	20

2	204	Intro to SQL	20
3	80	Structured Programming Techniq	204
4	120	Intro to Java Programming	80
...			
5	210	Oracle Tools	220

20 rows selected.

**LAB
15.2**

If you want to order the result by the DESCRIPTION column in alphabetical order, without destroying the hierarchical default order of the CONNECT BY clause, you use the ORDER SIBLINGS BY clause. It preserves the hierarchy and orders the siblings as specified in the ORDER BY clause.

```
SELECT LEVEL, LPAD(' ', 2*(LEVEL-1)) || c.course_no
       AS course_no,
       description, prerequisite AS pre
  FROM course c
 START WITH c.course_no = 20
CONNECT BY PRIOR c.course_no = prerequisite
 ORDER SIBLINGS BY description
```

LEVEL	COURSE_NO	DESCRIPTION	PRE
1	20	Intro to Computers	
2	147	GUI Programming	20
2	100	Hands-On Windows	20
2	204	Intro to SQL	20
3	80	Structured Programming Techniq	204
4	120	Intro to Java Programming	80
5	122	Intermediate Java Programming	120
6	124	Advanced Java Programming	122
6	125	JDeveloper	122
...			

20 rows selected.

Any other ORDER BY clause has the effect of the DESCRIPTION column now taking precedence over the default ordering. For example, the result of ordering by the DESCRIPTION column without the SIBLINGS keyword results in this listing. As you notice, the hierarchy order is no longer intact.

```
SELECT LEVEL, LPAD(' ', 2*(LEVEL-1)) || c.course_no
       AS course_no,
       description, prerequisite AS pre
  FROM course c
 START WITH c.course_no = 20
CONNECT BY PRIOR c.course_no = prerequisite
 ORDER BY description
```

LEVEL	COURSE_NO		DESCRIPTION	PRE
6	124		Advanced Java Programming	122
8		450	DB Programming in Java	350
5	144		Database Design	420
...				
2	140		Structured Analysis	20
3	80		Structured Programming Techniq	204

20 rows selected.

Ordering by the LEVEL pseudocolumn results in all the parents being grouped together, then all children, all the grandchildren, and so on.

```
SELECT LEVEL, LPAD(' ', 2*(LEVEL-1)) || c.course_no
       AS course_no,
       description, prerequisite AS pre
  FROM course c
 START WITH c.course_no = 20
CONNECT BY PRIOR c.course_no = prerequisite
 ORDER BY LEVEL
```

LEVEL	COURSE_NO		DESCRIPTION	PRE
1	20		Intro to Computers	
2	100		Hands-On Windows	20
2	142		Project Management	20
2	147		GUI Programming	20
...				
8		450	DB Programming in Java	350

20 rows selected.

LAB 15.2 EXERCISES

15.2.1 RESTRICT THE RESULT SET IN HIERARCHICAL QUERIES

a) Show the course number and course description of courses with course number 310 as a prerequisite. Make these records the root of your hierarchical query. Display all the courses that can be taken after these root courses have been completed as child records. Include the LEVEL pseudocolumn as an additional column.

b) Execute the following query. What do you observe about the result?

```
SELECT LEVEL, LPAD(' ', 6*(LEVEL-1)) ||course_no
       || ' ' ||description hier
  FROM course
 START WITH course_no = 310
CONNECT BY PRIOR course_no = prerequisite
     AND LEVEL <= 3
```

c) What does the following START WITH clause accomplish?

```
SELECT LEVEL, LPAD(' ', 3*(LEVEL-1)) ||course_no
       || ' ' ||description hier
  FROM course
 START WITH prerequisite IS NULL
CONNECT BY PRIOR course_no = prerequisite
```

15.2.2 .MOVE UP AND DOWN THE HIERARCHY TREE

a) Execute the following query, placing the PRIOR operator on
the PREREQUISITE column. How does the result compare to
the previously issued queries?

```
SELECT LEVEL, LPAD(' ', 6*(LEVEL-1)) ||course_no
       || ' ' ||description hierarchy
  FROM course
 START WITH course_no = 132
CONNECT BY course_no = PRIOR prerequisite
```

b) Write the SQL statement to display the following result.

```
LEVEL HIERARCHY
----- ------------------------------------
    5 310   Operating Systems
    4    130   Intro to Unix
    3       132   Basics of Unix Admin
    2          134   Advanced Unix Admin
    1             135   Unix Tips and Techniques

5 rows selected.
```

c) Insert the following record into the COURSE table and execute
the query. What error message do you get and why?
ROLLBACK the INSERT statement after you issue the SELECT
statement.

```
INSERT INTO course
   (course_no, description, prerequisite,
    created_by, created_date, modified_by, modified_date)
VALUES
   (1000, 'Test', 1000,
    'TEST', SYSDATE, 'TEST', SYSDATE)
```

```
SELECT course_no, prerequisite
  FROM course
 START WITH course_no = 1000
CONNECT BY PRIOR course_no = prerequisite


ROLLBACK
```

LAB 15.2 EXERCISE ANSWERS

15.2.1 ANSWERS

a) Show the course number and course description of courses with course number 310 as a prerequisite. Make these records the root of your hierarchical query. Display all the courses that can be taken after these root courses have been completed as child records. Include the LEVEL pseudocolumn as an additional column.

Answer: The START WITH clause starts the hierarchy with the prerequisite course number 310. The PRIOR operator identifies the COURSE_NO as the parent record for which all the children are retrieved.

```
SELECT LEVEL, LPAD(' ', 6*(LEVEL-1)) ||course_no
       || ' ' ||description hierarchy
  FROM course
 START WITH prerequisite = 310
CONNECT BY PRIOR course_no = prerequisite
    LEVEL HIERARCHY
--------- --------------------------------------------
        1 130    Intro to Unix
        2        132   Basics of Unix Admin
        3              134   Advanced Unix Admin
        4                    135   Unix Tips and Techniques
        2        330   Network Administration
        1 145    Internet Protocols

6 rows selected.
```

The START WITH condition returns two records, one for the Intro to Unix class and the second for Internet Protocols. These are the root records from the hierarchy.

```
START WITH prerequisite = 310
```

The PRIOR operator in the CONNECT BY clause identifies the COURSE_NO as the parent. Child records are those records with the same course number in the PREREQUISITE column. The following two CONNECT BY clauses are equivalent.

```
CONNECT BY PRIOR course_no = prerequisite
```

and

```
CONNECT BY prerequisite = PRIOR course_no
```

If you use the PRIOR operator on the PREREQUISITE column, you will reverse the hierarchy and travel in the opposite direction. You will see examples of this shortly.

Last, you need to add the LEVEL function as a single column to display the hierarchy level of each record. If you also want to show the hierarchy visually with indents, the combination of LEVEL and LPAD does the trick. Recall the syntax of LPAD:

```
LPAD(char1, n [, char2])
```

The LPAD function uses the first argument as a literal. If char2 is not specified, by default it will be filled from the left with blanks up to the length shown as parameter n. The following SELECT clause indents each level with six additional spaces. Obviously, you may choose any number of spaces you like.

```
SELECT LEVEL, LPAD(' ', 6*(LEVEL-1)) ||course_no
         || ' ' ||description hierarchy
```

The length for the first level is 0 (Level 1 − 1 = 0); therefore, this level is not indented. The second level is indented by six spaces (6 * (2 − 1) = 6), the next by twelve (6 * (3 − 1) = 12), and so on. The resulting padded spaces are then concatenated with the course number and course description.

b) Execute the following query. What do you observe about the result?

```
SELECT LEVEL, LPAD(' ', 6*(LEVEL-1)) ||course_no
         || ' ' ||description hier
  FROM course
 START WITH course_no = 310
CONNECT BY PRIOR course_no = prerequisite
     AND LEVEL <= 3
```

Answer: The LEVEL pseudocolumn restricts the rows in the CONNECT BY clause to show only the first three levels of the hierarchy.

```
    LEVEL HIER
--------- ------------------------------------------
        1 310  Operating Systems
        2     130  Intro to Unix
        3         132  Basics of Unix Admin
```

```
      3              330  Network Administration
      2         145  Internet Protocols
```

5 rows selected.

From the previous exercise you learned that the WHERE clause eliminates the particular row but not its children. You restrict child rows with conditions in the CONNECT BY clause. Here the PRIOR operator applies to the parent row and the other side of the equation applies to the child record. A qualifying child needs to have the correct parent and it must have a LEVEL number of 3 or less.

c) What does the following START WITH clause accomplish?

```
SELECT LEVEL, LPAD(' ', 3*(LEVEL-1)) ||course_no
       || ' ' ||description hier
  FROM course
 START WITH prerequisite IS NULL
CONNECT BY PRIOR course_no = prerequisite
```

Answer: This query's START WITH clause identifies all the root rows of the COURSE table. Those are the courses without any prerequisites.

While the START WITH is optional with hierarchical queries, you typically identify the root rows of the hierarchy. That's the starting point for all rows.

The next statement displays the result of a query without a START WITH clause.

```
SELECT LEVEL, LPAD(' ', 3*(LEVEL-1)) ||course_no
       || ' ' ||description hier
  FROM course
CONNECT BY PRIOR course_no = prerequisite
    LEVEL HIER
--------- -----------------------------------------------
      1 10   DP Overview
      2    230  Intro to Internet
      ...
      1 310  Operating Systems
      2    130  Intro to Unix
      3       132  Basics of Unix Admin
      4          134  Advanced Unix Admin
      5          135  Unix Tips and Techniques
      3       330  Network Administration
      2    145  Internet Protocols
      1 330  Network Administration
      ...
      1 130  Intro to Unix
      2    132  Basics of Unix Admin
      3       134  Advanced Unix Admin
```

```
4      135   Unix Tips and Techniques
2      330   Network Administration
1 132    Basics of Unix Admin
2      134   Advanced Unix Admin
3          135   Unix Tips and Techniques
1 134    Advanced Unix Admin
2      135   Unix Tips and Techniques
1 135    Unix Tips and Techniques
1 350    JDeveloper Lab
...
1 430    JDeveloper Techniques
1 450    DB Programming in Java
```

107 rows selected.

Though such a query is not very useful, it helps to understand why the records appear multiple times. When the START WITH clause is not specified, every record in the table is considered the root of the hierarchy. Therefore, for every record in the table, the hierarchy is displayed and the courses are repeated multiple times.

For example, the course number 135, Unix Tips and Techniques, is returned five times. From the root 310, Operating Systems, it is five levels deep in the hierarchy. It is repeated for the root course number 130, Intro to Unix, then for 132, Basics of Unix Admin, then for 134, Advanced Unix Admin, and finally for itself.

15.2.2. ANSWERS

a) Execute the following query, placing the PRIOR operator on the PREREQUISITE column. How does the result compare to the previously issued queries?

```
SELECT LEVEL, LPAD(' ', 6*(LEVEL-1)) ||course_no
        || ' ' ||description hierarchy
   FROM course
  START WITH course_no = 132
 CONNECT BY course_no = PRIOR prerequisite
```

Answer: The PREREQUISITE column becomes the parent and the COURSE_NO column becomes the child. This effectively reverses the direction of the hierarchy compared to the previously issued queries.

The result of the query shows all the prerequisites a student needs to take before enrolling in course number 132, Basics of Unix Administration.

```
LEVEL HIERARCHY
--------- ------------------------------------
    1 132   Basics of Unix Admin
    2       130   Intro to Unix
    3             310   Operating Systems
```

3 rows selected.

The student needs to take course number 310, Operating Systems, then course number 130, Intro to Unix, before taking the COURSE_NO 132, Basics of Unix Admin.

b) Write the SQL statement to display the following result.

```
LEVEL HIERARCHY
----- ------------------------------------
    5 310   Operating Systems
    4       130   Intro to Unix
    3             132   Basics of Unix Admin
    2                   134   Advanced Unix Admin
    1                         135   Unix Tips and Techniques
```

5 rows selected.

Answer: The rows show you the prerequisite courses for 135 as a root. The ORDER BY clause orders the result by the hierarchy level.

```
SELECT LEVEL, LPAD(' ', 2*(5-LEVEL)) ||course_no
          || ' ' ||description hierarchy
  FROM course
 START WITH course_no = 135
CONNECT BY course_no = PRIOR prerequisite
  ORDER BY LEVEL DESC
```

Because the result shows you the prerequisites, the PRIOR operator needs to be applied on the PREREQUISITE column. PREREQUISITE becomes the parent column.

```
CONNECT BY course_no = PRIOR prerequisite
```

The ORDER BY clause orders the records by the hierarchy LEVEL in descending order. The indentation with the LPAD function is different from previous examples. You now subtract the number 5 from each level and multiply the result by 2, resulting in the largest indentation for the root.

c) Insert the following record into the COURSE table and execute the query. What error message do you get and why? ROLLBACK the INSERT statement after you issue the SELECT statement.

```
INSERT INTO course
   (course_no, description, prerequisite,
    created_by, created_date, modified_by, modified_date)
VALUES
   (1000, 'Test', 1000,
    'TEST', SYSDATE, 'TEST', SYSDATE)


SELECT course_no, prerequisite
   FROM course
 START WITH course_no = 1000
CONNECT BY PRIOR course_no = prerequisite

ROLLBACK
```

Answer: The INSERT statement causes the course number 1000 to be its own parent and child. This results in a loop in the hierarchy and is reported by the hierarchical query.

```
SELECT course_no, prerequisite
   FROM course
 START WITH course_no = 1000
CONNECT BY PRIOR course_no = prerequisite

ERROR:
ORA-01436. CONNECT BY loop in user data



no rows selected
```

This is quite an obvious loop; because it is in the same record, the row is both the parent and the child. However, you can run the query without any error if you use the new Oracle 10*g* NOCYCLE parameter following CONNECT BY.

```
SELECT course_no, prerequisite
   FROM course
 START WITH course_no = 1000
CONNECT BY NOCYCLE PRIOR course_no = prerequisite
  COURSE_NO PREREQUISITE
---------- ------------
      1000         1000

1 row selected.
```

The new pseudocolumn CONNECT_BY_ISCYCLE lets you detect the offending row by displaying a value of one, otherwise it shows the value zero. Note the pseudocolumn only works when the NOCYCLE parameter of the CONNECT BY clause is specified.

```
SELECT CONNECT_BY_ISCYCLE, course_no, prerequisite
  FROM course
 START WITH course_no = 1000
CONNECT BY NOCYCLE PRIOR course_no = prerequisite
CONNECT_BY_ISCYCLE   COURSE_NO PREREQUISITE
------------------ ---------- ------------
                 1       1000         1000

1 row selected.
```

The next example displays another loop; it was generated when the foreign key constraint between the PREREQUISITE and the COURSE_NO column was temporarily disabled. Loops can be buried deep within the hierarchy and can be difficult to find when many rows are involved, unless you can use the CONNECT_BY_ISCYCLE pseudocolumn.

```
COURSE_NO PREREQUISITE
--------- ------------
     2000         3000
     3000         2000
```

LAB 15.2 SELF-REVIEW QUESTIONS

In order to test your progress, you should be able to answer the following questions.

1) The ORDER BY clause does not order the columns within a hierarchy, but it does order the columns in the order stated in the ORDER BY clause unless the SIBLINGS keyword is used.

   a) _____ True
   b) _____ False

2) Which column is the parent in the SQL statement below?

   ```
   CONNECT BY PRIOR emp = manager
   ```

   a) _____ The EMP column
   b) _____ The MANAGER column
   c) _____ None of the above

3) The CONNECT BY condition cannot contain a subquery.

   a) _____ True
   b) _____ False

4) Joins were not allowed in hierarchical queries in Oracle versions prior to 9*i*.

    a) _____ True
    b) _____ False

5) The pseudocolumn CONNECT_BY_ISLEAF displays zero if the row is the last branch of the hierarchy tree.

    a) _____ True
    b) _____ False

Answers appear in Appendix A, Section 15.2.

LAB
15.2

CHAPTER 15

TEST YOUR THINKING

The projects in this section are meant to have you utilize all of the skills that you have acquired throughout this chapter. The answers to these projects can be found at the companion Web site to this book, located at: *http://authors.phptr.com/rischert3e*. Visit the Web site periodically to share and discuss your answers.

1) Name other hierarchical relationships you are familiar with.

2) Change the prerequisite of course number 310 "Operating Systems," a root row in the hierarchy, from a null value to 145 "Internet Protocols". Write the query to detect the loop in the hierarchy using the CONNECT_BY_ISCYCLE pseudocolumn.

3) Why does this query not return any rows?

```
SELECT *
  FROM instructor
 WHERE REGEXP_LIKE(instructor_id, '[:digit:]')
```

no rows selected

4) Add a social security number column to the STUDENT table, or create a separate table with this column. Write a column check constraint that verifies that the social security number is entered in the correct ###-##-#### format.

EXPLORING DATA WAREHOUSING FEATURES

This chapter revisits some of the concepts and functionality discussed in previous chapters, namely the DECODE function, the CASE expression, and aggregate functions. You will expand on your existing knowledge and solve more complex queries.

Analytical functions allow you to explore information in ways never imagined before. These functions let you analyze data to determine rankings, perform complex aggregate calculations, and reveal period-to-period changes.

The WITH clause allows you to reuse the query result without having to reexecute the statement; this greatly improves execution time and resource utilization.

The CUBE and ROLLUP operators perform multiple aggregation levels at once. All this functionality offers you a glimpse into some of the incredibly powerful capabilities of Oracle's data warehousing features, which allow users to query large volumes of summarized data.

LAB 16.1

ADVANCED SQL CONCEPTS, ANALYTICAL FUNCTIONS, AND THE WITH CLAUSE

LAB OBJECTIVES

After this lab, you will be able to:
- ✔ Transpose a Result Set
- ✔ Utilize Analytical Functions and the WITH Clause

TRANSPOSE RESULTS

USING THE DECODE FUNCTION

The DECODE function permits you to perform not only powerful *if then else* comparisons but also allows you to transpose or pivot the results of queries. For example, the following query returns a listing of the number of courses held for each day of the week. The day of the week is formatted using the DY format mask.

```
SELECT TO_CHAR(start_date_time, 'DY') Day, COUNT(*)
  FROM section
 GROUP BY TO_CHAR(start_date_time, 'DY')
DAY  COUNT(*)
---  ---------
FRI         7
MON        17
...
TUE        12
WED        15

7 rows selected.
```

You can to transpose the result, effectively producing a Crosstab to display the result horizontally, with the days of the week as columns and a count below. This is accomplished if you nest the DECODE function within the COUNT function.

```
SELECT COUNT(DECODE(
       TO_CHAR(start_date_time, 'DY'), 'MON', 1)) MON,
       COUNT(DECODE(
       TO_CHAR(start_date_time, 'DY'), 'TUE', 1)) TUE,
       COUNT(DECODE(
       TO_CHAR(start_date_time, 'DY'), 'WED', 1)) WED,
       COUNT(DECODE(
       TO_CHAR(start_date_time, 'DY'), 'THU', 1)) THU,
       COUNT(DECODE(
       TO_CHAR(start_date_time, 'DY'), 'FRI', 1)) FRI,
       COUNT(DECODE(
       TO_CHAR(start_date_time, 'DY'), 'SAT', 1)) SAT,
       COUNT(DECODE(
       TO_CHAR(start_date_time, 'DY'), 'SUN', 1)) SUN
  FROM section
   MON   TUE   WED   THU   FRI   SAT   SUN
  ----- ----- ----- ----- ----- ----- -----
    17    12    15    19     7     5     4

1 row selected.
```

Recall the syntax of the DECODE function:

```
DECODE (if_expr, equals_search,
        then_result [,else_default])
```

Note: Search and result values can be repeated.

When each row of the expression TO_CHAR(start_date_time, 'DY') is evaluated, it returns the day of the week in the format DY, which is MON for Monday, TUE for Tuesday, and so on. If the DECODE expression is equal to the search value, the result value of 1 is returned. Because no ELSE condition is specified, a NULL value is returned.

The COUNT function without an argument does not count NULL values; NULLs are counted only with the wildcard COUNT(*). Therefore, when the COUNT function is applied to the result of either NULL or 1, it only counts those records with NOT NULL values.

USING CASE

Instead of the DECODE function, you can also write the statement with the equivalent CASE expression for an identical result.

```
SELECT COUNT(CASE WHEN TO_CHAR(start_date_time, 'DY')
          = 'MON' THEN 1 END) MON,
       COUNT(CASE WHEN TO_CHAR(start_date_time, 'DY')
          = 'TUE' THEN 1 END) TUE,
       COUNT(CASE WHEN TO_CHAR(start_date_time, 'DY')
          = 'WED' THEN 1 END) WED,
       COUNT(CASE WHEN TO_CHAR(start_date_time, 'DY')
          = 'THU' THEN 1 END) THU,
       COUNT(CASE WHEN TO_CHAR(start_date_time, 'DY')
          = 'FRI' THEN 1 END) FRI,
       COUNT(CASE WHEN TO_CHAR(start_date_time, 'DY')
          = 'SAT' THEN 1 END) SAT,
       COUNT(CASE WHEN TO_CHAR(start_date_time, 'DY')
          = 'SUN' THEN 1 END) SUN
  FROM section
```

USING A SCALAR SUBQUERY

The next query shows yet another way you can accomplish the same output. The drawback of this solution is that you execute seven individual queries; this is not as efficient as the DECODE or CASE, which executes only once against the table.

```
SELECT (SELECT COUNT(*)
          FROM section
         WHERE TO_CHAR(start_date_time, 'DY') = 'MON') MON,
       (SELECT COUNT(*)
          FROM section
         WHERE TO_CHAR(start_date_time, 'DY') = 'TUE') TUE,
       (SELECT COUNT(*)
          FROM section
         WHERE TO_CHAR(start_date_time, 'DY') = 'WED') WED,
       (SELECT COUNT(*)
          FROM section
         WHERE TO_CHAR(start_date_time, 'DY') = 'THU') THU,
       (SELECT COUNT(*)
          FROM section
         WHERE TO_CHAR(start_date_time, 'DY') = 'FRI') FRI,
       (SELECT COUNT(*)
          FROM section
         WHERE TO_CHAR(start_date_time, 'DY') = 'SAT') SAT,
       (SELECT COUNT(*)
          FROM section
         WHERE TO_CHAR(start_date_time, 'DY') = 'SUN') SUN
  FROM dual
```

Note: For very difficult queries where the result cannot be performed using any of the previously mentioned solutions, you may want to consider the creation of a temporary table to hold intermediate results. Creating temporary tables is discussed in Chapter 11, "Create, Alter, and Drop Tables."

ANALYTICAL FUNCTIONS

Why should you use analytic functions? Oracle includes a number of very useful functions that allow you to analyze, aggregate, and rank vast amounts of stored data. You can use these analytical functions to find out the top-*n* revenue-generating courses, compare revenues of one course with another, or compute various statistics about students' grades.

Although this lab does not discuss all of the available analytical functions, it does provide you with an overview of the most commonly used functions. You will gain an appreciation of their core functionality and usefulness, particularly with regard to the calculation of rankings or generation of moving averages, moving sums, and so on.

Analytical functions execute queries fairly quickly because they allow you to make one pass through the data, rather than writing multiple queries or complicated SQL to achieve the same result. This significantly speeds up query performance.

The general syntax of analytic functions is listed here:

```
analytic_function([arguments]) OVER (analytic_clause)
```

Note the use of the OVER keyword. It indicates that the function operates after the results of the FROM, WHERE, GROUP BY, and HAVING clauses have been formed.

The ANALYTIC_CLAUSE may contain three other clauses: A QUERY_PARTITIONING, ORDER_BY, or WINDOWING clause:

```
[query_partition_clause] [order_by_clause [windowing_clause]]
```

There are slight variations in the general syntax with certain functions whereby some require specific clauses and others do not. The QUERY_PARTITIONING clause allows you to split the result into smaller subsets on which you can apply the analytical functions. The ORDER_BY_CLAUSE is much like the familiar ordering clause; however, it is applied to the result of the analytic function. The WINDOWING_CLAUSE lets you compute moving and accumulative aggregates such as moving averages, moving sums, or cumulative sums by choosing only certain data within a specified window.

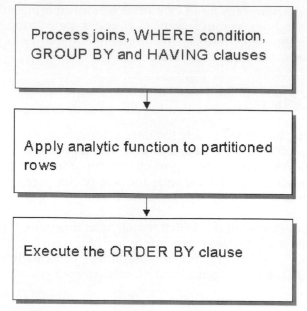

Figure 16.1 ■ Query processing steps with analytical functions.

QUERY PROCESSING WITH ANALYTICAL FUNCTIONS

Query processing with analytical functions is performed in several steps (see Figure 16.1). First, joins, WHERE, GROUP BY, and HAVING clauses are carried out. This result is then utilized by the analytic functions. If any partitioning clause is listed, the rows are split into the appropriate partitions. These partitions are formed after the GROUP BY clause, so you may be able to analyze data by partition, not just the expressions of the GROUP BY clause. If a windowing clause is involved, it determines the ranges of sliding windows of rows. The functions are based against the specified window and allow moving averages, sums, and so on. Analytical functions may have an ORDER BY clause as part of the function specification that allows you to order the result before the analytical function is applied. Last, if an ORDER BY clause is present at the end of the statement, the result set is sorted accordingly.

ANALYTICAL FUNCTION TYPES

Analytical functions can be categorized into various types: An overview of the different types is listed in Table 16.1. Ranking functions determine the ranking of a value (e.g., to determine the top three students based on their grade averages or to determine the first and last values of an ordered group). The reporting functions take the familiar aggregate function capabilities a step further by allowing you to aggregate values without the need for a GROUP BY clause. The windowing capability allows you to generate moving averages, cumulative sums, and the like.

Table 16.1 ■ **Type and Purpose of Analytical Functions**

Type	Purpose
Ranking	Compute ranking. Function examples are RANK, DENSE_RANK, NTILE, ROW_NUMBER.
Hypothetical Ranking	Determine the rank of hypothetical data values within a result set.
FIRST/LAST	Finds the FIRST and LAST value within an ordered group.
Reporting	Use aggregate functions such as SUM, AVG, MIN, MAX, COUNT, VARIANCE, or STDDEV. Also calculate ratios using functions as RATIO_TO_REPORT.
Windowing	Calculate moving averages and cumulative values using AVG, SUM, MIN, MAX, COUNT, FIRST_VALUE, LAST_VALUE. (Note: FIRST_VALUE and LAST_VALUE are only available within a WINDOWING_CLAUSE, unlike the FIRST/LAST function.)
Statistical	The MEDIAN function and the STATS_MODE function allow calculation of the median and the most frequently occurring value.
LAG/LEAD	These two functions allow you to specify an individual row relative to before or after the current row. The functionality is somewhat similar to windowing and very useful to compare period-to-period changes
Inverse Percentile	The value in a data set that is equal to a specific percentile. This functionality is beyond the scope of this book.
Linear Regression	Compute linear regression and other related statistics. These functions are beyond the scope of this book.

The LAG/LEAD functions allow you to easily see how much values changed from one period to another.

RANKING FUNCTIONS

In Chapter 7, "Subqueries," you explored the subject of top-*n* queries using an inline view and the ROWNUM pseudocolumn. Ranking functions allow for even more advanced functionality. As you read through this lab, you will learn about the differences between the ranking functions.

The first example of a ranking function is DENSE_RANK and the next query shows the ranking of the grades for student ID 254 in section 87. The grades are ranked by the lowest grade first. Notice the use of the ORDER BY clause within the analytical function.

```
SELECT numeric_grade,
       DENSE_RANK() OVER (ORDER BY numeric_grade) AS rank
  FROM grade
 WHERE student_id = 254
   AND section_id = 87
NUMERIC_GRADE          RANK
-------------     ----------
          71               1
          71               1
          75               2
...
          91               5
          98               6
          98               6
```

12 rows selected.

The NUMERIC_GRADE value of 71 is the lowest grade of the student; it holds rank number 1. The next higher grade, which is 75, holds rank number 2, and so on. The ORDER BY clause controls the ordering of the ranking. If you want the highest grade to have rank number 1, use DESCENDING in the ORDER BY clause. The default is ASCENDING. You may already have noticed one difference to the inline view; the DENSE_RANK function allows identical values to share the same rank.

To find out the three lowest grades of the student, rather than all the grades, you can modify the query by using the ranking function and an inline view as follows:

```
SELECT *
  FROM (SELECT numeric_grade,
               DENSE_RANK() OVER (ORDER BY numeric_grade)
               AS rank
          FROM grade
         WHERE student_id = 254
           AND section_id = 87)
 WHERE rank <= 3
NUMERIC_GRADE          RANK
-------------     ----------
          71               1
          71               1
          75               2
          76               3
```

4 rows selected.

To contrast this with the inline view solution discussed in Chapter 7, "Subqueries," you will only receive three rows. The lowest grade is listed twice and unlike the DENSE_RANK function, the ROWNUM pseudocolumn does not distinguish between grades that share the same values.

```
SELECT *
  FROM (SELECT numeric_grade
          FROM grade
         WHERE student_id = 254
           AND section_id = 87
         ORDER BY numeric_grade)
 WHERE ROWNUM <=3
NUMERIC_GRADE
-------------
           71
           71
           75

3 rows selected.
```

The next query shows you the revenue generated per course. It is based on a table named COURSE_REVENUE and its columns are defined as follows:

```
SQL> DESCR course_revenue
 Name                     Null?      Type
 ------------------------ --------   ------------
 COURSE_NO                NOT NULL   NUMBER(8)
 REVENUE                             NUMBER
 COURSE_FEE                          NUMBER(9,2)
 NUM_ENROLLED                        NUMBER
 NUM_OF_SECTIONS                     NUMBER
```

The REVENUE column holds the revenue generated by the respective COURSE_NO. The COURSE_FEE column shows the amount charged for enrollment in one individual course, the NUM_ENROLLED column stores the number of students enrolled in a specific course. The NUM_OF_SECTIONS column holds the number of sections per course.

This table is not part of the STUDENT schema, but can be created from the additional script available for download from the companion Web site.

RANK, DENSE_RANK, AND ROW_NUMBER

The next query illustrates the differences between the three different ranking functions: RANK, DENSE_RANK, and ROW_NUMBER. The simplest function of the three is the ROW_NUMBER, and it is listed as the last column in the result; it has similar functionality to the ROWNUM pseudocolumn. It sequentially assigns a unique number to each row starting with the number 1 based on the ORDER BY clause ranking of the revenue. Notice that when rows share duplicate revenue values, such as the course numbers 20 and 350, one of them arbitrarily gets the next number assigned.

```
SELECT course_no, revenue,
       RANK() OVER (ORDER BY revenue DESC)
         rev_rank,
       DENSE_RANK() OVER (ORDER BY revenue DESC)
         rev_dense_rank,
       ROW_NUMBER() OVER (ORDER BY revenue DESC)
         row_number
  FROM course_revenue
```

COURSE_NO	REVENUE	REV_RANK	REV_DENSE_RANK	ROW_NUMBER
25	53775	1	1	1
122	28680	2	2	2
120	27485	3	3	3
...				
240	14235	7	7	7
20	10755	8	8	8
350	10755	8	8	9
124	9560	10	9	10
125	9560	10	9	11
130	9560	10	9	12
142	8365	13	10	13
147	5975	14	11	14
310	4780	15	12	15
...				
204	1195	23	16	24

24 rows selected.

The RANK function assigns each row a unique number except for duplicate rows, which receive the identical ranking, and a gap appears in the sequence to the next rank. In the column labeled REV_RANK, course numbers 20 and 350 share the identical revenue and therefore obtain the same rank. You can observe a gap to the next rank.

The ranking function DENSE_RANK assigns duplicate values the same rank. The result of this function is displayed in the column labeled as REV_DENSE_RANK.

The syntax of the three functions is as follows:

```
ROW_NUMBER() OVER ([query_partition_clause] order_by_clause)
RANK() OVER ([query_partition_clause] order_by_clause)
DENSE_RANK() OVER ([query_partition_clause] order_by_clause)
```

The ORDER_BY_CLAUSE is required because it determines the ordering of the rows and therefore ranking. Although in the previous example no null values were present, you should understand that nulls are assumed to be equal to another null value. Just like the ORDER BY clause at the end of a SQL statement, you can include the NULLS FIRST or NULLS LAST clause to indicate the position of any nulls in the ordered sequence. If you need a refresher on NULLS FIRST or NULLS LAST, refer to Lab 5.2 in Chapter 5, "Aggregate Functions, GROUP BY, and HAVING."

The syntax includes the optional QUERY_PARTITION_CLAUSE. This option allows you to rank across portions of the result set as you see in the following examples.

PARTITIONING THE RESULT

The previous query generated the ranking over the entire result. The optional partitioning clause lets you create independent rankings and resets the rank whenever the partitioned values change. In the next query, the COURSE_FEE column is added to show the respective fee per course number. The ranking is now partitioned by a course's fee instead of the entire result. You will observe that the ranking changes after each value change in the COURSE_FEE column.

```
SELECT course_no, course_fee fee, revenue,
       RANK() OVER (PARTITION BY course_fee
          ORDER BY revenue DESC) rev_rank,
       DENSE_RANK() OVER (PARTITION BY course_fee
          ORDER BY revenue DESC) rev_dense_rank,
       ROW_NUMBER() OVER (PARTITION BY course_fee
          ORDER BY revenue DESC) row_number
  FROM course_revenue
```

COURSE_NO	FEE	REVENUE	REV_RANK	REV_DENSE_RANK	ROW_NUMBER
230	1095	15330	1	1	1
240	1095	14235	2	2	2
135	1095	4380	3	3	3
25	1195	53775	1	1	1
122	1195	28680	2	2	2
120	1195	27485	3	3	3
140	1195	17925	4	4	4
100	1195	15535	5	5	5
20	1195	10755	6	6	6
350	1195	10755	6	6	7
124	1195	9560	8	7	8
125	1195	9560	8	7	9
130	1195	9560	8	7	10

...

COURSE_NO	FEE	REVENUE	REV_RANK	REV_DENSE_RANK	ROW_NUMBER
204	1195	1195	20	13	21

```
24 rows selected.
```

The first step in the query execution is the forming of the partition, then for each distinct partition value the ORDER BY clause is executed. This example demonstrates the use of a single partitioned value, the COURSE_FEE column. You can partition over multiple values/columns by listing each individual expression and separating them with a comma in the partitioning clause.

Note: Do not confuse the partitioning clause in analytical functions with the concept of physically splitting very large tables or indexes into smaller partitioned tables and indexes. Table and index partitioning functionality is beyond the scope of this book and independent of analytical functions discussed in this lab.

NTILE

The NTILE function is another ranking function. You can use the NTILE function to divide data into buckets of fourth, thirds, or any other groupings. The next SELECT statement shows the result split into four buckets (4 quartiles or $4 \times 25\%$ buckets). Those in the first quartile of the revenue receive the number 1 in the NTILE column. The next quartile displays the number 2, and so on.

```
SELECT course_no, revenue,
       NTILE(4) OVER (ORDER BY revenue DESC) ntile
  FROM course_revenue
```

COURSE_NO	REVENUE	NTILE
25	53775	1
122	28680	1
120	27485	1
140	17925	1
100	15535	1
230	15330	1
240	14235	2
20	10755	2
...		
204	1195	4

24 rows selected.

The syntax of the NTILE function is as follows:

```
NTILE(expr) OVER ([query_partition_clause] order_by_clause)
```

Other less frequently used ranking functions are CUME_DIST and PERCENT_RANK. CUME_DIST determines the position of a specific value relative to a set of values, and PERCENT_RANK calculates the percent rank relative to the number of rows.

HYPOTHETICAL RANKING

Sometimes you may want to find out how a specific data value ranks if it was part of the result set. You can perform this type of what-if analysis with the HYPO-THETICAL RANKING syntax, which uses the WITHIN GROUP keywords. The next query determines the rank of the value 20,000 if it was present in REVENUE column of the COURSE_REVENUE table. As you see from the result of the query, it would have a rank of 4.

```
SELECT RANK(20000) WITHIN GROUP (ORDER BY revenue DESC)
        "Hypothetical Rank"
  FROM course_revenue
Hypothetical Rank
-----------------
                4

1 row selected.
```

The syntax for hypothetical ranking is as follows:

```
[RANK|DENSE_RANK|PERCENT_RANK|CUME_DIST](constant[, ...])
WITHIN GROUP (order_by_clause)
```

FIRST/LAST FUNCTIONS

The FIRST and LAST functions operate on a set of values to show the lowest or highest value within a result. The syntax of this function is:

```
aggregate_function KEEP
(DENSE_RANK {LAST|FIRST} order_by_clause)
[OVER query_partitioning_clause]
```

The next query displays for the GRADE table and SECTION_ID 99 a count of the number of rows with the highest and the lowest grades.

```
SELECT COUNT(*),
       MIN(numeric_grade) min, MAX(numeric_grade) max,
       COUNT(*) KEEP (DENSE_RANK FIRST ORDER BY numeric_grade)
        lowest,
       COUNT(*) KEEP (DENSE_RANK LAST ORDER BY numeric_grade)
        highest
  FROM grade g
 WHERE section_id = 99
```

COUNT(*)	MIN	MAX	LOWEST	HIGHEST
108	73	99	2	9

```
1 row selected.
```

This result indicates a total of 108 rows or individual grades. Of these rows, the lowest grade is 73 and the highest is 99, as computed with the familiar MIN and MAX functions. The query's last two columns apply the FIRST and LAST functions; two grade rows exist for the lowest grade of 73 and nine rows have 99 as the highest grade.

The purpose of the FIRST and LAST functions is that they allow you to ORDER BY one column but apply the aggregate to another column. This effectively eliminates the writing of a subquery that reads the same table yet again.

The equivalent statement to determine the result of the FIRST and LAST ranking functions would be this query, which makes multiple passes through the SECTION table.

```
SELECT numeric_grade, COUNT(*)
  FROM grade
 WHERE section_id = 99
   AND (numeric_grade IN (SELECT MAX(numeric_grade)
                            FROM grade
                           WHERE section_id = 99)

         OR
        numeric_grade IN (SELECT MIN(numeric_grade)
                            FROM grade
                           WHERE section_id = 99))

 GROUP BY numeric_grade
NUMERIC_GRADE    COUNT(*)
------------- ----------
          73          2
          99          9

2 rows selected.
```

MEDIAN

The analytical MEDIAN function returns the median or middle value. The syntax is as follows:

```
MEDIAN (expression) [OVER (query_partitioning_clause)]
```

The next SELECT statement returns the GRADE_TYPE_CODE and the NUMERIC_GRADE columns. The third column, labeled MEDIAN, displays the median of the NUMERIC_GRADE column partitioned by the GRADE_TYPE_CODE. The median for GRADE_TYPE_CODE 'FI' is 88 and for 'MT' is 77.

```
SELECT grade_type_code, numeric_grade,
       MEDIAN(numeric_grade) OVER (PARTITION BY grade_type_code)
       AS median
```

```
    FROM grade
  WHERE section_id = 150
GR NUMERIC_GRADE      MEDIAN
-- -------------    ----------
FI            77            88
FI            88            88
FI            99            88
MT            76            77
MT            77            77
MT            88            77
```

6 rows selected.

As indicated by the square brackets in the previously shown syntax, the OVER partitioning clause is optional. The next statement excludes the clause. It lists all the distinct grade type codes and the respective median.

```
SELECT grade_type_code, MEDIAN(numeric_grade)
  FROM grade
 GROUP BY grade_type_code
GR MEDIAN(NUMERIC_GRADE)
-- --------------------
FI                   85
HM                   85
MT                   88
PA                   87
PJ                   88
QZ                 85.5
```

6 rows selected.

If your statement needs to run against a database prior to Oracle 10g, you can compute the median with the PERCENTIL_CONT function.

STATS_MODE

The STATS_MODE function is a statistical function newly added to Oracle 10g along with a number of other useful statistical functions. The next statement illustrates the use of this function; it returns the value that occurs with the greatest frequency. In this instance, the function's parameter is the COST column and returns the value of 1195.

```
SELECT STATS_MODE(cost)
  FROM course
```

```
STATS_MODE(COST)
----------------
            1195
```

1 row selected.

To verify the result that 1195 is the most frequently occurring COST column value, you can run this query:

```
SELECT cost, COUNT(*)
  FROM course
 GROUP BY cost
 ORDER BY COUNT(*)
      COST   COUNT(*)
---------- ----------
      1595          1
                    1
      1095          3
      1195         25
```

4 rows selected.

The syntax is of the STATS_MODE function is as follows:

```
STATS_MODE(expr)
```

REPORTING FUNCTIONALITY

The reporting functionality allows you to compute aggregates for a row in a partition. The syntax is as follows:

```
{SUM|AVG|MAX|MIN|COUNT|STDDEV|VARIANCE}
    ([ALL|DISTINCT] {expression|*})
        OVER ([PARTITION BY expression2[,...]])
```

The next example lists the individual grades for each grade type for STUDENT_ID 254 enrolled in SECTION_ID 87. The last column labeled AVG displays the grade average for each grade type.

```
SELECT numeric_grade, grade_type_code,
       AVG(numeric_grade)
         OVER(PARTITION BY grade_type_code) AS avg
  FROM grade
 WHERE student_id = 254
   AND section_id = 87
```

```
NUMERIC_GRADE GR         AVG
------------- -- ----------
           91 FI          91
           91 HM        84.8
           75 HM        84.8
           98 HM        84.8
...
           91 HM        84.8
           76 MT          76
```

12 rows selected.

Notice that there is no GROUP BY clause, even though an aggregate function is used in the SELECT statement. The aggregate function is processed last and works over the GRADE_TYPE_CODE column partition. Effectively, the partitioning clause works similarly to the GROUP BY clause, as it groups those rows together and builds the aggregate for each one of the distinct value of the partition.

If you omit the partition as indicated with the empty set of parentheses, the aggregate is computed for all the rows of the result set as you see in the next query.

```
SELECT numeric_grade, grade_type_code,
       AVG(numeric_grade) OVER() AS avg
  FROM grade
 WHERE student_id = 254
   AND section_id = 87
```

```
NUMERIC_GRADE GR         AVG
------------- -- ----------
           91 FI 84.5833333
           91 HM 84.5833333
           75 HM 84.5833333
           98 HM 84.5833333
...
           76 MT 84.5833333
```

12 rows selected.

RATIO_TO_REPORT

The RATIO_TO_REPORT function is another reporting function; it computes the ratio of a value to the sum of a set of values. The syntax is as follows:

```
RATIO_TO_REPORT(expression) OVER
([query_partition_clause])
```

The next SQL statement illustrates the use of the function. The result of the RATIO column represents the ratio of the entire revenue because the partitioning clause is absent. The first row shows the total revenue of COURSE_NO 10 for 1195; the RATIO column indicates that the computed value represents 4.496284 percent of the entire revenue.

```
SELECT course_no, revenue,
       RATIO_TO_REPORT(revenue) OVER () AS ratio
  FROM course_revenue
 COURSE_NO     REVENUE        RATIO
---------- ---------- ----------
        10        1195 .004496284
        20       10755  .04046656
        25       53775   .2023328
       100       15535 .058451698
       120       27485 .103414542
...
       350       10755  .04046656
       420        2390 .008992569

24 rows selected.
```

WINDOWING

The WINDOWING clause allows you to compute cumulative, moving, and centered aggregates. A window has a defining starting and ending point. All the parameters in the windowing clause are always relative to the current row. A sliding window changes the starting or ending points depending on the definition of window.

A window that defines a cumulative sum starts with the first row and then slides forward with each subsequent row. A moving average has sliding starting and ending rows for a constant logical or physical range.

The next SELECT statement illustrates the computation of a cumulative average and a cumulative sum that is based on the values from the first row until and including the current row. The result shows the individual course numbers and their respective revenues. The CumAvg column shows the cumulative average and the CumSum column the cumulative sum.

```
SELECT course_no, revenue,
       AVG(revenue) OVER (ORDER BY course_no
         ROWS BETWEEN UNBOUNDED PRECEDING AND CURRENT ROW)
         "CumAvg",
       SUM(revenue) OVER (ORDER BY course_no
         ROWS BETWEEN UNBOUNDED PRECEDING AND CURRENT ROW)
         "CumSum"
  FROM course_revenue
```

COURSE_NO	REVENUE	CumAvg	CumSum
10	1195	1195	1195
20	10755	5975	11950
25	53775	21908.3333	65725
100	15535	20315	81260
120	27485	21749	108745
...			
350	10755	11451.5217	263385
420	2390	11073.9583	265775

24 rows selected.

Examine the third row with COURSE_NO equal to 25. The average was built based on the revenue values of COURSE_NO 10, 20, and 25, which have REVENUE column values of 1195, 10755, and 53775, respectively. The average of these three values is 21908.3333. The next row builds the average from the previously mentioned values plus the current value, which is 15535; divided by four this yields 20315. The value in the CumAvg column changes for each subsequent row.

The CumSum column is the cumulative sum and for each subsequent row it adds the revenue value to the previously computed sum.

The next example shows a centered average; it is computed with the row preceding the current row and the row following the current row. The column is labeled CentAvg. A moving average takes the current row and the previous row and the result is shown in the MovAvg column.

```
SELECT course_no, revenue,
       AVG(revenue) OVER (ORDER BY course_no
         ROWS BETWEEN 1 PRECEDING AND 1 FOLLOWING)
       "CentAvg",
       AVG(revenue) OVER (ORDER BY course_no
         ROWS 1 PRECEDING)
       "MovAvg"
  FROM course_revenue
```

COURSE_NO	REVENUE	CentAvg	MovAvg
10	1195	5975	1195
20	10755	21908.3333	5975
25	53775	26688.3333	32265
100	15535	32265	34655
120	27485	23900	21510
...			
420	2390	6572.5	6572.5

24 rows selected.

You can expand this functionality for any of the aggregate functions, not just averages. This allows you to compute moving sums, centered sums, moving min and max values, and so on.

The syntax of the windowing clause is as follows:

```
order_by_clause {ROWS|RANGE}
{BETWEEN
  {UNBOUNDED PRECEDING|CURRENT ROW|
   expression {PRECEDING|FOLLOWING}}
AND
  {UNBOUNDED FOLLOWING|CURRENT ROW|
   expression {PRECEDING|FOLLOWING}}|
   {UNBOUNDED PRECEDING|CURRENT ROW|expression PRECEDING}}
```

The ROWS and RANGE keywords allow you to define a window, either *physically* through the number of ROWS or *logically* such as a time interval or a positive numeric value in the RANGE keyword. The BETWEEN...AND clause defines the starting and ending point of the window and if none are specified, defaults to RANGE BETWEEN UNBOUNDED PRECEDING AND CURRENT ROW.

UNBOUNDED PRECEDING indicates the window starts at the first row of the partition and UNBOUNDED FOLLOWING indicates the window ends at the last row of the partition.

Besides the aggregate functions such as AVG, COUNT, MIN, MAX, SUM, STDDEV, and VARIANCE, you can use the FIRST_VALUE and LAST_VALUE functions, which return the first value and last value in the window, respectively.

LOGICAL AND PHYSICAL WINDOWS

As mentioned previously, a window can be defined as either a logical or a physical window. A physical window is defined with the ROWS keyword. A logical window uses the RANGE keyword. Table 16.2 highlights the main differences between logical and physical windows. You will explore these differences in the following exercises.

THE ORDER BY CLAUSE

The ORDER BY clause in a windowing clause is mandatory and determines the order in which the rows are sorted. Based on this order, the starting and ending points of the window are defined.

```
SELECT numeric_grade, grade_type_code,
       AVG(numeric_grade) OVER(ORDER BY grade_type_code)
       AS cumavg
```

Table 16.2 ■ Differences between Physical and Logical Windows

Physical Window	Logical Window
Specify window with the ROWS keyword.	Specify the window with the RANGE keyword.
Ability to specify the exact number of rows.	Logical offset that determines the starting and ending point of the window; this can be a constant (i.e., RANGE 5 PRECEDING), an expression that evaluates to a constant, or an interval (i.e., RANGE INTERVAL 10 DAYS PRECEDING).
Duplicate values in the ORDER BY clause do not affect the definition of the *current row*.	Duplicate values are considered the same for the purpose of defining the *current row*; therefore, the aggregate function includes all duplicate values, even if they follow after the current physical row.
Allows multiple ORDER BY expressions.	Only one ORDER BY expression is allowed.

```
    FROM grade
  WHERE student_id = 254
    AND section_id = 87
NUMERIC_GRADE GR     CUMAVG
------------- -- ----------
          91 FI         91
          91 HM 85.3636364
          75 HM 85.3636364
          98 HM 85.3636364
...
          76 MT 84.5833333

12 rows selected.
```

The SELECT statement computes the average of grades based on the GRADE_TYPE_CODE column. Notice the moving average changes upon each change in the GRADE_TYPE_CODE value. Because no windowing clause is specified, the window defaults to RANGE BETWEEN UNBOUNDED PRECEDING AND CURRENT ROW. Effectively this is a logical window. Therefore, the cumulative average value changes upon the change of the value in the GRADE_TYPE_CODE column.

 One of the keys to understanding logical windows is that the current row equals all the rows with the same ORDER BY values.

Again, in the next statement the windowing clause is missing but now there are four columns in the ORDER BY clause. These columns represent the primary key and make the values in the ORDER BY clause unique. In the CUMAVG_OVER_PK column, you notice that the average changes with each row. The PARTITION column is formed with a combination of the PARTITIONING clause and the WINDOWING clause. The rows are partitioned by GRADE_TYPE_CODE, and the cumulative average change is reset with each change in the partition.

```
SELECT numeric_grade, grade_type_code,
       grade_code_occurrence AS occur,
       AVG(numeric_grade) OVER(ORDER BY student_id,
         section_id, grade_type_code,
         grade_code_occurrence) AS cumavg_over_pk,
       AVG(numeric_grade) OVER(PARTITION BY
       grade_type_code
       ORDER BY student_id, section_id,
       grade_type_code, grade_code_occurrence)
       AS partition
  FROM grade
 WHERE student_id = 254
   AND section_id = 87
```

NUMERIC_GRADE	GR	OCCUR	CUMAVG_OVER_PK	PARTITION
91	FI	1	91	91
91	HM	1	91	91
75	HM	2	85.6666667	83
98	HM	3	88.75	88
98	HM	4	90.6	90.5
81	HM	5	89	88.6
71	HM	6	86.4285714	85.6666667
71	HM	7	84.5	83.5714286
81	HM	8	84.1111111	83.25
91	HM	9	84.8	84.1111111
91	HM	10	85.3636364	84.8
76	MT	1	84.5833333	76

12 rows selected.

INTERVALS AND LOGICAL WINDOW

The next SQL statement shows another example of the functionality of a logical window and the RANGE keyword. The resulting output of the statement lists the number of students that enrolled on specific dates. The sliding windowing functionality with the moving AVG function is applied to the last three columns named PREV 10 DAYS, NEXT 10 DAYS, and 20-DAY WINDOW.

The column PREV 10 DAYS indicates the average number of students that enrolled 10 days prior to the listed ENROLL_DATE. The starting point of the window is 10 days prior to the ENROLL_DATE of the current row and the ending point of the window is the current row. The next column labeled NEXT 10 DAYS is a window that defines itself from the current row until 10 days after the ENROLL_DATE. The column 20-DAY WINDOW shows a 20-day sliding window, starting with 10 days prior to the current row and 10 days after the current row.

```
SELECT TRUNC(enroll_date) ENROLL_DATE, COUNT(*) "# ENROLLED",
       AVG(COUNT(*))OVER(ORDER BY TRUNC(enroll_date)
        RANGE INTERVAL '10' DAY PRECEDING) "PREV 10 DAYS",
       AVG(COUNT(*))OVER(ORDER BY TRUNC(enroll_date)
        RANGE BETWEEN CURRENT ROW
        AND INTERVAL '10' DAY FOLLOWING) "NEXT 10 DAYS",
       AVG(COUNT(*))OVER(ORDER BY TRUNC(enroll_date)
        RANGE BETWEEN INTERVAL '10' DAY PRECEDING
        AND INTERVAL '10' DAY FOLLOWING) "20-DAY WINDOW"
   FROM enrollment
  GROUP BY TRUNC(enroll_date)
```

ENROLL_DA	# ENROLLED	PREV 10 DAYS	NEXT 10 DAYS	20-DAY WINDOW
30-JAN-03	11	11	17	17
02-FEB-03	14	12.5	20.6	19
04-FEB-03	13	16	22.8	19.8571429
07-FEB-03	20	17	23.4	20.625
10-FEB-03	22	19.75	24.4	22.375
11-FEB-03	24	20.6	27.2	23.8888889
13-FEB-03	25	22.8	28	25.125
16-FEB-03	26	23.4	29	25.4285714
19-FEB-03	25	24.4	30.5	26.3333333
21-FEB-03	36	27.2	36	27.2

```
10 rows selected.
```

Examine the first row; it displays 30-JAN-03 in the ENROLL_DATE column. You will notice that 11 students enrolled on the respective date. The average number of enrollments for the previous 10 days is computed by the nested AVG(COUNT(*)) function, which computes the average of the number of enrolled students per ENROLL_DATE within the last 10 days. Because this is the first row and there are no prior values, the average is equal to the number of enrolled students. Note that all the values in the ENROLL_DATE column are truncated to ensure only date not time values are considered.

All the cumulative window values change as you move forward within each subsequent enrollment date. For example, the row with the ENROLL_DATE value of 10-FEB-03 shows the average number of enrollments for the previous 10 days (including the current date) as 19.75. This value is computed by averaging the number of enrollments up to and including the 02-FEB-03 value. The value in the

NEXT 10 DAYS column is computed once again through the sliding window of 10 days after the current date and inclusive of the current row. This includes all the enrollments up to and including 19-FEB-03. The value in the 20-DAY WINDOW column includes the prior 10 days and the 10 days following the current date of the row.

Notice that the query shows the use of interval literals; remember that interval literals are expressed in the format:

```
INTERVAL n DAY|MONTH|YEAR
```

If you need to compute the time interval between two dates use the NUMTOYMINTERVAL or NUMTODSINTERVAL functions discussed in Chapter 4, "Date and Conversion Functions."

LAG/LEAD FUNCTIONS

The LAG/LEAD functionality allows you to get values from other rows relative to the position of the current row. The syntax is:

```
{LAG|LEAD}(expression[,offset][,default])
  OVER ([query_partition_clause] order_by_clause)
```

The LAG function will return one of the values of the previous rows, the LEAD function will return one of the values of the next rows. The optional OFFSET parameter identifies the relative position of the row; if no parameter is specified it defaults to 1. The optional default parameter returns the value if the offset falls outside of the boundaries of the table or the partition, such as the last and first rows. The LAG and LEAD functions do not have a windowing clause because the offset indicates the exact row.

The next SQL statement shows a useful example of the LAG function. The column labeled "This Month's Revenue" displays the revenue generated for the month in which an individual section begins. The column "Previous Month" is computed using the LAG function. The offset number is specified as 1, which indicates to always use the previous row's value. The "Monthly Change" column computes the change to the previous month by subtracting the value of the "This Month's Revenue" column from the value in the "Previous Month" column.

```
SELECT TO_CHAR(start_date_time, 'MM') "Month",
       SUM(cost) "This Month's Revenue",
       LAG(SUM(cost),1) OVER
         (ORDER BY TO_CHAR(start_date_time, 'MM'))
         "Previous Month",
       SUM(cost)-LAG(SUM(cost),1) OVER
         (ORDER BY TO_CHAR(start_date_time, 'MM'))
         "Monthly Change"
```

```
    FROM enrollment e, section s, course c
  WHERE e.section_id = s.section_id
    AND s.course_no = c.course_no
    AND c.cost IS NOT NULL
  GROUP BY TO_CHAR(start_date_time, 'MM')
```

Mo	This Month's Revenue	Previous Month	Monthly Change
04	59745		
05	98780	59745	39035
06	48695	98780	-50085
07	58555	48695	9860

4 rows selected.

ADVANTAGES OF ANALYTICAL FUNCTIONS

Analytical functions have a number of advantages. Unlike SELECT statements containing aggregate functions and the GROUP BY clause, they allow you to display summary and detail data together rather than writing separate queries. The next SELECT statements illustrate this advantage.

This query shows the average revenue per number of sections in a course.

```
SELECT num_of_sections, AVG(revenue)
  FROM course_revenue
 GROUP BY num_of_sections
```

NUM_OF_SECTIONS	AVG(REVENUE)
1	2987.5
2	10369.2857
3	7833.33333
4	10157.5
5	22107.5
6	27485
8	53775

7 rows selected.

The next statement allows you to show any of the table's columns; you are not limited to only the columns listed in the GROUP BY clause and you avoid the ORA-00937 or ORA-00979 errors. The result demonstrates a listing of both summary and detail data.

```
SELECT course_no, revenue, num_of_sections,
       AVG(revenue) OVER (PARTITION BY
         num_of_sections) AS avg_rev_per_cour
  FROM course_revenue
```

COURSE_NO	REVENUE	NUM_OF_SECTIONS	AVG_REV_PER_COUR
10	1195	1	2987.5
132	2390	1	2987.5
145	2390	1	2987.5
...			
147	5975	1	2987.5
134	2390	2	10369.2857
350	10755	2	10369.2857
...			
146	3585	2	10369.2857
...			
135	4380	3	7833.33333
...			
25	53775	8	53775

24 rows selected.

Analytical functions perform postprocessing on the result, which makes them very efficient and simple to use. Some analytical functions cannot be duplicated using any other SQL syntax. For example, the DENSE_RANK or moving and cumulative values cannot be computed without the use of the analytical clause in a statement.

THE WITH CLAUSE

The WITH clause, also referred to as the *subquery factoring clause*, offers the benefit of reusing a query when it occurs more than once within the same statement. Instead of storing the query results in a temporary table and performing queries against this temporary table, you can use the WITH clause; it gives the query a name and allows you to reference it multiple times. This avoids a reread and re-execution of the query, which improves overall query execution time and resources utilization, particularly when very large tables and/or joins are involved. The WITH clause also simplifies the writing of SQL statements. You most frequently use this type of query when querying against large volumes of data, such as in data warehouses.

The WITH keyword identifies that multiple SQL statements are involved. The following example determines the revenue generated by each instructor. The query result returns only those instructors and their respective revenue that have a greater than average revenue generated by all instructors combined.

```
WITH
revenue_per_instructor AS
(SELECT instructor_id, SUM(cost) AS revenue
  FROM section s, course c, enrollment e
 WHERE s.section_id = e.section_id
   AND c.course_no = s.course_no
 GROUP BY instructor_id)
```

```
SELECT *
  FROM revenue_per_instructor
 WHERE revenue > (SELECT AVG(revenue)
                    FROM revenue_per_instructor)
INSTRUCTOR_ID    REVENUE
-------------  ----------
          101       51380
          103       44215
          107       35745
          108       39235
```

4 rows selected.

The WITH clause creates a name for the "temporary" result called REVENUE_
PER_INSTRUCTOR. This result is then referred to in the subsequent SELECT
statements within the context of the original query.

Because the REVENUE_PER_INSTRUCTOR query involves a join and an aggregate
function, it is useful to examine the result of the join to ensure the accuracy of
the aggregate function.

```
SELECT instructor_id, cost, s.section_id, student_id
  FROM section s, course c, enrollment e
 WHERE s.section_id = e.section_id
   AND c.course_no = s.course no
 ORDER BY instructor_id
INSTRUCTOR_ID       COST SECTION_ID STUDENT_ID
-------------  ---------- ---------- ----------
          101       1195         87        256
...
          105       1195        152        138
          105       1195        152        144
          105       1195        152        206
          105       1195        152        207
          105       1195        144        153
          105       1195        144        200
          105       1095        113        129
          105       1195        105        202
          105       1195         91        232
          105       1195        105        263
          105       1195        105        261
          105       1195        105        259
          105       1195        105        260
          105       1195         83        124
          105       1195         91        271
...
          108       1195         86        102
```

226 rows selected.

For example, review INSTRUCTOR_ID 105. Effectively, the SUM function adds up all the individual values of the COST column resulting in a total of 19020. Adding the GROUP BY and the SUM function to the joined tables produces this output, which is identical to the result achieved by the REVENUE_PER_INSTRUCTOR query:

```
SELECT instructor_id, SUM(cost)
  FROM section s, course c, enrollment e
 WHERE s.section_id = e.section_id
   AND c.course_no = s.course_no
 GROUP BY instructor_id
```

INSTRUCTOR_ID	SUM(COST)
101	51380
102	24995
103	44215
104	29675
105	19020
106	21510
107	35745
108	39235

8 rows selected.

To determine the average revenue for all instructors, you nest the two aggregate functions AVG and SUM. The REVENUE_PER_INSTRUCTOR, however, reuses the previous result instead of executing the following query.

```
SELECT AVG(SUM(cost))
  FROM section s, course c, enrollment e
 WHERE s.section_id = e.section_id
   AND c.course_no = s.course_no
 GROUP BY instructor_id
```

AVG(SUM(COST))
33221.875

1 row selected.

Without the WITH clause, you will need to write the following statement, which effectively performs the reading of the tables and the join twice, once for the subquery and once for the outer query. This requires more resources and consumes more time than writing the query with the subquery factoring clause, particularly when large tables, many joins, and complex aggregations are involved.

```
SELECT instructor_id, SUM(cost) AS revenue
  FROM section s, course c, enrollment e
 WHERE s.section_id = e.section_id
   AND c.course_no = s.course_no
```

```
      GROUP BY instructor_id
   HAVING SUM(cost) > (SELECT AVG(SUM(cost))
     FROM section s, course c, enrollment e
    WHERE s.section_id = e.section_id
      AND c.course_no = s.course_no
    GROUP BY instructor_id)
```

 Do not confuse the WITH clause in subqueries with the START WITH clause used in hierarchical queries, discussed in Chapter 15, "Regular Expressions and Hierarchical Queries."

From the following statement, you will notice that you can also write this query using the analytical function discussed previously. As you have discovered throughout this book, there are often times when there are many ways to formulate a SQL statement. Knowing your options is useful and allows you to choose the most efficient statement.

```
   SELECT *
     FROM (SELECT instructor_id, SUM(cost) AS revenue,
                  AVG(SUM(cost)) OVER() AS avg
            FROM section s, course c, enrollment e
           WHERE s.section_id = e.section_id
             AND c.course_no = s.course_no
          GROUP BY instructor_id) t
    WHERE revenue > avg
```

INSTRUCTOR_ID	REVENUE	AVG
101	51380	33221.875
103	44215	33221.875
107	35745	33221.875
108	39235	33221.875

4 rows selected.

INTERROW CALCULATIONS

Oracle 10g added the ability to perform spreadsheet-like calculations useful for budgeting and forecasting. This allows the display of additional rows or calculations in the query result through the application of formulas in the MODEL clause of a SELECT statement. Following is a query example based on the MODEL_EXAMPLE table consisting of the columns COURSE, GENDER, YEAR, and ENROLL_NO, which store data about courses, gender, the enrollment year, and the enrollment figures respectively. (This table can be created based on the additional script available from the companion Web site.)

The data contained in this table contains only data for the year 2004, but the following example query result will show additional rows for the years 2005 and 2006. For those years, the query determines the projected enrollment numbers in the courses Spanish II and Spanish III based on the previous year's enrollment numbers. You need to keep in mind that these rows represent a query result, and the query does not update the MODEL_EXAMPLE table.

```
SELECT course, gender, year, s
  FROM model_example
 MODEL PARTITION BY (gender)
       DIMENSION BY (year, course)
       MEASURES (enroll_no s)
 (
  s[2005,'Spanish II'] = s[2004,'Spanish I'],
  s[2006,'Spanish III'] = ROUND((s[2005, 'Spanish II'])*0.80)
 )
 ORDER BY year, gender, course
```

COURSE	G	YEAR	S
Spanish I	F	2004	37
Spanish II	**F**	**2004**	**59**
Spanish III	**F**	**2004**	**3**
Spanish I	M	2004	3
Spanish II	**M**	**2004**	**35**
Spanish III	**M**	**2004**	**34**
Spanish II	F	2005	37
Spanish II	M	2005	3
Spanish III	F	2006	30
Spanish III	M	2006	2

10 rows selected.

The MODEL clause lists a PARTITION element that is much like the familiar partition in the previously discussed analytical functions query and defines the top-level grouping. The DIMENSION element identifies the key to the MEASURES cells, which hold numeric values. In this example the GENDER column is the PARTITIONed column, the DIMENSION columns YEAR and COURSE identify the groups within each partition. The MEASURE column is ENROLL_NO and is uniquely identified by the combination of partition and dimension columns.

The rule s[2005,'Spanish II'] = s[2004,'Spanish I'] is a definition of an assignment. A rule consists of references. The two-dimensional [2005,'Spanish II'] reference defines a single cell for the dimensions YEAR and COURSE. The measure s is an alias as defined in the MEASURE element. The left side of the assignment indicates the destination cell; the right side determines the values for it. In this instance, the destination cell with the year 2005 and the course Spanish

II does not exist in the MODEL_EXAMPLE table and is created in the result set by default; this action is referred to as UPSERT. The right side of the assignment states that the measure cell should be the same value as the value in year 2004 and for the course Spanish I. When you review the query result, you notice that two rows are created for this year; one for male and another for female.

The next rule, listed as s[2006,'Spanish III'] = ROUND((s[2005, 'Spanish II'])*0.80), defines that the enrollment number for Spanish III in year 2006 should be 80 percent of the enrollment for Spanish II in 2005 rounded to nearest whole number.

The previous statement's calculations are referring to specific individual cells. You can also specify ranges of cells, create loops, and so on. The next example illustrates the projection of enrollment figures for Spanish II for the years 2005 through 2007. The FOR loop creates these years. The measure values are based on previous year's value of Spanish II. The CURRENTV() function returns the current value of the YEAR dimension column, but because the function reads CURRENTV( )-1, it looks at previous year's value. The calculation ROUND((s [CURRENTV()-1,'Spanish II'])*1.1) assumes a 10 percent increase each subsequent year and is rounded to the nearest whole number.

```
SELECT course, gender, year, s
  FROM model_example
 WHERE course = 'Spanish II'
 MODEL PARTITION BY (gender)
       DIMENSION BY (year, course)
       MEASURES (enroll_no s)
 (
  s[FOR year FROM 2005 TO 2007 INCREMENT 1,
    'Spanish II']
  = ROUND((s[CURRENTV() 1,'Spanish II'])*1.1)
 )
 ORDER BY year, gender, course
```

COURSE	G	YEAR	S
Spanish II	F	2004	59
Spanish II	M	2004	35
Spanish II	F	2005	65
Spanish II	M	2005	39
Spanish II	F	2006	72
Spanish II	M	2006	43
Spanish II	F	2007	79
Spanish II	M	2007	47

8 rows selected.

CREATING YOUR OWN CUSTOM FUNCTION

So far you have used a variety of the rich offerings of Oracle's built-in functions. Using the PL/SQL language, you can write your own functions. Although this book will not discuss the PL/SQL language in detail, this brief section will offer you a glimpse into what a customized PL/SQL function can accomplish when used within a SQL statement.

Why would you write your own PL/SQL function? This functionality is quite useful in the case of complicated query logic because it allows you to easily call the function that hides the complexity of the logic. The next example shows a custom function that chooses the next business day if the passed date falls on a weekend day. The function queries the HOLIDAY table to make sure the next business day does not fall on a company holiday. You can use this function much like any of the single-row functions you have learned about.

The next example shows how the function called NEXT_BUSINESS_DAY works. As you can see it hides all the complexity of figuring out the date for you and simply returns the next business day.

```
SELECT next_business_day('10-AUG-2002')
  FROM dual
NEXT_BUSI
---------
12-AUG-02

1 row selected.
```

Because August 10, 2002 falls on a Saturday, the next business day is a Monday. Therefore, if you're trying to write a report to list the due dates of invoices and you must always display a business day as the due date, it is easier to use this function. Furthermore, it is simpler than writing a long CASE expression—and you may be unable to do this at all if you are working with an old Oracle version that does not support the CASE expression. Other statements can use the stored function and take advantage of the functionality. Additionally, a stored function ensures that subsequent changes to the logic are automatically applied to any statement that calls the function.

Following is the PL/SQL code that implements and stores the NEXT_BUSINESS_DAY function in the database.

```
CREATE OR REPLACE FUNCTION next_business_day(i_date DATE)
   RETURN DATE IS
   v_date DATE;
BEGIN
  v_date:=i_date;
  SELECT NVL(MAX(holiday_end_date)+1, v_date)
    INTO v_date
```

```
  FROM holiday
 WHERE v_date BETWEEN holiday_start_date AND holiday_end_date;
 IF TO_CHAR(v_date, 'DY') = 'SAT' THEN
    v_date:=v_date+2;
 ELSIF TO_CHAR(v_date, 'DY') = 'SUN' THEN
    v_date:=v_date+1;
 END IF;
 RETURN v_date;
EXCEPTION
 WHEN OTHERS THEN
  RETURN NULL;
END next_business_day;
/
```

Note that in previous Oracle versions, functions executed from a SQL statement required that they be wrapped inside a package—a type of PL/SQL object.

Clearly, writing your own custom functions simplifies the logic of complicated business rules and can overcome SQL limitations. However, you must keep in mind that the function will be executed for every row of the result set; the key is to eliminate as many rows as possible first before applying the function.

To learn more about the PL/SQL language, refer to *Oracle PL/SQL by Example* by Benjamin Rosenzweig and Elena Silvestrova (Prentice Hall).

LAB 16.1 EXERCISES

16.1.1 TRANSPOSE A RESULT SET

a) The following query result is a listing of all the distinct course costs and a count of each. Write the query to achieve the result.

```
     1095      1195      1595      NULL
--------- --------- --------- ---------
        3        25         1         1
```

1 row selected.

b) Build upon exercise a to include a range so the output looks like the following. Hint: You can write the query with the CASE expression or use the DECODE and SIGN functions.

```
1500 OR LESS MORE THAN 1500
------------ --------------
          29                1
```

1 row selected.

16.1.2 UTILIZE ANALYTICAL FUNCTIONS AND THE WITH CLAUSE

a) Modify the following query to display the top-3 revenue-generating courses. If there is a tie in the revenue, include the duplicates. Hint: Use an inline view to achieve the desired result.

```
SELECT course_no, revenue,
       RANK() OVER (ORDER BY revenue DESC)
         rev_rank,
       DENSE_RANK() OVER (ORDER BY revenue DESC)
         rev_dense_rank,
       ROW_NUMBER() OVER (ORDER BY revenue DESC)
         row_number
  FROM course_revenue
```

b) Based on the following statement, explain how the result of the AVG column is achieved.

```
SELECT numeric_grade AS grade, grade_type_code,
       grade_code_occurrence AS occurrence,
       AVG(numeric_grade) OVER(PARTITION BY grade_type_code
       ORDER BY grade_code_occurrence) AS avg
  FROM grade
 WHERE student_id = 254
   AND section_id = 87
```

GRADE	GR	OCCURRENCE	AVG
91	FI	1	91
91	HM	1	91
75	HM	2	83
98	HM	3	88
98	HM	4	90.5
81	HM	5	88.6
71	HM	6	85.6666667
71	HM	7	83.5714286
81	HM	8	83.25
91	HM	9	84.1111111
91	HM	10	84.8
76	MT	1	76

12 rows selected.

c) How would you formulate the question this query is attempting to solve?

```
SELECT e.*, SUM(diff) OVER (ORDER BY 1 ROWS BETWEEN
       UNBOUNDED PRECEDING AND CURRENT ROW) AS cum_sum
  FROM (SELECT TRUNC(enroll_date),
               TRUNC(enroll_date)-LAG(TRUNC(enroll_date),1)
               OVER (ORDER BY TRUNC(ENROLL_DATE)) DIFF
          FROM enrollment
        GROUP BY TRUNC(enroll_date)) e
```

TRUNC(ENR	DIFF	CUM_SUM
30-JAN-03		
02-FEB-03	3	3
04-FEB-03	2	5
07-FEB-03	3	8
10-FEB-03	3	11
11-FEB-03	1	12
13-FEB-03	2	14
16-FEB-03	3	17
19-FEB-03	3	20
21-FEB-03	2	22

10 rows selected.

d) Explain the result of this query.

```
WITH
num_enroll AS
(SELECT COUNT(*) num_students, course_no
   FROM enrollment e JOIN section s
 USING (section_id)
 GROUP BY course_no),
avg_stud_enroll AS
(SELECT AVG(num_students) avg#_of_stud
   FROM num_enroll
 WHERE num_students <> (SELECT MAX(num_students)
                          FROM num_enroll))
SELECT course_no, num_students
   FROM num_enroll
 WHERE num_students > (SELECT avg#_of_stud
                         FROM avg_stud_enroll)
   AND num_students < (SELECT MAX(num_students)
                         FROM num_enroll)
```

COURSE_NO	NUM_STUDENTS
20	9
100	13

120	23
122	24
124	8
125	8
130	8
140	15
230	14
240	13
350	9

11 rows selected.

LAB 16.1 EXERCISE ANSWERS

16.1.1 ANSWERS

a) The following query result is a listing of all the distinct course costs and a count of each. Write the query to achieve the result.

1095	1195	1595	NULL
3	25	1	1

1 row selected.

Answer: The answer requires the use of the DECODE function nested inside the aggregate function COUNT or you can write the query using the CASE expression.

```
SELECT  COUNT(DECODE(cost,  1095,  1))  "1095",
        COUNT(DECODE(cost,  1195,  1))  "1195",
        COUNT(DECODE(cost,  1595,  1))  "1595",
        COUNT(DECODE(cost,  NULL,  1))  "NULL"
   FROM course
```

Or:

```
SELECT  COUNT(CASE WHEN cost = 1095 THEN 1 END) "1095",
        COUNT(CASE WHEN cost = 1195 THEN 1 END) "1195",
        COUNT(CASE WHEN cost = 1595 THEN 1 END) "1595",
        COUNT(CASE WHEN cost IS NULL THEN 1 END) "NULL"
   FROM course
```

The transposed result uses the COUNT function to count the row only if it meets the search criteria of the DECODE function or CASE expression. The first column of the SELECT statement tests for courses with a cost of 1095. If this expression is equal to 1095, then the DECODE function or CASE expression returns the value

1; otherwise, it returns a NULL value. The COUNT function counts NOT NULL values; the NULL values are not included. Note that this is different from the way the COUNT(*) function works, which includes NULL values in the count.

The last column in the SELECT statement tests for courses with a NULL cost. If this condition of a NULL course cost is true, the DECODE function or the CASE expression returns a 1 and the row is included in the count.

You can also expand on the previous example to show all the course costs by prerequisite. Here, two courses with prerequisite 25 have a course cost of 1095 and 1195, respectively.

```
SELECT prerequisite,
       COUNT(DECODE(cost, 1095, 1)) "1095",
       COUNT(DECODE(cost, 1195, 1)) "1195",
       COUNT(DECODE(cost, 1595, 1)) "1595",
       COUNT(DECODE(cost, NULL, 1)) "NULL"
  FROM course
 GROUP BY prerequisite
```

PREREQUISITE	1095	1195	1595	NULL
10	1	0	0	0
20	0	5	0	0
25	1	1	0	0
. . .				
350	0	1	0	1
420	0	1	0	0
	0	4	0	0

17 rows selected.

The CASE expression can be used instead of the DECODE function. The query would then look similar to the following statement:

```
SELECT prerequisite,
       COUNT(CASE WHEN cost = 1095 THEN 1 END) "1095",
       COUNT(CASE WHEN cost = 1195 THEN 1 END) "1195",
       COUNT(CASE WHEN cost = 1595 THEN 1 END) "1595",
       COUNT(CASE WHEN cost IS NULL THEN 1 END) "NULL"
  FROM course
 GROUP BY prerequisite
```

It is best to use the CASE expression as it is always easier to understand than DECODE functionality. It also has the added benefit of being ANSI compatible. You should know about DECODE nonetheless because sometimes your SQL queries may need to run against an Oracle version prior to the implementation of the CASE functionality.

b) Build upon exercise a to include a range so the output looks like the following. Hint: You can write the query with the CASE expression or use the DECODE and the SIGN functions.

```
1500 OR LESS MORE THAN 1500
------------ --------------
          29              1
```

```
1 row selected.
```

Answer: The simplest query statement is achieved with the CASE expression. Otherwise use the SIGN function nested within the DECODE function to compare the values.

```
SELECT COUNT(CASE WHEN NVL(cost,0) <=1500 THEN 1 END)
       "1500 OR LESS",
       COUNT(CASE WHEN cost >1500 THEN 1 END)
       "MORE THAN 1500"
  FROM course
```

You can only express the same logic with the DECODE and SIGN functions.

```
SELECT COUNT(DECODE(SIGN(NVL(cost, 0) -1500), 1, NULL, 'A'))
       "1500 OR LESS",
       COUNT(DECODE(SIGN(NVL(cost,0) -1500), 1, 'A', NULL))
       "MORE THAN 1500"
  FROM course
```

To evaluate the function, read it from the inside out. Look at the first column of the SELECT statement. First, the NVL function is evaluated; if the cost equals NULL, a zero is substituted. The result of the expression NVL(cost, 0) – 1500 returns either a zero, a negative number, or a positive number. The SIGN function is applied to this expression and the SIGN function returns a 1 if the result of the expression NVL(COST, 0) – 1500 is positive. If the result is negative, the SIGN function returns a –1; if the result is zero, the SIGN function returns a zero. Based on the return value of the SIGN function, the DECODE function compares it to the search criteria.

For example, if the course cost of the row equals 1095, then the result of the expression 1095 – 1500 equals –405, a negative number. The SIGN function returns a –1. Therefore, the else condition of the DECODE function is executed, which returns the value 'A'. The COUNT function counts this record, because it is a NOT NULL value.

If the cost is greater than 1500, the expression SIGN(NVL(cost, 0) – 1500) returns a positive number, for which you find the search value of 1; then the resulting return value of the DECODE function is a NULL value. This row is not included in the count.

For the second column, which lists the costs greater than 1500, the same logic is repeated, but the search and resulting condition of the DECODE change accordingly.

Alternatively, you can write this with a SUM function to achieve the same result. Note that with the SUM function, the substitution value of the DECODE matters because it is added up. This is in contrast to the COUNT function, where only the NOT NULL values are counted, but the actual value does not matter.

```
SELECT SUM(DECODE(SIGN(NVL(cost, 0) -1500), 1, NULL, 1))
       "1500 OR LESS",
       SUM(DECODE(SIGN(NVL(cost, 0) -1500), 1, 1, NULL))
       "MORE THAN 1500"
  FROM course
```

While these crosstab queries are relatively easy to write using the DECODE or CASE functionality, you may encounter more complex query requirements where temporary tables can be helpful to reduce the complexity.

16.1.2 ANSWERS

a) Modify the following query to display the top-3 revenue-generating courses. If there is a tie in the revenue, include the duplicates. Hint: Use an inline view to achieve the desired result.

```
SELECT course_no, revenue,
       RANK() OVER (ORDER BY revenue DESC)
         rev_rank,
       DENSE_RANK() OVER (ORDER BY revenue DESC)
         rev_dense_rank,
       ROW_NUMBER() OVER (ORDER BY revenue DESC)
         row_number
  FROM course_revenue
```

Answer: Using an inline view you restrict the rows to only those where the values in the REV_DENSE_RANK column are 3 or less. The DENSE_RANK function is the better choice just in case some courses share the same revenue.

```
SELECT course_no, revenue, rev_dense_rank
  FROM (SELECT course_no, revenue,
               DENSE_RANK() OVER (ORDER BY revenue DESC)
                 rev_dense_rank
          FROM course_revenue) t
 WHERE rev_dense_rank <= 3
```

COURSE_NO	REVENUE	REV_DENSE_RANK
25	53775	1
122	28680	2
120	27485	3

3 rows selected.

BOTTOM-*N* RANKING

The bottom-*n* ranking is similar to top-*n* except now you change the order of the ranking. Instead of ordering the revenue by descending order, the ORDER BY clause is now in ascending order. The query to determine the bottom three revenue-ranking courses is listed here.

```
SELECT course_no, revenue, rev_dense_rank
   FROM (SELECT course_no, revenue,
                 DENSE_RANK() OVER (ORDER BY revenue ASC)
                 rev_dense_rank
            FROM course_revenue) t
  WHERE rev_dense_rank <= 3
```

COURSE_NO	REVENUE	REV_DENSE_RANK
10	1195	1
204	1195	1
132	2390	2
145	2390	2
420	2390	2
134	2390	2
146	3585	3
330	3585	3

8 rows selected.

b) Based on the following statement, explain how the result of the AVG column is achieved.

```
SELECT numeric_grade AS grade, grade_type_code,
       grade_code_occurrence AS occurrence,
       AVG(numeric_grade) OVER(PARTITION BY grade_type_code
       ORDER BY grade_code_occurrence) AS avg
  FROM grade
 WHERE student_id = 254
   AND section_id = 87
```

GRADE	GR	OCCURRENCE	AVG
91	FI	1	91
91	HM	1	91
75	HM	2	83
98	HM	3	88
98	HM	4	90.5
81	HM	5	88.6
71	HM	6	85.6666667
71	HM	7	83.5714286
81	HM	8	83.25
91	HM	9	84.1111111
91	HM	10	84.8
76	MT	1	76

12 rows selected.

Answer: The statement computes a cumulative average for each partition. The average is reset after the values listed in the partition clause change. The ORDER BY clause determines the definition of the window.

After the WHERE clause is executed, postprocessing with the analytical function takes over. The partitions are built first. The result shows three distinct values: FI, HM, and MT for final, homework, and midterm, respectively. After a change in partition, the average is reset.

It is easiest to follow the logic by examining the individual computations for each respective row. They are listed next to the result.

GRADE	GR	OCCURRENCE	AVG	
91	FI	1	91	/* (91)/1 */
91	HM	1	91	/* (91)/1 partition change*/
75	HM	2	83	/* (91+83)/2 */
98	HM	3	88	/* (91+83+98)/3 */
98	HM	4	90.5	/* (91+83+98+98)/4 */
...				
76	MT	1	76	/* (76)/1 partition change*/

12 rows selected.

You will notice that for the HM partition there are duplicates for the NUMERIC_GRADE column values (row 4 and 5 show 98). Because the column GRADE_CODE_OCCURRENCE is part of the ORDER BY clause and has different and ever-changing values, the cumulative average is computed for each row.

c) How would you formulate the question this query is attempting to solve?

```
SELECT e.*, SUM(diff) OVER (ORDER BY 1 ROWS BETWEEN
         UNBOUNDED PRECEDING AND CURRENT ROW) AS cum_sum
  FROM (SELECT TRUNC(enroll_date),
              TRUNC(enroll_date)-LAG(TRUNC(enroll_date),1)
               OVER (ORDER BY TRUNC(ENROLL_DATE)) DIFF
          FROM enrollment
        GROUP BY TRUNC(enroll_date)) e
```

TRUNC(ENR	DIFF	CUM_SUM
30-JAN-03		
02-FEB-03	3	3
04-FEB-03	2	5
07-FEB-03	3	8
10-FEB-03	3	11
11-FEB-03	1	12
13-FEB-03	2	14
16-FEB-03	3	17
19-FEB-03	3	20
21-FEB-03	2	22

10 rows selected.

Answer: Determine the difference in days between the distinct ENROLL_DATE values; only consider the date not the time values. In the result list the distinct ENROLL_DATE values, the difference in days between each value, and the cumulative sum of days in the last column.

d) Explain the result of this query.

```
WITH
num_enroll AS
(SELECT COUNT(*) num_students, course_no
   FROM enrollment e JOIN section s
 USING (section_id)
  GROUP BY course_no),
avg_stud_enroll AS
(SELECT AVG(num_students) avg#_of_stud
   FROM num_enroll
 WHERE num_students <> (SELECT MAX(num_students)
                          FROM num_enroll))
SELECT course_no, num_students
   FROM num_enroll
 WHERE num_students > (SELECT avg#_of_stud
                         FROM avg_stud_enroll)
    AND num_students < (SELECT MAX(num_students)
                          FROM num_enroll)
```

```
COURSE_NO  NUM_STUDENTS
---------  ------------
       20             9
      100            13
      120            23
      122            24
      124             8
      125             8
      130             8
      140            15
      230            14
      240            13
      350             9
```

11 rows selected.

Answer: The query will return those courses and the respective enrollment above the average enrollment per course, excluding any courses with the highest enrollment.

This query uses two inline queries NUM_ENROLL and AVG_STUD_ENROLL. The first query, called NUM_ENROLL, computes the number of enrolled students per course. The second query, labeled AVG_STUD_ENROLL, uses the previous query to determine the average number of students enrolled excluding the course with the highest enrollment. The last query shows the COURSE_NO column together with the number of enrolled students where the course has an enrollment that is higher than the average enrollment. Remember this average excludes the course with the highest enrollment. The last condition specifically excludes the course with the highest enrollment in the result as it would otherwise be included as it obviously has a higher than average enrollment.

As you discovered already, the SQL language allows many different ways of expressing a query and still achieving the same result. The differences often lie in the efficiency of the statement. The result can also be obtained using this query; notice that several joins are required with each execution of the condition, thus requiring more resources and time than simply re-using the temporarily stored query result. Furthermore, the WITH clause breaks down the problem into individual pieces, therefore simplifying the writing of complex queries.

```
SELECT course_no, COUNT(*) num_students
  FROM enrollment e JOIN section s
 USING (section_id)
 GROUP BY course_no
HAVING COUNT(*) > (SELECT AVG(COUNT(*))
                     FROM enrollment e JOIN section s
                    USING (section_id)
                    GROUP BY course_no
```

```
                      HAVING COUNT(*) <> (SELECT MAX(COUNT(*))
                                     FROM enrollment e JOIN section s
                                     USING (section_id)
                                     GROUP BY course_no))
    AND COUNT(*) <>(SELECT MAX(COUNT(*))
                        FROM enrollment e JOIN section s
                    USING (section_id)
                    GROUP BY course_no)
```

LAB 16.1 SELF-REVIEW QUESTIONS

In order to test your progress, you should be able to answer the following questions.

1) What value does the following expression return?

   ```
   DECODE(SIGN(100-500), 1, 50, -1, 400, NULL)
   ```

   a) _____ −400
   b) _____ 50
   c) _____ 400
   d) _____ −1
   e) _____ NULL

2) The difference between the RANK and DENSE_RANK functions is that DENSE_RANK leaves no gaps in ranking sequence when there are ties in the values.

   a) _____ True
   b) _____ False

3) If you use the RANK function without a partitioning clause, the ranking works over the entire result set.

   a) _____ True
   b) _____ False

4) The ROWS keyword in a windowing clause defines a logical window.

   a) _____ True
   b) _____ False

5) The presence of duplicate rows in an ORDER BY clause of a logical window will cause the analytical function such as an average to be computed for the rows with identical value.

   a) _____ True
   b) _____ False

6) The LAG and LEAD functions may have a windowing clause.

a) _____ True
b) _____ False

7) The FIRST_VALUE and LAST_VALUE functions only work with a windowing clause.

a) _____ True
b) _____ False

Answers appear in Appendix A, Section 16.1.

LAB 16.2

ROLLUP AND CUBE OPERATORS

LAB OBJECTIVES

After this lab, you will be able to:
✔ Use the ROLLUP, CUBE, GROUPING, and GROUPING
  SETS Capabilities

Oracle includes many enhancements to the GROUP BY clause that make aggregating data from many different perspectives simpler and more efficient. These enhancements come in the form of the ROLLUP and CUBE operators, the GROUPING function, and GROUPING SETS capabilities. The ROLLUP and CUBE operators allow you to create subtotals and grand totals by simply eliminating the need to run multiple queries against the data.

You will see how useful these capabilities are for analyzing data and discovering relationships between data elements. This functionality is primarily used in data warehousing environments with the goal of providing users with reporting and decision support functionality against summarized data.

End-user access is often accomplished with various querying tools that read this summarized data and allow users to "slice and dice" the information in any way they desire. As many companies are increasingly using their databases to gain competitive market advantage and to better support their customers as well as reduce costs, this capability allows you to uncover much information about the data.

Many software vendors offer various types of tools that present the summarized data in an easily understandable format to users; Oracle itself also supplies its own version of an end-user decision support software tool called Oracle Discoverer. While we will not discuss the capabilities and merits of such tools, we will illustrate the summarization capabilities of Oracle to discover relationships and information about the data. You will see that this functionality is quite powerful, extremely valuable, and yet very easy to use.

THE ROLLUP OPERATOR

The ROLLUP operator allows you to create subtotals and grand totals, also referred to as *super aggregate rows*, for various groupings and for all rows.

The table used for the exercises in this lab is called INSTRUCTOR_SUMMARY and is included in the supplemental tables you can download from the companion Web site. It contains summary data generated from the various tables in the STUDENT schema.

The DESCRIBE command lists the following columns. The primary key of the table consists of the INSTRUCTOR_ID, SEMESTER_YEAR, and SEMESTER_MONTH columns.

```
SQL> DESCR instructor_summary
Name                       Null?      Type
----------------------     --------   ----------------
INSTRUCTOR_ID              NOT NULL   NUMBER(8)
GENDER                                CHAR(1)
CAMPUS                                VARCHAR2(11)
SEMESTER_YEAR              NOT NULL   VARCHAR2(4)
SEMESTER_MONTH             NOT NULL   VARCHAR2(2)
NUM_OF_CLASSES                        NUMBER
NUM_OF_STUDENTS                       NUMBER
REVENUE                               NUMBER
```

The INSTRUCTOR_ID is identical to the familiar column in the INSTRUCTOR table. The GENDER column identifies the gender as either male (M), female (F), or unknown (U) If the title of an instructor is different than Mr., Mrs., or Ms. The CAMPUS column indicates the name of the campus where the instructor's office is located. The SEMESTER_YEAR and SEMESTER_MONTH columns display the year and month the instructor worked. The column NUM_OF_CLASSES holds the number of sections the instructor taught, the NUM_OF_STUDENTS shows the column number of students for all the sections, and the REVENUE column contains the revenue generated by the individual instructor for these classes.

Using the familiar GROUP BY clause, the following query produces a listing of instructors grouped by the GENDER, SEMESTER_YEAR, and SEMESTER_MONTH columns, including the total number of students taught.

```
SELECT gender, semester_year AS year,
       semester_month AS month,
       SUM(num_of_students) AS total
  FROM instructor_summary
 GROUP BY gender, semester_year, semester_month
```

```
G YEAR MO      TOTAL
- ---- --  ----------
F 2003 05          0
F 2003 06         16
F 2004 07         37
M 2003 06         45
M 2003 07         79
U 2003 05          0
U 2003 07         49

7 rows selected.
```

Based on the result, you notice that all the distinct occurrences of these three columns are summarized.

Instead of using the GROUP BY clause, the next query uses the ROLLUP operator. You will discover the formation of subtotals for each of the groups. Your individual result will not display the actual shading shown here; they only illustrate the location of the formed super aggregate rows.

```
SELECT gender, semester_year AS year,
       semester_month AS month,
       SUM(num_of_students) AS total
  FROM instructor_summary
 GROUP BY ROLLUP(gender, semester_year, semester_month)
G YEAR MO      TOTAL
- ---- --  ----------
F 2003 05          0
F 2003 06         16
F 2003           16 Subtotal for female in year 2003
F 2004 07         37
F 2004           37 Subtotal for female in year 2004

F                53 Subtotal for entire female gender
M 2003 06         45
M 2003 07         79
M 2003          124 Subtotal for male in year 2003

M               124 Subtotal for entire male gender
U 2003 05          0
U 2003 07         49
U 2003           49 Subtotal for unknown gender 2003

U                49 Subtotal for entire unknown gender

                226 Grand Total

15 rows selected.
```

Examining the result, you will observe some of the same rows as those shown in the previous GROUP BY query. What is different are additional rows. These additional rows indicate subtotals for the GENDER and YEAR columns, a subtotal for the GENDER column only, and a grand total column. The subtotals are formed for each change in value.

The first shaded set of summary rows indicates 16 female students for the year 2003 and 53 female students in total.

Notice that you only needed one query to generate different groupings of data. The individual groupings are: group #1: gender, year, and month; group #2: gender and year; group #3: gender; and group #4: grand total.

The number of columns or expressions appearing in the ROLLUP clause determines the number of groupings. The formula is $n + 1$ where n is the number of columns listed in the ROLLUP clause. Without the ROLLUP clause you would need to write four individual queries.

The first query is already listed at the beginning of this lab, but repeated together with partial output. This query represents the different individual rows grouped by the columns GENDER, SEMESTER_YEAR, and SEMESTER_MONTH.

```
SELECT gender, semester_year AS year,
       semester_month AS month,
       SUM(num_of_students) AS total
  FROM instructor_summary
 GROUP BY gender, semester_year, semester_month
G YEAR MO      TOTAL
- ---- --  -----------
F 2003 05           0
F 2003 06          16
...
U 2003 07          49

7 rows selected.
```

The second query lists the GENDER and SEMESTER_YEAR columns and computes the respective summary data.

```
SELECT gender, semester_year AS year,
       SUM(num_of_students) AS total
  FROM instructor_summary
 GROUP BY gender, semester_year
G YEAR       TOTAL
- ----  -----------
F 2003          16
F 2004          37
M 2003         124
U 2003          49

4 rows selected.
```

The third query is a listing grouped to give you a subtotal for the gender.

```
SELECT gender, SUM(num_of_students) AS total
  FROM instructor_summary
 GROUP BY gender
G        TOTAL
-        ----------
F             53
M            124
U             49
```

3 rows selected.

And the last query is the grand total for all the rows.

```
SELECT SUM(num_of_students) AS total
  FROM instructor_summary
     TOTAL
  ----------
       226
```

1 row selected.

The idea of the ROLLUP operator is that you don't need to write multiple queries and Oracle doesn't need to process the table multiple times, but rather does all the necessary work in one pass through the table. This is a very efficient and quick way to accomplish the desired result.

THE CUBE OPERATOR

The CUBE operator takes the formation of super aggregates yet another step further—it allows you to generate all the possible combinations of groups. If you have n columns or expressions in the GROUP BY clause, the CUBE operator generates 2^n groupings. The CUBE operator received its name from the different combinations that can be achieved from an n-dimensional cube. The next example illustrates the combinations based on the previously used query. The CUBE operator is now substituted for the ROLLUP operator.

```
SELECT gender, semester_year AS year,
       semester_month AS month,
       SUM(num_of_students) AS total
  FROM instructor_summary
 GROUP BY CUBE(gender, semester_year, semester_month)
G YEAR MO       TOTAL
- ---- -- ----------
F 2003 05            0
F 2003 06           16
F 2003              16
```

F	2004	07	37
F	2004		37
F		05	0
F		06	16
F		07	37
F			53
M	2003	06	45
M	2003	07	79
M	2003		124
M		06	45
M		07	79
M			124
U	2003	05	0
U	2003	07	49
U	2003		49
U		05	0
U		07	49
U			49
	2003	05	0
	2003	06	61
	2003	07	128
	2003		189
	2004	07	37
	2004		37
		05	0
		06	61
		07	165
			226

31 rows selected.

The shading around the rows indicates the new additionally formed subtotals. Observe a subtotal for GENDER and SEMESTER_MONTH, another for SEMESTER_YEAR and SEMESTER_MONTH, a subtotal for SEMESTER_YEAR only, and lastly a total by SEMESTER_MONTH.

The cube determined the 2^3 different combinations for the three columns, which results in a total of eight different subtotals. The ROLLUP already determined four and the CUBE added four more combinations.

DETERMINING THE ROLLUP AND CUBE COMBINATIONS

Assume you have three rollup groups in your GROUP BY ROLLUP clause listed like the following hypothetical columns named YEAR, MONTH, and WEEK.

```
GROUP BY ROLLUP (year, month, week)
```

You will get the following four rollup groups according to the $n + 1$ formula: group #1, which consists of year, month, and week; group #2, which shows year and month; group #3, which shows year; and group #4, which shows the grand total. Hierarchies such as time periods or sales territories (continent, country, state, county) lend themselves naturally to the ROLLUP operator, though you can obviously create your own or use your own combination of columns to roll up.

If you use the CUBE operator instead, you generate eight different combinations, all of which are listed in Table 16.3. Note the empty set of parentheses, (), indicates the grand total.

Table 16.3 ■ Grouping Combinations

Operator	Formula Grouping	Combinations
ROLLUP (year, month, week)	$n + 1$ $3 + 1 = 4$	(year, month, week), (year, month), (year), ()
CUBE (year, month, week)	2^n $2^3 = 8$	(year, month, week), (year, month), (year), (month, week), (year, week), (week), (month), ()

PARTIAL CUBE AND ROLLUP RESULTS

To exclude certain subtotals from the CUBE or the ROLLUP result, you can selectively remove columns from the CUBE or ROLLUP clause and place them into the GROUP BY clause or generate summaries based on composite columns. Although it is useful to know about these options, you may simplify this with the GROUPING SETS clause, discussed shortly.

Table 16.4 lists the partial ROLLUP and CUBE results when a column moves into the GROUP BY clause. The example uses three columns called YEAR, MONTH, and WEEK. Most notably, the summary grand total is missing from all the partial rollups.

Table 16.4 ■ Partial ROLLUP and CUBE Operations

GROUP BY Clause	Grouping Combinations
year, ROLLUP (month, week)	(year, month, week), (year, month), (year)
year, month ROLLUP (week)	(year, month, week), (year, month)
year, CUBE(month, week)	(year, month, week), (year, month), (year, week), (year)
year, month, CUBE (week)	(year, month, week), (year, month)

You can further group on composite columns. A composite column defined within this context is a collection of columns and is listed within a set of parentheses. As such, a composite column is treated as a single unit; this avoids any unnecessary aggregations for specific levels. The results of operations on composite columns are listed in Table 16.5.

Table 16.5 ■ Composite Column ROLLUP and CUBE Operations

Composite Columns	Grouping Combinations
ROLLUP ((year, month), week)	(year, month, week), (year, month), ()
ROLLUP (year), (month, week)	(year, month, week), (month, week)
CUBE ((year, month), week)	(year, month, week), (year, month), (week), ()
CUBE (year), (month, week)	(year, month, week), (month, week)

GROUPING SETS

Computing and displaying only selective results can actually be simplified with the GROUPING SETS extension of the GROUP BY clause. You explicitly state which summaries you want to generate. The following query applies the GROUPING SETS functionality to the example query drawn on previously.

```
SELECT gender, semester_year AS YEAR,
       semester_month AS month,
       SUM(num_of_students) AS total
  FROM instructor_summary
 GROUP BY GROUPING SETS
       ((gender, semester_year),    -- 1st Group
        (semester_month),           -- 2nd Group
        ())                         -- 3rd Group
 G YEAR MO      TOTAL
 - ---- -- ----------
 F 2003            16
 F 2004            37
 M 2003           124
 U 2003            49
        05          0
        06         61
        07        165
                  226

 8 rows selected.
```

The query produces three sets: one for the GENDER and SEMESTER_YEAR columns, a second for the SEMESTER_MONTH, and the last group is the grand total. Each individual set must be enclosed in parentheses; the empty set of parentheses indicates the grand total. The GROUPING SETS clause provides the advantage of reading the table once and generating the results at once and only for those summaries in which you are interested. GROUPING SETS functionality is very efficient and yet selective about the results you choose to report.

**LAB
16.2**

COMBINE GROUPING SETS

If you have many hierarchy groupings, you may not want to specify all the different groupings individually. You can combine multiple GROUPING SETS to generate yet more combinations.

The next example lists two GROUPING SETS clauses in the GROUP BY clause.

```
GROUP BY GROUPING SETS (year, month),
         GROUPING SETS (week, day)
```

The cross product results in the following equivalent groupings.

```
GROUP BY GROUPING SETS (
            (year, week),
            (year, day),
            (month, week),
            (month, day))
```

THE GROUPING FUNCTION

One of the purposes of the GROUPING function is that it helps you distinguish the summary rows from any rows that are a result of null values. The next query shows a CUBE operation on the columns SEMESTER_YEAR and CAMPUS. As it turns out, the CAMPUS column contains null values, and it is difficult to distinguish between the summary row and an individual row holding a null value.

```
SELECT semester_year AS year, campus,
       SUM(num_of_classes) AS num_of_classes
  FROM instructor_summary
 GROUP BY CUBE (semester_year, campus)
 ORDER BY 1
```

YEAR	CAMPUS	NUM_OF_CLASSES	
2003	DOWNTOWN	10	
2003	LIBERTY	19	
2003	MORNINGSIDE	29	
2003		10	Summary row or null?
2003		68	
2004	MORNINGSIDE	10	
2004		10	

DOWNTOWN	10	
LIBERTY	19	
MORNINGSIDE	39	
	10	Summary row or null?
	78	

12 rows selected.

The GROUPING function eliminates any ambiguities. Whenever you see a value of 1 in a column where the GROUPING function is applied, it indicates a super aggregate row, such as a subtotal or grand total row created by the ROLLUP or CUBE operator.

```
SELECT semester_year AS year, campus,
       SUM(num_of_classes) AS num_of_classes,
       GROUPING (semester_year) GP_YEAR,
       GROUPING (campus) GP_CAMPUS
  FROM instructor_summary
 GROUP BY CUBE (semester_year, campus)
 ORDER BY 1
```

YEAR	CAMPUS	NUM_OF_CLA	GP_YEAR	GP_CAMPUS	
2003	DOWNTOWN	10	0	0	
2003	LIBERTY	19	0	0	
2003	MORNINGSIDE	39	0	0	
2003		10	0	0	NULL value GP_CAMPUS
2003		68	0	1	
2004	MORNINGSIDE	10	0	0	
2004		10	0	1	
	DOWNTOWN	10	1	0	
	LIBERTY	19	1	0	
	MORNINGSIDE	39	1	0	
		10	1	0	NULL value GP_CAMPUS
		78	1	1	

12 rows selected.

When examining the result, you observe the columns where the GROUPING function is applied and has a value of zero or 1. The number 1 indicates that this column is a super aggregate row.

The first shaded area on the resulting output shows a zero in the GP_CAMPUS column; this indicates that the null value in the CAMPUS column is indeed a null. The next row lists the number one in the GP_CAMPUS column; this designates the row as a summary row. It lists 68 classes for all campus locations in 2003.

The second shaded row shows the number 1 in the GP_YEAR column. This indicates that the SEMESTER_YEAR column is an aggregate just like the previous three rows. That means the rows display the aggregate values for each individual campus for all years.

The last row contains the number 1 for both the GP_YEAR and the GP_CAMPUS columns. This indicates the grand total.

You can use the GROUPING function not only to determine if it's a generated row or null value, but to return certain rows from the result set with the HAVING clause. This is yet another way to selectively choose certain summary rows only.

```
HAVING GROUPING(campus) = 1
```

The GROUPING function can be utilized to add labels to the super aggregate rows. Instead of a blank column, a label such as 'GRAND TOTAL:' is displayed.

```
SELECT CASE WHEN GROUPING(semester_year) = 1
            AND GROUPING(campus) = 1 THEN 'GRAND TOTAL:'
       ELSE semester_year
   END AS year,
   CASE WHEN GROUPING(semester_year) = 1
            AND GROUPING(campus) = 1 THEN NULL
       ELSE campus
   END AS campus,
   SUM(num_of_classes) AS num_of_classes,
   GROUPING (semester_year) GP_YEAR,
   GROUPING (campus) GP_CAMPUS
 FROM instructor_summary
 GROUP BY CUBE (semester_year, campus)
```

YEAR	CAMPUS	NUM_OF_CLAS	GP_YEAR	GP_CAMPUS
2003	DOWNTOWN	10	0	0
2003	LIBERTY	19	0	0
2003	MORNINGSIDE	29	0	0
2003		10	0	0
2003		68	0	1
2004	MORNINGSIDE	10	0	0
2004		10	0	1
	DOWNTOWN	10	1	0
	LIBERTY	19	1	0
	MORNINGSIDE	39	1	0
		10	1	0
GRAND TOTAL:		78	1	1

```
12 rows selected.
```

 Remember you can also use the NVL or COALESCE function to test for null values and return a substitute value.

THE GROUPING_ID FUNCTION

If your query includes many GROUPING functions, you may want to consider consolidating the columns with the GROUPING_ID function. This function is not only similar in name and functionality but allows multiple columns as a parameter; it returns a number indicating the level of aggregation in the rollup or cube.

The GROUPING_ID returns a single number that identifies the exact aggregation level of every row.

```
SELECT semester_year AS year,
       campus,
       SUM(num_of_classes) AS num_of_classes,
       GROUPING (semester_year) GP_YEAR,
       GROUPING (campus) GP_CAMPUS,
       GROUPING_ID(semester_year, campus)
       AS GROUPING_ID
  FROM instructor_summary
 GROUP BY CUBE (semester_year, campus)
```

YEAR	CAMPUS	NUM_OF_C	GP_YEAR	GP_CAMPUS	GROUPING_ID
2003	DOWNTOWN	10	0	0	0
2003	LIBERTY	19	0	0	0
2003	MORNINGSIDE	29	0	0	0
2003		10	0	0	0
2003		68	0	1	1
2004	MORNINGSIDE	10	0	0	0
2004		10	0	1	1
	DOWNTOWN	10	1	0	2
	LIBERTY	19	1	0	2
	MORNINGSIDE	39	1	0	2
		10	1	0	2
		78	1	1	3

12 rows selected.

The GROUPING_ID function works just like the GROUPING function that generates zeros and ones. However, the GROUPING_ID function concatenates the zeros and ones and forms a bit vector, which is treated as a binary number. The GROUPING_ID returns the binary number's base-10 value. A value of 1 for each GROUPING column indicates that this is the grand total. This 11 binary number for the two-level column aggregation represents the number 3, which is returned by GROUPING_ID function. Zeros in all the columns of the GROUPING functions indicate that this is the lowest aggregation level.

Table 16.6 lists binary numbers and their numeric equivalent on the example of a four-column cube, representative of a GROUP BY clause such as CUBE(year, month, week, day). The column labeled GROUPING_ID displays the result of the

Table 16.6 ■ **Bit to Numeric Representation on the Example of a Four-Column CUBE**

GROUPING_ID	Numeric Equivalent	Bit-Vector Aggregation Level
0	0 0 0 0	(year, month, week, day)
1	0 0 0 1	(year, month, week)
2	0 0 1 0	(year, month, day)
3	0 0 1 1	(year, month)
4	0 1 0 0	(year, week, day)
5	0 1 0 1	(year, week)
6	0 1 1 0	(year, day)
7	0 1 1 1	(year)
8	1 0 0 0	(month, week, day)
9	1 0 0 1	(month, week)
10	1 0 1 0	(month, day)
11	1 0 1 1	(month)
12	1 1 0 0	(week, day)
13	1 1 0 1	(week)
14	1 1 1 0	(day)
15	1 1 1 1	()

GROUPING_ID function for each individual column; the bit-vector column indicates which bits are turned on and off. The new 10*g* BIN_TO_NUM function allows you to convert a binary value to a NUMBER. Every argument represents a bit in the bit vector.

```
SELECT BIN_TO_NUM(1,1)
  FROM dual
BIN_TO_NUM(1,1)
---------------
              3

1 row selected.
```

You can use the GROUPING_ID function for labeling columns as discussed previously. However, its primary use is the application of *materialized views*, an Oracle object that allows you to create and maintain aggregate summary tables. Storing pre-aggregate summary information is an important technique for maximizing query performance in large decision support applications. The effect of the creation of this materialized view is that data is physically stored in a table. Any changes to the underlying tables are reflected in the materialized view through various refresh methods. (Unlike views, discussed in Chapter 12, "Views, Indexes, and Sequences," materialized views require physical storage.)

```
CREATE MATERIALIZED VIEW instructor_sum_mv
STORAGE(INITIAL 5 M PCTINCREASE 0)
AS
SELECT semester_year AS year,
       campus,
       SUM(num_of_classes) AS num_of_classes,
       GROUPING_ID(semester_year, campus)
       AS GROUPING_ID
  FROM instructor_summary
 GROUP BY CUBE (semester_year, campus)
Materialized view created.
```

You must have the CREATE MATERIALIZED VIEW privilege to be able to perform this operation.

GROUP_ID FUNCTION

The GROUP_ID function lets you distinguish among duplicate groupings; they may be generated as a result of combinations of columns listed in the GROUP BY clause. The GROUP_ID returns the number zero to the first row in the set that is not yet duplicated; any subsequent duplicate grouping row receives a higher number, starting with the number 1.

```
SELECT semester_year AS year, campus,
       SUM(num_of_classes) AS num_of_classes,
       GROUPING_ID(semester_year, campus) GROUPING_ID,
       GROUP_ID()
  FROM instructor_summary
 GROUP BY GROUPING SETS
       (semester_year, ROLLUP(semester_year, campus))
```

YEAR	CAMPUS	NUM_OF_CLASSES	GROUPING_ID	GROUP_ID()
2003	DOWNTOWN	10	0	0
2003	LIBERTY	19	0	0
2003	MORNINGSIDE	29	0	0
2003		10	0	0
2004	MORNINGSIDE	10	0	0
		78	3	0
2003		68	1	0
2004		10	1	0

```
2003                      68         1         1
2004                      10         1         1
```

10 rows selected.

This query illustrates the result of the GROUP_ID function, which returns a zero for the first row; the subsequent identical group returns the number 1 in the GROUP_ID() column. You will see this in the last two rows of the result.

If you have complicated queries that may generate duplicate values, you can eliminate those rows by including the condition HAVING GROUP_ID() = 0.

LAB 16.2 EXERCISES

16.2.1 USE THE *ROLLUP, CUBE, GROUPING,* AND *GROUPING SETS* CAPABILITIES

a) Describe the effect of the following SQL statement and its resulting output.

```
COL SALUTATION FORMAT A5
COL "Area Code" FORMAT A9
COL "Reg.Month" FORMAT A10
SET pagesize 1000

SELECT salutation AS SALUTATION, SUBSTR(phone, 1,3)
       AS "Area Code",
       TO_CHAR(registration_date, 'MON') AS "Reg.Month",
       COUNT(*)
  FROM student
 WHERE SUBSTR(phone, 1,3) IN ('201','212','718')
   AND salutation IN ('Mr.', 'Ms.')
 GROUP BY ROLLUP (salutation, SUBSTR(phone, 1,3),
       TO_CHAR(registration_date, 'MON'))
```

SALUT	Area Code	Reg.Month	COUNT(*)
Mr.	201	FEB	34
Mr.	201	JAN	9
Mr.	201		43
Mr.	212	FEB	1
Mr.	212	JAN	1
Mr.	212		2
Mr.	718	FEB	72
Mr.	718	JAN	17
Mr.	718		89
Mr.			134

```
Ms.    201      FEB               27
Ms.    201      JAN                5
Ms.    201                        32
Ms.    212      FEB                2
Ms.    212      JAN                1
Ms.    212                         3
Ms.    718      FEB               52
Ms.    718      JAN               13
Ms.    718                        65
Ms.                              100
                                 234
```

21 rows selected.

b) Answer the following questions about the result set:

How many female students are there in total?
How many male students live in area code 212?
What is the total number of students?
How many female students live in the area code 718 and registered in January?

c) If the CUBE operator is used on the query in exercise a instead, how many different combinations of groups do you get? List the groups.

d) Describe the result of the following query using the GROUPING SET extension to the GROUP BY clause.

```
COL "Area Code" FORMAT A9
COL "Reg.Month" FORMAT A9

SELECT SALUTATION, SUBSTR(phone, 1,3) "Area Code",
       TO_CHAR(registration_date, 'MON') "Reg.Month",
       COUNT(*)
  FROM student
 WHERE SUBSTR(phone, 1,3) IN ('201','212','718')
   AND salutation IN ('Mr.', 'Ms.')
 GROUP BY
       GROUPING SETS
       ((SALUTATION, SUBSTR(phone, 1,3)),
        (SALUTATION, TO_CHAR(registration_date, 'MON')),
        ()
       )
SALUT Are Reg   COUNT(*)
----- --- --- ---------
Mr.   201              43
Mr.   212               2
Mr.   718              89
```

```
Ms.    201              32
Ms.    212               3
Ms.    718              65
Mr.            FEB     107
Mr.            JAN      27
Ms.            FEB      81
Ms.            JAN      19
                       234
```

11 rows selected.

e) Write the necessary individual queries to create the results similar to exercise d. There is no need to include the null values in the columns.

LAB 16.2 EXERCISE ANSWERS

16.2.1 ANSWERS

a) Describe the effect of the following SQL statement and its resulting output. (For space reasons, the code is not repeated here.)

Answer: The query generates summary totals for three different groupings of students by using the ROLLUP operator. This effectively creates groupings, which are counting rows in the STUDENT table. Four rollup groups are generated based on the columns: salutation, area code, and registration month (labeled "Reg.Month").

The first ROLLUP group is salutation, area code, and registration date; the second group is salutation and area code; the third is salutation; and the last is a grand total of all the rows. The shaded rows indicate the first occurrence of a group.

SALUT	Area Code	Reg.Month	COUNT(*)	
Mr.	201	FEB	34	Group #1
Mr.	201	JAN	9	
Mr.	201		43	Group #2
Mr.	212	FEB	1	
Mr.	212	JAN	1	
Mr.	212		2	
Mr.	718	FEB	72	
Mr.	718	JAN	17	
Mr.	718		89	
Mr.			134	Group #3
Ms.	201	FEB	27	
Ms.	201	JAN	5	

Ms.	201		32
Ms.	212	FEB	2
Ms.	212	JAN	1
Ms.	212		3
Ms.	718	FEB	52
Ms.	718	JAN	13
Ms.	718		65
Ms.			100

234   Group #4

21 rows selected.

b) Answer the following questions about the result set:

How many female students are there in total?
How many male students live in area code 212?
What is the total number of students?
How many female students live in the area code 718 and registered in January?

Answer: You can obtain all these answers by examining the result set.

The first question, "How many female students are part of the result set?", can be easily answered by looking at the result set. The correct answer is that there are 100 female students. Following is an excerpt of the output.

```
SALUT Area Code Reg.Month   COUNT(*)
----- --------- ----------  ---------
...
Ms.                              100
```

The next question about the male students living in area code 212 can be obtained from this row. As you can see the number of students is 2.

```
SALUT Area Code Reg.Month   COUNT(*)
----- --------- ----------  ---------
...
Mr.   212                          2
```

The total number of students satisfying the WHERE clause of the query can be obtained with the last row, the grand total row. There are 234 in total.

```
SALUT Area Code Reg.Month   COUNT(*)
----- --------- ----------  ---------
...
                                 234
```

Last, there are 13 female students who live in area code 718 and registered in January.

```
SALUT Area Code Reg.Month   COUNT(*)
----- --------- ---------- ---------
...
Ms.   718       JAN               13
```

c) If the CUBE operator is used on the query in exercise a instead, how many different combinations of groups do you get? List the groups.

Answer: There are three columns involved; therefore, there are 2^3 possible combinations, which translate to eight different groupings.

Group #1: Salutation, area code, registration date
Group #2: Salutation, area code
Group #3: Salutation
Group #4: Area code, registration date
Group #5: Registration date
Group #6: Salutation, registration date
Group #7: Area code
Group #8: Grand total

d) Describe the result of the following query using the GROUPING SET extension to the GROUP BY clause.

```
COL "Area Code" FORMAT A9
COL "Reg.Month" FORMAT A9

SELECT SALUTATION, SUBSTR(phone, 1,3) "Area Code",
       TO_CHAR(registration_date, 'MON') "Reg.Month",
       COUNT(*)
  FROM student
 WHERE SUBSTR(phone, 1,3) IN ('201','212','718')
   AND salutation IN ('Mr.', 'Ms.')
 GROUP BY
       GROUPING SETS
       ((SALUTATION, SUBSTR(phone, 1,3)),
        (SALUTATION, TO_CHAR(registration_date, 'MON')),
        ()
       )
SALUT Are Reg   COUNT(*)
----- --- --- ---------
Mr.   201          43
Mr.   212           2
Mr.   718          89
Ms.   201          32
Ms.   212           3
Ms.   718          65
Mr.       FEB     107
```

```
Mr.       JAN        27
Ms.       FEB        81
Ms.       JAN        19
                    234
```

11 rows selected.

Answer: The query result shows students with the salutations Mr. and Ms. that live in the area codes 201, 212, and 718. The GROUPING SETS extension to the GROUP BY clause allows you to selectively group specific information. There are three individual groups. The first set is salutation and area code and is indicated as a set with the enclosed parentheses. The next set is the registration month and the salutation is again enclosed in the parentheses. The third and last set is an empty set of parentheses; this indicates the grand total. The GROUPING SETS clause is very efficient as it queries the table once to generate the result.

e) Write the necessary individual queries to create the results similar to exercise d. There is no need to include the null values in the columns.

Answer: From the previous question, we already identified the three groupings, which then translate into three individual queries.

Query #1:

```
SELECT salutation, SUBSTR(phone, 1, 3), COUNT(*)
  FROM student
 WHERE SUBSTR(phone, 1,3) IN ('201','212','718')
   AND salutation IN ('Mr.', 'Ms.')
 GROUP BY salutation, SUBSTR(phone, 1, 3)
SALUT SUB  COUNT(*)
----- ---  ---------
Mr.   201        43
Mr.   212         2
Mr.   718        89
Ms.   201        32
Ms.   212         3
Ms.   718        65
```

6 rows selected.

Query #2:

```
SELECT salutation, TO_CHAR(registration_date, 'MON'),
       COUNT(*)
  FROM student
 WHERE SUBSTR(phone, 1,3) IN ('201','212','718')
   AND salutation IN ('Mr.', 'Ms.')
 GROUP BY salutation, TO_CHAR(registration_date, 'MON')
```

```
SALUT TO_  COUNT(*)
-----  ---  ---------
Mr.    FEB       107
Mr.    JAN        27
Ms.    FEB        81
Ms.    JAN        19
```

4 rows selected.

Query #3:

```
SELECT COUNT(*)
  FROM student
 WHERE SUBSTR(phone, 1,3) IN ('201','212','718')
   AND salutation IN ('Mr.', 'Ms.')
 COUNT(*)
 ---------
      234
```

1 row selected.

LAB 16.2 SELF-REVIEW QUESTIONS

In order to test your progress, you should be able to answer the following questions.

1) A query has the following GROUP BY clause. How many different groupings are visible on the result?

```
GROUP BY CUBE (color, price, material, store_location)
```

a) _____ 4
b) _____ 5
c) _____ 16
d) _____ 24
e) _____ Unknown

2) A query has the following GROUP BY clause. How many different groupings are visible on the result?

```
GROUP BY ROLLUP (color, price, material, store_location)
```

a) _____ 4
b) _____ 5
c) _____ 16
d) _____ 24
e) _____ Unknown

3) A return value of 1 from the GROUPING function indicates an aggregate row.

    a) _____ True
    b) _____ False

4) How many groups are generated by the following query.

```
GROUP BY GROUPING SETS((color, price), material, store_location)
```

    a) _____ 3
    b) _____ 4
    c) _____ 5
    d) _____ 16
    e) _____ Unknown

Answers appear in Appendix A, Section 16.2.

LAB 16.2

C H A P T E R   1 6

TEST YOUR THINKING

The projects in this section are meant to have you utilize all of the skills that you have acquired throughout this chapter. The answers to these projects can be found at the companion Web site to this book, located at: http://authors.phptr.com/rischert3e. Visit the Web site periodically to share and discuss your answers.

1) Write the question for the following query and answer.

```
SELECT COUNT(DECODE(SIGN(total_capacity-20),
            -1, 1, 0, 1)) "<=20",
       COUNT(DECODE(SIGN(total_capacity-21),
            0, 1, -1, NULL,
            DECODE(SIGN(total_capacity-30), -1, 1)))
            "21-30",
       COUNT(DECODE(SIGN(total_capacity-30), 1, 1)) "31+"
  FROM (SELECT SUM(capacity) total_capacity, course_no
          FROM SECTION
         GROUP BY COURSE_NO)
     <=20      21-30       31+
--------- --------- ---------
         2        10        16
```

```
1 row selected.
```

2) Determine the top three zip codes where most of the students live. Use an analytical function.

3) Explain the result of the following query.

```
SELECT 'Q'||TO_CHAR(start_date_time, 'Q') qtr,
       TO_CHAR(start_date_time, 'DY') day, COUNT(*),
       DENSE_RANK() OVER (
          PARTITION BY 'Q'||TO_CHAR(start_date_time, 'Q')
          ORDER BY COUNT(*) DESC) rank_qtr,
       DENSE_RANK() OVER (ORDER BY COUNT(*) DESC) rank_all
```

```
   FROM enrollment e, section s
  WHERE s.section_id = e.section_id
  GROUP BY 'Q'||TO_CHAR(start_date_time, 'Q'),
        TO_CHAR(start_date_time, 'DY')
  ORDER BY 1
QT DAY   COUNT(*)   RANK_QTR   RANK_ALL
-- ---  ---------- ---------- ----------
Q2 WED        42          1          1
Q2 THU        36          2          2
Q2 MON        30          3          3
Q2 TUE        28          4          5
Q2 FRI        15          5          7
Q2 SAT        13          6          8
Q2 SUN        13          6          8
Q3 MON        29          1          4
Q3 THU        20          2          6

9 rows selected.
```

CHAPTER 17

SQL
OPTIMIZATION

Throughout this book you find alternate SQL statements for many solutions. This chapter focuses on helping you determine the most effective SQL statement to efficiently and quickly return results. You gain an overview of the workings of the Oracle Optimizer and an understanding of SQL performance tuning techniques. The list of tuning suggestions in this chapter is by no means comprehensive, but merely a starting point. After you understand how to read the execution steps of SQL statements, you will have gained a better understanding of Oracle's optimization strategies and will be able to focus on tuning problem areas with alternate SQL statements and techniques.

L A B   1 7 . 1

THE ORACLE OPTIMIZER AND WRITING EFFECTIVE SQL STATEMENTS

LAB OBJECTIVES

After this lab, you will be able to:
- ✔ Read the Execution Plan
- ✔ Understand Join Operations and Alternate SQL Statements

Poor performance of a system is often caused by one or a combination of problems: poor database design, improper tuning of the Oracle server, and poorly written SQL statements. A well-thought-out database design has the greatest positive impact on database performance, followed by effectively written SQL statements, and then by tuning the Oracle server itself. This chapter focuses on writing effective SQL statements only.

The Oracle database server provides you with a number of tools that help you improve the efficiency of SQL statements. This chapter shows you how to obtain an *execution plan,* which is a sequence of the steps that Oracle carries out to perform a specific SQL command. You can change the execution plan by choosing an alternate SQL statement or by adding a *hint,* which is a directive to execute the statement differently. Using hints, you can force the use of a specific index, change the join order, or change join method. Before learning more about the execution plan and the query tuning tools, you must understand the basics of how a SQL statement is evaluated by the Oracle database server.

SQL STATEMENT PROCESSING

Before a SQL statement returns a result set, the server performs a number of operations that are completely transparent to the user. The first step is the creation of a cursor, an area in memory where Oracle stores the SQL statement and all associated information.

Next, Oracle parses the SQL statement. This entails checking the syntax for validity, checking if all the column and table names exist, and determining if the user has permission to access these tables and columns. Part of the parsing operation is also the determination of the execution plan.

Because parsing requires time and resources, there are ways to eliminate parsing when repeatedly executing similar statements. Oracle maintains a cache of recently executed SQL statements and their respective execution plan so if an identical statement has been used previously, it does not need to be re-parsed. This is accomplished by using bind variables, which are placeholders for values. If bind variables are used in a statement, the variable names must be associated with an actual value at execution time. More on bind variables is discussed shortly.

If bind variables are used, they are associated with the appropriate values. Next the SQL statement is executed. If the SQL statement is a query, the result needs to be fetched. Once all the rows are fetched, the cursor is closed. Figure 17.1 graphically shows an overview of these various steps.

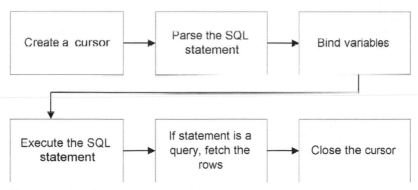

Figure 17.1 ■ Overview of SQL statement processing steps.

THE OPTIMIZER

The Oracle optimizer is part of the Oracle software; it examines each SQL statement and chooses the best execution plan for it. An execution plan consists of a sequence of steps that are necessary to execute your SQL statement. Oracle has two optimizers: the rule-based optimizer and the cost-based optimizer.

The rule-based optimizer is the optimizer employed by Oracle since its beginnings. It determines the execution plan through a number of rigid rules. While this optimizer continues to exist in Oracle 10*g*, Oracle will no longer support it.

The cost-based optimizer takes statistics into consideration to determine the best plan. These statistics include values such as the number of rows in the table and the selectivity of columns, among many other factors. The cost-based optimizer determines the best execution plan by calculating the estimated cost of various execution options and then uses the plan with the lowest cost as the chosen plan.

Statistics are gathered automatically in Oracle 10*g* and in prior Oracle versions this was accomplished through the DBMS_STATS procedure or the ANALYZE command. The statistics are stored in the data dictionary.

CHOOSING THE OPTIMIZER MODE

The cost-based optimizer has a number of optimizer modes. You can decide whether you want to optimize for best overall throughput (ALL_ROWS) or best response (FIRST_ROWS_*n*). The ALL_ROWS mode is most useful for reporting and batch processing whereas FIRST_ROWS is best for interactive applications to quickly retrieve the first *n* rows. Based on the chosen optimizer mode, the gathered statistics, and certain database initialization parameters, the Oracle optimizer chooses the best execution plan. See Table 17.1 for a listing of the optimizer modes.

You modify the optimizer mode on the database instance level in the database initialization file with the OPTIMIZER_MODE parameter, or for an entire session with an ALTER SESSION SET OPTIMIZER_MODE command. For an individual SQL statement, you can override it with a hint.

Table 17.1 ■ Optimizer Mode

Optimizer Mode	Explanation
FIRST_ROWS_*n*	The optimizer mode has the goal of retrieving the specified first *n* row(s). This mode is best for interactive programs that need to display *n* initial rows of data on a screen. This setting differs from the FIRST_ROWS mode in that you list the number of rows. The FIRST_ROWS optimizer goal without the specified number of rows is supported for backward compatiblity reasons.
ALL_ROWS	The goal is the best performance with minimal resources for retrieving all the rows.
RULE	This setting uses the rule-based optimizer. The presence of statistics is irrelevant. (While this feature still works, the setting is being desupported.)
CHOOSE	This option is available but being desupported with Oracle 10*g*, in previous version is relied on the presence of statistics in at least one of the accessed tables to choose the cost-based optimizer over the rule-based optimizer.

To find out the parameter settings in your initialization file, use the SQL*Plus SHOW PARAMETERS command. The next statement displays the parameters and their respective settings where the word OPTIMIZER in the parameter name. From the result you notice that this database instance has the default OPTIMIZER_MODE setting of ALL_ROWS.

```
SQL> SHOW PARAMETER OPTIMIZER
optimizer_dynamic_sampling   integer   2
optimizer_features_enable    string    10.1.0
optimizer_index_caching      integer   0
optimizer_index_cost_adj     integer   100
optimizer_mode               string    ALL_ROWS
```

KEEPING STATISTICS UP TO DATE IN ORACLE

Accurate statistics about the distribution of data is essential for good performance. Oracle automatically gathers statistics for objects that have stale or missing statistics and keeps these statistics up to date periodically. The statistics are stored in the data dictionary. Gathering of statistics is accomplished through a job called GATHER_STATS_JOB created automatically when the database was initially created. Oracle's internal job scheduler periodically runs this job at night during the week and on the weekend to check for stale or missing statistics. You can check if the job is running by executing this statement. Note you need to have access to the DBA_ dictionary views to query the view.

```
SELECT job_name, enabled, last_start_date
  FROM dba_scheduler_jobs
 WHERE job_name = 'GATHER_STATS_JOB'
JOB_NAME                ENABL LAST_START_DATE
----------------------- ----- -----------------------------------
GATHER_STATS_JOB        TRUE  26-JAN-04 10.00.02.109124 PM -08:00

1 row selected.
```

If you create a new index on a table or rebuild an existing one, Oracle 10*g* automatically collects the statistics. However, the statistics may be stale when 10 or more percent of the rows change due to INSERT, UPDATE, or DELETE operations. Oracle keeps track of the modifications in the USER_TAB_MODIFICATIONS data dictionary.

The USER_TAB_MODIFICATIONS data dictionary view shows the tables owned by the current user that are being monitored. Furthermore, it shows the volume of data modified since the last gathering of statistics. Please note that the number found in the INSERTS, UPDATES, and DELETES columns of the view is approximate and may not be populated for a few hours after the completion of the DML operation.

```
SELECT table_name, inserts, updates, deletes,
       timestamp
  FROM user_tab_modifications
TABLE_NAME        INSERTS UPDATES DELETES TIMESTAMP
---------------   ------- ------- ------- ---------
COURSE                  1       0       0 30-JAN-04

1 row selected.
```

If you prefer that Oracle does not collect modification statistics, your database administrator can change the STATISTICS_LEVEL initialization parameter to BASIC from the TYPICAL (default) or ALL value. (In versions before Oracle 10*g*, you needed to identify stale statistics by monitoring the data modifications in a table. This was accomplished with the ALTER TABLE statement and the MONITORING clause. This clause has been deprecated in Oracle 10*g* and the continued use of it does not have any effect on the monitoring whatsoever.)

MANUAL GATHERING OF STATISTICS

If you want to manually gather statistics (this may be useful after a large data load or mass update) or if you work with an Oracle 9*i* database, the following paragraphs explain some of the involved procedures you will need to execute. You can check for the presence of statistics by querying the data dictionary views ALL_TABLES and ALL_INDEXES. After statistics about a table or index are gathered, a number of columns in these data dictionary views will contain values. For example, in the USER_TABLES view, the column NUM_ROWS will contain the number of rows in the table, the average row length, and the date and time the statistics were last gathered.

```
SELECT table_name, num_rows, avg_row_len,
       TO_CHAR(last_analyzed, 'MM/DD/YYYY')
       AS last_analyzed
  FROM user_tables
TABLE_NAME          NUM_ROWS AVG_ROW_LEN LAST_ANALY
------------------- -------- ----------- ----------
INSTRUCTOR                10          85 12/23/2003
GRADE                   2004          49 12/23/2003
...
ZIPCODE                  227          53 12/23/2003

10 rows selected.
```

For indexes, you can review the number of rows, number of distinct keys, and the date and time the statistics were last updated. Other related data dictionary views will contain additional information, but querying the USER_TABLES and USER_INDEXES provides you with some of the most essential information.

```
SELECT index_name, num_rows, distinct_keys,
       TO_CHAR(last_analyzed, 'MM/DD/YYYY')
       AS last_analyzed
  FROM user_indexes
INDEX_NAME          NUM_ROWS DISTINCT_KEYS LAST_ANALY
----------------    -------- ------------- ----------
INST_ZIP_FK_I              9             4 12/23/2003
GR_GRTW_FK_I            2004           252 12/23/2003
...
CRSE_PK                   30            30 12/23/2003

20 rows selected.
```

In case no statistics are available for a table or index, Oracle 10*g* will estimate statistics during the execution of the statement based on a sample size. You will learn more about sample sizes shortly.

THE DBMS_STATS PACKAGE

The DBMS_STATS package is an Oracle-supplied PL/SQL package that generates and manages statistics for use by the cost-based optimizer; a few of the many procedures in the package to gather statistics are listed in Table 17.2.

Table 17.2 ■ DBMS_STATS Procedures That Gather Statistics

Procedure	Purpose
GATHER_TABLE_STATS	Gather table, column, and index statistics
GATHER_INDEX_STATS	Gather index statistics
GATHER_SCHEMA_STATS	Gather statistics for all objects in a schema
GATHER_DATABASE_STATS	Gather statistics for all objects in a database instance
GATHER_SYSTEM_STATS	Gathers system statistics about the CPU and I/O

Following are some examples on how you execute the procedures to collect statistics. The next statement gathers exact statistics for the COURSE table located in the STUDENT schema.

```
EXEC DBMS_STATS.GATHER_TABLE_STATS(ownname=>'STUDENT', tabname=>'COURSE');
PL/SQL procedure successfully completed.
```

The two parameters OWNNAME for the schema name and the TABNAME for the table name are required. The example uses the named notation syntax (ownname=>) to identify each parameter with the appropriate value. You do not need to list the parameter names OWNNAME and TABLENAME if you supply the

PL/SQL procedure the parameter values in the order in which the parameters are defined in the package.

```
EXEC DBMS_STATS.GATHER_TABLE_STATS('STUDENT', 'COURSE');
```

The procedure has additional parameters (e.g., ESTIMATE_PERCENT) that let you specify the sample percentage. If you don't specify the additional parameters, default values are assigned. In the previous examples, the ESTIMATE_PERCENT is not specified so the default is to compute the exact statistics.

If the different parameters do not fit on one line or if you want to separate each parameter, write the procedure call as follows:

```
BEGIN
  DBMS_STATS.GATHER_TABLE_STATS(
    ownname=>'STUDENT',
    tabname=>'COURSE',
    cascade=>TRUE);
END;
/
```

The procedure adds a third parameter, the CASCADE parameter and sets it to TRUE. This instructs the procedure to collect both table and index statistics simultaneously. To find out the different parameter names of a procedure, you issue the DESCRIBE command in SQL*Plus. It lists all the individual procedures available and their respective parameters. The In/Out column indicates if the procedure requires an input parameter or returns an output value. You can find out more information about each parameter and the respective default values in the *Oracle 10g PL/SQL Packages and Types References* manual.

```
SQL> DESCR DBMS_STATS
...
PROCEDURE GATHER_TABLE_STATS
Argument Name                 Type          In/Out Default?
--------------------------    -----------   ------ --------
  OWNNAME                     VARCHAR2      IN
  TABNAME                     VARCHAR2      IN
  PARTNAME                    VARCHAR2      IN     DEFAULT
  ESTIMATE_PERCENT            NUMBER        IN     DEFAULT
  BLOCK_SAMPLE                BOOLEAN       IN     DEFAULT
  METHOD_OPT                  VARCHAR2      IN     DEFAULT
  DEGREE                      NUMBER        IN     DEFAULT
  GRANULARITY                 VARCHAR2      IN     DEFAULT
  CASCADE                     BOOLEAN       IN     DEFAULT
...
```

A difference between Oracle 10*g* and Oracle 9*i* is that Oracle 9*i* did not automatically update the table and index statistics. Instead, users created scheduled SQL scripts with the cron job facility in Unix or "at" service in Windows. Another alternative was to use Oracle's built-in DBMS_JOB scheduler package.

EXACT STATISTICS OR SAMPLE SIZE

Statistics can be either computed exactly or estimated. Because calculating exact statistics may take a long time on very large tables, it is sometimes more practical to estimate sufficiently accurate statistics. For large tables, a sampling percentage size of 10 to 25 percent is often fine, or you can let Oracle determine the size of the sample.

MANAGING STATISTICS

Besides gathering statistics, the DBMS_STATS package includes procedures to modify, view, export, import, delete, lock, and restore statistics. For example, you can save the current statistics before gathering new statistics so you can restore them should the performance of the system be adversely affected. The statistics can also be copied from one database instance to another. This is useful if you want to test how your SQL statements behave in a different environment (e.g., test vs. production). You can also lock the statistics so they remain unchanged. Table 17.3 shows a few of the DBMS_STATS procedures that manage statistics for an individual table.

Table 17.3 ■ Selected DBMS_STATS Procedures

Procedure	Purpose
DELETE_TABLE_STATS	Deletes statistics for an individual table
CREATE_STAT_TABLE	Creates a table to hold statistics for import/export
LOCK_TABLE_STATS	Freezes the current statistics including indexes for an individual table.
UNLOCK_TABLE_STATS	Unlocks the table and index statistics.
RESTORE_SCHEMA_STATS	Restores all the statistics for a specified schema for a particular timestamp. This is useful if performance degrades and you want to restore the previous set of statistics.
EXPORT_TABLE_STATS	Exports statistics about an individual table so it may be used for a later import
IMPORT_TABLE_STATS	Imports table statistics into the data dictionary

TIMING THE EXECUTION OF A STATEMENT

If a SQL statement does not perform well, you need a baseline to compare the execution time of other alternative SQL statements. One simple way to accomplish this in SQL*Plus is to execute the SQL*Plus command SET TIMING ON. This command returns the execution time.

 Note that repeated executions of the same or similar statements take less time than the initial execution because the data no longer needs to be retrieved from disk since it is cached in memory. Just because you made a minor change to the statement doesn't mean the statement is actually running faster.

```
SQL> SET TIMING ON
SQL> SELECT COUNT(*)
       FROM student
  COUNT(*)
---------
       268

1 row selected.
Elapsed: 00:00:00.30
```

Tuning a SQL statement is effective only if your SQL statement executes against realistic data volumes and column distributions similar to what is expected in a production environment. For instance, the execution plan for a join involving two tables varies if the data in the test environment is 100 rows, but in production it is 50,000 rows. The Oracle optimizer also evolves with each subsequent version of the Oracle database, so having a test environment that closely resembles your production environment greatly aids in this process.

THE EXECUTION PLAN

The optimizer creates the execution plan, also referred to as the *explain plan.* It shows the individual steps the Oracle database executes to process a statement. You read the execution plan from the inside out, meaning the most indented step is performed first. If two steps have the same level of indentation, the step listed first is the first executed. Following is a SQL statement and its execution plan. You learn how to obtain such an output shortly. (Note that the ID column on the right is only a number identifying the step; it does not indicate the execution order in any way.)

```
SELECT student_id, last_name
  FROM student
 WHERE student_id = 123
```

```
------------------------------------------------------
| Id  | Operation                      | Name       |
------------------------------------------------------
|  0  | SELECT STATEMENT               |            |
|  1  |   TABLE ACCESS BY INDEX ROWID|  STUDENT   |
|  2  |     INDEX UNIQUE SCAN          | STU_PK     |
------------------------------------------------------
```

The first step performed is a lookup of the value 123 in the index STU_PK. Using the index entry, the row is retrieved from the STUDENT table via the ROWID, which specifies the location (datafile and data block) of the row. Table access is not required if the statement retrieves all the column values from the index. For example, if the statement required only the STUDENT_ID, the table access is unnecessary.

RETRIEVING THE EXECUTION PLAN

There are various ways to obtain an execution plan. This chapter discusses the use of the EXPLAIN PLAN FOR command in conjunction with the DBMS_XPLAN.DISPLAY package. Among the many other ways to retrieve the execution plan are the AUTOTRACE command in SQL*Plus, which is discussed on the companion Web site, the Oracle TKPROF utility shown in the *Oracle DBA Interactive Workbook* by Melanie Caffrey and Douglas Scherer, and any of the popular third-party tools listed in Appendix H, "Resources."

DBMS_XPLAN

Using the EXPLAIN PLAN FOR command and the DISPLAY function of the DBMS_XPLAN package, you can list the explain plan in an easy to read format. The DISPLAY function retrieves the execution plan and runtime statistics based on the V$SQL_PLAN and V$SQL_PLAN_STATISTICS data dictionary tables. The next statement shows how you can create the explain plan with the EXPLAIN PLAN command.

```
SQL> EXPLAIN PLAN FOR
  2   SELECT student_id, last_name
  3    FROM student
  4   WHERE student_id = 123
  5  /
Explained.
```

Afterwards, you can retrieve the plan using this DISPLAY function.

```
SELECT *
  FROM TABLE(DBMS_XPLAN.DISPLAY)
```

```
PLAN_TABLE_OUTPUT
-----------------------------------------------------------------------
-----------------------------------------------------------------------
|Id|Operation                      |Name    |Rows|Bytes|Cost (%CPU)|Time     |
-----------------------------------------------------------------------
| 0|SELECT STATEMENT               |        |   1|   12|   2  (50)|00:00:01|
| 1| TABLE ACCESS BY INDEX ROWID|STUDENT|   1|   12|   2  (50)|00:00:01|
|*2|  INDEX UNIQUE SCAN            |STU_PK |   1|     |   1 (100)|00:00:01|
-----------------------------------------------------------------------

Predicate Information (identified by operation id):
---------------------------------------------------
PLAN_TABLE_OUTPUT
-----------------------------------------------------------
   2 - access("STUDENT_ID"=123)
```

13 rows selected.

If your result does not fit the display of your screen, you can enter the following SQL*Plus commands to increase the line size and to suppress any headings.

```
SET LINESIZE 130
SET PAGESIZE 0
```

UNDERSTANDING COST, ROWS, AND BYTES VALUES

In the previous explain plan you noticed a number of columns; they provide more detail about each individual step. The COST value is a number that represents the estimated number of disk I/O and amount of CPU and memory required to execute the desired action. The cost helps you determine how involved each step is so you can focus on tuning the steps with the highest cost. The cost is determined using estimated amounts of memory, input/output, and CPU time required to execute the statement, and certain Oracle initialization parameters. The number of ROWS shows the cardinality of the step (i.e., how many rows the optimizer expects to process at this step).The BYTES column shows the size in bytes expected for the step.

The DISPLAY function without any parameter includes statistics. If you want to display only the minimum plan information, use the BASIC parameter as in the next statement.

```
SELECT *
  FROM TABLE(DBMS_XPLAN.DISPLAY(null, null, 'basic'))
```

```
--------------------------------------------------
| Id  | Operation                    | Name       |
--------------------------------------------------
|   0 | SELECT STATEMENT             |            |
|   1 |   TABLE ACCESS BY INDEX ROWID| STUDENT    |
|   2 |     INDEX UNIQUE SCAN        | STU_PK     |
--------------------------------------------------
```

8 rows selected.

The DISPLAY function has three parameters, and the syntax is as follows:

```
DBMS_XPLAN.DISPLAY
  (table_name IN VARCHAR2 DEFAULT 'PLAN_TABLE',
  statement_id IN VARCHAR2 DEFAULT NULL,
  format IN VARCHAR2 DEFAULT 'TYPICAL')
```

The first allows you to specify the name of the table where the plan is stored. By default, the explain plan is stored in the PLAN_TABLE. The second parameter lets you include a STATEMENT_ID; this is useful if execute the EXPLAIN PLAN command with a SET STATEMENT_ID clause to identify between different statements. If you do not specify a value, the DISPLAY function returns the most recent explained statement. The third and last parameter permits you to change the display output of the plan. The BASIC value shows the operation ID, the operation, and the object name. The TYPICAL option is the default and includes the predicate (WHERE clause). The ALL choice displays all available data including column information (column projection) and data related to the Oracle parallel server, if applicable.

Please note that while most explain plans in this book do not show the row, cost, and bytes columns due to space reasons, you should display them when tuning a statement as these values provide useful details about each individual step.

HINTS

If you are not satisfied with the optimizer's plan, you can change it by applying hints. Hints are directives to the optimizer. For example, you can ask to use a particular index or to choose a specific join order. Because you know the distribution of the data best, sometimes you can come up with a better execution plan by overriding the default plan with specific hints. In certain instances this may result in a better plan. For example, if you know that a particular index is more selective for certain queries, you can ask the optimizer to use this index instead.

Following are examples of useful hints. The hint is always enclosed by either a multiline comment with a plus sign (/*+ */) or a single line comment with a plus sign (--+).

The following statement uses an index hint to scan the STU_ZIP_FK_I index on the STUDENT table. This index is actually a poorer choice than the STU_PK index, but the example demonstrates how you can override the optimizer's default plan.

```
SELECT /*+ INDEX (student stu_zip_fk_i) */ student_id,
       last_name
  FROM student
 WHERE student_id = 123
-----------------------------------------------------------
| Id  | Operation                   | Name          |
-----------------------------------------------------------
|   0 | SELECT STATEMENT            |               |
|   1 |   TABLE ACCESS BY INDEX ROWID| STUDENT      |
|   2 |     INDEX FULL SCAN         | STU_ZIP_FK_I  |
-----------------------------------------------------------
```

In Table 17.4 you see some of the frequently used hints. You will use some of them in the exercises throughout this lab.

Table 17.4 ■ Popular Hints

Hint	Purpose
FIRST_ROWS(n)	Return the first n rows as quickly as possible.
ALL_ROWS	Return all rows as quickly as possible.
RULE	Unlike any of the other hints, this hint uses the rule-based optimizer instead of the cost-based optimizer. Any additional hints are ignored.
INDEX(tablename indexname)	Use the specified index. If an alias is used in the FROM clause of the query, be sure to list the alias instead of the tablename.
ORDERED	Joins the tables as listed in the FROM clause of the query.
LEADING(tablename)	The specified table is the first table in the join order.
USE_MERGE(tablename)	Use the sort-merge join method to join tables.
USE_HASH(tablename)	Use the hash join method to join tables.
USE_NL(tablename)	Use the nested loop join method; the specified table name is the inner table.

INCORRECTLY SPECIFYING HINTS

If you incorrectly specify the hint, the optimizer ignores it and you are left to wonder why the hint does not work. Here is an example of the index hint specified incorrectly.

```
SELECT /*+ INDEX (student stu_zip_fk_i) */ student_id,
       last_name
  FROM student s
 WHERE student_id = 123
```

```
-----------------------------------------------------
| Id | Operation                    | Name      |
-----------------------------------------------------
|  0 | SELECT STATEMENT             |           |
|  1 |  TABLE ACCESS BY INDEX ROWID | STUDENT   |
|  2 |   INDEX UNIQUE SCAN          | STU_PK    |
-----------------------------------------------------
```

Instead of the table name STUDENT, the table alias s should be used because an alias is used in the FROM clause of the statement. This incorrect hint causes the optimizer to use a different index.

Your hint may also be ignored if you use the FIRST_ROWS hint in a query that contains a GROUP BY clause, aggregate function, set operator, the DISTINCT key word, or an ORDER BY clause (if not supported by an index). All these Oracle key-words require that the result or sort is first determined based on all the rows before returning the first row.

JOIN TYPES

Determining the type of join and the join order of tables has a significant impact on how efficiently your SQL statement executes. Oracle chooses one of four types of join operations: Nested Loop Join, Sort-Merge Join, Hash Join, or Cluster Join. This lab discusses only the first three, which are the most popular ones.

NESTED LOOP JOIN

With the nested loop join, the optimizer picks a driving table that is the first table in the join chain. In this example, the driving table is the ENROLLMENT table. A full table scan is executed on the driving table and for each row in the ENROLL-MENT table; the primary key index of the STUDENT table is probed to see if the WHERE clause condition is satisfied. If so, the row is returned in the result set. This probing is repeated until all the rows of the driving table, in this case the ENROLLMENT table, are tested.

The execution plan of a nested loop join looks like the following.

```
SELECT /*+ USE_NL(e s) */ *
  FROM enrollment e, student s
 WHERE e.student_id = s.student_id
```

```
----------------------------------------------
|Id|Operation                    |Name        |
----------------------------------------------
| 0|SELECT STATEMENT             |            |
| 1| NESTED LOOPS                |            |
| 2|  TABLE ACCESS FULL          |ENROLLMENT  |
| 3|  TABLE ACCESS BY INDEX ROWID|STUDENT     |
|*4|   INDEX UNIQUE SCAN         |STU_PK      |
----------------------------------------------
```

Note that the execution plan for a nested loop is read differently from the other execution plans because it contains a loop. The access to the STU_PK index, the most indented row, is not read first, but rather is probed for every row of the driving ENROLLMENT table.

The nested loop join is typically the fastest join when the goal is to retrieve the first row as quickly as possible. It is also the best join when you access approximately 1 to 10 percent of the total rows from the tables involved. This percentage varies depending on the total number of rows returned, various parameters in your Oracle initialization file, and the Oracle version. But it gives you a general idea of when this join is useful.

 The selection of the driving table is essential to good performance of the nested loop join. Making the driving table return the least number of rows is critical for probing fewer records in subsequent joins to other tables. Therefore, eliminate as many rows as possible from the driving table.

SORT-MERGE JOIN

To perform this join, a full table scan is executed for each table. In the following SQL statement, the entire ENROLLMENT table is read and sorted by the joining column, and then the STUDENT table is scanned and sorted. The two results are then merged and the matching rows are returned for output. The first row is returned only after all the records from both tables are processed.

This join is typically used when the majority of the rows are retrieved, the join condition is not an equijoin, when no indexes exist on the table to support the join condition, or when a USE_MERGE hint is specified.

```
SELECT /*+ USE_MERGE (e, s)*/ *
  FROM enrollment e, student s
 WHERE s.student_id = e.student_id
```

```
-------------------------------------------------
| Id  | Operation            | Name             |
-------------------------------------------------
|  0  | SELECT STATEMENT     |                  |
|  1  |   MERGE JOIN         |                  |
|  2  |     SORT JOIN        |                  |
|  3  |       TABLE ACCESS FULL| ENROLLMENT     |
|  4  |     SORT JOIN        |                  |
|  5  |       TABLE ACCESS FULL| STUDENT        |
-------------------------------------------------
```

HASH JOIN

The hash join is available only in the cost-based optimizer. Oracle performs a full table scan on each of the tables and splits each into many partitions in memory. Oracle then builds a hash table from one of these partitions and probes it against the partition of the other table. The hash join typically outperforms the sort-merge join.

```
SELECT /*+ HASH_JOIN */ *
  FROM enrollment e, student s
 WHERE s.student_id = e.student_id
```

```
-------------------------------------------------
| Id  | Operation            | Name             |
-------------------------------------------------
|  0  | SELECT STATEMENT     |                  |
|  1  | HASH JOIN            |                  |
|  2  |   TABLE ACCESS FULL| ENROLLMENT        |
|  3  |   TABLE ACCESS FULL| STUDENT           |
-------------------------------------------------
```

BIND VARIABLES AND THE OPTIMIZER

If you repeatedly execute the same statement with only slightly different values in the WHERE clause, you can eliminate the parsing with the use of bind variables, also referred to as *host variables*. For example, if the users of your program repeatedly issue this query, but substitute a different phone number each time, you should consider substituting the literal value with a bind variable.

```
SELECT last_name, first_name
  FROM student
 WHERE phone = '614-555-5555'
```

The use of the bind variable eliminates the parsing of the SQL statement. This overhead is significant when you have many users on a system. Bind variables are prefixed with a colon. The new statement with a bind variable looks like this:

```
SELECT last_name, first_name
  FROM student
 WHERE phone = :phone_no
```

The :PHONE_NO bind variable gets a new value assigned whenever the user issues the statement. The statement with the bind variable is already parsed and the execution plan is determined and therefore ready for execution (see Figure 17.1).

The next example illustrates the use of a bind variable in SQL*Plus. The VARIABLE command creates a bind variable. The next PL/SQL block assigns the variable a value, which is 914-555-5555.

```
SQL> VARIABLE phone_no VARCHAR2(20)
SQL> BEGIN
  2     :phone_no :='914-555-5555';
  3   END;
  4   .
SQL> /
```

PL/SQL procedure successfully completed.

The subsequent execution of the SQL statement using the bind variable associates the assigned value with the variable and returns the correct row.

```
SQL> SELECT last_name, first_name
  2     FROM student
  3    WHERE phone = :phone_no
  4   /
```

LAST_NAME	FIRST_NAME
Mwangi	Paula

1 row selected.

Bind variables are advantageous in applications where the same statement is executed repeatedly. At the first invocation of the statement with the bind variables, the optimizer looks at the selectivity of the value and determines the best possible execution plan. In repeated executions of the statement, no peeking at the value takes place. This assumes that every value associated with the bind variable has the same selectivity.

In a scenario where the statement is executed with a literal value instead, the next statement's literal values may be more selective and result in a more favorable execution plan.

In general, you should use bind variable if the same statements are executed frequently and the difference in the selectivity between the different values is minimal. This is typically the case in transaction processing oriented environments—the use of bind variable results in time and resource savings due to the elimination of the parsing step.

This is in contrast to data warehousing environments where the queries are long running or of an ad-hoc nature and therefore executed infrequently. Therefore, the use of literals is preferred because the optimizer can make a better determination about the most efficient execution plan. Also, the parsing time is negligible in comparison to the execution time.

HISTOGRAMS

For table columns where the data is not uniformly distributed, Oracle 10*g* automatically creates histograms. For example, Oracle may determine that the values of a particular column are distributed as 10 percent with values of >=500 and 90 percent with values of <500. The histogram for this skewed data allows the optimizer to better understand the distribution of data. Note the optimizer cannot utilize the histograms if you use bind variables.

SQL PERFORMANCE IMPROVEMENT TIPS

There are a few good habits to adopt when you write SQL statements. Keep the following list of suggestions in mind when diagnosing performance problems, writing or rewriting SQL statements.

- Functions applied to indexed columns in the WHERE clause do not take advantage of the index unless you use the MIN or MAX function. For example, a function-based index is useful for case-independent searches instead of the UPPER function on the search column. If you always apply the TRUNC function to columns of the DATE datatype, consider not storing the time portion in the column as this information is probably irrelevant. Implicit type conversions can also cause Oracle to cast a value to another datatype, thus preventing the use of the index, as you will see in the exercises later.

- Use analytical functions where possible instead of multiple SQL statements as it simplifies the query writing and requires only a single pass through the table.

- Build indexes on columns you frequently use in the WHERE clause but keep the performance trade-offs of DML statements in mind. Adding an index can also adversely affect the performance of other SQL statements accessing the table. Be sure to test your scenarios carefully.

- Drop indexes that are never or very infrequently used. If you find that a specific index is only used for month-end processing, it may be advantageous to drop the index and only rebuild it shortly before the month-end job. Do not forget to gather statistics after you create the index. The use of some indexes may not be apparent; for example, some foreign key indexes may only be used to prevent locking issues (see Chapter 12, "Views, Indexes, and Sequences"). As with any change, be sure to carefully test to avoid any adverse impact.

- Consider restructuring existing indexes. You can improve the selectivity by adding additional columns to an index. Alternatively, you can change the order of columns in a composite index.

- Full-table scans may at times be more efficient than the use of indexes if the table is relatively small in size as Oracle can read all the data with one I/O operation.

- If you are retrieving more than 5 to 20 percent of the rows, a full table scan may also be more efficient than retrieving the rows from an index.

- When joining tables using the nested loop join, make sure to choose the table that returns the fewest number of rows as the driving table. You can enforce this with the ORDERED hint.

- Consider replacing the NOT IN operator with the NOT EXISTS operator and eliminate as many rows as possible in the outer query of a correlated subquery.

- If you have very large tables, consider partitioning the tables. This is a feature found only in the Oracle Enterprise edition.

- If your queries involve aggregates and joins against large tables, you can use materialized views to pre-store results and refresh them at set intervals. Oracle has a set of advisor procedures that help you design and evaluate the benefits of materialized views.

- Make sure you did not forget the joining criteria so as to avoid the building of a Cartesian product.

- Rebuild indexes periodically to improve the performance of the index. This is accomplished with the ALTER INDEX indexname REBUILD command. Use this particularly after many DELETE statements have been issued. Starting with Oracle 10*g*, statistics are automatically collected as part of the rebuild or the creation of a new index.

- Make sure statistics for your tables and indexes are periodically gathered and after heavy DML activity. Missing or inaccurate statistics are a common source of performance problems. Sometimes volume and distribution of your data change and your statistics may require updating, in particular if you are using Oracle versions prior to 10*g*.

- Review the result of the execution plan carefully to determine the cause of any performance problem; examine execution steps involving a large number of rows or high cost. Use hints to tune the statement and make sure the hints are valid. Do not use hints that have no effect, such as a FIRST_ROWS hint on a statement with an ORDER BY clause because the ORDER BY sort operation needs to be processed first before any rows are returned.

- Use the CASE expression to avoid visiting tables multiple times. For example, if you need to aggregate rows that have different WHERE conditions within the same table, you can use the CASE expression to aggregate only those rows that satisfy the necessary condition.

- SQL optimization is not just useful for queries, but also for delete, update, and insert operations. Too many indexes can slow down DML as the indexed column(s) need to be deleted or updated (if the indexed column values change) or values need to be inserted. However, indexes are beneficial for updates and deletes particularly if the WHERE clause refers to an indexed column. This retrieves the row quickly. Missing foreign key indexes are a frequently overlooked problem; they are needed because not only they are frequently used in queries, but also because they can cause locking issues discussed in Chapter 12, "Views, Indexes, and Sequences."

- Make sure you test your SQL statements carefully in a representative test environment where the data distribution, data volume, and hardware setup is similar to a production environment. Be sure to make a copy of your statistics with the DBMS_STATS. EXPORT_SCHEMA_STATS procedure. In case the performance degrades after analyzing, you can restore the old statistics with the DBMS_STATS.IMPORT_SCHEMA_STATS.

THE SQL TUNING ADVISOR

Oracle 10g implemented a new tool that greatly aids the tuning process; it is called the SQL Tuning Advisor. It offers an automated approach to tuning and it removes some of the guesswork by recommending specific actions that will benefit an individual statement or set of statements. Instead of trying out the previously mentioned tips and hints, the SQL Tuning Advisor incorporates these tips and recommends suggestions to improve the statement. This feature is accessible through the Oracle Web-based Enterprise Manager and is part of Oracle's strategy to simplify many complex database administration and tuning tasks. You will see that having the background knowledge acquired from the beginning of this chapter helps you evaluate the recommendations of the tool and provides you with an better understanding of the Oracle functionality. The URL to logon to the Enterprise Manager is in the format of http://machine_name:5500/em. Figure 17.2 shows the logon screen that connects with the STUDENT user and the SYSDBA privilege. (Please note that the SYSDBA privilege is not required to perform SQL statement tuning tasks. Alternatively, you can login with SYSMAN account and the password you set up during the installation.)

If the STUDENT or another account you want to use does not have SYSDBA privileges, you can grant this privilege. The following statements illustrate the necessary steps for the SYSTEM user to provide this privilege to the STUDENT user.

```
SQL> CONNECT system AS SYSDBA
Enter password: ****
Connected.
SQL> GRANT sysdba TO student
Grant succeeded.
```

Figure 17.2 ■ Enterprise Manager log on screen.

After the successful logon, you will be presented with a screen similar to Figure 17.3. It shows the Database Home page from which you can get access to the Advisor Central link located on the bottom of the page below the heading Related Links.

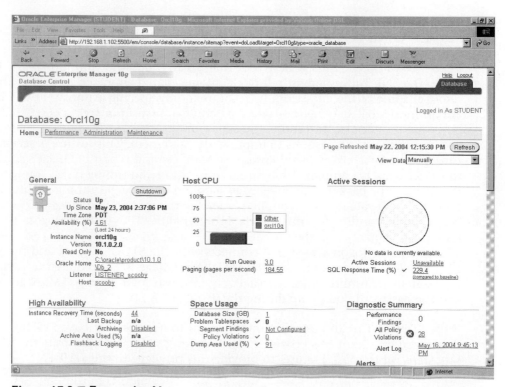

Figure 17.3 ■ Enterprise Home page.

Choose the SQL Tuning Advisor Links link, which will take you to a page similar to Figure 17.4. You can choose the sources for SQL statements to tune. For example, you can pick the Top SQL statements to review and tune.

ORACLE
Enterprise Manager   Help Logout

Database: orcl > Advisor Central > SQL Tuning Advisor Links
SQL Tuning Advisor Links
SQL Tuning Advisor is used to analyze individual SQL statements and makes recommendations for improving its performance. It can be launched from the following
places. You can click on one of the following sources, which will lead you to a data source where you can tune SQL statements using SQL Tuning Advisor.
Top SQL
SQL Tuning Sets
Snapshots
Baselines

Help | Logout

Copyright © 1996, 2003, Oracle. All rights reserved.
About Oracle Enterprise Manager Database Console

Figure 17.4 ■ **SQL Tuning Advisor links.**

The SQL Tuning Advisor takes one or multiple statement and returns recommendations for the statements. You can choose between a limited or comprehensive scope (see Figure 17.5). The comprehensive scope includes a SQL Profile, and you can specify a time limit for the task.

SQL Tuning Options

Cancel   OK

Task name Task 1
Description
STS Name test
STS Description

SQL Statements

Previous 1-1 of 1 Next

SQL Text	Parsing Schema
select count(*), sum(status0), sum(status1), min(decode(snap_id, :bid, e_time, b_time)), max(e_time), sum when max(e_time) > min(b_time) then 1 else 0 end, ...	SYS

Scope

○ Limited. Analysis without SQL Profile recommendation. Takes about 1 second per statement.
◉ Comprehensive. Complete analysis including SQL Profile. May take a long time.
   Total Time limit 30   Minutes

Start

◉ immediately
○ Later
   Date Jan-26-2004
         (example: Dec-12-2002)
   Time 8 ▾ 18 ▾ 00 ▾ ○ AM ◉ PM

Cancel   OK

Help | Logout

Copyright © 1996, 2003, Oracle. All rights reserved.
About Oracle Enterprise Manager Database Console

Figure 17.5 ■ **SQL Tuning Options page.**

This will create a task to review the statement and return a set of recommendations. Once the task is complete, you can view the changes to the statement (see

Figure 17.6). You can accept the tuning recommendation by creating a SQL profile.

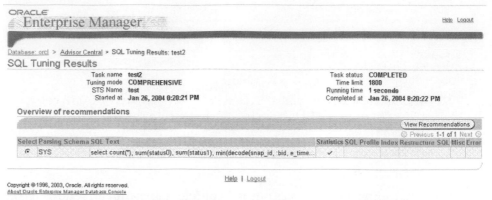

Figure 17.6 ■ SQL Tuning Results page.

SQL PROFILE

A SQL profile is for an individual statement, and it consists additional statistics. The profile is stored in the data dictionary and will be used in together with the regular statistics the next time the statement is invoked. The advantage of SQL profiles is that you avoid modifying the underlying statement, which is particularly valuable with packaged applications where you do not have the ability to access and change the SQL statement.

THE SQL ACCESS ADVISOR

Another advisor within the Oracle Enterprise Manager is the SQL Access Advisor. It offers help by suggesting materialized views and indexes to create and/or drop based on a hypothetical or actual workload. The sources of the workload can be collected through Enterprise Manager. Both database administrators as well as application developers will find this advisor very helpful because it offers additional suggestions to further optimize an individual application.

LAB 17.1 EXERCISES

17.11.2 READ THE EXECUTION PLAN

a) Describe the result of the following query.

```
SELECT index_name, column_name, column_position
  FROM user_ind_columns
```

```
WHERE table_name = 'STUDENT'
ORDER BY 1, 3
```

b) Generate an explain plan for the following SQL statement. What do you observe about the use of the index?

```
SELECT *
  FROM student
 WHERE student_id <> 101
```

c) Create an index called STU_FIRST_I on the FIRST_NAME column of the STUDENT table. Then execute the following SQL statement and describe the result of the execution plan.

```
SELECT student_id, first_name
  FROM student
 WHERE first_name IS NULL
```

d) Execute the following SQL query and describe the result of the execution plan.

```
SELECT student_id, first_name
  FROM student
 WHERE UPPER(first_name) = 'MARY'
```

e) Examine the following SQL queries and their respective execution plans. What do you notice about the use of the index? Drop the index STU_FIRST_I afterward.

```
SELECT student_id, first_name
  FROM student
 WHERE first_name LIKE '%oh%'
```

Id	Operation	Name
0	SELECT STATEMENT	
1	TABLE ACCESS FULL	STUDENT

```
SELECT student_id, first_name
  FROM student
 WHERE first_name LIKE 'Joh%'
```

Id	Operation	Name
0	SELECT STATEMENT	
1	TABLE ACCESS BY INDEX ROWID	STUDENT
2	INDEX RANGE SCAN	STU_FIRST_I

f) Execute the following SQL query and describe the result of the execution plan.

```
SELECT *
  FROM zipcode
 WHERE zip = 10025
```

g) Explain why the following query does not use an index.

```
SELECT *
  FROM grade
 WHERE grade_type_code = 'HW'
```

17.1.2 UNDERSTAND JOIN OPERATIONS AND ALTERNATE SQL STATEMENTS

a) Given the following SELECT statement and the resulting execution plan, determine the driving table and the type of join performed.

```
SELECT --+ FIRST_ROWS(10)
       i.last_name, c.description, c.course_no
  FROM course c, section s, instructor i
 WHERE c.course_no = s.course_no
   AND s.instructor_id = i.instructor_id
   AND s.section_id = 133
```

Id	Operation	Name
0	SELECT STATEMENT	
1	NESTED LOOPS	
2	NESTED LOOPS	
3	TABLE ACCESS BY INDEX ROWID	SECTION
4	INDEX UNIQUE SCAN	SECT_PK
5	TABLE ACCESS BY INDEX ROWID	COURSE
6	INDEX UNIQUE SCAN	CRSE_PK
7	TABLE ACCESS BY INDEX ROWID	INSTRUCTOR
8	INDEX UNIQUE SCAN	INST_PK

b) The following alternate SQL statements result in the respective execution plans. What differences do you observe?

```
SELECT *
  FROM student
 WHERE student_id NOT IN
       (SELECT student_id
          FROM enrollment)
```

```
-------------------------------------------------
| Id | Operation            | Name       |
-------------------------------------------------
|  0 | SELECT STATEMENT     |            |
|  1 |  FILTER              |            |
|  2 |   TABLE ACCESS FULL  | STUDENT    |
|  3 |   TABLE ACCESS FULL  | ENROLLMENT |
-------------------------------------------------
```

```
SELECT *
  FROM student s
 WHERE NOT EXISTS
       (SELECT 'X'
          FROM enrollment
         WHERE s.student_id = student_id)
```

```
------------------------------------------------
| Id | Operation            | Name     |
------------------------------------------------
|  0 | SELECT STATEMENT     |          |
|  1 |  FILTER              |          |
|  2 |   TABLE ACCESS FULL  | STUDENT  |
|  3 |   INDEX RANGE SCAN   | ENR_PK   |
------------------------------------------------
```

```
SELECT student_id
  FROM student
MINUS
SELECT student_id
  FROM enrollment
```

```
-------------------------------------------------
| Id | Operation             | Name       |
-------------------------------------------------
|  0 | SELECT STATEMENT      |            |
|  1 |  MINUS                |            |
|  2 |   SORT UNIQUE         |            |
|  3 |    TABLE ACCESS FULL  | STUDENT    |
|  4 |   SORT UNIQUE         |            |
|  5 |    TABLE ACCESS FULL  | ENROLLMENT |
-------------------------------------------------
```

c) Show the execution plan for the following SELECT statements and describe the difference.

```
SELECT student_id, last_name, 'student'
  FROM student
UNION
SELECT instructor_id, last_name, 'instructor'
  FROM instructor
```

```
SELECT student_id, last_name, 'student'
  FROM student
UNION ALL
SELECT instructor_id, last_name, 'instructor'
  FROM instructor
```

LAB 17.1 EXERCISE ANSWERS

17.1.1 ANSWERS

a) Describe the result of the following query.

```
SELECT index_name, column_name, column_position
  FROM user_ind_columns
 WHERE table_name = 'STUDENT'
 ORDER BY 1, 3
```

Answer: The result of the query shows a listing of all indexes on the STUDENT table and the order in which the columns are indexed. In this example, both indexes are single-column indexes.

INDEX_NAME	COLUMN_NAME	COLUMN_POSITION
STU_ZIP_FK_I	ZIP	1
STU_PK	STUDENT_ID	1

```
2 rows selected.
```

b) Generate an explain plan for the following SQL statement. What do you observe about the use of the index?

```
SELECT *
  FROM student
 WHERE student_id <> 101
```

Answer: The index is not used in this query; every record is examined with the full table scan instead.

```
-------------------------------------------
| Id | Operation        | Name    |
-------------------------------------------
|  0 | SELECT STATEMENT |         |
|  1 | TABLE ACCESS FULL| STUDENT |
-------------------------------------------
```

Inequality conditions, such as <>, !=, or any negation using NOT typically never make use of an index.

c) Create an index called STU_FIRST_I on the FIRST_NAME column of the STU-DENT table. Then execute the following SQL statement and describe the result of the execution plan.

```
SELECT student_id, first_name
  FROM student
 WHERE first_name IS NULL
```

Answer: The query does not make use of the index on the FIRST_NAME column because NULL values are not stored in the index. Therefore, a full table scan is executed.

```
CREATE INDEX stu_first_i ON student(first_name)
Index created.
```

The subsequently issued query results in this execution plan:

```
----------------------------     ----------------
| Id  | Operation           | Name      |
----------------------------------------------
|  0  | SELECT STATEMENT    |           |
|  1  |   TABLE ACCESS FULL| STUDENT   |
----------------------------------------------
```

If you expect to execute this query frequently and want to avoid a full table scan, you may want to consider adding a row with a default value for FIRST_NAME such as 'Unknown'. When this value is inserted in the index, a subsequently issued query, such as the following, uses the index.

```
SELECT student_id, first_name
  FROM student
 WHERE first_name = 'Unknown'
```

The index is not efficient, however, if you expect a significantly large number of the values to be 'Unknown'. In this case, retrieving values through the index rather than the full table scan takes longer.

d) Execute the following SQL query and describe the result of the execution plan.

```
SELECT student_id, first_name
  FROM student
 WHERE UPPER(first_name) = 'MARY'
```

Answer: The query does not make use of the index on the FIRST_NAME column.

```
-------------------------------------------
| Id  | Operation          | Name         |
-------------------------------------------
|  0  | SELECT STATEMENT   |              |
|  1  |   TABLE ACCESS FULL| STUDENT      |
-------------------------------------------
```

The UPPER function can be used in the SQL statement if you are unsure in which case the first name was entered.

The query returns records with the values of MARY, Mary, or combinations thereof. Each time you modify an indexed column, the use of the index is disabled. The solution is to create a function-based index. For more information on this topic, refer to Chapter 12, "Views, Indexes, and Sequences."

e) Examine the following SQL queries and their respective execution plans. What do you notice about the use of the index? Drop the index STU_FIRST_I afterward.

```
SELECT student_id, first_name
  FROM student
 WHERE first_name LIKE '%oh%'
```

```
-------------------------------------------
| Id  | Operation          | Name         |
-------------------------------------------
|  0  | SELECT STATEMENT   |              |
|  1  |   TABLE ACCESS FULL| STUDENT      |
-------------------------------------------
```

```
SELECT student_id, first_name
  FROM student
 WHERE first_name LIKE 'Joh%'
```

```
-----------------------------------------------------------
| Id  | Operation                    | Name              |
-----------------------------------------------------------
|  0  | SELECT STATEMENT             |                   |
|  1  |   TABLE ACCESS BY INDEX ROWID| STUDENT           |
|  2  |    INDEX RANGE SCAN          | STU_FIRST_I       |
-----------------------------------------------------------
```

Answer: The first query does not make use of the index on the FIRST_NAME column because the index cannot determine the index entries. The second query allows the use of the index.

You may experience that the second query does not use an index. The optimizer may determine that the table is so small it is more efficient to simply read the entire table. However, if the table contains a larger data set, the optimizer will make use of the index.

Drop the index from the schema to restore the schema to its original state.

```
DROP INDEX stu_first_i
Index dropped.
```

f) Execute the following SQL query and describe the result of the execution plan.

```
SELECT *
  FROM zipcode
 WHERE zip = 10025
```

Answer: The query does not make use of the primary key index on the ZIP column.

```
----------------------------------------
| Id  | Operation          | Name       |
----------------------------------------
|  0  | SELECT STATEMENT   |            |
|  1  |   TABLE ACCESS FULL| ZIPCODE    |
----------------------------------------
```

The full table access is used because the datatypes between the ZIP column and the number literal do not agree. The ZIP column is of VARCHAR2 datatype to store leading zeros for zipcodes such as 00706, and the literal in the WHERE clause is a NUMBER. This query is an example of when Oracle performs an implicit conversion. Oracle converts the ZIP column to a NUMBER and, therefore, disables the use of the index. If the WHERE clause is written as follows, it uses the index.

```
WHERE zip = '10025'
-----------------------------------------------------------
| Id  | Operation                    | Name               |
-----------------------------------------------------------
|  0  | SELECT STATEMENT             |                    |
|  1  |   TABLE ACCESS BY INDEX ROWID| ZIPCODE            |
|  2  |    INDEX UNIQUE SCAN         | ZIP_PK             |
-----------------------------------------------------------
```

g) Explain why the following query does not use an index.

```
SELECT *
  FROM grade
 WHERE grade_type_code = 'HW'
```

Answer: The GRADE_TYPE_CODE column is not the leading column on any index of the GRADE table.

```
-----------------------------------------
| Id  | Operation          | Name  |
-----------------------------------------
|   0 | SELECT STATEMENT   |       |
|   1 |   TABLE ACCESS FULL| GRADE |
-----------------------------------------
```

The following query shows the indexes on the GRADE table. As you see, the GRADE_TYPE_CODE is a column in two different indexes but is never the leading column, nor are any of the leading columns in the WHERE clause of the query.

```
SELECT index_name, column_name, column_position
  FROM user_ind_columns
 WHERE table_name = 'GRADE'
 ORDER BY 1, 3
```

INDEX_NAME	COLUMN_NAME	COLUMN_POSITION
GR_GRTW_FK_I	SECTION_ID	1
GR_GRTW_FK_I	GRADE_TYPE_CODE	2
GR_PK	STUDENT_ID	1
GR_PK	SECTION_ID	2
GR_PK	GRADE_TYPE_CODE	3
GR_PK	GRADE_CODE_OCCURRENCE	4

6 rows selected.

The following query makes use of the index GR_GRTW_FK_I because the leading edge of the index is in the WHERE clause.

```
SELECT *
  FROM grade
 WHERE grade_type_code = 'HW'
   AND section_id = 123
```

And this query uses the primary key index GR_PK.

```
SELECT *
  FROM grade
 WHERE grade_type_code = 'HW'
   AND section_id = 123
   AND student_id = 567
```

 Oracle's skip scan feature improves index scans when the leading portion of the index is not specified. Essentially, scanning an index is faster than scanning the table, and the skip scanning feature splits the index into smaller subindexes. These different subindexes show

the number of distinct values in the leading index. The feature is most useful when there are few distinct values in the leading column of the index. The explain plan will indicate if Oracle took advantage the skip scan feature to access the data.

17.1.2 ANSWERS

a) Given the following SELECT statement and the resulting execution plan, determine the driving table and the type of join performed.

```
SELECT --+ FIRST_ROWS
        i.last_name, c.description, c.course_no
  FROM course c, section s, instructor i
 WHERE c.course_no = s.course_no
   AND s.instructor_id = i.instructor_id
   AND s.section_id = 133
```

```
----------------------------------------------------------------
| Id  | Operation                          | Name       |      |
----------------------------------------------------------------
|  0  | SELECT STATEMENT                   |            |      |
|  1  |   NESTED LOOPS                     |            |      |
|  2  |    NESTED LOOPS                    |            |      |
|  3  |     TABLE ACCESS BY INDEX ROWID|  SECTION   |      |
|  4  |      INDEX UNIQUE SCAN             |  SECT_PK   |      |
|  5  |     TABLE ACCESS BY INDEX ROWID|  COURSE    |      |
|  6  |      INDEX UNIQUE SCAN             |  CRSE_PK   |      |
|  7  |     TABLE ACCESS BY INDEX ROWID |  INSTRUCTOR |     |
|  8  |      INDEX UNIQUE SCAN             |  INST_PK   |      |
----------------------------------------------------------------
```

Answer: The driving table of this nested loop join is the SECTION table.

The following steps are performed by this query: The index SECT_PK is probed for the SECTION_ID of 133 and one record in the SECTION table is accessed. Then, the index CRSE_PK on the COURSE table is checked for the COURSE_NO matching the row. The row is retrieved to obtain the DESCRIPTION. Finally, the instructor index INST_PK is used to find a match for the INSTRUCTOR_ID from the initial row in the SECTION table, and then the corresponding record in the INSTRUCTOR table is retrieved. You can influence the join order with the ORDERED or the LEADING hint. This can have a significant impact on performance.

Comparing the execution time of the nested loop to the sort-merge join or the hash join probably will not show a great variance for the data within the STUDENT schema, but if you are joining larger tables, the differences may be significant.

b) The following alternate SQL statements result in the respective execution plans. What differences do you observe?

```
SELECT *
  FROM student
 WHERE student_id NOT IN
        (SELECT student_id
           FROM enrollment)
```

```
--------------------------------------------
| Id | Operation           | Name           |
--------------------------------------------
|  0 | SELECT STATEMENT    |                |
|  1 |  FILTER             |                |
|  2 |   TABLE ACCESS FULL | STUDENT        |
|  3 |   TABLE ACCESS FULL | ENROLLMENT     |
--------------------------------------------
```

```
SELECT *
  FROM student s
 WHERE NOT EXISTS
        (SELECT 'X'
           FROM enrollment
          WHERE s.student_id = student_id)
```

```
--------------------------------------------
| Id | Operation           | Name           |
--------------------------------------------
|  0 | SELECT STATEMENT    |                |
|  1 |  FILTER             |                |
|  2 |   TABLE ACCESS FULL | STUDENT        |
|  3 |   INDEX RANGE SCAN  | ENR_PK         |
--------------------------------------------
```

```
SELECT student_id
  FROM student
MINUS
SELECT student_id
  FROM enrollment
```

```
--------------------------------------------
| Id | Operation           | Name           |
--------------------------------------------
|  0 | SELECT STATEMENT    |                |
|  1 |  MINUS              |                |
|  2 |   SORT UNIQUE NOSORT|                |
|  3 |    INDEX FULL SCAN  | STU_PK         |
|  4 |   SORT UNIQUE NOSORT|                |
|  5 |    INDEX FULL SCAN  | ENR_PK         |
--------------------------------------------
```

Answer: The NOT IN subquery does not take advantage of the index on the ENROLL-MENT table, but the NOT EXISTS query does. The MINUS operator has a completely different execution plan.

The NOT IN operator can be very inefficient, but newer versions of Oracle frequently replace the full tablescan with an antijoin, which does take advantage of the index. If your statement needs to run against older versions of Oracle, consider replacing it with a NOT EXISTS if the performance is not satisfactory. The NOT EXISTS operator takes advantage of the index on the ENROLLMENT table. You should keep in mind that you want to eliminate as many rows as possible in the outer query of the NOT EXISTS correlated subquery so the repeated execution of the inner query is minimized. The execution plan of the MINUS operator does not look very impressive but can actually be one of the fastest ways to retrieve the result, especially when a large number of records is involved.

 Always consider alternative SQL syntax when writing queries and tune your SQL statements with a representative data set. If the distribution of the data changes, so will the statistics, and the optimizer may favor a different execution plan.

c) Show the execution plan for the following SELECT statements and describe the difference.

```
SELECT student_id, last_name, 'student'
  FROM student
UNION
SELECT instructor_id, last_name, 'instructor'
  FROM instructor

SELECT student_id, last_name, 'student'
  FROM student
UNION ALL
SELECT instructor_id, last_name, 'instructor'
  FROM instructor
```

Answer: The UNION statement involves an additional sort, which is not performed on the UNION ALL statement.

```
SELECT student_id, last_name, 'student'
  FROM student
UNION
SELECT instructor_id, last_name, 'instructor'
  FROM instructor
```

Id	Operation	Name
0	SELECT STATEMENT	
1	SORT UNIQUE	
2	UNION-ALL	
3	TABLE ACCESS FULL	STUDENT
4	TABLE ACCESS FULL	INSTRUCTOR

```
SELECT student_id, last_name, 'student'
  FROM student
UNION ALL
SELECT instructor_id, last_name, 'instructor'
  FROM instructor
-----------------------------------------------
| Id  | Operation            | Name           |
-----------------------------------------------
|  0  | SELECT STATEMENT     |                |
|  1  |  UNION-ALL           |                |
|  2  |   TABLE ACCESS FULL| STUDENT         |
|  3  |   TABLE ACCESS FULL| INSTRUCTOR      |
-----------------------------------------------
```

Whenever possible, avoid any unnecessary sorts required by the use of UNION or DISTINCT.

LAB 17.1 SELF-REVIEW QUESTIONS

In order to test your progress, you should be able to answer the following questions.

1) The rule-based optimizer requires tables to be analyzed.

   a) _____ True
   b) _____ False

2) An ORDERED hint can influence the join order of SQL statements using the cost-based optimizer.

   a) _____ True
   b) _____ False

3) The join order of tables is important for good performance of the nested loop join.

   a) _____ True
   b) _____ False

4) An execution plan is always read from the bottom to the top and then from the inside to the outside.

   a) _____ True
   b) _____ False

5) Incorrectly written hints are treated as comments and ignored.

   a) _____ True
   b) _____ False

Answers appear in Appendix A, Section 17.1.

CHAPTER 17

TEST YOUR THINKING

> The projects in this section are meant to have you utilize all of the skills
> that you have acquired throughout this chapter. The answers to these
> projects can be found at the companion Web site to this book, located at:
> *http://authors.phptr.com/rischert3e*. Visit the Web site periodically to share and discuss
> your answers.

1) Given the following execution plan, describe the steps and their order
of execution.

```
SELECT c.course_no, c.description,
       i.instructor_id
  FROM course c, section s, instructor i
 WHERE prerequisite = 30
   AND c.course_no = s.course_no
   AND s.instructor_id - i.instructor_id
```

```
-------------------------------------------------------------
| Id  | Operation                       | Name            |
-------------------------------------------------------------
|   0 | SELECT STATEMENT                |                 |
|   1 |  NESTED LOOPS                   |                 |
|   2 |   NESTED LOOPS                  |                 |
|   3 |    TABLE ACCESS BY INDEX ROWID  | COURSE          |
|   4 |     INDEX RANGE SCAN            | CRSE_CRSE_FK_I  |
|   5 |    TABLE ACCESS BY INDEX ROWID  | SECTION         |
|   6 |     INDEX RANGE SCAN            | SECT_CRSE_FK_I  |
|   7 |   INDEX UNIQUE SCAN             | INST_PK         |
-------------------------------------------------------------
```

2) Describe the steps of the following execution plan.

```
UPDATE enrollment e
   SET final_grade =
       (SELECT NVL(AVG(numeric_grade),0)
          FROM grade
         WHERE e.student_id = student_id
           AND e.section_id = section_id)
 WHERE student_id = 1000
   AND section_id = 2000
0 rows updated.
```

```
---------------------------------------------------------
| Id  | Operation                       | Name          |
---------------------------------------------------------
|  0  | UPDATE STATEMENT                |               |
|  1  |  UPDATE                         | ENROLLMENT    |
|  2  |   INDEX UNIQUE SCAN             | ENR_PK        |
|  3  |    SORT AGGREGATE               |               |
|  4  |     TABLE ACCESS BY INDEX ROWID | GRADE         |
|  5  |      INDEX RANGE SCAN           | GR_PK         |
---------------------------------------------------------
```

3) The following SQL statement has an error in the hint. Correct the statement so Oracle can use the hint.

```
SELECT /*+ INDEX (student stu_pk) */ *
  FROM student s
 WHERE last_name = 'Smith'
```

APPENDIX A

ANSWERS TO SELF-REVIEW QUESTIONS

CHAPTER 1
Lab 1.1 ■ Data, Databases, and the Definition of SQL

Question	Answer	Comments
1)	a	
2)	b	A table must always have at least one column. Rows are not required.
3)	b	SQL is a language. For example, SQL*Plus is a software program (which you will learn about in Chapter 2, "SQL: The Basics") that allows you to use SQL language to interact with the database.
4)	a	Most database systems are multiuser systems.
5)	a	

Lab 1.2 ■ Table Relationships

Question	Answer	Comments
1)	b	The entity relationship diagram is a logical model that doesn't deal with physical tables yet, but instead with entities and attributes.
2)	a	Another cardinality notation used to depict a one-to-many relationship is 1:M or 1:N.
3)	a	
4)	b	The schema diagram or physical model is derived from the logical data model.
5)	b	Actually, when you denormalize you reintroduce redundancy.

851

6)	b	The logical database design is one of the steps in the database development life cycle that ends with the actual physical database implementation. SQL works with the physical database implementation.
7)	a	
8)	a	

Lab 1.3 ■ The STUDENT Schema Diagram

Question	Answer	Comments
1)	a, c	
2)	a	
3)	b	The number of rows is completely independent of the number of columns in a table.
4)	b	The SECTION table has COURSE_NO and INSTRUCTOR_ID columns as foreign keys.
5)	a	Each individual database system software may have limits constrained by the hardware and software. It is not uncommon to have tables exceeding 10 million rows.
6)	b	A primary key may never contain NULL values.
7)	a	
8)	c	The table has at least three foreign key columns. Some foreign keys may consist of multiple columns.
9)	a	
10)	a	An example of a foreign key that allows null values is the ZIP column on the INSTRUCTOR table.
11)	a	The prevention of orphan rows, thereby preserving the parent–child relationship between tables, is key to the success of a relational database design.

CHAPTER 2

Lab 2.1 ■ The SQL*Plus Environment

Question	Answer	Comments
1)	a	The DESC command is an easy way to find out about the structure of a table; that is, column names, datatypes, and if a column allows NULL values or not.
2)	b	SQL*Plus is not necessary to connect to Oracle. You may use other types of software that allows database connectivity. You can also use *i*SQL*Plus, which only

requires a Web browser. As with any database connection you will obviously need a valid user ID and password.

3)   a

4)   a

5)   a

Lab 2.2 ■ The Anatomy of a SELECT Statement

Question	Answer	Comments
1)	a	
2)	a	To show all the columns, it is easiest to use the asterisk wildcard character (*).
3)	b	The asterisk is used for the column list only.
4)	a	A column with the COURSENO does not exist on the COURSE table.

Lab 2.3 ■ Editing a SQL Statement

Question	Answer	Comments
1)	b	Only the most recent statement is saved in the buffer.
2)	a	Note that the forward slash must be in a separate line and start at the first position.
3)	b	You can save a file anywhere you have permission to access the drive.
4)	b	The SQL*Plus START command executes a file; the RUN command or the forward slash executes the contents of the buffer.

Lab 2.4 ■ The WHERE Clause: Comparison and Logical Operators

Question	Answer	Comments
1)	b	Comparison operators can compare multiple values, such as the IN operator, which compares against a list of values.
2)	b	The BETWEEN operator is inclusive of the two values specified.
3)	a	Testing for nulls must be done using the IS NULL operator. This query will not return any rows!
4)	a	The LIKE operator cannot compare against a list of values.

5)	b	This query is valid. Alternatively, the <> operator or the WHERE clause NOT state = 'NY' can be used.
6)	b	Because the comparison operator is the equal sign (=), not the LIKE operator, it looks for a last name exactly equal to 'SM%', including the % sign. If you use the LIKE operator instead, then last names beginning with the uppercase letters SM are returned.

Lab 2.5 ■ The ORDER BY Clause

Question	Answer	Comments
1)	b	The order should be SELECT, FROM, WHERE, ORDER BY.
2)	b	The default ORDER BY sort order is ascending.
3)	a	There is no error in this statement.
4)	b	The query does not contain an error.
5)	a	Typically yes, the exception is the use of the DISTINCT keyword in the SELECT clause.

CHAPTER 3

Lab 3.1 ■ Character Functions

Question	Answer	Comments
1)	b	For example, the INSTR function, which converts single values, requires two parameters and may have optional parameters.
2)	a	You will see other uses of the DUAL table throughout this book.
3)	a	
4)	a	You may not apply a function to the table name in the FROM clause of a SQL statement.
5)	a	The RTRIM right trims characters. If a parameter is not specified, it trims spaces.
6)	c	The LENGTH function returns the length of a string.
7)	a	
8)	a	This is in contrast to the aggregate functions where one or more rows are involved. Aggregate functions are discussed in Chapter 5, "Aggregate Functions, GROUP BY and HAVING."
9)	c	The SUBSTR function returns a specified portion of a character string.

10)   b   Usually character functions return a datatype of CHAR or VARCHAR2; however, the INSTR and LENGTH functions return a number.

Lab 3.2 ■ Number Functions

Question	Answer	Comments
1)	a	
2)	b	The ROUND function works on the DATE, the NUMBER, and the floating-point datatypes. It can also take a string consisting of numbers as a parameter, providing it can be implicitly converted into a NUMBER datatype.
3)	b	This SELECT statement subtracts the CAPACITY columns from each other. It is perfectly valid to use another column rather than a literal, as we used in most other examples. The result of the query will not make much sense in this case, resulting in zero values. If any of the CAPACITY column values contains a null value, the result is another null.
4)	c	Most functions return a null with a null argument. There are a few exceptions such as the REPLACE and NVL functions.

Lab 3.3 ■ Miscellaneous Single-Row Functions

Question	Answer	Comments
1)	a	Any calculation with a null always yields null. If you want to avoid this behavior, you can use the NVL function to substitute another value.
2)	b	If the datatypes are different, Oracle attempts to convert the substitution expression's datatype to the input expression's datatype. If this is not possible, the function returns an error as in this example. The text literal "None", which is the substitution expression, cannot be converted into the input expression's NUMBER datatype. The corrected statement looks like this: `SELECT NVL(TO_CHAR(cost), 'None') FROM course.`
3)	b	The UPDATE command (discussed in Chapter 10, "Insert, Update, and Delete"), updates data in the database. Any of the functions you have learned about so far will not modify the value in the database.

4) a

5) b The DECODE function is permitted in any SQL statement where functions are allowed.

6) a The CASE expression is allowed anywhere expressions are allowed including ORDER BY clauses or inside functions.

7) b The functions in this lab can be used on most datatypes. For example, the NVL function is most frequently used on DATE, NUMBER, and VARCHAR2 datatypes.

CHAPTER 4

Lab 4.1 ■ Applying Oracle's Date Format Models

Question	Answer	Comments
1)	a	The TRUNC function, without a format model, sets the timestamp to midnight. TRUNC can also take a NUMBER datatype as a parameter.
2)	b	The TO_DATE function is required instead. For example, SELECT TO_DATE('01/12/2000','MM/DD/YYYY') FROM dual.
3)	d	The case is identical to the case of the format mask. The format mask DY returns MON, Day returns Monday and padded to nine spaces, DAY returns MONDAY.
4)	e	The fill mode (fm) prevents any blank padding between December and 31. The date format element suffix th adds the ordinal number.
5)	b	Note the minutes (MI) are displayed as months (MM) instead. This is a mistake beginners often make by confusing the month (MM) format with the minutes (MI) format.

Lab 4.2 ■ Performing Date and Time Math

Question	Answer	Comments
1)	a	You need to supply a negative value as a parameter. For example, the following statement subtracts one month from the current date: SELECT ADD_MONTHS (SYSDATE,-1) FROM dual.
2)	a	You compute this by multiplying 24 hours by the 4 quarters of every hour. You can verify this with the following query: SELECT TO_CHAR(SYSDATE, 'HH24:

MI'), TO_CHAR(SYSDATE+1/96, 'HH24:MI') FROM
dual.

3)   c   The NEXT_DAY function takes two parameters: a date and a day of the week. Sunday, January 9 is the next Sunday after January 2, 2000.

4)   c   The ROUND function rounds not just numbers, but also dates. Here the ROUND function's format model is not listed; therefore, it rounds to the nearest date. Because the time is before noon, it rounds to the current date. If the time is after noon, the next day is returned.

Lab 4.3 ■ Understanding Timestamp and Time Zone Datatypes

Question	Answer	Comments
1)	c	The FROM_TZ function returns a TIMESTAMP WITH TIME ZONE datatype.
2)	a	The ALTER SESSION command can, among other things, change the individual's session time zone.
3)	a	The date and time are stored in the database server's own time zone, but the result is displayed in the individual user's respective time zone.
4)	a	The time zone displacement value, also called the time zone offset value, is the difference in hours and minutes between the local time and UTC (Coordinated Universal Time).
5)	a	
6)	a	

Lab 4.4 ■ Performing Calculations with the Interval Datatypes

Question	Answer	Comments
1)	b	The TO_YMINTERVAL function converts the text literal to an INTERVAL YEAR TO MONTH datatype instead.
2)	b	The NUMTODSINTERVAL function returns a INTERVAL DAY TO SECOND datatype.
3)	b	You can use the EXTRACT function on INTERVAL datatypes.
4)	b	The interval literal is valid.

Lab 4.5 ■ Converting from One Datatype to Another

Question	Answer	Comments
1)	d	Solution d results in an error because 'A123' cannot be converted to a NUMBER. (Note, Oracle versions prior to 9i may return an error message on statement e because the TO_CHAR function expects a NUMBER or DATE datatype, not a character datatype. The passed literal 'A123' is assumed to be a NUMBER and Oracle attempts to implicitly convert the literal to a NUMBER; therefore an error is returned.)
2)	c, d, e	These are all valid, including e, but solution e does not show all the digits because the passed parameter exceeds the specified precision. Solutions a and b are invalid NUMBER masks; solution b also misses a single quote at the end of the format mask.
3)	a	It is always best to explicitly specify the datatype and not to rely on Oracle's implicit conversion.
4)	a	Conversion functions operate on a single row at a time.
5)	b	Changing the query as follows will correct the error.

```
SELECT *
  FROM conversion_example
 WHERE course_no = CAST(123 AS VARCHAR2(3))
```

CHAPTER 5

Lab 5.1 ■ Aggregate Functions

Question	Answer	Comments
1)	c	Only AVG, COUNT, and SUM are aggregate functions. ROUND is a single-row function.
2)	c	The aggregate function MAX determines the most recently modified record for the ENROLLMENT table. If a null value is returned, the value March 12, 2005 is substituted.
3)	a	Typically, aggregate functions work on groups of rows, but can also be applied to a single row. For example, the following two statements return the same result. SELECT MAX(modified_date) FROM zipcode WHERE zip = '10025'; SELECT modified_date FROM zipcode WHERE zip = '10025'.

4)	a	The asterisk is not a permissible argument for the AVG function.
5)	b	It computes the average capacity of only the DISTINCT capacities of the SECTION table.
6)	b	The statement is correct and shows an example of an expression as an argument of an aggregate function. The values in the CAPACITY columns are multiplied by 1.5, then the aggregate function SUM is applied.

Lab 5.2 ■ The GROUP BY and HAVING Clauses

Question	Answer	Comments
1)	b	Only the SECTION_ID column. The other columns contain aggregate functions, which are computed based on the grouping by SECTION_ID.
2)	a	It is syntactically correct to do this, but it is redundant because GROUP BY implies distinct values.
3)	a	Aggregate functions are not allowed in the WHERE clause unless they are part of a subquery. (See Chapter 7 for more on subqueries.)
4)	b	One row, because all the NULL values are grouped together. Although one NULL does not equal another, in a GROUP BY clause they are grouped together.
5)	a	The SQL statement is correct. You do not need to list the columns of the GROUP BY clause in the SELECT list as well. This type of query is typically not very useful because this individual example displays only the value of the COUNT function and not the column by which the group is formed. The result of the query looks like the following output.

```
COUNT(*)
----------
         1
...
         1

28 rows selected.
```

CHAPTER 6

Lab 6.1 ■ The Two-Table Join

Question	Answer	Comments
1)	f	The alias is incorrect on the STUDENT table's ZIP column.
2)	d	Lines 2 and 5 are incorrect. In line 5 the STUD.ZIP column does not exist; it needs to be changed to S.ZIP to correspond to the STUDENT table's alias s listed in the FROM clause. Line 2 lists a nonexistent SZIP column. Change it to S.ZIP for the query to work.
3)	b	The table alias is just another name to reference the table.
4)	a	The equijoin tests for equality of values in one or multiple columns.
5)	c	The column W.GRADE_TYPE_CODE_CD is misspelled and needs to be changed to W.GRADE_TYPE_CODE for the query to work.
6)	b	The NULL value from one table does not match the NULL value from another table; therefore, the records are not included in the result.
7)	a	The USING clause assumes the equality of the values and identical column names. If you want to specify inequality or the join columns do not share the same name, use the traditional WHERE clause or use the ON clause. For more on inequality in joins refer to Chapter 9, "Complex Joins."
8)	a	The natural join does not allow any USING or ON clause. The common column names are assumed to be the joining criteria.
9)	b	This is not required, but is often included to understand the result set.

Lab 6.2 ■ Joining Three or More Tables

Question	Answer	Comments
1)	b	This statement has the correct join criteria between the tables SECTION, COURSE, and INSTRUCTOR. Note, the COURSE table is not necessary to show the instructors assigned to sections.
2)	c	You get this error if you list two columns with the same name. Resolve it by prefixing the column with a table name or a table alias.

3)   b   Multicolumn joins need to have all the common columns listed. Some joins do not follow the primary/foreign key path because either a foreign key relationship does not exist or a shortcut is used to obtain the information.

4)   a   The SECTION_ID column has the wrong table alias; change it to E.SECTION_ID or G.SECTION_ID instead.

5)   a   The most common type of join is the equijoin, which is based on the equality of values. This is typically expressed with the equal (=) sign, or in ANSI syntax with the NATURAL JOIN or INNER JOIN together with the USING clause or the ON condition. You will explore nonequijoin conditions, self-joins, and outer joins in Chapter 9, "Complex Joins."

6)   a   Remember the n − 1 formula? In the case of multicolumn keys, you may have additional conditions in your WHERE clause or multiple columns in your ANSI join ON or USING clause.

CHAPTER 7

Lab 7.1 ■ Simple Subqueries

Question	Answer	Comments
1)	a	A subquery with the ORDER BY clause results in an error, except for inline views discussed in Lab 7.3.
2)	b	Subqueries can also be used in other types of SQL statements. Most frequently, they are used in SELECT statements or in INSERT, DELETE, or UPDATE statements.
3)	a	The most deeply nested subquery is executed first. This is in contrast to the correlated subquery, which executes the outer query first, then repeatedly executes the inner subquery for every row of the outer query.
4)	c	The IN operator allows multiple rows.
5)	a	You can compare column pairs by enclosing them in parentheses and comparing them to the subquery using the IN operator. Make sure the datatype and column pairs match on both sides of the IN operator.

Lab 7.2 ■ Correlated Subqueries

Question	Answer	Comments
1)	a	The NOT EXISTS operator tests for NULL values, in contrast to the NOT IN operator which does not.
2)	a	For every row of the outer query, the inner query is executed.
3)	a	They result in the same output, although one may execute more efficiently than the other.
4)	b	The query looks only for enrolled students that have no corresponding record in the GRADE table for the particular section.
5)	a	The join may repeat some of the values from the child table and applying the aggregate function to these rows may not yield the correct result. Therefore, check the result of the join first!

Lab 7.3 ■ Inline Views and Scalar Subquery Expressions

Question	Answer	Comments
1)	a	
2)	b	A scalar subquery returns a single column and single row.
3)	b	Inline views, unlike regular views, are not stored in the data dictionary.
4)	b	It is a pseudocolumn, appearing as though it was an actual column in the table, but it is not.
5)	a	Just like other types of views, this is allowed.

Lab 7.4 ■ ANY, SOME, and ALL Operators in Subqueries

Question	Answer	Comments
1)	b	The first query tests if the number 6 is unequal to any of the values in the list. It is unequal to the number 9 and therefore the query returns the value `True`. The second query checks if the number 6 is not in the list of values. The value is included, and the query returns `no rows selected`.
2)	a	The two queries return the identical result.
3)	a	These operators can be used interchangeably.
4)	a	ANY, SOME, and ALL operators allow you to compare a list of values with the comparison operators. The IN operator tests for equivalency of values only.

CHAPTER 8

Lab 8.1 ■ The Power of UNION and UNION ALL

Question	Answer	Comments
1)	a	The UNION set operator already performs a sort and only lists distinct values.
2)	b	The ORDER BY clause is always the last clause in a set operation.
3)	b	A UNION set operation does not eliminate rows; rather, it combines rows from each SELECT statement, eliminating duplicates only. An equijoin returns only rows where values from each table are equal.
4)	b	You can UNION any tables as long as you conform to the rules of the UNION operation; that is, the same number of columns and the same datatype.
5)	a	One of the rules of set operations is that the number of columns must be the same, as well as the datatypes of those columns.

Lab 8.2 ■ The MINUS and INTERSECT Set Operators

Question	Answer	Comments
1)	b	The two SELECT statements result in two different sets of data.
2)	a	The SELECT statements in a set operation can be any SELECT statements.
3)	b	The datatype of the columns must agree.
4)	a	All set operators, except UNION ALL, eliminate duplicate values, so DISTINCT is not needed.

CHAPTER 9

Lab 9.1 ■ Outer Joins

Question	Answer	Comments
1)	a	The OR operator is not allowed in the outer join. The result is an error message such as this one: ORA-01719: outer join operator (+) not allowed in operand of OR or IN.
2)	a	The IN operator may not be used. The error message is identical to the one in question 1. Note that the new ANSI join syntax overcomes some of these limitations.

3)	a	The Oracle outer join operator indicates from which table you want to display NULLs for nonmatching values. Alternatively, this can be expressed with the ANSI outer join syntax or a UNION.
4)	d	You cannot write a full outer join with two (+) outer join operators. You need to write two outer join statements and combine the result with the UNION set operator or use the ANSI full outer join syntax.

Lab 9.2 ■ Self-Joins

Question	Answer	Comments
1)	b	Any kinds of joins do not have to follow the foreign/primary key path. But you have to carefully examine the result to make sure it is correct. Otherwise, it could result in a Cartesian product.
2)	b	You can join a table to itself without a recursive relationship, (e.g., to determine data inconsistencies).
3)	b	Such restrictions do not exist.
4)	a	
5)	a	Yes, an alias is required.

CHAPTER 10

Lab 10.1 ■ Creating Data and Transaction Course

Question	Answer	Comments
1)	b	Only DDL or DCL commands issue implicit commits.
2)	b	
3)	b	You can insert multiple rows by selecting from another table.
4)	a	
5)	b	Only committed changes can be seen by all users. The session issuing the change can always see the change.
6)	a	

Lab 10.2 ■ Updating and Deleting Data

Question	Answer	Comments
1)	a	If the rows have not been committed to the database, they can be restored. In Oracle 10*g* you can attempt to restore it with the FLASH BACK command.
2)	a	

3)	b	Queries never place locks on rows. The exception is the SELECT FOR UPDATE command; it retrieves the rows and explicitly locks them.
4)	b	Reading uncommitted data is called "dirty reads." Oracle only shows data that has been committed and achieves read-consistency by reading old data from the rollback (or undo) segments to present the user a picture of how the data looked at the time the query started.
5)	a	If the same session issues a DCL or DDL command instead of a ROLLBACK or COMMIT, it will force an implicit commit and therefore release the lock on the row.

CHAPTER 11

Lab 11.1 ■ Creating and Dropping Tables

Question	Answer	Comments
1)	a	The primary key consists of multiple columns.
2)	a	When the CREATE TABLE statement uses the AS SELECT keywords to select from another table or tables, the SELECT statement can contain a join of multiple tables.
3)	b	The foreign key constraints of the child tables are dropped, but not the child tables themselves.
4)	a	
5)	b	You can create a table from another regardless if the table has rows or not.
6)	a	Any DDL commands, such as CREATE TABLE, ALTER TABLE, TRUNCATE TABLE, issue an implicit commit.
7)	a	If the foreign key column is defined as nulls allowed, a null value is also acceptable.
8)	b	Ideally, primary key values should be generic and never subject to changes; otherwise, this requires updates to the corresponding foreign key columns.
9)	a	The INITIAL extent specifies the storage allocation when the table is initially created. Once the data is entered and the space filled, Oracle will automatically allocate another extent in a size indicated with the NEXT parameter.
10)	a	

11)	b	The maximum allowable value is 9.99. For a column defined as NUMBER(3,0), the largest value can be 999.

Lab 11.2 ■ Altering Tables and Manipulating Constraints

Question	Answer	Comments
1)	a	The syntax should not include both keywords CONSTRAINT and PRIMARY KEY. The correct syntax is either ALTER TABLE tablename DROP CONSTRAINT followed by the constraint name, or ALTER TABLE tablename DROP PRIMARY KEY.
2)	b	The ADD keyword is used to add columns or constraints to a table, whereas the MODIFY keyword is used to change characteristics of a column.
3)	a	You can only add a NOT NULL constraint if the referenced column contains values or the table is empty.
4)	b	The ALTER TABLE...DISABLE PRIMARY KEY command is an example of the command used without the name of the constraint.
5)	b	A column's datatype can also be changed to a compatible datatype, such as from a VARCHAR2 to CHAR.

CHAPTER 12

Lab 12.1 ■ Creating and Modifying Views

Question	Answer	Comments
1)	a	
2)	a, b	
3)	e	
4)	a	Views must follow a number of rules to be updatable. This view allows inserts and updates and deletes referencing the STATE column, but not to the MODIFIED_DATE column. If you are in doubt, query the data dictionary view called USER_UPDATABLE_COLUMNS.
5)	a	You can list only certain columns in a view, and/or you can restrict the view with the WHERE clause for specific rows.
6)	a	You can choose to keep the name or create a different name; however, expressions require a column alias.

Lab 12.2 ■ Indexes

Question	Answer	Comments
1)	c, d	A concatenated index typically outperforms individual column indexes. However, as with any query, you need to know how many rows you expect to retrieve with the criteria. If you retrieve a large number of records, the full table scan may outperform the retrieval from the index. Oracle's optimizer will automatically make this determination. If you create a concatenated index, choose the column order carefully. If you have a choice, choose the most selective column first; that is, the column with the most distinct values. Starting with Oracle 9*i*, a new feature called skip scan can overturn these "old" rules. Be sure to test your options carefully to determine the best performance.
2)	b	Indexes can slow down INSERT, UPDATE, and DELETE operations. Retrieving data from an index may take more time if the retrieved data set is relatively large because both table and index need to be accessed.
3)	a	These columns are often listed in the WHERE clause and therefore accessed frequently. Indexing these columns improves the performance of joins and locking.
4)	a	
5)	b	Nulls are not stored in a B-tree index; therefore, a search for null values will not use the index. However, a concatenated index will store nulls as long as the leading column of the concatenated index is not null.
6)	a	Indexes are not only useful for SELECT statements, but also for UPDATE and DELETE statements to quickly locate the record. Note that INSERT, UPDATE, and DELETE operations on columns containing indexes are much slower because the index needs to be updated with the changed or newly inserted values.

Lab 12.3 ■ Sequences

Question	Answer	Comments
1)	a	
2)	b	It is best to use a generated value for a primary key, such as from a sequence, because it is generic, not subject to any change, and prevents duplicates or null values.
3)	a	

4)   b   These two objects are independent of each other. For
                         example, you can use the same sequence for multiple
                         tables.

5)   a

CHAPTER 13

Lab 13.1 ■ The Oracle Data Dictionary Views

Question	Answer	Comments
1)	a	
2)	a	Other object types are also listed in this view.
3)	a	
4)	b	The ALL_TABLES view shows only the tables accessible to a user.
5)	a	

Lab 13.2 ■ Advanced SQL*Plus Commands

Question	Answer	Comments
1)	a	
2)	b	The CHR(10) function issues a line feed.
3)	a	
4)	a	Note that the $ command is not available on all operating systems.
5)	a	
6)	a	Rather than retyping the same commands over again, dynamic SQL scripts, also referred to as master/slave scripts or SQL to generate SQL, simplify this task.

CHAPTER 14

Lab 14.1 ■ Users, Privileges, Roles, and Synonyms

Question	Answer	Comments
1)	b	A user's objects can be dropped with the CASCADE keyword at the end of the DROP USER statement.
2)	a	
3)	a	System and object privileges cannot be granted or revoked in the same statement. However, system and object privileges, in separate statements, can be granted to or revoked from a single role.

4)	b	Both system and object privileges can be granted to a user through a role.
5)	b	Dropping a role has no effect on the underlying objects.
6)	a	
7)	b	DCL commands implicitly issue a COMMIT, much like DDL commands.

CHAPTER 15

Lab 15.1 ■ Regular Expressions

Question	Answer	Comments
1)	b	The REGEXP_LIKE operator cannot be used in the SELECT clause of a statement, otherwise you will get the error message ORA-00904: "REGEXP_LIKE": invalid identifier
2)	e	The quantifier is invalid because the minimum value of '4' is greater than the maximum value of '1'.
3)	b	The regular expression is looking for characters that are not digits with a minimum length of at least 1 character and a maximum of 5 characters. This pattern must end the expression. The nondigit characters are "ABC" and the replacement does not occur because the pattern is not found in the supplied input string.
4)	a	
5)	a	The query will result in the ORA-12729: invalid character class in regular expression error message. The POSIX classes are case-sensitive and must be spelled exactly as listed.
6)	a	The query will show 'CD' as a result because the '+' operator will look for the one or more upper case letters. The query specifies no starting position or occurrence; therefore, the default is the first starting position and the first occurrence.
7)	a	The two regular expressions are equivalent for Latin numbers. However, if you need to support other characters sets, this will not hold true.

Lab 15.2 ■ Hierarchical Queries

Question	Answer	Comments
1)	a	
2)	a	The PRIOR operator determines the parent.
3)	a	
4)	a	
5)	b	The CONNECT_BY_ISLEAF pseudocolumn display the value of 1, if it's a leaf of the hierarchy tree, otherwise it displays 0.

CHAPTER 16

Lab 16.1 ■ Advanced SQL Concepts, Analytical Functions, and the WITH Clause

Question	Answer	Comments
1)	c	
2)	a	
3)	a	
4)	b	The ROWS keyword defines a physical window.
5)	a	
6)	b	LAG and LEAD do not need a windowing clause, the position is defined with the offset value.
7)	a	

Lab 16.2 ■ ROLLUP and CUBE Operators

Question	Answer	Comments
1)	c	The formula to determine the number of different combinations for the CUBE operator is 2^n. With four columns the answer is 2^4, which equals 16.
2)	b	The formula for ROLLUP is $n + 1$. With four columns there will be a total of five groupings.
3)	a	A super aggregate row generated by the CUBE or ROLLUP operator will return the number 1 with the GROUPING function
4)	a	These are three sets. The first set is a combination of the columns COLOR and PRICE as indicated with the parentheses around the columns. The second group is MATERIAL and the last group STORE_LOCATION.

CHAPTER 17

Lab 17.1 ■ The Oracle Optimizer and Writing Effective SQL Statements

Question	Answer	Comments
1)	b	
2)	a	
3)	a	The join order has a significant impact on performance.
4)	b	It is read from the inside to the outside. If two statements have the same level of indentation, the topmost statement is read first. The exception to this rule is the nested loop join.
5)	a	

APPENDIX B

SQL FORMATTING GUIDE

SQL formatting guidelines are a set of written instructions, similar to a stylesheet in publishing, that help programmers determine what the program code should look like. The main rule is *consistency*—once you have decided on the style, use it rigorously.

Why have guidelines? The major benefit of standardized formatting is ease of reading. This is particularly important if someone else has to maintain, upgrade, or fix your programs. The easier a program is to read, the easier it is to understand, and the faster changes can be made. This ultimately saves time and money.

CASE

SQL is case insensitive. However, there are guidelines to follow when writing SQL, for the sake of readability:

- Use UPPER case for SQL commands and keywords (SELECT, INSERT, UPDATE, DELETE, ALTER, etc.), datatypes (VARCHAR2, DATE, NUMBER), functions (COUNT, TO_DATE, SUBSTR, etc.), and SQL*Plus commands (CONNECT, SET, etc.).
- Use lowercase for column and tables names, as well as variable names.

FORMATTING SQL CODE

White space is important for readability. Put spaces on both sides of an equality sign or comparison operator. All examples in this book use a monospaced font (Courier) that makes the formatting easier to read. Proportionally spaced fonts can hide spaces and make it difficult to line up clauses. Most text and programming editors use monospace fonts by default.

Placing the various clauses of a statement in a separate line helps outline the structure of a statement. Following are formatting examples used throughout this book.

IN QUERIES

For SELECT statements, right-align keywords (SELECT, FROM, WHERE, the ORDER of ORDER BY), as in this example:

```
SELECT *
  FROM course
 WHERE prerequisite IS NULL
 ORDER BY course_no
```

IN DML STATEMENTS

For DML statements, right-align keywords (the INSERT of INSERT INTO, VALUES, SELECT). List columns on a separate line, indenting the open parenthesis two spaces. Align columns underneath each other, putting only a few columns on each line, as in this example:

```
INSERT INTO zipcode
  (zip, created_by, created_date,
   modified_by, modified_date)
VALUES
  ('11111', USER, SYSDATE,
   USER, SYSDATE)
```

IN DDL STATEMENTS

When using CREATE TABLE and defining columns, or using ALTER to alter a table, indent the second line and all other lines thereafter by two spaces, as in this example:

```
CREATE TABLE toy
  (description         VARCHAR2(15) NOT NULL,
   last_purchase_date  DATE,
   remaining_quantity  NUMBER(6))
```

When creating a table from another, right-align keywords (CREATE, SELECT, FROM, WHERE), as in this example:

```
CREATE TABLE jan_99_enrollment AS
SELECT *
  FROM enrollment
 WHERE 1 = 2
```

COMMENTS

Comments are very important when writing SQL code. Comments should explain the main sections of the program or SQL statement and any major logic or business rules that are involved or nontrivial.

Suggestion: Use the '--' comments instead of the '/*' comments. It is easier to comment out a set of code for debugging using the '/*' comments if the code has only '--' comments. This is because you cannot embed '/*' comments within '/*' comments.

APPENDIX C

SQL*PLUS COMMAND REFERENCE

UNSUPPORTED SQL*PLUS COMMANDS IN *i*SQL*PLUS

*i*SQL*Plus does not support some of the SQL*Plus commands; they are simply not applicable and if you issue the command it will raise an SP2–0850 error message. Table C.1 lists these unsupported commands.

Table C.1 ■ Unsupported SQL*Plus Commands in Oracle 10g

Command	Purpose
CLEAR SCREEN	Clears screen of commands.
EDIT	Set the default editor.
EDITFILE	Sets the default file name for the EDIT file. The default file name in the Windows environment is afiedt.buf.
SET FLUSH	Setting FLUSH off allows the operating system to buffer the output.
GET	Loads a file into the SQL buffer.
HOST	Executes an operating system command from within SQL*Plus.
PASSWORD	Changes the password without displaying the password on the screen. In *i*SQL*Plus you can click on Preferences, Change Password instead.
SAVE	Saves the contents of the SQL buffer to a file.
SET SHIFTINOUT	Used only for terminals that display shift characters.
SET SHOWMODE	SQL*Plus system variable display mode.

(continued)

Table C.1 ■ Unsupported SQL*Plus Commands in Oracle 10g (cont.)

Command	Purpose
SET SQLBLANKLINES	Controls if blank lines are allowed within a SQL command or script.
SET SQLCONTINUE	Controls the line continuation prompt when a command doesn't fit in a line and needs to be continued. The default continuation character is a hyphen (-).
SET SQLNUMBER	Sets numeric sequence for subsequent prompt lines.
SET SQLPREFIX	Changes the SQLPREFIX character from the default value of # to another non-alphanumeric character.
SET SQLPROMPT	Changes the default SQL> prompt.
SET SUFFIX	Sets the default file extension for SQL*Plus scripts.
STORE	Saves all the settings of the SQL*Plus environment in a file.
SET TAB	Sets how SQL*Plus formats using either white spaces or tab characters.
SET TERMOUT	Controls the terminal output.
SET TIME	Shows the current time.
SET TRIMOUT	Allows trailing blanks at the end of each displayed line.
SET TRIMSPOOL	See SET TRIMOUT.
SPOOL	Allows recording of commands in a file.

FORMATTING OUTPUT IN SQL*PLUS

The SQL*Plus COLUMN command allows you to change the column heading and format the query result. These formatting options are useful within SQL*Plus and allow for better readability.

FORMATTING THE QUERY RESULT

To allow a better viewing of the query result, you can use the COLUMN command with the FORMAT clause to change the formatting of the column. The syntax of the COLUMN command is as follows:

```
COLUMN columnname FORMAT formatmodel
```

The COLUMN keyword can be abbreviated as COL. The column name indicates the name of the column or the column alias. If you choose a mixed case column alias or one that contains spaces, you must enclose it with double quotes.

The format model allows for formatting of numeric and alphanumeric columns. For alphanumeric columns, it consists of the letter A and a column width. Numeric columns allow formatting for $ signs and commas.

To format the alphanumeric LAST_NAME column of the STUDENT table to a width of 20 characters, you would issue the following command:

```
COLUMN last_name FORMAT A20
```

The A20 format model indicates that you want the column formatted in alphanumeric format with a maximum width of 20 characters. If any value does not fit within the column, it will wrap. If you prefer that the values get truncated, use the SET WRAP OFF command or the TRUNCATED option of the FORMAT command.

```
COLUMN last_name FORMAT A5 TRUNCATED
```

Optionally, you can also wrap whole words with the COLUMN command.

```
COLUMN description FORMAT A20 WORD_WRAPPED
```

The effect on text such as "Intro to the Basic Language" is as follows:

```
Intro to the Basic
Language
```

Following is an example of a numeric format model that formats the COST column with a leading dollar sign and separates the thousands with a comma.

```
COL cost FORMAT $9,999.99
```

The result of this format model on different values is shown as follows:

```
  945.99    $945.99
 1945.99  $1,945.99
10945.99 ##########
```

Notice that the last value cannot fit within the specified column width of the format model and SQL*Plus indicates this overflow with a pound (#) symbol for each allowed digit.

Alphanumeric values are displayed left-justified and numeric values are shown as right-justified.

To display the current attributes of a column, you use the COLUMN command with the column name.

```
COLUMN cost
COLUMN     cost ON
FORMAT     $9,999.99
```

To show the attributes of all columns, enter the COLUMN command without a column name or alias. To reset the display attributes to their default, use this syntax:

```
COL cost CLEAR
```

To reset the display attributes for all columns, issue the CLEAR COLUMNS command.

You can temporarily suppress the display attributes and return them to the default values with this syntax:

```
COL cost OFF
```

To restore the attributes use the COL cost ON command.

To give another column the same attributes as an existing column's attributes, you can copy the attributes with the LIKE clause of the COLUMN command. The FIRST_NAME column obtains the identical display attributes.

```
COL last_name FORMAT A10
COL first_name LIKE last_name
```

CHANGING THE COLUMN HEADING

You can change the column heading with the HEADING clause of the COLUMN command. The syntax is as follows:

```
COLUMN columnname HEADING columnheading
```

To display a heading over more than one line, you use the vertical bar (|) where a new line begins.

```
COL last_name HEADING STUDENT|LAST|NAME
```

```
STUDENT
LAST
NAME
--------
Crocitto
Landry
```

SQL*PLUS LINE EDITOR EDITING COMMANDS

This section is not applicable for *i*SQL*Plus. SQL*Plus stores SQL and PL/SQL commands (not SQL*Plus commands) in the SQL*Plus buffer.

To edit SQL*Plus commands that have been entered at the SQL*Plus command prompt, simply backspace over the command. SQL and PL/SQL commands that have been stored in the SQL*Plus buffer may be edited from within SQL*Plus using the SQL*Plus editing commands listed in Table C.2.

Table C.2 ▪ SQL*Plus Editing Commands

Command	Abbreviation	Purpose
Append text	A text	Add text at the end of a line
Change /old/new	C /old/new	Change old to new in a line
Change /text	C /text	Delete text from a line
Clear Buffer	CL Buff	Delete all lines
Del	(none)	Delete a line
Input	I	Add one or more lines
Input text	I text	Add a line consisting of text
List	L	List all lines in the SQL buffer
List n	L n or n	List 1 line
List *	L *	List the current line
List Last	L Last	List the last line
List m n	L m n	List a range of lines (m to n)

USING THE SQL*PLUS LINE EDITOR
TO SAVE AND RETRIEVE FILES

To save the current contents of the SQL*Plus buffer to a command script, use the SAVE command. An .sql extension is attached to the filename by default.

```
SQL> SAVE create_table_cat
```

To save the contents of the SQL*Plus buffer to a filename that already exists, use the SAVE command with the REPLACE option.

```
SQL> SAVE create_table_cat REPLACE
```

USING AN EDITOR TO CREATE A COMMAND SCRIPT

If you want to retrieve a file and place the contents of a command script into the SQL*Plus buffer, use the SQL*Plus GET command.

```
SQL> GET create_table_cat
```

If you have a set of commands (SQL*Plus, SQL, or a combination of the two) that may be used more than once, it is strongly recommended that you store them in a command script. A command script is a text file that can be run from the SQL*Plus command prompt:

```
SQL> @create_table_cat.sql
```

Or you can run it from the operating system command prompt. The next command runs SQL*Plus from the Windows operating system command line and connects via the STUDENT account and the LEARN password. It automatically also runs the file CREATE_TABLE_CAT.SQL file located in the c:\guest directory. The .sql extension is optional.

```
C:\>sqlplus student/learn @c:\guest\create_table_cat.sql
```

Instead of a file name you can also use an URL such as http://alice/myscripts/create_table_cat.sql.

USING AN EDITOR THAT IS EXTERNAL TO SQL*PLUS

To use your default operating system editor, type EDIT at the SQL*Plus prompt. EDIT loads the contents of the SQL*Plus buffer into the default editor.

You can start and create a new file with the EDIT command, which will invoke the editor.

```
SQL> EDIT
```

To load an already existing file with the user-supplied filename, that file will be opened for editing. SQL*Plus will supply the extension .sql by default.

```
SQL> EDIT create_table_cat
```

CHANGING THE DEFAULT EDITOR

To load the SQL*Plus buffer contents into a text editor other than the default, use the SQL*Plus DEFINE command to change the value of the variable, _EDITOR, to contain the name of the new editor.

```
SQL> DEFINE _EDITOR = ED
```

SQL*PLUS COMMANDS

The following are just some of the most commonly used commands available for use with SQL*Plus. Some of them are discussed in Chapter 2, "SQL: The Basics" and Chapter 13, "The Data Dictionary and Advanced SQL*Plus Commands." This listing is not intended to be a thorough guide to SQL*Plus commands, and some of the listed commands take additional parameters. Note that certain SQL*Plus commands can be toggled on or off (e.g., ECHO and FEEDBACK commands) or changed from one value to another with the SET command. (e.g., the LINESIZE command). All of the current values of the commands can be viewed when you type SHOW ALL at the SQL*Plus prompt. *i*SQL*Plus allows you to execute many of the commands or alternatively change settings the Preferences menu. The command's description will note if a command has an equivalent *i*SQL*Plus Preference menu option or if the command is not applicable. Note the letters appearing in square brackets are optional.

```
@ ("at") and @@ (double "at" sign)
```

The "at" symbol (@) precedes a file name to run a SQL script. It is equivalent to the START command; for example: @@filename[.ext]. An @@ command runs a nested command file and runs in the same directory path as the calling script. Instead of passing a file name, you can alternatively use an URL such as @http://scooby:1521/myscript.sql or @ttp://acme.com:1521/script2.sql. *i*SQL*Plus only supports the URL format. (Do not confuse the @ START command with the connect identifier. The @ connect identifier is used in conjunction with the CONNECT command mentioned in Chapter 14, "Security.")

```
&variablename
```

The ampersand (&) symbol is used as a substitution variable. Use the SET DEFINE OFF command to turn off the use of the ampersand as the substitution variable.

```
&&variablename
```

The double ampersand symbol (&&) is also a substitution variable, but it avoids reprompting. The variable is declared for the duration of the SQL*Plus session. Use UNDEFINE to undefine the variable and allow for reprompting.

```
/
```

The forward slash is entered at the SQL*Plus prompt to execute the current SQL statement or PL/SQL block in the buffer.

```
ACC[EPT] variablename
```

The ACCEPT command reads a line of input and stores it in a user variable.

```
A[PPEND]
```

The APPEND command appends text at the end of a line.

```
C[HANGE]
```

The CHANGE command changes text on the line indicated by following the CHANGE command with a forward slash, the old text, another forward slash, and the new text.

```
CL[EAR] BUF[FER]
```

The CLEAR BUFFER command clears all lines of a SQL statement from the buffer.

```
CL[EAR] COL[UMNS]
```

The CLEAR COLUMNS command clears all formatting of columns issued previously during the current session.

```
CL[EAR] SCR[EEN]
```

The CLEAR SCREEN command clears the entire screen of all commands. This command is not available in *i*SQL*Plus; use the Clear button instead.

```
COL[UMN]
```

The COLUMN command shows the display attributes for all columns. To show a specific column, use COLUMN columnname. To reset the attributes, use the COLUMN columnname CLEAR command. Also refer to the FORMAT command.

```
CONN[ECT]
```

When the CONNECT command is followed by a user ID, password, and the connect identifier (if any), it allows you to connect to the Oracle database as another user, and it closes the active session for the current user. You can also use the DISCONNECT command to close an active session.

```
COPY
```

Allows you to copy results between tables or databases. It allows you to create or append rows to existing tables or create new tables.

```
DEF[INE] [variablename]
```

The DEFINE command defines a SQL*Plus variable and stores it in a CHAR datatype variable. You can use a number of predefined variables. For example, _USER shows the current user name, _CONNECT_IDENTIFIER displays the connect identifier (DB name), or _DATE to display the current date. These predefined variables are useful in SQL scripts or in the SET SQLPROMPT command. Without a variable name, it shows all the defined variables. SET DEFINE defines the substitution character—by default the ampersand symbol (&). SET DEFINE OFF turns the use of the substitution character off.

```
DEL
```

The DEL command deletes the current line in the buffer.

```
DESC[RIBE]
```

The DESCRIBE command describes the structure of a table, view, or stored object, detailing its columns and their datatypes and lengths. (See also SET DESCRIBE DEPTH.)

```
ED[IT] [filename.ext]
```

The EDIT command invokes the editor specified in SQL*Plus, opening a file with the current SQL statement. You can edit a specific file by executing the EDIT command followed by a filename. This command is not available in *i*SQL*Plus.

```
EXIT
```

The EXIT command disconnects the current user from the database and closes the SQL*Plus software. This command does not end your session in *i*SQL*Plus; use the Logout icon to end your session and to free up resources on the server.

```
EXE[CUTE] statement
```

The EXECUTE command executes a single PL/SQL statement.

```
FOR[MAT] formatmodel
```

The FORMAT command, together with the COLUMN command, specifies the display format of a column. For example, COL "Last Name" FORMAT A30, or COL cost FORMAT $999.99, or COL description FORMAT A20.

```
GET filename[.ext]
```

Loads a file into the SQL buffer. This command is not available in *i*SQL*Plus.

```
HELP [topic]
```

The HELP command accesses the SQL*Plus help system.

```
HO[ST]
```

The HOST command executes an operating system command without exiting SQL*Plus. Depending on the operating system, ! or $ can be specified instead of the HOST command. This command is not available in *i*SQL*Plus.

```
I[NPUT]
```

The INPUT command adds one or more lines to the current SQL statement. This command is not available in *i*SQL*Plus.

```
L[IST] [n|n m|n *|n LAST|*|*n| *LAST|LAST]
```

The LIST command lists the contents of the buffer. L n lists line n; n m lists lines n through m; n* lists lines n through the current line (as indicated by an asterisk); n LAST lists line n through the last line; * lists the current line; *n lists the current line through line n; * LAST lists the current line through the last line.

```
PASSWORD [username]
```

Change the password without displaying it. This command is not available in *i*SQL*Plus.

```
PRI[NT] [variable]
```

Displays bind variable created with the VARIABLE command.

```
PROMPT [text]
```

The PROMPT command sends the specified message or a blank line to the user's screen.

```
REM[ARK]
```

The REMARK command begins a comment in a command file.

```
REP[LACE]
```

The REPLACE command is used in conjunction with the SAVE command to save a SQL statement to an existing file and overwrite it. The syntax is: SAVE filename[.sql] REPLACE.

```
RUN
```

The RUN command lists and executes a SQL command in the SQL buffer.

```
SAV[E] filename[.ext]
```

When followed by a file name, the SAVE command saves the file to the operating system. A directory can be specified. This command is not available in *i*SQL*Plus.

```
SET AUTO[COMMIT]
```

The AUTOCOMMIT command can be set for a session to automatically commit all DML statements, rather than having to issue an explicit COMMIT command. The equivalent *i*SQL*Plus setting can be changed in Preferences → Script Execution → Commit Changes.

```
SET DEFINE [ON|OFF]
```

The DEFINE command turns the use of the substitution character on and off. See also DEFINE command. The equivalent *i*SQL*Plus setting can be changed in Preferences → Script Execution → Substitution Variable Prefix.

```
SET DESCRIBE [DEPTH [1|N|ALL] [LINENUM [ON|OFF]] [INDENT
[ON|OFF]]
```

The SET DESCRIBE DEPTH command allows the SQL*Plus DESCRIBE command to recursively describe the different levels of an object. The equivalent *i*SQL*Plus setting can be changed in Preferences → Script Formatting → Describe Objects.

```
SET ECHO [OFF|ON]
```

The ECHO command controls whether the commands in a SQL*Plus script are shown when the script is executed. The equivalent *i*SQL*Plus setting can be changed in Preferences → Script Formatting → Display Commands.

```
SET FEED[BACK] [6|n|OFF|ON]
```

The FEEDBACK command displays the number of records returned by a query when a query selects at least n records. The equivalent *i*SQL*Plus setting can be changed in Preferences → Script Formatting → Display Record Count.

```
SET LIN[ESIZE] [80|n]
```

The LINESIZE command sets the number of characters that SQL*Plus displays on a line before beginning a new line. The equivalent *i*SQL*Plus setting can be changed in Preferences → Script Formatting → Line Size.

```
SET PAGES[IZE] [14|n]
```

The PAGESIZE command sets the number of lines from the top title to the end of the page. A value 0 suppresses SQL*Plus formatting information such as headings. The equivalent *i*SQL*Plus setting can be changed in Preferences → Interface Configuration → Output Page Setup.

```
SET PAU[SE] [OFF|ON|text]
```

The PAUSE command allows control of scrolling and text displayed during pause. In *i*SQL*Plus this displays the Next Page button. You can change the setting in Preferences → Interface Configuration → Output Page Setup. Note the PAUSE command is not supported in *i*SQL*Plus versions prior to Oracle 10*g*.

```
SET SQLPROMPT
```

The SET SQLPROMPT command changes the SQL*Plus prompt. This command is not available in *i*SQL*Plus. You may find it convenient to change the prompt if you frequently switch user accounts and set it to the current login account with the SET SQLPROMPT _USER> command.

```
SET TIME [ON|OFF]
```

The TIME command shows the current time. This command is not available in *i*SQL*Plus.

```
SET TIMING [ON|OFF]
```

The TIMING command turns on/off the display of timing statistics. The equivalent *i*SQL*Plus setting can be changed in Preferences → Script Formatting → Timing Statistics.

```
SET TERM[OUT] [OFF|ON]
```

The TERMOUT command controls the display of output. This command is not available in *i*SQL*Plus.

```
SET VER[IFY] [OFF|ON]
```

The VERIFY command controls whether SQL*Plus lists text of a command before and after SQL*Plus replaces substitution variables with values. The equivalent *i*SQL*Plus setting can be changed in Preferences → Script Formating → Display Substitution Variables.

```
SHO[W] ALL
```

The SHOWALL command lists the value of all SQL*Plus system variables. The SHOW USER command is also useful to display the current login name.

```
SHUTDOWN
```

The SHUTDOWN command shuts down an Oracle database instance.

```
SPO[OL] {filename[.ext] [CRE[ATE]|REP[LACE]|APP[END]]|OFF|OUT}
```

When you issue the SPOOL command followed by a file name, all commands subsequently issued in SQL*Plus are written to the file. The SPOOL OFF command stops writing to the file. If you do not specify an extension, the default extension is LIS or LST. In Oracle 10*g* added CREATE, APPEND, and REPLACE options whereas in prior versions you could only create or replace a file. This command is not available in *i*SQL*Plus.

```
START {filename[.ext]|url}
```

When followed by a file name, the START command executes the file. This is the same as the @ symbol. In *i*SQL*Plus only the URL format is supported.

```
STARTUP
```

The STARTUP command starts up an Oracle instance and optionally mounts and opens the database.

```
UNDEFINE variablename
```

The UNDEFINE command deletes a user variable that was explicitly defined with the DEFINE command or implicitly with the & or && substitution variables.

```
WHENEVER OSERROR
```

The OSERROR command exits SQL*Plus if an operating system command generates an error. In *i*SQL*Plus it returns to the workspace.

```
WHENEVER SQLERROR
```

The SQLERROR command exits SQL*Plus if an SQL command generates an error. In *i*SQL*Plus it returns to the workspace.

APPENDIX D

STUDENT DATABASE SCHEMA

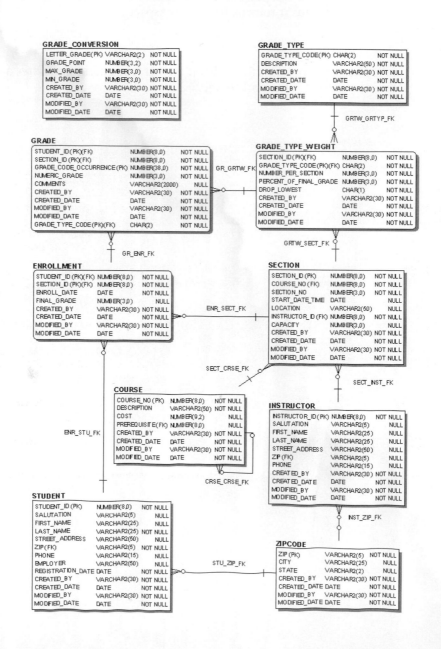

TABLE AND COLUMN DESCRIPTIONS

COURSE: Information for a course

Column Name	Null	Type	Comments
COURSE_NO	NOT NULL	NUMBER(8, 0)	The unique ID for a course.
DESCRIPTION	NULL	VARCHAR2(50)	The full name for this course.
COST	NULL	NUMBER(9,2)	The dollar amount charged for enrollment in this course.
PREREQUISITE	NULL	NUMBER(8, 0)	The ID number of the course which must be taken as a prerequisite to this course.
CREATED_BY	NOT NULL	VARCHAR2(30)	Audit column—indicates user who inserted data.
CREATED_DATE	NOT NULL	DATE	Audit column—indicates date of insert.
MODIFIED_BY	NOT NULL	VARCHAR2(30)	Audit column—indicates who made last update.
MODIFIED_DATE	NOT NULL	DATE	Audit column—date of last update.

SECTION: Information for an individual section (class) of a particular course

Column Name	Null	Type	Comments
SECTION_ID	NOT NULL	NUMBER(8,0)	The unique ID for a section.
COURSE_NO	NOT NULL	NUMBER(8,0)	The course number for which this is a section.
SECTION_NO	NOT NULL	NUMBER(3)	The individual section number within this course.
START_DATE_TIME	NULL	DATE	The date and time on which this section meets.
LOCATION	NULL	VARCHAR2(50)	The meeting room for the section.
INSTRUCTOR_ID	NOT NULL	NUMBER(8,0)	The ID number of the instructor who teaches this section.
CAPACITY	NULL	NUMBER(3,0)	The maximum number of students allowed in this section.
CREATED_BY	NOT NULL	VARCHAR2(30)	Audit column—indicates user who inserted data.
CREATED_DATE	NOT NULL	DATE	Audit column—indicates date of insert.
MODIFIED_BY	NOT NULL	VARCHAR2(30)	Audit column—indicates who made last update.
MODIFIED_DATE	NOT NULL	DATE	Audit column—date of last update.

STUDENT: Profile information for a student

Column Name	Null	Type	Comments
STUDENT_ID	NOT NULL	NUMBER(8,0)	The unique ID for a student.
SALUTATION	NULL	VARCHAR2(5)	This student's title (Ms., Mr., Dr., etc.).
FIRST_NAME	NULL	VARCHAR2(25)	This student's first name.
LAST_NAME	NOT NULL	VARCHAR2(25)	This student's last name.
STREET_ADDRESS	NULL	VARCHAR2(50)	This student's street address.
ZIP	NOT NULL	VARCHAR2(5)	The postal zip code for this student.

PHONE	NULL	VARCHAR2(15)	The phone number for this student, including area code.
EMPLOYER	NULL	VARCHAR2(50)	The name of the company where this student is employed.
REGISTRATION_DATE	NOT NULL	DATE	The date this student registered in the program.
CREATED_BY	NOT NULL	VARCHAR2(30)	Audit column—indicates user who inserted data.
CREATED_DATE	NOT NULL	DATE	Audit column—indicates date of insert.
MODIFIED_BY	NOT NULL	VARCHAR2(30)	Audit column—indicates who made last update.
MODIFIED_DATE	NOT NULL	DATE	Audit column—date of last update.

ENROLLMENT: Information for a student registered for a particular section (class)

Column Name	Null	Type	Comments
STUDENT_ID	NOT NULL	NUMBER(8,0)	The unique ID for a student.
SECTION_ID	NOT NULL	NUMBER(8,0)	The unique ID for a section.
ENROLL_DATE	NOT NULL	DATE	The date this student registered for this section.
FINAL_GRADE	NULL	NUMBER(3,0)	The final grade given to this student for all work in this section (class).
CREATED_BY	NOT NULL	VARCHAR2(30)	Audit column—indicates user who inserted data.
CREATED_DATE	NOT NULL	DATE	Audit column—indicates date of insert.
MODIFIED_BY	NOT NULL	VARCHAR2(30)	Audit column—indicates who made last update.
MODIFIED_DATE	NOT NULL	DATE	Audit column—date of last update.

INSTRUCTOR: Profile information for an instructor

Column Name	Null	Type	Comments
INSTRUCTOR_ID	NOT NULL	NUMBER(8)	The unique ID for an instructor.
SALUTATION	NULL	VARCHAR2(5)	This instructor's title (Mr., Ms., Dr., Rev., etc.).
FIRST_NAME	NULL	VARCHAR2(25)	This instructor's first name.
LAST_NAME	NULL	VARCHAR2(25)	This instructor's last name.
STREET_ADDRESS	NULL	VARCHAR2(50)	This instructor's street address.
ZIP	NULL	VARCHAR2(5)	The postal zip code for this instructor.
PHONE	NULL	VARCHAR2(15)	The phone number for this instructor, including area code.
CREATED_BY	NOT NULL	VARCHAR2(30)	Audit column—indicates user who inserted data.
CREATED_DATE	NOT NULL	DATE	Audit column—indicates date of insert.
MODIFIED_BY	NOT NULL	VARCHAR2(30)	Audit column—indicates who made last update.
MODIFIED_DATE	NOT NULL	DATE	Audit column—date of last update.

ZIPCODE: City, state, and zipcode information

Column Name	Null	Type	Comments
ZIP	NOT NULL	VARCHAR2(5)	The zip code number, unique for a city and state.
CITY	NULL	VARCHAR2(25)	The city name for this zip code.
STATE	NULL	VARCHAR2(2)	The postal abbreviation for the U.S. state.
CREATED_BY	NOT NULL	VARCHAR2(30)	Audit column—indicates user who inserted data.
CREATED_DATE	NOT NULL	DATE	Audit column—indicates date of insert.
MODIFIED_BY	NOT NULL	VARCHAR2(30)	Audit column—indicates who made last update.
MODIFIED_DATE	NOT NULL	DATE	Audit column—date of last update.

GRADE_TYPE: Lookup table of a grade type (code) and its description

Column Name	Null	Type	Comments
GRADE_TYPE_CODE	NOT NULL	CHAR(2)	The unique code that identifies a category of grade (e.g., MT, HW).
DESCRIPTION	NOT NULL	VARCHAR2(50)	The description for this code (e.g., Midterm, Homework).
CREATED_BY	NOT NULL	VARCHAR2(30)	Audit column—indicates user who inserted data.
CREATED_DATE	NOT NULL	DATE	Audit column—indicates date of insert.
MODIFIED_BY	NOT NULL	VARCHAR2(30)	Audit column—indicates who made last update.
MODIFIED_DATE	NOT NULL	DATE	Audit column—date of last update.

GRADE_TYPE_WEIGHT: Information on how the final grade for a particular section is computed. For example, the midterm constitutes 50 percent, the quiz 10 percent, and the final examination 40 percent of the final grade

Column Name	Null	Type	Comments
SECTION_ID	NOT NULL	NUMBER(8)	The unique ID for a section.
GRADE_TYPE_CODE	NOT NULL	CHAR(2)	The code that identifies a category of grade.
NUMBER_PER_SECTION	NOT NULL	NUMBER(3)	Identifies how many of these grade types can be used in this section (i.e., there may be three quizzes).
PERCENT_OF_FINAL_GRADE	NOT NULL	NUMBER(3)	The percentage this category of grade contributes to the final grade.
DROP_LOWEST	NOT NULL	CHAR(1)	Is the lowest grade in this type removed when determining the final grade? (Y/N).
CREATED_BY	NOT NULL	VARCHAR2(30)	Audit column—indicates user who inserted data.
CREATED_DATE	NOT NULL	DATE	Audit column—indicates date of insert.

MODIFIED_BY	NOT NULL	VARCHAR2(30)	Audit column—indicates who made last update.
MODIFIED_DATE	NOT NULL	DATE	Audit column—date of last update.

GRADE: The individual grades a student received for a particular section (class)

Column Name	Null	Type	Comments
STUDENT_ID	NOT NULL	NUMBER(8)	The unique ID for a student.
SECTION_ID	NOT NULL	NUMBER(8)	The unique ID for a section.
GRADE_TYPE_CODE	NOT NULL	CHAR(2)	The code that identifies a category of grade.
GRADE_CODE_OCCURRENCE	NOT NULL	NUMBER(38)	The sequence number of one grade type for one section. For example, there could be multiple assignments numbered 1, 2, 3, etc.
NUMERIC_GRADE	NOT NULL	NUMBER(3)	Numeric grade value (e.g., 70, 75).
COMMENTS	NULL	VARCHAR2(2000)	Instructor's comments on this grade.
CREATED_BY	NOT NULL	VARCHAR2(30)	Audit column—indicates user who inserted data.
CREATED_DATE	NOT NULL	DATE	Audit column—indicates date of insert.
MODIFIED_BY	NOT NULL	VARCHAR2(30)	Audit column—indicates who made last update.
MODIFIED_DATE	NOT NULL	DATE	Audit column—date of last update.

GRADE_CONVERSION: Converts a number grade to a letter grade

Column Name	Null	Type	Comments
LETTER_GRADE	NOT NULL	VARCHAR(2)	The unique grade as a letter (A, A−, B, B+, etc.).
GRADE_POINT	NOT NULL	NUMBER(3,2)	The number grade on a scale from 0 (F) to 4 (A).
MAX_GRADE	NOT NULL	NUMBER(3)	The highest grade number that makes this letter grade.
MIN_GRADE	NOT NULL	NUMBER(3)	The lowest grade number that makes this letter grade.
CREATED_BY	NOT NULL	VARCHAR2(30)	Audit column—indicates user who inserted data.
CREATED_DATE	NOT NULL	DATE	Audit column—indicates date of insert.
MODIFIED_BY	NOT NULL	VARCHAR2(30)	Audit column—indicates who last made update.
MODIFIED_DATE	NOT NULL	DATE	Audit column—date of last update.

APPENDIX F

ADDITIONAL
EXAMPLE TABLES

Throughout this book some exercises made use of tables not part of the STUDENT schema diagram listed in Appendix D, "STUDENT Schema Diagram." These additional tables can be created in your STUDENT schema by downloading the script sql_book_add_tables.sql from the companion Web site located at: http://authors.phptr.com/rischert3e. The purpose of these additional tables is to illustrate SQL concepts that could otherwise not be shown within the available data and datatypes in the STUDENT schema.

TABLE AND COLUMN DESCRIPTIONS

CHAPTER 3: CHARACTER, NUMBER, AND MISCELLANEOUS FUNCTIONS

GRADE_SUMMARY: Shows the use of the **COALESCE** function

Column Name	Null	Type	Comments
STUDENT_ID	NULL	NUMBER(8,0)	The unique ID for a student.
MIDTERM_GRADE	NULL	NUMBER(3)	Midterm grade of a student.
FINALEXAM_GRADE	NULL	NUMBER(3)	Final grade of a student.
QUIZ_GRADE	NULL	NUMBER(3)	Quiz grade of a student

FLOAT_TEST: Helps demonstrate the use of the BINARY_FLOAT datatype

Column Name	Null	Type	Comments
TEST	NULL	BINARY_FLOAT	Test column.

CHAPTER 4: DATE AND CONVERSION FUNCTIONS

DATE_EXAMPLE: Holds data to illustrate the use of datetime-related datatypes

Column Name	Null	Type	Comments
COL_DATE	NULL	DATE	Holds data in the DATE datatype.
COL_TIMESTAMP	NULL	TIMESTAMP(6)	Holds data in TIMESTAMP datatype with a 6-digit precision for fractional seconds.
COL_TIMESTAMP_W_TZ	NULL	TIMESTAMP(6) WITH TIME ZONE	Holds data in TIMESTAMP WITH TIME ZONE datatype.
COL_TIMESTAMP_W_LOCAL_TZ	NULL	TIMESTAMP(6) WITH LOCAL TIMES ZONE	Holds data in TIMESTAMP WITH LOCAL TIME ZONE datatype.

CONVERSION_EXAMPLE: Helps demonstrate the effect of Oracle's implicit datatype conversion

Column Name	Null	Type	Comments
COURSE_NO	NULL	VARCHAR2(9)	Course number.

MEETING: Shows the use of the OVERLAP operator

Column Name	Null	Type	Comments
MEETING_ID	NULL	NUMBER(10)	The unique ID for a meeting.
MEETING_START_DATE	NULL	DATE	The meeting's starting date and time.
MEETING_END_DATE	NULL	DATE	The meeting's ending date and time.

CHAPTER 9: COMPLEX JOINS

T1: Illustrates outer joins and full outer joins

Column Name	Null	Type	Comments
COL1	NULL	NUMBER	Column holds numeric data.

T2: Illustrates outer joins and full outer joins

Column Name	Null	Type	Comments
COL2	NULL	NUMBER	Column holds numeric data.

CHAPTER 10: INSERT, UPDATE, AND DELETE

INTRO_COURSE: Similar in structure to the COURSE table and used to show examples of insert statements

Column Name	Null	Type	Comments
COURSE_NO	NULL	NUMBER(8, 0)	The unique ID for a course.
DESCRIPTION	NULL	VARCHAR2(50)	The full name for this course.
COST	NULL	NUMBER(9,2)	The dollar amount charged for enrollment in this course.
PREREQ_NO	NULL	NUMBER(8, 0)	The ID number of the course that must be taken as a prerequisite to this course.
CREATED_BY	NULL	VARCHAR2(30)	Audit column—indicates user who inserted data.
CREATED_DATE	NULL	DATE	Audit column—indicates date of insert.
MODIFIED_BY	NULL	VARCHAR2(30)	Audit column—indicates who made last update.
MODIFIED_DATE	NULL	DATE	Audit column—date of last update.

GRADE_DISTRIBUTION: Used to demonstrate multi-table INSERT statements

Column Name	Null	Type	Comments
SECTION_ID	NULL	NUMBER(8)	The unique ID for a section.
GRADE_A	NULL	NUMBER(4)	Number of students with grade of A.
GRADE_B	NULL	NUMBER(4)	Number of students with a grade of B.
GRADE_C	NULL	NUMBER(4)	Number of students with a grade of C.
GRADE_D	NULL	NUMBER(4)	Number of students with a grade of D.
GRADE_F	NULL	NUMBER(4)	Number of students with a grade of F.

GRADE_DISTRIBUTION_NORMALIZED: Helps illustrate the use of the multi-table INSERT statements

Column Name	Null	Type	Comments
SECTION_ID	NULL	NUMBER(8)	The unique ID for a section.
LETTER_GRADE	NULL	VARCHAR(2)	The unique grade as a letter (A, A-, B, B+, etc.).
NUM_OF_STUDENTS	NULL	NUMBER(4)	Number of students.

EMPLOYEE: Holds employee information

Column Name	Null	Type	Comments
EMPLOYEE_ID	NULL	NUMBER	The unique ID for an employee.
NAME	NULL	VARCHAR2(10)	Employee's name.
SALARY	NULL	NUMBER	Employee's salary.
TITLE	NULL	VARCHAR2(10)	Employee's job title.

EMPLOYEE_CHANGE: Contains changes to the EMPLOYEE table for the purpose of showing INSERT/MERGE functionality

Column Name	Null	Type	Comments
EMPLOYEE_ID	NULL	NUMBER	The unique ID for an employee.
NAME	NULL	VARCHAR2(10)	Employee's name.
SALARY	NULL	NUMBER	Employee's salary.
TITLE	NULL	VARCHAR2(10)	Employee's job title.

SECTION_HISTORY: Lists historical data from the SECTION table to help illustrate the use of the multi-table INSERT command

Column Name	Null	Type	Comments
SECTION_ID	NOT NULL	NUMBER(8,0)	The unique ID for a section.
START_DATE_TIME	NULL	DATE	The date and time on which this section meets.
COURSE_NO	NOT NULL	NUMBER(8,0)	The course number for which this is a section.
SECTION_NO	NOT NULL	NUMBER(3)	The individual section number within this course.

CAPACITY_HISTORY: Holds historical data from the SECTION table related to the CAPACITY column; used to show the use of the multi-table INSERT command

Column Name	Null	Type	Comments
SECTION_ID	NOT NULL	NUMBER(8,0)	The unique ID for a section.
LOCATION	NULL	VARCHAR2(50)	The meeting room for the section.
CAPACITY	NULL	NUMBER(3,0)	The maximum number of students that can be enrolled in this section.

TA: Helps illustrate a correlated update problem

Column Name	Null	Type	Comments
ID	NULL	NUMBER	The unique ID the table.
COL1	NULL	VARCHAR2(4)	The column holds alphanumeric data.

TB: Helps illustrate a correlated update problem

Column Name	Null	Type	Comments
ID	NULL	NUMBER	The unique ID the table.
COL2	NULL	VARCHAR2(4)	The column holds alphanumeric data.

CHAPTER 15: REGULAR EXPRESSIONS AND HIERARCHICAL QUERIES

ZIPCODE_EXAMPLE: Helps illustrate regular expression examples

Column Name	Null	Type	Comments
ZIP	NULL	VARCHAR2(5)	Zipcode column.

CHAPTER 16: EXPLORING DATA WAREHOUSING FEATURES

COURSE_REVENUE: Contains data about the total revenue per course, the total number of students enrolled, and the number of sections for this course

Column Name	Null	Type	Comments
COURSE_NO	NULL	NUMBER(8, 0)	The unique ID for a course.
REVENUE	NULL	NUMBER	The revenue for this course.
COURSE_FEE	NULL	NUMBER(9,2)	The course fee (course cost) of this course.
NUM_ENROLLED	NULL	NUMBER	The number of students enrolled in this course.
NUM_OF_SECTIONS	NULL	NUMBER	The number of sections for this course.

INSTRUCTOR_SUMMARY: Holds revenue and enrollment information by instructor, year, and month

Column Name	Null	Type	Comments
INSTRUCTOR_ID	NOT NULL	NUMBER(8,0)	The ID number of the instructor who teaches this section.
SEMESTER_YEAR	NOT NULL	VARCHAR2(4)	Semester year in which this instructor teaches.
SEMESTER_MONTH	NOT NULL	VARCHAR2(2)	Month in which the instructor teaches.
GENDER	NULL	CHAR(1)	Gender.
CAMPUS	NULL	VARCHAR2(11)	Campus location.
NUM_OF_CLASSES	NULL	NUMBER	Number of sections.

NUM_OF_STUDENTS	NULL	NUMBER	The number of enrolled students.
REVENUE	NULL	NUMBER	This column holds the generated revenue amount, which is computed by multiplying the course cost by the number of enrolled students.

MODEL_EXAMPLE: Contains data that help illustrate interrow calculation examples

Column Name	Null	Type	Comments
COURSE	NULL	VARCHAR2(30)	The name of a course.
GENDER	NULL	CHAR(1)	Gender of student enrolled in course.
YEAR	NULL	NUMBER	The year enrolled.
ENROLL_NO	NULL	NUMBER	The number of enrolled students.

NAVIGATING THROUGH THE ORACLE DOCUMENTATION

WHY DO YOU NEED TO READ THIS APPENDIX?

After reading this book and performing the exercises, you will have gained significant experience and knowledge with the Oracle database. Congratulations! Not every topic and syntax option can be discussed in this book; otherwise, it would have several thousands of pages. The emphasis is on highlighting the most commonly used features. What do you do to learn more about a particular topic or what if you have further questions? One of the ways to research the answer is to consult the Oracle supplied documentation.

Another reason you may need to refer to the Oracle documentation is when versions change (an inevitable fact of software development). Additional features are often added and existing functionality enhanced. Perhaps you are working with a previous Oracle version and want to check if certain features are available. As you can see, there are many reasons why reading the documentation is unavoidable.

WHERE DO YOU FIND THE ORACLE DOCUMENTATION?

The Oracle documentation can be installed using Oracle's installer program, or you can look up the documentation on the OTN (Oracle Technology Network) Web site. The OTN site is Oracle's own site that contains a wealth of information, including the documentation, and is geared towards developers and DBAs. Before you can access the site, you must register (registration is free). The URL for OTN is http://otn.oracle.com. After you register, you can find all Oracle documentation (including previous Oracle versions) at this URL: http://otn.oracle.com/documentation/index.html. You can also use this link: http://tahiti.oracle.com.

After you navigated through the different options, you will receive a screen similar to Figure G.1, which shows the Getting Started screen.

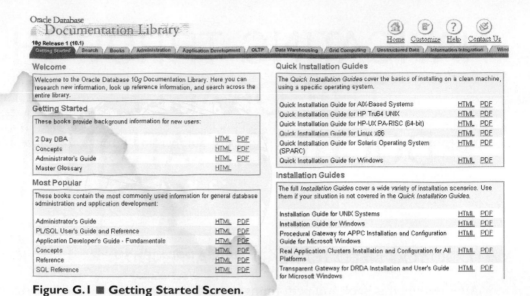

Figure G.1 ■ Getting Started Screen.

The Getting Started screen organizes the various manuals. For example, you will find a section that lists manuals useful for new users and another lists all the installation manuals.

If you already know in which book you will find the needed information, you can click directly on any of the tabs organized by the different topics located on the

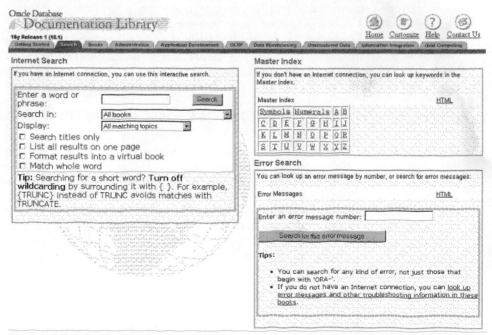

Figure G.2 ■ Search Screen.

top of the screen. Most manuals can be viewed and downloaded in PDF format, if you care to print the information or keep it on your local machine.

If you do not know in which manual to look for the desired topic, you want to click on the Search tab (Figure G.2). This tab is divided into three different sections. On the left side is a menu that lets you jumpstart your search for specific words or phrases. On the right, you can lookup keywords in the Master Index, which contains the index entries for all books. The box on the lower right of the screen allows you to enter an error message number and retrieve the cause and recommended action.

JUMPSTART YOUR SEARCH

The left side of the search tab presents a Search box that allows you to enter a word or phrase you want to search for in either upper or lowercase. If you already know the specific Oracle documentation you are looking for, you can choose from a selected list of books.

You can enter a phrase or an individual word. Multiple words or phrases can be connected with AND to query for items that contain both words—this is useful if your initial search result yielded too many matches. You can also use the OR and the NOT Boolean operators to improve your search results.

The search result presents a listing of books and the number of matching topics in each. You can then read the books and matches you consider most relevant. The most widely used books are listed first. When you have chosen a book, the search result is listed in alphabetical order.

If you are unsure which book is the best choice, you can click on the Format results into a virtual book checkbox to format the search results into a virtual book. This may make it easier to read the search results. It also presents introductory material first.

On top of the Search tab, you will find a Help icon. When you click on this icon, you will find useful tips on using the search features.

ORACLE DOCUMENTATION TITLES

It is useful to know what topics are covered in the various Oracle manuals. Table G.1 lists of the most commonly used manuals and the major topics covered in each.

Table G.1 ■ Selected Oracle Documentation Titles

Book	Contents
2 Day DBA	This book describes the essentials of administering a database. It explains the key tasks in an easy-to-read format.
Administrator's Guide	Basic database administration tasks, such as creating new databases; starting up and shutting down a database, managing the files, backup and recovery, storage management; creating, altering, and dropping database objects, managing users and permissions.
Application Developer's Guide—Fundamentals	This guide is one of the most useful Oracle documentation books. It contains a wealth of information from a developer's perspective. Information such as the management of database objects, the selection of datatypes, and the enforcement of data integrity via constraints is discussed. You will find information about choosing an indexing strategy for good performance as well as an introduction into application security and a discussion of PL/SQL triggers.
Application Developer's Guide - Object-relational Features	This book discusses the various object-oriented features available within the Oracle database and how you can map relational data to objects.
Backup and Recovery Basics	This book details backup and recovery strategies to ensure adequate protection of your database.
Concepts	This manual discusses the Oracle architecture and its core concepts and is intended for database administrators and database application developers. It explains the details of data blocks, tablespaces, the data dictionary, the database instance with startup and shutdown, the different types of database objects, data types, triggers, and dependency amongst objects, data integrity and security.
Data Warehousing Guide	This book covers the issues evolving around designing, building and maintaining a data warehouse. It explains the analytical functions and discusses data transformation and loading.
Enterprise Manager Concepts	This manual includes all the basics about Oracle's Enterprise Manager.
Error Messages	You will find most error messages in this manual, except for SQL*Plus SP2 errors. You will find those in the SQL*Plus User's Guide and Reference. Other product-specific errors are also found in the respective Oracle product manuals.
Installation Guide for Windows or Installation Guide for Unix Systems	An installation guide to installing the Oracle software for the individual operating system environment (e.g., Windows, Unix).

Table G.1 ■ Selected Oracle Documentation Titles (*continued*)

Book	Contents
Performance Tuning Guide and Reference	This manual is concerned with tuning SQL statements and the Oracle database for optimal performance. The various methods illustrate how you can collect performance statistics on your database and how to tune SQL statements.
Reference	The dynamic and static data dictionary views are listed in this book along with the Oracle initialization parameters for the initialization file (init.ora).
SQL Reference	This is an alphabetical reference to all SQL commands. Furthermore, it contains a list of all functions, operators, and expressions. Diagrams show and explain the different syntax options. If you are unsure of a command's syntax options, this is the manual to consult.
Platform Guide for Windows	This text discusses the implementation of Oracle on Windows platforms.
PL/SQL Packages and Types Reference	Information about the procedures and functions of Oracle-supplied packages appear in this manual. For example, you find examples and parameter listings about collecting statistics with the DBMS_STATS package in this book.
SQL*Plus User's Guide and Reference	Guide to SQL*Plus including all SP2 error messages. Contains a listing of all SQL*Plus commands and formatting options.

ERROR MESSAGES

The Oracle Error Messages manual, together with the SQL*Plus User's Guide and Reference manual, lists the most common error messages. Error messages are usually prefixed with a three-letter code that indicates the program that issued the error. It also gives you an indication in which manual to look for the error or which of Oracle's products causes the error. Most error messages are found in the Oracle Error Messages manual; however, some product-specific errors are found in each product's individual manual (i.e., SP2 errors are found in the SQL*Plus User's Guide and Reference manual). Table G.2 lists the most common error message codes.

Table G.2 ■ Common Oracle Error Message Codes

Message Prefix	Oracle Software
ORA	Oracle server message
TNS	Oracle Net messages
SP2	SQL*Plus message
EXP	Export utility message
IMP	Import utility message
SQL*Loader	SQL*Loader message
OSD	Windows-specific message
KUP	External table message
RMAN	Recovery Manager message
PLS	PL/SQL message

READING ORACLE SYNTAX DIAGRAMS

In Chapter 3, "Character, Number, and Miscellaneous Functions," you were introduced to a variant of the BNF (Backus-Naur Form) style syntax (see Table 3.1).

You will notice that most of Oracle's manuals now show the graphic syntax diagrams. To read such a diagram, you should follow the path of the line, starting from the left to the right. Keywords such as commands are in uppercase and inside rectangular boxes. Required syntax always appears on the main path; an optional choice is listed above the main path. Multiple choices are indicated through multiple paths either on or above the main path.

Figure G.3 lists the partial syntax diagram of the CREATE INDEX command. As you see, the CREATE INDEX command allows for a number of choices. You can choose between the syntax options CREATE INDEX, CREATE UNIQUE INDEX, and CREATE BITMAP INDEX. The UNIQUE and BITMAP keywords are optional and let you create different types of indexes.

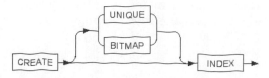

Figure G.3 ■ Excerpt of CREATE INDEX syntax.

Figure G.4 shows you additional syntax conventions on the example of the VAL-UES clause of the INSERT command. Inside circles you will find punctuation, operators, and delimiters such as commas or parentheses. Object names, expressions, parameters, and variables appear in lowercase and inside ovals. If you are allowed to choose more than one option, the diagram has a loopback path that lets you repeat the choices. In this example, expression or the DEFAULT keyword within the set of parentheses may be repeated but are separated from each other by a comma.

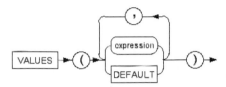

Figure G.4 ■ The VALUES clause of an INSERT command.

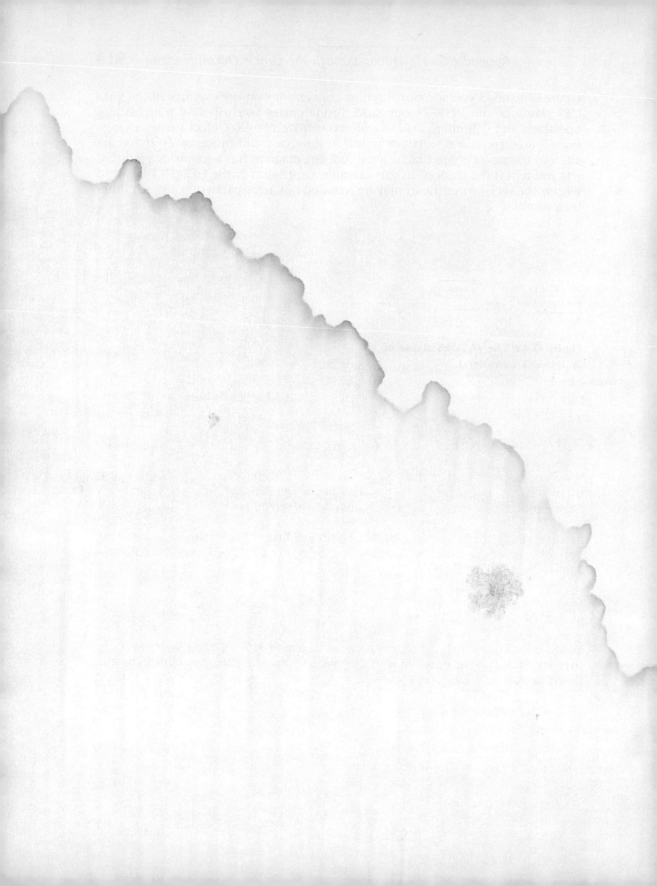

APPENDIX H

RESOURCES

This appendix lists Oracle-related Web sites where you will be able to explore topics in greater detail and find information beyond the scope of the book. Because Web links always change, also refer to the companion Web site located at http://authors.phptr.com/rischert3e for up-to-date listings and additions. The companion Web site also features a bulletin board to exchange messages.

USEFUL ORACLE-RELATED WEB SITES

A well-organized Oracle portal called *Oracle FAQ* features extensive links to many useful Oracle related sites. This is an informative site for further research on Oracle topics. You can find it at http://www.orafaq.com.

At http://www.jlcomp.demon.co.uk/faq/ind_faq.html, a U.K. site, you will find helpful answers to questions categorized by various subjects such as database administration, SQL, or PL/SQL.

ORACLE NEWSGROUPS

You can search through the following newsgroups with the Google search engine: http://groups.google.com. Often the answer to your question may already be out there. Be sure to check it out.

comp.databases.oracle.tools
comp.databases.oracle.misc
comp.databases.oracle.server
comp.databases.oracle.marketplace

If you want to subscribe to a very active Oracle mailing list, you join the ORACLE-L list by sending an email to ListGuru@fatcity.com with the word SUBSCRIBE in the message body.

ORACLE'S OWN WEB SITES

Oracle's home page is located at http://www.oracle.com.

The Oracle Technology Network (OTN) offers free product downloads, discussion forums, white papers, sample code, documentation, and technical articles on a variety of Oracle related issues. You can find the site at http://otn.oracle.com. The site requires registration, but is free.

Tom Kyte at Oracle runs a forum for frequently asked questions at http://asktom .oracle.com/.

Oracle has a new Oracle by Example (OBE) series, which offers tutorial type instruction for read-world problems: http://otn.oracle.com/obe/start/index.html. Along with it you will find also the 2-day DBA manual useful for beginning DBA topics—located at http://otn.oracle.com/obe/2day_dba/index.html.

Oracle support via Metalink is available only if you purchase an Oracle support contract.

http://www.oracle.com/support
http://metalink.oracle.com/index.html

To find answers regarding SQL*Plus on OTN visit http://otn.oracle .com/tech/sql_plus/. There you will be able to ask questions and review previous postings, including a FAQ on SQL*Plus and *i*SQL*Plus.

You will also see various forums on OTN where you can pose questions; you can visit them at http://www.oracle.com/forums/.

ALTERNATIVE SQL*PLUS SOFTWARE TOOLS

This book uses SQL*Plus and *i*SQL*Plus as execution environments because one of these tools is always available with every Oracle installation. There are many excellent tools on the market that make you wonder how you could have ever lived without them. These tools often feature an easy-to-use editor and a graphical execution environment with a browser showing all the database objects. You can easily execute queries, generate execution plans for SQL statements, export and import tables, and reverse-engineer the DDL for existing objects. We recommend that you download one of the trial versions to help you determine the suitability for you individual needs. Following is a list of popular vendors. The ORAFAQ Web site, which is located at http://www.orafaq.com/tools/index.htm, lists many more including a comparison chart.

PL/SQL Developer by Allaround Automations:
http://www.allroundautomations.nl/plsqldevaddons.html

RapidSQL by Embarcadero Technologies: http://www.embarcadero.com

SQL Navigator and Toad by Quest Software: http://www.quest.com

DATABASE DESIGN SOFTWARE

Besides Oracle's own Designer tool, there are a many vendors that offer tools that allow you to create logical and physical data models for Oracle databases. Following are a few of the popular vendors.

DeZign by Datanamic: http://www.datanamic.com

ER/Studio: http://www.embarcadero.com

ERwin Data Modeler by Computer Associates: http://www.cai.com

USER GROUPS

Joining a user group is one of the best ways to gain knowledge and experience using Oracle. Be sure to check out the group in your geographical area.

International Oracle User Group: http://www.ioug.org

Search Oracle's Web site for a listing of all user groups:
http://www.oracle.com/corporate/overview/usergroups.html

Oracle Development Tools User Group: http://odtug.com

ORACLE-RELATED PUBLICATIONS

SELECT Magazine, a publication of the IOUG user group:
http://www.selectonline.org

Oracle Magazine, a free Oracle publication that contains technology articles as well as tips and techniques: http://www.oramag.com/publications

ACADEMIC RESOURCES

Mailing list and repository related to using Oracle in an academic teaching environment: http://mail.uindy.edu/mailman/listinfo/oracle_in_academia

Other useful sites are http://www.isfacdir.org/ and http://www.magal.com/iswn/teaching/database/ for database-related teaching materials.

Oracle Academic Initiative (OAI): http://oai.oracle.com

Oracle Workforce: http://workforce.oracle.com

BOOKS

Following is a list of titles that allow you to explore advanced subjects in further detail.

SQL for Smarties: Advanced SQL Programming by Joe Celko; Morgan Kaufman Publishers, Inc., 1995. Excellent coverage of many advanced SQL topics.

SQL Puzzles & Answers by Joe Celko; Morgan Kaufman Publishers, Inc., 1997. This book contains many clever and humorous real-life examples and solutions.

Oracle SQL High-Performance Tuning, 2nd edition, by Guy Harrison; Prentice Hall, 2001. An excellent resource if you want to know more about writing efficient SQL statements and getting the most out of your database.

Oracle PL/SQL by Example, by Benjamin Rosenzweig and Elena Silvestrova; Prentice Hall, 2004. This book is the logical choice to take you to the next level of Oracle knowledge. It is based on the same workbook pedagogy as this book, with exercises and labs. It is a perfect introduction into the PL/SQL language.

Oracle Design by Dave Ensor and Ian Stevenson; O'Reilly, 1997. The book is primarily centered around Oracle 7 (a newer companion book called *Oracle 8 Design Tips* is also available). However, a number of the excellent design tips contained within still hold true.

Mastering Regular Expressions by Jeffrey E. F. Friedl; O'Reilly, 2002. Detailed explanations of regular expressions.

ORACLE DATATYPES

This appendix lists Oracle's most commonly used built-in datatypes. Note that some of the datatype mentioned have additional datatypes to support specific national character sets such as NCLOB or NVARCHAR2.

Oracle supports intermedia datatypes, spacial (geographic) data, the ANY type where a datatype is not known and can be dynamically configured, and the XML types. These datatypes can be used in conjunction with C/C++, Java, or PL/SQL.

Oracle's PL/SQL language has some of the same datatypes as listed in Table I.1, but in some cases, PL/SQL places certain restrictions on manipulation and size. If you are working with datatypes within the PL/SQL language, please refer to *Oracle PL/SQL by Example* by Benjamin Rosenzweig and Elena Silvestrova for more details.

Table I.1 ■ Oracle's Most Commonly Used Built-In Datatypes

Datatype	Explanation
NUMBER [optional precision,[optional scale]]	Oracle stores zero, positive, and negative fixed- and floating-point numbers. The allowable values for precision are 1 to 38 and for the scale −84 to 127. If you don't specify the precision or scale, the magnitude of the number is between $1.0\ 10^{-130}$ and $9.9\ ...\ 9 \times 10^{125}$ (38 nines followed by 88 zeroes) with 38 digits of precision.
BINARY_FLOAT	Holds floating point numbers in 32-bit format. Floating point numbers support infinity and NaN (not a number). The datatype is new in Oracle 10*g*.

(continued)

Table I.1 ■ Oracle's Most Commonly Used Built-In Datatypes (continued)

Datatype	Explanation
BINARY_DOUBLE	The 64-bit double-precision floating data point number implementation. Together with the BINARY_FLOAT datatype, this datatype is new in Oracle 10*g* and and implements most of the the IEEE standard for floating point numbers. Floating-point computation using the BINARY_FLOAT and BINARY_DOUBLE datatypes are more efficient than with the NUMBER datatype.
VARCHAR2 (size)	Variable length character string with a maximum size of 4,000 characters (or bytes). A length must always be specified.
CHAR [optional size]	Fixed character length data with maximum size of 2,000 characters; the default size is 1. Any space not used by the stored text is padded with blanks.
LONG	Character datatype with a maximum storage capacity of 2 gigabytes. LONGs are subject to a number of restrictions and Oracle recommends you convert data from this datatype to CLOBs, as the LONG datatype is desupported starting with Oracle 10*g*.
CLOB	This stores large text objects. Use this instead of the LONG datatype. Also useful for storing XML objects.
DATE	Stores date and time including seconds from January 1, 4712 BC to AD December 31, 9999.
TIMESTAMP [optional seconds precision]	Same as DATE but includes fractional seconds precision from 0 to 9 digits. The default is 6.
TIMESTAMP [optional seconds precision] WITH TIME ZONE	Same as TIMESTAMP, including the time zone displacement value.
TIMESTAMP [optional seconds precision] WITH LOCAL TIME ZONE	Same as TIMESTAMP WITH TIME ZONE, except time is displayed in session's time zone and stored in the database's time zone.
INTERVAL YEAR [optional year precision] TO MONTH	Period of years and months. The optional precision may range from 0–9, with a default value of 2.
INTERVAL DAY [optional day precision] TO SECOND [optional fractional seconds precision]	Period of time in days, hours, minutes, and seconds. The default day precision is 2 with acceptable values from 0 to 9. The default fractional seconds precision is 6 with acceptable values from 0 to 9.

(continued)

Table I.1 ■ Oracle's Most Commonly Used Built-In Datatypes (*continued*)

Datatype	Explanation
ROWID	Represents the unique address of a row in a table, displayed in hexadecimal format. Typically used in conjunction with the ROWID pseudocolumn. See Chapter 12, "Views, Indexes, and Sequences," for more information on ROWID.
RAW (size)	Raw binary data with maximum length of 2,000 bytes. Useful for small binary data such as graphics.
LONG RAW	Same as RAW except holds up to 2 gigabytes. Used for binary data such as graphics, sounds, or documents. Oracle recommends that you convert LONG RAWS to binary BLOB columns as they have fewer restrictions than a LONG RAW.
BLOB	Stores unstructured binary large objects. Often used for graphic images, video clips, and sounds. Unlimited size LOB support for Oracle 10*g* and based on a DB_BLOCK size from 2 to 32 K, the size limit is 8 to 128 terabytes.
BFILE	Points to large binary file stored outside of the database. Oracle can read the file only, not modify it. Oracle requires appropriate operating-system-level read permissions on the file.

INDEX

928

929

930

TOMORROW'S SOLUTIONS FOR TODAY'S PROFESSIONALS

Prentice Hall Professional Technical Reference

| Browse | Book Series | What's New | User Groups | Alliances | Special Sales | Contact Us |

Search | Help | Home

Quick Search

PTR Favorites

Find a Bookstore

Book Series

Special Interests

Newsletters

Press Room

International

Best Sellers

Solutions Beyond the Book

Shopping Bag

Keep Up to Date with
PH PTR Online

We strive to stay on the cutting edge of what's happening in professional computer science and engineering. Here's a bit of what you'll find when you stop by **www.phptr.com**:

What's new at PHPTR? We don't just publish books for the professional community, we're a part of it. Check out our convention schedule, keep up with your favorite authors, and get the latest reviews and press releases on topics of interest to you.

Special interest areas offering our latest books, book series, features of the month, related links, and other useful information to help you get the job done.

User Groups Prentice Hall Professional Technical Reference's User Group Program helps volunteer, not-for-profit user groups provide their members with training and information about cutting-edge technology.

Companion Websites Our Companion Websites provide valuable solutions beyond the book. Here you can download the source code, get updates and corrections, chat with other users and the author about the book, or discover links to other websites on this topic.

Need to find a bookstore? Chances are, there's a bookseller near you that carries a broad selection of PTR titles. Locate a Magnet bookstore near you at www.phptr.com.

Subscribe today! Join PHPTR's monthly email newsletter! Want to be kept up-to-date on your area of interest? Choose a targeted category on our website, and we'll keep you informed of the latest PHPTR products, author events, reviews and conferences in your interest area.

Visit our mailroom to subscribe today! **http://www.phptr.com/mail_lists**